MECHANICAL TO DIGITAL PRINTING IN SCOTLAND:
The Print Employers' Organisation

MECHANICAL TO DIGITAL PRINTING IN SCOTLAND:
The Print Employers' Organisation

John Gennard
Emeritus Professor
Strathclyde Business School
Glasgow

Edinburgh
Scottish Printing Archival Trust in association
with Graphic Enterprise Scotland 2010

First published in Great Britain by the Scottish Printing Archival Trust (SC no: 012320) in association with Graphic Enterprise Scotland in 2010.

ISBN: 978-0-9563043-1-5

Design by Lunaria
www.lunaria.co.uk

Cover lino-cut illustration by Owain Kirby
www.owainkirby.co.uk

Set in Adobe Garamond and Proxima Nova

Printed by Bell & Bain
www.bell-bain2.demonweb.co.uk

The publishers are especially grateful to Bell & Bain and Antalis McNaughton for their in-kind contribution to this book.

CONTENTS

Contents

Contents

Contents

Contents

Contents

Contents

Contents

LIST OF FIGURES AND TABLES

LIST OF MAIN ABBREVIATIONS

ACAS	Advisory Conciliation and Arbitration Service	**HNC**	Higher National Certificate
ACP	Association of Correctors of the Press	**HND**	Higher National Diploma
ASLP	Amalgamated Society of Lithographic Printers and Auxiliaries of Great Britain and Ireland	**IPF**	Irish Printing Federation
		LEC	Local Enterprise Companies
ASTMS	Association of Scientific, Technical and Managerial Staffs	**LMPA**	London Master Printers Association
		LSC	London Society of Compositors
BFMP	British Federation of Master Printers	**LTS**	London Typographical Society
BIPIC	British and Irish Printing Industries Council	**MCTS**	Monotype Casters and Typefounders Society
BPIF	British Printing Industries' Federation	**MOC**	Mother of the Chapel
		MSC	Manpower Services Commission
CBI	Confederation of British Industries	**MSP**	Member of the Scottish Parliament
CEEP	European Centre of Employers and Enterprises providing Public services	**NAT**	National Arbitration Tribunal
COSHH	Control of Substances Hazardous to Health	**NATSOPA**	National Society of Operative Printers and Assistants
CPI	Consumer Prices Index	**NPB&I**	National Board for Prices and Incomes
EU	European Union	**NCEO**	National Confederation of Employers' Organisations
FOC	Father of the Chapel	**NEDO**	National Economic Development Office
GMB	General, Municipal, Boilermakers and Allied Trade Union	**NGA**	National Graphical Association
GPMU	Graphical, Paper and Media Union	**NJIC**	National Joint Industrial Council
		NS	Newspaper Society
HMSO	Her Majesty's Stationery Office	**NTO**	National Training Organisation

NUPB&MR	National Union of Printing, Bookbinding and Machine Rulers	**SLADE**	Society of Lithographic Artists, Designers, Engravers and Process Workers
NUPB&PW	National Union of Printing, Bookbinding and Paperworkers	**SMPS**	Society of Master Printers of Scotland
NUPT	National Union of Press Telegraphists	**SNPA**	Scottish Newspaper Publishers' Association
NUWDAT	National Union of Wallcoverings, Decorative and Allied Trades	**SOGAT**	Society of Graphical and Allied Trades
		SPEF	Scottish Print Employers Federation
P&KTF	Printing and Kindred Trades Federation	**SSC**	Sector Skills Councils
PEET	Printing Equipment Education Trust	**STA**	Scottish Typographical Association
PEF	Printing Education Forum	**SVQ**	Scottish Vocational Qualifications
PIRA	Printing Industry Research Association	**TA**	Typographical Association
PMMTS	Printing Machine Managers Trade Society	**TEC**	Training and Enterprise Councils
PPITB	Printing and Publishing Industry Training	**TOPS**	Training Opportunities Scheme
		TSA	Training Services Agency
REACH	European Community Regulation (EC 1907/2006): Registration, Evaluation, Authorisation and restriction of Chemical substances.	**TUC**	Trades Union Congress
		UFI	University for Industry
		UNICE	Union of Industrial and Employers' Confederations of Europe
		USDAW	Union of Shop, Distributive and Allied Workers
SCOTVEC	Scottish Vocational Education Council		
SGA	Scottish Graphical Association	**VAT**	Value Added Tax
SGB	Scottish Graphical Branch of SOGAT (82)	**YMP**	Young Master Printer
SGD	Scottish Graphical Division of SOGAT (75)	**YTS**	Youth Training Scheme
SJIC	Scottish Joint Industrial Council		

GLOSSARY OF TERMS

Balancing time: any employee losing time (for example by arriving late) must, if working overtime on that day, make up that time at ordinary rates before the overtime rate became payable. If no overtime was worked, pay for lost time would be deducted at the ordinary rate. Each day stood by itself, and time lost on one day could not be made up later in the working week.

Bronzing: process of adding a metallic finish to printed matter. The bronze was dusted onto a surface previously treated with glue where it was to accept the bronze.

Call money: extra payment to staff required to work overtime which is (a) not continuous from the usual hour of ceasing work, or (b) which starts not less then two hours before the usual time for starting work

Composition: the process of assembling type into lines then pages for letterpress printing

Docket: form filled in by individual employees, showing the time taken for each job, and the amount of output

Double demy: a size of paper 35 x 22.5 inches (572 x 889mm). Also used to describe a printing machine for which this is the maximum size of sheet

Electro: short for electrotype. A relief printing plate made by depositing a shell of copper on a mould of the forme of type and/or illustration blocks.

Em: the square of the body of any size of type, thus used as a unit of measurement.

En: half the width of an em, and the width of an average type character

Father of the Chapel: the Chapel was the traditional name given to a meeting of printers, and following from this the chief official was known as the Father or Mother of the Chapel

Flong: material used to make the mould in the stereotyping process

Galley: open-ended tray on which the compositor places type matter line by line as it is set

Gold foil blocking: the process of stamping a design onto a book cover using gold leaf and a press

Gravure: see photogravure

Half-tone: illustration reproduced from an original that has been photographed through a ruled glass screen, producing an image composed of equally spaced dots that vary in size according to the varying tones of the original

Interlocutor: decree of a Scottish court

Journeyman: worker who has completed his apprenticeship in the trade

Large Post 15lb: 'Large Post' is a traditional size of paper sheet: 419x533mm or 16½x21 inches. 15lb refers to the substance of the paper: in this case 15 pounds (Imperial weight) per ream of 500 sheets paper

Letterpress: printing done from raised type or blocks

Lithography: process of printing from a flat surface, based on the principle that oil and water do not mix. Ink is applied selectively to the printing surface by chemically treating image areas to attract ink and non-image areas to attract water. Offset lithography means that the image is 'offset' from plate to blanket, and from there to the paper.

Machine extras: additional sums, paid over and above the basic wage, for operating larger or more complex printing machines, or attachments to them. By 1980, machines were classified according to a formula, which took into account such things as sheet size and running speed.

Minicomputer: a medium-sized computer, more powerful than a personal computer, but smaller than a main-frame.

Negative spotter: one who corrects the spots and other small blemishes on the negative film image to be used for printing

Photogravure: an intaglio process, where the image is etched and therefore sunk below the surface. The original copy is photographed to produce a negative from which a positive is made. This is printed down onto a sensitised gelatine-coated surface known as carbon tissue. After exposure this is mounted on a copper cylinder and developed. It is then varnished, dried and etched to create to surface used for printing.

Piece rate: rate of pay related to the amount of work produced

Plate grainers: see Stone and plate preparers

Process work: preparation of the printing surface by photographic and/or chemical means, enabling the reproduction of continuous tone originals, known as 'half-tone' illustrations. Light tones appear as tiny dots, darker tones as larger dots

Stab rate: shorthand for the 'established rate for the job'

Stereo or stereotype: letterpress printing surface cast in type metal from a mould, created from a forme of composed type

Stone and plate preparers: workers who prepared the surface of the stones or plates used for lithographic printing. The surface had to be roughened to retain moisture and to provide a surface to which the image will adhere. The depth of the grain also influenced the length of life of the plate

Stop-cylinder: sheet-fed cylinder press in which the paper-carrying impression cylinder stops revolving after completing one revolution and is stationary during the return of the bed bearing the forme

Straight-on working: a form of overtime. The agreement between the Scottish Alliance and the STA for 1925 states that 'When a man works straight on more than one hour after the normal stopping time, he shall be paid an extra half-hour at his rate of wages' (Clause 3, page 4).

Tea money: rate paid to anyone required to work overtime in the evening for not less than one hour after the usual hour of closing unless notice is given on or before the previous day.

Teletype: transmitter/receiver for telegraph messages

Time rate: payment by time worked, not volume of work produced. It can be an hourly rate, a weekly wage or a monthly salary.

PREFACE

In January 2005, I was commissioned by the Scottish Print Employers Federation and the Scottish Printing Archival Trust to produce an official history of the evolution and development of the collective organisation of Scottish printing employers to mark their centenary in 2010. The mechanisation of typesetting and printing in the late nineteenth century and the early twentieth century had led to a massive expansion of both commercial and book printing. There was no comprehensive record of this period and the purpose was to produce one while records and memories still remained.

My objective has been to tell the story of the printing employers' organisation in Scotland within the context of the growth of printing companies in Scotland and their links with publishers, the development of craft unions and the response of employers to organised labour and the impact of technical change on industry organisation, labour relations and society. The Scottish Print Employers Federation gave me open and free access to all its records and those of its predecessors – the Scottish Alliance, the Scottish Alliance of Master Printers and the Society of Master Printers of Scotland – and an entirely free hand to write the history as I found it. Any views expressed in this history are entirely my own without any influence or censorship by the Scottish Print Employers Federation.

I have arranged the history in five parts. The first deals with the growth and development of the printing industry in Scotland from the establishment in 1507 of the first printing press in Edinburgh to 1890. The second part deals with the Scottish Alliance of Employers in the Printing and Kindred Trades covering the period 1890 to 1953, whilst the third section deals with the period of the Scottish Alliance of Master Printers (1953 to 1960). The fourth part examines the growth and development of the Society of Master Printers of Scotland over the period 1960 to 1990. The next part deals with Scottish Print Employers Federation and relates to the period 1990 to 2009. The final part covers Graphic Enterprise Scotland from 2009 to date. Within parts 2, 3 ,4 and 5 a thematic approach is taken – decision-making structures, financial developments, relationships with the English and Welsh Master Printers' body, the provision of core services to member firms and relationships with trade unions. Taking a thematic approach is not without its limitation in that it involves overlapping, going backwards and forwards in chronology and any division into separate compartments is unreal historically.

The history has been written from the official records of the Scottish Alliance, the Scottish Alliance of Master Printers, the Society of Master Printers of Scotland

and the Scottish Print Employers Federation – minutes of the Executive Board, the report of the Executive Board to the annual general meeting, Circulars to member firms, the Constitution and Rules, annual accounts and balance sheets, minutes of the Industrial Relations, Finance and Education and Training Subcommittees of the Executive Board, the *Scottish Alliance Bulletin* (July 1919 to June 1927) and the *Scottish Digest* which was issued quarterly between January 1961 and May 1964. Face-to-face interviews were conducted with present and past leading officials and Presidents. In addition, the Scottish Printing Archival Trust histories of the Edinburgh (1990), Glasgow (1994), Dundee and Perth (1996) and Aberdeen and the Northern Counties (2000) printing industries provided a great deal of information, particularly for Chapter 1. John Child's book *Industrial Relations in the British Printing Industry* (1967) and that of Ellic Howe *The British Federation of Master Printers, 1900-1950* (1950) were also indispensable sources of reference for the early chapters of this history.

I wish to express my great appreciation of the kindness and constant helpfulness of Jim Raeburn, Bob Hodgson and Patrick Mark who all made constructive comments on every chapter. A very big thank you is owed to Helen Williams for cataloguing and organising appropriately the archive materials of the Scottish Print Employers Federation and its forerunners, for reading and correcting the manuscript and for dealing with the publication.

A debt of gratitude is also owed to Jean Peebles and especially to Debbie Campbell, who both diligently and cheerfully word processed numerous drafts of the manuscript.

Lastly, research work inevitably impinges upon family life and thanks for understanding in this matter and are due to Anne, John, Julie, Paul and Lilly

John Gennard
October 2010

FOREWORD

This book is a culmination of six years work by John Gennard, produced through painstaking analysis of a massive volume of documentation accumulated since 1910, and by face-to-face interviews with significant individuals associated with the organisation.

The story told is a fascinating one, which wends its way through history from the installation of the first printing press in Edinburgh in 1507 to the effects and implications of modern digital printing of today.

Although our organisation was founded only in 1910, John explains in some detail the development of printing in Scotland to that date and the very significant technological changes brought about by the introduction of mechanical typesetting at the end of the nineteenth and early twentieth centuries. He demonstrates clearly how these changes radically affected the economics of printing and the effects on people in print and the development of organised labour.

Indeed, the original reasons for the formation of the Scottish Alliance of Masters in Printing and Kindred Trades on 8th November 1910 are identified as the introduction of mechanical composition through the Linotype and Monotype machines, the growth of the trade union membership and power, the creation of a national federation of print unions and the need to deal with the issue of product market competition based on price-cutting between Scottish Master Printers.

The author takes you carefully through the name changes to the Scottish Alliance of Master Printers 1953, Society of Master Printers of Scotland 1960, the Scottish Print Employers Federation 1990 and to Graphic Enterprise Scotland 2008. At each change he indicates the socio-economic dynamics coming into play and how they are all associated with technological change, organised labour, collective agreements, and government policy and legislation.

One of the significant themes throughout the history is that, despite the name changes, the role of the organisation has changed little. Core services of negotiation of collective agreements with the trade unions, the training of apprentices and political lobbying still remain with us today. The author also outlines technological changes such as direct to plate, direct to press, digital printing and the progressive amalgamation of the trade unions into Unite the union, as a modern day version of the 'raison d'être' of the organisation.

A recurring feature of the story is our relationship to other print employers' organisations, elsewhere in the UK. Scotland had been a founder member of the

BFMP but in 1910 formed its own organisation. It progressively developed its autonomy in finance, conditions of membership, its own collective agreements and over the years pulled out of areas of influence at the BFMP, such as representation on the governing council and major sub-committees. It is particularly apt since John explains the ups and downs of a fractious relationship with the BFMP and its successor organisation, not finally settled until 1984.

Membership numbers have also changed in line with the economic changes encountered in our history. Membership was at its peak in the 1950s and 1960s, but since then it has been in decline through liquidations, takeovers and amalgamations. However, as John illustrates, the organisation has always managed to attract new members and he points out that one of the objectives of GES today is to recruit new full and associate members, together with developing new services in line with members' business requirements. Success to date has been limited and the industry still exhibits the commercial pressures of poor margins, falling demand, a strong pound, overcapacity and downward pressure on pricing. John also adds the new challenges of e-procurement and new media.

John skilfully portrays our history over the past 100 years, chronicling our passage through the growth of printing companies in Scotland, the development of craft unions, the response to organised labour and the impact of technical change on individuals, organisations and labour relations. This work will be of interest to any social historian but, in particular, to anyone with any connection to the printing industry.

The book is a testimony to the scholarship of the author and to the people in the organisation and industry over the past century. We have survived by reacting to changes in printing and the commercial factors within Scotland and the UK

Bob Hodgson
Director

Chapter 1

THE GROWTH AND DEVELOPMENT OF THE PRINTING INDUSTRY IN SCOTLAND, 1507 – 1890

This chapter first traces the development of the Scottish printing industry and the rise of its foremost printing firms from the establishment of the first printing press in Scotland in 1507 to the period immediately prior to the introduction of mechanical composition. It then analyses, over the same period, the technological developments in the letterpress and lithographic printing processes. The third section examines wages and other employment conditions in the Scottish printing industry during the nineteenth century. Finally the chapter examines industrial relations developments in the industry pre-1890, including the emergence of trade unions.

The Origins of Printing in Scotland
a. Pre-Industrial Revolution
i. Edinburgh

The early history of printing in Scotland centred on Edinburgh, which at the beginning of the sixteenth century was the seat of government and of the monarchy and of the country's trade and commerce. Printing existed on mainland Europe from the mid-fifteenth century. The first printing press in England had been established in Westminster, by William Caxton, in 1476. It was not until 1507 that printing came to Scotland. In September of that year King James IV granted a patent to Walter Chepman and Androw Myllar to print the laws of Scotland, Acts of Parliament, chronicles, mass books and portable breviary.[1]

At the request of James IV, Chepman and Myllar imported a printing press from France which they located in the Cowgate district of Edinburgh. Chepman, a man of property, well-known to the King, provided the capital to start the business and the Cowgate premises. Myllar, on the other hand, provided the technical know-how, having acquired printing skills in Rouen in France. William Elphinstone, Bishop of Aberdeen, persuaded James IV to issue the patent as he wanted an authentically Scottish form of service to replace the current English one. The *Aberdeen Breviary*, written by Bishop Elpinstone was the 'jewel' of the Chepman-Myllar press being published in two volumes, one in 1509 and the other in 1510. Elphinstone's hope for their general use in Scotland did not materialise.

The economic turmoil following James IV's death at the Battle of Flodden in 1513 affected adversely the development of printing in Edinburgh. Royal patronage ended and, after the death around 1511 of Androw Myllar, no printer of significance existed in Edinburgh until Thomas Davidson started a printing business there in the late 1520s. He was the first Scottish printer to use roman type in printing *Strena*, a poem written in 1528 to celebrate the accession of King James V. In 1541 he was commissioned to print the Acts of Parliament.[2]

The years leading up to and including the Reformation, saw an increase in the number of printers, and printed material, fuelled by the outbreak of debate, argument and accusation. Satirical poetry and drama, for example, were used by reformers to expose the alleged ignorance of the Roman Catholic clergy.[3] As a result, in 1551 the Scottish printing press became highly regulated when a law decreed nothing be printed without a licence. Failure to obtain a licence carried the penalty of the seizure of goods and banishment. However, continued attempts by the Scottish Parliament and the Church to control the output of the printing industry implied the decree was ineffective. The decree and the post-Reformation period, nevertheless, depressed the output of the Scottish printing press and curtailed its development.

In the mid-sixteenth century, the printing of the Bible was a major part of Edinburgh's printing activities. Complaints by John Knox, and other reformers, of the high costs of imported Bibles culminated in Thomas Bassandyne printing the first Bible in Scotland. In 1561, with his partner Alexander Arbuthnot, he reprinted the Geneva Bible. The New Testament appeared under Bassandyne's imprint in 1576 and the Old Testament under Arbuthnot's in 1579. To finance the Bassandyne/Arbuthnot Bible project, every parish in Scotland contributed £5 in return for which the Privy Council provided a Bible. When the project was completed in 1579 the Scottish Parliament decreed every household paying £300 of yearly rent and every proprietor worth £500 in land and goods must purchase a Bible. To enforce this law an appointed individual visited every parish and had to be shown a Bible with the owner's name on the fly-leaf.

Up to 1710 printing in Edinburgh was closely associated with the Scottish monarchy. Royal patents confined printing to select individuals. Robert Waldegrave was a good example. Appointed the King's Printer, he produced the first book in Britain on maritime jurisprudence entitled *The Sea Law of Scotland* and in 1597 printed the works of King James VI, one of which was so sensitive it was only distributed amongst the King's trusted servants. The Union of the English and Scottish Crowns in 1603, and the subsequent departure of the Court to London, removed a major source of patronage and the number of books printed in Edinburgh in the years immediately following 1603 fell sharply. The industry, however, survived. The demand from the church, the universities, the law courts and private individuals ensured a viable market for book printing. Scottish intellectuals were also well served by the Scottish printing industry typified by the printing in 1614 of John Napier's book on logarithms and in 1633, of the first Scottish edition of the Authorised Version of the Bible printed by Robert Young, printer to Charles I. It arrived at a time of religious tension and uncertainty and the edition which included illustrative plates proved highly controversial. This tension gave rise to a twenty-year cycle (1639-1660) of war, famine, instability, invasion and repression during the Bishops' Wars of 1639 – 1642, through the English Civil War to the invasion and occupation of Scotland by Cromwell. This environment was not conducive to the writing of books, never mind their printing.

From 1671 to 1711 Scottish printing was dominated by the Anderson family. In 1671 Andrew Anderson was appointed the King's Printer by Charles II and given the sole right to print all books in Scotland. Nobody else could print without his permission. Despite his monopoly position, he printed little and when he died in 1676 his wife Agnes (who reverted to her maiden name of Campbell) took over the business and pursued the monopoly ruthlessly, prosecuting anyone who printed materials without her permission. Her forty-year domination of Scottish printing was a period of legal disputes, appeals, allegations of bad workshop practice (for example the employment of apprentices rather than journeymen) and accusations of poor quality work. She was criticised for producing incorrect Bibles and books and for being motivated solely by making money.[4] Agnes Campbell's monopoly over Scottish printing ended when, on the expiry of her patent, it was awarded to James Watson (her major opponent) and Robert Freebairn, both Edinburgh printers who convinced the King of the necessity to revive the high standards and good name of Scottish printing.

ii. Aberdeen

The spread of the printing press outside of Edinburgh proceeded slowly. Presses were installed in Dundee in 1547, in St Andrews in 1552, in Stirling in 1571 and in Aberdeen in 1622. Edward Raban introduced printing to Aberdeen on becoming printer to Aberdeen Town Council and to the University, a position he held until 1649. Over a twenty-seven-year period he produced 150 publications ranging over a wide field.[5] Among these were hornbooks and his *Almanac*. The former were single leaf protected by a layer of horn, and used by children in school classrooms. The *Almanac*, first published in 1623, was printed annually and due to its success pirated by other printers. Raban was succeeded by James Brown whose printed output was insignificant.

In 1661 John Forbes and his son became Aberdeen Town Council and University Printer. Their success was based on the annual production of 50,000 copies of the *Aberdeen Almanac* first published by Raban. Its continuing success encouraged pirated editions. Forbes complained to the Privy Council which in 1684 forbade the pirating of the *Aberdeen Almanac*.[6] In 1736 the printer to the Aberdeen Town Council and the university became James Chalmers who specialised in printing local sermons but no books of significance came from his press. His outstanding achievement was founding the *Aberdeen Journal* whose first issue was 29 December 1747 to 5 January 1748 and was the forerunner of today's *Press and Journal*. The monopoly of printing in Aberdeen ended in 1752 when Francis Douglas and William Murray opened their printing office. In contrast to James Chalmers, who preferred the stability offered by town council and university printing, the Murrays were entrepreneurs printing a wider range of products, particularly books. They published in 1761 the first magazine in Aberdeen entitled *The Aberdeen Magazine*.

iii. Glasgow

Despite having a university and being an episcopal see, Glasgow in the sixteenth and seventeenth centuries was a comparatively small place. Printing had existed in Scotland for 130 years before the first press arrived in Glasgow. In 1638 the Glasgow magistrates invited George Anderson to transfer his printing activities from Edinburgh to Glasgow, to print the proceedings of the General Assembly of the Church of Scotland to be held there in November 1638.[7] Anderson printed in Glasgow until his death in 1647. In 1661 the Glasgow Town Council granted municipal patronage to Robert Sanders who printed in Glasgow until his death in 1694. Between 1661 and 1672 he adopted the title of 'The Town's Printer' and from 1672 to 1684 that of 'Printer to the City and the University'. There was never more than one printer working in Glasgow until the second decade of the eighteenth century. In 1738, 100 years after printing in Glasgow began there were only three printers in the city – Alexander Miller, William Duncan and James Duncan. The Duncans went into partnership in 1718 but by 1720 were printing separately. They printed mainly religious tracts.

iv. Dundee/Perth

There is uncertainty over the date when printing began in Dundee but it is thought to have been 1547 when John Scott set up the first press in the town. There was little expansion of printing in the town over the next two centuries.[8]

In Perth printing began in 1715 with the arrival of Robert Freebairn. After participating in a failed Jacobite attempt to capture Edinburgh Castle he fled the city, joining the Jacobite Army at Perth where he established the town's first printing press to print Jacobite proclamations. The Earl of Mar had ordered the transfer of this printing press to Perth from Aberdeen. After Freebairn there was little printing in Perth until 1770 when George Johnston installed his press from Aberdeen.

b. Post-Industrial Revolution

The period 1850 to 1900 was relatively peaceful and printing first revived and then expanded. The collapse of the Anderson/Campbell monopoly in Edinburgh saw a growth in the number of printing shops and improvements in the general quality of print work. During the late eighteenth and the early nineteenth centuries Edinburgh was a centre for printing and publishing and for the trades allied to printing, for example – typefounding, engraving, bookbinding, stereotyping and, in the Midlothian area, paper manufacture. In 1745 there were five printing presses in Edinburgh but by 1799, twenty seven. A growing demand for books was a development from which printers benefitted.

The Industrial Revolution brought fluctuations in economic activity. There was a close relationship between the peaks and troughs in general industrial activity and those of the printing industry. Demand for its products fell during recession and increasing unemployment. The printing industry was not linked to the economic fluctuations of Scotland's capital industries (eg steel, shipbuilding) in which economic cycles were the greatest. It suffered less in economic recession than those industries as it catered chiefly for domestic markets where consumer demand was relatively more stable than in export markets. In the second half of the nineteenth century the industry was also influenced by events of direct concern. Two such examples were the repeal of Stamp Duty in 1855 and the abolition of paper duty in 1861. The book trade was affected adversely by increased competition consequent upon the repeal of these two taxes.

The Industrial Revolution witnessed a growing demand for new reading materials such as magazines, periodicals and newspapers rather than books. Industrialisation saw the Scottish book trade suffer as publishing moved towards London. The connection between the Edinburgh print industry and the London publishing houses was, however, maintained with many printing offices relying for their work on orders placed by London publishing houses.

i. Edinburgh

In Edinburgh, printers played a part in the general spirit of enquiry and of intellectual activity connected with the Industrial Revolution. An example was the academic Thomas Ruddiman who became in 1728 printer to the College of

Edinburgh. Another was Patrick Neill, a renowned botanist, who established in 1762 the firm of Balfour & Neill which became, upon Balfour's retiral in 1765, Neill & Company. Until its demise in 1973 Neill & Company was amongst Edinburgh's foremost printing firms. In the 1750s Alexander Donaldson, an Edinburgh bookseller, played a leading part in the production of cheap editions of popular works, an activity copied by London publishers. In 1771 William Smellie edited the first edition of the *Encyclopaedia Britannica* printed in Edinburgh by Carruthers and Bell with extensive copperplate illustrations. The book became a source of repeat work for Edinburgh printers. Smellie, in 1787, printed the Edinburgh edition of Burns' poems. James Pillans, an apprentice of William Smellie, admitted his son Hugh as a partner in a firm which became known as J. Pillans & Son. A separate business had been founded by another son, John, and the two merged in 1827 to become H & J Pillans.

Thomas Oliver began his printing career in a humble way, composing type on his mother's hearthstone. Twenty years later, in 1808, he took on as a partner a bookbinder called George Boyd, forming one of the most famous of Edinburgh's printing firms. Originally Oliver & Boyd worked closely with James Hogg, John Galt and Thomas Carlyle specialising in the printing of Scottish poetry. By 1836 it was the first firm in Edinburgh combining printing, bookbinding and publishing on a large scale within a single building. Another Edinburgh print firm, T & A Constable Ltd, had its origins at this time forming a joint printing and publishing enterprise. In 1835 the company became the King's Printer, doing so again in 1869. In 1859 it became the printer to Edinburgh University. James Ballantyne and Co., founded in 1796 in Kelso, moved to Edinburgh in 1802. They printed and published the poems and novels of Sir Walter Scott. Ballantyne's was a typical printing firm in nineteenth century Edinburgh, enjoying a close relationship with author and publisher, a reputation for high quality work, and producing a large output of books. Another famous Edinburgh printing firm – R & R Clark Ltd – created in 1846, played a prominent role in Edinburgh book printing enjoying close relationships with authors such as Robert Louis Stevenson, Rudyard Kipling and George Bernard Shaw.[9]

1837 saw the formation one of the best known Edinburgh printing houses. Originally founded as William Oliphant & Co a new partnership took over in 1841 when the firm became known as Murray and Gibb, renamed Morrison & Gibb in 1879, a title retained until its closure in 1985. A company closely associated with Edinburgh book printers was the bookbinders Hunter & Foulis Ltd founded in 1857 as William Hunter & Co.[10] Douglas A Foulis took over the firm in 1925 and it became known as Hunter & Foulis Ltd in 1946. It thus remained a family business becoming one of the largest publishers' bookbinders in the UK. By the 1890s bookbinding was undertaken for well known publishers such as J Bartholomew & Son, Hutchinson & Co, Methuen & Co, T & A Constable, Hodder & Stoughton and Kegan Paul and Whitaker.

ii. Glasgow

Significant developments in Glasgow book printing took place from 1740, after which there were seldom fewer than eight presses in the city. Two important presses were those of Robert and Andrew Foulis and Robert Urie. Robert Foulis, appointed Glasgow University Printer in 1743, specialised in high quality printing of classical works. Care, accuracy and the beauty of the typography were the characteristics of his work. While other printers provided products demanded by the general public, the Foulis press published classical books in Latin, Greek, English, French, Spanish and Italian. The work was in the forefront of European printing. This major contribution to the development of printing in Glasgow happened during a period of sustained economic activity and expansion for the city. It was the heyday of the 'tobacco lords' and the beginning of the development of Glasgow and the Clyde as a trading centre. Andrew Foulis junior is credited with the development of stereotyping, a process which played an important part in the production, on a large scale, of cheap editions of books for which there was a popular demand. The process invented by William Ged, an Edinburgh goldsmith in 1725, had been rejected by the industry. It was reintroduced successfully by Andrew Foulis and Alexander Tilloch in 1782.

The nineteenth century saw Glasgow University Press continue appointing a printer to the University. Early in the century new print firms were forming. Foremost amongst these were Blackie & Son and William Collins, names that became known worldwide and remained in existence almost to the end of the twentieth century. For Blackie & Son, formed in 1809, the 'numbers trade' was a major activity. Books in paperbound sections, called 'numbers' were sold by subscription. The sections were modestly priced and paid for one by one thereby putting books within the financial reach of relatively poor people. Although the 'number' trade formed a significant part of Blackie's production, the firm also published Bibles.

In 1819 William Collins (Printers and Publishers) was established. Dr Chalmers, a local preacher, whose sermons were renowned throughout Scotland, became dissatisfied with his publishers and transferred his work to William Collins and his brother, with whom he entered into a partnership. They bought out Chalmers and the company became known as Wm Collins Sons & Co. In 1824 Collins published its first dictionary and in 1842 obtained a licence to print and publish the Bible. Further growth of printing in Glasgow was seen in 1831 when James Bell and Andrew Bain founded the firm of Bell & Bain, which today still remains one of the oldest established printers in Glasgow, specialising in printing technical and scientific books. Another long surviving Glasgow firm, J & J Murdoch, had its origins in 1844. It developed into a major company, producing high quality labels for mineral water bottles and litho trade work for letterpress printers and stationers.

The second half of the nineteenth century saw consolidation and expansion of printing and publishing in Glasgow. Apart from the development of technology, the expansion was generated by the development of municipal libraries from 1850, repeal of the newspaper tax in 1855, the removal of excise duty in 1861 and population growth in the city. There were new demands for educational, travel and scientific books, encyclopaedias and dictionaries. As the population of Glasgow grew from 77,000 in 1800 to 333,000 in 1850, printing expanded. It was estimated that in the 1850s there were 300 hand presses and 120 driven by steam power. The Education Acts of 1870 (England and Wales) and 1872 (Scotland) making elementary education compulsory for all children, created an unprecedented demand for the printing of school and of children's books. The second half of the nineteenth century also saw the emergence of print firms still printing in Glasgow today. John McGavigan who started in Glasgow as a general printing shop in 1860 later extended to specialist screen printing. John McCormick & Co started in 1890 as a bookbinding and paper ruling company and continues to operate today from a city centre location. John Watson & Co continues in business there after 200 years.

iii. Dundee/Perth/Aberdeen

Although there had been little printing over the previous two centuries, from the middle of the eighteenth century Dundee developed into a leading Scottish print centre. In 1829 James Chalmers introduced the first lithographic works to Dundee and is well known as the designer of the first adhesive postage stamp in 1834. In 1865 the *Dundee Directory* listed eleven printers which had increased to thirteen by 1874 and by 1900 to twenty five. At the beginning of the nineteenth century the Valentine family was connected with the weaving industry. In 1840 James Valentine moved into printing, engraving and photography. Two of his sons (George and William) subsequently entered the business, developing it to international standards. In 1906 Valentine's labour force was 600, having been thirty in 1886. In 1903 Valentine claimed 25% of the UK postcard market.[11] In 1886 William Burns and his friend William Harris formed Burns & Harris as stationers, booksellers and printers, engaged in both letterpress and lithographic processes. They expanded their general print trade activities, one of their most successful developments being the printing of coloured labels for distillers, the jam and confectionery trades.

The main contribution to printing in Perth in the eighteenth and nineteenth centuries was came from the Morison family, starting with Robert the elder, who combined bookselling with being postmaster of Perth in the first half of the eighteenth century. The family connections with printing continued unbroken until, at the age of forty five, David Morison retired from the business and left Perth. Between 1773 and 1800 over forty book titles were printed on the Morison press. Another rising print firm in 1830 in Perth was Woods which gained a reputation for high quality printing and for satisfying the growing demand for postage stamps. In the twentieth century the firm diversified into printing auction catalogues. Farquhar & Son started printing in Perth in 1870, becoming best known as bookbinders and paper makers. In the 1950s they moved into continuous stationery and general print. Late nineteenth century and the early twentieth-century printing in Perth was influenced by Samuel Cowan who printed the *Perth Advertiser* but developed the general printing side of his business employing at one time over 100 compositors, many being women. His staff were mainly employed on book printing for London publishers. The company went bankrupt in 1907.

In 1768 Francis Douglas was replaced as the second printer in Aberdeen by John Boyle, who printed, like Douglas, the works of Pope, Swift and Voltaire and minor religious publications. His best known work was the family Bible published in two parts during 1769-71. This was the only complete Bible published in Aberdeen. The last notable printer in Aberdeen in the eighteenth century was Andrew Shirrefs but a number of printing failures, for example his *Caledonian Magazine* between 1786 and 1790, discouraged him and he left Aberdeen in 1791 to print in Edinburgh. By the mid-1830s there were twelve printing firms in Aberdeen City. Prominent among these were John Avery & Co, James Chalmers and G & R King. From its beginnings the Aberdeen University Press specialised in typesetting, including foreign languages and mathematical work.

Technological Developments
a. Letterpress Printing
From 1507 to the 1890s the dominant printing process in Scotland was letterpress, which used type or blocks as a raised surface to be printed. Letterpress printing was originally performed on platen machines in which the type remained stationary but later by machines in which the type bed reciprocated. The first stage of the process involved compositors arranging separate letters by hand to form words and lines of text, and subsequently distributing used type to the type case. This required considerable manual dexterity. Mechanical composition did not enter the Scottish printing industry until the 1890s. The second stage of the letterpress process applied ink to the surface to be printed. This process, called presswork, was done by pressmen. The operation of the presses relied heavily on manual strength.

Before the Industrial Revolution the average printing office employed small numbers. The master printer did most of the work himself assisted by one or two journeymen and apprentices. The amount of capital necessary to start a small print shop offered no barrier to the entrepreneur. The Industrial Revolution extended greatly the size of the Scottish printing industry, brought a decline in illiteracy and a diffusion of useful knowledge. It brought mechanisation to the press room whilst leaving composition unaffected. New technology was introduced into the press room as a gradual process. Iron and steam, the basis of the Industrial Revolution, entered the Scottish printing industry in the early nineteenth century. Steam presses became a feature from 1815. The iron presses which replaced wooden presses, were stronger, more accurate and a bigger sheet could be printed with less effort. The first revolutionary invention in the press rooms was the cylinder printing machine powered by hand and then by steam. These machines involved type placed on a flat bed, the print impression given by a cylinder and the inking of the forme done automatically by rollers. They could produce over 1,000 impressions per hour.

In the first half of the nineteenth century many small printing shops in Scotland still used wooden presses powered by hand. Power-driven printing machinery was introduced only in restricted offices in Edinburgh and Glasgow. In the second half of the nineteenth century technological developments in the jobbing and book sectors of the industry were less spectacular than in newspapers. Many smaller offices continued using the old iron hand-powered presses such as the Stanhope, Albion and Imperial. From the 1860s, small platen machines, such as the Cropper, either treadle or power operated, were introduced into jobbing offices. Flatbed machines with a cylinder impression, the most widely used being the Wharfedale, were first manufactured in the 1850s. These operated on the 'stop-cylinder' principle, producing around 1,000 to 1,500 impressions per hour but printed only on one side of the sheet. Perfecting machines were later introduced which printed on both sides of the sheet from two reciprocating type beds and two impression cylinders, the sheets reversed in their movement between the two cylinders, by either small drums or grippers. In the nineteenth century, technological innovations in the press room thus went from hand presses to cylinder machines driven by manual labour and to mechanically powered presses.

During the second half of the nineteenth century the majority of Scottish printing firms were private family businesses (see above). Book printing was concentrated in the large firms but the printing of posters, bills, circulars, tickets and other commercial work was undertaken by many businesses. Gradually the average number of workers employed per printing shop increased, until by 1900 at least one print firm in Glasgow employed nearly 2,000 people.[12]

Bookbinding operations comprised forwarding (folding, collating and sewing the printed sheets together) and finishing (attaching the case to the sewn sections, applying the title and decoration, gilding etc). The typical bindery shop employed only a few workmen, equipment was negligible and a journeyman could, with relative ease, become a master bookbinder. The small master bookbinders were independent companies fulfilling orders for customers, in some cases from their own homes. By 1850, however, bookbinding was a significant activity in both Glasgow and Edinburgh. The emphasis was on publishers' binding with books bound for special customers. By the 1850s cloth binding had largely superseded leather binding. Cloth was first used in 1822 in London by Archibald Leighton, whose father came from Aberdeen. In the early days of the use of bookcloth the bookbinder bought white calico in Manchester, sent it to London for dyeing and then to another firm to be calendered. By the 1870 this was no longer the case, with cloth purchased locally. It was not until 1832 it was possible to gold foil block a cloth-bound book.

In a typical bindery in the mid-nineteenth century, there was no gas lighting and when the employees in the winter months worked into the hours of darkness, a single candle or 'dip' in a tin candlestick provided the main illumination for each employee. The typical hand-operated machines were stamping presses, standing screw presses, hand cutting machines, laying and finishing presses, piercing machines, bevelling machines and glue pots. Robert Leighton in London pioneered steam-driven machinery for bookbinding and from the 1860s the revolutionary Caledonian Paper Cutting Machine was introduced by Scottish bookbinding companies. Other new equipment introduced in the second half of the nineteenth century included power-driven sewing machines, hydraulic presses, rolling machines, backing machines and gilding presses.

b. Lithographic Printing

Lithography was invented by a Bavarian artist and engraver Alois Senefelder in 1798. He discovered that by drawing on a smooth slab of calcareous stone, he could take prints from his drawings. This process was simpler than engraving which involved the cutting of the image to be printed into the surface of a copper plate from which prints could be taken. The invention itself gave the name to the process. The Greek words 'lithos', a stone and 'graphein' to write. In 1820 Mr Robertson established first lithography company in Scotland in Edinburgh.

James Chalmers introduced the first lithographic print works to Dundee in 1829 and became renowned as the designer, in 1834, of the first adhesive postage stamp. In 1851 Andrew Drummond set up the first litho business in Kirkcaldy.[13] The lithographic process was developed in Glasgow in the 1820s, although the name of the first printer to use litho in Glasgow is uncertain. However in March 1902, Thomas Murdoch presented to the Old Glasgow Club a paper entitled 'The Early History of Lithography in Glasgow', listing some names of printers involved in the process. These included Hugh Wilson, Maclure, MacDonald & Co (established in 1836) and Gilmour & Dean (formed in 1846). Maclure, MacDonald & Co were the first UK firm to use steam power for lithographic printing.[14] Gilmour & Dean supplied bank notes to all the Scottish banks but by the latter half of the twentieth century specialised in high quality labels primarily for the spirits industry.

Between 1860 and 1870 the cylinder press entered lithography. Previously presses were hand-operated. A bed carrying the printing stone with the sheet of paper laid on the top was covered by a leather tympan and all passed under a boxwork scraper which pressed tightly onto the stone making the print. The cylinder press by opening up quality printing, enabled lithographic printing to expand.

Compositor at the case.
Reproduced courtesy of the Scottish
Centre for the Book,
Edinburgh Napier University.

Employment Conditions
a. Wages and Hours of Work
i. The Edinburgh Interlocutor

In 1803 Edinburgh compositors received permission from the Sheriff for a meeting, from which a request for an increase in wages was made to the employers. The request went to the Law Courts which initially rejected the compositors' demands. They appealed to the Court of Session and in 1804 the Lord President, Ilay Campbell issued an interlocutor in favour of the compositors. The employers' appeal against the decision was rejected. The 1805 *Scale of Prices* for composing work now had legal backing. The Edinburgh compositors argued to the Court that in recent years the cost of living had risen by 33⅓% but their wages had not increased since 1792. Their memorandum for an increase concluded:

> …that their wages are the same as those given half a century ago while the price of living has risen more than one third. But the memorialists think themselves entitled to a rise of one quarter, as required to place them in the same state of comfortable luxury relative to the price of the articles of subsistence as formerly, as necessary to place them in a relative level with other workmen, both skilled and unskilled and as fully justified by the particular articles of labour which they are called upon to perform of the skill, knowledge, unremitting attention, long education and injury to health which are the requisites and concomitants of their employment…[15]

The *Scale of Prices* granted by the Interlocutor were:

> All work considered as common be cast up at 4½d per 1,000 ens including heads and directions.

Session-Work and Jobs be paid at the rate of 5½d per 1,000 ens.

All Dictionaries done in the manner of a Lexicon be paid at 5d per 1,000; but not to extend to Dictionaries of Science, or such as, from their nature, can be considered only as common matter.

Pamphlets of five sheets and under be paid one shilling per sheet above what they come to by letter for furniture and extra trouble.

All worker here to fore paid double (Greek and Scheme) take a proportionate advance according to the first proposition.

All work printed in a foreign language, though common type, be paid at 5d per 1,000.

All works done on Nonpareil be paid at 5d per 1,000 and on Pearl at 5½d per 1,000.

Grammars and School Books where Roman and Italic words occur alternatively, with braces, different justifications, etc be paid at 5½d per 1,000.

Newspapers be considered as liable to a proportionate advance according to the first proposition.

The employers reacted to the Interlocutor *Scale of Prices* by trying to avoid some of its high charges, by introducing a 'time system' of payment, together with piece-rate payment systems, with a consequent downward pressure on earnings. The scale nevertheless ensured industrial calm but the economic problems following the Napoleonic War meant the 'Interlocutor Scale' was overtaken by events.

ii. General Wage Increases

By 1849 the average wage of a skilled printer in Scotland was 15s 6d per week for a working week of at least sixty six hours. Over the decade 1852 to 1862 there were changes to wage rates. In 1853 the Scottish Typographical Association (STA) persuaded employers in Edinburgh and Glasgow the minimum wage be 25s 0d per week and outside these two cities 20s 0d. For ten years this remained the going wage rate but outside Edinburgh and Glasgow the wage rate was always less than 20s 0d, despite STA efforts to secure this rate. This period saw the end of an employer practice that had developed in Edinburgh after the 1847 strike of paying a person on the time-rate system more than the recognised minimum wage rate in return for which their hours of work were determined at the employer's discretion.

The period 1862 to 1870 saw increases in rates of pay throughout the whole Scottish printing industry. The increases were first achieved in Edinburgh with Glasgow soon following. In a series of increases in all sectors of the industry between 1862 and 1867 Edinburgh and Glasgow received similar enhancements in time and piece-rates. The time-rate for book and jobbing compositors became 27s 6d and the piece-rate 5½d per 1,000 ens. During the same period a general increase in wages also took place outside Glasgow and Edinburgh. By 1869 the STA objective of a 22s 0d per week minimum outside Glasgow and Edinburgh was exceeded in many areas. For example the time-rate in Greenock, Hamilton and Paisley was 25s 0d per week.

Further wage increase demands were made in 1870, reaching their peak with the Edinburgh strike of 1872. Glasgow triggered a round of wage increases by gaining in 1871 an increase for the book and jobbing sections. In 1872 print workers in Glasgow claimed a fifty-one-hour working week. Although this was achieved in daily morning newspapers, in other sectors of the industry in Glasgow a reduction only to fifty four hours per week was achieved along with the establishment of a time-rate of 30s 0d per week and a piece-rate of 6¾d per 1,000 ens.

In Edinburgh the STA gave highest priority to securing reductions in hours of work rather than increases in wages. Hours of work were reduced to fifty seven per week in 1865 and in 1871 the unions claimed a fifty-one-hour working week. The employers offered a reduction to fifty four hours with an increase of ½d per 1,000 ens on piece-rates. The union accepted the offer on an interim basis but in 1872 submitted a claim for the book printing and jobbing sector for a fifty-one-hour working week, an increase of ½d per 1,000 ens on piece-rates and for increased overtime rates. The employers rejected the claim and a three-month strike involving 750 employees, ensued. The Edinburgh employers minimised the impact of the strike by the introduction of non-union employees recruited in England, apprentices and female compositors. Eventually the employees returned to work accepting the employers' offer to enhance the time-wage and overtime rates. In the Edinburgh book and jobbing sections, the employment conditions of compositors were less favourable than those in Glasgow.

Reductions in hours of work to fifty one also took place in Aberdeen, Dumbarton, Dundee and Perth. In other areas of Scotland hours of work were reduced, varying between fifty four and fifty six. In Alloa weekly hours remained sixty. In Greenock the time-rate became the Glasgow rate of 30s 0d per week. Over the period 1872 to 1890 there was little change in wages and hours of work. Glasgow gained further advantage over Edinburgh as the time-rate increased to 32s 6d. Edinburgh's print workers claim for an increase of ½d per 1,000 ens on all piece-rates in the book section met with only partial success.

The economic situation throughout this period was depressed, a situation that did not favour improvements in employment conditions. In many industries, other than the printing industry, employees in this period accepted wage cuts. Attempts by a small number of Scottish printers to increase hours of work and/or reduce pay rates were unsuccessful. The majority of print employers, however, made no attempts to behave in this way.

During the nineteenth century a feature of wages in the Scottish printing industry was their relative stability over long periods. This was an advantage in times of deflation where in other industries wage cuts were implemented. Gillespie reports the 1886 *Wage Census* showed the relative position of printers to other skilled trades in a favourable light. The weekly rate in Glasgow was 32s 6d and in Edinburgh 30s 0d. The weekly rate for masons, on summer hours, was 29s 9d in both Edinburgh and Glasgow whilst engineering fitters in Glasgow received 27s 6d.

iii. Piece- and Time-Rates – the Edinburgh System

The continuation of the piece-rate system in Edinburgh contrasted with the situation elsewhere in Scotland. The explanation was said to be that the 1805 Interlocuter gave the scale a status it lacked elsewhere. A feature of Edinburgh book printing houses was the existence of a mixed payment system in which both piece- and time-rates operated in the same establishment. The Edinburgh employers considered some charges in the scale too high. To circumvent these they employed a number of men on an 'established wage' basis, by whom the highest priced work was undertaken. The least remunerative work was given to the piece-work employees. The result was the work done by time-rate employees, calculated at piece-rates, was worth more than the time-rate wage, whilst that done by the piece-rate workers gave average earnings considerably below the time-rate. This payment system led to claims of favouritism by employers in the distribution of work leading to grievances and ill-feelings between time-rate paid and piece-rate paid employees.

The position was made worse in that some employers gave preference in the allocation of work to apprentices and, after the 1872 strike, to female compositors. The system provided an incentive to employers to increase the number of apprentices they employed. They were usually employed on the simplest work which was often the best paid, in return for a relatively small rate of pay. The effect of the mixed payment system was to depress the average earnings of the majority of Edinburgh compositors.

iv. The Employment of Apprentices

During the late eighteenth and early nineteenth centuries, the Scottish printing industry expanded and many employers preferred to employ boy labour rather than journeymen. The restriction of apprentices was a major objective of the General Typographical Association of Scotland formed in 1836 and of the subsequent National Typographical Association. The frequent occurrence of large-scale unemployment in the nineteenth century, focussed attention increasingly on what print employees regarded as its root cause, namely the unlimited increase in the number of apprentices recruited by the employers.

For the print trade unions, the solution lay in restricting the number of apprentices to which employers could offer employment. In 1842 Edinburgh compositors petitioned their employers arguing the 'apprentice problem' arose from the growth of small masters and the resulting decline in the profits of 'reputable employers'. Although printing expanded rapidly the work was increasingly undertaken by boys instead of by craftsmen who as a result set themselves up as master printers. The consequent product market competition drove down print product prices. The Scottish print employers opposed the compositors' attempts to restrict the intake of apprentices to one for every three journeymen employed. The union was unable to enforce this policy and in 1850 there were in total 954 journeymen and 550 apprentices in the six towns of Dundee, Edinburgh, Glasgow, Kilmarnock, Perth and Stirling while for the whole of Scotland the estimated numbers were 1,500 journeymen and 1,200 apprentices.[16]

In 1858 the STA adopted the policy 'that branches shall fix the ratio of apprentices for their own guidance but in no case shall the minimum be lower than two apprentices to the firm and one apprentice to every two journeymen thereafter'. The policy was largely ignored by the employers. Throughout the 1860s the STA tried to remedy the 'apprentice question' around three approaches – the number allowed to enter the industry be restricted, a reduction in the length of the apprenticeship, and the abolition of apprenticeships. The main debate centred around the first two options, with the majority view emerging that the apprenticeship be reduced in length. Again STA policy had only limited success. In 1862 the number of apprentices in the six towns mentioned above had increased to 917 and that of journeymen to 1380. In Edinburgh the ratio of apprentices to journeymen had increased to 60% compared with 55% in 1850. In 1860 thirty three book and jobbing offices employed 133 journeymen and 136 apprentices. Outside of Glasgow and Edinburgh it was common practice to dismiss a man on the completion of his apprenticeship and replace him by two apprentices.

In 1872 the STA changed its policy allowing one apprentice to every three journeymen and one to the firm but again except in larger Scottish towns employers ignored the policy. The STA policy of restriction had, until the last decade of the nineteenth century, limited success. The restriction of numbers strategy was more successful post-1890 following the introduction of mechanical composition machines, which required better trained employees, resulting in a reduction in the number of apprentices employed. Mechanical composition made the STA's apprentice restriction policy, for so long a dead letter, effective.

v. Female compositors

By the 1860s women were seeking employment in less dangerous, but more skilful tasks, of the composing room. These women, from higher income group families, desired paid work not, as with women from the working classes, from necessity. The pressure for women to enter the composing room was initially seen by compositors as the work of social reformers, a view reinforced by the failure in 1865 of the Caledonian Press established in 1861 by the Scottish National Institution for Promoting the Employment of Women in the Art of Printing, a philanthropic body. Eight girl apprentices had been employed with three journeymen tutors.

The situation was fundamentally changed by the unsuccessful 1872 compositors' strike. The striking compositors were replaced by non-union labour and by women and an outcome of the strike was the continued employment of women by major Edinburgh printing firms on rates of pay less than those for men. By 1875 there were, in Edinburgh book and jobbing houses, 100 female compositors in direct competition with journeymen. By 1890 the employment of women in Edinburgh composing rooms was widespread. Robert Clark of R & R Clark claimed the distinction of training Fanny McPherson as the first woman compositor in Great Britain. Women compositors remained in employment and the STA accepted the reality of the situation. In 1886, the union accepted the employment of women in the composing room, and admitted them into membership, provided they were paid the same as men. Edinburgh remained a major exception to this policy. There, the reality could not yet be changed and by 1890 a pool of female compositors remained in competition with the STA journeymen.

Industrial Relations Pre-1890

a. Employees

When the numbers employed in print offices increased, chapel organisation emerged through which journeymen printers exercised self-government.[17] Membership was compulsory. Journeymen became members when engaged by the master printer and apprentices on finishing their training. The head of the chapel was called the Father and its income came from entry fees, fines for breaching chapel rules and general contributions. The chapel disciplined men through fines and provided help in times of misfortune. It was a democratic workplace institution with authority to make rules on a range of issues relating to the organisation of production and the personal conduct of its members. Originally 'chapels' included both masters and men but the increasing employment size of print workplaces resulted in the separation of master printers and employees.

In 1799, compositors in Edinburgh elected a standing committee thought to be the earliest example of employee organisation in the Scottish printing industry. Trade unions were illegal under the Combination Acts of 1799 but continued, often under the disguise of a friendly society. The standing committee functioned as a trade body via its informal nature. It met in taverns and workplace issues were discussed, disputes reported and decisions taken which were implemented by the chapels. A trade society proper amongst Edinburgh journeymen printers was formed between 1826 and 1836 but trade unionism in the Edinburgh print trade only prospered after 1840.

A trade society was instituted in Glasgow in 1817. It had three objectives. First to provide financial support for members required to leave the city in search of employment. Second, to furnish money to such members as could find employment in the city and third to co-operate with other places in exposing irregular work and maintaining a friendly interaction throughout the trade. The Glasgow Trade Society was concerned with the relief of unemployment under the tramping system but had a watching brief over wage rates. The society recruited only journeymen and the entrance fee and the monthly contribution was 6d. Under the tramping system an unemployed member received a card confirming their position as a member and travelled on foot around the country searching for work. On presentation of his card at each place visited they received food and lodging and in the absence of work a sum of money to help them on their way. This was sometimes supplemented by the charity of members of local chapels. If, on the completion of the tour of the branches, they failed to gain permanent employment, they returned to their home town and society. The Glasgow Trade Society *Regulations* provided a member setting out in search of work with 15s 0d or if married 21s 0d. A tramp visiting Glasgow received 7s 0d provided they were a member of a similar society. The sum of 5s 0d was paid to strangers who had not had an opportunity to become a member of a similar society provided they were 'free of professional opprobrium'.

The first attempt at Scotland-wide employee organisation in the printing industry was in 1836 when the General Typographical Association of Scotland was formed in August of that year. The Glasgow Trade Society played a major role in the formation of the General Typographical Association although Edinburgh was the main centre of the Scottish printing industry and the number employed there exceeded that of Glasgow. The General Typographical Association sought uniform rates of pay, to regulate the number of apprentices and to equalise the pay of pressmen and of compositors. In 1843 the General Typographical Association had 700 members in fifteen branches, including Aberdeen, Dumfries, Edinburgh, Glasgow, Kelso, Kilmarnock, Montrose, Perth and Stirling. The Association's members faced problems of unemployment, straining its finances severely and making amalgamation a necessity.

In July 1844, the General Typographical Association of Scotland merged with the National Typographical Association which covered England, Ireland and Wales. It comprised five districts – of which Scotland was its Northern District. Each district was governed by a board. The Association sought to support and maintain members on strike and unemployed, and replace the 'tramping system' with a system of unemployment benefit. The Northern Board, administered by the Edinburgh Society, reached agreement with the employers on a minimum wage rate of 25s 0d per week in all places within ten miles of Edinburgh and Glasgow and elsewhere 20s 0d. 1846 severely strained the National Typographical Association finances. Trade was depressed and there were numerous disputes.

The Association's funds became badly depleted. By December 1846 the Northern Board had little or no funds, and the 'death blow' was the 1847 Edinburgh strike. The financial viability of the National Typographical Association required a radical revision of its rules and practices. Although this happened, it proved impossible to keep the Association viable and in 1848 it collapsed.

Of the fifteen typographical societies in Scotland only two – Edinburgh and Glasgow – survived the collapse of the National Typographical Association. The Aberdeen Society announced its inability to carry on before the Northern Board was dissolved. The Edinburgh Society had suffered badly and it was 1851 before it again became financially viable. The first attempts to re-form a Scottish association came from the Glasgow Society in January 1849. Trading conditions at the time were poor and attempts to revive a Scotland-wide skilled printers' organisation proved premature. In 1851 however, the Glasgow Society formed a committee reviving the Scottish Association. In December 1851 the Edinburgh Society approved the Glasgow Society's scheme and was followed quickly by the Kilmarnock and Paisley Societies. In November 1852 a delegate meeting was held in the Angus Temperance Hotel, Glasgow at which unanimous approval was given to the formation on 1 January 1853 of the Scottish Typographical Association (the STA).

b. Employers
i. Glasgow
Concerned by the rise of trade unionism, the Glasgow printing employers in 1837 formed the Glasgow Master Printers Association to defend their economic interests. In February 1837 the General Typographical Association of Scotland sought parity of pay for pressmen and compositors and in pursuit of this objective the Glasgow pressmen drew up a scale of prices based on rates prevailing over the last ten years in the main print houses in Glasgow. The employers opposed this demand and to reduce the influence of the General Typographical Association formed the Glasgow Master Printers Association. The employers' association agreed a number of policies including not to employ any members of the union. They also agreed that to protect their interests, members dismiss immediately all journeymen who were members of the union and refuse to employ apprentices who had left the office of another member without permission. The Glasgow Master Printers Association resolved to protect themselves against unjust attempts by journeyman to increase wages and restrict the number of apprentices and to support measures to promote a 'General Association of the Master Printers' throughout the United Kingdom. Workmen received notices to quit from a number of offices and sixty five journeymen and sixty apprentices were involved in the dispute. The union urged its members in Scotland to resist this challenge but the Glasgow Master Printers realised the outcome would influence significantly its future. The union imposed a levy of 5% of their wages on members to assist those involved, or affected by the dispute but unfortunately nothing was recorded about the dispute or its outcome.[18]

ii. Edinburgh

The creation of Northern District Board of the National Typographical Association in 1844 has been credited with the creation of the Master Printers Association in Edinburgh. Growing opposition by the employers to the activities of the Edinburgh Society led in October 1846 to thirty eight Edinburgh employers issuing a three part *Declaration*:

(1) No journeyman be taken into employment who either leaves or threatens to leave his employer on 'strike'.
(2) No journeyman be taken into employment without producing a certificate from his last employer.
(3) In all cases Masters prefer to employ Non-Unionists rather than Unionists.

In January 1847, the thirty eight members entered into dispute with the STA Edinburgh Society. On 27 January 1847 the employers' association requested the union accept the three resolutions on the penalty of dismissal and when it refused, 150 men were dismissed in early February. The union could only provide financial assistance to its members by asking those in other parts of Scotland to pay double subscriptions. This burden proved too heavy for most members to bear. The employers recruited sufficient non-union labour, mostly from England, to replace the strikers and to continue to supply their customers' orders. On 13 October 1847 the strike was terminated. The union was financially ruined and collapsed.

iii. Disputes

Over the period 1853 to 1871 relationships between the STA and the Master Printers Associations of Glasgow and Edinburgh were constructive. 1872, however, saw a major dispute in the industry. Again the venue was Edinburgh, with a strike over a reduction in the hours of work and a pay increase involving between 700 and 800 men and which lasted for three months. In September 1872 the STA presented a claim to the Edinburgh Masters Printers Association for a fifty-one-hour working week with an increase of ½d per 1,000 on piece-rates. In addition, pay improvements were sought for overtime working and for author's corrections. In October the Edinburgh Master Printers Association rejected the union's demands. The union imposed an overtime ban and gave fourteen days notice to strike from 1 November 1872. Further if no settlement was reached before the end of the fortnight's notice an advance of 2s 6d on the time-rate was a condition of any subsequent settlement. Towards the end of the notice period the union modified its claim, offering to accept any reductions in hours of work by instalments over a period of eighteen months with a reduction of one hour immediately. The overtime rate claim was reduced but to offset these concessions the weekly time-rate was to increase to 30s 0d. The employers offered to concede the 30s 0d wage and the reduced advance in overtime rates but refused to consider any reductions in hours or improvements in piece-rates.

The notices having expired some 750 men came out on strike, their number including compositors and machine minders. While the Edinburgh strikers, and in general Scottish compositors and pressmen, remained loyal to their union the employers replaced the strikers with non-union men chiefly from England and with apprentices and women compositors. By mid-February 1873 there were over 700 non-union men, women and apprentices in employment in the Edinburgh print industry and the STA had little option but to call off the strike on the terms offered at its start by the Edinburgh Master Printers Association. Although most of the strikers were immediately re-employed, a by-product was the establishment of women in the skilled grades of work in the Edinburgh print industry. In June 1873, fifty women compositors were employed in the city and in the following years their number increased.

Summary

The printing press was introduced into Edinburgh in 1507 when a patent was granted by King James IV to Walter Chepman and Androw Myllar. Its introduction into the rest of Scotland proceeded slowly. The beginning in Edinburgh in 1507 was followed by St Andrews in 1552, Stirling in 1571, Aberdeen in 1622 and in Glasgow in 1638 when the General Assembly of Scotland wanted the record of their decisions printed. These towns had no factories of any size. The printshops were small, one man or two at the most and it was not unusual for a printer to collect his tools and move from one place to another. Some of the well-known printing companies were started in the nineteenth century including Wm Collins Sons & Co, Bell & Bain. T & A Constable, R & R Clark, Blackie & Son, Valentine & Sons, Burns & Harris and Farquhar & Son. From 1507 to 1890 the dominant printing process in Scotland was letterpress.

In the nineteenth century technological innovations in the press room went from hand presses to cylinder machines driven by mechanically powered presses. The lithographic process was introduced into Scotland in the 1820s. During the period 1507 – 1890 in the Scottish printing industry, wages were relatively stable over long periods but the relative position of Scottish print workers to other skilled trades was favourable. The 1872 Edinburgh compositors' strike in the Edinburgh book trade resulted in women compositors establishing themselves as skilled employees, albeit at a lower wage than a skilled male employee.

Unionisation in the Scottish printing industry has its roots back to 1799 whilst 1853 witnessed the establishment of the Scottish Typographical Association. In response to the rise of trade unionism the master printers in Edinburgh and Glasgow established their own collective organisations to provide a counter weight to this growth of trade unionism.

Notes

1   A breviary is a book containing the service for each day, to be recited by those in orders of the Roman Catholic Church.

2   *A Reputation for Excellence: A History of the Edinburgh Printing Industry.* Edinburgh: Scottish Printing Archival Trust, Merchiston Publishing, 1990.

3   See Sarah C. Gillespie (1953). *The Scottish Typographical Association, 1853-1952.* Glasgow: MacLehose, p5.

4   Op cit, p7.

5   *A Reputation for Excellence: A History of the Aberdeen Printing Industry.* Edinburgh: Scottish Printing Archival Trust, Merchiston Publishing, 2000.

6   Op cit p3.

7   *A Reputation for Excellence: A History of the Glasgow Printing Industry.* Edinburgh: Scottish Printing Archival Trust, Merchiston Publishing, 1996.

8   *A Reputation for Excellence: A History of the Dundee and Perth Printing Industries.* Edinburgh: Scottish Printing Archival Trust, Merchiston Publishing, 1996.

9   In 1946 when George Bernard Shaw was approached by Penguin for permission to publish a series of ten of his plays Shaw stipulated one condition: that 'Clarks of Edinburgh must do the printing'. 100 copies of each were produced in record time.

10   Douglas A Foulis took over the company in 1925 and it became Hunter and Foulis Ltd in 1946. A milestone in the company's long history was its take-over of Henderson & Bisset in 1968. *See A Hundred Years of Publishers' Bookbinding, 1857-1957.* Edinburgh: privately printed for Hunter & Foulis, 1957.

11   Valentine & Sons merged with John Waddington in 1960. The postcard line ended in 1970 and for a period the firm concentrated on greeting cards. Valentine's closed down in October 1994.

12   *A Reputation for Excellence: A History of the Glasgow Printing Industry,* Edinburgh: Scottish Printing Archival Trust, Merchiston Publishing, 1996, p11.

13   See J. H Allen (1998), *Allen the Lithographers.* Kirkcaldy: Inglis Allen.

14   See *A Reputation for Excellence: A History of the Glasgow Printing Industry.* Edinburgh: Scottish Printing Archival Trust, Merchiston Publishing, 1994, p17.

15   See S.C. Gillespie (1953), *A Hundred Years of Progress: The Record of the Scottish Typographical Association, 1853-1952.* Glasgow: MacLehose, p23.

16   Op cit p92.

17   The explanation of the term 'chapel' is unknown. Some attributed it to the fact that Caxton set up his press in a small chapel attached to Westminster Abbey. Others have seen in it as a symbol of the close association of the early printing industry with the Church and theological writings.

18   See S.C. Gillespie (1953), *A Hundred Years of Progress: The Record of the Scottish Typographical Association, 1853-1952.* Glasgow: MacLehose, p29.

Part 1

THE SCOTTISH ALLIANCE OF EMPLOYERS IN THE PRINTING AND KINDRED TRADES, 1910-1952

Chapter 2

THE SCOTTISH ALLIANCE IN THE MAKING

This chapter examines why, in 1910, the Scottish Alliance of Masters in the Printing and Kindred Trades was formed. The main reasons included the economic expansion of the industry, the introduction of mechanical composition, the growth of trade union membership and power, and the creation of a national federation of print unions. Faced with changes in technology and the growing militancy of the unions, the Scottish print employers realised that to counteract this they required to create their own Scotland-wide collective organisation.

Introduction

Prior to 1890, the relative balance of bargaining power in the Scottish industry lay with the employers due to persistent unemployment in the industry, the introduction of power-driven presses and the unfavourable legal environment in which trade unions operated. The Combination Acts (1799) outlawed trade unions and though these were repealed in 1825 trade unions had no legal right to exist until the Trade Union Act (1871), or freedom to undertake peaceful picketing in industrial disputes until the Conspiracy and Protection of Property Act (1875). To retain their relatively superior bargaining power, Scottish print employers sought continually to reduce their costs of production, mainly by replacing the employment of highly skilled labour with untrained, female and apprentice labour.

The period 1890 to 1914 saw the relative balance of bargaining power and, therefore, the outcome of labour/management relations move in favour of print employees, due to the economic expansion of the industry, the introduction of mechanical composition, the growth of membership amongst craft print unions, the rise of 'new' unions of semi-skilled workers and the creation in 1902 of a national federation of print trade unions. Faced with changes in technology and the growing union militancy, master printers in the UK realised if they were to counteract collective union power, they must form collective organisations. The print employers in 1901 created a UK-wide collective organisation entitled the British Federation of Master Printers (BFMP) to resist the steady 'encroachment' of union rules on management prerogative. In 1910 the Scottish print employers formed a Scotland-wide body – the Scottish Alliance of Masters in the Printing and Kindred Trades. Although this Alliance affiliated to the British Federation of Master Printers it retained a significant degree of financial and industrial relations autonomy. It was created, inter alia, to take labour out of competition, to counterbalance print union power and to eliminate product market competition based on price cutting between Scottish master printers.

Economic Expansion of the Industry

Over the period 1890 to 1914 the demand for printed products in Scotland grew steadily, due amongst other things to the expansion in population. The introduction of compulsory education and the emergence of an increasing number of newspapers and periodicals also contributed. The reduction in the cost of books, stemming from the mass production of both printing and binding opened a large untapped market for cheap editions of books which became core business for many Scottish printing houses. Improvements in colour printing and photographic reproduction coincided with the rapid development of poster and display advertising. This gave a stimulus to the jobbing printing trade.

A feature of company organisation in the Scottish printing industry over the period 1890 to 1914 was the growth of larger production establishments. For example, the Parkside factory of Thomas Nelson and Sons in Edinburgh produced as routine work, over 30,000 volumes of books daily but could in an emergency double this output. Up to 1900 book printing relocated from London to Edinburgh where production costs were lower resulting from the employment of women compositors at lower pay rates than for male compositors. After the introduction of mechanical composition, Edinburgh master printers had to employ higher quality labour so that improved, and better quality, output offset increased overheads for capital charges. Edinburgh's competitive advantage in book production relative to London and the home counties began its decline from this time. Lagging in the installation of newer machines Edinburgh lost its share of the London publishers' book printing market to English provincial towns just outside London.

The period 1890 – 1914 witnessed a significant growth in employment in the Scottish printing industry. In 1891 the industry employed 36,000 of which 1,000 were women. By 1901 the number of employees had increased to 44,000 of which 20,000 were women. At the time of the formation of the Scottish Alliance the total number of employees was 56,000 of which 25,000 were women. Over the period 1891 to 1911 total employment in the industry rose by 20,000. In percentage terms there was a bigger increase in the employment of women relative to men. The employment of men increased by 32% but that of women by 79%.[1]

Technological Change

Mechanical composition first appeared in Scotland in the 1860s but it was not until the last decade of the nineteenth century that composing machines were widely used. By 1914 the technical revolution in composing was virtually complete. The major newspaper houses in Scotland were using Linotype machines and all the main book printing houses used Monotype machines. The transition to mechanical composition was swift after centuries of hand composition and in just two decades, for larger print offices, it was complete.

Composing machines invented pre-1890 were not economically viable compared with hand composition. They did not justify the capital investment. The earliest composing machines consisted of racks of letters connected with a keyboard. As the operator pressed the keys appropriate letters slid down a guide and were arranged in a line. On relatively simple composing work the operator could compose three times quicker than by hand but distribution of previously used metal type was time-consuming because of the need to arrange the letters the right way up in the racks. To make the earlier composing machines economical, master printers sought to have them operated by juvenile labour. Opposition from the STA, however, made this practice possible only in non-union printing houses.

The position changed with the arrival of the Linotype machine which proved not only workable but economical and practical and was the first typesetting machine in general use. The machine was first used in the USA in 1886 but there is no reference to when, or where, it was first introduced into Scotland. Trade union records first make reference to Linotype machines in 1890 when a dispute arose following their introduction into the office of the *Scottish Leader* in Edinburgh. Linotype machines consisted of a rack of brass matrices released by a keyboard mechanism and assembled into a line. When the operator pressed a lever the line of matrices was presented to a mould into which molten metal was then forced. The result was a line of type or 'slug' ready for assembly with other lines to form a galley. After the 'slug' had been cast the matrices were returned mechanically to their respective channels ready for use again. A large element in the cost of hand composing was distributing the type after use, an operation which cost about one quarter as much as the actual composition. The Linotype machine eliminated this expense for after printing the slugs were returned to the melting pot. Linotype established itself in the large Scottish newspaper houses, but was not introduced into the Scottish book and jobbing printing industry where production costs were a more important consideration than in newspaper publishing.

The second mechanical composing machine coming into general use in the last decade of the nineteenth century was the Monotype machine. It was first introduced into Scotland in 1899 in the *Glasgow Mail* office. The machine had two parts – a keyboard which punched holes in a continuous reel of paper and a casting machine, which produced individual letters. When the punched strip of paper from the keyboard was fed into the caster, compressed air forced through the holes guided a matrix into position over the mould and the required letter was then cast and moved out into the line. The machine cast spaces of the correct width to justify each line. It could be used as a simple typecaster and as a variety of typeface matrices were developed it eventually superseded the older typecasting equipment. As a typesetting machine, Monotype was in widest use in the Scottish bookwork and general printing industries. Although its output in terms of quality and quantity was comparable with the Linotype machine, its drawback was higher labour costs in that, unlike the Linotype two employees were required to operate it. On the other hand, the paper ribbon could be stored cheaply and be used an indefinite number of times, making the Monotype composing machine particularly suitable for bookwork where later printings or editions might be required.

Initially the introduction of composing machines caused the displacement of labour. By 1900, however, it was accepted that the employment impact of the machines had not been as bad as first feared. The expansion of the industry absorbed the men displaced and print companies outside Glasgow and Edinburgh began to recruit fewer apprentices rather than displace journeymen. In the case of compositors in Scotland there is no record of them opposing their introduction. As Gillespie remarked

> …When a perfected composing machine eventually arrived it was operated by STA members who were successfully protected against any general influence of cheap labour. Much of the credit for this situation was due to the long heralded but much delayed arrival of the composing machine. Compositors were not, therefore, unprepared for its arrival nor had they failed to learn from others the futility of opposing it…

In the press room there was not the same spectacular technological developments. The flatbed machine with a cylinder impression, such as a Wharfedale or Miehle, continued in general use. Over the period 1896 to 1914 lithographic printing was revolutionised by the development of offset printing in which the print was transferred to a rubber blanket cylinder before being applied to the paper. This process removed many technical difficulties and machine speeds increased to an average of between 1,500 and 3,000 copies per hour. As composing machines became more widespread, Scottish printers considered the appropriate rate of pay for the employees operating them. In 1891 the STA adopted two rules for the staffing of composing machines.[2] First the machines be operated solely by time-served craftsmen and recognised apprentices. Second no compositor be paid piece-work on composing machines until they were able to earn the time rate. Pay rates for operating composing machines were contained in house agreements.

There were a few areas where attempts were made by employers to operate their composing machines with cheaper female labour. Edinburgh had the largest number of female compositors prior to the introduction of composing machines. Aberdeen had a similar situation but on a smaller scale whilst in the late 1890s there were attempts to employ female labour in Dundee and Perth. Edinburgh had between 700 and 800 women compositors most of whom were being transferred from hand composition to mechanical machines, particularly Monotype machines. The rate paid to these women was less than half the rate for men. The employers felt uplifted when an arbiter rejected, in 1903, the STA Glasgow branch argument in support of a wage increase, that the presence of female compositors in Edinburgh affected adversely the Glasgow print companies' ability to compete with Edinburgh print firms.

In 1906 the print employers in Aberdeen and in Edinburgh opened negotiations with the STA over the employment of female compositors. In 1907, agreement was reached in Aberdeen under which employers accepted no further introduction of women to skilled jobs. The agreement was only reached after a fifteen week strike and one Aberdeen print house preferring to manage without unions. In the same year the number of women compositors employed in Dundee had been reduced to two whilst in 1909 the print employers in Perth reported no female labour was employed in the town at rates below those received by men. In 1909 the STA Edinburgh branch submitted a claim to the Edinburgh Master Printers Association 'that from 1 January 1910 there shall be no further introduction of females into the trade in Edinburgh nor any importation of female compositors from other centres and in future machine composition be solely undertaken by male union labour'. There followed a lengthy dispute which was not settled until September 1910 after strike notices tendered by members of all printing and kindred trade unions in Edinburgh.

The 1910 agreement contained four main provisions:
(1) women already employed in the composing room would remain
(2) no new recruits be taken on before 30 June 1916
(3) new keyboarding on composing machines be operated by union labour and 50% of make-up and corrections be undertaken by males.

(4) the STA Edinburgh Branch would make no claims for advances in hours of work or wages within the next three years.

Although the ban on the recruitment of female apprentices was originally for a period of six years it became permanent. All female compositors in the Edinburgh trade at this time had been apprenticed before the 1910 agreement and represented declining employment in the trade. In 1911, the STA created the Edinburgh Female Compositors Society. By 1918 female compositors in Edinburgh were fully organised and in the same year granted a vote on STA affairs. In 1920 the Edinburgh Female Compositors Society was given representation on the STA Executive council and in 1922 merged into the STA Edinburgh branch.

The Growth of Print Trade Unions
a. The Craft Unions

Over the period 1890 to 1914 the membership of the STA grew from 3,000 to 5,000, an increase of 67%. The membership of the lithographic pressmen's union, the Amalgamated Society of Lithographic Printers and Auxiliaries of Great Britain and Ireland (ASLP) grew steadily. In 1860 an organisation for litho printers entitled the Central Association of Lithographic and Copper-plate Printers was formed. It comprised seven societies – Belfast, Dublin, Edinburgh, Glasgow, Liverpool, Manchester and Sheffield. On 20 August 1862 the Central Association held its annual meeting, which lasted four days, in McArthur's Temperance Hotel, Trongate, Glasgow. The meeting discussed the possible amalgamation of the various Societies comprising the Central Association but postponed a decision on the matter. The Glasgow Society delegates for example were not prepared to vote in the issue.[3] In 1880, however, the then nine societies of the Central Association amalgamated to become the Amalgamated Society of Lithographic Printers and Auxiliaries of Great Britain and Ireland. Branches were established in Glasgow, Edinburgh and Dundee. The skilled litho machine managers' organisation had developed from a series of local societies into a national union with branches in Great Britain and Ireland.

In September 1885 the Society of Lithographic Artists, Designers, Engravers and Process Workers (SLADE) was formed.[4] It had a total membership of 252 in ten local societies, known as branches. None of these branches had been in Scotland. The membership of SLADE continued to grow and by 1888 three branches (Aberdeen – eighteen members; Edinburgh – ten members; and Glasgow – thirty four members) existed in Scotland. SLADE represented employees working in the origination stage of the lithographic printing process and process engraving. Like their counterparts in the machine room they were members of a UK-wide union.

b. The Bookbinders

In 1833, the Glasgow Society of Bookbinders advocated the formation of a national union of bookbinders to improve co-ordination and co-operation between its different local societies. In the mid 1830s most bookbinding centres had their own societies including Edinburgh and Glasgow. In 1835 the

Bookbinders' Consolidated Relief Fund brought together all local bookbinder societies outside London. Although the Glasgow Society joined the Consolidated Fund the Edinburgh Society stayed outside. The Consolidated Relief Fund was a benefit society to provide financial support to bookbinders travelling the country in search of work. In 1840 it changed its name to the Bookbinders' Consolidated Union concerned with the improvement of the employment conditions of bookbinders as well as the relief of its unemployed members. In 1872 the Consolidated Union enlarged its title to the Bookbinders and Machine Rulers Consolidated Union to recognise that machine rulers were a significant section within the union. In 1872 the Edinburgh Union Society of Journeymen Bookbinders, founded in 1822, dissolved itself and transferred membership into the Consolidated Union. By 1872 the Edinburgh branch had 265 members and the minimum rate of pay was 27s 0d per week whilst the Glasgow branch had 233 members and a minimum weekly pay rate of 28s 0d per week.[5]

The Bookbinders Consolidated Union was reluctant to organise women employed in bookbinding departments. As a consequence the National Amalgamated Society of Printers, Warehousemen and Cutters began organising women, leading to conflict with the Consolidated Union. In January 1911 the four different unions catering for bookbinders – the Consolidated Union, the London Consolidated Society, the Vellum Binders Society and the Daywork Bookbinding Society – merged as one national union called the National Union of Bookbinders and Machine Rulers. Scottish print employers now dealt with a nationally-based bookbinders' trade union organisation.

c. Semi-Skilled

One impact of the technological change implemented in the industry over the period 1890 to 1914 was the formation of unions by unskilled workers. Their members had little of the all-round training and nothing of the apprenticeship experience of skilled journeymen. The semi-skilled worker unions had aspirations which often conflicted with those of the craft union, which still desired to keep labourers, boys and women from access to the higher skilled and higher paid jobs. After 1890 the print craft unions witnessed, with mixed feelings, the growth of the Print Labourers Union which became the National Society of Operative Printers and Assistants (NATSOPA), of the Union for Warehousemen, Cutters and Assistants and of the National Union of Paper Mill Workers. The first named mainly confined its organisation to machine room assistants in newspapers and had little presence in Scotland.

In 1889 Alfred Evans founded the Printers' and Stationers' Warehousemen, Cutters and Assistants Union catering for non-craft men in printers or stationers' warehouses. These unloaded, stacked, sorted, cut and folded the paper. The objectives of the union included obtaining a minimum wage of 32s 0d per week for bookbinders' cutters, of 30s 0d per week for warehousemen and cutters, of 24s 0d per week for a warehouse assistant and a minimum of time and a quarter for overtime; to provide unemployment benefit; to reduce the hours of work and to regulate relationships between employers and workmen. On 1 January 1900 the National Amalgamated Society of Printers' Warehousemen and Cutters was formed via a merger of the Printers' and Stationers' Warehousemen, Cutters and Assistants and the Amalgamated Society of Printers' Warehousemen formed in 1893 by a marriage of the Caxton Society and the London Society of Warehousemen. The National Amalgamated Society established a branch in Glasgow. In 1914 the union merged with the National Union of Paper Mill Workers which had been established in 1890 to form the 15,000 member National Union of Printing and Paper Workers.[6]

d. The Printing and Kindred Trades Federation

In March 1890, George Kelley, General Secretary of the ASLP, wrote to all the printing and kindred trade unions proposing a conference of printing trades unions with the view to forming a federation. A conference was held in Manchester on 8 September 1890 to which the STA sent representatives. A subsequent meeting, held in 1891, agreed to establish an organisation to be called the Printing and Kindred Trades Federation (P&KTF). Its objectives would include combining for trade purposes and to secure unity of action amongst its affiliated unions. It would seek to establish more uniform working conditions throughout the industry and to co-ordinate union policies, especially during conflicts with employers. It would not, however, interfere in the internal management of any affiliated union nor with its rules and customs.

The London craft unions refused to join a national trade union federation preferring to form their own. The P&KTF started, therefore, as a purely non-London organisation. As neither the London or non-London P&KTF had an independent source of income their activities were confined to encouraging trade union co-operation. The STA joined the non-London based P&KTF in 1891 but withdrew the following year. This action followed a P&KTF decision to seek a reconciliation between the STA Edinburgh branch and the Edinburgh Machine Men who had seceded from the STA in 1874 arguing their affairs interests were not receiving adequate attention within the existing decision making structures of the STA.[7] Although this issue was not finally resolved until 1907 the STA rejoined the P&KTF. A conference was arranged in December 1900 between the London Federation and the non-London Federation. It decided in favour of the formation of a national federation with a strike fund based on the principle that support be given to each union from the funds of all. The new constitution agreed for a national Printing and Kindred Trades Federation came into being on 1 January 1902. It was, amongst other things, to secure unity of action amongst its affiliated unions and to prevent the occurrence of strikes but had no power to negotiate wages on behalf of its affiliates. It could bargain collectively on behalf of its affiliates on hours of work, holidays, pensions and apprentices' wages. The decision of the printing unions to establish a national federation was a significant factor in the decision of the printing employers to establish in 1900 the Federation of Master Printers and Allied Trades of the United Kingdom. The STA had played a leading part in the negotiations to form a national federation of printing union. This role was recognised in the appointment of John Templeton, the STA General Secretary, as the first Vice-President of the National Printing and Kindred Trades Federation.

Industrial Relations Problems, 1890 – 1911
a. The STA

In the 1890s the STA sought improvements in wages, hours and other employment conditions. The lead was taken by its Glasgow branch which established a time rate of 34s 0d for a fifty-two-and-a-half-hour week. Its Edinburgh branch obtained a rate of 32s 0d per week for a fifty-two-and-a-half-hour week and an increase of ¼d per 1,000 on the piece rate. The STA's Greenock and Paisley branches established the Glasgow rate. In 1903 the STA Glasgow branch claimed an increase of 3s 6d per week. The claim went to arbitration but was rejected by the arbiter on the grounds that in Edinburgh rates of pay were 2s 0d per week lower for a longer working week. The arbiter considered a further rise in Glasgow rates relative to Edinburgh would result in Glasgow losing work to Edinburgh. The Glasgow branch renewed its claim in 1907 and after protracted negotiations secured an increase of 1s 6d per week with a further 6d the following year. This was the first increase the Glasgow Master Printers Association had granted since 1891.

The Glasgow STA branch was, in the period 1890 – 1911, concerned about payment to members operating the new composing machines. In 1904 it submitted a claim to the Glasgow Master Printers Association for a wage of £2 for Monotype operators, an objective achieved in 1905. In the following year a new scale for mechanical composition in book printing and the jobbing trade was approved. As part of the general wage advance, in 1907 the rate for mechanical composition was increased by 2s 0d while a further increase of 3s 0d was granted in 1914.

In 1901 the Glasgow Branch sought a forty-eight-hour working week but in the face of the opposition from the Glasgow Master Printers Association, accepted a reduction to fifty hours with forty eight and a half hours for night shift workers. By 1902 over half the STA membership enjoyed a fifty-hour week. In Edinburgh hours of work remained at fifty two and a half. Gillespie reported the outcome of wage changes in Glasgow over the period 1890 to 1914 as:

> ...the outcome of the improvements in Glasgow during this ten year period was to establish a stab rate for book and jobbing of 38/- for a fifty-hour week, an increase of 4/- over the period, with no reduction in hours; for composing machines the rates were 45/- and 43/- for Monotype...[8]

During the period 1890 to 1914 pay rates in Edinburgh lagged behind those of Glasgow. In 1908 hours of work in Edinburgh were reduced to fifty per week with an increase of ½d on time rates. In 1910 the Edinburgh Master Printers Association reached an agreement with the STA Edinburgh Branch under which the union accepted a three-year moratorium on claims for hours, wages and other terms of employment in return for the employers reducing the employment of female compositors. By 1914 in the Scottish printing industry the lowest wage rate was 27s 6d per week in print offices in Dingwall whilst in Cupar, Stranraer and Wick the weekly rate was 28s 0d. In Greenock and Paisley the Glasgow rate of 30s 0d prevailed whilst most employees in the industry throughout Scotland worked a fifty-hour week. As a result the STA was not a signatory to the 1911 P&KTF/BFMP agreement for the phased introduction of a reduction of hours of work to fifty one.

b. The Lithographers

In 1890, members of the ASLP Glasgow branch claimed an increase in the minimum rate of 25s 6d to 30s 0d per week. When the two sets of representatives met the employers offered an increase of 1s 2d per hour. This was rejected by the union which said they would accept nothing less than their original demand of 30s 0d per week. At a further meeting the employers refused to improve their original offer, following which a number of individual litho employers conceded the union claim. One of these conceding companies was a member of the employers' negotiating team. The dispute was then quickly settled on the following terms:

(1) apprentices on the expiry of their apprenticeship be paid 27s 6d per week for one year;

(2) all journeymen whose salary at present was 27s 0d or less be paid 27s 6d per week for one year;

(3) journeymen whose salary at present was less than 30s 0d per week but more than 27s 6d be paid 30s 0d per week for fifty one hours or 29s 0d for fifty four hours in place of 27s 6d for fifty one hours and 32s 0d for fifty four hours in place of 30s 0d for fifty one hours.[9]

In 1903 the ASLP aimed to fix the rate of wages for its members operating rotary machines at 55s 0d per week in London and at 45s 0d outside of London and was prepared to take industrial action to enforce the policy. The Glasgow and West of Scotland Master Lithographers Association resolved 'that members leaving one situation for another should not receive a higher wage than that they had been in receipt of during the last six months in their previous situation'. This resolution irritated Glasgow ASLP members. They sought a meeting with the employers but when no response resulted, an ultimatum was issued to the Master Lithographers Association that if they continued with their policy a claim would be made that the minimum rate be raised from 34s 0d to 36s 0d. After consideration the Master Lithographers Association withdrew their resolution and the matter was resolved peacefully.[10]

In 1890 the Paisley litho employers were faced with a demand for a reduction of weekly hours from fifty seven to fifty one to obtain parity with conditions in Glasgow which was only seven miles away. At a meeting of employers and employees a compromise was agreed that hours of work be reduced to fifty three and a half. By 1900 in Glasgow litho printers had weekly hours of fifty one but owing to the letterpress and bookbinding hours being still fifty four, litho craftsmen worked in shops where the other kindred trades worked fifty two hours but they received 2s 0d more per week. In 1900 the working hours of litho printers in Aberdeen were reduced from fifty one to fifty per week on condition 'that the men in the printing and allied trades unions hereby agree to keep time so that a full week of fifty hours shall be worked. If this condition is not implemented by the employees the employers reserve the right to return to fifty one hours'.

c. Bookbinders

The major industrial relations event over the period 1890 – 1911 was the dispute between Wm Collins Sons & Co, Glasgow and the Glasgow branch of the Bookbinders Consolidated Union over employment in the bindery of lower paid female labour. In 1896, the 229 female employees of the company were paid rates between 6s 0d and 8s 0d per week. The union's Glasgow branch wished to call a strike over the issue of lower paid labour but the national union did not consider the branch organisationally or financially capable to undertake such action. It persuaded the Glasgow branch to agree to employ a 'Special Organiser' for six weeks to undertake organising work in Glasgow.

In 1897, Wm Collins Sons & Co forced the issue. At a meeting of employees Mr Collins announced he wanted to know whether they approved (or disapproved) of a letter sent by the Special Organiser to a certain religious body. When the employees expressed their approval, the company stated that due to the interference by the Organiser of the Bookbinders Consolidated Union with its customers, its bookbinding department was non-union and any worker who disliked this action was free to resign from the company. The employees submitted their resignations but the national union disclaimed responsibility for the men's action. Nevertheless it supported the Glasgow branch and advised its branches throughout Great Britain to support Glasgow financially. This they did on a generous scale. The union's branches sent delegations to Wm Collins Sons & Co, to Parliament and to the press whilst the national union provided strike benefit at 15s 0d per week. By September 1898 the dispute had absorbed nearly a third of the national union's total funds.

The dispute was not settled until June 1900, following the intervention of the union's Bradford Branch. The Bradford Trades Council questioned whether the 'Fair Contracts Resolution' of the Bradford School Board was being observed by Collins in its production of school books. An inquiry was held but it deferred 'to give the parties at variance an opportunity to close the breach and arrange for future amicable working'.[11] A conference held in Glasgow on 23 June 1900 between representatives of Wm Collins Sons & Co, the Bradford Trades Council, the Glasgow branch and the head office of the Bookbinders Consolidated Union resulted in agreement. The union withdrew the Special Organiser's letter of 1897 and signed a statement to the effect that the firm was managed on similar lines to other bookbinding departments in Glasgow. In return the company pledged to pay all bookbinders and machine rulers the minimum rates of wages paid by members of the Glasgow Master Bookbinders Association and that when vacancies occurred they would recruit employees via the union.

In reality the dispute had not been settled. By 1901 the number of union members in the firm was only six. The union was critical of the company's application of the agreement, particularly the recruitment of future labour needs via the union, and its members were again pressing for strike action against the company. The national union raised its grievance with the Chairman of the Bradford School Board, explaining the 'supposed' agreement was not operating as intended because its parties had widely different views of what they considered they had agreed. In 1903 the Wm Collins Sons & Co dispute was satisfactorily resolved. By this time there were twenty five union members working in the company which gave an assurance that it had no objection to its employees becoming union members. In return the union was to make no further applications for improvements in wages and other employment conditions for a period of five years. The union accepted reluctantly the deal hoping over the next five years to at least double its membership in the company.

d. The Printing and Kindred Trades Federation

In 1908, the P&KTF submitted a claim to the BFMP for a forty-eight-hour working week arguing the work of employment in the printing industry was onerous, arduous and monotonous so a reduction in hours of work would result in a higher standard of work. In presenting the claim the P&KTF argued the introduction of new machinery had enhanced labour productivity and the employees should share in the benefits of this improvement. The BFMP rejected the claim declining to negotiate on the question. A conference was held in 1909 between the BFMP and the P&KTF with the former refusing to take the matter any further. In November the P&KTF again pressed for a conference but the BFMP again rejected the claim arguing many printing offices were non-union so any concessions might place unionised houses at an even greater competitive disadvantage than at present.

In September 1910, the P&KTF submitted a claim to the BFMP for a fifty-one-hour working week from 1 January 1911 and for a forty-eight-hour working week from exactly a year later. At this point the STA withdrew from the UK-wide campaign to secure the forty-eight-hour working week. It preferred to postpone any industrial action as the prospect of the P&KTF paying strike benefit for thousands of men had serious consequences for the financial viability of the P&KTF. The London unions, left to pursue the forty-eight-hour working week on their own, struck to achieve this objective on 6 February 1911. Three English provincial printing unions made an agreement with the BFMP in March 1911 whereby in towns working fifty two hours or less hours of work were reduced in May 1911 to fifty one hours.

In towns working fifty two and a half and fifty three hours, working time was reduced by one hour in May 1911 and to fifty one hours in May 1912. Towns working fifty four hours and above saw reductions to fifty three hours in May with one further hour per year until a fifty-one-hour working was reached.

In Scotland, a campaign for the reduction of hours had started in 1901. In Glasgow weekly working hours were fifty – less than in the BFMP/P&KTF 1911 agreement but in Edinburgh remained at fifty two and a half per week. By 1914 half the employees in the Scottish printing industry enjoyed a fifty-hour working week. In 1911 the ASLP Edinburgh branch requested a forty-eight-hour week and an increase in wage rates. Both were refused by the Edinburgh and East of Scotland Master Lithographers Association. The ASLP instructed its members to hand in their notices but this was followed by lockout notices from the employers. The ASLP attended a conference at which the employers agreed a wage increase but hours of work remained unchanged.[12]

The Formation of Employers' Associations
a. The British Federation of Master Printers (BFMP)

Confronted with growing print union membership and market power, printing employers in Britain concluded they required their own collective organisation as a countervailing power to the unions. 15 April 1901, saw the formation of the British Federation of Master Printers and Allied Trades of Great Britain and Ireland.[13] The idea of the Federation was conceived in Glasgow in 1897. When the London Master Printers Association was founded in 1890, there was talk of extending its organisation to embrace the whole of Great Britain and Ireland but nothing came of it. In 1897 there were two main collective organisations of print employers in Glasgow – the Glasgow Master Printers Association and the Glasgow and West of Scotland Master Lithographers Association. The latter organisation proposed a British- and Irish-wide federation of litho print employers, with a head office in Leeds, for exchanging information on wages and other conditions of employment and to assist member firms when disputes occurred with employees and their trade union. Nothing came of this initiative but in 1899 the Glasgow and West of Scotland Master Lithographers Association issued a circular to all master printers' associations in the country. A conference at Leeds, or some other convenient venue, was suggested. The circular was distributed under the signature of Walter McLean, President of the Association. Originally it was intended the meeting be restricted to lithographers but it was eventually agreed to include letterpress printers.

The conference was duly held in Leeds on 9 October 1899 and delegates attended from master printer organisations from London, Manchester, Glasgow (Walter McLean), Birmingham, Sheffield, Derby, Leeds, Bradford and Burnley. The conference accepted the London Master Printers Association proposal to federate into one collective organisation all the Master Printers Societies in Great Britain and Ireland for their mutual benefit. A committee was formed to draft a constitution.

Over eighteen months passed before the draft constitution was approved at a meeting in Leeds held on 15 April 1901. The British Master Printers Federation's first official meeting took place on 28 May 1901, at which Walter McLean from Glasgow and West of Scotland Master Lithographers Association was elected to its governing council. He became President of the BMPF in 1904.[14]

The BFMP performed three major functions. First it engaged in political lobbying and kept watch on parliamentary bills likely to affect the interests of master printers. The first years of the twentieth century saw the intervention of many state and local bodies in the conduct of business, for example the Workmen's Compensation Act (1897).[15] Given this increasing government intervention it was crucial employers had an industrial pressure group to protect, and advance, their interests amongst political decision makers. It was also important for master printers to have an organisation to help them find their way through the growing complexity of government regulations. Second, it negotiated collectively on behalf of master printers with the trade unions and by so doing took 'wages out of competition' by setting national minimum standards applicable to all member firms of the BFMP. Third, it established a proper costing system for the industry to eliminate unsound price-cutting between master printers. It formulated a set of rules to protect master printers from the unreasonable demands of their customers.

b. The Scottish Alliance of Masters in Printing and Kindred Trades

Confronted with growing trade union membership, the rise of national print union organisations, a national federation of print trade unions, and the industrial relations problems of the early twentieth century, Scottish printing employers recognised they required a collective organisation to resist the steady 'encroachment' of union rules into managerial prerogatives. To this end Scottish employers played a major role in bringing into being in 1901 the British Federation of Master Printers (BFMP) and then in 1910 the Scottish Alliance of Masters in the Printing and Kindred Trades.

At the time of the formation of the BFMP there existed in Scotland four main printing employers' associations. At the meeting held on 22 December 1876 at 87 St Vincent Street, Glasgow there was a proposal, unanimously accepted, that an association of Master Printers of Glasgow be founded. The catalyst for this meeting was a demand from print journeymen in the city for an increase in wages. Having agreed to establish a Master Printers association the employers considered the request for a wage increase but unanimously agreed to reject it. The objective of the Glasgow Master Printers Association 'shall be mutual confidence respecting matters affecting the trade and joint action when needful or advisable'. In November 1892 the Scottish Association and the STA set up an arbitration committee to consider any disputes arising from the interpretation of the price scale or other matters. The committee consisted of three employer representatives and three employee representatives. In the early years of the twentieth century the litho print employers of Glasgow created the Glasgow and West of Scotland Master Lithographers Association. They were quickly followed by Glasgow bookbinding employers who created the Glasgow Master Bookbinders Association. All three Glasgow print employers' associations were located in offices in St Vincent Street.

In 1846 the master printers of Edinburgh established the Edinburgh Master Printers Association. Its objectives were fourfold:

(1) to discuss matters of common interest to the trade in Edinburgh and its neighbourhood with a view to concerted action
(2) to monitor legislation as may affect the trade's interest and to take action if necessary
(3) to maintain uniformity of working hours, customs and rates of wages and
(4) to ensure members did not employ any apprentice (male or female) from the establishment of another member without a note from his or her last employer certifying he or she is free to change employers.

Like the Glasgow Master Printers Association, the Edinburgh Master Printers Association decision-making machinery consisted of an executive council and an annual general meeting serviced by office bearers such as a president, vice-president, treasurer and secretary. Any member company in dispute with their employees contacted the Association Secretary who submitted the matter to the Executive Council or, after May 1899, under a collective agreement with the STA, to the Arbitration Committee. This committee, consisting of three employer and three employee representatives was mutually agreed on 12 May 1899. Before the turn of the century, the Edinburgh litho employers, to combat growing union power, formed the Edinburgh and East of Scotland Master Lithographers Association. About the same time the Edinburgh bookbinders, like their counterparts in Glasgow, formed the Edinburgh Master Binders and Machine Rulers Association.

The first decade of the twentieth century witnessed the formation of collective bodies of print employers outside of Glasgow and Edinburgh. The Dundee Master Printers Association was formed followed by the creation of the Association of Master Printers and Lithographers of Dundee and District. In November 1906 the Master Printers of Kirkcaldy agreed to be 'banded together in the same union' and sought the BFMP advice on how to achieve this. In 1908 they joined the Edinburgh and East of Scotland Master Lithographers Association. The master printers of Greenock also combined to create the Greenock Master Printers Association. Printers in Falkirk, Perth and Stirling were co-operating with each other in resisting trade union power but did not create any formal collective master printers' organisation.

The forming of a Scottish federation of masters in the printing and kindred trades had occupied the minds of master printers in Edinburgh and Glasgow for some time. This took practical shape in October 1910 when a meeting of delegates from the existing Master Printers, Master Lithographers, Master Bookbinders Associations and other interested parties was convened to further this aim.

A notice from Edward M. Murray, Honorary Secretary of the Edinburgh Master Printers Association, dated 4 October 1910, proposed a Scottish federation of masters in the printing and allied trades and urged support for a Scotland-wide printing employers' organisation in the following terms:

> The Scottish Alliance of Masters in the Printing and Kindred Trades
>
> ...A strong feeling exists in this and other towns that no time should be lost in amalgamating and strengthening all forces at the disposal of the masters in the above trades.
>
> If the Association is in sympathy with this movement we invite you to send two delegates to a conference to be held in Edinburgh at a date which will be intimated later.
>
> This Federation will in no sense be antagonistic to the Federation of the United Kingdom of Great Britain and Ireland but, on the contrary, it is hoped it will greatly add to its power and effectiveness.
>
> Kindly fill in the enclosed circular and send it to me by return...

The meeting to consider the establishment of a Scottish Alliance was held on 8 November 1910 at the North British Station Hotel, Edinburgh at 2.30 pm and attended by delegates from the Association of Master Printers of Dundee (one), Edinburgh (two delegates), Glasgow (two delegates) and Greenock (two), the Master Lithographer Associations of Dundee and District, Edinburgh and East of Scotland and Glasgow and the West of Scotland (three) the Association of Master Bookbinders and Machine Rulers of Edinburgh (three delegates) and Glasgow Master Bookbinders Association. In addition there were representatives, but unaffiliated to any master printers' association, from Falkirk, Perth and Stirling printers and from the Edinburgh Stereotypers and the Edinburgh Process Engravers (two delegates). In total twenty three delegates were present. Duncan Cameron from the Edinburgh Master Printers Association was unable, for business reasons, to attend the 8 November 1910 meeting but sent a letter of apology and in which he expressed support for the creation of the Scottish Federation. He considered such action as the only effective means to counteract the growing power of the trade unions which 'it must be admitted have already compelled us to accept obnoxious conditions and whose inequitable demands show no sign of abating'.[16] He hoped the meeting would recognise the necessity for an organising secretary who would devote their whole time to organising master printers for the protection of their businesses.

The delegates were received by Walter Blaikie, President of Edinburgh Master Printers Association. It was proposed by David Cumming (President of the

Edinburgh and East of Scotland Master Lithographers Association) and seconded by George Stewart (Edinburgh Master Bookbinders and Machine Rulers Association) that Mr Blaikie take the chair and Mr Thomlinson (President, Glasgow Master Printers Association) be the Vice-Chair. The Chair explained that from recent industrial relations problems in Edinburgh had sprung the desire to to consult with colleagues in the trade in different parts of the country on the advisability of mutually strengthening and protecting each other. The general tenor of the meeting was that unless the proposed federation had powers over its members and could bind the different interests together in collective bargaining, the setting up of a federation would be pointless. The Acting Secretary intervened once or twice in the debate to give evidence from his enquiries amongst the strongest federations of masters in other industries in the country. He gave instances where the masters had been successful in disputes with their operatives because the strength of the collective organisation of the employers was acknowledged by both sides. Delegates made the point if the Scottish Alliance were to be established 'it must be one from which every member would draw strength in his dealings with the men'. Further opinions were expressed by the delegates as to having the services of a secretary, who would gain the confidence of the employers and the respect of the men. One delegate remarked 'At meetings we bark but don't bite subsequently and therefore there should be a mandatory obligation on our members in case of desertion' while another argued a federation would be useless if it did not have sanctions to enforce its policies.

The general feeling was that if the federation could be started on the right lines there was a great possibility of its success. Mr Thomlinson (Glasgow) seconded by Frank Mudie (D. C. Thomson & Co Ltd, Dundee) moved successfully the following resolution:

> …That this meeting of delegates from the various Associations of Masters in the Printing and Allied Trades of Scotland resolves to constitute the Scottish Federation of Masters in the Printing and Allied Trades for the purposes of mutual help and protection…

Given that the word 'federation' might be confused with other bodies, George Stewart of Edinburgh's suggestion the word 'alliance' be substituted was agreed. The meeting then appointed interim office bearers, an executive council, a treasurer and acting secretary.

In April 1911 Mr F H Bisset was appointed Secretary of the Scottish Alliance on an annual salary of £350 whilst offices were acquired in Frederick Street, Edinburgh at an annual rent of £45. A first draft of the constitution was prepared and issued at the end of May to the Master Associations of Edinburgh, Glasgow, Dundee, Greenock and Falkirk. In the light of these views a second draft was

Address presented by the Edinburgh Branch of the Printing & Kindred Trades Federation to the first Secretary of the Scottish Alliance, F H Bisset, in 1918

issued at the end of June 1911. The third, and final, draft, owing to the necessity of adjusting, reconciling and safeguarding the various interests and due to the holiday season, was only issued at the end of October. The constitution and rules of the Alliance were then adopted by all the local associations and companies then in membership. By the end of 1911 sixty five individual firms had taken out membership whilst nine local associations were in membership.[17]

The status of the Scottish Alliance vis-a-vis the British Federation of Master Printers was not easily settled. It was not until 1912 that agreement on this matter was reached. The Alliance would have six representatives on the BFMP Council but retained autonomy in financial and industrial relations matters. In his presidential address to the 1912 BFMP annual conference Walter Blaikie from T & A Constable, Edinburgh explained

...Scotsmen would take more interest in an organisation which they could consult for themselves in Edinburgh or Glasgow than they would do if they had to go all the way to London and perhaps be considered as provincial which they do not like...

Mr Blaikie asked the meeting to accept the Scottish Alliance and promised delegates the Alliance's members were with the Federation 'heart and soul'.[18] Mr Blaikie was elected President of the BFMP at its May 1912 meeting for the forthcoming year. He also achieved eminence as an authority on Scottish Jacobite history and, in particular the Rebellion of 1745.

The Alliance Resists the Unions
a. Piece Work in Edinburgh
In June 1912 the Edinburgh Typographical Association presented to the Master Printers of Edinburgh a request that piece working be abolished from 1 August 1913. The Master Printers rejected the demand but expressed a willingness to meet the union to discuss improving the employment conditions of piece workers. A conference followed but failed to produce satisfactory results with the STA refusing to consider proposals for improving the position of piece workers, repeating its demand for the abolition of piece work. The Edinburgh Master Printers Association, which considered this a breach of the 1911 agreement, indicated, with the approval of the Scottish Alliance that, failing the immediate withdrawal of the demand, lockout notices be issued forthwith. Two days later a letter was received from the Edinburgh Typographical Association stating its members, due to the threat of immediate lockout, had withdrawn their demand for the abolition of piece work.

b. The Employment of Females and Unskilled Male Labour
In September 1912 the Scottish District Council of the NUPB&MR presented a demand to every bookbinder and machine ruler in Scotland requesting agreement to proposals regarding the employment of females and unskilled male labour in bookbinding and paper ruling. The claim was considered by the local associations in the various districts but all agreed as the issue had national, rather than local implications, it be remitted to the Scottish Alliance to reply to the union on their behalf. The Scottish Alliance appointed a special committee, representative of the binding and ruling trades, to investigate the matter. On receipt of the committee's report the Scottish Alliance told the NUPB&MR its proposals were radical and would affect prejudicially the binding and ruling trades in Scotland. They had no alternative but to decline the union's claim.

The NUPB&MR, thereupon, suggested an exchange of views to which the Scottish Alliance agreed. A conference was held at which the two sides agreed to report progress to their constituents and thereafter meet again on 10 January 1913. The Executive Board repeated its position that although they were anxious to remove any real grievances they considered the demarcation of labour desired by the NUPB&MR a serious hindrance to the maintenance and development of the bookbinding and ruling trades in Scotland. The union's Scottish District Council described the Scottish Alliance's stand as 'extremely arbitrary' leaving them no choice but to take the fullest action in defence of their interests. The NUPB&MR national executive backed this decision and 600 of its members in Scotland were withdrawn from their employment after a ballot in favour of such action by 708 votes to 119. The strike lasted from early November until a settlement was reached on 17 December 1913.

Under this agreement a conciliation committee was appointed, consisting of equal numbers of representatives from the Scottish Alliance and the Scottish District Council of the NUPB&MR to consider grievances brought forward in Scotland by either side. Every future dispute was referred to this committee which reported to the Scottish Alliance and to the Scottish District Council of the union. Until this report had been published no aggressive action was to be taken by either side. This Conciliation Committee was an acceptance by both sides that they wished to see peaceful settlement of disputes. In future where a machine was introduced which replaced qualified male labour, the man in charge of the machine should be paid the standard rate and it be recommended by the Scottish Alliance to its members that qualified tradesmen had the first claim upon all machinery introduced in the future which displaced qualified male labour. In approving the agreement the Executive Board resolved 'that the thanks of the Board be accorded to the employers concerned for the united and successful resistance taken by them to the demands of the bookbinders union'.

c. The Proposed New Rules of the STA, 1912
The most serious business of the Scottish Alliance in 1912 was the dispute over the proposed new working rules of the STA. At its 1911 delegate meeting the STA adopted a series of radical alterations to its working rules with employers. These included a reduction of the maximum amount overtime permitted from twelve to nine hours per week, the abolition of suspension and employers to be required to give one week's notice before introducing short-time working. In 1912 STA branches attempted to enforce these new working rules without submitting them to the local print employers' association for consideration. At the insistence of its local associations the Scottish Alliance sought a conference with the STA on the proposed new rules. Despite an exchange of correspondence, extending over four months, the efforts of the Scottish Alliance to secure a conference had to be abandoned. It then informed the STA no new working rules which had not been mutually agreed would be recognised by its member firms.

Meanwhile protracted negotiations were taking place between the Glasgow Master Printers Association and the Glasgow branch of the STA. On 17 December 1912 the Glasgow branch of the STA informed the Glasgow Master Printers it would not enter further negotiations but would implement the new working rules immediately. Communication between the Glasgow Master Printers and the Edinburgh Master Printers followed and on 24 December 1912 the Scottish Alliance, at the request of the two local associations informed the union that failing the withdrawal of its intention to implement unilaterally the new proposed working rules, or to attend a joint conference, lockout notices would be issued in Glasgow and Edinburgh. In the light of this, joint conferences were held between the parties on 14 and 27 January 1913. These proved abortive and lockout notices were posted by the Glasgow and Edinburgh Master Printers Associations affecting some 2,500 workers representing from 85 to 90% of the members of the STA in its Glasgow and Edinburgh branches. The employers considered placing their work in other towns and to recruiting non-union labour.

At this stage the P&KTF asked the Scottish Alliance for a conference. A three-day-long conference took place in February 1913 resulting in an agreement embodying the items the Glasgow and Edinburgh employers had sought to defend. Its main provisions were:
(1) henceforth all new, or alterations in existing, rules, which may effect mutual interests not be introduced without mutual agreement,
(2) the 1912 rules be subject to a joint conference
(3) no new working rules or alterations be introduced before the end of 1913, unless by mutual agreement and
(4) the lockout notices were withdrawn pending a settlement of the rules in dispute.
As a result of conferences held in April 1913 the mutually approved working with the STA became for the first time, embodied in a national agreement, signed in January 1914. Thereafter changes to the union's rules relating to working conditions became the subject of joint negotiations and only if mutually approved, enshrined in a national agreement.

These three disputes demonstrated how quickly the Scottish Alliance secured recognition as the national organisation of the printing and allied trades employers in Scotland.

Summary
This chapter has analysed the reason for the formation of the Scottish Alliance of Masters in the Printing and Kindred Trades. Confronted by growing union power, based on the economic expansion of the industry, the implementation of mechanical composition and increasing union membership (including amongst semi- and unskilled workers) and industrial relations difficulties (including the P&KTF demand for a forty-eight-hour week) the Scottish printing employers accepted they required a collective organisation to counter the steady encroachment of the unions onto managerial prerogatives. On 8 November 1910, twenty three delegates to a meeting held in Edinburgh established the Scottish Alliance of Masters in the Printing and Kindred Trades to counterbalance the

growing power of the print trade unions. The Scottish Alliance in its role in the Edinburgh piecework dispute (1913), the employment of female and unskilled labour dispute (1912) and the 1912 STA working rules dispute soon secured recognition as the national organisation of the print employers in Scotland.

Notes

[1]   See Gillespie, S. C. (1953) Scottish Typographical Association, 1853 to 1952. Glasgow: MacLehose, p111.

[2]   Op cit, p113, 115-116.

[3]   See Sprout, T. (1930) *The History and Progress of the Amalgamated Society of Lithographic Printers and Auxiliaries of Great Britain and Ireland, 1880-1930*. Manchester: Jubilee Souvenir

[4]   See *Society of Lithographic, Artists, Designers, Engravers and Process Workers: A Record of Fifty Years, 1885-1935*. London, 1935

[5]   See Bundock, C. J. (1953) *The National Union of Printing, Bookbinding and Paperworkers*, Oxford: Oxford University Press.

[6]   The National Union of Papermill Workers organised all male and female workers above sixteen years of age employed within the gates of a paper mill. It sought to be an industrial union.

[7]   For a more detailed account of this dissatisfaction see Gillespie, S. A. (1953) *Scottish Typographical Association, 1853 – 1952*. Glasgow: MacLehose, pp122-125.

[8]   Op cit, p155.

[9]   This meant an advance of 2s 0d for a year and another 2s 6d at the end of twelve months. The difference in hours was accounted for by the solely lithographic establishments working only fifty one hours whereas in houses where both lithographic and letterpress were working the letterpress and binders hours were fifty seven hours per week. In such shops the lithographers worked three hours more than their own fifty one hours but three less than the kindred trades but at 2s 0d more per week. These were just some of the anomalies of the time.

[10] See Sprout, T. (1930) *The History and Progress of the Amalgamated Society of Lithographic Printers and Auxiliaries of Great Britain and Ireland, 1880-1930*. Manchester: Jubilee Souvenir, Manchester, p41.

[11] For a more detailed account of the dispute see Bundock, C. J. (1958) *The National Union of Printing, Bookbinding and Paperworkers*, Oxford University Press, pp 57-68 and pp63-65.

[12] See Sprout, T. (1930) *The History and Progress of the Amalgamated Society of Lithographic Printers and Auxiliaries of Great Britain and Ireland, 1880-1930*. Manchester: Jubilee Souvenir, p50.

[13] For a detailed analysis of why this happened see Howe, E. (1950) *The British Federation of Master Printers, 1900-1950*. London: British Federation of Master Printers

14 The BFMP held its Annual Convention in Glasgow in 1903 and again in 1908.

15 This made employers liable to pay compensation and the case of industrial injuries resulting from certain employments.

16 See Minutes of Scottish Alliance Executive, 17 January 1911.

17 These were the Edinburgh Master Printers Association; Association of Master Printers of Glasgow; Association of Master Bookbinders and Machine Rulers of Edinburgh; the Glasgow and West of Scotland Master Lithographic Association; the Edinburgh and East of Scotland Master Lithographers Association; the Master Printers of Falkirk; the Association of Master Printers and Lithographers of Dundee and District; the Greenock Master Printers' Association and the Association of Master Bookbinders and Machine Rulers of Glasgow.

18 See Howe, E. (1950) *The British Federation of Master Printers, 1900-1950.* London: British Federation of Master Printers, p32.

Chapter 3

**THE GROWTH AND DEVELOPMENT
OF THE ALLIANCE: 1910 – 1952**

This chapter explains the evolution and development of the decision-making structure – local associations, annual general meetings, Executive Board, office bearers, the Young Master Printer movement – of the Scottish Alliance of Masters in the Printing and Kindred Trades. It then analyses the relationship between the Scottish Alliance and the British Federation of Master Printers, based on the 'settlements' of 1912 and 1919. The third section of the chapter explains the financial structure of the Alliance covering trends in the annual subscription paid by its member firms and in its expenditure pattern. The final section outlines the core services provided by the Alliance to its members namely political lobbying, the selection, education and training of apprentices, and costing and estimating designed to stimulate the study of cost to check excessive price-cutting which threatened the economic well-being of the industry.

Membership

Following its formation, Alliance membership increased steadily. Firms were admitted into membership to the appropriate local association. Member companies paid their membership fee to the Scottish Alliance head office in Edinburgh. The working expenses of the local associations were funded by the Edinburgh head office. By 1919 the Scottish Alliance claimed a membership of 90% of printing companies in Scotland.[1] No firms, of any importance, were outside its jurisdiction. Membership was weakest amongst printing companies in the north of Scotland.

Table 3.1
Member Companies Joining the Scottish Alliance

Date	Number of Companies Joining
1912	66
1913	35
1918	66
1919	149
1920	70

Source: Alliance: Finance Committee

Some companies remained outside the Alliance which urged strongly upon its local associations the importance of securing into membership all employers in their district. In its report to the Alliance's 1918 annual general meeting, the Executive Board emphasised the necessity for 100% organisation amongst printers in Scotland. When print companies were asked why they remained non-members, the main response was the company had no industrial relations problems and therefore membership was unnecessary. The Alliance countered by pointing out that in many cities police patrolled the streets and on the whole seem to do little. The police service was required, for without it crime would become rampant and life and property unprotected. The Alliance argued

> ...it is the same with the Alliance. Just because national affairs seem to be going smoothly and you happen to have no trouble in your office at the moment does that mean you can scrump the Alliance and save your subscriptions?[2]

By 1921, ten years after its formation, the Scottish Alliance was undoubtedly the recognised authority speaking for printers for the whole Scottish industry. This contrasted to its early days when it only secured recognition by strong action. Ten years on, wages and working rules for the letterpress section of the industry were regulated by collective agreements between the Alliance and the STA so any employer outside the Alliance had no influence in the making of those agreements. As a strong and united body the Scottish Alliance could deal with every matter impinging on the interests of its members and in doing so gained the respect of all concerned.

In April 1926 the Scottish Alliance established a special committee to consider (1) the possibility of an agreement whereby all workers would be in a union and all employers members of the Scottish Alliance, (2) non-union companies and membership of the Alliance and (3) the 'open shop' principle. In October the committee reported. On the first issue it concluded no agreement be made giving 100% organisation of both employers and employees although it expressed sympathy with the aspiration. The committee recommended non-union employers be admitted into membership so long as they conformed to fair employment conditions and their membership was approved by the appropriate Alliance local association. On the issue of 'open shops' the committee recommended the Scottish Alliance did not support the principle. All three recommendations of the special committee were accepted by the Alliance.

In June 1931 the Alliance considered whether its present title be shortened. In March 1932 a motion at the Executive Board to change the title of the Alliance to the Scottish Alliance of Master Printers was moved and seconded. A second motion proposed the title remain unchanged. After much discussion the Executive Board decided to retain the existing title.[3]

In 1941, the Scottish Alliance extended its membership beyond conventional printing firms when it accepted into membership the Printing Department of the Glasgow Corporation. This appeared unlikely when the Corporation first announced its intention to undertake its own print work rather than have it done in the general jobbing industry. In December 1934, the Glasgow Corporation had established a department to manufacture, provide and supply the stationery, printing and bookbinding requirements of the Corporation, its committees, and the school requisites of its Education Department. The Scottish Alliance obtained the opinion of counsel on the Corporation's action. On being advised it was 'ultra vires' an 'Action of Supervision and Interdict' was raised in the name of the Alliance President, Robert Pinkerton Graham who was a ratepayer of Glasgow. The action was unsuccessful as was an appeal to the Court of Session. The cost to the Alliance of this legal action against the Glasgow Corporation decision to undertake its own printing and bookbinding amounted to £552. £175 had already been received towards the sum leaving the net cost at £337[4]. In 1941 the Glasgow Corporation's Print Department's application for membership of the Alliance was accepted, its Executive Board seeing no reason why the application be refused.

Constitutional Issues
a. Internal Decision-Making
Member firms became either constituents of a local association or of an affiliated association. The management of the Scottish Alliance was the responsibility of the Executive Board which had a number of standing subcommittees, for example Finance, and of ad hoc committees to deal with specific issues.

The elected office bearers were the President, Vice-President, Treasurer and all were ex-officio members of the Executive Board which was serviced by a secretariat under the direction of the Secretary. Member firms sent representatives to the annual general meeting held in March or April of each year. Additional to these internal constitutional issues, was the financial and industrial relationship between the Scottish Alliance and the British Federation of Master Printers.

i.   The Alliance Local Associations

In 1912, the Alliance accepted applications for affiliation from the Edinburgh Master Printers Association (February), the Association of the Master Bookbinders and Machine Rulers of Edinburgh (February), the Falkirk and District Master Printers (March), the Association of the Master Printers of Glasgow (March), the Association of Master Bookbinders and Machine Rulers of Glasgow (March), the Glasgow and West of Scotland Master Lithographers Association (April) and the Association of Master Printers and Lithographers of Dundee and District (July). In 1914, the annual general meeting of the Alliance asked the Executive Board to consider the question of bringing the local associations (branches) more closely into contact with the Alliance head office in Edinburgh. In October 1914 an application for affiliation from the Dumfries and Galloway Master Printers Association was accepted.

The 1916 annual general meeting instructed the Executive Board to submit to local associations a scheme for consolidation as branches of the Scottish Alliance. As a result, any local association or association of employers in the specified print trades, all of whose members were members of the Scottish Alliance, were constituted as a branch of the Alliance. Local associations embraced into membership all local members of the Alliance but could not admit into membership print employers who were not members of the Alliance. All subscriptions by companies to local associations ceased and working expenses incurred by associations were, in future, to be paid from the general funds of the Scottish Alliance. It was anticipated the establishment of local associations would consolidate and strengthen the Scottish Alliance. To finance the working expenses of local associations from Alliance general funds the annual subscription to the Alliance was increased from ½ d per £1 of wages paid to ¾d per £1 with a maximum subscription of £75 and a minimum of 10s 0d.

In 1916, the Association of Master Printers and Lithographers of Dundee and District and the Association of Master Printers of Dundee merged to form the Dundee Printing and Kindred Trades Employers Association which in February 1917, became the first reconstituted local association of the Alliance. The merger of the Edinburgh Master Printers Association, the Edinburgh and East of Scotland Master Lithographers Association and the Association of Edinburgh Master Binders and Machine Rulers created the Edinburgh Printing and Kindred Trades Employers Association which, in March 1917, became a local association of the Scottish Alliance. Also in 1917, the Glasgow Master

Printers Association was reconstituted as the Glasgow Printing and Kindred Trades Employers Association which then became a local association. In the following year, the Edinburgh and Glasgow local associations were permitted to change their constitutions to allow engravers have a separate section. At the same time, the Edinburgh Association changed its rules to admit stereotypers and electrotypers into a separate section of membership.

The Aberdeen Employers Association was granted local association status in March 1918 and three months later the Perth Master Printers Association became the Perth Local Association. In November 1918, the Kilmarnock Master Printers Association convened a meeting to consider the formation of an association of master printers in Ayrshire. The outcome was the creation of the Ayrshire Printing and Kindred Trades Employers Association which in February 1919 became the Ayrshire Local Association. 1919 also witnessed the Scottish Borders District Printing and Kindred Trades Employers Association becoming a local association. In March 1920, the Fifeshire Printing and Kindred Trades Employers Association, resulting from the efforts of the Kirkcaldy Master Printers to create an organisation for the whole of Fife, was constituted as an Alliance local association. In October of the same year, the Glasgow Trade Lithographers Employers Association affiliated to the Scottish Alliance. In April 1919, the Forfarshire and District Printing and Kindred Trades Employers Association was constituted a local association. By this time, the Greenock Master Printers had also become a local association.

In November 1922 print employers in the north of Scotland, outside of Aberdeen, held a meeting in the Station Hotel, Inverness. There were representatives from Peterhead to Inverness and from Inverness to Wick. Those present unanimously agreed to form the Northern Counties Printing and Kindred Trades Employers Association.[5] In 1923 it became the Northern Counties Local Association. The Scottish Alliance now had a local association network covering the whole of Scotland. A meeting of print employers in the Lanarkshire District held on 7 April and 24 May 1926 adopted the following resolution:

> that the members of the Scottish Alliance of Employers in the Printing and Kindred Trades in the Lanarkshire District now in General Meeting assembled resolved (1) to form an Association to be called the Lanarkshire District Printing and Kindred Trades Employers Association and (2) to adopt the Constitution and Rules of the said Association.

That the Lanarkshire District Printing and Kindred Trades Employers' Association resolves to apply to be constituted as a branch of the Scottish Alliance of Employers in the Printing and Kindred Trades, accepts the Constitution and Rules of the Alliance and undertake to abide by and conform to the same[6]

The April 1926 meeting of the Scottish Alliance Executive Board constituted the Lanarkshire District Printing and Kindred Trades Employers as its Lanarkshire Local Association.

In 1918, the Scottish Alliance, given its growing influence in the Scottish printing industry permitted separate sections to be adopted in its Edinburgh and Glasgow associations for copperplate engravers, electro- and stereotypers and litho artists and designers. In the Scottish Alliance itself, a section devoted to the interests of manufacturing stationers was established. Following negotiation with the Envelope Makers and Manufacturing Stationers Federation, an arrangement was made whereby a 'Manufacturing Stationers' section of the Scottish Alliance would act as the Scottish District Council of the Manufacturing Stationers Federation. All questions of hours, wages and working conditions would be handled by the Scottish Alliance with other trade matters being managed in co-operation with the Manufacturing Stationers Federation on whose council the Scottish Alliance had representation. These arrangements proved advantageous to the Scottish Alliance because as its Scottish District Council, it dealt successfully with issues affecting this branch of the printing industry.

In 1918 the Scottish Newspaper Proprietor's Association (SNPA) affiliated to the Scottish Alliance. It represented the interests of weekly newspapers. Its members also undertook general printing work to utilise fully their productive capacity. Twenty eight years later in November 1946, a special committee of the Scottish Alliance proposed alterations to the constitution of the SNPA, which was in conflict with the Scottish Alliance constitution. The matter was resolved in May 1947 when the Alliance and the SNPA agreed the latter appointed three representatives to the Alliance Executive Board instead of the current two and when matters of special interest to the SNPA were discussed with the STA two SNPA representatives would be on the Scottish Alliance delegation.

ii. The Annual General Meeting

The annual general meeting was held in March or April at which the annual report of the Executive Board was considered and approved, and to which an audited 'Statement of Accounts' for the preceding year ending 31 December was submitted. The annual general meeting also elected the Scottish Alliance office bearers, namely a President, Vice-President and Treasurer and considered any other competent business. The office bearers could stand for re-election at the next annual general meeting but no office bearer could hold the same office for more than three consecutive years. Special general meetings could be called by the Scottish Alliance Secretary on the requisition of the President or of the Vice-President or of any three Executive Board members or on a requisition made in writing by seven members of the Alliance stating the business to be considered. An extraordinary general meeting for a special emergency could be called at short notice by the Scottish Alliance Secretary on the requisition of the President.

At general meetings each member had one vote plus one additional vote for every £1 of aggregate subscription paid by the member firm in respect of the preceding year ending 31 December. No member had more than twenty five votes. Every partner or director of a member firm, or any individual appointed and empowered to represent the member company, could attend, and participate, in general meetings but the vote of any member firm could only be exercised by one individual. The annual general meeting was chaired by the President or in their absence the Vice-President. The chair of the annual general meeting had a casting vote as well as a deliberative vote.

iii. The Executive Board

The business of the Scottish Alliance was managed by an Executive Board, the membership of which consisted of representatives from local associations and affiliated associations. Each association appointed one representative and an additional representative for every £20,000 of aggregate wages paid to the Scottish Alliance during the preceding year ended 31 December, provided that the wages of no member firm exceed £24,000 per annum. Members of the Executive Board were appointed annually in January or February. Similarly substitute representatives were appointed by associations to fill vacancies occurring, and to attend and vote at meetings of the Executive Board and its committees in case of representatives being unable to attend. The 1921 annual general meeting agreed past Presidents, so long as eligible for election to the Executive Board, continue as ex-officio members of the board, unless a general meeting decided otherwise. This change ensured the Executive Board had available at all times the wisdom and experience of past Presidents. Prior to this rule change, the immediate past President continued as a member of the Executive Board until the following annual general meeting.

The Executive Board had plenary powers in the management of the affairs of the Alliance. This included the management of its property, the investment of its funds, the disposal of such funds, the raising, pursuing and defending actions at law and delegating all, or any of its powers or duties, to a committee or committees. The office bearers were ex-officio Trustees of the Scottish Alliance in whose names were invested its whole property portfolio. It was necessary to give the office bearers this status when the Scottish Alliance decided, in 1924, to purchase its head office at 12 Hill Street, Edinburgh. The Scottish Alliance had moved, in May 1919, to this location from 66 Frederick Street, Edinburgh, to obtain larger office accommodation and to permit its Edinburgh Association to be housed in the Alliance head office.

The Executive Board also appointed an auditor who had to be a professional accountant. board meetings were called by the Alliance Secretary on the request of the President, or of the Vice-President or of any three board members or in writing by any seven members of the Scottish Alliance stating the business to be discussed. Seven members formed a quorum at board meetings which were chaired by the President and in their absence the Vice-President, failing which by any board member elected to chair the meeting. At board meetings each member had one vote but the chair also had a casting vote.

iv. Committees
Each year the Executive Board following the annual general meeting elected members to serve on its standing committees. There was an Emergency Committee – which the President chaired and a Finance Committee chaired by the Treasurer. The board could appoint ad hoc committees for specific purposes. Every committee, whether standing or ad hoc, had authority to fill vacancies occurring in their numbers. The President was an ex-officio member of all committees.

Over the period 1920 to 1952 the Scottish Alliance established two additional standing committees. The Costing Committee, founded in 1911, promoted accurate and scientific costing. The British printing industry was amongst the first in the country to take up costing with enthusiasm. It was the first industry to devise and to adopt a uniform industry-wide costing system. In 1929, the Executive Board appointed a subcommittee consisting of the President (John Wylie), Vice-President (Theodore Watt) and William Maxwell, Robert Kilpatrick and Dr James MacLehose to consider establishing a Labour Negotiating Committee as a standing committee. The subcommittee, after taking into account the increase in the number of duties falling upon the President and the many calls on his time recommended the establishment of a standing Negotiating Committee consisting of five members plus the President. The Negotiating Committee members were subject to reappointment every year but the committee had the power to add to its numbers. The Executive Board accepted the recommendation of a standing Negotiating Committee to deal with any new claims from the print unions for changes to existing wages and conditions of employment. Dr MacLehose was appointed first Chair of the Negotiating Committee.

v. Officers and Premises
The Executive Board appointed the Scottish Alliance Secretary, who was responsible for its administration. The Alliance's first Secretary was F H Bisset, who in 1918 resigned the post on accepting employment with Wm Collins Sons & Co. Bisset enhanced the industrial and political influence of the Scottish Alliance and secured its organisational base. He impressed the print union officials with his straightforward dealings and earned their respect by an ability to understand their point of view. Mr Bisset was succeeded as Scottish Alliance Secretary by Mr R T Wishart, MA, BL, Secretary of the Insurance Committee for the Burgh of Edinburgh, at a salary of £500 per annum. He retained this position for thirty five years. Despite being held in wartime, the 1945 annual general meeting made a presentation to him in recognition of his then twenty five years service as Secretary of the Alliance. The Executive Board Meeting of 25 January 1948 accepted the suggestion of the President (J Gilchrist Johnston),

Past Presidents and the office bearers that the Alliance appoint an assistant secretary and in June 1948 Barrie Abbott took up this post.

The Scottish Alliance head office in 1911 was located at 66 Frederick Street, Edinburgh at an annual rent of £45. The Secretary could spend up to £75 towards office equipment and installed a telephone at an annual rent of £11 5s 0d. From Whitsunday 1919 the Frederick Street premises were vacated and the Alliance moved to 12 Hill Street, Edinburgh on a five year lease. This substantially increased accommodation space and permitted the housing of the Edinburgh Association. In 1923, the Executive Board approved the purchase of Hill Street at a price not exceeding £2,000.

vi. Contact with Member Firms

The Executive Board kept member firms up-to-date on its activities. The membership pre-1914 was mainly concentrated in the larger towns. Meetings were frequent and member firms were in touch personally with what was happening at Scottish Alliance headquarters in Edinburgh. Over a two-year period (1917 to 1919) the membership doubled and now existed in the most remote country districts of Scotland including the Shetland Isles. It was clear by mid-1919 that the industry tradition of wages and hours changing perhaps once in a ten-year period, had gone. In response to these changes, the Executive Board decided in mid-July 1919 to produce the *Scottish Alliance Bulletin*, issued periodically to keep member firms in touch with the work of the Alliance head office and to inform them on matters of general interest to the industry. The first issue of the *Bulletin* was July 1919 but on the grounds of cost was discontinued after the June 1927 issue.

A second method of communicating directly with member firms was the introduction in 1936 of a conference, held each October, to which all member firms were invited. It provided an opportunity for the Board to hear the views of the members on the Alliance's activities. The second annual meeting was held at Callander during the first weekend of October 1937. These conferences brought member firms and the Executive Board together with more time for an exchange of views and opinions than was possible in a formal meeting. The outbreak of the Second World War, however, made it impossible to continue these annual gatherings.

In December 1924, the Executive Board, again in the interests of greater understanding and trust between head office and its associations established a visitation committee which would visit associations. Associations arranged the meeting which the Visitation Committee would attend so there was time for the members of the committee, apart from the formal meeting, to discuss issues with individual member firms of the association. Again to help improve relationships between Alliance member firms and its Executive Board, the President and Secretary of associations were invited occasionally to meet with Scottish Alliance office bearers to exchange views on matters affecting the industry.

Founding conference of the Scottish Young Master Printers Group, held at St Andrews in 1928. R T Wishart, Secretary of the Scottish Alliance, is seated second from the left.

vii. The Young Master Printer Movement (YMP)

During the summer of 1925, a member of BFMP had asked Percy Michael to give his son some tuition on the work of the Federation. It occurred to H H Potts that similar instruction might be of use to a larger number of YMPs. The Home Counties Alliance of the BFMP took up the idea and arranged a YMP conference for September 1925. In early 1926 the Lancashire and Cheshire Alliance did the same and later in that year YMP Conferences were held in the Yorkshire Alliance, the South Western Alliance and the two Welsh Alliances. In February 1927 the London Alliance held a YMP conference attended by 180 delegates.

a. Founding Conference

Between 4 to 7 May 1928, the Scottish Alliance held a YMP conference at St Andrews attended by thirty three young men who were either members of Alliance firms or whose training was with the object of being promoted to partnership, director or secretaryship. They were drawn from a wide area extending from Aberdeen to Dumfries. The conference, which was an experiment, was successful from both a business and a social perspective. The YMPs quickly recognised they had much in common with their competitors and many new friendships were formed. The presentations at the conference were given by experienced master printers who were experts in their fields. They had to know their subjects thoroughly as the discussion and questions which followed each address displayed the keenness and enthusiasm of the YMPs and augured well for the future of the industry and the Scottish Alliance.

Following suggestions from this conference the Alliance Executive Board at its meeting on 5 June 1928 made six important decisions concerning the development of the YMP movement in Scotland:

(1) a YMP conference be held annually
(2) the YMP movement be developed locally in the different associations of the Alliance
(3) topics be suggested by the Alliance Executive Board for discussion at local meetings and then put on the agenda for the YMP annual conference
(4) lectures of a technical nature be given in the larger towns and cities but with invitations to attend such lectures being sent to members of the Alliance in neighbouring associations
(5) notices of such meetings be addressed specifically to YMPs who attend the annual conference and copies of the *Bulletin*, or literature of a technical nature issued by the Alliance be sent to young master printers in addition to copies sent to the firm
(6) having gained a greater knowledge of the Alliance and its values and objectives the YMPs endeavour to secure 100% organisation of YMPs.

The YMP movement was originally for the sons of master printers, and other young people who were working in a firm in membership of the Alliance, and whose training was directed to becoming a master printer, business partner, director or company secretary. In 1951, an amendment was made to this definition, as it was believed it excluded some young men employed in the industry from eligibility for membership. The definition was reworded to include those who had the 'intention that they qualify for the position of master printer or partner or director or general manager or secretary or any other position of trust and leadership in management'. The Scottish printing industry needed to improve the quality of its management and the Alliance Executive Board saw the YMP movement as an important component of management development as well as a mechanism to hear the voices of those who would some day have responsibility for the management of printing businesses and of carrying on the work of the Scottish Alliance.

In 1929, the Scottish YMP movement received official recognition from the Scottish Alliance when its Executive Board invited officers of YMP of Scotland to attend board meetings and to participate in its deliberations. In 1933, the YMP Group Committee became a standing committee of the Executive Board. This was a useful link giving the board the opportunity of gaining the views of those likely to be involved in the future in the work of the Alliance. In 1932, a constitution and rules for the YMP was drawn up under which the Scottish Group Committee meet quarterly and held an annual conference. There was to be a local YMP group in each of the associations. Local YMP groups were formed in 1928 in Edinburgh and Glasgow. There were not, however, in the late 1920s/early 1930s, sufficient numbers of young men in other associations to support the creation of YMP local groups.

b. Conferences

In May 1929, the YMP Conference was held in Turnberry and compared favourably with the inaugural conference of 1928. Those attending developed the friendships first made twelve months previously and formed new friendships. The YMP played a greater part at the conference as principal speakers than at the previous one. In 1932 a successful conference was held at Taymouth Castle at which the presentations, and subsequent debate, centred on production technology developments with the principal speaker being from the Printing Industries Research Association. The 1950 conference of the Scottish Group was held at Pitlochry and the attendance was the largest since the end of the Second World War. Addresses were given on aspects of the general theme 'Practical Management' with one session devoted to the experiences of the Anglo-American Letterpress Printing Productivity Team which visited the USA in 1950 to investigate why the USA printing industry was more productive than the UK industry. This visit was part of the UK government 1950 initiative to improve the performance of the British economy by sending a TUC and employers' central bodies delegation to the USA to ascertain why the USA economy performed better than the UK. This USA visit resulted in the formation in the Anglo-American Council on Productivity. Other subjects debated at the Pitlochry conference included methods of increasing productivity, time and motion study, costing, industrial safety, the attitude of trade unions to productivity and applied psychology.

c. Other YMP Activities

In addition to the annual conference the Scottish YMP conducted inquiries into aspects of the industry. In 1930, for example, they conducted an inquiry into the average operational times of hand-fed double demy Wharfedale machines engaged in letterpress work. The inquiry was to ascertain if it were possible to secure sufficient records to enable a statement of average operational times on lines similar to the average hourly cost rates issued by the Scottish Alliance Costing Committee. The success of the experiment led to records of other machines being obtained.

The Scottish YMP movement participated regularly in the BFMP YMP Summer School, the first of which was held in Edinburgh on 16 July 1934. The school was attended by fifty young men some of whom attended throughout its whole four weeks whilst others stayed for either the first or last fortnight. The curriculum included subjects not available in other course of instruction in Scotland and covered costing, estimating, economics, accountancy, salesmanship, factory management and business administration. This summer school was a success and became a regular feature in the education and training of YMP. The success of the first YMP national summer school was due to the work of Alex S Calder, the Secretary of the Edinburgh Printing and Kindred Trades Employers Association[7].

d. Local Groups

The Edinburgh and Glasgow YMP groups held regular meetings at which lectures and talks on problems affecting the printing industry in Scotland were followed by discussion and debate. Although by 1952 the YMP movement was firmly established in Scotland and local group meetings held as required in Edinburgh and Glasgow the Executive Board always felt there were still young men in the industry eligible for membership who failed to enrol as YMP. This was an untapped potential and the Executive Board appealed frequently to its member firms which had young male managers eligible for membership of the Scottish YMP Group to give them facilities to attend local meetings and the annual conference.

b. External : Relationships with BFMP
i. The 1912 Settlement

In 1912, agreement was reached between the BFMP and the Scottish Alliance agreement on their constitutional relationship. First, the direct relationship between the Scottish local associations and the BFMP ceased. In future the Scottish Alliance would represent their interests at the BFMP. Second, affiliation fee payments by individual local associations to the BFMP would end. The Scottish Alliance would pay an annual fee of £50 to the BFMP. Third, the local associations would no longer have representation on the BFMP Council. In future the Scottish Alliance would appoint from its members a number of representatives to the BFMP Council equal to, or approximately equal to, the present number. Fourth, the BFMP monthly *Circular* would be sent in bulk each month to the Alliance head office and then be distributed in Scotland by the Alliance along with any of its own communications. Any other BFMP's communications for Scotland would be sent through the head office of the Alliance. These constitutional arrangements were accepted by the BFMP Council at its June 1912 meeting. The six representatives from the Edinburgh and Glasgow local associations at that time members of the BFMP Council became the Scottish Alliance representatives on that Council. In addition the Alliance Secretary, F H Bisset became a member of the BFMP Costing Committee. Although the Scottish Alliance affiliated to the BFMP it retained autonomy on finance and on industrial relations matters. The Alliance had representation on other BFMP Committees including its Labour Committee, Labour Negotiating Committee, Finance Committee, Costing Committee, Legislation Committee, Public Relations Committee and YMP Committee.

Relationships with the BFMP cooled in April 1915 following publication in the BFMP's monthly *Circular* of an article analysing the state of the Edinburgh printing trade. The Scottish Alliance was annoyed the article appeared without any consultation with it. The 14 April 1915 Executive Board instructed the Scottish Alliance Secretary to write to the BFMP making three points. First, the article should not have been included in the *Circular* and second, there be a reply to the article by the Secretary of the Edinburgh Association and this be included in the next BFMP Circular. Third, in future matters directly relating to Scotland included in the *Circular* be submitted to the Scottish Alliance before their publication. The BFMP replied merely noting the Alliance views.

ii. The 1919 Settlement

Over the next four years the relationship between the BFMP and the Scottish Alliance remained cool but in summer 1919 following negotiations between the two organisations at the BFMP annual conference in Blackpool a satisfactory basis for future relationship was agreed.[8] The Scottish Alliance retained full control of its own finances, conditions of membership and on all matters pertaining to the printing industry in Scotland. On trade union matters the Scottish Alliance would, where possible, negotiate with BFMP representatives reserving the right to vary any terms proposed in so far as they related to Scotland. It was also agreed that for consultation or negotiation purposes with any trade union, the BFMP and the Scottish Alliance would each nominate annually their members to form a joint executive committee. The Scottish Alliance representation on the BFMP Council was increased to eight with voting powers on questions general to both England and Scotland. The Alliance agreed in future to contribute a fixed sum of £250 annually to the BFMP's funds and in return receive copies of all literature issued by the BFMP.

This new 'settlement' in BFMP/Scottish Alliance relationships was necessary because of the changing position in the industry whereby the settlement of wages and other employment conditions were now settled nationally instead of purely local and/or applicable to Scotland only. This changed situation necessitated more frequent attendance of the Scottish Alliance representatives in London with the concomitant of heavy travelling expenses. But for these representatives in certain cases attending to the affairs of their own business when in London, the cost to the Scottish Alliance would have been higher. There was a need for a closer relationship with the BFMP but still having regard to the differences between the English and the Scottish printing industries and the position of the relative unions.

Scots did hold high office in the BFMP. In 1920, Dr James MacLehose became Vice-President whilst two years later the BFMP held its annual general meeting in Glasgow. Dr MacLehose was a prominent figure in the BFMP as well as the Scottish Alliance of which he was President from 1913-16. He was both President of BFMP and Chairman of the NJIC in 1921-1922. He was Chairman and Managing Director of Robert MacLehose & Co Ltd, Glasgow. As an 'elder statesman' of the industry, no important steps were taken by either the Scottish Alliance or the BFMP without the President first ascertaining his view or seeking his guidance and counsel. Other Presidents of the Scottish Alliance who became President of the BFMP were William Maxwell (R & R Clark, Edinburgh) in 1929, Theodore Watt (The Rosemount Press, Aberdeen) in 1937 and Hope Collins (Wm Collins Sons & Co) in 1948. In addition,

Duncan Sillars (Valentines of Dundee) and Alliance President (1944-1946) became Chair of the BFMP Technical Committee for the period 1947-48.

Despite this 'new settlement' the 1921 Annual Report of the Scottish Alliance Executive Board to the tenth annual general meeting reported:

> ...the relationship of the Alliance to the British Federation of Master Printers has given the Board cause for considerable concern during the past year and a Special Committee was appointed to examine into the matter...

This committee, after several meetings and careful investigation of the question, unanimously recommended to the Executive Board to continue the relationship agreed in 1919. The BFMP on the invitation of the Scottish Alliance, held its 1921 annual meeting and its Cost Conference in Glasgow. Both these events helped improve England/Scotland relationships.

As well as their constitutional relationship the financial link between the BFMP and the Scottish Alliance was sensitive. The 1912 constitutional settlement included the Scottish Alliance paying an annual fee to the BFMP of £50. The 1919 settlement saw this sum increased to £250. Twelve months later the sum was increased to £500 in return, inter alia, for the BFMP representing the interests of the Scottish Alliance in the National Confederation of Employers Organisations. Previously the Scottish Alliance had affiliated directly to the Confederation. In 1951 the Scottish Alliance Finance Committee reviewed the annual subscription to the BFMP which by now was £550. The committee argued comparisons between what the Scottish Alliance paid relative to other BFMP Alliances were irrelevant. The Scottish Alliance financed its own costing service, did not recover from the BFMP the expenses involved in the attendance of Scottish Alliance representatives at meetings in London and conducted negotiations with the unions on its own. After discussing the Finance Committee's report the Scottish Alliance Executive Board increased its current contribution to the BFMP to £750 provided that in its annual accounts the BFMP made clear the special position of the Scottish Alliance relative to its other Alliances. The Federation agreed.

Financial Issues

The main source of income for the Alliance was the annual subscription paid quarterly by its member firms. Minor sources of income were entrance fees, interest from investments, recovered income tax and sundry receipts, including commission. The sums of money received from members' subscriptions over the period 1920-1944 is shown in Table 3.2. The annual subscription related to the amount of wages a member firm paid. It was calculated on the wages of workers, apprentices and foremen employed in Scotland by a member firm involved in any branch of the printing, including artists and warehouse staff but not the wages of the office staff.

Table 3.2
The Scottish Alliance
Membership Contribution Income (1920 – 1944)

Date	Income (£)
1920	6,069
1921	6,569
1925	5,962
1930	5,517
1931	5,472
1932	5,132
1933	4,970
1934	4,937
1935	4,887
1936	4,838
1937	4,954
1938	5,095
1939	4,934
1940	4,702
1941	4,385
1942	4,509
1943	4,819
1944	4,721

Source: Alliance: Finance Committee

In 1919, the annual subscription paid by members was ½d per £ of wages paid by the member firms with a minimum subscription of 1s 0d. These rates had been payable since April 1912. The 1916 annual general meeting raised the subscription rate to ¾d per £ of wages and that the maximum annual contribution to £75 per year and the minimum 10s 0d. This stemmed from the decision that the ordinary expenses of constituted local associations be met from Alliance central funds. The Executive Board held on 8 July 1919 examined carefully the finances of the Alliance. Given the additional expenditure involved in the payment for members attending conferences and BFMP Council meetings in London, and other expenses necessary for the development of the effectiveness of the Alliance, an increase in the annual subscription was proposed to 1d per £ of wages paid by the member firms and that the minimum annual subscription be £1. The scale of expenses allowed for attending conferences and meetings in London by the members from the Glasgow and Edinburgh Association was fixed at £1l for a one day meeting and £1 11s 6d for each additional day. These proposals were accepted by the 1920 annual general meeting. In February 1924, the Executive Board rejected moves to reduce the annual subscription but accepted contributions for the 1924/1925 fiscal year remain unchanged.

In 1944, of the 337 firms in membership of the Scottish Alliance, seventy five (some 25%) paid the minimum subscription and ten the maximum. During the inter-war years and those of the Second World War the finances of the Alliance declined. Since 1925, subscription income fell from £5,967 to £4,839 in 1936 with an increase to £4,952 in 1937. Its income fell because of wage reductions, closure of businesses, mergers and take-overs and resignations. From 1928, except for 1929, 1939 and 1942, expenditure exceeded income. This deteriorating financial position led the Executive Board in November 1945 to ask its Finance Committee 'to investigate the present and future funds of the Alliance with a view to making recommendations to the Board'. In December 1945 the Finance Committee submitted its report. It explored the possibility of reductions in expenditure but concluded changes in the financial conditions prevalent since the Second World War made economies on 1938 levels of expenditure impossible. It considered the Alliance had been financially managed well in the past. The report's main recommendation was the annual rate of subscription payable by member firms continue at 1d per £ wage paid with a maximum contribution of £150 and a minimum of £2. These proposals were approved by the 1946 annual general meeting.

The main expenditure of the Alliance included staff salaries, travelling expenses to attend BFMP meetings, the costing system, technical education, the annual affiliation fee to the BFMP and local association working expenses. In 1920, the Scottish Alliance increased its annual subscription to the BFMP to £500. A Reserve Fund had by the end of 1919 had grown to £500 and by 1927 to £4,000. In August 1924 the Executive Board approved a Finance Committee recommendation that 10% of subscription income received from member firms finance technical education. This policy was reaffirmed in 1927. Fourteen years later, in March 1941, the Alliance agreed for the current year special grants to local associations for expenditure on technical education be increased to £200 in the case of the Edinburgh Association and that up to 16% of the annual subscription be available to other associations if required. It was also agreed that in future expenditure on technical education be a call on local association income and not the Alliance head office budget.

Expenditure exceeded income in 1934, 1935, 1936, 1937, 1940 and 1941. The total deficit accumulated in these six years was £710. Income exceeded expenditure in 1933, 1938, 1939, 1942, 1943 and 1944. The total surplus in these six years was £1,162. Despite this, there were significant reductions in certain items of expenditure. Travel expenses in 1937 amounted to £526 but only £191 in 1944. Travel costs including attending quarterly meetings of the BFMP and its committees and the National Joint Industrial Council were £616 in 1931 but by 1921 had reached £1,117.

Services to Members

The Scottish Alliance of Employers in the Printing and Kindred Trades provided five core services to its members – political lobbying; advice and assistance; costing and estimating; selection, recruitment and training of apprentices; and industrial relations. The Alliance gave advice to members on a wide range of issues such as commercial contracts, copyright law, derating, import/export duties, patent laws, pension and superannuation schemes, customer relations, imprint, libel laws and insurance. In industrial relations the Alliance negotiated, on behalf of its members, agreements covering wages and other employment conditions, provided advice on devising and implementing employee relations procedures and assisting member firms manage employee grievances and disciplinary situations.

a. Political Lobbying

Political lobbying services were mainly provided through the affiliation to the BFMP, whose Legislation Committee kept a watchful eye to protect the interests of the printing industry on legislation proposed by the UK Parliament. State legislation and the activities of government departments required consideration by the Executive Board. An example was the Alliance's opposition to the intention in 1920 of the Board of Trade to bring gold leafing within the scope of the Safeguarding of Industries Act. In the early 1950s the Alliance was active with the BFMP in trying to secure the removal of purchase tax on educational stationery. The Alliance urged its members to approach their MPs to draw their attention to the anomalies and hardship the tax caused.

In 1918, the Alliance became a member of the National Confederation of Employers Organisations (NCEO) formed to secure the co-operation throughout the country of various employers' organisations in dealing with labour relations matters and to achieve greater co-ordination of policy in dealing with such questions. The establishment of a National Joint Industrial Council in 1919 emphasised the need to create an organisation which could represent effectively all the employers' organisations and enable their representatives to articulate to government the view of all employers throughout the UK. The Scottish Alliance believed when the NCEO welded together its declared policies it would receive support both inside, and outside, Parliament. In 1920, the Alliance withdrew from membership of the NCEO leaving the BFMP, a much bigger voice within the organisation, to represent its interests there.

b. Selection, Education and Training of Apprentices

In 1932 the Executive Board appointed a committee to examine the National Joint Industrial Council (NJIC) and the Edinburgh Association schemes for the selection, education and training of apprentices to formulate a common scheme for the whole of Scotland. The committee's proposed scheme finished up being a combination of the best of NJIC and of the Edinburgh schemes. The proposed scheme, with minor amendments was approved by the Alliance and adopted by the Scottish NJIC. In approving the scheme the Executive Board stipulated its adaptation by Alliance associations be not compulsory but be subject to adaptation to meet local requirements. The Edinburgh Association had had three years experience of the workings of its scheme which its members regarded of great benefit. The new scheme did not remove the employer's right to choose the apprentice but gave facilities to satisfy themselves the young boy they selected had the physical and mental capacities to qualify from his seven years training as an efficient journeyman. The new scheme was accepted, by the STA, the ASLP and National Society of Electrotypers and Stereotypers (NSES). All the print unions co-operated fully with the employers to ensure that a high standard of new entrants was recruited to the different sections of the industry.

By 1934, the Scottish-wide scheme was operative in Glasgow, Aberdeen, Ayrshire and Edinburgh. By this date twenty one boys had been examined in Aberdeen of which nineteen were of the approved standard. In Edinburgh, where a scheme had operated since 1930, 498 boys were examined and 295 judged to have reached the required standards of the different sections of the industry. 1934 also saw the first examinations in Glasgow sat by thirty boys of which eighteen reached the approved standard. Scottish print employers reported satisfaction with the examination and the improved standard of the type of boy now entering the industry. In some areas of Scotland it was not possible to adopt the Scotland-wide scheme and employers introduced their own arrangements for the educational examination. In 1936 the scheme was extended to Dundee when its College of Art established a small 'state of the art' department for the training of personnel for skilled jobs in composition and letterpress and lithographic printing. The College provided for training in layout and commercial art. Its student catchment area covered Dundee, Angus, North Fife and Perthshire. Even so, the Scottish Alliance remained concerned about the absence of the 'Selection, Recruitment and Training of Apprentice Scheme' outside the four large Scottish cities[9].

c. Costing and Estimating

The costing movement was inaugurated in February 1913 by the BFMP. The Scottish Alliance Secretary, Mr Bisset, represented the Alliance on the Federation Costing Committee and took an active interest in its work. In February 1913 a Scottish 'Cost Conference' lasting two days took place. It was hoped the conference would stimulate the study of cost by the printing trades in Scotland and be a check upon the excessive price-cutting which threatened to undermine the economic basis of the Scottish printing industry. In Glasgow and Edinburgh the Master Printers Employers Associations established local Costing Committees. The Alliance Secretary conducted costing and estimating classes in Edinburgh and Glasgow. The Scottish Alliance costing system proved useful for attracting firms into membership. Many firms installed the system and the number of firms operating on sound cost lines enabled the Alliance member firms to establish with greater accuracy local hourly rates which were benefitted the trade in general. The ability to arrive via the Scottish Alliance system at exact costs during periods of rapid change provided considerable savings for the industry.

In 1922, the Alliance appointed Mr F V Nicholls as the Cost Accountant. By 1924, 131 print firms in Scotland were using the Scottish Alliance costing system. This represented 28% of the membership and only one other BFMP Alliance had a higher percentage. Eighty of the systems inspected by the Cost Accountant complied with BFMP principles. By 1926 the number of firms using the costing system had reached 153 and the Alliance Costing Committee believed each additional installation made for correct estimating and the elimination of unfair competition. In the mid 1930s, the Cost Accountant called on all members to revise their system as well as installations. An increasing number of companies instructed, on an annual basis, the Cost Accountant to revise their costings. The Costing Committee was pleased that the advice of the Cost Accountant was sought in both technical and administrative matters, and that a large number of check estimates were prepared. In the mid-1930s the Cost Committee became concerned about the lack of uniformity in estimating. The majority of complaints to the Costing Committee were about price-cutting arising from bad estimating rather than from a deliberate intention to sell below cost.

In 1937, the Costing Committee estimated the increase in the industry's costs arising from the introduction of a forty-five-hour working week in that year was 5½%. This related only to operation costs and did not include increases in the price of paper and other materials or to enhanced printing and transport charges. The committee also advised on the actual increase in costs related to any specific contract and to the nature of the work. One problem was no two companies were affected to the same extent by the changes in conditions in the print industry. This made giving advice on general questions of cost difficult. In September 1940 the Costing Committee advised member firms the effect upon costs of the increase in wages granted in August 1940 by the National Arbitration Tribunal (NAT) along with other increases amounted to an increase in costs of 10%.

During 1947, the BFMP Costing Committee changed the emphasis of its operations from installation work to the education and training of cost clerks and others. The Alliance offered help to any local associations wishing to conduct costing classes in their area and offered to provide a teacher prepared to take the classes. Help took the form of training the trainer and providing them with a standard syllabus and teaching aids. Costing and estimating classes were also offered at Heriot-Watt College, Edinburgh, the Stow College School of Printing, Glasgow and the College of Art, Dundee. In 1951 Mr F V Nicholls, Cost Accountant to the Alliance since 1923, retired and was succeeded at the start of 1952 by George W Llewellyn who had had considerable costing experience from his employment with a firm in Yorkshire.

In 1950, the Alliance Costing Committee considered the question of plant values for costing purposes. The continual increase in the prices of new machinery necessitated the need to build up a plant replacement reserve fund. For this purpose the committee recommended existing plant be valued at 75% of present day prices for new machinery and depreciation calculated on that amount be included in working expenses when calculating hourly cost rates. In the case of old machinery which might never be replaced, member firms were advised the same type of special consideration be given.

The purpose of the costing system was to prevent competition between printers based on price-cutting. The depression of the 1920s affected adversely the behaviour of some print employers. The Alliance Executive Board was concerned some print employers were pursuing a policy of 'reckless' price-cutting, resulting in many instances selling their products below cost. The Alliance was adamant such a policy, if continued, would only bring irretrievable disaster to both the price-cutting employer and their competitor print firms. In its 1921 report to the annual general meeting the Executive Board appealed to members to show loyalty towards each other arguing the installation, and working, of the costing system in every office was an essential step towards the elimination of the short-sighted policy of selling below cost. In 1929 the Costing Committee again considered the sensitive problem of price-cutting following complaints from a number of associations. The Committee advocated a more general application of the costing system as the best remedy and if estimates were based on facts derived from costing records this would help eliminate extreme low tenders which damaged the industry and were the direct cause of many requests for estimates. The Executive Board, on the advice of its Costing Committee, issued the following statement to its members:

> ...The Executive Board of the Scottish Alliance condemn the practice of price cutting and calls upon members to do their utmost to preserve prices that will be fair and reasonable to both the producer and the customer...[10]

In short a more general application of the costing system was the best method of combating the evils of product market competition based on cutting prices.

During the middle and late 1930s the Executive Board and its Costing Committee continued to be perturbed by the practice of some member firms quoting uneconomic prices for work. The Alliance condemned this action of quoting prices for work below cost. It advocated its associations review the matter to secure agreement amongst members honourably to support and to defend fair prices. In addition it urged member firms to discuss costs and prices with one another and offered the services of its Cost Accountant in any such discussions especially when doubts arose over what constituted an economic price. The elimination of uneconomic prices, the correction of errors in estimating, and the treating of sources of waste and inefficiencies in the workplace, were some of the ways in which the costing system was of value to member firms.

The policy of the Costing Committee contained five basic elements:
(1) the installation of the costing system, done by the Alliance Cost Accountant, be a service to member firms without charge.
(2) revisions of installations be undertaken by the Cost Accountant at a suitable charge.
(3) the Cost Accountant provided advice, and help, on technical matters.
(4) the Cost Accountant be not expected to teach costing a part of his duties, but he should co-operate fully with the costing tutors in educational institutions in Edinburgh, Glasgow and elsewhere to ensure those colleges were up-to-date and complied with costing examination requirements.
(5) close co-operation between member firms and the Alliance's Costing Department was essential.

While the Alliance Cost Accountant operated solely in Scotland and was under the direction of the Alliance office bearers he also worked closely with the BFMP Cost Accountant. He attended BFMP Costing Committee meetings in London. The BFMP Cost Accountant visited Scotland once or twice a year at the expense of the Scottish Alliance.

Summary

Membership of the Alliance grew strongly following its formation in 1910 and by 1926 it had local associations in Aberdeen, Ayrshire, Central Counties, Dundee, Dumfries, Edinburgh, Fifeshire, Forfarshire, Glasgow, Greenock, Lanarkshire, Perth and the Scottish Borders. Its decision making structure consisted of member firms, local associations, the Executive Board on which members represented their association and not their individual company and the annual general meeting. The chief official of the Scottish Alliance was the Secretary and as it grew in membership it developed mechanisms to communicate directly with member firms, for example by an annual conference open to all members and not just representatives. In the late 1920s, the Young Master Printer movement began in Scotland, becoming an important component in the development of future executive managers and owners in the industry.

The Scottish Alliance had a unique constitutional relationship with the BFMP relative to other BFMP Alliances. It had autonomy in that it controlled its own finances, conditions of membership and collective agreements. It remained an affiliated body of the BFMP with representation on its governing council and major subcommittees. It paid an annual subscription to the BFMP the amount of which was subject to periodic negotiation.

The main source of income for the Scottish Alliance was the annual subscription which was based on the amount of 'production worker' wages paid by the member firms although there was a minimum and maximum subscription payable. The major items of expenditure were staff salaries, technical education, affiliation fee to BFMP, working expenses of the associations, travel expenses and the operating costs of its costing system. During its lifetime, the financial position of the Scottish Alliance remained basically sound.

The core services the Alliance provided were political lobbying, advice and assistance, the negotiation of collective agreements with the trade unions, the selection, recruitment and training of apprentices and a costing and estimating service. This last service raised the awareness amongst member firms of the importance of the costing systems and procedures and their role as a check upon excessive price-cutting which during the inter-war years was a real threat to the economic stability of the Scottish printing industry.

Notes

1 See *Scottish Alliance Bulletin*, No. 1, July 1919.
2 See Scottish Alliance Bulletin, No. 13, July 1923.
3 See Minutes of the Executive Board Meeting, held on 8 March 1932.
4 See Minutes of the Executive Board Meeting, held on 30 July 1936.
5 By 1922 the Alliance had twelve branches – Aberdeen, Ayrshire, Central Counties, Dundee, Dumfries, Edinburgh, Fifeshire, Forfarshire, Glasgow, Greenock, Perth and Scottish Borders.
6 See Minutes of the Executive Board Meeting, held on 29 April 1926.
7 See Howe, E. (1950) *The British Federation of Master Printers, 1900-1950*. London: British Federation of Master Printers, p139.
8 Op cit, p145.
9 See Report of the Executive Board to the Twenty-eighth Annual General Meeting, March 1939.
10 See report of the Executive Board to the Nineteenth Annual General Meeting, March 1930.

Chapter 4

THE FIRST WORLD WAR, 1914 - 1918

This chapter examines the performance of the Scottish printing industry under the special conditions of the First World War. It analyses the UK government control over the industry's raw material supplies, particularly paper and over labour force redeployment to the army and munitions production via the direction of labour, conscription and the dilution of labour. Second, the chapter explains how the increasing cost of living, particularly food, led to claims from the unions for general wage increases and/or war bonuses. Although this brought friction between the Scottish Alliance and the print unions, in most instances it was settled amicably although on occasions industrial disputes arose. Part three of the chapter examines these infrequent disputes.

The Industry Under War Conditions

During the war, managing a printing company in Scotland became progressively more difficult. The trade suffered from diminished output, increased production costs, serious shortage of labour and restriction of paper supplies. The industry experienced an unprecedented scarcity of workers and a considerable rise in the cost of living led to labour unrest. Initially the war led to a fall in demand for the output of the industry and to increased production costs leading to increasing unemployment and short-time working. At the beginning of 1915 unemployment amongst print union members in Scotland was 10%. This labour surplus was soon absorbed as increasing numbers of print workers volunteered for the forces, were transferred to employment in the munitions industries and in 1917 conscripted into the forces. The labour surplus of the early war years had become a labour shortage leading to problems of craft dilution and the search for alternative supplies of labour. By the end of 1915 unemployment amongst Scottish print workers was less than 2% and the employers, faced with a labour shortage, pressed the unions to relax some of their restrictive working practices. In addition as the war progressed the industry experienced a steady decrease in the available supply of raw materials it required. Government control and direction of the economy tightened. The cost of living rose significantly each year leading to demands from the unions for an increase in wages.

The immediate impact of the First World War was a fall in demand for print work causing a sharp increase in unemployment. Where the volume of work was falling and the payment for that work uncertain companies introduced short-time working. As confidence returned, Scottish printing revived. A further factor at work was the hope the industry would capture some of the £350,000 worth of imported printed products into the UK from Germany. After the initial shock of the outbreak of war subsided, there was a scramble for printing work with a revival of competitive price-cutting. The Alliance warned its members that the price of raw materials would rise significantly and this, coupled with an increase in short-time working, would cause production costs to rise. The Alliance urged its members not to engage in price-cutting but to adopt accurate costing and estimating procedures. It was, however, unable to control the behaviour of its members in this regard despite the Secretary, Mr Bisset, giving a series of costing lectures at the technical college in Glasgow under the auspices of the Glasgow Association Costing Committee. The increased production costs were reflected in increased prices for print work causing a further decline in demand. The consequence of falling demand was increased short-time working and raised unemployment amongst Scottish print employees.

Government Control
a. Labour
In manpower terms, the Scottish printing industry was not regarded by the government as essential to the war effort, being seen as a 'luxury' industry. Printing jobs were not classified as reserve occupations. As a result, the labour surplus of the opening days of the war soon disappeared as the industry's workforce was redeployed by employees volunteering for the armed forces, their compulsory direction into the munitions industries and in 1917 conscription. In February 1916 a survey conducted by the Alliance amongst its members showed 45% of the total number of male workers, irrespective of age, employed in the printing industry immediately before the outbreak of war were now in colours. No other industry had a better record.[1] Scottish print workers had left the workshop for the battlefields in large numbers. By the end of 1916 some

50% of males employed in the Scottish printing industry before the war were either serving in the armed forces or working in the munitions industry. The departure of apprentices, particularly from lithographic departments, to serve in the forces caused problems. For many years the employers had complained of undue restriction of apprentices by the unions and now the unions objected to the places of enlisted apprentices being filled by new apprentices. The employers considered not to replace would seriously prejudice their prospects of later retaining British work which had been previously sent to Germany and of pushing German litho printers from the position they formerly held in foreign and colonial markets. In 1915 an agreement was reached between the Alliance and the STA to prevent the exceptional conditions of wartime resulting in a large influx of apprentices into the industry. Under the agreement the number of apprentices permitted to a firm was to be that existing in August 1914. Apprentices on active service were regarded as being in the employment of the firm for the purposes of determining the apprentice ratio. The replacement of apprentices in the armed forces was permitted only where the apprentice had served not more than one year of their apprenticeship or was within one year of its completion before they joined the forces.

By the autumn of 1915, the labour surplus had become an acute shortage. The Alliance and the trade unions became concerned with issues of dilution and regulating the influx of low paid labour. The government by late 1915, seeking to recruit into the armed forces some 30,000 men per week, began asking printing employers throughout the UK about the extent to which women could replace their male employees. The government was informed that before women could replace men they would require appropriate training and in addition, craft print union opposition to substituting women would have to be overcome.

The process of substituting young people for adults, women for men, semi-skilled for skilled, is known as the 'dilution of labour'. In the circumstances of the First World War, the aim was to make the fullest use of whatever type of labour was available in order to release for military service as many fit men as possible. By the end of 1915, the labour situation with respect to the armed forces was so acute that government officials met with the Council of the BFMP on which the Scottish Alliance had representation. Both the BFMP and the Scottish Alliance pointed out they could make no further economies in the use of printing employees unless the unions were prepared to relax their demarcation rules. At this stage the print unions were recovering from a year of relatively high unemployment and were apprehensive about the consequences of a reduction in paper imports. They were not in the mood to make concessions on demarcation.

At the insistence of the Home Office the BFMP approached the P&KTF and in April 1916 they reached agreement setting out general principles to govern the circumstances in which the print unions would suspend their recognised trade rules and customs when they could not supply skilled labour. Subject to the proviso that pre-war conditions be restored as soon as possible after the armistice, P&KTF-affiliated unions, including the STA, agreed the following clause:

> ...During the war and for such subsequent period as may be necessary to enable the unions to supply labour the unions agree to such suspension of rules and customs as may be necessary to secure the carrying on of the trade.
>
> The agreement shall come into operation only when, and for so long, as the unions are unable to supply labour. It shall be regarded purely as a war emergency and pre-war conditions shall be reverted to when the war is over...

In addition, the agreement guaranteed every employee joining the forces would be reinstated, when the war ended, in their previous position where this was possible provided they were capable of still discharging their duties. Where dilution was introduced by the employment of women those already employed in the trade were given first preference to undertake skilled work but if a reduction of staff became necessary the women dilutees would be the first to be dismissed. Any dispute arising under the agreement was referred to an arbitration committee comprised of representatives from both parties with the power to appoint an independent chair in the case of deadlock.

Questions of remuneration, demarcation and other details were left for settlement between the Scottish Alliance, the STA and the UK-wide unions with members in Scotland. Negotiations over the dilution of labour between the Alliance and print unions in Scotland followed the April 1916 agreement. The Alliance and the bookbinders' union in Scotland made an agreement which the employers considered of assistance to the bookbinding trade. In other parts of the industry, as in other parts of the UK, little progress was achieved in implementing dilution proposals owing to the unhelpful attitude of the unions.

In the larger Scottish cities, print employers obtained substantial benefit by the conclusion of agreements with the Advisory Committee or military representatives to the Military Service Tribunal, providing for the exemption from military service of print workers in those branches of the trade where labour shortages were most acute. By the spring of 1917 the labour needs of the armed forces remained inadequate and the government introduced conscription. The government released a number of munitions worker every month for the army and substitution officers at the Labour Exchange called upon local employers to provide men for the munitions industry. Since occupations in Scottish printing and allied trades were not restricted occupations, the industry was expected, under the government's direction of labour policies, to release existing employees to work in munitions factories.

b. Raw Materials

A further problem for Scottish print employers during the First World War was an increasing shortage of raw materials, especially paper. In 1915, the government announced the prohibition of the import of two thirds of the normal supplies so as to secure increased shipping space. The 'Prohibition of Imports (Paper etc.) Proclamation' (February 1916) prohibited from 1 March 1916 the importation into the United Kingdom of all materials for the manufacture of paper, cardboard (including strawboard, plasterboard, mill board and wood pulp board) and all printed publications exceeding sixteen pages in length, imported otherwise than as single copies through the post. The government appointed a commission to grant licences, and to arrange for the importing and distribution of bulk supplies among paper makers and paper users. Its chairman was Sir Thomas Whittaker MP, a director of insurance companies, whilst the remaining ten members were connected with the newspaper, book, printing and paper making trades. The BFMP appointed an advisory committee to assist the licensing authority. This committee immediately argued the printing trade was inadequately represented on the commission. In order supplies be fairly allocated, the year ending 31 December 1914 was taken as the basis.

By mid-1916, the paper shortage was becoming increasingly serious. From 1917, the paper restriction order prohibited the production of posters exceeding 600 square inches. Newspaper content bills were not to be printed and the use of paper for direct mail advertising was limited severely. In 1918, the government replaced the Paper Commission with a Paper Controller. By spring 1918 only 50% of the normal pre-war quantities of paper and pulp were being imported.

c. Other Matters

In April 1917, the Director of Materials informed the BFMP that he was authorised to issue permits for the purchase of lead to the extent of five tons during the months of April and May. Supplies of zinc were also commandeered by the government and the use of flour for paste in bookbinding prohibited. In the summer of 1917, the UK printing industry received an allocation of ten tons of printing metal for the use by firms during the months of June to August. The lithographic trade was permitted five tons of zinc in six months, a like weight of used plates to be found in exchange. In January 1918, Scottish print firms were pressurised by government to release metal for the manufacturing of shrapnel. The government had established a committee for the release of printers' metal and this body fixed the prices paid for scrap metal.

Government restrictions were found in areas other than the supply of raw materials. In 1915 the government abolished the half penny postage rate on printed matter but following representations from the BFMP that increased prices on this class of mail would hit printers hard, the government reversed this decision. Parliament decided the voters' list should not be printed but since some Scottish firms had already commenced work on the list it was expected they would suffer a heavy loss. Prompt action by the BFMP and the Alliance secured compensation for the member firms concerned. Restrictions of one sort or another continued to be imposed on the industry and in June 1917, the Board of Trade banned the publication of new periodicals. The government had already, in support of the war effort, taken over a number of printing works.

The government controls during the war years of labour and raw materials supplies were unpopular with Scottish print employers. The Alliance Executive Board's report to the 1917 annual general meeting complained the difficult conditions under which the industry operated were made steadily worse by:

> ...the effect of new Government restrictions, excellent no doubt in their purpose but irritating and anomalous in their incidence and most unsettling and prejudicial to the trade in their ambiguity and the constant amendment of their provisions...

The shortage of skilled labour and raw materials meant that during the war the Scottish printing industry could not satisfy the demand for its products. There were insufficient skilled workers available. Supplies of raw materials were almost unobtainable. Customers could not be confident their orders would be delivered. As a result some organisations, for example, local authorities, developed their own in-house printing capacity to secure their printing requirements whilst the UK government established its own printing works – the Stationery Office – to print ration books. After the end of the war not all of this work returned to the industry.

Wage Movements

From the beginning of the second year of the war, owing to increases in the cost of living, skilled labour shortages and the expanding economic activity, claims by print unions for either an advance of wages or for a war bonus became general throughout the industry in Scotland. In the early years of the war, the unions accepted small increases as war bonuses to meet increases in the cost of living. Applications for increases were made by the STA and the Scottish branches of UK-wide unions with members in Scotland. The years 1915 to 1918, saw repeated wage increases although they were not as high as they might have been, but for the excessive amounts of overtime worked and the consequent high levels of earnings. Wages rose steadily in all parts of Scotland and in some years, for example 1916, two increases of wages were conceded within a period of six months. While the abnormal external environment in which the industry operated during the First World War led to labour discontent there were few serious disputes.

The Alliance, under the Presidencies of Dr James MacLehose (1913-1916) and James S Waterston (1916-1919), at first grudgingly granted wage increases for fear of creating an awkward precedent but later granted larger increases in the spirit of compromise and later still even larger increases in the assurance member firms would more than recover these increases as a retail prices increased.

a. The Scottish Typographical Association

The immediate impact of the outbreak of war was to halt a number of wage increase claims which had been submitted by various STA branches. As the war progressed the manpower demands of the armed forces and the munitions industries eliminated unemployment from the Scottish printing industry creating a shortage. This, together with a rising cost of living, especially food stuffs, produced numerous demands from STA members for wage increases. In autumn 1915 deadlock was reported between the STA Edinburgh branch and the Edinburgh Master Printers Association over a claim for a wage increase. The Alliance's Executive Board refused the union's request for a conference arguing they did not consider deadlock had been reached and conciliation contained in their collective agreement had not been exhausted. In October 1915, the employers agreed to a conference with the union, chaired by an independent person, Sheriff MacKenzie, at which an agreement was reached.

In June 1916, the Glasgow Master Printers Association received a wage increase demand from the Glasgow STA branch of 5s 0d per week and for a reduction in the working week for all grades to forty eight hours. In September, the Glasgow Master Printers offered a war bonus of 2s 0d per week which proved acceptable to the Glasgow branch. 1916 also saw the Aberdeen Master Printers Association grant a war bonus increase of 2s 0d per week to STA Aberdeen branch members for the duration of the war and for three months thereafter. A war bonus of 1s 6d per week was granted, as opposed to 2s 0d to the members of the Dundee and Greenock branches of the STA. In Edinburgh in 1916, STA members accepted a war bonus of 2s 0d per week to male members and 1s 6d to women members. In Perth, the Perthshire Printing and Kindred Trades Association conceded a 2s 6d per week increase in the minimum grade rate for STA members to give the weekly wage of 37s 0d and a 2s 0d war bonus whilst in Galashiels and Selkirk the minimum weekly wage was enhanced to 35s 0d per week. In February 1917, the minimum weekly wage of STA members in Falkirk increased by 3s 6d per week making a weekly wage of 36s 0d. In the same month the Glasgow Master Printers Association granted a further war bonus of 3s 0d to STA members giving a weekly wage of 40s 0d plus a 5s 0d per week war bonus. In April 1917, the Edinburgh employers' association granted a further war bonus of 3s 0d giving a weekly wage of 37s 0d plus a 6s 0d per week war bonus. In the same month, the Dundee Printing and Kindred Trades Association conceded a further war bonus of 3s 0d to give a weekly wage of 30s 0d plus a weekly war bonus of 5s 0d.

During the First World War, the wage increases gained by Scottish printing employees ranged from a low of 16s 0d in Forfar to a high of 32s 0d in Dundee. In Glasgow in the book and jobbing sector employees' wages increased by 30s 0d to give a weekly wage rate of 68s 0d with 73s 0d and 75s 0d for those operating composing machines. In Edinburgh during the First World War the weekly wage rate increased by 31s 0d to 66s 0d. The rate for those employed on mechanical composition rose to 68s 6d per week giving a total increase over the war of 30s 0d. Outside of Glasgow and Edinburgh, Greenock and Paisley secured the Glasgow weekly rate of 68s 0d. By the end of the war the weekly rate in Forfar was 46s 0d and that in both Banff and Hawick 47s 6d per week.

b. Bookbinders and Machine Rulers

In April 1914 the Alliance received, from the Scottish District Council of the National Union of Bookbinders and Machine Rulers, a claim for an increase of 3s 0d per week on the current minimum rate in the bookbinding and related trades throughout Scotland. The Alliance Executive Board, after consulting with its local associations replied stating due to the losses caused to the trade through the recent strike the request could not be considered. The union's response was to write a letter of protest to the Executive Board.

At its meeting on 14 April 1915, the Executive Board declined to consider any increase in wages from any union during the war. The Secretary of the Alliance wrote to the Secretary of the Scottish District Council of the Bookbinders and Machine Rulers Union stating:

> ...that while the Board sympathised with the position of his members the state of the trade arising out of the war made it quite impossible for them to consider any question of increasing wages during the war and that while the Board was prepared to have a Conference if desired by his Council, they did not consider that any good purpose could be served by such a Conference...[2]

On 27 April 1915 a conference was held between the Alliance and the Scottish District Council at which the former was prepared to reconsider wage rates and other employment conditions in the event of the economic state of the industry becoming satisfactory after the war. The Scottish District Council asked the Alliance to reconsider its policy not to grant a wage increase during the war but the Alliance again emphasised it saw no valid reason to change its policy. In response the Bookbinders Union members decided, by ballot, further steps be taken to secure an advance in wages. They submitted a claim for an increase of 6s 0d per week in the minimum rate throughout Scotland with an advance of 10% on piece rates. In October 1915 the Alliance offered to increase the bookbinding minimum wage throughout Scotland by 2s 0d and to bargaining adjustment to piece rates on a house by house basis. This was subject to a conference with the Scottish District

Council at which the question of time recording and temporary modification of working conditions be discussed. At the conference held on 15 December 1915, the Alliance's offer was rejected. Following a further conference in early 1916 the union accepted the employers' offer when the latter dropped their preconditions.

In June 1916, the Scottish District Council submitted to the Alliance a claim for an increase of 5s 6d per week on the present minimum rate with corresponding increases in piece rates. The Alliance responded that they were only prepared to review wages when satisfactory arrangements had been agreed concerning the temporary dilution of labour and for this information to be provided to employers so as to ascertain the true cost of work. At a meeting with the Scottish District Council of the union held on 21 September 1916 agreement was reached. There was an increase of 2s 6d per week on the standard minimum rate. In return the union accepted the keeping of 'time records' and of records of work undertaken during the year. The agreement was ratified by the union on 30 September 1916.

In November 1917, the Alliance again received a claim from the Scottish District Council for an increase in wages. The Aberdeen, Edinburgh, Glasgow and Dundee associations of the Alliance[3] all opposed granting any wage increase. The bookbinders had received an increase in August 1917 and the Alliance's opposition to a further increase was that no changes in circumstances had taken place since August to justify this. Second the employers considered any question of a wage increase was a matter for the proposed Scottish Wages Board when established. Nevertheless, the Alliance offer to meet with the union in conference was rejected. The Scottish print employers considered the union's claim in conjunction with those recently received from the Glasgow branch of the P&KTF, the Edinburgh and Dundee branches of the ASLP, the Edinburgh branch (Women's Section) of the NUP&PW and from the Dundee branch of the STA. The Alliance suggested these claims be considered on a co-ordinated basis at a conference between the union and itself.

Early in 1918, the Scottish District Council sent a letter to the Alliance seeking the equalisation of bookbinding wages with those of other trades in the industry. At a conference held in March between the Alliance and Scottish District Council, the former objected to the principle of parity with other trades, owing to the complications that might arise with these other sections. So the union was informed the employers saw the matter of one for consideration by the proposed wages board when it was established. In July 1918, the Scottish District Council submitted a new claim:
(1) there be to all male members of the union a 20s 0d per week increase in wages.
(2) the weekly increase for all female members presently in receipt of 15s 0d per week and over, be 10s 0d.
(3) the weekly increase for all female members in receipt of a weekly wage of less than £15 be 5s 0d per week.

(4) payment be made for all statutory holidays and

(5) the employers consider levelling up male bookbinder wages to those of other allied trades in the Scottish printing industry.

At a conference held on 29 August 1918, the Alliance repeated the view they could not improve their offer but were prepared to refer the matter of parity to the Committee on Production with the following terms of reference:

> ...That the Committee on Production be asked to give a decision on the facts submitted by the Scottish Alliance of Master Printers in the Printing and Kindred Trades and the Scottish District Committee of the National Union of Bookbinders and Machine Rulers as to the claim by the union that the wages of their male members be levelled up to those of the other allied trades...

On 13 December 1918, the Alliance received a letter from the Ministry of Labour stating the bookbinders claim on levelling up the wages of their male members to those of other trades had been referred to the Interim Court of Arbitration for determination. The court awarded parity with other trades in the industry by granting an increase of 1s 6d per week on the minimum wage of the male members of the Bookbinders and Machine Rulers Union.

c. The ASLP

In May 1915, to minimise the occurrence of industrial action, Scottish Alliance and the ASLP extended the Lithographic Trade Conciliation Board to the whole of Scotland. It was a body to which disputes between the two parties could be referred for possible settlement. Under its constitution there were seven trade union representatives and seven employer representatives. The Alliance representative were to be drawn two from Edinburgh, two from Glasgow and one each from Dundee, Greenock and Aberdeen local associations. The board originally covered only Edinburgh and Glasgow. The Conciliation Board, along with that for the STA and the bookbinders helped keep relationships between the Alliance and the unions in the Scottish industry constructive and in a spirit of moderation.

In October 1915 the ASLP submitted a claim for a wage increase. Although the Alliance rejected the claim it attended a conference at which it offered to increase the minimum weekly wage rate of 37s 0d per week to 39s 0d. The union rejected the offer and imposed an overtime working ban in both Glasgow and Edinburgh. In February 1916 a conference was held under the chairmanship of the Chief Industrial Commissioner and at which a settlement was reached. In September 1916, the Edinburgh ALSP branch claimed an increase in wages. The employers were prepared to offer a war bonus of 2s 0d per week subject to discussions on the dilution of labour and an increase in output. The war bonus of 2s 0d was accepted by the ASLP Glasgow and Edinburgh branches. Later in 1916, the 2s 0d per week war bonus was also granted by the Alliance to the ASLP branches in Dundee and Greenock.

In early 1917 the Aberdeen ASLP branch received an increase of 3s 0d as a war bonus making the minimum rate in that town 36s 0d plus 3s 0d war bonus. The 3s 0d war bonus was also granted to their employees by the Glasgow and Edinburgh Associations of the Scottish Alliance making the minimum rate in both cities 40s 0d plus a war bonus of 5s 0d. In June 1917, the ASLP Edinburgh and Glasgow branches submitted a wage demand for an across-the-board increase of 10s 0d per week. The demand was regarded as premature, but the Alliance met with the two branches to exchange views. In light of this demand and the probability of similar claims from other unions, the June 1917 meeting of the Alliance Executive Board requested the Board of Trade enquire into the wages paid in the whole of the Scottish printing industry. The Alliance committed itself to give every assistance to such an enquiry. In September 1917, a wages conference was held, involving representatives of the Alliance, the ASLP and the NUPB&MR, under the chairmanship of the Chief Industrial Commissioner. The parties failed to reach an agreement but accepted that the ASLP case be decided by the Chief Industrial Commissioner whose decision would bind both parties. In the case of the bookbinders, the Commissioner was to make a recommendation which would be favourably considered by both parties. Subsequently, in both cases the Chief Industrial Commissioner awarded a wage increase of 4s 0d per week which was accepted by all the parties concerned.

d. Printing and Kindred Trades Federation

Under the P&KTF constitution, in places where two or more branches of affiliated unions existed such unions were to co-operate and form a local federation. P&KTF local federations existed in Glasgow and Edinburgh co-ordinating the organisation of print employees there. At either national or local level, the P&KTF could not negotiate wages on behalf of its affiliates. It did, however, bargain on their behalf on hours of work, holidays, pensions, etc. In the later stages of the First World War its affiliates gave it authority for the duration of the war only, to bargain on their behalf on wage matters.

In March 1918 the Glasgow local federation submitted a claim for:
(1) an increase of 10s 0d per week for all members of its affiliated unions including apprentices aged eighteen years and over,
(2) a 5s 0d per week increase to apprentices under eighteen years of age,
(3) the increases be effective from 25 March 1918 and
(4) the employers reply to the claim before 16 March.

The Glasgow Master Printers rejected it, considering to grant it would merely trigger other wage demands. It rejected the claim on the grounds the cost of living had not increased since the last pay increase, the matter be dealt with at the national level and if a conference were arranged then the Chief Industrial Commissioner of the Board of Trade be involved.

The Glasgow Master Printers sought the opinion of the Alliance who advised them to meet with P&KTF representatives to:

(1) clarify the grounds upon which the increase in wages was being sought,
(2) tell them their demand be refused as a local one and
(3) see how far they should go deferring action until the national demand was made.

The Alliance also advised the results of any conference be communicated to its other associations. A conference of representatives of the Alliance and the P&KTF took place on 7 August 1918. The P&KTF said its affiliates could accept nothing less than the proposed 10s 0d per week increase. The Alliance responded by arguing the Glasgow Master Printers could not agree to any advance but were prepared to submit the issue to the proposed wages board or to the Committee on Production. This suggestion was rejected by the P&KTF which passed the following resolution:

> ...That we adhere to the 10/- requested. That we are not prepared to recommend to our members that the question be submitted to the Committee on Production but suggest that you again consult your members and meet us on Wednesday next week, to continue Conference...[4]

The Alliance attended a further conference held on 14 August 1918 at which it submitted a revised offer. Male workers received an increase of 7s 6d per week and senior apprentices 3s 6d. Female workers currently receiving a weekly wage of more than 17s 6d receive an increase of 3s 6d per week. Female employees currently earning 17s 6d per week or less to receive a weekly increase of 2s 0d. If acceptable these proposed increases would be implemented on 26 August 1918. The offer was rejected by the unions. At a conference held on 5 September 1918 the employers agreed:
(1) to recommend an increase of 10s 0d per week to male workers with no alteration on the increased offer already made to other workers,
(2) the claim of the Edinburgh female compositors be remitted to the Edinburgh Local Association,
(3) in districts where female compositors were paid the standard wage of the STA branch they receive the increase proposed for male workers, namely 10s 0d per week and,
(4) the increases be payable on the first pay day after 16 September 1918.
This revised offer was accepted by P&KTF affiliates.

e. The Wages Board

The sectional wage movements of the First World War period led to steps towards national level negotiations and agreements in Scotland. The initiative was taken by the Alliance who discussed the question of determining wages on a Scotland-wide basis with the Ministry of Labour. The catalyst for this action was two wage increases in Edinburgh, Glasgow, Aberdeen, Dundee and Perth resulting from the activities of the P&KTF. A conference was convened in the North British Station Hotel at the end of July 1917 with Sir George Askwith acting as independent chair and with representatives of the Alliance and the trade unions present. The meeting considered the possibility of national negotiations for the Scottish printing industry and the establishment of a Scottish wage board.

An amicable settlement on wages was reached but, more importantly, the conference passed a resolution agreeing the principle that wages be dealt with nationally and recommending the establishment of a committee to consider, and draw up, a constitution for a joint wages board[5]. Mr Bisset for the Alliance and John Richardson of the STA were appointed joint secretaries to the committee. The dominant view at the February 1917 conference was national agreements would be more productive, responsible, broad-minded and fairer to the industry than was the case under the existing system of local/district wage movements.

Progress towards the establishment of a Scottish wages board was slow. There were several follow up conferences, and negotiations were not helped in that the NUPB&MR was not at this stage a member of the P&KTF, whilst the National Society of Electrotypers and Stereotypers did not accept the need for a wages board for Scotland. In March 1918, the bookbinders' union rejoined the P&KTF and the NSES and dropped its opposition to the principle of a wages board. The constitution of the Wages Board for the Printing Industry in Scotland was approved by both sides of the joint committee and subsequently the trade unions. By the end of 1918 the board was finally established but did not become operable until 14 January 1919. The unions agreed any claim from one union to the board be initially submitted to the Workers' Panel which would consult with other sections of the industry so a common claim went to the board.[6]

The board consisted of an equal number (eight) of representatives of the Scottish Alliance and the trade unions in Scotland affiliated to the P&KTF. The board could be terminated by either side giving the other six months notice in writing. The board adjusted from time to time, by mutual agreement, the minimum wages paid and the maximum hours worked in each branch of the industry in Scotland. All changes in wages or hours of work decided by the board took effect from the first pay day of the third month following the date of the meeting at which the proposed changes were first considered. The board met within twenty one days of notice being received by the secretary of either side, such notice to state clearly the purpose of the meeting. The board could adjourn for a period not exceeding fourteen days to enable representatives to report to, and to consult, with their constituents. In the event of a settlement not being reached either side could request a further meeting of the board within fourteen days. Such meetings chaired by a mutually agreed individual. If the parties could not agree an independent chair the Ministry of Labour appointed one. The independent chair had no power to arbitrate on differences between the parties. He could only give an opinion or make a recommendation(s). When the Chairman of the Wages Board was from the employers' side the

Vice-Chairman was from the employees' side and vice versa. Each side appointed its own secretary. No strike, lock out or other aggressive or coercive action was to be taken by either side on any matter of wages or hours until the matter had been considered by the board. Should the board adjourn no industrial action was to be taken by either party during the period of the adjournment.[7]

Industrial Disputes

Whilst the abnormal conditions of the First World War led to a considerable amount of labour unrest, there were only two major disputes during the period in the Scottish printing industry, one of which was in progress when war was declared in August 1914. This had begun in July 1914 and involved a strike of female workers who were members of the Warehousemen and Cutters Union employed by John Horn Ltd, Glasgow. It ended on 1 September 1914. The second dispute involved a strike of the stone and plate preparers in Edinburgh who were members of the National Society of Operative Printers and Assistants (NATSOPA). This dispute resulted in a lockout of all print workers in both Glasgow and Edinburgh.

a. John Horn

The female members of the Warehousemen and Cutters Union employed by John Horn of Glasgow struck on Saturday 4 July 1914, alleging victimisation of one of their fellow workers. The circumstances of the case had been considered by the executives of the three Glasgow associations of employers (Master Printers, Lithographers and Master Bookbinders) at a meeting on 30 June 1914 at which Horn's proposal to accept the employees' strike notices was unanimously approved. It was agreed to support the company in dismissing the individual employee, to recommend the Executive Board of the Alliance give their support to John Horn and they compensate the company for any financial losses which they might sustain from the strike. At subsequent meetings of the Edinburgh Master Printers Association and the Edinburgh Lithographers Association similar decisions were made. After a full debate on the proposed strike, the Alliance Executive Board at its meeting on 9 July 1914 agreed the following resolution.

> ...The Executive Board of the Scottish Alliance, having considered the strike of some 50 female employees of Messrs John Horn Ltd, Glasgow, on the grounds that one of their fellow workers had been victimised, is satisfied that the services of the girl, T. Smyth were dispensed with in the ordinary way of business and that there was no victimisation. The Board unanimously agrees 1) to give Messrs Horn all necessary support and instructs the Secretary accordingly and 2) that Messrs Horn be compensated for losses sustained by them in the dispute.

In mid-July the STA Glasgow branch instructed its members not to handle or undertake work belonging to Messrs Horn. The Glasgow Master Printers

Association responded by saying any member of the STA Glasgow branch who declined to undertake work given them would be immediately suspended. The Glasgow Master Printers Association claimed the union's behaviour was a breach of the current mutually agreed working rules. On the outbreak of war, at a time when the strike had virtually collapsed, a communication was received from Sir George Askwith, Chief Industrial Commissioner to the Board of Trade asking the dispute be submitted to an independent enquiry. The Alliance agreed to this request. On 1 September 1914 the independent enquiry was held at the Central Hotel, Glasgow chaired by Sheriff A O M Mackenzie who decided that the employee involved, Theresa Smyth, had been dismissed fairly. This brought the dispute to an end. The Alliance Executive Board reported at its meeting on 23 December 1914 the cost of the strike at Horns had been £190 which would not be met from the funds of the Alliance but by voluntary subscriptions from Edinburgh and Glasgow printing companies and by a direct payment from the funds of the Glasgow Master Printers Association.

b. The Stone and Plate Preparers' Dispute[8]

This dispute led to a lockout of the whole printing trade in both Edinburgh and Glasgow and was the most serious in which the Scottish Alliance had been involved since its inception. The lithographic stone and plate preparers were members of NATSOPA which was not recognised by the Scottish Alliance. In October 1915, NATSOPA lodged a claim that the pay rates of stone and plate preparers in Edinburgh be increased to 29s 0d per week. The Alliance refused to acknowledge the claim as they did not recognise NATSOPA. The seventeen stone and plate preparers tendered their notices but the twenty who were non-union members continued to work. ASLP members refused to accept stones polished by non-union employees. In November 1915, in Edinburgh the ASLP withdrew its objection to accepting stones polished by non-unionists but said it would not accept stones from men engaged to fill the places of the employees on strike. Twenty four Edinburgh firms, employing 80% of the members of the ASLP Edinburgh Branch, pledged to lock out union members with effect from 13 November 1915. Glasgow and Edinburgh Master Printers Associations agreed not to consider any further wage demands until the difficulties with the ASLP in Edinburgh had been resolved.

Prior to the strike, attempts by the P&KTF to try to organise a conference between the Alliance and NATSOPA failed. In February 1916, the ASLP Edinburgh branch informed the Edinburgh Master Lithographers Association that its members with effect from 4 March 1916 refused to handle stones or plates prepared by non-union labour. The Edinburgh Master Lithographers Association referred the matter to the Alliance urging them to take a general, not local or sectional, view as the action of the ASLP Edinburgh branch was at the insistence of the P&KTF. The Scottish Alliance, considering itself now in dispute with the P&KTF, called upon its members in Edinburgh and Glasgow to post to all members of unions affiliated to the P&KTF suspension notices. This resulted in some 700 STA members being locked out as well as 400 members of the bookbinders' union and sixty members of the ALSP. The dispute varied in duration from two to five weeks.

The Board of Trade intervened. There were two conferences between the Scottish Alliance and the P&KTF with Sir Thomas Munro acting as independent chair and conciliator. The first conference lasted twelve hours but produced no constructive result. A week later a second conference, lasting ten hours, was held. Eventually a settlement was reached under which the lockout notices were withdrawn, and eleven stone and plate preparers reinstated at a minimum wage of 28s 0d, increasing to 29s 0d three months later. Some thirty six men were now employed in Edinburgh as stone and plate preparers, twelve of which (all unionists) had been granted the 29s 0d weekly wage whilst working during the strike.

The Edinburgh unions had supported the eleven striking stone and plate preparers but Glasgow had not become involved until the lockout notices were issued in March 1916. ASLP Glasgow branch members therefore sought, before returning to work, some guarantee from employers that in future no lockout would take place in the lithographic trade in Glasgow owing to industrial problems in another area. Two conferences were held resulting in agreement that in future no strike or lockout would take place in the Glasgow lithographic trade until both sides had reflected on the situation. Should no agreement be reached, a second meeting with an independent chairman would be held within eight days to consider the matter further.

The stone and plate preparers' dispute of 1915/16 was at the time the most serious in which the Alliance had been involved since its formation. The Alliance considered but for the precipitate and aggressive action taken by the P&KTF the dispute would not have lasted as long as it did. The 1916 Annual General Meeting of the Scottish Alliance was told:

> ...Certain features of the dispute indicate a deliberate effort amongst sections of workers to effect a disruption of the Alliance, an effort which it is hardly necessary to add, met with no success but had rather the contrary effect. Your Board have to emphasis that in the dispute they had no quarrel with any Scottish union or any breach of any union, the trouble emanating entirely from labour organisations south of the border...[9]

Summary
During the First World War (1914-1918), member firms of the Scottish Alliance, although ably led by its Presidents (Dr James MacLehose and James S Waterston), experienced initially a decline in economic activity, and a labour surplus. With the deployment of the industry's workforce into the army first by volunteers and subsequently conscription and into the munitions industry,

the labour surplus became a scarcity. The Scottish print industry faced a constant drain on its labour force by the demands of the army. In a further attempt to release fit young men for the army, the government pressurised print employers to substitute older people for young, women for men and unskilled for skilled and to conclude a labour dilution agreement.

The war years were characterised by a shortage of raw materials, especially paper. There was a steady decrease in the availability of every kind of raw material required. The industry's output was severely reduced relative to pre-August 1914. Government regulations and restrictions were prejudicial to the Scottish print industry and their continual amendments were a source of irritation to member firms of the Alliance. The steady increase in the cost of living, especially foodstuffs, led to labour unrest which for the most part was resolved without industrial action. The main exception was the 1915-1916 strike of stone and plate preparers in Edinburgh which resulted in a lockout of all litho print employees in Glasgow and Edinburgh. The wage increases of this period were either flat rate pay increases and/or smaller increases in the form of war bonuses.

Notes

[1] See Report by the Executive to the Sixth Annual General Meeting of the Scottish Alliance of Masters in the Printing and Allied Trades, April 1917.

[2] See Minutes of the Meeting of the Executive Board, 14 April 1915.

[3] The Aberdeen employers' association did not become a branch of the Alliance until March 1918.

[4] See Minutes of the Meeting of the Executive Board, 9 August 1918.

[5] See Report by the Executive Board to the Seventh Annual General Meeting of the Scottish Alliance of Masters in the Printing and Allied Trades, Glasgow, April 1918.

[6] See S C Gillespie (1953), *A Hundred Years of Progress: The Record of the Scottish Typographical Association*, 1853 to 1952. Glasgow: MacLehose, p158.

[7] There was also an Addendum to the Constitution of the Wage Board which stated: 'It is mutually agreed that it is desirable that all employers in the industry in Scotland should be members of the Scottish Alliance of Employers in the Printing and Kindred Trades and that all workers members of the appropriate trade union and that every endeavour be made to carry this into effect'.

[8] For a more detailed description and analysis of this dispute see T Sproat (1930) *The History and Progress of the ASLP, 1880-1936*. Manchester: Jubilee Souvenir, pp59–61 and C J Bundock (1958), *The National Union of Printing, Bookbinding and Paperworkers*, Oxford: Oxford University Press, p101.

[9] See Report by the Executive Board to the Fifth Annual General Meeting of the Scottish Alliance of Masters in the Printing and Allied Trades, Glasgow, June 1916.

Chapter 5

RELATIONSHIPS WITH THE TRADE UNIONS 1919- 1939: EXTERNAL ENVIRONMENT

This chapter outlines the economic and technological environment in which collective bargaining in the Scottish printing industry took place over the period 1919 to 1939. It starts by pointing out there were no dramatic technological developments implemented during the inter-war years but some important developments took place with the mechanisation of bookbinding. Second, the chapter traces the beginning of what became, after the Second World War, an alternative to the conventional printing industry based on the use by non-printing companies of small office printing machines. The chapter then reports the extent of unemployment in the Scottish printing industry in the period 1919 to 1939, pointing out although it was high relative to previous time periods, it was only one half of the level of that experienced by other industries in Scotland. Next the new industrial relations institutions – the Scottish Wages Board, the National Joint Industrial Council and the Scottish Joint Industrial Council – established by the employers and unions in the Scottish printing industry to avoid destructive open industrial conflict are examined. The chapter then notes the change in attitude, particularly of the STA, to the organisation of women and the industry's lesser skilled employees. Finally, the chapter evaluates the impact of the General Strike of May 1926 on the industry.

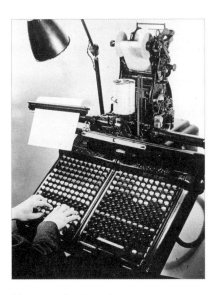

Monotype keyboard.
Reproduced courtesy of the Scottish Centre for the Book, Edinburgh Napier University.

Monotype caster.
Reproduced courtesy of the Scottish Centre for the Book, Edinburgh Napier University.

Industrial Developments

a. Technological

In the inter-war period there were no technical developments in the Scottish printing industry as dramatic as the introduction in the 1890s of mechanical composition and high-speed presses. There was, however, continuous search for greater machine speeds, greater accuracy and the development of ancillary machinery such as mechanical feeders and anti-setoff devices. An important new printing technique which developed between the two world wars was photogravure, a process well suited to meet consumer demand for the production of illustrated periodicals and glossy women's magazines which were becoming increasingly popular.

The most important technological development during the inter-war years in the printing industry was the mechanisation of bookbinding. One machine now performed all operation in making a cloth case whilst another did all of the 'forwarding' operations – folding, gathering and stitching in one run through. Cutting and trimming were speeded up by the use of three-knife trimmers. Blocking of the cases (printing of the titles etc.) was speeded up by power-driven machines. Part of the reason for the mechanisation of bookbinding was the union's policy of raising wage rates, especially those of women. Before the First World War many semi-skilled bookbinding tasks were performed by women or girls. After the war many women joined a union – often to the disgust of the old craftsmen – and their rates became standardised. There were, however, many other factors at work including the increasing demands of an educated population for cheap books, changes in publishers' practices, the growth of commercial and municipal libraries and the need to replace equipment worn out during the war. When the trade journals of the 1920s carried eye-catching advertisements stressing the improved capabilities of the new machines, of American design, most of the larger bookbinding offices decided to invest in them.

These changes posed potential industrial relations problems. Although the unions were not opposed to the introduction of new machinery they had a policy that as a matter of principle the machine operator be a member of the same union as the hand craftsman whose job the machine had replaced. As the Scottish print employers were content to operate such a policy, the 'control of the machine' did not become a matter of dispute. A second potential industrial relations problem was the extra payment an operator should receive for operating new machinery. The unions argued operators should have extra pay to compensate for the additional skill, responsibility or strain. They sought agreement on a schedule of extras payable for each type of machine. When these had been standardised, the unions claimed it was be relatively simple to determine the rate for a new machine by comparing it with one of the known ones. Constant disputes over machine rates were avoided when the employers and the unions agreed a procedure for determining the machine extras. All negotiations were to be on a UK basis, adjustments on a flat-rate basis, employees trained to operate new machines to receive half of the extra for the first six months and there be no change in the staffing of machines without consultation with the unions.

b. An Alternative Printing Industry

The inter-war period saw the growth of what Scottish print employers were to refer to as 'the alternative printing industry'. The Scottish Alliance *Bulletin* of October 1919 put this trend down to two factors.[1] First, during the war the public had to economise on its printing demands and discovered in many instances they could live without their previous printed products or could substitute something less expensive than their traditional printing requirements. For example some public bodies had the minutes of their meetings typewritten and their annual printed statements discontinued. Second, the high cost of printing caused organisations to discontinue their demand for printing work and to install their own small office printing appliances. It was common knowledge the high price of print meant long-standing customers were now doing without. The printing of catalogues was greatly reduced and in some cases terminated. In 1919, the Royal Technical College in Glasgow (now the University of Strathclyde) suspended printing of its *Calendar*, owing to its high costs. The *Calendar*, of which several thousand copies were printed each year, was over 400 pages. In manufacturing and commercial houses, jobbing sheets, memoranda and similar jobs which formerly were placed in jobbing print shops, in the inter-war years were increasingly produced by former customers on Roneo or Gestetner type duplicating machines within their own workplaces. These machines were operated by young girls at rates of pay and other employment conditions below those operating in the traditional printing industry.

In 1919 the President of the Scottish Alliance (James Paterson) received a request from the print employers' association in the Kirkcaldy district asking that protest be made against their public authority typing the voters' roll instead of printing. In Elgin and other authorities in northern Scotland the valuation rolls were switched from printing to being typewritten. In December 1934 the industry received a profound shock when the Glasgow Corporation established its own department to manufacture and supply the stationery, printing and bookbinding requirements of the Corporation and its committees, including exercise books and school requisites of its Education Department.[2]

The inter-war period witnessed print employers in Scotland, and the rest of the United Kingdom, discussing the merits and demerits of the UK central government maintaining its own printing works. The Stationery Office works at Harrow was set up in 1918 for the printing of ration books. There was dismay amongst printing companies when it became apparent the Stationery Office would be a permanent fixture. By early 1922 it employed 800 people. The Scottish print employers through affiliation to the BFMP, continued to question, unsuccessfully, whether the country could afford to retain a state printing works when its work could be done as efficiently and cheaper, in privately owned printing offices. The UK government on 16 June 1923, appointed a Committee of Inquiry into the Government Printing Works. Its report, published in March 1927, recommended apart from strictly confidential work, all printing required by the UK government be put out to open competition. Where the Stationery Office could show an estimated saving in comparison to the lowest tender price received from a private print firm the work was allocated to the government press. The government accepted this recommendation.

The inter-war years witnessed the beginning of another source of lost work for the Scottish printing industry, namely import penetration. Increasingly many new and existing school books in the English language were typeset and printed in India.

c. Unemployment

In the inter-war years the Scottish printing industry experienced high unemployment and changes in the composition of its workforce. The return to peacetime conditions brought expansion in the volume of business, chiefly as a result of completing the arrears of work accumulated during the war period. Few, if any, industries were as successful as Scottish printing in tackling, and overcoming, the difficulties of reinstating returning soldiers to their pre-war employment positions. In reality, the industry was more suited to peace and industrial development than to war and its accompanying destruction. By the end of 1920 the immediate post-war economic boom conditions had turned into economic depression. Printing, nevertheless, continued to be an industry with expanding employment opportunities. Unemployment was approximately half as high as the average for all other industries in Scotland. There was a setback in 1931, and it would be wrong to think print workers in Scotland escaped the impact of the Great Depression of the 1930s. They suffered higher levels of unemployment than print workers in other parts of the UK. In 1932 the percentage of unemployed print workers in Scotland was twice that for certain areas in England. The Alliance Executive Board report to the twenty third annual general meeting held in March 1934 blamed the relatively higher wages in Scotland.

> ...It is not open to question that the great difference between the wages in the larger Scottish branches and those in the competitive areas in England is the principal reason for the higher ratio of unemployment in Scotland...

The unemployment of the Great Depression affected adversely the morale of some employers in the industry and the Alliance became concerned some of its member firms adopted a policy of price-cutting, including selling their print products below cost. The Alliance warned against such a pricing policy and sought to convince them the installation, and working, of the Costing System in every office was an essential step towards elimination of the self-defeating policy of selling below cost.

To protect the economic well-being of the Scottish printing industry and to increase its employment opportunities, some Alliance members advocated all Scottish printing work be confined to Scotland. At the January 1936 Executive Board, James M'Kelvie argued this proposition suggesting the matter be considered by the Scottish Development Council. The Executive Board set up a small committee to investigate the matter. It reported to the January 1937 meeting of the Executive Board recommending that in view of the amount of work done by Scottish-based print companies for English local authorities the best policy would be not to make any official approach to the Scottish Development Council. The Executive Board accepted this view.[3] There was also a body of opinion amongst some Alliance members that economic recovery, and a consequent fall in unemployment would come through a combination of absolute cuts in wages, the removal of restrictions on working conditions and the reduction of special payments such as machine extras. In short, a reduction in production costs.

The print unions advocated the Scottish printing trade would only be revived by shortening the working week to share the existing work more equitably between workers, by a reduction in the apprentice ratio to reduce the supply of labour entering the industry and by the abolition, or severe restriction, of overtime working. These were, at the time, the traditional trade union remedies for reducing employment. They failed to realise the inter-war years' depression was related to economic adjustments and its reversal required radical fiscal and financial measures beyond the ability of trade unions to deliver.

During the inter-war years the Scottish printing industry saw a marked change in the proportion of compositors and machine men employed. In 1925 there were 4,905 compositors and machine men employed in the industry. Of these 68% were compositors. By 1951 the number of compositors and machine men in the industry had fallen to 4,554 and of this total 60% were compositors. In Edinburgh the number of compositors employed fell from 1,040 in 1913 to 607 in 1951 – a fall of 42%. The corresponding figures for machine men were 628 and 447 – a fall of 29%. The main factor at work was the relative decline in the Edinburgh book trade which had been a staple feature, for many years, of the Edinburgh printing industry.

Recognition by the STA after the First World War that female compositors were a reality in the Edinburgh printing industry, saw a gradual improvement in their status and a reduction in the pay gap between the male and the female compositor. Women recruited to replace male compositors during the First World War were paid the male rate which was higher than that paid to female compositors employed pre-war in Edinburgh and Aberdeen. The number of female compositors recruited in the war was small and soon after its end, those receiving the full male rate had all retired or been replaced. Throughout most of the 1919 to 1939 period women compositors were only found in Aberdeen and Edinburgh. Under the national agreements signed immediately after the end of the First World War they received 70% of the male rate. They could only accept employment outside Aberdeen and Edinburgh if paid the full male rate.

The New Industrial Relations Institutions

The inter-war years saw the emergence of three new industrial relations institutions for the Scottish printing industry. On 14 January 1919 the Scottish Wages Board for the Printing Industry was founded with the objective of adjusting, from time to time, by mutual agreement, the minimum wage paid and the maximum hours worked in the industry. The Board ceased to function in 1924. In July 1919 the National Joint Industrial Council (NJIC) for the printing industry held its initial meeting. It was formed as a co-operative organisation of employers and trade unions. Its constitution included a branch industrial council for Scotland known as the Scottish Joint Industrial Council (SJIC) to deal with matters affecting the industry in Scotland. The SJIC was inaugurated at a meeting in Glasgow on 29 November 1922. Basic wages and working conditions were regulated by a series of national agreements. The method of regulating relationships between the Alliance and the print unions in Scotland for settling disputes (for example conciliation boards) remained basically unchanged throughout the twenty-year period. Apart from the May 1926 General Strike, the feature of the industrial relations of the Scottish printing industry was the absence of deep-seated hostility between the employers and employees and the infrequency of open hostility.

a. The Scottish Printing Industry Wages Board

The first steps towards national negotiations in Scotland were taken by the Scottish Alliance which anticipated the Whitley Report published in 1917, which advocated, inter alia, national agreements. At their request a conference was held in Edinburgh in 1917 with representatives of the unions. Sir George Askwith from the Ministry of Labour acted as the independent chair. The meeting considered the possibility of national wage negotiations for the Scottish printing industries and agreed the establishment of a Scottish Wages Board. Progress to these ends was slow with over a year of negotiations and conferences. By 1918 a constitution for a Scottish Printing Industry Wages Board was agreed.

The board was constituted on 14 January 1919 but problems with the NSES and the bookbinders union meant the workers panel of the board was not agreed until 1 August 1919. The board consisted of eleven representatives from each side of the industry. The employers' representatives were the Alliance Secretary (R T Wishart), the Alliance President, the Chair of the Executive Board plus three representatives from its Edinburgh association, two from its Glasgow association and one each from the Aberdeen and Dundee associations plus a representative of the interests of its smaller associations. The National Union of Journalists' application for membership of the workers' panel of the board was rejected in 1920 and in 1924 because of Scottish Alliance opposition on the grounds that Scottish Newspaper Proprietors Association who dealt with the NUJ were not board members.

The problems amongst the unions in determining membership of the workers' side of the board caused difficulties with ratification of the 1919 *Hours and Holiday National Agreement* made between the BFMP and the P&KTF whereby working hours for the printing trades in the UK were reduced to forty eight per week. There was also payment to employees for six statutory holidays together with a week's holiday in the summer. This agreement became operative on 3 March 1919. Constitutionally the agreement, as far as Scotland was concerned, should have been referred to the Scottish Wages Board for ratification or amendment. Unfortunately the STA and the Scottish branches of the UK-wide unions, by still having to finalise the workers' side of the board, effectively made the board inoperative and prevented the '*Hours and Holiday Agreement*' being considered by the board. The Alliance, in view of the inadequate time available for separate Scottish negotiations and recognising the advantages of securing, for the first time in the history of the industry, uniformity throughout the whole UK on hours and holidays, waived the constitutional point of consideration by the wages board and put into operation in Scotland on 3 March the BFMP/P&KTF *Hours and Holiday Agreement*. The Scottish Alliance had representation on the BFMP Joint Labour Committee which had negotiated the agreement.

Although the STA was a staunch supporter of the wages board several of the unions with headquarters outside Scotland, but with branches in Scotland, were less enthusiastic. They considered the board duplicated wage negotiations in England and Wales and it was expensive to send national officials to Scotland to attend meetings of the board. These unions began to indicate they might withdraw from the board. In March 1923 the ASLP announced its withdrawal and ceased to nominate its representatives to the board. In April 1924, the NUPB&PW gave six month's notice of its intention to resign from the board. By December 1924 there were only two trade unions in membership of the board and on 9 December 1924 the Scottish Printing Industry Wages Board was dissolved.

For six years the wages board had played an important part in the negotiations which had taken place regarding both increases, and decreases, in wages. It was a matter of regret for the Scottish Alliance that the board had ceased to exist.[4] The principle of national negotiation in Scotland did not die with the demise of the wages board. All wage matters continued to be settled for Scotland by negotiations between the Scottish Alliance and the unions in Scotland except for the period of the Second World War when Scotland participated in wage negotiations involving the BFMP and the P&KTF. After 1945 Scotland re-established its autonomy for wage negotiations.

b. The National Joint Industrial Council (NJIC)

In 1915 a letter to the *Newspaper Owner and the World* suggested trade unions co-operate with employers' organisations in enforcing standard costing methods to determine prices. In the course of further correspondence and discussion the idea of co-operation for wider purposes than suppressing price-cutting gradually gained ground. Comprehensive schemes for 'trade betterment' were advanced by supporters amongst both employers and unions.[5] In 1917, a conference of representatives of unions and employers held in Belfast discussed ways and means of securing greater co-operation for printing betterment and the meeting resolved:

> that this conference endorses the principle of greater co-operation between employers and workers for printing trade betterment and pledge themselves to support and encourage a scheme for giving effect to this decision.

The Belfast Conference took place shortly before the government's Whitley Report was published in June 1917. This report recommended the formation 'for each industry an organisation representative of employers and working people to have as its objective the regular consideration of matters affecting the progress and well being of the trade from the point of view of all those engaged in it, so far as this is consistent with the general interest of the community'. Joint Industrial Councils were to be formed by the voluntary action of the existing organisations in each industry. The BFMP already had a Betterment of Relations Committee and this body met with P&KTF in July 1917. Although an informal meeting each side brought forward proposals for a joint industrial council. The next meeting passed unanimously a resolution approving the creation of a national joint industrial council and establishment of a joint subcommittee to devise a constitution which would subsequently be submitted to both sides for approval. Many meetings took place throughout the succeeding months of 1917 and the early months of 1918. By April 1918 the two sides had reached agreement on the constitution and functions of the proposed council. Problems regarding representation on the Council of the Newspaper Society and of the NUPB&MR meant the draft constitution was not approved by the BFMP and the unions until early 1919. The first meeting of the National Joint Industrial Council took place on 1 July 1919. In the printing industry, adoption of a Whitley scheme was facilitated by the high degree of organisation amongst its employers and employees.

The Joint Industrial Council was formed as co-operative organisation of employers and trade unions. It was an association of employers who were members of the Federation of Master Printers and Allied Trades of the United Kingdom (BFMP). Non-union companies, though they could join the BFMP could not be represented on the Joint Industrial Council. The trade unions had to be affiliated to the Printing and Kindred Trades Federation (P&KTF). No organisation not supportive of the objects of both Federations was eligible for membership of the Joint Industrial Council. The National Executive of the Joint Industrial Council consisted of equal numbers of employers and employees with both the BFMP and the P&KTF electing their own representatives. Of the employer representatives two seats were for employers from Scotland. The chair of the Joint Industrial Council rotated annually from one side to the other. When the chair was with the employers' side the vice-chair came from the union side and vice versa.

The NJIC had four main objectives:
(1) co-operation between employers and employees to reduce reckless price-cutting
(2) an extension of joint consultation between workers and management
(3) an improvement in the health and safety of workers and
(4) the elimination of industrial stoppages by the provision of conciliation.
The decision-making machinery of the council was of a joint nature from top to bottom. At the workplace its presence was seen in 'workers advisory committees' with representatives of both management and workers. Management and workers also elected members of the district joint committees which sent representatives to the annual convention, which was two-way channel of communication between the Executive Council and individual firms. In this way district joint committees were linked to the NJIC in London or with the branch council for Scotland. The annual convention was an open forum for the discussion of the general problems of the industry.

At the national level the NJIC had four main committees – the Health Committee, the Apprenticeship Committee, the Organisation Committee and the Conciliation Committee. The Health Committee did valuable educational work, seeking to improve the hygienic standards of printing offices. The Apprenticeship Committee was concerned to reform the apprenticeship system in the interests of both employers and employees. It advocated radical ideas of scientific selection and thorough technical education. The Organisation Committee encouraged organisation on both sides of the industry.

Paragraph twenty five of the NJIC constitution governed disputes. The 'dispute rule' was simple:

> No strike, lock out or other aggressive action shall take place in any locality until the matter in question has been placed before, and considered, by the District Committee and failing a settlement being arrived at, has been remitted to the National Council which shall meet to consider the question within six days.

The promotion of good relationships between employers and employees, the recognition of mutual interests and the investigation of methods of settling any differences were important objects of the NJIC. To further these a conciliation committee was established. Disputes were referred first to a district committee (if one existed) then to the Conciliation Committee and finally to the full council. The voluntary acceptance of the recommendation(s) of the Conciliation Committee was a fundamental principle accepted by both sides of the councils. The Conciliation Committee was highly successful in preventing the breakdown of negotiations on several critical occasions. Most disputes which came before the Conciliation Committee were over the interpretation and application of the National Agreement.

c. The Scottish Joint Industrial Council (SJIC)

One of the first decisions of NJIC was the formation of a branch council for Scotland. The Scottish Alliance believed the formation of a Scottish branch of then JIC of the Printing and Allied Trades of the UK would result in Scottish employers and employees having a better understanding of each other's difficulties, particularly those which were of a peculiarly Scottish nature. Many difficulties had to be cleared away before the SJIC held its initial meeting in Glasgow on 29 November 1922, by which time the ASLP and the NSES had dropped their objections to the draft constitution. It would have seriously affected the value of the council had these two unions remained in opposition but minor adjustments to the proposed constitution were sufficient to enable the two unions to approve it.

Its constitution mirrored the national one. The board consisted of forty eight members of which twenty four were drawn from the Scottish Alliance and twenty four from the various print unions affiliated to the P&KTF and having members in Scotland. At the initial meeting of the board the President of the Scottish Alliance (Robert Wilson) was appointed the first chair of the SJIC and the General Secretary of the STA its first vice-chair. The Secretary of the Alliance (R T Wishart) was appointed joint secretary to the board. The quarterly meetings of the SJIC took place in various towns in Scotland. Its main committees, whose functions were the same as those of the national body, were the General Purposes, the Organisation, the Health, the Unemployment, the Apprentice and Technical Education and the Conciliation Committees. The meeting of the SJIC enabled valuable discussion of differences of opinion expressed on the subjects under review and focussed attention on non-contentious matters to the mutual advantages of employers and employees. Much good work was done in its committees.

Three district committees were proposed – Eastern (Edinburgh, Fife and eastern border towns), Northern (Dundee, Perth, Forfarshire, Aberdeen and the north) and Western (Glasgow, west of Scotland, Ayrshire and Dumfriesshire). The district committees, by the free exchange of opinion, concentrated on matters of joint interest and on improving existing relationships between employers and workers in the same district. Both sides of the SJIC reported back to the Organisation Committee that instead of its proposed three committees there be four, there being a separate committee for Aberdeen and the north. At the meeting on 13 March 1924 the Organisation Committee's proposal for four districts (Northern, Central, Eastern and Western) was accepted and it was left to each panel to make arrangements for the selection of representatives to serve these district committees. This never happened and the Organisation Committee's attempts to establish district committees proved unsuccessful, although matters were not helped by financial difficulties.[6]

The ASLP, whilst willing to participate in district committees in Scotland, was not prepared to be a member of the SJIC. Both the employer and employee panels regretted this position. The ASLP confirmed at the SJIC meeting held in Glasgow on 9 May 1923 its intention to leave the Council whereupon the Scottish Council adopted the following resolution.

> …that this Council is of the opinion that there can be no Scottish branch of the NJIC unless all bodies affiliated nationally and having a Scottish membership are affiliated to the Scottish branch…

Concern for the future of the SJIC increased when the NSES gave notice of their intention of withdrawing.
On 31 July 1923 a special meeting of the SJIC was called involving representatives from the NJIC, the ASLP and the NSES. A long discussion took place on the difficulties the ASLP and the NSES faced in becoming members of the SJIC.

The chief difficulties stressed by each of the two unions were that of expense and of a fear the duplication of national machinery in Scotland might lead to confusion. The difficulties centred around the disputes clause in the SJIC constitution. A subcommittee from both sides of the council sought some agreement whereby the two unions would be happy to become parties to the Scottish JIC. It did not prove easy to draft a form of words to overcome the ASLP and NSES fears but ultimately all parties accepted the subcommittee's recommendation that the constitution be changed from:

> Conciliation Committee – Chairman, Vice Chairman and Joint Secretary with 3 representatives from each panel chosen by the respective Chairman and Secretary of the Panel.

to:

> Conciliation Committee – Chairman, Vice Chairman and Joint Secretaries with four representatives chosen by each of the respective disputants from the panel of the Scottish Council or the National Council or the joint panels of the Scottish and National Council.

The SIJC meeting held on 26 September 1923 was the first time the Council had present representatives from all the unions.

In January 1924 following the STA's decision to form an 'Auxiliary Section' it withdrew from the P&KTF. As a result it ceased to qualify for membership of the SJIC and the NJIC. The absence of the STA from the SJIC limited the usefulness of that body. Good work continued to be undertaken, and meetings of the council provided opportunities for both employees and employers to take a broader view of the general welfare of the industry in an atmosphere different from that of a conference where one side considered a specific request from the other. The SJIC Organisation Committee wrote to the Alliance suggesting a three party policy conference under the auspices of the Alliance to explore how to resolve the differences dividing the STA from the other unions affiliated to the P&KTF. The Alliance took up the suggestion and a three party conference was held on 30 November 1926. As a basis for a settlement the Alliance proposed
(1) it be recognised for the organisation of employees the STA has an Auxiliary Section;
(2) in the larger cities the sphere of operations of the Auxiliary Section be men and women employed in letterpress printing;
(3) in the smaller towns the Auxiliary Section be given a free hand to recruit as members any workers in the industry and
(4) in the larger cities the NUPB&PW have as their sphere of influence male and female employees in all other sections of the industry.
The STA could not accept condition (2). It was contrary to their Auxiliary

Section constitution which claimed the right to organise non-craft workers in every print office in Scotland. This meant, for example, any bookbinding office which employed a compositor or a machineman was regarded as a printing office and the same applied to litho print offices.

The efforts of the Alliance to secure a settlement between the STA and the P&KTF-affiliated unions proved unsuccessful. In May 1927 the STA requested recognition by the Alliance of its Auxiliary Section on the same basis as granted to it as a craft union. The Alliance had worked hard to create the conditions by which harmony could be restored between the STA and P&KTF affiliates so the P&KTF could again be all-embracing and the STA rejoin the SJIC. Unfortunately the STA had sought something the Alliance was not prepared to concede. It refused to recognise the STA's Auxiliary Section on the same basis as it recognised the STA 'proper', as it covered workers for which it had agreements with other unions. It was also bound by the SJIC resolution the Alliance would not make an agreement with a union which would adversely affect any of the unions in membership of the SJIC without first consulting them. The Scottish Alliance was a constituent part of the BFMP which did not want recognition granted to the STA Auxiliary Section.

In 1928 the STA reached an amicable settlement covering the jurisdictional boundaries between its Auxiliary Section and the NUPB&PW. The STA, after an absence of four years, resumed membership of the P&KTF and thereby the SJIC and NJIC. By early 1929 the SJIC again held within its membership all the print unions in Scotland and became once again a power of good on behalf of the industry as a whole. This was illustrated in 1931 when, for pragmatic reasons it made amendments to its constitution to facilitate its workings and to allow disputes to be considered by its Conciliation Committee without reporting them to the National Committee in the event of a failure to agree.

Changing Attitudes of the Print Unions to Organisation

Union organisation in the Scottish printing industry after the First World War was not radically different from that of 1914 except the number of union members had increased. Throughout the inter-war period the Alliance recognised and negotiated with the STA and the Scottish District Councils of the ASLP, the NSES and the NUPB&PW. SLADE would not enter into national agreements, preferring to negotiate house agreements with individual employers. In 1920, the National Union of Printing Bookbinding and Machine Rulers amalgamated with the National Union of Printing and Paper Workers to form the National Union of Printing, Bookbinding and Paper Workers (NUPB&PW) with over 100,000 members making it the largest union in the industry. It recruited into membership skilled crafts such as bookbinders, pressmen and warehousemen, semi-skilled male assistants and women and girls working in paper mills, stationery firms and bookbinding shops. Some 60%

of its membership were women. The growth in print union membership in the years immediately after the end of the First World War was mainly amongst women and semi-skilled workers. When the economic expansion of 1919 – 1920 was replaced by economic recession and then the Great Depression, the resulting unemployment caused print union membership to decline.

Less apparent, however, was the change in attitudes to union organisation. The disruption of traditional workplace practices made necessary by labour shortages in the final stages of the First World War had demonstrated many old demarcation lines restricting the work of women and 'unskilled men' could not be justified on grounds of technical inability. These workers were determined to retain the employment opportunities the war had given them and had been organised with much success. The craft print unions realised their pre-1914 hegemony could not be regained. The lithographic printers amalgamated with the stone and plate preparers. The NSES recruited stereotypers' assistants whilst the bookbinders abandoned their opposition to women trade unionists and established a Women's Section. The STA amended its Rule Book to provide for an Auxiliary Section of assistants and women.

These activities aroused the suspicion of the Printers' Warehousemen and Cutters' Union and NATSOPA although this union was not recognised by the Alliance. These unions suspected the sudden interest in organising assistants and women was due less to philanthropy than a desire to control a potential alternative labour supply. The immediately post-war years were thick with jurisdictional disputes that threatened the authority of the P&KTF. Despite poaching on its membership territory by the craft unions, the NUPB&PW emerged under capable leadership as one of the strongest unions in the industry.

The need for a body to arbitrate on inter-union rivalry meant the P&KTF, during the inter-war years, grew in importance. The factor explaining its enhanced status was the print unions need for a single body to articulate their interests to the government, the BFMP and the Scottish Alliance on national issues such as the utilization of manpower and the post-1918 resumption of the apprenticeship system. Illustrative of the change in the authority of the P&KTF was its negotiation in 1919 and in 1937 of the *Hours and Holiday Agreement* covering the whole industry.

The General Strike
In 1925, the coal miners were threatened with wage reductions and increased hours of work. The Trades Union Congress (TUC) pledged support to the miners' unions to the extent if necessary of calling sympathetic strikes by other unions. The latter were put into several categories – 'front line', 'second line' etc. The printing unions were categorised into 'front line'. In May 1926, the TUC called its affiliates out on sympathy strike in support of the coal miners arguing 'it is the

miners facing the wage cut this time but it could be you next time'. Negotiations between the coal owners and the miners' unions collapsed and the miners were locked out. At the eleventh hour officials from the TUC were in conference with the government hoping to avoid major industrial conflict. At this crucial stage the members of the compositors' chapel at the *Daily Mail* office refused to set an editorial which contained, they felt, misrepresentations of the issues at stake. On this pretext the government broke off negotiations forcing the TUC either to back down or call a sympathy strike. Reluctantly the TUC called out the 'front line' unions on 3 May 1926. The General Strike lasted ten days. It was called off when the miners' leaders refused to accept a compromise solution.

On the morning of 3 May when it became clear following the TUC recommendation the Scottish printing industry would be involved in the sympathy stoppage, the Alliance pointed out to the STA the clauses in the national agreement which set out the procedural stages to be followed before any aggressive action was taken. The Scottish Alliance Emergency Committee dealt immediately with any developments. Late on the afternoon of 3 May 1926, the Alliance received a telephone communication from the STA saying it would implement the recommendation of the TUC and instruct its members to stop work that night. This information was immediately telegraphed to all Alliance local association secretaries advising their members to open as usual the next day. The BFMP Emergency Committee acted on similar lines with reference to the UK-wide print unions. A formal protest was made by the Alliance to the STA complaining they were acting in breach of procedure. The Scottish Alliance Emergency Committee was in two places, one part in Glasgow and the other in Edinburgh. Each half met daily during the stoppage discussing the numerous problems which developed. Despite transport difficulties, the two halves of the Emergency Committee met in Edinburgh on 11 May 1926. By telephone and telegram the Alliance Emergency Committee kept in contact with the BFMP Emergency Committee and Alliance associations were advised of developments as and when necessary. A circular letter briefly setting out the position was issued on 6 May to all Alliance member firms and a second circular was ready for issue when on 12 May, the TUC called off the General Strike.

A meeting of the Alliance Executive Board was held in Glasgow on 13 May. The President, William Maxwell, reviewed the position that had developed during the strike and explained the contents of the notice which the BFMP was asking members to display at works entrances. The STA was not at this time affiliated to the P&KTF so it was necessary for the Alliance to tell the STA Executive the terms of re-engagement of its members. Discussion between the Alliance and the STA took place as to the conditions under which its members would be permitted to return to work. Representations were made to the Alliance head office by some member firms that before any resumption of work took place there be changes to the existing *Mutual Rules Agreement* covering short-time working and staffing of machines. Suggestions were also made that the

Hours and Holidays Agreement be cancelled.. After considerable discussion the Scottish Alliance Emergency Committee was authorised to meet the STA to discuss the resumption of work on the following conditions:

(1) no lightning strikes in future

(2) it was impossible to take back every man immediately and the suspension clause of the *Mutual Working Rules Agreement* would operate

(3) no victimisation against those who had continued to work during the strike and

(4) the STA refrain from entering print shops and threatening employers.

The STA would report to the Executive Board of the Scottish Alliance if they had complaints as to how member firms implemented the 'Return to Work' Agreement. The STA requested the immediate resumption of full-time employment for all men (including those in daily newspapers with whom the Scottish Alliance had no connection) who were in employment on the night of 3 May. The Alliance discussed the union's demands but agreement was quickly made as to the terms upon which STA members would return to work. There was little change to the conditions agreed by the Alliance Executive Board at its meeting earlier in the day. On the advice of BFMP, the Alliance instructed member firms to exhibit at their works entrance the following notice:

> Re-engagement as required will be at the individual's former rate
> of pay but on a day to day basis pending final national settlement
> in their respective trades.[7]

On Friday 14 May 1926 the STA accepted the Alliance's conditions for the resumption of work by its members. The Alliance agreed to take back within one week all men who were employed on Monday 3 May 1926. During the four weeks thereafter, any of the men after two day's employment could be suspended. In addition the STA agreed not to victimise any member firms of the Alliance, undertook not to victimise any employee who remained at work or returned to work during the strike and accepted in the event of finding conditions in any office which they considered unsatisfactory they would not threaten the employer but report the matter to the Alliance. In addition the Alliance wanted a commitment from the STA that it would not, at any future date, take part in a lightning strike. Membership of the TUC prevented the STA giving this commitment but it agreed in all disputes it would act strictly in accordance with its national agreements with the employers concerned. The issue went to a ballot of STA members. They voted overwhelmingly in favour of adhering to national agreements at all times and in all cases. The ballot paper had contained two questions. First, should national agreements with the employers be adhered to at all times and in all cases? Second, should workers obey recommendations from the Trades Union Congress or any other body which would violate national agreements? 3,575 members voted in favour of the first question. Only 244 voted in favour of the second question.

Few difficulties arose with the resumption of work but the settlement aroused adverse criticism from print companies in certain areas, particularly Dundee. The broad view taken by the Alliance was that its action had been justified by results. The STA appreciated the Alliance's action in making the resumption of work as easy as possible and relations between individual employers and their employees quickly returned to the same friendly basis existing before 3 May. The Alliance President (William Maxwell) in his opening address to the Executive Board meeting of 17 June 1926 said an honourable settlement had been made with the STA without humiliation of the men and it would result in better relationships between the parties in the future.

The return to work arrangements for print workers in Scotland in membership of UK-wide unions with branches in Scotland, were the result of negotiations between the BFMP and the P&KTF. A provisional agreement was reached on 15 May on the basis of which, work was generally resumed. Negotiations reached a final agreement on 27 May 1926. Considerable delay took place with some of the unions in ratifying the agreement, but by 13 July 1926 all unions had ratified the agreement. Under this affiliate members of the BFMP were recommended to give preference, as and when required, in engagement to former employees who left work during the General Strike. In return the unions agreed that, in future, no chapel meetings would be held during working hours.

The General Strike and the protracted coal dispute brought some difficult problems in their train. These occasioned many conferences and meetings of the Conciliation Committee. A few member firms of the Alliance declared their offices 'open' houses. To resolve this matter, lengthy discussions were held between the Alliance and the STA. It was not possible in all cases to resolve the matter and several firms became non-union but in more than 90% of printing offices in Scotland the status quo before the General Strike was resumed. The General Strike made surprisingly little difference to the practice of industrial relations in the Scottish general printing industry. The SJIC and NJIC survived. The unions accepted national agreements held with employers had to be adhered to until changed by mutual agreement. The Alliance membership had had no desire to humiliate its employees believing conciliation and co-operation be the principles upon which industrial relationship returned to their pre-General Strike quality. It was in Scottish newspaper offices that, post the General Strike, printing union organisation suffered. Prominent amongst newspaper firms which decided to operate as non-union shops were George Outram Ltd and D C Thomson of Dundee.

Summary

This chapter has examined the external environment in which the Scottish Alliance and the print unions in Scotland related to each other during the inter-war years. There were no major technological revolutions compared to the introduction of mechanical composition of the late 1890s/early 1890s. There was, however, continuous search for faster machines and development of ancillary machinery such as mechanical feeders. The most significant technological development was the mechanisation of bookbinding.

The inter-war years saw the beginning of what later became known as 'the alternative printing industry' based on non-printing firms installing their own small office printing machines or as with Glasgow Corporation establishing its own full-blown print and binding works. This development was the result of companies during the First World War economising on their use of the printed word and after the end of the war, the high cost of printing.

The end of the First World War witnessed a boom in which the Scottish printing benefited followed by an economic slump and the Great Depression. Printing in Scotland, nevertheless continued to expand and unemployment in the printing industry was half that for other Scottish industries. It would be incorrect, however, to think that print workers in Scotland escaped the impact of the Great Depression. In 1932 unemployment amongst Scottish print workers was lower than for other industries in Scotland but was over twice that for print workers in certain parts of England. Some employers saw the answer to the unemployment problem being cuts in production costs (for example wage reductions) whilst the unions saw the answer in shorter working hours including less overtime and reduction in the number of apprentices entering the industry.

The outstanding feature of the industrial relations of the Scottish printing industry during the inter-war years was the relative infrequency of open industrial conflict. This situation was due to many factors but contributing was the rise of a number of new industrial relations institutions. In 1919, the Scottish Wages Board of the Printing Industry came into being with the objective of adjusting, periodically by mutual consent, the minimum wage to be paid and the maximum hours worked in the industry. The board ceased to operate in 1924. In 1919 the National Joint Industrial Council for the Printing Industry was formed as a co-operative organisation of employers and trade unions. One of its objectives was the elimination of industrial stoppages by the provision of conciliation procedures. An initial decision of the NJIC was to form a branch council for Scotland which became known as the Scottish Joint Industrial Council holding its initial meeting in November 1922. It performed the same function as the NJIC.

The inter-war years also saw a change in the attitude of trade unions as to the workers they were prepared to organise. The suspension of the traditional workplace practices in the later years of the war illustrated that the old demarcation lines which had traditionally limited the work traditionally done by women and unskilled men could not be justified on grounds of their technical ability. These workers wanted to retain the employment position the war had given them. The craft unions sought to organise these workers. The STA, for example, established an 'Auxiliary Section' which recruited assistants and women. This change of attitude in the part of craft unions led to inter-union disputes in which the P&KTF gained a reputation of being a fair arbitrator.

1926 saw the Scottish printing industry affected by the General Strike which was in reality a sympathy strike by the trade union movement in support of the coal mining unions which had called their members out on strike against employer attempts to cut their wages. The General Strike lasted ten days. The Alliance was upset the print unions had called their members out on strike in breach of existing collective agreements. Following the end of the General Strike, as a condition of their employees returning to work, Alliance member firms sought assurances that, in future, the unions would adhere at all times to the agreement to which they were signatories. In the Scottish printing industry, relationships returned quickly after the end of the General Strike to their pre-strike levels.

Notes

[1] See the Scottish Alliance *Bulletin*, No. 2, October 1919.
[2] See Report by the Executive Board to the Twenty fourth Annual General Meeting, March 1935.
[3] See Minutes of the Executive Board Meeting, 26 January 1937.
[4] See Report of the Executive Board to the Fourteenth Annual General Meeting, March 1925.
[5] See Child, J. (1967) *Industrial Relations in the British Printing Industry*. London: Allen & Unwin, p254.
[6] See the Scottish Alliance, *Bulletin*, No. 17, June 1925.
[7] See Minutes of the Executive Board meeting held 13 May 1926.

Chapter 6

RELATIONSHIPS WITH THE TRADE UNIONS 1919- 1939:
WAGE MOVEMENTS

The chapter begins by outlining changes in the basic rates of pay in national wage agreements concluded in the inter-war years. The second part explains the wage grading system introduced in 1922. The chapter then traces negotiations between the Scottish Alliance and the print unions over employment conditions to apply solely in Scotland. The final section examines payments and staffing for employees operating certain new machines and relationships between the Alliance and the NUPB&PW.

Changes to the National Agreement

In 1919, national wage claims replaced local wage claims and national agreements local agreements. The former contained basic terms and conditions for the industry throughout Scotland. During 1919 and 1920, the Scottish Wages Board granted four increases to the national basic wage. Between 1921 and 1922, flat rate wage reductions, totalling £1, were made to the basic national rate of pay. No other flat rate increases, or decreases, occurred to national agreement conditions during the inter-war years. This was despite the Scottish print employers' attempts to impose further reductions in the depressed trading conditions of the early 1930s.

a. Basic Increases

On 1 August 1919, the STA and the P&KTF-affiliated unions with members in Scotland presented a claim to the Scottish Alliance for an increase of 16s

0d per week for all males and females performing the same class of work. The unions justified the claim on the grounds that wages paid in the printing industry were too low in view of the long apprenticeship and standard of education required in comparison to other trades, the increase in prices since the end of the war and that print workers desired a higher standard of living. The employers offered an increase of 7s 0d per week to letterpress printers, litho printers, litho artists, operators and assistants and female compositors but offered no increase for apprentices. Sir Thomas Munro who had been appointed independent chairman of the Scottish Wages Board considered the employers' offer, given the circumstances of the time, fair and reasonable. The wages board, therefore, granted a wage increase of 7s 0d from September 1919. It awarded, from January 1920, a further weekly increase of 7s 6d for male workers and of 3s 6d to female workers.

During 1920, two wage negotiations took up much of the Alliance's time. The first was an application lodged on 12 April 1920 by the Scottish group of the P&KTF and the STA for an advance of 22s 6d per week for all adult male and female workers doing the same class of work and an increase of 15s 0d per week for all other adult female workers. Although these negotiations were initiated in Scotland, towards the end of May 1920 the UK-wide unions with branches in Scotland joined their application with that which P&KTF was pursuing nationally with the BFMP. At conferences in London both the BFMP and the P&KTF-affiliated unions, with the exception of the Typographical Association (TA), recommended to their members a wage increase of 10s 0d per week to all adult male workers and of 3s 6d per week to qualified women workers with a proportionate increase in the pay of apprentices and learners, effective from 12 June 1920. An extraordinary general meeting of the Alliance was held on 31 May 1920 at which there was a record attendance and at which its representatives on the Scottish Wages Board were authorised to make the same offer to workers in Scotland. Difficulties arose in England with the TA but they ultimately accepted the 10s 0d increase. The settlement remained unacceptable to TA members in Manchester and Liverpool and industrial unrest in these two cities culminated in TA members there ceasing work on 28 August. Print employers throughout the country considered it essential to support the print employers in the two cities and Alliance member firms made considerable contributions towards the Liverpool and Manchester Print Employers Guarantee Fund.

The Liverpool and Manchester dispute was no sooner over than claims from the print unions for an advance of 15s 0d per week for men and 7s 6d for women occupied the attention of the BFMP and the Alliance. All the print unions in Scotland on this occasion put forward their claim through the P&KTF. The Alliance, in light of the slump in trade, strenuously opposed any further increase in wages. This view did not receive the support of the BFMP but the attitude of the Scottish Alliance went a long way towards preventing the BFMP offer of 5s 0d being increased.[1] The unions at the beginning of October 1920 refused to consider the 5s 0d offer but ultimately accepted it, to operate from 15 November 1920.

b. Wage Reductions

In May 1921, the Scottish Alliance (and the BFMP) sought a wage reduction of 15s 0d per week for men and of 5s 6d for women to put the industry on a sound footing given the poor state of business. The unions rejected the employers' offer to cut the reduction to 10s 0d per week for men and to 3s 6d for women. Following a NJIC meeting agreement was reached on a weekly reduction of 7s 6d implemented in two instalments of 5s 0d on 1 October 1921 followed by a further reduction of 2s 6d from 7 January 1922. The reduction for women was to be 3s 0d per week in two stages, one of 2s 0d and one of 1s 0d.

Immediately following the second instalment of the reduction being implemented the Alliance made strong representation to the BFMP that steps be taken to secure further reductions in wages. The BFMP in February 1922 intimated to all the unions they wished to review the wage position. The Scottish Alliance made similar representations to the Scottish Wages Board and to the STA and to the Scottish branches of the UK-wide unions. Meetings took place with the unions and with the Scottish Wages Board but the outcomes were unsatisfactory to the Scottish Alliance. The unions were not prepared to recognise the gravity of the existing economic situation and indicated their policy was uncompromising refusal to consider the necessity for a wage reduction. The position of the Alliance was that if the cost of living returned to pre-First World War levels wages be increased, provided the economic conditions of the industry could fund such an increase. In the present situation the priority was placing the Scottish print industry on a sound basis.

On 28 March 1922, the Executive Board of the Alliance viewed with great concern the economic state into which the printing trade had fallen as a result of the postponement of a readjustment downwards of wages. It urged on the BFMP the necessity of immediate arrangements for a series of wage reductions which would put printing costs onto a sound economic basis. It also argued the industry had no other means by which it might be revived and reiterated its deeply held opinion that if this resulted in a general stoppage of work throughout the industry the employers would have to show a united and solid front. This view of the Executive was confirmed the following day at its 1922 annual general meeting when the Alliance pressed strongly upon the BFMP and the unions the necessity of a substantial reduction in wages. A conference was held with the Scottish Wages Board at which the Alliance proposed a wage reduction of 15s 0d per week implemented in instalments. At a subsequent meeting (2 May 1922) the wages board recommended a reduction of 15s 0d by three instalments – 5s 0d each in June, July and August. The unions, except for the ASLP and the NSES accepted the recommendation on condition no further reduction in wages occurred during 1923.

The ASLP, which had absented itself from the Wages Board, meetings rejected the agreement. After due consideration the lithographic employers gave notice to implement similar reductions to those introduced into letterpress houses. A strike of ASLP members resulted and after a stoppage of three weeks a settlement was reached providing for a weekly reduction of ASLP members' wages of 12s 6d in four instalments – 5s 0d in July 1922, 2s 6d in October 1922, 2s 6d from January 1923 and a further 2s 6d from July 1923. Negotiations with the NSES resulted in an agreement of a weekly wage reduction of 6s 0d in two instalments – 4s 0d from 28 October 1922 and 2s 0d from 6 January 1923. Without exception the Alliance members employing litho employees loyally supported the Alliance during this difficult period. Their united stand made the litho and other unions recognise the employers were determined, owing to the force of circumstances, wages be reduced. As a result of the settlement with the ASLP, the Alliance received a request from the STA that their agreement of 2 May 1922 be on the same basis as the ASLP settlement. An emergency general meeting of the Scottish Alliance, held on 12 July 1922, agreed the first two reductions of 5s 0d recommended by the Wages Board should stand but that the third be cut from 5s 0d to 2s 6d effective 6 January 1923 and stabilised throughout 1923.

The stabilization of wages to the end of 1923 was beneficial to the Scottish printing industry enabling customers to place orders with confidence and enabling print firms to give firm estimates of the price of job.[2] The Alliance favoured the continuation of the wage stabilization policy but in January 1924 the STA lodged a claim with the wages board for a general increase in wages and a change of the grading system. The employers side of the wages board rejected the claim arguing no convincing arguments had been presented to justify the STA's request for a general wage increase. On 10 October 1924, in the face of strong Alliance opposition, the STA withdrew its claim for a general wage increase.

c. Reduction in Costs of Production 1931/1933
By 1931, economic activity in the Scottish printing industry was depressed and the February 1931 Executive Board meeting of the Alliance agreed to consider the present rate of wages paid to all sections of the industry with a view to a reduction being negotiated. In July 1931 the Alliance accepted, in view of the national economic situation, a general relaxation in working rules and conditions take place, including a demand for an all-round reduction in wages. A committee was appointed to investigate present rules and working conditions agreed with the various unions to secure some relaxation in their operation. In January 1932, the Alliance endorsed the BFMP Labour Negotiation Committee stance that the P&KTF be approached immediately to consider the urgent necessity, in the interest of all concerned in the industry,

---

for a reduction in production costs by means of a general reduction in wages and the removal of restrictive working conditions.

1932 was a year of severe economic difficulty in all sections of the Scottish printing industry. As previously noted, the percentage of unemployed print workers in Scotland was twice that for such workers in certain areas of England. During the year, the Alliance began negotiations with all printing unions to secure a reduction of production costs by a 15% reduction in wages, by the removal of certain restrictions on working conditions and a scaling down of 'extra' payments. The BFMP conducted the negotiations with the unions, with Scotland represented on the BFMP's Labour Committee by Dr MacLehose. In Scotland, negotiations were between the Scottish Alliance team led by Dr MacLehose and the STA. The issues were the same in both sets of negotiations. Early in 1932 BFMP asked for a conference with the P&KTF to discuss reducing costs and stimulating demand for printing products. The P&KTF replied it had no authority to negotiate wage reductions but was prepared to discuss how production costs might be reduced. After several abortive conferences the BFMP advised each union separately it wished to negotiate alterations to their national agreement. All the individual unions refused this demand for a reduction in wages. The terms of their reply showed the unions had been in consultation with one another and their agreed policy was to refuse to agree any reduction in wages by negotiation.

In July 1932, the Scottish Alliance wrote to the STA saying that it had considered for some time the serious effects on the Scottish printing industry of the worldwide depression. The situation had become so serious the Alliance proposed a conference to explore the possibilities, in the general interests of the industry, of arriving, by mutual agreement, at some means of reducing production costs and of increasing trade in the industry. In September 1932 the Alliance proposed to the STA:

(1) a reduction in wages and short-time arrangements,

(2) assistants be recognised in the foundry but be paid at a lower rate of wages than journeymen,

(3) lost time be balanced against overtime in the week,

(4) no call money be paid where employees were warned before leaving work they may be called back into work and no call money be paid on a Sunday,

(5) employees required to start work two hours before their usual starting time be not entitled to call money,

(6) where the provisions of local rules conflicted with the national agreement the latter to were to prevail and,

(7) the 'more favourable conditions' clause be deleted from the national agreement.

Negotiations dragged on but their outcome was a general refusal by the STA to consider the Scottish Alliance's seven propositions. In both the BFMP and the Scottish Alliance negotiations the unions managed to prolong the negotiations on reductions on production costs to such an extent that before any conclusion could be reached, the worst of the economic depression in the industry had passed. There were clear signs of economic recovery. The crisis had passed and in 1934 unemployment in the industry fell substantially. The efforts of the BFMP and the Alliance to enforce wage and other production cost reductions during the Great Depression had been thwarted by the unions' stubbornness and procrastination.

Wage Grading Scheme

To secure greater uniformity in wages rates the STA in 1919 submitted proposals for the grading of towns and districts in Scotland. This 'wage grading system' was to provide wage differentials between the same class of workers in different towns. The towns were classified into grades according to their size, their importance as a printing centre, the character of the neighbourhood and the local cost of living. The claim was the subject of a number of conferences. The draft working rules submitted by the STA in 1920 proposed wages be regulated on the basis of a radius from certain large towns. This would, the Scottish Alliance argued, result in anomalies similar to those already existing but the Alliance gave an undertaking to examine the grading question. In June 1921 the STA submitted, via the Wages Board, to the Scottish Alliance a proposal for a grading scheme on lines similar to that of 1919. The proposed scheme placed all towns and districts in three groups with a differential of 5s 0d between the highest and the lowest grades. The Alliance set up a special committee with representatives from each district, to draw up an alternative scheme as the STA's proposals were not acceptable. The committee found nineteen different rates of wages in the printing industry. To decide on the merits of the case put forward by the representatives of each town and district proved a difficult matter. In 1922 after protracted negotiations a 'wages grading scheme' was agreed under which was divided into five grades (Grade I and Ia, Grade II, Grade III, Grade IV and Grade V). The difference between the wage rate agreed for Grade I and Grade V was 12s 0d.

The scheme became operable in June 1922 and existed for one year without revision. Further, a condition of the wage decreases of 1922 and 1923 was that no further wage alterations take place before January 1924. In the meantime, complaints from STA branches regarding the wage grading scheme began to mount. Many claimed they should have been placed in a higher grade. Edinburgh, for example, was not included in Grade I but in Grade Ia with a rate of 2s 0d below Glasgow.

Later in 1924, the STA presented a new grading scheme to the wages board for the approval by the employers side. The proposals incorporated a flat-rate increase of 2s 6d for all grade rates. Although the Scottish Alliance rejected the proposal, the employer panel of the wages board intimated if there were anomalies in the grading scheme and they were identified the Alliance would consider suggestions for their removal. The workers' side of the board, however, confined their arguments to the generality rather than specificity and indicated no cases where they considered anomalies existed in the grading scheme.

In the absence of an agreement, the matter proceeded to the SJIC. Further negotiations took place between the Alliance and the STA and in October 1924 a new grading scheme was approved but with no flat-rate increase to existing rates. Under the scheme the number of grades was reduced to four, narrowing the pay differential between the top grade towns and the bottom grade towns to 9s 0d. Edinburgh was included in Grade I. The Alliance approved the revised grading scheme whilst the STA membership voted by 2,366 votes to 912 to accept the scheme. Throughout the prolonged negotiations, the Alliance strenuously contested the grounds of the STA claims with reference to most places Although protests were received from some member firms in several of the areas affected, the Alliance was satisfied the best possible outcome had been achieved.[3]

In 1938, the STA proposed a single uniform wage grade for Scotland. The union argued that since the present rates were fixed in 1924 changes had occurred which not only gave rise to anomalies but reduced differences in the cost of living between various parts of the country. The Scottish Alliance rejected the proposal but was prepared to set up a committee to inquire into the wage grading system. In May 1938 the STA submitted amended proposals providing for two grades of wages for Scotland with a differential of 3s 0d. The union sought wage increases in practically every town in Scotland except for those already in Grade I. The Alliance, after consulting with its members, said it could not accept the STA regrading proposals but were prepared to discuss anomalies if these were forwarded by the union. It was not prepared to agree to two grades nor to the elimination of Grade IV. By the end of 1939 the STA had still to submit to the Alliance alleged wage grading anomalies although it announced it was still pressing for the adoption of their revised scheme of two grades for Scotland.

Difficulties arose with the ASLP over the question of grading wages. In 1922, it put a claim to the Scottish Alliance there be only one rate of pay applicable to the whole of Scotland for its members. The Alliance supported, as in England and Wales, three grades of pay for litho printers in Scotland. The ASLP initially rejected a three grade scale but after protracted negotiation accepted it. The Alliance believed although the amount of money at stake was small the principle involved was of considerable importance to the whole industry.[4]

Mutually Agreed Working Rules

In addition to the negotiation of national agreements with the print unions operating in the Scotland, the Scottish Alliance also concluded agreements with them providing uniform working conditions for their members throughout Scotland. These agreements were referred to as 'mutual working rules'.

a. The STA

In 1920, the STA Delegate Meeting approved proposals to alter working conditions and the ratio of apprentices to journeymen in the trade. These were presented to

---

the Scottish Alliance with an intimation that they become operative at the start of 1921. Most of the proposed working conditions rule changes were unacceptable to the Alliance. It could not, for example accept the proposal that the STA have discretionary power to refuse to allow overtime working. An alternative proposal that overtime working be restricted to six hours per week was countered by one from the Alliance that normal overtime working be restricted to thirty hours per month and emergency overtime work be agreed only after consultation with the chapel and the local union branch. It was eventually agreed normal overtime be limited to twenty seven hours in any calendar month and to nine hours in any week. On the issue of short-time working both the Scottish Alliance and the STA accepted that three days be the minimum period of notice required for the introduction of short-time working applicable to the whole of Scotland. The STA claim that night shift be four hours less than the day shift was also unacceptable but it was eventually agreed that the night shift be forty six working hours per week with no payment for meal breaks taken during the night. The STA proposal for the abolition of piece work from the industry found no support with the Scottish Alliance and so it was withdrawn by the STA. The rules, including the establishment of a conciliation committee, were finally agreed in April 1921. For the first time in the history of the Scottish printing industry mutual working rules and uniform conditions with respect to STA members applied to the whole of Scotland.

The changes to mutual rules applicable to the whole of Scotland could now only be made with the consent of the Scottish Alliance. This was a major achievement. It would no longer be possible for small local employers' associations to be compelled to grant conditions to union members contrary to the conditions prevailing elsewhere. Much attention had been given to the framing of these rules. That the time spent had been worthwhile was borne out by the fact that despite a period of stress and strain through which the industry had been passing only two meetings of the conciliation committee were necessary to deal with questions which arose under the rules.

During 1923 the Conciliation Committee, under the mutual rules with the STA, was frequently called upon to adjust differences which arose between member firms and the STA. In the majority of cases these differences were due to misunderstandings. The fact they were all amicably adjusted demonstrated the value of the Conciliation Committee to the industry. The recommendations of the Conciliation Committee were almost without exception accepted and implemented by the Scottish Alliance and the STA.

The outstanding issue for the Scottish Alliance in 1925 was negotiation with the STA over working conditions rules. The changes proposed by the STA were of such a radical nature it seemed almost impossible that any agreement could be achieved. Many days were spent by the Alliance Negotiating Committee in conference with the STA and in meetings with its member companies.

After negotiations with the STA extending over more than one year the revised national rules affecting working conditions were finally agreed on 10 September 1925. The main contentious issues in the bargaining sessions were the short-time rule, the ratio of apprentices and the staffing of machines. The STA pressed for the total abolition of the short-time working provision whilst Alliance, acting on a mandate from their constituents, were equally adamant that provision for short-time be retained in the rules. The STA argued the operation of the short-time rule created dissatisfaction throughout Scotland, undermined the loyalty of employees to their firms and created a bad atmosphere in the different printing offices. The STA claimed there were cases where some of their members were on short-time working and yet others in the same office, but in a different department, were periodically working overtime. The Alliance position remained that it was necessary to make provision for short-time working, as on occasions shortage of work meant it was impossible to employ men for the full forty eight hours a week. Only after a vote of Alliance membership showed they were not willing to take a stoppage of work in Scotland to secure retention of the former rule, did the Alliance reluctantly decide to authorise its Negotiating Committee to accept the STA position that the short-time working rule be accepted. The apprentice ratio was maintained and mutually satisfactory provisions were included to apply in any town in which unemployment might at any time happen to be abnormal.

The 1923 STA Delegate Meeting instructed the union to put forward to the Scottish Alliance claims for alterations to mutual working rules and conditions. Several member firms considered this claim was a response to the Scottish Alliance proposals for a reduction in production costs (see above). The Alliance said such thoughts were misguided as many of the demands were similar to, or only slight modifications on, claims that had been rejected by the Scottish Alliance in the past few years.[5] As some of the amendments proposed by the STA were radical, the Alliance held meetings of all its local associations so every member had an opportunity of expressing their opinion as to whether any of the STA's claims be conceded. The local association meetings were well attended and the unanimous view was the proposed amendments be rejected as they would result either in increased the costs of production or add to the existing difficulties in completing work. The Scottish Alliance therefore informed the STA it could not agree to its proposed amendments to the national working rules. The STA accepted the Alliance's view.

Subsequent to the 1936 STA Delegate Meeting the Scottish Alliance was asked by the union to consider a number of proposed changes to the existing agreement on working rules and conditions. These proposed alterations covered hours, overtime working, rates of payment, the ratio of apprentices, facilities for training, staffing of machines, rates of wages to machine men operating certain classes of machines and the wages of readers. The member firms of the Alliance were consulted about these changes. The dominant view was existing agreements were equitable subject to the need for certain minor amendments. Several proposals were scrutinised in negotiating conferences between the Alliance and the STA in an atmosphere of a mutual desire to further the welfare of the industry. Negotiations were postponed pending settlement of the reduction in working hours question (see Chapter 7) but resumed in September 1937 when the STA pressed for many radical changes which the Alliance could not accept. An agreement to amend the existing agreement was reached on 29 December 1937 and became operative on 31 January 1938. The important changes related to rules dealing with emergency overtime working, the ratio of apprentices to journeymen, the adoption of a scale of merit payments to men having special skill, extra payment to men specially engaged as readers and a method of payment to casual workers which removed existing difficulties surrounding their holiday payments.

b. The ASLP

The standardisation of STA working rules and conditions throughout Scotland had benefitted Alliance member firms compared with the uncertain position which had previously existed. Against this background, the Alliance gave favourable consideration to a request in 1924 from the Scottish District Council of the ASLP to devise mutual by-laws covering the whole of Scotland for the litho section of the Scottish printing industry. Agreement was reached and came into effect on 3 November 1925. Under the agreement no employee, except a member of the ASLP, was permitted to do lithographic work whilst no female employee was to be employed in any branch of the trade recognised as the jurisdiction of litho printers. Overtime worked up to midnight was to carried a 50% premium whilst that worked after midnight and Saturdays was to be paid at double time. Night shift was to be forty six hours per week with a premium of 25% on the day rate. In the event of any firm resorting to short-time working or suspension, three days notice was to be given and a further three days before any further reduction in hours could take place. No man was to resign their present employment without giving, or receiving, a fortnight's notice. Employees unable to attend work because of sickness, or any other cause, were to inform their employer within twenty four hours of the reason for their absence. Employees failing to comply with this procedure were to be reported to the ASLP branch secretary to be dealt with as the branch decided. All questions as to the interpretation of these Scottish Alliance/ASLP by-laws, and all differences between the parties were to be considered by a conciliation committee, consisting of three representatives from the Alliance and three from the ASLP Scottish District Council and the respective secretaries. None of these by-laws were to be changed without mutual consent.

In the mid-1930s several minor difficulties arose with the ASLP in connection with overtime working and the interpretation of the Scottish by-laws agreement. These were adjusted locally and the services of the Conciliation Committee were not required. An understanding was reached between the Alliance and the ASLP on certain points including engagement of employees, short-time and overtime working over which there had been some friction between the parties. The necessity for employers to guard against complacency was demonstrated at the end of 1934. The ASLP issued a book of rules to its members in which there was a clause stating no overtime be paid at less than one hour and not less than an hour for part of any succeeding hour. When the Alliance protested to the ASLP, the union said the revised overtime working rule had been included by mistake. The ASLP then advised its members that the rules were non-effective.

During 1935 a conference held between the Scottish Alliance and the Scottish District Council of the ASLP considered the existing by-laws agreement. As a result amendments were agreed. These dealt with breakdowns in suspensions, men working during their dinner break and the payment of an allowance for tea money where the necessity for overtime working had not been made known to employees before the dinner break.

c. Auxiliary Workers

In 1924, the STA created an Auxiliary Section into which recruited lesser skilled and women workers. This caused strained relations with other unions, especially the NUPB&PW and ultimately led the STA to withdraw from the P&KTF and the SJIC. In 1926, the Scottish Alliance appointed a special committee to investigate the whole question of the probable effects of an STA Auxiliary Section and to minimise the impact of inter-union disputes so the Scottish industry would not be affected adversely by industrial disputes not of the Alliance's making. Acting on the recommendation of this committee the Scottish Alliance arranged a conference between itself, P&KTF unions and the STA. This three party conference was held in November 1926 to which the Scottish Alliance submitted certain points to form the basis of discussion. The STA refused to accept a tripartite approach and the conference was adjourned. A further meeting with the STA was held in January 1927 but unfortunately without the results the Alliance hoped. The STA said it was seeking for its Auxiliary Section the same recognition status as accorded by the Scottish Alliance to itself.

In 1928, the STA and the NUPB&PW reached an agreement over the jurisdiction of the membership of their respective organisations. The prominent feature of the agreement was there would not be any dispute as to which union a worker could join. In the light of this the Scottish Alliance recognised the STA Auxiliary Section on the same basis as the existing agreement between itself and bookbinding union. The Scottish Alliance was not to be seen as party to the agreement between the STA and NUPB&PW.

In 1929, the dominant issue taking up the time of the Scottish Alliance was a request from the STA, jointly with the NUPB&PW, for a set of rules regulating the working conditions of auxiliary workers. The two unions suggested these rules be based on those at present applicable to compositors and machinemen. The proposals were submitted to the local associations of the Alliance for consideration. On receiving the opinion of its local associations the Scottish Alliance informed the STA and the NUPB&PW there was unanimous objection to the new conditions which the two unions sought to impose on the industry. The Alliance considered the existing working conditions in all the sections of the industry were the result of long years of experience of their peculiar requirements and if the terms of the suggested agreement were implemented, for instance, to the bookbinding or warehousing sections the results would be disastrous.[6]

The Scottish Alliance Negotiating Committee with co-opted members representing all interested sections of the Alliance and led by Dr MacLehose met the two unions in conference. The unions explained they were not proposing the rules be applicable to the bookbinding section of the industry but were meant to cover auxiliary workers in the printing section only. A discussion on the general position took place and the difficulty of distinguishing between a warehouse and a bindery was emphasised. There was difficulty in obtaining from the unions a clear statement of the classes of labour to whom the proposals would apply. Ultimately the NUPB&PW withdrew from the negotiations saying they wished the existing 1925 agreement between the Alliance and itself to be the agreement covering the working rules and conditions of their members in Scotland. The STA wished a separate set of rules for their auxiliary members and submitted proposals which had previously been presented to the Scottish Alliance. It was possible, but not without considerable difficulties, to reach an agreement with the STA covering working rules for its Auxiliary Section on all points with the exception of the 'no short time and no suspension' rule. After consulting with its local associations the Alliance accepted the STA position after it was agreed the application of the rules be limited to those wholly employed as assistants in case rooms or letterpress machine rooms in the four cities (Aberdeen, Dundee, Edinburgh and Glasgow) and to auxiliary workers in other areas and who were not wholly or mainly under a supervision of STA skilled craftsmen. In signing the agreement the Alliance made it clear they were not 'surrendering' any claims they might have in the future to have the short time clause removed or amended.

Machine Issues

The collective agreements between the Alliance and the STA and the Scottish District Councils of the ASLP, NSES and the NUPB&PW contained minimum extra payments, supplementary to the basic rate to employees in charge of certain machines. The unions claimed the operators of these machines should have extra pay to compensate them for the additional skill, strain and responsibility involved. Machine extras were set out in the agreement as a schedule of extras payable for each type of machine.

In 1924, there were negotiations between the BFMP, Alliance and the ASLP over the rates of wages payable to men working flatbed offset machines. Representatives of the Scottish Alliance attended these negotiations and the meetings of the Conciliation Committee of NJIC. The ASLP claimed the rates of pay for their members operating flatbed offset machines had not been fixed when the national agreement was concluded in 1919 and the men operating these machines were entitled to a supplementary payment of 5s 0d above the minimum wage rate. The employers argued these machines did not justify any additional pay. The majority of men operating the machines were receiving merit money in addition to the minimum rate and in most cases the merit payments were in excess of 5s 0d. Instructions were twice issued by the ASLP to their members to refuse to work the machines unless the additional 5s 0d was paid. The first instructions were withdrawn in many cases before stoppage notices had been given and in all cases before notices expired. Negotiations resumed but no settlement was reached and stoppage notices were again tendered by the men in a number of firms. Before these notices expired, negotiations and intervention by the JIC conciliation machinery resulted in agreement whereby the rate for flatbed offset machines from 2 April 1925 was an additional 4s 0d above the minimum scale of wages. It was agreed the ASLP request negotiations in twelve months time with regards to the additional 1s 0d.

In 1929, the Alliance received a claim from the STA for the grading of letterpress machines, together with claims for extra wages for operating certain machines and for restrictions on working conditions. These claims were considered at three lengthy conferences with the STA and at numerous meetings of the Alliance Negotiating Committee. The position taken by the Alliance was they approved of the recognition of merit and the payment of merit money but were opposed to a person being paid a rate above the minimum because they were an operator on a particular class or size of machine. Although the Alliance was opposed to the general principle of grading machines it was prepared to devise a scheme that was acceptable to both itself and the STA and which could be implemented without involving an increase in printing costs.

The Alliance considered the STA proposals for payments for operating certain machines and concluded they would seriously harm sections of the industry. After consultation with its member firms mostly likely to be affected and after considering the minimum rates being paid by member firms possessing these letterpresses machines, an offer of extra rates on specified machines was made to STA representatives. The union said the offer was inadequate but the Alliance stressed they would not increase their offer. The STA, realising it was not possible at the present time to persuade the Alliance to depart from its position withdrew indefinitely its claim for the grading of letterpress machines.

In 1930, the Scottish Alliance raised the question with the STA of the staffing of small auto-fed and fast-running machines. The STA pointed out when the national mutual rules and working conditions were renegotiated in 1925 machines such as the Vertical Miehle, the Kelly Press and auto-fed platens, etc were not considered by the negotiators. After the question was considered at three conferences, the Alliance and the STA appointed a joint expert committee to investigate the staffing of the machines concerned and to prepare a report. During 1931, this joint committee visited several works and studied the machines in operation under normal working conditions. It was hoped an agreement would be reached but the STA maintained they could not agree either to any differentiation between the various classes of small auto-fed machines or that they be staffed according to the class of work on which they were being employed. The STA claimed all auto-fed machines of fifteen by ten inches and over be staffed on the basis of one man to one machine and one man to two auto-fed platens. The Scottish Alliance rejected this argument.

Difficulties arose during the early 1930s in a number of printing offices over the introduction of small auto-fed cylinder machines and auto-fed platen machines. In March 1934, the Alliance submitted proposals to the STA for the staffing of these machines. At a conference in November the union re-tabled their proposals which had been rejected by the Scottish Alliance in May 1934. While accepting a proposal from the Alliance concerning process colour work on cylinder machines, made in an effort to remove difficulties there might be with such work, the STA tabled a new demand regarding colour printing on platen machines. Little progress was made and the STA requested a meeting of the conciliation committee of the SJIC. This committee which met in February 1935, after hearing evidence from both parties and examining suggestions which had been made at the various conferences, issued in February 1935 recommendations on the staffing of small auto-fed machines. These were not entirely satisfactory to the Alliance but in the hope of reaching a mutually acceptable settlement of an issue which had remained unresolved for four years, the Alliance accepted the conciliation committee's recommendations. The STA refused to accept the recommendations and suggested amendments which the Alliance considered would have made the position worse than if the union's May 1934 proposals had been implemented. The STA asked the issue be submitted to the NJIC Conciliation Committee which advised both parties accept the recommendation of the SJIC Conciliation Committee. A further seven months lapsed before the STA concluded an agreement on this basis. It endorsed the SJIC Conciliation Committee recommendations with an undertaking the training of apprentices would be safeguarded and they would not be employed for long periods on small auto-fed machines.

In the early stages of the negotiations on rotary machines the STA suggested differentiation based on the number of operations which could be done on a machine. It became clear to the Alliance and the union that an agreement on such lines would lead to serious anomalies and be inequitable in its operation. An unsuccessful attempt was thereafter made to frame an agreement in general terms. The STA referred the matter to a conciliation committee of the Scottish JIC. This committee, after taking evidence from both sides recommended the parties meet again. At the ensuing conference a tentative agreement was concluded covering several points, including that rotary machines currently in operation should continue to be staffed as at present. The year-long negotiations with the STA over the staffing of rotary machines and small auto-fed machines was brought to a close when an agreement was signed in May 1935. This introduced a new principle into the agreements between the Alliance and the STA. In future in the event of the two parties being unable to agree on the manner in which any rotary machine be staffed provision now existed for calling in an independent chair to work with a joint committee and to issue a recommendation as to how the problem might be resolved.

In autumn 1931, NUPB&PW approached the Alliance for a conference on the rates of wages paid to men employed on certain machines in the binding and ruling sections of the industry. The union requested extra rates which had been agreed to in England and had been operating for several years now be made applicable in Scotland. Again, the Alliance could not accept the NUPB&PW's claim and rejected the principle of automatic application to Scotland of more favourable situations in England.

In 1935 the Alliance refused to enter into agreement with the Bookbinders Union to provide for the payment of extras on certain classes of machines. The NUPB&PW argued the BFMP *Power Machine Agreement* signed in March 1925, and subsequent agreements, applied to Scotland. A SJIC conciliation committee ruled these agreements did not apply to Scotland and any agreement applicable to Scotland be negotiated between the Alliance and the Bookbinders' Union. The NUPB&PW asked the Alliance if it were prepared to negotiate such an agreement. The Alliance explained they were satisfied to enter into an agreement on the lines suggested but they considered it not in the best interests of the employers and the employees in the industry. By the outbreak of the Second World War no further developments had taken place with reference to the NUPB&PW request that a power machine agreement, applicable to Scotland, be concluded.

The NUPB&PW

In 1925 the Scottish District of the Bookbinders' Union approached the Alliance claiming the wages of bookbinding and machine rulers be as those of letterpress printers. The union based its argument on the grounds these members had served a seven year apprenticeship, the Court of Arbitration's opinion was that wages of bookbinders and machine rulers be equal to those of printers and that the alteration in printers' wages in certain areas had created difficulties for their members. The Alliance pointed out the position of printers had only changed in certain towns and that in some areas, prior to the introduction of the wage grading scheme, the binders had higher pay than the printers.

The Alliance offered an agreement that wages paid under the grading system for bookbinders and letterpress printers be the same from the April 1926. It was not prepared to grant increases to any person in receipt of earnings as high as in the new proposed grading scheme and there be no change in present piecework rates and in no case should any increase from the agreement exceed 1s 6d per week. Agreement was concluded at the end of December 1925 and from April 1926 the minimum rates of pay of the bookbinder, machine ruler and typographical workers were the same in the different districts of Scotland.

In 1932, NUPB&PW met the Alliance in conference concerning the ratio of apprentices in bookbinding and machine ruling departments. The union claimed in calculating the number of apprentices to which a firm was entitled, the number of journeymen in the two departments be added together. The Alliance took the position it was the practice in Scotland to treat the two departments separately in calculating the number of apprentices. At the same time the Alliance intimated an anxiety to secure adequate training for boys and said if the NUPB&PW considered in any case the training was inadequate they would to meet with local representative to discuss the matter.

Under a national agreement between the Scottish Alliance and the NUPB&PW a wage of 58s 6d was paid to printers, packers and general assistants, provided they were over twenty one years of age, with not less than one year's experience of warehouse work. In 1934 the union submitted a claim to the Alliance the clause be deleted from the agreement under which the employer could pay a labourer whatever wage he chose if he was under twenty one years of age, or during his first year in the trade if over twenty one years. It was pointed out to the Alliance by the NUPB&PW some employers failed to observe the terms of the agreement to pay the agreed rate after a year's work experience. The Scottish Alliance considered 58s 6d was too high for that class of labour but so long as the agreement existed its terms must be observed. A suggestion to the union there be a reduction in this standard rate was, to say the least, unacceptable. The Alliance then offered two scales of wages providing for a three-year period for those commencing over eighteen years of age and a two-year period for those commencing over twenty one years of age, followed by the standard rate. This was accepted by the union.

During 1938, conferences were held throughout the year with the NUPB&PW and the Alliance covering limitations on overtime working, overtime rates, payment of extras to casual workers, demarcation of labour between men and women, juniors, piece work and a claim for extras on a machine. Agreement was reached that the double-day shift agreement with the STA, namely both the morning and afternoon shifts be paid the same rate of wages, should apply to NUPB&PW members. The Alliance was adamant it could not meet the union's request on demarcation, payment of extras and overtime restrictions but did conclude an agreement with the union covering piece work, the employment of junior girls and of the employment of casual workers.

Summary

During 1919, the Scottish Alliance negotiated with the STA and the Scottish District Councils of the ASLP, NSES and the NUPB&PW national agreements covering basic terms of employment. These agreements were not confined to craftsmen. They covered all groups of employees. The different wage rates in these agreements involved two major principles. First, they fixed skill differentials between different classes of workers in the same town. Second, they established differentials between the same class of workers in different towns – the 'wage grading system'. The majority of national agreements to which the Scottish Alliance was party covered basically the same ground and were negotiated in a similar manner.

During the inter-war period, there were two alterations to the national agreements. First, in 1921, the Alliance achieved wage reductions which though relatively substantial, left the real purchasing power of the rates considerably higher than in 1920. Attempts by the Alliance in 1931/32 to achieve reductions in production costs were thwarted by the unions dragging out negotiations for a sufficient period of time that the industry's economic downturn recovered. Second, throughout the inter-war period, all the unions obtained extra payments for their members operating machines requiring special skills or extra responsibility or discomfort.

In addition to the negotiation of national agreements, the Alliance concluded agreements providing uniform working conditions for their members throughout Scotland. These were known as national working rule agreements. The 1921 agreement with the STA meant for the first time in the history of the Scottish printing industry, national working rules and uniform conditions with respect to the letterpress side of the industry now applied to the whole of Scotland. Similarly, agreements were negotiated between the Scottish Alliance and the ASLP providing Scotland-wide mutually agreed working rules and employment conditions for the lithographic section of the industry. Both agreements provided for a conciliation committee to settle peacefully disputes arising from the application and interpretation of the agreed working rules. Much time was spent on the drafting of the rules but this paid off because despite the economic difficulties of the industry during the inter-war years meetings of the conciliation committees were infrequent. The framing of national working rules applicable to the whole of Scotland and agreeing that changes could only be made with the mutual consent of the Alliance and the unions was a notable achievement. No longer could a small local association to be compelled to grant conditions to union members out of keeping with conditions elsewhere.

Another notable feature of industrial relations in the industry over the period 1919-1939 was the relative absence of hostility and the infrequency of open conflict between the Scottish Alliance and the print unions. One reason was that in the inter-war years, unemployment in the printing industry was about half that for Scotland as a whole.

Notes

[1] See Report by the Executive Board to the Tenth Annual General Meeting, Edinburgh, 1921.

[2] See Report of the Executive Board to the Thirteenth Annual General Meeting, Glasgow, 1924.

[3] See Report by the Executive Board to the Fourteenth Annual General Meeting, Perth, 1925.

[4] See Report by the Executive Board to the Twelfth Annual General Meeting, Edinburgh, 1923.

[5] See Report by the Executive Board to the Twenty Second Annual General Meeting, Edinburgh, March, 1933.

[6] See Minutes of the Executive Board Meeting held 28 November 1929.

Chapter 7

HOURS AND HOLIDAYS, 1919 - 1939

The last chapter examined wage movements in the Scottish printing industry during the inter-war period. This analyses changes in holiday entitlement and standard weekly working hours during the same period. There were two major alterations to standard working hours – one in 1919 and one in 1937. The chapter begins by examining the events leading to the 1919 *Hours and Holiday Agreement*. The second part outlines how the 1937 *Hours and Holiday Agreement* was reached and implemented.

Introduction

In Scotland hours and holidays were negotiated between the BFMP and the P&KTF with the Alliance having representation on the BFMP Labour Negotiating Committee. For the STA and the other print unions in Scotland, a forty-eight-hour working week had long been a bargaining objective. The P&KTF hours and holiday movement of 1910-11 failed to achieve this goal and its affiliates remained dissatisfied with a fifty-one-hour working week. There was now a desire amongst printers for an annual week's holiday with pay, and payment for statutory holidays such as Christmas Day, Good Friday and other bank holidays. Improvements in hours and holidays were a lower collective bargaining priority during the First World War but from 1918 the P&KTF-affiliated unions gave priority to reducing working hours. The majority view was for a forty-eight-hour week but some unions wanted forty four, or even forty. Shorter hours, the unions hoped, would reduce unemployment, improve health and provide more leisure time for mental and physical recreation. Employers, it was contended, should not retain all the benefits of the productivity improvements stemming from the implementation of labour-saving machinery. The Scottish Alliance had a different perspective seeing reduction in working time as increasing production costs, causing shortages of labour and reducing the competitiveness of the Scottish printing industry.

The 1919 Hours and Holiday Agreement

The individual print unions jealously guarded their autonomy to determine their own members' pay rates and gave the P&KTF no authority to bargain these. In the case of holidays and hours of work, however, the affiliates were content for it to negotiate collectively on their behalf. In 1919, the P&KTF submitted a claim to the BFMP for a forty-eight-hour working week, payment for statutory holidays and a week's annual holiday. The hours reduction claim of 1910-11 had been prolonged with a grave danger of a national strike. In 1919 an agreement was reached after a number of conferences characterised by 'reasonableness, moderation and remarkable goodwill on both sides'.[1] There was much give and take over matters of contention. The National Union of Bookbinders and Machine Rulers was not, in 1919, a member of the P&KTF and was not represented at the bargaining table. The BFMP recommended to its members the union's members be entitled to the benefits of any new agreement.

A conference was held in London in January 1919 involving the BFMP and P&KTF to consider the latter's demand for a forty-eight-hour week, a summer holiday and payment for statutory holidays. Any P&KTF agreement made had to embrace Scotland. At the conference the standard working week of forty eight hours was agreed and there be payment, in the year, for six statutory holidays. The issue of payment for a week's summer holiday was deferred to another meeting. The Alliance decided to send its Secretary, Mr Bisset to the BFMP Labour Subcommittee meeting to be held in London on 30 January to make clear the position as regards Scotland, namely hours and holidays questions could only be dealt with by the Scottish Printing Industry Wages Board. The Alliance also discussed at length hours, holidays and wages in Scotland and adopted the following resolution[2].

> Hours and Wages
> ...that the views of the branches be obtained forthwith on the calling of an early meeting of the Wages Board with a view to the general revision of wages and the institution of a reduced uniform working week in the trade in Scotland...

> Holidays
> That the question of payment for statutory holidays be remitted to the branches for consideration...

British Federation of Master Printers: Young Master Printers' Summer School, held in Edinburgh, July – August 1934

The Alliance Secretary, Mr Bisset, duly informed the BFMP as to the its view as to the applicability to Scotland of any BFMP/P&KTF agreement on hours and holiday. In February 1919 the Alliance agreed to the negotiations for a reduced working week in Scotland but the P&KTF claim for payments for statutory and summer holidays be rejected. It was agreed to refer the question to the Scottish Printing Industry Wages Board. The Alliance then received a letter from the Secretary of the Scottish district of the P&KTF containing on behalf the Aberdeen, Edinburgh, Glasgow and other Scottish P&KTF districts, a claim for a forty-hour week with no reduction in wages and payment for all holidays, including one week during the summer. The letter also requested a conference to consider the claim, to be held before 20 February 1919.

In the meantime the BFMP and the P&KTF reached a new *Hours and Holiday Agreement* to come into effect on 3 March 1919. It provided for a forty-eight-hour week, payment for statutory holidays and for a paid week's summer holiday. The agreement laid down the standard working week in all departments of forty eight hours. The time of starting work remained unchanged unless agreement was reached in each shop on alternative arrangements. The same condition applied to any change in workshop practice. To compensate piece workers for the loss of earnings due to the reduction of hours, piece rates were subjected to an interim increase of 5% until permanent adjustments were made. At least six days in each year were to be national holidays. If employees were required to work on any of these days they were entitled to extra pay for that day as well as a day's holiday with pay at a later date.

Each employee was entitled to one week's annual holiday, to be taken between 31 March and 30 September and to receive the time-rate for such week, or in the case of a piece worker the average of their weekly earnings over the past six months. A minimum period of continuous employment of six months with the present employer was necessary to qualify for paid holiday entitlements. Any employee leaving a firm was entitled to a day's pay for every two months' of completed service since the preceding 30 June the base date for all calculation of holidays. A joint committee was established to adjudicate on any differences arising from the interpretation and application of the agreement.

The Secretary of the Alliance, Mr Bisset, wrote to the Director of the BFMP asking for the precise terms of the resolution at its council meeting ratifying the agreement and/or of the unsuccessful amendment moved by representatives of the Scottish Alliance. The reply stated that the motion was 'that the provincial agreement as to hours and holidays be approved and that the question of Scotland being included be left in the hands of the Joint Committee'. It said the Scottish amendment to the motion was 'that pending negotiations as to the question of hours and holidays in Scotland through the Scottish Printing Industry Wages Board or otherwise this agreement shall not operate in Scotland'. This amendment to the motion received only the four votes of the Scottish representatives on the BFMP Council and was declared lost.

The Scottish Alliance faced problems in maintaining its policy that the BFMP/P&KTF 1919 *Hours and Holiday Agreement* should not operate in Scotland, as hours and holiday changes were a matter for the Scottish Printing Industry Wages Board. The Chair and Secretary of the P&KTF at the 30 January 1919 conference in London had formally stated that the *Hours and Holiday Agreement* must include Scotland and would be operative in Scotland on 3 March 1919 whether accepted by the Scottish Alliance or not. There was also the problem that the unions, including the STA, had not yet appointed their representatives to the workers side of the Scottish Printing Industry Wages Board, and in the view of John Robertson, Joint Secretary to the board, although the board had been duly constituted on 14 January 1919 it could not meet until the changes suggested to its constitution had been approved by its constituents. In short, the attitude of the unions made it impossible for the question of hours and holidays be considered timeously by the Scottish Printing Industry Wages Board. However, it was desirable to have a uniform arrangement for hours and holidays throughout the UK and complications would arise in the event of unions affiliated to P&KTF claiming a forty-eight-hour working week in Scotland on 3 March 1919. There were further complications in that the STA put in a claim for a forty-hour working week and the Scottish District Council of the Bookbinders Union for a forty-four-hour week. In the light of these complications the Alliance, given inadequate time was available for separate negotiations and recognising the advantages of securing, for the first time in the history of the industry, uniformity on the two important issues of hours of work and holidays, waived the technical point of separate consideration. It decided to implement the BFMP/P&KTF *Hours and Holiday Agreement* from 3 March 1919. The Alliance recognised the value of pragmatism over strict adherence to principle.

The ink was hardly dry on the 1919 *Hours and Holiday Agreement* when the P&KTF decided, at its annual conference in April 1919, to claim a working week of forty four hours (day shift) and forty hours (night shift). The forty-eight-hour working week, it was argued, had been so long in coming it was now felt to be out of date. A ballot showed an overwhelming majority of members of P&KTF-affiliated unions favoured pursuing a further reduction in working hours. In February 1920 the BFMP opened negotiations with the P&KTF over the possibility of a further reduction in working hours. The unions presented their case in a lukewarm manner realising there was little chance of concessions being granted by the BFMP[3]. They found difficulty in refuting the BFMP arguments. The employers made it clear their member firms would not offer any further reductions in hours of work. It was too soon after the forty-eight-hour agreement. The UK and the Scottish printing industry needed to enhance their production levels, manpower was in short supply and production costs were increasing. In the light of the BFMP and the Scottish Alliance strong stance against further reductions in working time, the P&KTF shelved any further demands for reductions in hours of work and increases in paid holiday entitlement. Hours were not, in fact, to be changed again until 1937.

The 1920 annual general meeting of the Alliance adopted a resolution, remitted to the Executive Board, to consider the termination of the 1919 *Hours and Holiday Agreement* and to compensate the employees for loss of holiday entitlement by monetary payments. When the Alliance Executive considered the matter, the suggestion did not receive any support and the motion fell. The 1932 annual general meeting also was critical of the 1919 *Hours and Holiday Agreement* and carried the following motion:

> That the Alliance Board be asked to impress upon the Federation the necessity of a modification of the Hours and Holiday Agreement so that only those people who by long service and good behaviour and loyalty have deserved it should be entitled to be paid for holidays and the provisions of the Agreement whereby pro rata allowances are paid to temporary workers should be abolished...

At its meeting on 1 June 1932 the Alliance Executive Board decided not to forward the resolution to the BFMP. A member of the board then proposed the BFMP seek the abolition of the *Hours and Holiday Agreement* but on being put to the vote the proposal was rejected.

In 1932/1933 the Scottish Alliance sought to restore the demand for printed products by seeking a reduction in wage costs and/or a relaxation of restrictive working practices. The 1933 annual general meeting also saw changes to the 1919 *Hours and Holiday Agreement* playing a part in lowering production costs. Some delegates considered the agreement required reconsideration and be amended as an urgent necessity. They wished to see the Scottish Alliance representatives on the BFMP Council press for such a review. Other delegates urged the Alliance to have the agreement scrapped; there were also voices which argued no action. The meeting nevertheless passed a motion instructing the Alliance representatives on the BFMP Council to press for a review of the agreement and for its eventual termination. Nothing happened as a result of the 1933 annual general meeting adopting this policy.

The 1937 Hours and Holiday Agreement

It was not until the 1930s the print unions, as part of their policies for reducing unemployment, moved hours and holidays further up their collective bargaining agenda. The stronger unions continually pressed the P&KTF to seek negotiations for shorter hours. The P&KTF officers, knowing the precarious financial state of some of its affiliates, refused to take any steps that could lead to a serious dispute. The print unions believed a reduction in hours would help solve the unemployment caused by increasing mechanisation and rationalisation, whilst the speeding up of production put greater strain on the members. The 1931 annual meeting decided that a special conference be held. This was held in January 1933 and concluded that to lessen unemployment and to enable all to share in the benefit of increased output resulting from rationalisation there be a reduction of working hours, a further restriction on overtime working and of the intake of apprentices.

Just before this conference the BFMP and the Alliance requested from the unions reductions in the cost of production, including wage reductions and the relaxation of some working practices. Given the worsening economic depression in the industry P&KTF accepted there was little likelihood of the employer conceding further reductions in working hours. The unions used their desire for less working time to reply to the employers case that further reductions in working hours could not be afforded. They even raised their demand to a forty-hour working week 'in view of the continued unemployment'. The P&KTF was part of a national and international movement on the part of trade unions to reduce unemployment which was a worldwide phenomenon. The P&KTF, until 1936, did little other than pass annual resolutions in favour of reduced working hours. The P&KTF did not force the issue as the International Labour Office was expected to recommend a forty-hour working week be introduced in selected pilot industries. The British print unions hoped their industry would be selected, but this proved not to be the case.

By 1935 the worst of the economic depression had passed and BFMP and Alliance proposals of 1932/3 for reductions in production costs had been withstood by

---

the unions. The P&KTF believed the time was now right for stronger efforts to reduce working hours. It balloted its affiliated unions in the issue. In February 1936 the result showed a large majority in each union (and 86% overall) in favour of demanding a forty-hour week without reduction in pay and supporting any action necessary to achieve it. The P&KTF had submitted to the BFMP on 10 January 1936 a claim for a reduction in the standard working week from forty five to forty hours, that there be no proportionate reduction in wages and overtime rates be paid for all work beyond forty hours per week. The Alliance immediately recommended rejection of the P&KTF application.[4]

a. The Negotiations

A conference to discuss the P&KTF claim was held on 10 March 1936. The P&KTF said their present application was for a forty-hour working week and all its affiliated unions had been consulted and the majority in favour of the claim being tabled was the greatest they had ever known. The P&KTF outlined its arguments in favour of reducing working hours, the main one being the desirability that workers have more leisure time, financed from the benefits of the implementation of the improved methods of production introduced into the industry during the past two decades. The P&KTF also argued their members were not prepared to wait for the outcome of international conferences on the subject of the forty-hour week. Since 1919 the industry had seen remarkable efforts to speed up machinery and to reduce the amount of labour employed. The P&KTF negotiators saw no opportunity of reducing unemployment other than by shortening the hours of work and pointed out that while the industry had been depressed it had not been appropriate to seek a reduction in working hours. Now in the light of the changed economic circumstances of the industry the time was right to seek a further reduction in working hours which could be granted with advantage by master printers.

Having consulted with their members, the BFMP and the Alliance rejected the P&KTF claim on a number of grounds:
(1) a reduction in hours would result in an increase of printing costs and a consequential reduction in the demand for print products.
(2) if a reduction in hours of work led to a demand for additional qualified labour it was not available. There would be an even more acute shortage of labour.
(3) any increase in printing costs would lead to commercial work at present being done by printers, being undertaken by duplicating machines and similar equipment. A large quantity of printing would be removed from the legitimate printing industry and be undertaken by large customers under employment conditions of a lower standard than those prevailing in the industry.
(4) the present conditions of employment in the industry were as good as or better than those of craftsmen in other industries.
(5) the complaints of customers regarding the prejudicial effects of conditions in the print industry as affecting their own industries would be accentuated.

(6) the employers argued printing offices where the employment conditions were unfair in comparison with those found in unionised plants would increase both in number and size.

The BFMP and the Alliance were prepared to make concessions to the P&KTF in return for some concessions from the P&KTF-affiliated unions, for example, the relaxation of apprentice ratios and of overtime limits. The P&KTF refused to discuss these issues, arguing they were not within its authority but were the preserve of its individual affiliate unions. The negotiations ended in deadlock. Three conferences were held in October 1936 but no breakthrough was achieved. The P&KTF reaffirmed its demand for a forty-hour week and informed the BFMP it intended to call a special meeting of the NJIC. The Joint Labour Committee of the BFMP upon which there were two representatives from the Scottish Alliance, met on 24 September 1936 and agreed the NJIC intervene but pointed out the correct procedure was to involve the assistance of the NJIC Conciliation Committee rather than call a special meeting of NJIC. The P&KTF accepted this suggestion.

The NJIC Conciliation Committee met on 14 December 1936. Its finding was as follows:

> ...The Conciliation Committee having considered the complete deadlock which exists between the P&KTF and the BFMP and the Newspaper Society on the application of the P&KTF for a forty hour week for the printing industry, recommends that the parties meet again, without reference to their respective mandates to consider the possibility of reaching an agreement on some new basis satisfactory to both side...[5]

The BFMP Council and the Alliance Executive Board accepted this finding and appointed a special committee of fifteen members of the Joint Labour Committee to consider the problems facing the industry and empowered to negotiate with the P&KTF. Following the recommendation of the Conciliation Committee, four conferences were held between 15 February and 10 March 1937 involving the special committee.

At the first conference the employers stated the possibility of reaching agreement depended on the extent to which the unions co-operated in building a new basis which was both practically and economically possible for the industry. The BFMP then outlined proposals designed to help employers address the problems of increased costs and the shortage of skilled labour arising from the implementation of further reductions in working hours. At the second meeting the P&KTF argued their mandate was confined to negotiating on hours of work and other issues were the sole preserve of the employers and the individual unions. The P&KTF pressed for a further meeting of the NJIC Conciliation

Committee but the employers preferred a further conference saying, if the P&KTF agreed to this, they would make a definite offer at the conference on reduction of hours. At the third conference a draft agreement was submitted by the employers in which a reduction of hours for day workers from forty eight to forty six per week was proposed in return for the unions relaxing working rules concerning apprentices, overtime and agreeing a stabilisation clause of three years. The P&KTF expressed disappointment with the offer arguing they hoped the BFMP would have made an offer of a forty-four-hour working week. At a fourth conference the BFMP retabled their offer of a reduction in working hours of two hours and no more. The P&KTF rejected the offer of a forty-six-hour working week, requesting a special meeting of the NJIC.

b. The Agreement

The NJIC meeting of 14 April 1937 recommended both parties resume negotiations. A series of meetings took place but the BFMP stuck to their forty six hours offer. The P&KTF on 23 April informed the BFMP it would ballot its affiliated unions on the question 'Are you in favour of handing in notices failing an amended offer for a forty-four-hour week for the industry?' In the light of this development the BFMP made an improved offer of a forty-five-hour working week. The P&KTF Executive meeting of 28 April recommended acceptance of the forty-five-hour working week for day workers. The members of the P&KTF-affiliated unions were balloted on the employers' offer and the result, announced on 21 July 1937, showed that 85,593 had voted in favour of acceptance with 26,552 against, a majority of 59,041. This ended the negotiations on a reduction in the length of the working week which had begun on 10 January 1936.

The 1937 *Hours and Holiday Agreement* came into force on 4 October 1937. Weekly working hours became forty five for day workers and forty three for night workers. In return the print unions made certain concessions whereby the overtime maximum hours was increased by the same number of hours by which the working week was reduced, namely to twenty two hours per fortnight. The P&KTF-affiliated unions accepted a 'stabilisation' clause whereby except in the event of a considerable increase in the cost of living or any national or international agreements regarding hours, neither side would request 'a major alteration of any agreement which will materially affect the cost of production' during the next three years.

This stabilisation clause was resented by the STA whose members had gained less than the others owing to the prevalence of shorter working hours in Scotland relative to England and Wales. The STA's policy was a forty-hour working week. Its members voted against acceptance of the 1937 *Hours and Holiday Agreement* but as an affiliate member of the P&KTF accepted the majority decision. The stabilisation clause precluded the STA from seeking major alterations in the national agreement to which it was a party for the next three years.

The resulting changes in the hours of working in the industry were implemented with remarkable smoothness and in only a few cases was a discussion between the Alliance and a trade union necessary.[6] The Scottish Alliance accepted alterations to piece rates so that piece-rate workers did not suffer loss of earnings from the introduction of the reduced working week. The necessary adjustments were achieved amicably within individual book and jobbing houses.

Summary

During the inter-war years, there were two major changes to the standard working week in Scottish printing industry. The national *Agreement* made between the BFMP and the P&KTF, providing for a working week in the UK printing industry of forty eight per week and for payment of six statutory holidays and for a weeks' holiday in the summer came into operation on 3 March 1919. Constitutionally, the agreement should have been referred to the Scottish Printing Industry Wages Board. The Alliance realising the advantages of obtaining uniformity throughout the UK on hours of work and holiday entitlement, decided on pragmatic grounds not to insist on this.

In 1936, the P&KTF submitted a claim for a forty-hour working week. On several occasions the negotiations almost broke down but agreement was reached in 1937 on a forty-five-hour working week. This agreement was accepted by a substantial majority on a ballot vote of all P&KTF-affiliated unions but the Scottish Alliance learned the STA members had voted against acceptance, but as an affiliate of the P&KTF accepted the majority of view. The resultant change of hours of work was implemented smoothly in the industry.

Notes

[1]   See J Child, *Industrial Relations in the British Printing Industry*. London: Allen & Unwin, p228.
[2]   See Minutes of the Executive Board, 29 January 1919.
[3]   See Howe, E (1950) *The British Federation of Master Printers, 1900-1950*. London: British Federation of Master Printers, p69.
[4]   See Report of the Executive Board to the Twenty Sixth Annual General Meeting, Edinburgh, 1937.
[5]   See Howe, E (1950) *The British Federation of Master Printers, 1900-1950*. London: British Federation of Master Printers, pp127-28.
[6]   See Report of the Executive Board to the Twenty Seventh Annual General Meeting, Glasgow, 1938.

Chapter 8

THE SECOND WORLD WAR, 1939 - 1945

This chapter examines the role of the Scottish Alliance in the Second World War (1939-1945) a period in which four Presidents (Robert Wylie, John B Bartholomew, W Hope Collins and Duncan Sillars) protected and advanced the interests of member firms in difficult circumstances. The first part examines the industrial relations issues arising from air raids on the civilian populations of the major towns and cities of Scotland. The chapter then outlines the impact of the shortage of raw materials, especially paper supplies, on Scottish print firms whilst the next section examines the industry's adjustment to the government Defence Regulations requiring any print firm to undertake print work the government directed.

The fourth part of the chapter considers the labour shortage arising in the industry from conscription and the direction of labour into the munitions industry. It then analyses how the Scottish Alliance relieved the manpower shortage problems by persuading the print unions to relax restrictive working practices, to accept dilution of skilled labour and agree placement and recruitment of apprentices called up to serve in HM Armed Forces. The Second World War period saw increases in the cost of living leading to frequent demands from the print unions for increases in their members wages. The final part of this chapter assesses the outcome of the ensuing wage negotiations.

Introduction

During the Second World War the problems faced by the Scottish printing industry were much the same as those of the First World War. At first there was dislocation and unemployment followed by gradual adjustments to war conditions with shortages of labour and materials. There was government rationing, the control of raw materials, conscription into the armed forces, and transfer and compulsory 'direction' of labour from printing, a less essential wartime industry, into munitions industries and civil defence. This resulted in a labour shortage and the necessity for relaxation of union working rules and for the dilution of labour. The Second World War period witnessed rising production costs, increasing living costs, frequent demands from the unions for wage increases and problems of replacing and reinstating apprentices.

The Scottish printing industry was more seriously affected by the Second, than by the First World War. Shortages of materials were more severe, government control and rationing more stringent and labour shortages more acute whilst air raids destroyed or damaged a number of printing offices and killed or injured many civilians. The 1939-1945 War was more of a 'total' war than 1914-18. Having experienced the First World War, the Scottish printing industry adjusted to war-time conditions for the second time more quickly and efficiently.

It is not possible to give anything like a full explanation of the Scottish Alliance's many war-time activities regarding labour supply, employment conditions, conscription, transfer of print workers into essential war industries, appropriate replacement of apprentices, the dilution of labour, air-raids, paper rationing, government controls and meeting with government departments and committees etc. This work was done through either the Scottish Alliance Emergency Committee, the BFMP, or the NJIC War Emergency Standing Committee. This was due largely to the government which, on the grounds of time and expediency, wished to deal only with one organisation representing the whole printing industry. Most of the industry's problems were dealt with by agreements between the P&KTF and the BFMP through a series of wage agreements dealing with short-time working, air raids, relaxation of union working rules, labour dilution, transfer of workers, apprentice replacements, wage increases and working hours. Initially the P&KTF experienced some difficulty in Scotland where the STA had established its own tradition of negotiating with the Scottish Alliance and was loathe to concede its autonomy in wage matters to the P&KTF. The other print unions in Scotland were, however, content to let the P&KTF negotiate with the BFMP on the understanding any agreement reached would be applicable in Scotland. The STA's 'nationalist' tendency was overcome when the P&KTF set up a special Scottish Advisory Committee to deal with conditions in Scotland. The Scottish Alliance was happy to participate in UK-wide negotiations with representation on the BFMP National Negotiating Committee.

James MacLehose who chaired the Scottish Alliance Labour Committee was a member of the BFMP War Emergency Labour Committee.

Air Raids

On 29 August 1939, the BFMP invited the P&KTF to discuss the impact of the likely war situation on the industry. The next day they reached an agreement entitled *Agreement on Emergency Conditions* in which it was accepted in dealing with the many difficulties that would arise there be a general spirit of accommodation between the employers' and employees' organisations and between the employers and the employees in each establishment.[1] Further clauses made provision for the transfer of work and workers to other districts, for rearrangement of hours of work to permit work being done during day shift, for payment of wages for time lost in air raid alerts, for short-time work with proportionate reduction in wages in each establishment and for the establishment of a Joint War Emergency Committee.

Although the STA Executive Council refused to accept the *Agreement on Emergency Conditions* was applicable to their members, the Alliance Emergency Committee negotiated with the STA an agreement on similar lines to the national one. These two agreements helped the industry over the early war period but their operation proved unsatisfactory in certain respects to both sides. There were disputes over overtime payments and short-time working. The STA, for example, wanted to impose upon Scotland a short-time working week of not less than forty hours and wanted short-time working arrangements to be a matter between each management and chapel. The STA wanted employers to give at least a week's notice to put their workers on short time. The Alliance considered short-time hours should be paid at thirty six and not forty and the minimum period of notice from an employer to the workforce to implement short-time working be three days.

The Scottish Alliance and the BFMP complained about paying full wages for the first hour of suspension of work and payment of half wages thereafter for time spent in the air-raid shelters and wanted to reduce all hours to half pay. The emergency agreement contained no procedure for the settlement of disputes. Negotiations between the P&KTF and the BFMP to amended the *Agreement on Emergency Conditions* failed and on 2 June 1940 it was terminated having lasted nine months. With this, no arrangements existed for payment for lost time during air raids and air raid warnings. A national agreement had been made on 27 May 1940 dealing with working time lost through air raids and air raid warnings. This agreement was accepted by the Scottish Alliance and the STA. On the appeal of the government that business should carry on after the siren until it was clear enemy attack was imminent, an agreement to this effect was made on 24 September 1940 between the BFMP and the P&KTF (known as the War Agreement No 2).

This scheme could be adopted by mutual agreement – the desire of management and a majority vote of the workers. Where the scheme of working until warning of imminent danger was given by a roof spotter was adopted, employers paid full wages for time lost. Where work was suspended due to enemy action employees received half pay. Other clauses made provision for suspension of work through air raid damage to premises and plant, for transference of workers to other districts and for rearrangement of working hours to utilize as much winter daylight as possible.

The law of Scotland and that of England differed so far as the contract of employment was concerned when premises were inadvertently destroyed or made unsuitable for the conduct of business. The Alliance said it could not accept the 24 September 1940 agreement dealing with payments on destruction of premises or suspension of work due to enemy damage. The STA took the position that they were not prepared to accept the agreement regarding short-time working and instructed its members to continue working under the 27 May 1940 agreement. Subsequent experiences of air raid warnings in Scotland led initially in February 1941 to an interim agreement between the Alliance and the STA. In March 1942, the 24 September 1940 agreement was amended to meet Scottish employment law requirements and the Alliance and the STA accepted it then apply to Scotland. As enemy bombing grew more severe, the Defence Regulations 'fire watching' became in January 1941 compulsory. In February 1941 the BFMP and the P&KTF signed War Agreement No. 4 providing inter alia, a scheme for the transfer of labour from areas where owing to damage to printing offices by enemy action there might be a surplus of workers. It recommended married and unmarried men with similar work responsibilities, who might be transferred with the authority of their trade union, receive the grade rate of the town to which they were sent plus a subsistence allowance of 3s 0d a day.

Rationing of Paper and Other Materials

Control of the use of paper during the war lay with the Paper Control Department of the Ministry of Supply. At the end of October 1939 it raised the maximum prices of paper to 60% above their pre-war level and all stocks and supplies of wood pulp were placed at the disposal of the Ministry of Supply. In February 1940 the threat of paper rationing became a reality. The Control of Paper Order No 8 gave printers, for the period 3 March - 1 June 1940, a maximum of 60% of the total quantity (by weight) of paper supplied to any individual during the equivalent period in 1939. In March 1940 the Paper Control Department issued a draconian order. The paper ration was reduced, retrospectively from 3 March, by half to 30% of the amount purchased in 1939. The normal pre-war consumption of paper in the UK had been over three million tons of which one million tons were imported. Of the two million tons made in this country, 80% of the raw material was imported from Scandinavia.[2]

Within a month of reducing the paper ration to 30% of the pre-war consumption level, the Paper Control Department issued a series of orders which hit the industry hard. Order No 14 abolished rationing, whilst licence Order No 16 imposed far-reaching restrictions on the manufacture and use of paper. The issue of new periodicals and certain types of posters and circulars was prohibited. The use of wrapping and packaging materials were severely restricted. The manufacture of paper goods, ranging from handkerchiefs to confetti, was forbidden. The industry by April 1940 was in real danger of a paper famine. In October 1940, largely due to joint representations by the BFMP and the P&KTF, the industry received slight relaxation of paper rationing. The small concessions mainly affected the use to which paper might be put and did not increase the amount of paper available to the industry. For example, an advertiser could distribute up to 56lbs in weight of circulars in a three months' period although the manufacture of paper drip mats remained prohibited.

Paper Order No 32 came into force on 21 April 1941. Further restrictions were imposed on the use of paper. The aggregate weight of advertising circulars which could be distributed in any three months was reduced, from 50% to 15% of the weight distributed in the corresponding months of the year ending 31 August 1939. Loose advertising inserts in newspapers and periodicals were prohibited. Programmes for entertainment, horse racing, sports and athletic meetings were reduced from 200 to eighty square inches. Labels were not to exceed twenty square inches. Paper Control Order No 36, published only the day before it became operable on 12 November 1941, was issued without warning, or prior consultation, with the BFMP. Many printers, commercial users of printed goods, advertisers, calendar, diary and greeting card makers and others only learned a new order was in force by reading the newspapers. The immediate impact was the disruption of large numbers of printing jobs in various stages of progress, particularly in advertising. Many print orders in Scotland were entirely prohibited from the date of the order resulting in heavy financial losses for the printers concerned. The Ministry of Supply was not helpful to the industry although it did allow printing work that had actually been started to the extent of 'spoiling the paper' be completed within reasonable time after 12 November 1941. The printing of guide books was entirely prohibited. The maximum size of posters was reduced by half to 1,200 square inches in area although the Ministry refused to give an official definition of what constituted a poster. Advertising circulars were also effectively banned.

Further paper control restrictions came into effect in March 1943.[3] The size of cheque forms, dividend warrants and headed letter paper was reduced. For business headings the maximum size was to be fifty seven square inches and the maximum substance Large Post 15lbs. On 26 September 1944 the President of the Board of Trade announced the first concessions in paper rationing. The allocation for book publishers was increased from 30% to 42½% of their 1939 usage.

During the Second World War, the government restricted the supply of other raw materials needed to produce printed products. Immediately on the outbreak of war the government imposed a complete prohibition of the sale of aluminium for use as litho plates. The government in November 1941 rationed turpentine which was essential for the manufacture of printing inks and then chrome (yellow) inks of good quality ceased to be obtainable whilst the supply of the more expensive inks was severely limited. The capture of Malaya by the Japanese meant the loss of Malayan tin for the war effort, so in March 1942 the Ministry of Supply told the BFMP it called upon the printing industry to supply large quantities of its metal to essential war industries. The target for the industry was set at 7,000 tons. Each individual printer in Scotland was required to send to the Scottish Alliance details of the approximate total weight of metal held by them on 15 April 1942. The BFMP pointed out to all its Alliances and to the Scottish Alliance, that unless sufficient tonnage was delivered to refiners, against prices agreed between the BFMP and the refiners, the Ministry would resort to compulsion. Fortunately this course of action was unnecessary and the industry contributed 4,000 tons of metal to the war effort.

Government Printing Work and Other Orders

In September 1941 the Controller of HMSO was appointed a 'competent authority' under Defence Regulations and given power to require any printing firm to undertake any work according to his directions, to fix the price to be paid for it and to take over any printing office. Before the official announcement was made the Controller of the HMSO, Sir William Cooling, met the officers of the BFMP and assured them he had no desire to exercise his new powers and was confident he would be able to enable the government's demand for printing work to be met by co-operation with the BFMP. Unfortunately this proved not to be the case.

Dissatisfaction existed in Scotland over the amount of government printing done there. Member firms of the Alliance considered the allocation to Scotland of printing orders stemming from the national emergency situation of the war unfair. A memorandum from the Scottish printing industry on government printing contracts was sent to all Scottish MPs suggesting they press for
(1) not less than 1/10 of government printing be allocated to Scotland and
(2) tenders be on the basis of delivery 'ex-works'.
Scottish MPs, regardless of party affiliation, raised a number of questions in the House on the matter but in a statement to the House the Financial Secretary to the Treasury refused to accept that tenders be invited on an 'ex-works' basis.[4] The government remitted the issue of the allocation of printing contracts to the HMSO Contracts Committee under the chair of F H Haynes. In May 1941 the committee reported. It considered in view of the present economic conditions in the industry it was an inappropriate moment to take the matter further. The government kept the HMSO Contracts Committee in being in case at a later date it was considered desirable to restore it.

In September 1941 yet another controller, this time one new to the printing industry, came into the scene. He was the Controller-General of Factory and Storage Premises and required almost limitless floor space for factory units and storage. Here again, although he had power of requisition there was the desire to work with the BFMP in dealing with the printing industry.

In 1942, the industry was faced with additional government controls and regulations this time in the packaging sector of the industry. The Control of Packing Order No 1 (1942) stated when packaging materials were printed they could be put 'twice through the machine' and no more. If an employer had a machine which could print several colours at once so much the better if the customer wanted colourful packaging. The order was very detailed. For example, it specified a long list of containers ranging from those destined for the reception of 'Bacteriological virus rodent exterminators' down to receptacles for 'Moustache and eyebrow pomade'.

The 1940 proposal of the Chancellor of the Exchequer to apply the new purchase tax to almost every class of printed matter met with opposition from the UK printing industry. The Chancellor, in the face of intense political lobbying by the BFMP, made some concessions. He agreed to withdraw the proposed tax of one-sixth on newspapers, periodicals, trade catalogues, price lists, printed books, posters, pamphlets and leaflets. The Scottish Alliance considered the tax had numerous anomalies, was unfair, was confusing and was hastily conceived and ill-considered. Matters were not helped in that government had made the printer an unpaid tax collector for the Treasury at a time when many printers were harassed by air-raids and by a lack of clerical staff. The regulations covering the implementation of the tax were quite complex and did not help matters. They infuriated Alliance member firms whose owners and/or senior managers found it difficult enough to cope with simple day-to-day affairs.

Transfer of Print Workers to the Armed Forces and Munitions

The immediate impact of the outbreak of war in 1939 on the Scottish printing industry was an economic depression. In the general print and book trade, existing orders were cancelled, publications suspended, advertisements cut back whilst firms introduced short-time working, dismissed employees or closed down. There was a shortage of paper, printing metal and other materials. Printing workers in Scotland became unemployed. As in the First World War this initial labour surplus soon became an acute labour shortage. Large numbers of print workers volunteered or were conscripted into the armed forces whilst many went into civil defence work or to work in munitions and armament factories. This left a depleted labour force, mostly of older men, to produce the essential wartime printing under the difficulties of air raids, blackouts and fire watching.

After the fall of France in June 1940, the government acquired emergency powers and began to regulate national industry, making efforts to increase production of munitions, armaments and aircraft and to rein back less essential trades such as printing. From now on the government control of paper, metals, ink and all forms of printing became severe, if not draconian. The printing industry was pressurised to transfer employees to war work. In June 1940 the Ministry of Labour met with representatives of the BFMP and the P&KTF at which the question of the co-operation of printing trade workers in the war effort was discussed. The scheme agreed at this meeting, to achieve this objective, was a voluntary one and was not approved by the NJIC although that body on 15 June 1940 issued an 'urgent appeal to employers and workers to facilitate the transfer of manpower to the armaments industry'. The main feature of the voluntary scheme was that local committees of employers and trade unions would co-operate with Employment Exchanges in transferring print workers, especially the unemployed, to essential industries in which their skills could be readily used. By October 1940 the transfer of unemployed print workers to work in munitions factories was complete.

By 1943, the government had scraped the industry's manpower resources dry for three years. On 31 March 1943 the government, at a joint meeting of the BFMP and the P&KTF, told the master printers the industry had to release a further 13,000 of their employees for work in the war industries. They were informed a high proportion of the 13,000 employees required would have to be found from a limited number of geographical areas. There was a real risk many printing works in these areas would close. The potential loss of 13,000 employees meant an industry which had already lost much of its labour force would experience a further drastic reduction. The NJIC War Emergency Committee examined the practicality of the Board of Trade proposals. This convinced both employers and trade union leaders it would be impossible to maintain printing production and the essential service required by other industries in some areas if the scheme were implemented. The NJIC asked the Board of Trade to reconsider its scheme, arguing the withdrawal of labour from the industry through existing procedures operated by the Ministry of Labour would provide a reasonable flow to meet the special requirements of the war industries. The Board of Trade accepted the NJIC's case and withdrew its proposed scheme.[5]

In September 1944 by which time the defeat of Germany was only a matter of time, thought was given as how to manage the economy from a wartime to a peacetime one. The NJIC submitted a memorandum to the Ministry of Labour on the release of printing workers from munitions, other war industries and civil defence. It argued the industry's labour force was no longer capable of meeting the demands for essential printing. With the end of the war in sight every government department and public authority was speeding their reconstruction plans. The war industries were gearing up for a return to peacetime production and every scheme and plan had to be printed before it could be implemented. Under the circumstances the NJIC argued the industry be granted 'first class priority' in the release of labour from the munitions industries. The NJIC's proposal to the Ministry of Labour met with some success when in November 1944 the Director General of Manpower said arrangements had been made under which certain urgent demands in respect of Stationery Office work would be met by the withdrawal of nominated ex-printing operatives from war work for transfer back to the industry. Furthermore, men and women who became surplus in other industries, or who were released from the armed forces would return to the printing industry unless they were urgently required for other purposes.

During the Second World War, the Scottish printing industry lost a significant part of its workforce by transfer to munitions industries, to civil defence and by conscription into the armed forces. In December 1940 the 'reserved' age for printing trade workers, hitherto thirty, was raised to thirty five. The calling up of men under thirty five, coupled with the large number that had already left the industry, caused an acute labour shortage at a time when there were increasing demands for printing for essential purposes from the expanding war industries. So concerned were the BFMP and P&KTF about the situation a joint deputation met, on 14 February 1941, the Parliamentary Secretary to the Ministry of Labour. The deputation pointed out the industry was essential to the war effort and there existed an acute shortage of labour made more difficult because the degree of specialisation in the industry meant skilled workers were not interchangeable. They also argued that an increasing demand for work of national importance was falling upon the industry's seriously depleted staff, and the industry was at the point where it was unable to meet the printing requirements of the government and the war industries. The government merely noted the industry's position.

In the spring of 1941 the government revised the Schedule of Reserved Occupations and Protected Work but it left the reserved maximum age of many occupations in printing at thirty five. But for the successful lobbying activities of the Labour Committee of the BFMP this age might have been raised to forty one. In December 1941, the Schedule of Reserved Occupations was again drastically revised. It provided for the gradual abolition of almost all reservations, fundamentally changed the procedure for making applications for deferment and restricted the grounds on which deferment might be granted. Only individual cases would now be considered. Applications would no longer be submitted to the appropriate government department but would be sent to the local Labour Exchange for consideration by the newly formed Manpower Boards. The National Service Act (1941) made men between the ages of forty one and fifty inclusive and, with certain exceptions, women liable for service with the armed forces or civil defence, as and when royal proclamations covering their age groups were issued. Men over military age (forty one) came under the Registration for Employment Order and could be directed to war work.

The unemployment and short time working in the first year of the war gave way by the end of 1940 to a labour shortage which become more acute in 1941.

Despite government restrictions on paper and printing there was still much essential printing to be done. With an older workforce, the industry at times struggled to complete essential printing orders. The shortage of materials and manpower meant printers could not continue to undertake printing work for long-standing customers where that work was not essential to the war effort. Their customers sought alternative ways of getting the work done. The industry lost some long-standing traditional work that never came back to the industry after the war. In Scotland the tendency of local authorities to stop printing valuation rolls became a serious matter for some member firms of the Alliance. In 1942 Ayr County Council, in spite of representation by the Scottish Alliance, produced the Valuation Roll by methods other than conventional printing. Later in the same year the Perth and Glasgow town councils did the same.

However, the production of a complete register of electors for the 1945 general election presented the UK and Scottish printing industries with one of the largest problems faced during the war years. Over thirty million names had to be set, involving large amounts of mechanical composition and composing room work. Given the industry's labour situation in December 1944 the delivery of this task on time was beyond the capacity of the British printing industry. The BFMP consulted with the print unions including the STA to discover the number of ex-print workers employed in civil defence and then informed HMSO that to deliver on time (7 May 1945) 900 additional men were required by no later than 8 January 1945. The Ministry of Labour decided not to direct men back to the trade but to release workers who wished to return to the printing industry, and could be spared from their present jobs, to assist with the printing of the Voters Roll. These men were allowed to join their old firms but if their own particular company was not to be engaged on this class of work they were sent to work at other firms in their locality. Over thirty million names out of thirty three million were undertaken by the general printing industry. The HMSO dealt with the balance through the London daily newspapers and their provincial production offices.

The Dilution of Labour

During 1941 as more and more men and women of military age were conscripted into the armed forces and others transferred to essential war industries, the supply of labour to the Scottish printing industry fell short of demand and for the rest of the war the industry had to cope with an acute labour shortage. To solve the manpower shortage both the Ministry of Labour and the Scottish Alliance urged relaxation of restrictive union rules and the 'dilution of labour'. To prevent government compulsion the BFMP and the P&KTF negotiated in February 1941 War Agreement No. 3 permitting, on certain conditions, variations of agreements and trade union rules and customs. The agreement set out the general principles to govern 'dilution' agreements between employers' organisations and individual unions:

(1) any agreement on relaxation of union rules, trade customs or collective agreements be negotiated by the individual unions.

(2) any variations agreed apply only for such time as the unions were unable to supply the required labour. At the end of hostilities, pre-war conditions would resume.

(3) where women took the place of men 'reasonable preference' would be given to women already in the trade.

(4) employees joining the forces or national service were as far as possible to be reinstated after the war.

(5) if an employer reduced their staff they must dispense first with 'dilutee' labour. A joint committee of the BFMP and the P&KTF arbitrated on disputes arising from the agreement.

Following the settlement of general principles to governing dilution agreements, the Scottish Alliance began negotiations with the separate unions for such agreements. On 9 September 1941, the Alliance and the NUPB&PW reached an agreement providing for the dilution of labour in the bookbinding section of the industry. It provided for the variation of trade agreements, rules, customs and practices within establishments and the substitution of women or unskilled men for craftsmen when the union was unable to supply men. Throughout the war period the agreement operated satisfactorily and was viewed by both the Alliance and the union as of benefit to the industry.

The situation with the STA was very different. It opposed the dilution of labour, particularly by the introduction of female labour. The report of the Scottish Alliance Executive Board to the 31st annual general meeting held in Glasgow remarked:

> Negotiations with the Scottish Typographical Association for some scheme of substitution of female labour for male labour and the suspension of certain peacetime restrictions for the duration of the war have produced meagre results.

In its annual report to the 1943 annual general meeting the Executive Board complained again of the STA being unhelpful in accepting the substitution of men by women and accused it of being more concerned with guarding its pre-war conditions and practices than anticipated during a national crisis. In August 1942 the Scottish Alliance informed the Ministry of Labour it had raised, with the STA, some eighteen months previously the question of substitution of male labour by female labour and that it could not be held responsible for the delay in the implementation of the substitution of male employees by females.

Apprentices: Placement and Reinstatement

Another problem on the outbreak of war was the replacement and reinstatement of apprentices called into the armed forces. Reinstatement could not really be settled until the end of hostilities was in sight. Replacement was therefore the immediate problem. The STA proposed in September 1939 no apprentices be started during the war. This was rejected by the Scottish Alliance who argued where but for military service, a boy would have completed their apprenticeship they be replaced by a new apprentice. The nationwide print unions with members in Scotland operated under national agreements concluded by the P&KTF and the BFMP covering the reinstatement and replacement of apprentices on war service. They permitted limited replacement but the scheme was unacceptable to the STA because of its policy of a moratorium on apprentices during hostilities.

The Scottish Alliance's position was that where a boy, but for military service, would have completed his apprenticeship, he should no longer be reckoned in the number of apprentices attached to an office. The STA argued any boy who left the industry as an apprentice for the armed forces must return to the industry as an apprentice and in the meantime must be included in the number of apprentices attached to the office. The Alliance Negotiating Committee stressed the employers had no desire to overload the industry with apprentices but it was essential progressive recruitment for the present and future manpower requirements of industry continued. They advised the STA they were prepared to set up a joint committee to consider all applications for starting a composing room or machine room apprentices. If the STA refused to go forward with such a joint committee, a committee of the Scottish Alliance would itself consider cases and decide the merits of each individual application.

With the STA sticking to its policy of moratorium on apprentices for the duration of the war and the Scottish Alliance equally determined a limited introduction of apprentices was necessary the SJIC Conciliation Committee considered the issue. Its decided against a complete ban on apprentices and it instructed both sides of the industry to confer and formulate an agreement. As a result in September 1942 a wartime agreement between the Scottish Alliance and the STA was made governing the reinstatement and replacement of apprentices during the war. It established the principle that some inflow of apprentices into the industry during the war was essential, and covered the training and reinstatement of apprentices after the ending of hostilities as well as the admission of apprentices during the war years. A new scale of apprenticeship ratios was approved as follows – one apprentice to two journeymen, two to five, three to ten, four to fifteen thereafter rising by one apprentice and five journeymen up to a total of ten apprentices to forty five journeymen. One additional apprentice was to be permitted for every ten journeymen above forty five. Apprentices on active service counted as part of the permitted ratio and replacements could only be made if an apprentice died on active service or indicated in writing they would not be returning to the printing trade. If, however, five years of the apprenticeship had been completed before enlistment, a new apprentice could be started at the time. As a result of the agreement the restriction on the entry of apprentices was more severe, but more effective, than during the First World War. Gillespie gives some idea of its extent pointing out that between 1940 and 1944 firms in the six largest branches of the STA started 158 apprentices compared with 575 in the five year period prior to 1940.[6]

By mid-1944, under the September 1942 agreement, fifty eight apprentices had started. A dispute arose over the interpretation of the agreement. The STA contended the agreement meant all apprentices, apart from those who had completed five years prior to enlisting, be counted in the number of apprentices attached to a firm for apprentice ratio purposes. The Alliance held for apprentice ratio purposes, apprentices serving with the armed forces whose apprenticeship under normal conditions would have expired, were excluded. The dispute was submitted to the SJIC Conciliation Committee which confirmed the view of the Scottish Alliance. The STA refused to accept the finding and later refused to attend a meeting of the NJIC Conciliation Committee. The national committee issued a finding which, like that of the Scottish committee, upheld the view of the Scottish Alliance. In spite of this finding, the STA members employed by Wm Collins Sons & Co tendered strike notices when a composing and machine room apprentice were started. When the dispute was reported to the Ministry of Labour and National Service the notices were withdrawn to allow negotiations to proceed. The outcome was the STA accepted the Scottish Alliance interpretation of the September 1942 Agreement.

Wage Movements
a. General Increases
In October 1939 the STA claimed a weekly wage increase of 15s 6d for journeymen, 11s 6d for woman compositors, 11s 6d for male auxiliary workers and 6s 6d for auxiliary female workers. The Scottish Alliance rejected the claim on three grounds.

(1) The wages and conditions of employment in the Scottish printing industry gave its employees a high standard of living compared with workers in other industries. No wage increase could be granted towards enhancing employment standards.

(2) As the Scottish printing industry was suffering a great reduction in the volume of work from the effects of the war. It was unable under present circumstances to grant a cost of living bonus.

(3) Should the cost of living continue to rise the Alliance was prepared to reconsider its position if there be an improvement in demand for print products.

At the same time an application for a new bonus of 10s 0d per week for adult male workers, 7s 6d for women and 4s 0d for juveniles was submitted to the BFMP by the P&KTF on behalf of all the other print unions. The BFMP War Emergency Committee met with the P&KTF at two conferences and informed them, for similar reasons to those influencing the Scottish Alliance, they could not grant the request. The P&KTF claim was based on the increase in the official cost of living index since the outbreak of the war from 155 (1 December 1939) to 173, a rise of nearly 12%. The P&KTF stressed its claim was to maintain the standard of living of print workers and not gain them real wage increases.

The STA claim was referred to SJIC Conciliation Committee which issued its findings on 1 April 1940. It recognised an increase in the cost of living had taken place but in the present state of the industry in Scotland, considered no increases in wages could be justified unless adopted on a UK-wide scale. The Scottish Alliance accepted this finding but the STA did not. The matter was then referred to the NJIC Conciliation Committee which met on 2 May 1940. While it understood wage negotiations were normally conducted directly between the STA and the Scottish Alliance it recommended there was, in the present national difficulties, a relationship with the national wage movement which might influence the future wage negotiations of the parties. The Alliance accepted this finding and informed the STA they were prepared to merge the Scottish negotiations with the UK-wide negotiations over a war bonus. The STA balloted its membership as to whether its claim be further pressed or it should join the P&KTF movement for a war bonus. The vote was in favour of the latter. This was the first time the STA asked the P&KTF to negotiate for them on wages. In all subsequent general wage increases during the war the STA was part of UK-wide negotiations between the BFMP and the P&KTF.

On 18 June 1940 the BFMP and the P&KTF met again and the latter said it proposed to refer the matter to the new National Arbitration Tribunal (NAT) set up by the Ministry of Labour and National Service. The BFMP welcomed this, especially as its findings would be binding on the UK printing industry. The NAT met on 13 August 1940 and the industry's war bonus claim was the first case in the UK considered by it. It awarded men and women on men's work a weekly increase of 5s 0d, other women 2s 6d and male and female juveniles 1s 6d. Few difficulties arose in implementing the award but it was unclear from the terms of the award whether female compositors in Aberdeen or Edinburgh were entitled to the 5s 0d granted to men or to 70% of that in accordance with the agreement with the STA regulating the relationship of the two rates of pay. The question was submitted to the NAT for interpretation. Its decision was that female compositors in Aberdeen and Edinburgh were entitled to the full 5s 0d advance.

On 30 July 1941, an application for a further general increase in wages was made to the BFMP by the P&KTF on behalf of its affiliated unions, including the STA. The application was for varying rates of increases according to the basic wage of the individual with greater increases claimed for lower paid workers. The amount in question ranged from a 6s 0d advance where the basic grade rate was 90s 0d or over, up to 14s 0d where the basic grade rate was under 60s 0d with proportionate increases for women and juveniles. The Scottish Alliance participated in the national negotiations, having representation on the BFMP Labour Negotiating Committee. It agreed that any increase granted be flat-rate for men with proportionate increases for women and juveniles, and any wage negotiations should not be subject to individual employers having the option to increase weekly hours.

The consensus amongst print employers throughout the UK was opposition to differential increases. On 4 November 1941 the P&KTF accepted on behalf of affiliated unions (including the STA) a 5s 0d per week increase in pay for men, for women on men's work and for female compositors, a 3s 6d increase for other women and 2s 0d for apprentice males and women learners. The STA indicated it could not be a party to clause six of the agreement (working of overtime). The Scottish Alliance considered the position at a meeting on 12 November 1941 and decided the agreement be implemented forthwith stressing both itself and the STA were bound by the terms of the November 1941 agreement. This position was reported to the BFMP as the validity of the whole agreement was at stake. The BFMP, the P&KTF and the NJIC all indicated their view that the STA was bound by the agreement. In the face of this pressure for ensuring the negotiated agreement was upheld, and implemented, the STA reluctantly accepted the agreement.

In March 1943 the P&KTF, submitted a claim for a weekly wage increase of 20s 0d for all adult workers, both men and women, and for 15s 0d for apprentices and juniors. The P&KTF justified its claim on the basis the wages of workers in the printing trade had not kept pace with those received by employees in other industries, particularly those in the war industries and the print employers, despite all current difficulties, were making good profits and could afford to meet the unions' demands. The 1943 annual general meeting of the Scottish Alliance unanimously recommended the BFMP reject the claim completely, to indicate to the P&KTF no counter offer would be forthcoming from the employers' side and to suggest, on account of the wide gulf between their respective positions, and subject to a reference to the NJIC, the dispute be referred to the NAT. On 21 April 1943 the BFMP told the P&KTF they had rejected the claim, intimated no counter offer would be made and suggested the matter be referred to the NJIC and ultimately to the NAT.[7]

The NAT issued its award on 21 June 1943, the hearing having taken place on 17 June. The claim for a weekly increase of 20s 0d for men and women on men's work was rejected and no increase granted. Other women were awarded a weekly increase by the NAT. No increases were given to juveniles since the P&KTF and the BFMP had withdrawn that issue from the dispute. On 24 June 1943 the BFMP and the P&KTF signed War Agreement No 7 which gave 3s 0d per week extra to female juveniles. The award gave rise to dissatisfaction amongst the unions and the Scottish Alliance was approached shortly after the NAT award by the STA for a general increase in wages to all its members. The Alliance took the view it had to adhere to the terms of the award. Applications for individual wage increases were made by other unions to the BFMP. Meantime the STA, in an endeavour to further their aims imposed, following a ballot of the membership, an overtime ban and disrupted normal methods of production in the industry. Their actions were in breach of agreement between the Scottish Alliance and the STA and contrary to the constitution of the SJIC. A finding to this effect was issued by the SJIC Conciliation Committee on 16 September 1943 which recommended the STA withdrew the instructions and act in accordance with constitutional procedure. The STA, which failed to appear before the Conciliation Committee, ignored the finding. Subsequently following discussions in London, the ban on overtime by the STA and the aggressive action by other print unions in England was withdrawn to allow negotiations to resume at the UK level.

At a wage conference in October 1943 the BFMP offered an increase of 5s 0d in men's minimum wage rates but offered nothing for the women or juveniles. The P&KTF presented a counter offer of a weekly advance of 7s 6d to men and women on men's work and 3s 6d to women. The BFMP said they accepted the P&KTF's proposition and would grant male juveniles an increase of 3s 0d and a further increase of 2s 6d to the women who had received 4s 0d under the NAT award. There was, however, a condition. The wage increases were to be regarded as stabilised and no further collective increases of wages were to be claimed during the period of the war and for twelve months afterwards so long as the cost of living remained at its present, or approximately, its present figure. This stabilisation clause much influenced the Scottish Alliance to ratify the agreement. All P&KTF-affiliated unions balloted on the BFMP proposals which were accepted and embodied into War Agreement No 8 operable from the first day in November 1943.[8] With the issue of wages now settled, it was possible for both sides of the Scottish printing industry to give thought to the reconstruction of the industry and postwar difficulties.

b. Regrading

While joining with the P&KTF for the negotiation of general increases in wages, the STA secured additional increases for some of its members through changes to the wage grading scheme. In July 1942 the STA applied to the Scottish Alliance for a uniform rate of wages to be paid to compositors and machine men throughout Scotland. On 21 July 1942 the Scottish Alliance proposed the division of Scotland into three grades. The present Grade I be retained at 87s 6d. The existing Grades II and III be combined as Grade II at a weekly rate of 84s 6d. Grade IV would become Grade III with a weekly rate of 81s 6d. Galashiels, Hawick and Selkirk be moved into the new Grade III. The Scottish Alliance proposed Aberdeen be placed in the Scheme as Grade Ia at a weekly rate of 86s 0d.

The three grades offer was rejected by the STA. The Alliance and the STA failed to reach agreement both on the number of grades and the respective placing of towns. These questions were referred to the SJIC Conciliation Committee. This committee met on 24 November 1942 but was adjourned until 2 December 1942 when it issued its findings. It recommended that Aberdeen be placed in Grade I and that there be three grades of wages (see Table 8:1).

Table 8.1
The Wage Grading System : 1942

Occupation	Grade I	Grade II	Grade III
Compositors and Machine men	87s 6d	84s 6d	81s 6d
Female Auxiliary	41s 0d	39s 6d	38s 6d
Male Auxiliary	70s 0d	68s 0d	66s 6d

The Scottish Alliance accepted the Conciliation Committee's findings as did the STA although it pressed for Kilmarnock and Perth to be raised to Grade I status. The Alliance argued these two towns stay in Grade II but if that would result in delaying a settlement of the grading scheme, it was prepared to see the matter go to an independent body. The STA did not press its claim that Kilmarnock and Perth be upgraded into Grade I.

c. Apprentices' Wages

In July 1943 the Scottish Alliance negotiated a separate agreement with the STA covering the wages of apprentices. Apprentices were to receive wages expressed as a percentage of the minimum rate of a journeyman. There was a sliding scale, according to whether the apprenticeship was for five, six or seven years and with successive annual increments. Where a boy was apprenticed for seven years his initial wage was 20% of a journeyman, rising to 60% in his seventh year. This agreement was a milestone. In the past, the percentage rates had been on the basis of a recommendation from the Scottish Alliance. The agreement was a major concession of principle by the employers. For the first time they recognised that the STA's interest in apprenticeship was more than merely that of a restrictive ratio/quota.

Summary

For most of the Second World War the government's impact on the Scottish printing industry was restrictive. Manpower was withdrawn from the industry by transfer to munitions and civil defence work and by conscription into the armed forces. This led by 1941 to a labour shortage in the industry. Government control of paper, metals, inks and all other print raw material became very severe. The Controller of the HMSO had powers to takeover any print works and require it undertake any work he directed. Both the Scottish Alliance and the unions realised there would eventually be a need for the replacement of craftsmen by semi-skilled employees and for men by women. In February 1941, the BFMP, the Scottish Alliance and the P&KTF reached an agreement on general principles to govern dilution schemes.

During the Second World War the P&KTF played a greater part in negotiations of wages applicable in Scotland. The STA yielded autonomy reluctantly and only because of the emergency conditions. During 1939-1945, there were three (1940,

1941 and 1943) general flat-rate increases in wages followed by two years of stabilisation. In addition, the period saw the number of wage grades in Scotland reduced to three and a ground-breaking agreement linking the pay of apprentices to set percentages of the craft rate.

The Second World War had little impact on the industry's industrial relations institutions and procedures. The SJIC continued to operate and the national agreements survived the war with their main terms substantially intact. This was in contrast to what happened after the end of the First World War when there was a fundamental change to the industry's industrial relations system. Local agreements were replaced by national agreements, the BFMP, Scottish Alliance and P&KTF emerged more powerful and the NJIC was established. The Second World War period was in industrial relations terms a stable period.

Notes

[1]   See E Howe (1950) *The British Federation of Master Printers*. London: British Federation of Master Printers, p149.

[2]   But Norway was now in German hands and Sweden and Finland were cut off. A month or two earlier the British paper mills had been working to capacity. Now many of them were closed for want of raw materials.

[3]   By this time the number of Paper Orders had reached 59.

[4]   See Minutes of the Executive Board for their meeting of 26 February 1941, and 25 March 1941 and 4 June 1941.

[5]   In 1939 the UK printing industry had employed some 270,000 people. By July 1942 some 100,000 had left the industry for the services or war work and by March 1943 a further 8,000 had departed. Unfortunately no figures are available solely for Scotland.

[6]   See S C Gillespie (1953) *A Hundred Years of Progress: The Record of the Scottish Typographical Association, 1853 to 1952*. Glasgow: MacLehose, p192.

[7]   The Employment and National Arbitration Order of 1940 resulted from recommendations given to the Ministry of Labour by the British Employers Confederation and the TUC. Its purpose was to find the best means of 'removing general wage problems from the field of controversy during the then critical period of the War and of settling trade disputes without interruption'. It introduced unilaterally compulsory arbitration to settle industrial disputes during the war.

[8]   See Report by the Executive Board to the Thirty Third Annual General Meeting, Glasgow, March 1944.

Chapter 9

THE POST-SECOND WORLD WAR SETTLEMENT 1946-1952

This chapter begins by outlining the economic, social and political context in which the Scottish printing industry operated after the end of the Second World War. It shows how the Labour government elected in the 1945 general election took essential industries into public ownership and established a framework of social security. The second part examines the P&KTF 1946 claim for a general increase in wage rates, whilst part three explains the 1946 negotiations for a forty-hour working week and a fortnight's paid annual holiday. The chapter then tells the story of how, by a long and tortuous path over the period 1947 to 1951, the Scottish printing industry established a stable wage structure for the following five years. The fifth section of the chapter explains changes to the 'Wages Grading Scheme' whilst the penultimate section traces changes in the mutually agreed working rules and employment conditions. The final part of the chapter analyses the Scottish Alliance's efforts to manage the manpower shortage, particularly of compositors, existing in the industry in the immediate post-Second World War period.

Economic and Social Context

The Second World War distorted the UK economy. It required the contraction of the production in non-essential industries, the sale of overseas investments and the restriction for non-essential industries of capital equipment. The 1945 general election saw the election of a Labour government under the premiership of Clement Attlee. It was re-elected in the 1950 general election but voted out of office in the October 1951 election in favour of a Conservative government under the leadership of Winston Churchill. The Attlee government attempted to transform the UK economy by taking key, privately-owned industries such as coal, transport, fuel and power, into public ownership within the framework of social security extended to every man, woman and child in the country. The Labour government sought to maintain full employment, stabilise the cost of living, increase UK exports and decrease its imports, to reconstruct the economy's basic industries and services and to improve the productivity of industry.

The standard of living of the UK population depended on the UK having a positive balance of payments, meaning that it was exporting more than it was importing. The UK imported foodstuffs to feed its people and raw materials to manufacture into goods then sold in overseas markets. To pay for essential imports, it had to earn the means from the sale of exported goods and services such as shipping and insurance. In 1945, the UK had a severe balance of payment deficit. To close the gap, the Labour government increased industrial production and the proportion sold overseas, and increased labour productivity per head through the activities of the National Production Advisory Council on Industry, the Anglo-American Council on Productivity and the Committee on Industrial Productivity. The Anglo-American Council promoted economic well-being by a free exchange of industrial knowledge and experience to improve industrial efficiency. The Committee on Industrial Productivity advised on the form and scale of research effort necessary to increase industrial productivity.

An important part of the Attlee government's attempt to increase industrial production, to improve the quality and quantity of UK exports and to reduce the volume and value of imports was its programme of nationalising key sectors of the privately-owned economy. A nationalised industry has a legalised product market monopoly. The legislation creating such industries specified only one company could supply the service concerned. It was illegal for competitors to enter the market. The customer had no choice from whom they purchased the goods or services concerned. Over the period 1945-1951, the Labour government nationalised coal, gas, electricity, road haulage, railways, civil aviation, and iron and steel.

As production increased following the end of the Second World War, employment levels improved and the Labour government delivered its full employment goal. Over the period 1948-1952, the average level of unemployment in the UK was 2%. By 1951, industrial and agricultural production was 40% higher than pre-war levels. The volume of exports was 65% above their mid-1939 level. Despite this improved performance, balance of payment problems continued. The redistribution of manpower resources to export and import substitution industries took longer than anticipated leaving export industries short of essential labour. In 1947, a severe winter dislocated the supply of fuel with a consequent disruption of production and government export targets were not met. The UK government had insufficient gold and foreign currency reserves upon which to draw to fund the gap between its export income and its import expenditure. In 1949, the UK had only £1.3 million gold and foreign currency reserves which by 1952 had only risen to £1.7 million. By 1948, inflationary pressures were beginning to affect the UK economy reflected in relative increases in UK export prices and relative decreases in the price of imports. The government was concerned this would lead to employers granting wage increases not matched by increases in productivity, giving rise to a situation of too much money chasing too few goods and fuelling further inflation. In 1950, matters became more difficult with the outbreak of the Korean War which lasted until 1953. Many countries feared the outbreak of a third world war and the world demand for raw materials increased rapidly, causing their price to rise, feeding into UK import prices and stoking further inflationary pressures in the UK economy.

To tackle these problems, the Labour government maintained some of the wartime controls over the economy, for example the 'control of engagement' order providing employers may not engage or seek to engage employees otherwise than through a Local Employment Exchange or an employment agency approved for that purpose. To reduce food imports, bread rationing, which had not existed in the war years, was introduced. The government maintained considerable control over the allocation of raw materials to industry giving priority to firms requiring additional resources for export orders. In November 1949, to stimulate the growth of exports and the growth of import substitution industries, the government devalued the pound from £1 = $4 to £1 = $2.80. This increased the price of imported goods adding further to the inflationary pressures. In February 1948, the Prime Minister made a statement to the House of Commons on 'Personal incomes, costs and prices' subsequently issued as a White Paper. The statement drew attention to the country's economic difficulties and said there were no grounds for general increases in pay, although there might be exceptional circumstances where an increase could be justified, for example to attract employees into export-centred industries. Collective bargainers were expected to accept as a general principle a temporary stop to further increases in personal incomes from whatever source they came.[1]

The Attlee governments introduced a welfare state providing collective insurance against the disruption of family life. In July 1948 a system of social protection was introduced, embracing a comprehensive scheme of national insurance (the National Insurance Act 1946) for sickness, unemployment, industrial injuries and disease, maternity and child benefit, care of widows and orphans and retirement pensions for the aged. The Poor Law was replaced by a 'humane, enlightened and wisely conceived system of national assistance for the needy who fell below the floor established by the national insurance scheme'. On the same day, the National Health Service Act (1946) was implemented. It provided a complete national health service for every member of an insured person's family. The service was available to everyone free of charge at point of need.

The incoming Conservative government of 1951, accepted the welfare state provision of the Attlee government and made no attempt to change it. On economic matters, it shared the same objectives – full employment, control of inflation, a balance of payments surplus and economic growth – but its means of managing the economy had some marked differences. The Conservative government (1951-1955) of Winston Churchill removed government restrictions and regulations on industry, commerce and individuals in what it described as a 'bonfire of controls'. It lowered income tax and bank rates, and denationalised the road haulage and the iron and steel industries.

The 1946 Wage Increase

On 3 September 1945 the BFMP received a request for a wage increase from the P&KTF, despite War Agreement No. 8 of November 1943 containing provision that there be no further collective applications for wage increases during the period of the war and for twelve months thereafter so long as the cost-of-living index remained at or near its present figure. A temporary increase in the cost-of-living index figure from 102 to 107 in May 1945 gave the P&KTF a reason for approaching the BFMP on the issue of wages. Repudiation of the agreement was not supported by any print union but there was dissatisfaction amongst their members in that increases granted in wages in other industries had resulted in some unskilled men now earning higher wages than print craftsmen. The P&KTF claim therefore, was that the total wage increases during the year in the printing industry compared unfavourably with wages advances in other industries. The P&KTF did not state the exact amount of wage increase claimed.

The Scottish Alliance accepted if the full period of wage stabilisation were allowed to expire the industry would face wage demands from individual unions. Such negotiations would create a similar condition of uncertainty as followed the 1914-1918 War and would have prevented Scottish firms planning for the future. Negotiations therefore started between the BFMP and the P&KTF in which the Scottish Alliance representatives played their part. On 31 October 1945 the BFMP offered weekly increases of 7s 6d to men, 5s 6d to women and 3s 6d to boy and girl learners. The offer was rejected by the P&KTF. On 3 December 1945 the BFMP improved its offer to 8s 6d per week to men and to women on men's work, 7s 6d to adult women and 4s 0d to boy and girl juniors. The P&KTF accepted these proposed increases and in return agreed wages be stabilised until 30 June 1947. The agreement operated from the first pay day of January 1946.

The 1946 Hours and Holiday Agreement

The 1937 *Hours and Holiday Agreement* provided a forty-five-hour working week and a stabilisation period of three years on claims for further improvements. When this expired in 1940 the country was at war so the P&KTF postponed reopening negotiations. On 25 February 1946 P&KTF made a claim to the BFMP for a forty-hour working week and a fortnight's annual holiday with pay in addition to statutory bank holidays. On 12 March the BFMP reply referred to the Labour government's appeal for increased production and commented this could not be dissociated from claims for a reduction in working hours and an increase in holidays. The BFMP and the P&KTF met on 1 May 1946 at which the latter set out its reasons for their positions. The Scottish Alliance was unanimously opposed to a reduction in working hours and to an increase in holidays and considered these issues UK ones which should not be treated as a matter for an individual industry or part of an industry.[2]

The P&KTF argued its claim was practical and motivated by the desire amongst print employees for more leisure time. It considered the benefits of increased productivity stemming from changed methods of production, including faster machines, should not accrue solely to the customers in lower prices but some be passed the employees as enhanced employment conditions. The P&KTF said the granting of its claim would provide additional leisure time for print workers which would have a beneficial effect on their health and the productivity of the labour force. It also considered the implementation of its claim would not result in having to recruit additional manpower to maintain production. Additional supplies of labour were available from:
(1) the present unemployed in the industry,
(2) members still in His Majesty's forces or otherwise away from the trade and
(3) the transfer of redundant employees from the newspaper section of the industry where the demand for labour had fallen owing to reduction in pagination.
The P&KTF also argued no better incentive to maximum production could be provided than by a reduction in working time. Finally the P&KTF said the 1937 agreement was a compromise on the demand for a forty-hour working week and placed an obligation on it to review the issue three years after the implementation of the 1937 Agreement.

The BFMP saw many reasons why it could not accede to the claim for either a forty-hour working week or for two weeks' holiday with pay. They argued that to introduce at the present time such a change would not benefit the industry and would conflict with the current economic needs of the country. To concede the claim was not practical. The printing industry needed to increase its production whereas conceding the P&KTF's claim would lead to a fall in the volume of production. The BFMP also contended the industry's labour supply was insufficient to meet the existing demand for printed products. The shortage of women employees, was particularly acute. The Second World War saw the accumulation of work and the economic prospects facing the industry were good, provided a balanced labour force was secured to maintain production. The BFMP considered the P&KTF hours and holiday claim was inappropriate because the printing industry was essentially a service industry to other industries whose output per man-hour had fallen relative to 1939 standards. The BFMP contended, in reality, conceding the claim for extra overtime would not increase print workers' leisure time but merely their overtime earnings. Finally the BFMP argued that growing competition from office printing machines militated against any increase in printing costs.

On 28 May 1946 the P&KTF claim was rejected. It expressed disappointment at the BFMP attitude but agreed to refer the matter to a NJIC conciliation committee. This met on 26 June 1946 and, after hearing the evidence of the two sides, issued the following recommendation:

> ...Having heard the parties and after very careful consideration the Committee recognises that a state of deadlock exists in the negotiations on the application for a 40 hour week and a fortnight's holiday with pay and recommends that the situation be reported without delay to the full meeting of the JIC...

A special meeting of the NJIC, held on 11 July, noted the difference between the BFMP and the P&KTF rested on the practicability of altering working conditions at the present time. It recommended the issue be referred to the recently constituted standing committee of the NJIC on Employment and Production. This committee met on 16 July 1946 but was unable to break the deadlock. The industry's conciliation machinery for the avoidance of disputes had been exhausted.

On 22 July the P&KTF, dissatisfied with the slow progress being made, instructed its affiliated unions to operate an overtime ban from 12 August 1946 and to ballot their members for strike action. On the same day the BFMP informed the Ministry of Labour a serious prospect of an industrial dispute existed. A joint meeting was held at the Ministry on 29 July under the chairmanship of the Chief Industrial Commissioner, who emphasised the need to resume negotiations. After a lengthy discussion, in separate panels, the deadlock was broken on the understanding the P&KTF instructions for an overtime ban and a strike ballot be withdrawn. The BFMP offered:
(1) a fortnight's annual holiday with pay, in addition to bank holidays from the beginning of 1947,
(2) from 1 January 1947 a reduction of one hour per week in the standard working week to 44,
(3) the establishment of a fact-finding committee under an independent chair and
(4) the hours question to be further examined in the light of the conclusions of the fact-finding committee.

The P&KTF rejected these proposals. The Scottish Alliance told the BFMP that although it disapproved of the offer it had made, it would leave the matter to its representatives on the BFMP Negotiating Committee, but no further reduction to the suggested forty four be made. It was prepared to accept strike notices in support of this position. The Scottish Alliance was, however, content to cede the fortnight's holiday.[3]

As the date for the start of the overtime ban came near the BFMP on 7 August improved its offer to
(1) a fortnight's holiday with pay from 19 July 1947,
(2) a five day week, subject to a mutual house or local agreement,
(3) a reduction of normal hours to forty three and a half to operate from 1 January 1947 and
(4) a review of the position in June 1947.
Again, the offer was conditional on the P&KTF withdrawing its proposed overtime ban and strike ballot. The P&KTF considered the offer inadequate and the overtime ban came into force on 12 August 1946.

On 15 August, the Ministry of Labour met with both sides. The BFMP said they were not prepared to negotiate under duress. The P&KTF said they were not prepared to lift the overtime ban unless the employers accepted a fortnight's holiday from 1 January 1947 and a forty-two-and-a-half-hour week from 1 October 1946. Given these two positions, the Minister of Labour appointed a Court of Inquiry 'to inquire into the nature and circumstances of the dispute and to report'.[4] The Court of Inquiry took evidence from the unions affiliated to the P&KTF and from the BFMP over a period of ten days concluding with two lengthy submissions by the parties. During the court hearings the unions conducted their strike ballots which resulted in a five to one vote in favour of strike action. The Court of Inquiry published its report on 24 September 1946.[5]

The court took the view that in the general printing industry 'the demands on production are at present very large and so far as we can foresee, are likely to continue to be very large for some appreciable time to come'. It also reported that in spite of the availability, at the present time, of an increase in the industry labour force this would only be secured by recruitment to the industry, of women and girls. The court considered some reduction of hours of work would be beneficial to the productive capacity of the individual worker. It also considered that within the general printing industry the reduction of hours together with other adjustments in employment conditions would not give any increase in aggregate production in the near future even when account was taken of any effective net increase of the labour force. The court also considered there would be a substantial loss of production if the claims of the trade unions were granted in full but, given the circumstances in the industry and on the evidence available to it, the Court was unable to quantify this loss. It concluded the granting of a fortnight's annual holiday with pay was practicable at the present time but the reduction of the working week from forty five to forty was impractical. The Court gave no clear indication of what reduction in weekly working hours it thought feasible.

Following the Court's report the BFMP and the P&KTF resumed negotiations but they soon again reached deadlock. When an industrial stoppage appeared likely the Ministry of Labour made a dramatic intervention. On 27 September 1946 the BFMP and the P&KTF were called at short notice to the Ministry of Labour and told the Cabinet had decided the previous evening radical measures were to be taken to ensure publication of the Register of Electors and other official election printing in time for the November municipal elections. The government threatened to issue Defence Regulations compelling workers to work on producing the Electoral Register and list of voters and ordering workers if necessary to work overtime. This dramatic government action changed the course of the dispute. On 30 September the P&KTF told the Ministry it had recommended its affiliated unions to withdraw immediately the overtime ban, on the condition negotiations resume at once.

On the following day the BFMP offered two weeks' holiday with pay in addition to the statutory holidays and a forty-three-and-a-half-hour working week. It also admitted the stabilisation clause in the 1946 wage agreement was unpopular with employees and was now prepared to offer an increase in wages immediately and to withdraw the stabilisation clause. The employers proposed weekly pay increases of 10s 0d to craftsmen, 8s 0d to other adult males and 7s 6d to adult women. A conference of trade union executives, held on 9 October, recommended acceptance of this offer. The acceptance in a ballot by the union's members of the offer was notified to the BFMP at the end of October. Initially the STA refused to withdraw the overtime ban but after discussion with Scottish Alliance, its membership voted to accept the offer so ending the dispute.

The 1946 *Hours, Holiday and Wage Agreement* was ratified by all the P&KTF-affiliated unions on 28 October 1946. It provided:
(1) two weeks' holiday with pay,
(2) a forty-three-and-a-half-hour working week and a five day week, the latter subject to variation by house or local agreements,
(3) cancellation of the stabilisation clause in the January 1946 *Wages Agreement*,
(4) wage increases of 10s 0d to male craftsmen, 8s 0d to other adult males and 7s 6d to adult women,
(5) apprentices and juveniles to receive the appropriate percentage of the increase to journeymen and

(6) acceptance of the principle of a forty-two-and-a-half-hour week with the consequent amendment of the *Hours and Holiday Agreement* 'when the necessary adjustments for adequate recruitment into the industry have been made with the unions concerned and when the labour situation has sufficiently improved to enable the industry to meet its obligations to the community'.

During this 'Hours and Holiday' dispute, the BFMP (and the Scottish Alliance) had stood firm for nearly two months against the trade unions' aggressively enforced overtime ban. Even after the Court of Inquiry published its report the Alliance and the BFMP continued to support 'the principle of free negotiation unhampered by action of an aggressive or coercive nature'. The wisdom of the BFMP and the Alliance refusal to reduce working hours beyond the figure which their negotiators were prepared to accept before the P&KTF tried to enforce their claim by industrial action, had been justified by subsequent events. After this dispute, heavy overtime was worked in the Scottish printing industry which was still unable to meet demands of all its customers.

Search for a Wage Structure, 1947 – 1951

a. 1947

Early in 1947, the STA lodged a claim for an increase in wages of 9s 0d per week so the wages of its craft members equalled the highest rate of pay to any other P&KTF-affiliated union. It also claimed the women's rate be increased to 75% of the male bookbinders rate. There was some delay before the Scottish Alliance considered the claim by which time wage increases were being sought by the other print trade unions with members in Scotland, justified on the grounds of the rising cost of living. The NUPB&PW claimed an increase of 22s 0d per week for bookbinders, machine rulers, warehousemen and porters whilst the ASLP and the NSES claimed weekly increases of 10s 0d. There was also the claim by the P&KTF on behalf of its affiliates that double-day shift and night shift be reduced to thirty seven and a half hours per week and paid in the case of night shift at at a premium of 50% and that of double day shift at 33.33% above the normal basic rate. The BFMP and the Scottish Alliance sought the co-operation of the P&KTF in the creation of a co-ordinated wage structure for the industry. The purpose was to remove anomalies over a period of years and simplify the various individual union agreements which had become unduly complex. The Scottish Alliance told the STA it would only negotiate via the BFMP and a special general meeting of the Alliance held on 6 November 1947 adopted the following resolution:

> ...That this Special General Meeting of the Scottish Alliance is of the opinion that, as claims for wage alterations have been received from all unions having members in Scotland, it is not practicable to deal separately with the claims that have been received from the Scottish Typographical Association.

Resolves to discuss the wage claims through the organisations of the BFMP and the P&KTF and in the event of any union, having members in Scotland deciding to be a party to any such discussions, resolves to withstand any action that may be taken by a union to enforce its demands upon the Scottish printing and kindred trades.[6]

The Scottish Alliance favoured a national settlement of any wage claim rather than deal piecemeal with demands of individual unions. The STA was, at this stage, not prepared to work through the P&KTF and repeated its desire to deal directly with the Scottish Alliance. In protest against the Scottish Alliance's policy of only negotiating through the BFMP, the STA imposed from 22 November 1947 a ban on all overtime working. The Scottish Alliance referred the matter to a conciliation committee of the SJIC which on 28 November awarded that the action of the STA in imposing a ban on overtime without bringing the matter in dispute before the SJIC was aggressive action contrary to the constitution of the JIC. The STA was urged by the Conciliation Committee to withdraw the overtime ban. The Scottish Alliance and the STA were also recommended to reflect on their respective positions.

Meanwhile, little progress was made in negotiations between the BFMP and the P&KTF to agree a wage structure for the industry. On 25 November the P&KTF said they were not authorised to enter into negotiations with the BFMP so on 2 December 1947 the BFMP Labour Negotiating Committee decided to negotiate with individual unions. The Scottish Alliance accepted the Conciliation Committee recommendation to reflect on its position and announced it was now prepared to meet with the STA on the condition it withdrew the overtime ban and other working restrictions. The overtime ban was lifted and the STA and the Scottish Alliance resumed negotiations on 24 December 1947. Early in 1948, an increase of 9s 0d per week was agreed for STA craftsmen, of 7s 6d to auxiliary male workers of 3s 0d to auxiliary female workers with an additional 2s 6d per week to women with three years experience and a further 2s 6d to women with five years or more experience.

b. 1948
Another attempt to negotiate a wages structure started in England at the beginning of 1948. Collectively the unions submitted proposals for a settlement of all outstanding claims based on a craft rate of 140s 0d for London and of 130s 0d for Grade I towns in the provinces and existing differentials between craft, unskilled and women remain. In Scotland the P&KTF proposed a weekly wage increase of 16s 6d for all workers, except for NSES members who claimed an increase of 6s 6d. The BFMP regarded the P&KTF proposals too expensive but an adjournment for a week to 4 February 1948 gave it an opportunity to consider the unions' proposals. The Scottish Alliance held a special general meeting on 28 January

1948 at which members confirmed their confidence in their representatives on the BFMP Negotiating Board. On 4 February when negotiations resumed, the Prime Minister made a statement to the House of Commons contained in a White Paper entitled *Statement on Personal Incomes, Costs and Prices* appealing to collective bargainers to conclude zero wage increase agreement. The immediate effect of the *Statement* was an adjournment of the negotiations. When they resumed the BFMP offered increases of 15s 0d per week to journeymen in London and 16s 6d in the English provinces and Scotland with a view to an immediate settlement with all P&KTF affiliates and which would operate on the pay day of that week. When the unions rejected the BFMP offer, it declined to continue negotiations.

Following this breakdown, the STA submitted the offer to their members who accepted it by 3,507 votes to 1,279. An agreement between the Scottish Alliance and the STA was then concluded on 20 February 1948. Members of the NUPB&PW in Scotland also accepted the BFMP/Scottish Alliance offer of an increase of 16s 6d. The ASLP, having rejected the offer, considered itself in dispute with the print employers. The Ministry of Labour referred the dispute to the NAT which awarded a weekly increase of 15s 0d for ASLP members in London and 9s 0d in the English provinces and Scotland effective from 10 March 1948. In the same month, the BFMP concluded an agreement with the NSES increasing their weekly rates of pay by 8s 6d. The Scottish Alliance made an agreement with the NSES providing for a weekly increase in the basic rate of 7s 6d, making it equivalent to the recognised Linotype rate in Scotland. The Alliance agreement differed from the English and Welsh agreement in that it did not allow employers to absorb the basic increase against existing merit payments. The Scottish Alliance Executive Board took the view merit money was a matter for agreement between individual firms and their individual employees and should not come within the remit of the Alliance or the print unions.

The NSES agreement disturbed craft parity with the STA and in June 1948 the STA lodged a claim with the Scottish Alliance to re-establish parity with the NSES. The Alliance argued such parities could not be established and sustained by fragmented negotiations but only by the creation of a rational wage structure for the industry. In October 1948 the STA agreed to join the P&KTF in considering the desirability and practicability of setting up a wage structure for the industry. The Scottish Alliance favoured this development and participated in national level discussions with BFMP to devise a wage structure to apply to the whole of the UK. Unfortunately, although from the employers' point of view such a structure was desirable, the printing unions were unable to agree amongst themselves a possible structure. The STA indicated that in future it proposed to negotiate directly with the Scottish Alliance. In the meantime, in November 1948 SLADE members in Scotland received weekly increases of 9s 0d, subject to no increase for members working solely in linoleum. SLADE had received the increase granted to other unions in the first quarter of the year.

c. 1949

In December 1948, the BFMP wrote to the P&KTF explaining two things. First, the employers wished an assurance that if a wage structure were negotiated, the unions would recognise it for a number of years, enabling it to 'bed in'. Second, there was an urgent need to improve productivity in the industry and for union co-operation in devising, and applying, incentive schemes which would result in increased earnings without increasing the cost of the printed product to the consumer. On 27 January 1949 the P&KTF held a conference of its thirteen affiliated unions. After a lengthy meeting it was decided each union be asked to inform the P&KTF whether it was prepared to continue consideration of a UK wage structure. On 1 March 1949 a letter was sent to the BFMP saying that 'owing to the inability of the P&KTF to secure harmony in the views of the individual unions regarding a wage structure, the P&KTF is unable to proceed with the movement for such a structure'. The reality was that both the P&KTF affiliates and the BFMP accepted a wage structure was desirable. The unions just could not agree amongst themselves what this should be. Both the employer and employee collective bodies accepted that to move once and for all from the 'leap-frogging' claims of the individual unions which caused instability in the industry could only be to their mutual advantage.

Soon after the P&KTF letter, the BFMP received a request for a joint conference from four unions (ASLP, NUPB&PW, NATSOPA and the TA) indicating their desire to negotiate jointly for their members, including those in Scotland, via the BFMP. It was agreed BFMP draw up a proposed wage structure as the basis for negotiations with the four unions. The memorandum prepared by the BFMP would not apply in all its details to Scotland. The Scottish Alliance opposed any increase in wages but was prepared to reconsider this position providing a genuine wage structure covering all unions could be obtained. The BFMP proposed a weekly wage increase in the Grade I provincial rate of 8s 6d and hoped to bring all unions into a logical wage structure. A conference with the four unions took place on 5 July 1949. The BFMP proposals were sent to all other unions, including the STA, with the suggestion they formed the basis for an agreed wage structure for the industry. The ASLP immediately rejected the BFMP's proposals. The TA submitted counter proposals which mainly related to wage grading. When the BFMP rejected the TA proposals, the union threatened to take industrial action. The Scottish Alliance was prepared to offer the STA the basic rate in accordance with the proposed structure and to negotiate directly with the STA points of detail which were dealt with in mutual rules. On 29 August 1949, a conference was held to which all the print unions were invited. After some discussion the P&KTF informed the BFMP it was not prepared to discuss further the employers' proposals for a wage structure.

The TA imposed industrial action which was strongly resisted by English employers but did not affect Scottish print employers. Ultimately, following intervention by the Ministry of Labour, a draft agreement was reached which the TA submitted to a ballot of their members. This gave a weekly increase of 8s 6d on the minimum rate of Grade I towns. Subsequently the Scottish Alliance and the STA resumed direct negotiations. There had always existed differences between the wage grading system and machine extra payments in England and Scotland and the Scottish Alliance did not want to depart from the present wage grade system in Scotland with the existing difference of 3s 0d. By November 1949, an agreement had been reached. It provided an increase of 8s 6d per week on all minimum rates leaving the adjustment of merit money payments to the individual employer and employee. In the same agreement provision was made for an increase to females of 2s 6d with an additional 6s 0d to females with five years experience after completing training. Apart from wages the agreement provided for the encouragement, both by the Scottish Alliance and the STA, of incentive schemes to improve the industry's efficiency and productivity. In addition the period of apprenticeship was reduced from seven to six years and arrangements made for an extra bonus of eighty five apprentices to be introduced over and above the agreed quotas.

The negotiations involving the STA and the Scottish Alliance were more complicated than those in England as the agreement between the BFMP and the TA covered only compositors and machine managers. In Scotland the STA represented many women and male auxiliary workers who in England were members of either the NUPB&PW or NATSOPA. The Scottish Alliance accordingly offered an agreement on similar lines to that with the STA to the NUPB&PW. This was accepted on a ballot vote of their Scottish members and the agreements with the STA and the NUPB&PW came into operation on 28 November 1949 and 5 December 1949 respectively.

d. 1950

In July 1949 the ASLP refused to be a party to an agreement with the BFMP on similar lines to that of the TA. It objected to incentive payment schemes and an increase in the number of apprentices or to a reduction of the period of apprenticeship. Negotiations between the Scottish Alliance and the ASLP recommenced but by April 1950 no agreement had been reached. The Scottish Alliance continued to support the BFMP's Joint Labour Committee policy that no settlement be reached in Scotland until one had been concluded in England. The Alliance reserved its right to make its own arrangements with the ASLP as regards wage grading and mutual working conditions. The ASLP gave notice of termination of their agreements but claims for varying amounts of wage increases were made by its branches and chapels to individual firms. An application was made to the Scottish Alliance for an increase of wages of 8s 6d per week for all its members in Scotland, including its stone and plate preparers' section. The Scottish Alliance refused to enter negotiations until normal working was resumed. Some chapels imposed overtime bans without giving the employer the appropriate period of notice. Before this could happen the ASLP dispute with the BFMP was referred on 10 July 1950 to the NAT. The Tribunal issued its award on 18 July and an agreement between the ASLP and the BFMP was reached on the basis of this award. The agreement included provision for weekly increases of 8s 6d and 7s 6d to the journeymen and stone and plate preparers respectively in Grade I, the establishment of two grades of pay in Scotland, the reduction of the apprenticeship period from seven to six years and a clause promoting increased production and the installation of incentive schemes. Arrangements were made for starting 120 apprentices (thirty to Scotland) throughout Britain, outside the normal ratio and for the upgrade of a small number of suitable men to craft status.

In March 1950, the London Society of Compositors (LSC) made a claim to the London Master Printers' Association for a considerable wage increase. In May the LSC gave notice of withdrawal from the NJIC, banned overtime and imposed other aggressive measures. The dispute was referred to the NAT which issued its award on 20 June 1950. It provided an increase of 3s 6d subject to a lifting of an overtime ban. The minimum compositor rate for London would become 143s 6d. The LSC refused to recognise the award and continued its industrial action, and in August nearly 4,000 LSC members were dismissed because of the introduction of restrictive practices in breach of established customs and practices in the industry. The LSC members returned to work on 13 September 1950 and both sides requested a Court of Inquiry be appointed by the Minister of Labour to consider the dispute and that pending the court's report, negotiating between the parties be adjourned. On 21 October 1950 the Court issued its findings. After negotiations a new agreement came into effect in London from 20 November 1950.[7] It raised the minimum rate for London to 155s 0d and stated merit money and house-rate payments be absorbed in the increased minimum rates. Stability of wages and employment conditions for five years were agreed subject to a cost-of-living sliding scale. The agreement provided for a block of additional apprentices and late entrants and for an increase in the normal apprenticeship ratio.

The Court made suggestions affecting other sections of the industry. It was realised other trade unions would inevitably press for increased wages. The BFMP took the initiative and offered increases in wages linked with conditions on additional manpower, greater production and a period of stabilisation. A conference with the P&KTF representing all print unions, including the STA, was held on 13 December 1950. The BFMP put forward proposals which included a weekly increase of 11s 6d in the minimum rates of craftsmen, 8s 6d for semi-skilled and unskilled men and 6s 0d for women. Each case was subject to the absorption of merit money or house-rates to the extent of the increase in the basic rates and on condition satisfactory arrangements were made for increased manpower, a period of stabilisation and increased production. The BFMP proposed a cost-of-living bonus on a sliding scale with six-monthly adjustments.

e. 1951

The BFMP and the P&KTF met on 27 February 1951 when eight unions including the STA, the NUPB&PW, and the NSES were present. The unions proposed higher rates of which those that affected Scotland were for a weekly increase of 14s 0d for craftsmen, of 24s 0d for women and of 17s 6d for unskilled men. It was also claimed women receive 1s 0d per point, the same as men under the cost-of-living sliding scale. The unions opposed the absorption of merit money. The Scottish Alliance adopted the position that in any settlement with the P&KTF, or with the individual unions, agreement on additional manpower was of prime importance and that no settlement on wages be implemented until specific agreements on manpower were made.[8] This attempt to secure a UK-wide agreement on a basic wage structure for the industry with all the unions failed. In March 1951, several unions, including the STA and the ASLP, withdrew from the national negotiations.

In April 1951, the STA submitted claims to the Scottish Alliance for an across-the-board increase of 15%, the present three wage grades in Scotland be discontinued and a new Grade I rate operate throughout Scotland. On 1 May 1951, the Alliance made clear to the STA there could be no agreement on wages until the manpower situation had been settled. On 26 May 1951, the Scottish Alliance and the STA made an agreement providing for:

(1) Additional apprentices – there be a special extra allowance of sixty compositors and twenty machine room apprentices over and above the present quota.

(2) Co-operation for increased production. Employers and members of the STA were encouraged to co-operate in taking all practicable steps making for greater productivity and efficiency.

(3) Increase in basic rates. There was a weekly increase of 12s 6d to craftsmen, of 10s 0d to non-craft and of 8s 0d to women. This gave a basic Grade I rate for compositors and machine men of 143s 6d.

(4) A cost-of-living sliding scale bonus based on the cost-of-living index figure published monthly by the Ministry of Labour to be adjusted half yearly (May and November). For each point rise or fall in the Retail Prices Index from the base figure of 114 (its level in September 1950) the bonus be increased (or decreased) by 1s 0d for men and 9d for women per week. This bonus was a flat addition to the week's pay and was excluded for the calculation of overtime and shift rates.

(5) The rates and other conditions in the agreement remain in force for a period of five years from 16 November 1950 and thereafter until six months notice, by either side, to terminate it had expired.

During the remainder of 1951, the Scottish Alliance concluded agreements with the ASLP, the NSES, SLADE, the NUPB&PW under which the basic Grade I craft rate became 143s 6d per week. These agreements covered five main topics – an increase in basic rates, a cost-of-living sliding scale bonus, additional apprentices, co-operation for increased production and a five-year period of stabilisation from November 1950. These agreements although negotiated separately with individual unions, brought into existence a wage structure for the industry. The basic rate increases and the cost-of-living sliding scale bonus were influenced, to a considerable extent, by the report of the Court of Inquiry.

A number of member firms criticised the Scottish Alliance for entering into wage agreements based on movements in the Retail Prices Index. In general the Alliance's Executive Board was satisfied such agreements were in the best interests of the Scottish printing industry. In its report to forty second annual general meeting, the Executive Board defended the cost-of-living bonus:

> ...There may be minor fluctuations in costs but these are easily estimated and the position is a more satisfactory one than constant negotiations with unions and uncertainty as to the probable result of such negotiations...

Grading Schemes

In 1951 the STA lodged a claim for a revision of the *Wage Grading Scheme*. The aim was one grade for all its members throughout Scotland. The Scottish Alliance rejected the claim but proposed the present Grade III be abolished and existing Grade III towns be upgraded to Grade II at the existing grade rate providing there was no STA demand for the upgrading of Grade II towns to Grade I. The Scottish Alliance was prepared to consider any anomalies the union alleged existed in the present Grade II classified towns. The STA had proposed that Alloa, Ardrossan, Ayr, Dumfries, Dunfermline, Falkirk, Galashiels, Kirkcaldy and Stirling current Grade II towns be upgraded to Grade I. The STA also sought to establish the principle it be whole STA branches as distinct from specific towns that be upgraded. The Scottish Alliance rejected the principle of grading according to branches rather than towns.

After much discussion the Scottish Alliance Executive Board accepted two grades in Scotland instead of the existing three. It met again with the STA and reached a settlement on specific towns at present in Grade II which might be upgraded to Grade I. Alva, Ardrossan, Ayr, Dunfermline, Falkirk, Kirkcaldy and Stirling became Grade I towns. The STA accepted that Alloa and Galashiels remain Grade II towns but pressed successfully to upgrade Dumfries to Grade I. The Scottish Alliance did concede the STA claim Aberdeen be upgraded to Grade I. On 7 March 1952 the STA and the Scottish Alliance signed an agreement to operate from the first pay day in April 1952 providing in Scotland for two grades (Grade I and II) of pay with a wage differential of 3s 0d.[9] All towns in Grade III were raised to Grade II and eight Grade II towns to Grade I. The NUPB&PW had for many years sought there be only one grade of wages in Scotland applicable to all craftsmen. Shortly after the Alliance/STA agreement for two grades of wages the same agreement was made with the NUPB&PW.

Wharfedale press. Photography by Bob Woods.

Courtesy of Queanbeyan Printing Museum, New South Wales, Australia.

Working Rules

In May 1951 the Scottish Alliance and the NSES reached an agreement covering working rules and conditions. It covered the whole of Scotland and replaced the local agreements previously in force. In addition to reducing the apprenticeship period to six years provision was made for the training to craft status of adult men between the ages of twenty and twenty three years.

In April 1947 negotiations took place between the Scottish Alliance and the STA on amendments to the mutual rules affecting working conditions. The proposed STA changes were considered by the Scottish Alliance to affect detrimentally the Scottish printing industry's economic interests. The Alliance suggested minor amendments to the STA proposals that proved acceptable to the union which also agreed to a joint investigation to frame general principles for incentive payment schemes for application at house level. Despite lengthy negotiations, agreement was still only made on relatively minor matters. The STA indicated they preferred to continue working under the existing mutual rules. Towards the end of 1949, the STA mutual rules negotiations were resumed. In entering these negotiations the Scottish Alliance stressed they would make no concessions which might increase production costs. Minor amendments were, however, agreed and came into operation in mid-1950.

In September 1952 the ASLP Scottish District Council lodged a claim for changes to the existing by-laws agreement regarding extra payments for working on bronzing, for tea money and for night shift and double shift working. The Scottish Alliance Negotiating Committee was given a mandate to reach a settlement at the rates already applying in England but in no circumstances at rates higher than those already agreed in Scotland with the STA. In December 1952 the Scottish Alliance accepted where a member of the union was employed on double-day shift they would work on average up to forty two hours on an hourly rate equivalent to 20% above the normal day hourly rate, including machine extras and merit money. They also agreed the machine man responsible for, and other ASLP members engaged on, bronzing to receive 2d per hour extra above the minimum rate of the branch for each hour, or part of an hour, when engaged on that work. The Alliance agreed to give two weeks notice to end double-day shift working after six weeks working on that shift. The Scottish Alliance would not give extra payments for tea money but would recommend to member firms that as long a period of notice as possible be given when asking an employee to work overtime. It was adamant it would not increase payments for working night shift.

In 1944, due to wage stabilisation, the only wage question considered by the Scottish Alliance was a claim from NUPB&PW regarding wages paid to females operating guillotine machines in Aberdeen and Kirkcaldy. The employment of women on guillotines in these towns went back to the nineteenth century. When the Alliance refused to consider the claim, the matter went to the Conciliation Committee of the SJIC. Its finding was the parties had agreed in September 1942 the wage rates of guillotine operators on the assumption such machines were operated solely by males. It further recommended the Scottish Alliance and the NUPB&PW make an agreement on wages to be paid to females operating guillotines and arrangement be made for the ultimate elimination of female labour from the operation of guillotine machines. In May 1946 an agreement was made between the Scottish Alliance and the NUPB&PW providing for:

(1) 77½% of the male rate be paid to competent women engaged full-time on guillotines
(2) women engaged occasionally be paid 6d per hour extra with a guarantee of a minimum extra of 10s 0d per week if the women did not do any cutting during the week
(3) the full female rate (77½% of the male rate) be paid if women engaged intermittently in cutting exceeded twenty seven hours in any working week and
(4) from the date of ratification of the agreement no more women be introduced to guillotine work.

The Manpower Situation

The STA at the outbreak of the Second World War proposed a ban on the entry of apprentices to the composing and the machine rooms. Only after prolonged negotiations was an agreement concluded in September 1942 providing, under certain conditions, for the replacement of apprentices who had completed five years of their training prior to enlistment into the Armed Forces. By the end of the war 145 apprentices had been recruited under the 1942 agreement. At the same time the Scottish Alliance, approached the STA to consider the present and future manpower position of the Scottish printing industry. At the first meeting in September 1945 the Scottish Alliance submitted figures showing, after allowing for apprentices started, retirals, death in service and unemployed STA members, the shortage of manpower at the end of 1951 would be 716 employees.

The STA argued consideration of the manpower situation be postponed until after June 1946. This was unacceptable to the Alliance. The STA contended given the number of apprentices still in the armed forces there would be, in the future not a shortage of labour, but a surplus. Ultimately discussions between the Alliance Secretary and the President and General Secretary of the STA resulted in a mutually agreed manpower shortage figure of 502. These discussions had revealed two important issues. First, the strong opposition by the STA to allow apprentices to be started in any department where only one journeyman was employed. Second, the union claimed employers should bear the burden of seeing employees surplus to requirements receive financial protection and/or regain employment by the employer, by reducing working hours. In February 1946, an arrangement was reached between the Scottish Alliance and the STA as to the method of calculating the average number of men employed during the proceeding fifty two weeks, for calculating apprenticeship ratios. Journeymen returning from the armed forces were immediately counted as if they had been re-employed for a year.

The Scottish Alliance, during the years immediately following the end of the Second World War, was conscious of the prevailing shortage of manpower in all sections of the Scottish printing industry and had worked to find some solution to the problem. In preliminary discussions it became clear it would be difficult to persuade certain unions, who admitted to having no unemployed members, there be recruitment of many new entrants. The unions constantly pointed to their experiences of unemployment between the two world wars when they paid out large sums of money to their members in unemployment benefit. During 1947/8, a relatively larger number of apprentices entered the letterpress section of the industry than had done so for many years. This could not make up for the reduced entry between 1939 and 1947. There was no lack of boys wishing to become apprentices in the industry but many employers complained many did not match the standards the industry required. If this was the case, it reflected the reduced standard of education during the war years, from it which it was expected to take many years to recover.[10]

The Scottish Alliance took, on 1 July 1948, a census of the manpower position for all sections of the industry. It revealed many firms in all sections were not employing their full quota of apprentices and that there were 231 fewer compositors, twenty two fewer machine men, twenty four less stereotypers and seventy six fewer lithographers compared with 1 July 1939 census. The Scottish Alliance responded to the census results by urging its members to take up their full quota of apprenticeship in every department and to seek meetings with the print unions to discuss ways of reducing the manpower shortage, for example by lowering the period of the apprenticeship from seven years to six and a bonus intake of apprentices over and above the normal apprentice ratios. In 1948 an agreement was made with the NUPB&PW, that the apprenticeship period of bookbinders and machine rulers be reduced from seven years to six. Expectations that similar agreements could be made with the other print unions in Scotland did not materialise until 1951.

By early 1950, the manpower position, particularly in the letterpress and lithographic section of the industry continued to be a cause of concern to the Scottish Alliance. Unfortunately, in the November 1949 negotiations with the STA to permit the introduction of dilutees into the Scottish printing industry collapsed. The Alliance Executive Board deplored this and its April 1950 general meeting adopted unanimously the following resolution:

> ...the Scottish Alliance of employers in the printing and kindred trades deplores the failure of the Scottish Typographical Association to produce an adequate labour force in the case and machine room sections resulting in serious loss of work to the Scottish printing trade and demands that where craftsmen cannot be supplied by the STA auxiliaries be introduced meantime until such time as craftsmen became available.

The STA agreed to additional apprentices, as a long term policy to help ameliorate the manpower shortage, but the Scottish Alliance's view was that additional apprentices, although helpful, could not solve the fundamental manpower shortage problem. The manpower position, despite the 1949 agreements with the STA and the NUPB&PW and the 1950 agreement with the ASLP which permitted the introduction of a limited number of apprentices outside the ratio, continued to be a cause of disquiet to the Alliance.

In June 1950 the Alliance Negotiating Committee made it clear to the STA the union had an equal responsibility with the Alliance to maintain the viability of the Scottish printing industry which had suffered too long from a shortage of skilled operatives. The STA made no satisfactory reply the Scottish Alliance's case. In view of the national negotiations proceeding at that time and in which the employers were only prepared to trade wage increases for satisfaction on manpower no further separate action with the STA was taken.

In November 1950 an inquiry into the manpower shortage was undertaken and as a result, figures for the whole of the Scottish Alliance membership were obtained. These emphasised again the seriousness of the position. Since 1939, throughout the world, the printing industry had been expanding. In various European countries the number employed in the industry had increased by amounts ranging from 9% to 45%. In Britain the numbers had decreased by 5.6%. In Scotland the number of craftsmen employed by the same members of the Scottish Alliance have since 1938 declined in the composing room by 18%, by 5% in the machine room and by 15% in the lithographic department.

The Scottish Alliance urged its member firms to examine regularly the number of apprentices in their various departments and employ the full quota of apprentices to which they were entitled under the agreements with the trade unions. Any firm entitled to additional apprentices which they did not want to recruit was to inform the Scottish Alliance Secretary so arrangements could be made for the additional apprentices to be transferred to other firms willing, and able, to offer them training opportunities. Given the obligations under the manpower clauses of the 1951 collective agreements, a manpower enquiry was undertaken in November 1952 similar to those undertaken in 1950 and 1951. This survey demonstrated, yet again, the need of member firms to give the highest priority to their apprenticeship intake policy. Some 15% of journeymen employed in Scotland were over sixty years of age and if replacements were not forthcoming the manpower shortage and its attendant difficulties would continue. During 1952, in certain sections of the trade, the number of qualified journeymen employed declined but the number of apprentices in the trade increased.

At the time of the 1951 enquiry, members were asked to supply details of all apprentices employed so that a central apprentice register for each section of the trade could be set up in the Scottish Alliance head office. From this register, the Alliance office could supply for the guidance of its local association secretaries, at regular intervals, a list of firms which had apprentice vacancies. To ensure the central register was effective, when a member firm recruited an apprentice they were to supply to the Alliance head office details of the apprentice's name, age, date of starting and department in which employed. There was an understanding with the STA that intention to start a composing or machine room apprentice be sent to the Scottish Alliance Office ten days before the proposed start date.

Summary

The economic context in which the Scottish printing industry operated in the immediate post-Second World War years was difficult. Economic policy was geared towards allocating resources to export- and import-orientated industries of which printing was not part. From 1945 to October 1951, a Labour government transformed the UK economy, on the basis of taking key industries (eg coal, gas, electricity and transport) in the economy from private hands into public ownership within the framework of social security protection for all citizens. Although full employment was achieved, the major economic problem remained achieving a positive balance of payments. This meant restricting, in many cases by rationing, economic resources for private consumption and for industries such as printing. Increased industrial production brought full employment but led to inflationary pressures. This was made worse by the devaluation of the pound sterling against the dollar in November 1949. In a further attempt to restrain inflation, the government in February 1948 exhorted collective bargainers to restrain their pay settlements to zero. The incoming Conservative government of October 1951 retained the welfare state and the commitment to maintain full employment. It removed government restrictions, direct control over industry and dealt with inflation by interest rate and income taxes. It denationalised the iron and steel and road haulage industries.

In 1946, following industrial action and a Court of Inquiry, the Scottish printing industry saw the introduction of a forty-three-and-a-half-hour working week worked over five days and two weeks holiday with pay. Over the period 1947 to 1951, the industry arrived at a settlement of basic rates and conditions for the following five years (to November 1955). Behind the evolution of this wage structure lay many inter-union problems such as the appropriate differentials between skilled and semi-skilled employees, and between London and the rest of the UK, and the appropriate wage for women in relation to male wages. The Alliance and the BFMP favoured a united and co-ordinated wage structure for the industry. The print unions, including the STA, were unable to agree amongst themselves a wage structure. The craft unions, for example, feared that by joining a collective movement for a wage structure their interests would be swamped by the larger non-craft unions and thus jeopardise their future ability to advance the employment conditions of their members.

In December 1950, the BFMP (and the Scottish Alliance) offered to P&KTF-affiliated unions increases in wages in return for additional manpower, measures to improve productivity and efficiency, a cost-of-living bonus and a five-year stabilisation of wages and other employment conditions. In March 1951, the STA announced their withdrawal from the P&KTF wage negotiations, and in April 1951 approached the Scottish Alliance unilaterally for a wage agreement. The Alliance was only prepared to make an agreement if the STA agreed to an increase in the supply of labour. In May 1951, the Scottish Alliance and the STA reached an agreement providing increases in basic rates plus a cost-of-living bonus in return for the union permitting additional apprentices, encouraging its members to co-operate with all steps taken by employers designed for greater productivity and efficiency and a five-year stabilisation period for employment conditions. During the remainder of 1951, the Scottish Alliance made agreements on the same lines with the ASLP, the NSES, SLADE and NUPB&PW. These five agreements, although they were negotiated separately with the individual unions, brought into existence an agreed wage structure for the Scottish printing industry.

In the period 1945 to 1952 the Scottish Alliance was aware of the shortage of manpower in all sections of the industry and it worked hard to find solutions to the problem. It began a regular census of the manpower situation for all sections of the industry and to negotiate with the print unions an increase in the supply of labour via changes to the apprenticeship ratio, by reducing the period of apprentices, by a bonus intake of apprentices over and above the normal apprentice ratios and by the introduction of dilutees.

Notes

[1] See *Statement on Personal Incomes, Costs and Prices*, Cmnd 7321, HMSO, London, 1948.

[2] See Minutes of the meeting of the Executive Board, 22 May 1946.

[3] See Minutes of the meeting of the Executive Board, 6 August 1947.

[4] A Court of Inquiry is a procedure authorised under the Industrial Courts Act 1919, as a means of informing Parliament and the public of the facts and causes of a dispute. A Court of Inquiry was not primarily an arbitrative, mediation or conciliation body though it is expected its findings would help lead to a settlement.

[5] See *Report of a Court of Inquiry into the nature and circumstances of a dispute between the British Federation of Master Printers and the Printing and Kindred Trades Federation,* Cmnd 6912, HMSO, September 1946.

[6] See Minutes of Special General Meeting of the Scottish Alliance of Employers in the Printing and Kindred Trades, 6 November 1947.

[7] See *Report of a Court of Inquiry into the causes and circumstances of a dispute between the London Master Printers' Association and the London Society of Compositors,* Cmnd 8074, HMSO, October 1950.

[8] See Minutes of the meeting of the Executive Board held on 7 March 1951.

[9] Following the revision of the Grading Scheme in April 1952 the following towns were in Grade I – Aberdeen, Airdrie, Alexandria, Alva, Ardrossan, Ayr, Barrhead, Beith, Bellshill, Clydebank, Coatbridge, Dalkeith, Dumbarton, Dumfries, Dundee, Dunfermline, Edinburgh, Falkirk, Glasgow, Greenock, Hamilton, Helensburgh, Johnstone, Kilmarnock, Kilsyth, Kirkcaldy, Kirkintilloch, Motherwell, Paisley, Perth, Port Glasgow, Renfrew, Rutherglen, Stirling and Wishaw.

[10] See Report by the Scottish Alliance Executive Board to the Thirty Seventh Annual General Meeting, Glasgow, 30 March 1948.

Part 2

THE SCOTTISH ALLIANCE OF
MASTER PRINTERS, 1953-1960

Chapter 10

THE GROWTH AND DEVELOPMENT OF THE
SCOTTISH ALLIANCE OF MASTER PRINTERS, 1953-1960

This chapter begins by explaining the technological developments in production techniques in the 1950s in the Scottish printing industry, particularly the development of photocomposition and the growth of an alternative printing industry based on the installation of small office printing machines by non-printing companies in the public and financial sectors. The chapter then explains the reasons for the change of name from the Scottish Alliance of Employers in the Printing and Kindred Trades to the Scottish Alliance of Master Printers. It then examines the growth in membership in the Alliance and developments in its internal decision-making machinery – associations, office bearers, the Young Master Printer Group, etc. The chapter next outlines financial and industrial relationships with the BFMP. The fifth section explains developments in the Scottish Alliance income and expenditure whilst its penultimate part examines the core services provided to member firms. The final section outlines the rationale behind changing the organisation's name to the Society of Master Printers of Scotland.

Developments in the Industry

During the life time of the Scottish Alliance of Master Printers the major technological change in the Scottish printing industry was the replacement of mechanical composition by photocomposition. This involved setting on film or paper rather than the manipulation of metal type. It changed the nature of the work rather than the number of compositors required, but increased output and productivity considerably. The task of the hand compositor changed from the assembly of metal type and blocks to paste up or assembly of film. Hot metal was a letterpress process and was mutually incompatible with lithographic techniques based on film and paper. Photocomposition was the key to the rise of the lithographic printing process at the expense of the letterpress process. This trend accelerated in the 1970s with the introduction of computerised composition. Mechanical compositors found photocomposition created new employment opportunities as 'qwerty' keyboard operators or as photocomposer operators.

For the Scottish Alliance phototypesetting presented union demarcation problems. The STA claimed, in accordance with the past custom of the trade, their members operate the photocomposing keyboard and output units and also make corrections and do the make-up before handing over these materials to other employees. They claimed to do with film whatever they did with hot metal. They argued using a photographic composing machine was more than just preparing film to be pasted up in another department. It required knowledge of typography and the background of make-up and layout which was the compositor's training and thus these machines should remain their craft.

SLADE, on the other hand, argued typographical union members should handle work only up to the production of the undeveloped film or paper after which all tasks be carried out by SLADE and ASLP members. SLADE argued when an individual touched the keyboard instead of tapping out type, they beat out pulses that became photographic film. SLADE contended their members, and not STA members, develop, assemble, make up the pages and print down for plates. Photosetting, for SLADE, involved photography and had nothing to do with typography. They saw little point in allowing STA members to do work that had always been the preserve of SLADE members. The handling of film was the exclusive right of the litho unions and since no metal type was involved, STA members forfeited their traditional rights to undertake the correction, make-up and imposition of their own composition.

On 4 April 1958 a meeting took place between the BFMP and the six unions (STA, LTS, TA, Monotype Casters and Typefounders Society [MCTS], ASLP and SLADE) directly interested in photocomposition. This meeting considered a draft formula which it was hoped would provide the basis for the settlement of the staffing of photocomposition machines. The formula proposed that the operation of photocomposition keyboards and output units, correction of errors up to galley proof stage and the make-up of pages and advertisement be the work of typographical unions. This was the bulk of hot metal compositors' work. The insertion of half-tones and illustrations was to be the work of SLADE members. The proposed formula was acceptable to the BFMP and the Scottish Alliance. Although not every Alliance member firm was satisfied with the formula it did ensure the avoidance of inter-union disputes over claims as to which members operated photosetting machines.

The 1950s saw an increase in installations of small offset printing machines such as Multilith and Rotaprint in both the printing industry and outside the industry. The introduction of office printing machines began in the 1930s but after the Second World War the number of installations accelerated. This expansion into commerce, particularly banks and insurance companies, government departments and local government took work away in ever increasing amounts from the conventional printing trade. In February 1952, the Scottish Alliance sent a circular asking member firms to provide information of cases they knew of where office printing machines had been installed with the consequent loss of work. In April 1952, the circular results revealed office printing machines were operated by twenty five Scottish local authorities, thirteen banks and insurance companies and eighty three commercial firms.[1] The type of work and machines being used varied greatly. In the majority of cases the machines were operated by females. By 1959 it was estimated in the UK the number of small offset printing machines in use was 15,000, of which 15% were installed in organisations outside the printing industry. Local authorities in Scotland were using these machines to print, inter alia, domestic rate demands, accounts, stationery, note paper and committee and council meeting minutes. Although this work was of a relatively simple nature, small offset machines were capable of printing first class work when installed in printing offices.

Why had this expansion in the installation of small offset machines outside of the Scottish printing industry taken place? Since the end of the Second World War the industry had experienced expanding demand for printed matter which the industry could not meet. The industry was not seen as essential to achieving a balance of payment surplus and always struggled to persuade government to release raw materials to it. There were long delays in the completion of orders so customers began to place their orders abroad whilst others established their own in plant printing capacity rather than satisfy their printing requirements from the jobbing trade. Scottish print employers could not meet demand because of the shortage of skilled labour. The STA and the other craft print unions in Scotland were unwilling to make manpower concessions, for example, the admission of adult trainees, to enable Scottish print firms to satisfy the expanding customer demand. An important factor in the growth of commercial firms, local authorities and government departments in installing Multilith and Rotaprint machines was to obtain a better service than could be obtained from the conventional jobbing printer.

There were two other factors in the development of in-plant printing by organisations outside of the Scottish printing industry. First the production of certain kinds of printing was cheaper on office offset machines than machines used for that class of work in the traditional printing industry. The employees employed on office printing machines outside the industry were paid at rates below those payable in the conventional printing industry. Second employers who established their own in plant printing capacity, had the advantage over the jobbing printer that their output was not subject to Purchase Tax as was the case with conventional printing companies. The then Purchase Tax regulations relating to offset printing and stationery were a serious burden on the traditional printing industry.

When the Scottish Alliance was informed a local authority or some other organisation outside the industry were installing small offset printing machines, it would approach them to persuade them not to do so and to give print orders to a bona fide printing firm. This approach met with little success. For example, when the Alliance's attention was drawn, in July 1958, to the proposed use of a Multigraph machine by the Dunfermline Town Council for the printing of their committee minutes it approached the Council to point out the adverse consequences of its proposed action to the Scottish printing trade. The pleading proved unsuccessful. The Scottish Alliance in July 1958 discussed steps the industry might take to safeguard the interests of member firms when organisations outside the industry installed small office printing machines. It concluded each case had to be treated separately and that the Scottish Alliance Secretary would give members the necessary guidance in any individual case.

In the early 1950s the Scottish print employers, recognising the growth of in-plant printing outside the industry was a common concern with the print unions, accepted the matter be considered by the SJIC. Whenever a report was received by the SJIC that a local authority was contemplating the installation of a small office printing machine, efforts were made by the local printers and union representatives, often acting as a JIC district committee, to dissuade local authorities. This approach also met with little success.

Regrettably it took the printing unions in Scotland a long time to reach agreement on staffing levels and wage rates for employees operating Multilith, Rotaprint and Multigraph machines within the printing industry. It took time for member firms of the Scottish Alliance to recognise the benefits of installing such machines as items of their own equipment staffed by male or female auxiliaries or journeymen as the work required. In this way, they provided their customers with a speedy and efficient service competitive as to cost relative to non-print companies. The print unions generally agreed Multilith and Rotaprint were offset litho machines to be operated by ASLP, and their assistants be members of the appropriate assistants' unions. They also accepted Multigraph machines be staffed by members of the letterpress union.

In England and Wales in December 1952, the TA and the ASLP settled their demarcation problems concerning whose members staff small offset machines. TA members were to operate these machines on the condition they became associate members of the ASLP. Based on TA members becoming ASLP associate members, it was possible for employers to operate small offset printing machines staffed by TA members when no ASLP members were available. A similar agreement between the ASLP and the STA was not reached in Scotland until June 1962.

In October 1954 the Scottish Alliance signed an agreement with the STA covering the staffing of office printing machinery. It related to staffing levels and to wage rates in letterpress and was only applicable in those printing houses which did not employ ASLP members. In 1952 the Scottish Alliance had reached an agreement with the ASLP whereby Multilith, Rotaprint and Multigraph machines be staffed by male or female auxiliaries or by journeymen. There were difficulties between the ASLP and the STA over the latter's agreement with Scottish Alliance on the staffing of small offset machines. The dispute was referred to P&KTF Arbitration Board but the STA declined to co-operate with the Board. The P&KTF urged the STA to meet with a P&KTF delegation so its view of the matter could be placed before them. The STA considered no useful purpose would be served by receiving a P&KTF delegation.[2] This uncertainty as to staffing levels and wage rates for small offset machines in printing houses where only STA members were employed continued until June 1962 when an agreement on this issue, similar to that between the ASLP and TA in England and Wales, on this issue was agreed between the ASLP and STA.

Scottish Alliance of Master Printers

The 1953 annual general meeting of the Scottish Alliance voted to change the name of the organisation from the Scottish Alliance of Employers in the Printing and Kindred Trades to the Scottish Alliance of Master Printers. It was considered the previous title did not sufficiently denote the Scottish Alliance was different from the other twelve Alliances in England and Wales federated to the BFMP. These Alliances, unlike the Scottish, did not have financial and industrial autonomy to negotiate their own collective agreements, to provide their own costing service to members nor to meet their own expenses when their representatives attended BFMP Council, committee and section meetings. It was felt that the title Scottish Alliance of Master Printers was sufficiently different from the Alliances in England and Wales to denote the Scottish Alliance, given its financial and industrial autonomy, was unlike other member organisations affiliated to the BFMP.

The Scottish Alliance of Master Printers had a high degree of membership. Over 90% of printing firms in the Scottish printing industry were in membership. It had members throughout Scotland including rural areas as well as the cities of Glasgow, Edinburgh, Dundee and Aberdeen. In 1955, the Alliance had 376 firms in membership of which 120 were in the Glasgow association and eighty two in Edinburgh. The Aberdeen association had twenty six member firms and the Ayrshire and Dundee branches twenty each. The smallest branch was the

Scottish Borders with only three members. In 1960, at the end of the life of the Scottish Alliance of Master Printers, it had 329 member firms of which 104 were in the Glasgow Association and seventy six in the Edinburgh Association. The fall in membership relative to 1955 was due to resignations and expulsions stemming from the 1959 UK-wide stoppage in the general printing and provincial newspaper industry.

In the summer of 1959, the Scottish Alliance was involved in a six-week dispute between the BFMP and the affiliated unions of the P&KTF over the latter's demand from the unions for a forty-hour working week and for a 10% increase in wages. Some companies settled with the unions outside of the main negotiations. Print firms breaking ranks from the BFMP and the Scottish Alliance either resigned or were expelled from membership. Fifteen firms representing 426 employees and paying in subscription fees £465 resigned from the Alliance. A further thirty eight firms employing 363 employees and paying in affiliation fees £635 were suspended from membership. The dispute was settled in August 1959 and in the following autumn the Scottish Alliance considered what action to take against those member firms which during the dispute, either resigned or were put in suspension because they acted 'contrary to the interests of the Alliance'.

In November 1959, the Alliance decided no approach be made to those firms which had resigned but the views of local associations be obtained regarding those firms under suspension before any final decision was made on their future membership. At its January 1960 meeting the Alliance Executive Board, decided the membership of firms which had acted 'contrary to the interests of the Alliance' during the 1959 dispute be terminated. It agreed if those firms affected by this decision, and those which had resigned during the dispute, applied for readmission to the Alliance, their position be considered by the local association concerned which would make to the Scottish Alliance an appropriate recommendation. In short any question of re-admission to membership would be a matter in the first instance for the Scottish Alliance local association. In the end, the final total of firms leaving the Scottish Alliance because of resignations and expulsions arising from the 1959 dispute was thirty eight. The approximate loss in subscription income from these firms was £1,100 per annum.[3]

Constitutional Issues
a. Internal Decision-Making
i. Local Associations
The change of title to the Scottish Alliance of Master Printers was merely a change of name. There were no changes to its decision-making machinery. These remained local associations, affiliated associations, the Executive Board, the Annual General Meeting, office bearers, paid employees (the Secretary etc)

and the general membership. There were, however, consequential changes. For example in 1954 at their Annual Meeting the local associations accepted they alter their official titles to conform with the change of name of the Alliance agreed at its 1953 Annual General Meeting. The Edinburgh association, for example, became the Edinburgh Master Printers Association whilst the Glasgow association became the Glasgow Master Printers Association. The Greenock association became the Greenock Masters Printers Association. In short, the local associations all followed the example of the Executive Board and in all cases became known as 'Master Printers Associations'. In August 1955 the Forfarshire Master Printers Association transferred their membership to the Dundee and Aberdeen Master Printers Association, as appropriate.

The Presidents of the Scottish Alliance of Master Printers (Alastair M Stewart, Frank L Paton, James S Waterston and John Murdoch) continued the tradition of visiting the associations at their annual general meetings and receiving a warm welcome. On these visits, the President was usually accompanied by the Secretary, the Assistant Secretary and the Cost Accountant, with a view to their introduction to members who were not in close contact with the work of the Alliance's Executive Board.

To develop closer links between Scottish Alliance head office and the membership, the Alliance convened a weekend conference in the autumn of 1959, attended by representatives of all member firms. The industrial dispute meant the conference was delayed until March 1960 when it was held at the Turnberry Hotel. There was a varied programme and main addresses were by Sir John Simpson, Controller of HMSO and C L Pickering, HM Inspector of Printing Schools, both of whom were heard with interest.

ii. Officials
On 20 May 1953 R T Wishart retired as Secretary to the Scottish Alliance. He had held the position for thirty five years. The record of his service almost served as the history of the growth of the Scottish Alliance from its humble beginning to its position in 1953. Throughout his term of office 'R T', as he was known, amassed an amazing fund of knowledge of the organisation and the operation of all sections of the trade which, as members knew to their benefit, was there for the asking. As Secretary, Mr Wishart represented the Scottish Alliance in London at Federation meetings for the whole of his service and served, since its inception in 1922, as Joint Secretary of the Scottish Branch of the JIC. In addition, Mr Wishart represented the Alliance for many years on the Edinburgh Local Employment Committee where his service was recognised in 1950 with the award of MBE. In 1929 he had become a Justice of the Peace for the City of Edinburgh.

In the light of Mr Wishart's retirement, the President's and the Finance Committee reviewed the Alliance's staff position. The 1 July 1953 the Executive Board confirmed unanimously the four recommendations from the two committees presented to it by the President Alastair M Stewart. First, in view of Mr Wishart's long service, he be paid a supplementary pension. Second, W Barrie Abbott, currently the Scottish Alliance Assistant Secretary be appointed Secretary of the Alliance from 21 May 1953. He was born in Peebles and was a chartered accountant. He was employed in London on professional accounting and legal work before joining the Scottish Alliance. He also held a Bachelor of Law degree from the University of Edinburgh. He remained Secretary to the Scottish Alliance until 1984. Third, S G Coutts, currently secretary of the Edinburgh Master Printers Association be, in addition to his duties in that association, be appointed as Assistant to Barrie Abbott from 24 May 1953. Four, the Cost Accountant be paid on a salary scale. In June 1954 the Scottish Alliance provided the Secretary (Barrie Abbott) with the use of a car for Alliance business.[4]

In September 1953, Robert Wilson died. He had been associated with the Alliance from its inception and was its President from 1922-1924. He acted as Honorary Secretary to the meeting of delegates from the various printing associations in Scotland which decided on 8 November 1910 that the Scottish Alliance of Employers in the Printing and Kindred Trades be formed. Mr Wilson continued as Honorary Secretary until the appointment of F H Bisset as Secretary in April 1911. In his long connection with the Scottish printing industry, he held every possible office in the Edinburgh Association and the Scottish Alliance.

In November 1959 Mr Coutts, the Alliance Assistant Secretary and Edinburgh Master Printers Association Secretary informed the Executive Board he would retire with effect from the end of November 1959, from these positions. A selection committee specially appointed to deal with the selection of his successor unanimously agreed Mr T Lorimer, a qualified solicitor, be appointed as Edinburgh Association Secretary and Scottish Alliance Assistant Secretary with effect from 30 November 1959. He was appointed on an equal basis between the Alliance and the Association.

iii. Young Master Printers

Throughout the lifetime of the Scottish Alliance of Master Printers, the Young Master Printers movement remained active although the number of members fell during the period 1953 to 1960 inclusive which was a cause of concern. A major factor in this decline was the high number of retirements of senior members of the group. They were not replaced by younger members. In January 1960, the Scottish Alliance had 325 member firms, fifty seven of which had members in the Scottish YMP Group. The total number of members in the group was seventy five. The concern of the Alliance Executive Board with the membership of the YMP Group was seen in its frequency of advice in its report to the annual general meeting that member firms ensure all suitable young men in the industry were nominated as members of the group, and subsequently encouraged to participate fully in YMP activities, not only in the interests of the individual but of the firm and the industry as a whole.

An important part of the YMP Group's activity was its annual conference, held every autumn. During the conference presentations were made on a wide range of topics. Over the period 1953 to 1960 these included the history of the YMP movement, marketing, financial management, developments within the industry and methods of improving the flow of work and materials through the factory. In 1957, for the first time in ten years no Scottish YMP Group conference was held. The group conference was revived in autumn 1958 with a meeting held at North Berwick and met in 1959 and 1960. In 1953, the twenty fifth annual conference of the YMP was held. There was a large attendance of former and present YMPs who had held office in the Scottish Alliance and the associations. This demonstrated the vital role the YMP movement played in the Scottish printing industry. Another activity of the YMP Group was its annual general meeting which, after the important business had been conducted, was followed by factory visits. For example, in 1953, the attendees of the annual general meeting visited Blackwood, Morton & Sons, carpet manufacturers and Saxone Shoe Co.

Another important part of the YMP Group's work was the undertaking of specific projects. In 1956 the group prepared a report on apprentice selection in Scotland covering the number of apprentices recruited each year, the number of candidates passing successfully through the selection procedure, was there any standard selection procedure in use? was the procedure a variation of the National JIC scheme or was a different procedure used? The project examined how many apprentices were taken into firms by direct sponsorship rather than through a formal selection procedure. Were candidates interviewed and given any written tests? The report was considered by the Scottish Alliance Executive Board which asked the Scottish YMP Group to continue its investigations into apprentice selection procedures and to make appropriate recommendations for consideration by the Board.

The Edinburgh and Glasgow YMP Groups, as opposed to the Scottish YMP Group, held regular meetings. The Glasgow group had considerable success in stimulating interest and recruitment but reduction in the membership of the Edinburgh group restricted its activities. By the late 1950s membership of the Edinburgh group was again increasing and in the session 1959/60 both the Glasgow and Edinburgh Groups offered interesting programmes.[5]

b. Relationship with BFMP

The Scottish Alliance of Master Printers played an active part in the work of the BFMP whose business was managed, and controlled, by a 110-person Council on which the Alliance had six representatives. The Alliance was also represented on the standing committees of the BFMP including the following committees: Finance, Organisation, Legislation, Labour, Costing, Education and Training, and the Young Master Printers. Peter J W Kilpatrick from the Scottish Alliance Executive Board was first Vice-Chair of the BFMP Costing Committee and subsequently its Chair. Duncan C Sillars who had been President of the Scottish Alliance from 1944-1946, was Chair of the BFMP Technical Committee for several years but in 1952 resigned. Hope Collins from Wm Collins Sons & Co, a past President of the BFMP, took over the duties of this important committee and subsequently became the Assistant Honorary Treasurer of the BFMP. In 1955, Hamish A MacLehose from the eponymous Glasgow printing firm became BFMP President. Representation on BFMP committees and the holding of key offices in the BFMP by senior members of the Scottish Alliance meant a greater understanding between the two bodies.

In 1951, the Scottish Alliance increased its subscription to the BFMP from £500 per year to £750, provided that in its annual accounts the BFMP inserted a note making clear the special position of the Scottish Alliance relative to its other alliances. The increased subscription was paid in 1951 and 1952 but the agreed note had not been inserted in the BFMP annual accounts. The Scottish Alliance discussed the matter with the BFMP's Secretary and agreed as a matter of policy no further action be taken in this matter. In July 1956 the Scottish Alliance raised its annual subscription to the BFMP to £1,000 per annum. It was again suggested there be clarification in the BFMP accounts as to the nature of the amount paid annually by the Scottish Alliance.

In 1956 a dispute arose in England and Wales between the BFMP and the TA and LTS (see Chapter 12). Negotiations were resumed following the publication of the report of the Court of Inquiry set up by the Ministry of Labour. The Scottish Alliance admired the firm stand taken by BFMP members, particularly in London and they sent a message of congratulations and encouragement to the London Master Printers Association. On 12 March 1956 with respect to the dispute in England the BFMP established a Disputes Assistance Fund into which its members paid a levy of ½d per £ of wages paid during the year 1955. The Scottish Alliance in March 1956 recommended to the annual general meeting a similar levy in support of the fund would be made in Scotland. The annual general meeting of March 1956 approved the following motion:

> ...As a contribution towards the Federation Disputes Assistance Fund, a Special levy should be paid by each member. Such a levy should be at the rate of ½d in the £ on the wages paid by the members during 1955...

By July 1956, 293 members of the Scottish Alliance had paid a total £10,633 in 'Special Levy' payments in support of the BFMP Assistance Fund. By the end of 1956 the sum had risen to £11,377. In March 1957 the Scottish Alliance transferred the sum of £1,000 per annum from its General Fund to that of the BFMP subject to clarification of the position of the Scottish Alliance regarding access to the resources of the fund and that no change be made in the short run to the Alliance subscription rates. By February 1959 352 member firms of the Scottish Alliance had contributed £11,573 as special levy payments into the BFMP Disputes Assistance Fund. During the 1959 dispute over an increase in wages and a reduction in working hours, four grants from the fund totalling £850 were made to members of the Scottish Alliance associations of Edinburgh, Lanarkshire and Glasgow (two grants). The Alliance agreed in February 1960 to pay at the end of March the usual sum of £1,000 into the Disputes Assistance Fund but took the view further capital payments into the Fund would be unnecessary in the future and the BFMP be informed of this.

In 1957 the BFMP reviewed its procedure for negotiating collective agreements with individual unions and the P&KTF, given the experience gained in the 1955/56 wage negotiations. After consultation with its Negotiating Committee the Scottish Alliance sent a response to the BFMP on 26 June 1957. It pointed out from its experiences in Scotland it was essential the BFMP developed a less unwieldy procedure for dealing with wage negotiations. It argued the BFMP place greater reliance on a smaller negotiating committee with the necessary authority from the BFMP Council to negotiate an agreement within certain parameters. The Scottish Alliance considered it essential the smaller negotiating committee appreciated the views of the BFMP membership and enjoyed their confidence. It also stressed any reformed negotiating committee have an understanding of the views of the unions with which they bargained.

The Scottish Alliance submission then explained the procedure used in Scotland for negotiating with the unions pointing out its Executive Board was responsible for these negotiations and was Scottish equivalent in labour negotiation to the BFMP Council. The Scottish Alliance Executive Board gave wide authority to its Negotiating Committee which had a membership of fifteen. This committee in turn delegated responsibility for the actual negotiation to a subcommittee, which had five members (chair of the Negotiating Committee, Deputy Chair of the Negotiating Committee, the President, the Vice-President and a representative of the Scottish Newspaper Proprietors Association). This practice of delegating to a small subcommittee was also adopted for consideration of any matters arising from the operation of union agreements. The Scottish Alliance told the BFMP that this negotiating procedure had been developed over the last decade and was considered by member firms to have brought substantial benefits, particularly the promotion of goodwill and trust with the trade unions. In addition, the Scottish Alliance's evidence remarked it was interesting that a number of the print unions had adopted the Alliance practice of delegating to smaller groups the conduct of the actual negotiations but reporting back to a wider constituency.

The Scottish Alliance response to the BFMP Consultation Paper on reforming the negotiation procedure noted better communications between the BFMP and its members and vice versa were important not only for information and consultation purposes but to engender confidence by the membership in those protecting their interests in the negotiations. The Scottish Alliance response accepted settlements applicable to England and Wales impacted directly in Scotland. It was recognised if a situation arose whereby the BFMP was unable to obtain a settlement with one or more of the unions but the Scottish Alliance could, then the Alliance would not delay making that settlement. Such situations were likely to be unusual but could arise from differences in the speed of operation in Scotland where the number of firms were smaller in comparison to England, rather then from fundamental differences of view.

The Scottish Alliance response was welcomed in principle by the BFMP Council although it was critical of parts of it. As a result, in December 1957 the BFMP's President and the Scottish Alliance President (James M Waterston) met to discuss outstanding matters around the Scottish Alliance's response. A revised labour negotiations procedure was finally approved by the BFMP Council in January 1958 and incorporated the following paragraph regarding the special position of Scotland:

> The lack of any sign that the STA contemplates amalgamation, together with the traditional differences between Scottish and English practice, appears to make complete integration of English and Scottish negotiations very difficult except on general matters.

The Alliance considered, in the interests of both sets of employers, the highest degree of integration and consultation take place before proposals were made to the unions in either country. Where integration was not practicable the Scottish Alliance committed itself to confer with BFMP whilst retaining the right to vary any terms that may be proposed insofar as those terms affected Scotland.

Finances

Table 10:1 shows the income and expenditure of the Scottish Alliance of Master Printers for the years 1953 to 1960 inclusive. The main sources of income were members' subscriptions, interest from investments, entrance fees and sundry receipts. The main items of expenditure were salaries and national insurance payments, administration expenses, travel expenses, the Costing System, BFMP subscriptions and staff superannuation payments. The main assets of the Alliance was its headquarters, 12 Hill Street, Edinburgh which had been purchased in 1924 and valued in 1960 at £1,300. The Scottish Alliance had an investment portfolio which in 1953 had a market value of approximately £10,040, in 1957 of £12,385 and by end December 1960 of £12,536.

Table 10:1
Scottish Alliance of Master Printers Income
and Expenditure: 1953-1960

Date	Income (£)	Expenditure (£)	Surplus (£)
1953	14,255	11,943	+2,312
1954	14,074	13,056	+1,018
1955	14,901	13,928	+973
1956	16,572	15,894	+678
1957	16,927	15,577	+1,350
1958	17,430	15,981	+1,449
1959	13,176	17,800	-4,624
1960	19,169	17,752	+1,387

Source: Annual Accounts and Balance Sheet

In February 1960 the Alliance Finance Committee, examined the accounts for the past year, and estimated income and expenditure for the year 1960, predicting a deficit of £2,000 for the year unless there was a considerable increase in income. Since 1947 when the last increase in subscriptions had been agreed, wages for journeymen had increased by over 100% whereas in the same period the total income of the Alliance had increased by under 70%. The 1959 accounts, because of the major industrial dispute in the industry in that year, showed expenditure had exceeded income by £4,600. The Finance Committee considered if the Scottish Alliance's financial position was to remain on a sound basis income had to increase to take account of a drop of £1,000 per annum occasioned by termination of membership of thirty eight firms because of their behaviour in the 1959 dispute and to provide adequately for the normal rate of expansion in Scottish Alliance's services to members.

The Scottish Alliance Finance Committee, after careful consideration, recommended to the Executive Board and to the 1960 annual general meeting the present maximum limit of annual subscriptions be increased from £150 to £250 and the minimum be raised from £2 to £5 per annum. The committee had been influenced by a number of factors of which the most important was the maximum subscription had remained at £150 since 1947 and as a result, increases in Scottish Alliance income had been borne by a diminishing number of members not affected by a maximum subscription limit which had been established when the general level of prices and costs were only some three fifths of their 1960 level. The Finance Committee recommended the amount of maximum and minimum subscriptions be set, in future, by the Executive Board rather than the annual general meeting. This recommendation was accepted by the Executive Board whilst the 1960 annual general meeting decided unanimously the maximum and minimum annual subscriptions be altered from £150 to £250 and from £2 to £5 respectively.

In April 1960 the Scottish Newspaper Proprietors Association (SNPA) made an approach for an increase in the amount paid by the Scottish Alliance to the association in respect of SNPA firms which were also in membership of the Alliance. Discussions took place between representatives of the two bodies after which it was agreed there be integration of the secretariat of the Association and the Scottish Alliance. Barrie Abbott would become secretary of the SNPA and in future the Scottish Alliance pay to the Association a fixed percentage (approximately 2%) of the subscriptions received from dual members. These proposals were accepted by the Executive Board at its meeting held on 6 April 1960.

Services to Members

The Alliance continued to provide industrial relations services to its member firms. It bargained, and then serviced on their behalf, collective agreements with the STA and the UK-wide print unions with members in Scotland, particularly the ASLP and the NUPB&PW. It represented the industrial relations interests of its members on the BFMP Labour Committee, NJIC and the SJIC. The Scottish Alliance assisted member firms in the management of their employee grievances, of unsatisfactory performance of their employees and general advice on industrial relations matters. These were valued services by member firms, the vast majority of which were too small and lacking in resources to have their own personnel departments.

Another important service to member firms was political lobbying of national governments, via the BFMP, and of local government. Throughout its lifetime, the Scottish Alliance of Master Printers, via the BFMP Purchase Tax Joint Standing Committee, made efforts to convince the UK government of the anomalies caused by existing Purchase Tax regulations as they affected printing and stationery products. The tax was seen as a serious burden on the industry. Representations were made to the Chancellor of the Exchequer that the industry be relieved of the tax. In 1958 agreement was reached whereby hospitals operating under the National Health Service were to obtain printed paper stationery free of tax from registered printers. Some success was also achieved in minor items such as labels and partly printed leaflets. Although Purchase Tax on stationery was reduced from 30% to 25% in the 1959 budget the BFMP and the Scottish Alliance considered it a matter of regret this 5% reduction was no greater than the rate on other goods formerly taxed at 30%.

The majority of apprentices entering the Scottish printing industry went through a formal selection procedure but away from the industrialised areas, firms selected young people directly for apprenticeship. Selection schemes for apprentices operated in Ayrshire, Aberdeen and district, Dundee and district[6], Edinburgh and district and Glasgow and district. Approximately 280 candidates for apprenticeships came forward each year and 75% were assessed as suitable for entry into the industry. Selection procedures varied in detail in the different areas. The selection procedure was administered jointly by the Scottish Alliance and the P&KTF. The selection procedure involved many factors including a school report, medical record, education attainment (English, arithmetic and general knowledge), intelligence, colour vision and a general medical examination.

In the 1960s the quality of applicants for an apprenticeship was high, reflected in the high pass rate at a high standard and the successes registered in the City and Guilds of London Institute examinations. These were national in character and provided independent assessment of the training of printing apprentices. The percentage of passes in Scotland was above the average for the United Kingdom. The Scottish Alliance also monitored the training and equipment available in the various technical colleges. In 1959 day release schemes were operating in Aberdeen and Dundee whilst discussion began to establish a similar scheme in Dumfries.

An important service to member firms was costing and estimating. Following normal practice each year many member firms were visited by the Cost Accountant (George W Llewellyn) and practically all, except those in the outlying districts of Scotland, were seen at least once by him. These periodic visits by the Cost Accountant proved well worthwhile not only in stimulating interest in costing but in keeping members, particularly in the 'country areas' in touch with Alliance headquarters. Given the dominance of the industry by small firms the Scottish Alliance stressed the importance to its members of keeping records to show the cost of every job produced.

Whilst the need for accurate costing was recognised by member firms, the Scottish Alliance policy was that only regular calls from the Cost Accountant could ensure the advantage of improved costing methods, particularly to the smaller firms. The Alliance believed it was valuable, both to individual members, and to the trade generally, that these visits continued. Member firms often commented that the clerical work involved in operating the Costing System was too great for small firms. This was often shown to be an illusion and to be outweighed by the advantages gained by the proper use of the system.

A major activity of the Costing Department was the installation and revisions of the Costing System. A number of firms used the services of the Cost Accountant to review and revise their costing systems at regular intervals but many more member firms might have made use of the service had they given a higher priority to keeping their costing rates up to date. In 1953, thirty one installations and revisions of the Costing System were undertaken by Scottish Alliance members. In 1958 the number was thirty and in 1959 twenty. Member firms who had their costings reviewed every year (or at more frequent intervals) by the Cost Accountant and who based their costs on up to date budgets, had the means of controlling their expenditure, could produce monthly profit and loss statements, know how their businesses were faring and could take any required remedial action in good time if it became necessary. In March 1959, the Alliance increased the fees charged to member firms for cost revisions by the Alliance Cost Accountant from £3 3s 0d per hour to £5 5s 0d per hour.

Costing and estimating classes were held at the Heriot Watt College, Edinburgh, the Stow College School of Printing, Glasgow and the College of Art, Dundee. The BFMP also provided correspondence courses in both subjects. In May 1953 the first Estimating Stage 1 Examination was held in Scotland and there were 147 candidates. The results were satisfactory. The Scottish results in the Costing examinations, however, were poor. In 1958 over 400 candidates sat the BFMP examination in Costing, Estimating and Preliminary Technical Knowledge and the national pass rate was 50%. Of the twenty seven Scottish examinees eleven were successful. In 1959 there were 650 candidates for the BFMP examination and again the national pass rate was 50%. Of the thirty four Scottish candidates twelve were successful.

In 1958, the Scottish Alliance Costing Department introduced two new schemes – Management Ratios Scheme and Method Study. The former was at first well supported in Scotland but by 1959 support had reduced considerably. A similar trend was noted in England and Wales. The ratios calculated by the scheme showed how effective a firm was in comparison with others in the same section of the industry. In March 1958, the Alliance decided the responsibility for the introduction and practice of Method Study lay with individual member firms, and recommended each member firm of a reasonable size send a junior executive for training in the implementation of Method Study. It also agreed the Scottish Alliance's role in the furtherance of Method Study be confined mainly to education and advice but the Cost Accountant be available to
(1) advise member firms on the subject of Method Study
(2) assist the member firm's own Method Study Officer with their investigations and
(3) give practical help with Method Study to the smaller member firms.[7]
As a result of the clauses in the wage agreements concluded in 1959 covering Method Study, the Scottish Alliance organised a conference on the subject over the weekend of 29/31 January 1960. The conference was attended by sixty six people representing thirty five firms. Its objective was to stimulate an awareness of what Method Study was, and what it could do.

The Chair of the Scottish Alliance Costing Committee (Peter J W Kilpatrick) and the Cost Accountant regularly attended meetings of the BFMP Costing Committee. These meetings dealt with the launching of the Management Ratios Scheme, a report on costs and prices of printing in European countries, the possible adoption of one costing system for all European countries, mechanised costing and a report on the impacts on costs of the decrease in operating allowance on industrial premises.

Change of Name Again

In October 1959 the Scottish Alliance Executive Board decided:

> it was agreed that a Special Committee should be appointed by the Office Bearers to examine questions of the future policy on the part of the Alliance including the suggestions made at the meeting and to report...

This special committee on future policy placed its recommendations before the 14 January 1960 meeting of the Executive Board. It contained four recommendations:

(1) the responsibility for the welfare of the Scottish printing and weekly newspaper industry rested with those directly concerned with it.

(2) while co-operation between the Scottish Alliance and the BFMP was beneficial to both, and should continue, the autonomy of the Alliance be more fully recognised than in recent years.

(3) as confusion continued to exist regarding the position of the Scottish Alliance and other Alliances within the BFMP the name of the Scottish Alliance be changed.

(4) the BFMP office bearers be appraised of these recommendations by W Hope Collins and Hamish A Maclehose at the meeting of the BFMP General Purposes Committee to be held on 9 December 1959.

The Alliance Executive Board accepted the Future Policy Committee recommendations.

Hope Collins and Hamish MacLehose duly met the BFMP officers and informed them of the decisions of the Alliance's Future Policy Committee. The BFMP saw no difficulty in the change of name of the Alliance provided the word 'Federation' was not in the new name. The President (John Murdoch), the Secretary (Barrie Abbott) and the Alliance Cost Accountant (George Llewellyn) then visited local associations to explain, and discuss, the decisions of the Future Policy Committee. The first two recommendations, on the need for Scotland to look after the interest of the industry and exercise of 'autonomy', met with general approval. The proposed change of name caused difficulty.

There was a general feeling the suggested new name, namely Scottish Master Printers, was not satisfactory and there was something incomplete about it. In a number of meetings with local associations, it was proposed the word 'Federation' be substituted for 'Alliance' even though it was explained this would not be welcome to the BFMP. It was strongly suggested at two association meetings that there be no change of name unless it was to 'Federation' and the BFMP be 'made' to change the name of the English Alliances.

This was clearly impracticable. There was general agreement a change of name was desirable. The Secretary of the Alliance (Barrie Abbott), after further consideration to a new name, advised there would be good grounds for the use of the word 'Society'. There was already the Newspaper Society which represented provincial newspapers in England and its position as regards BFMP Joint Labour Committee was akin to the Scottish Alliance. He suggested the word 'Society' could be used in one of the following ways:

- The Scottish Master Printing Society
- The Scottish Society of Master Printers
- The Society of Master Printers of Scotland

The forty ninth annual general meeting of the Scottish Alliance held in Glasgow on 6 April 1960 unanimously agreed its name be changed to Society of Master Printers of Scotland. The change was accepted on the basis it would prevent confusion with other printing trade organisations in England which did not make collective agreements with the print unions on their own account but did so through the BFMP headquarters in London.[8]

Summary

During the lifetime of the Scottish Alliance of Master Printers, the major technological change in the Scottish printing industry was the move to replace mechanical composition by photocomposition. This involved setting on film or paper rather than the manipulation of type. It caused inter-union disputes between the STA and the litho craft unions (ASLP and SLADE) but they did reach a demarcation agreement in the spring of 1958. The 1950s saw an increase in the installations of small offset printing machines both within the printing industry and outside it (the financial sector, local authorities and central government). This created an alternative printing industry which took bread-and-butter work from the Scottish general printing industry. The Scottish Alliance was unsuccessful in persuading non-printing companies to return this work to the industry.

The 1953 annual general meeting changed the name of the Scottish print employers' organisation to the Scottish Alliance of Master Printers. The new title denoted the Scottish Alliance was different from the other member Alliances affiliated to the BFMP. The change of title involved no changes to the decision-making machinery of the Alliance. This remained members, local associations, the Executive Board, the annual general meeting and office bearers. R T Wishart, the Secretary of the Alliance, retired in May 1953 after thirty five years in the position. He was replaced by Barrie Abbott who remained Secretary to 1984. The Young Master Printers movement remained active, with its annual conference and the undertaking of specific projects, being central to its work.

Relationships with the BFMP were constructive. Scottish Alliance representatives played an active part in the subcommittees of the BFMP, occupied major offices of the BFMP including President and provided influential evidence to the BFMP consultation paper on reforming its negotiating procedure with the individual printing unions and the P&KTF. The financial basis of the Scottish Alliance was sound. A major increase in membership subscriptions, the first since 1947, occurred in 1960. Another financial reform in 1960 was that membership subscription would, in future, be set by the Executive Board rather than the annual general meeting.

The core services provided to member firms were the negotiation of collective agreements with the unions, political lobbying particularly to obtain more favourable Purchase Tax arrangements for the Scottish printing industry, the selection of apprentices and costing and estimating. This last service included the installation and revising of the cost system in member firms to enable 'proper' costing and pricing of jobs rather than companies compete with each other by uninformed price-cutting. In 1958, the Costing Department introduced two new services – a Management Ratios Scheme and Method Study.

In January 1960, the Scottish Alliance Committee on Future Policy recommended, inter alia, as confusion continued to exist regarding the Scottish Alliance and other Alliances within the BFMP, the name of the Scottish Alliance be changed, this time to the Society of Master Printers of Scotland (SMPS).

Notes

1   See Minutes of the Meeting of the Executive Board, 30 April 1952.
2   See *Annual Report 1954 and Report of Administrative Council*, May 1955, Printing and Kindred Trades Federation, p14.
3   See Minutes of the Meeting of the Executive Board, 23 February 1960.
4   See Minutes of the Finance Committee, 23 June 1954.
5   See Report by the Scottish Alliance Executive Board to the Forty Ninth Annual General Meeting, Glasgow, April 1960.
6   This district included Angus, North Fife, Perth and the county of Perthshire.
7   See Minutes of the Meeting of the Executive Board, 26 March 1958.
8   See Press Notice, 'Change of Name of Alliance', Scottish Alliance of Master Printers, Edinburgh, 7 April 1960.

Chapter 11

RELATIONSHIP WITH TRADE UNIONS: SCOTLAND

This chapter begins by looking at an important industrial relations institution in the Scottish printing industry, the Scottish Joint Industrial Council (SJIC). The next section examines the relationship between the Scottish Alliance of Master Printers and the STA, the NUPB&PW, the NSES and the ASLP and negotiations over mutual working rules to apply in Scotland. The final part of the chapter outlines the efforts of the employers to deal with acute staffing shortages and their impact on the industry.

The Scottish and National Joint Industrial Councils

The SJIC and its Aberdeen and Glasgow District Committees held, until 1959, regular meetings. The attendance was generally satisfactory. A number of meetings of the SJIC Organisation Committee took place to raise awareness of the council. In March 1953, the SJIC remitted to its employer and employee panels a report of a conference on office printing machinery held in November 1952. At the conference, both employers and employees said they had a direct interest in the work produced by these machines coming under the control of the industry. The employers' panel recommended in March 1953 two things. First, steps be taken to eliminate existing restrictions on the staffing of office machines, subject only to the trade union membership of the operator. Second, action be taken to end the unfair discrimination against the industry by existing Purchase

Tax legislation. These employer recommendations were put to the SJIC meeting of 18 March 1953 at which the employees' panel agreed discussion on the report be deferred for three months, so the P&KTF could consider the staffing of office printing machines.

In March 1958, the SJIC learned that, in addition to office printing machines, camera and platemaking equipment had been installed in the HMSO premises at Sighthill, Edinburgh and was operated by clerical staff. After local investigation the matter was referred to the National JIC. Its joint secretaries reported in September 1958 they met with Sir John Simpson, Controller of HMSO who had told them a Duplicating Department using small offset litho machines had been established. The joint secretaries reported in early 1958 there were throughout the HMSO some 350 small offset litho machines and fifty cameras of various sizes in use all over the country, including Scotland and Northern Ireland. The headquarters of the Stationery Office had a large duplicating department and there were seventy four installations in other government departments. At the December 1958 meeting of the NJIC three issues were agreed.

(1) Grave concern was felt not only at the situation disclosed in HMSO by the report of the National JIC secretaries, but that in England the existing situation represented developments that had built over many years.

(2) The NJIC did not regard the situation in HMSO to be satisfactory. The SJIC was anxious to know the steps which the NJIC might take to deal with the situation.

(3) The NJIC be aware of the SJIC's views so that it could be considered along with the National Secretaries' report.

There was, however, in reality, little the NJIC or the SJIC could do about the HMSO office printing machine problem and the situation continued.

In 1957, discussion took place over revising the NJIC conciliation procedures. Local disputes had been dealt with satisfactorily under the present conciliation procedure but it had been ineffective in national wage disputes. The printing unions were anxious some procedure be laid down which would operate in national disputes even if aggressive action had taken place. The BFMP, and the Scottish Alliance, on the other hand, were of the view the joint secretaries be required to take action only when there was prevailing disturbance of, or departure from, normal conditions of working. In October 1957 the BFMP and the P&KTF approved an amendment to the NJIC constitution to provide for the continuance of existing conciliation procedures in local and national disputes. In future, in cases of national disputes arising from the breakdown in negotiations for revision of agreements, the joint secretaries would arrange some form of conciliation or arbitration. It was recognised in a national dispute, if either party took aggressive action, or failed to comply with normal conditions of working, it be accepted the JIC conciliation machinery had been exhausted.

In October 1959 both sides of the NJIC agreed, in the light of the experience of the 1959 dispute, that the effectiveness of the NJIC be subjected to a searching review. A constitutional committee, consisting of eleven representatives from the unions and from the employers' side, was set up to consider this matter and to make recommendations. No further meetings of the NJIC would be held until the subcommittee had reported. The employers' side of the subcommittee produced a draft new constitution which proved unacceptable to the employee representatives.

No meetings of the SJIC had been held since the 1959 dispute. The STA informed the P&KTF that as most of the business of the NJIC concerned problems in England and Wales, it would not participate in any reformed constitution for the NJIC agreed between the BFMP and the P&KTF. It did say in the event of a reformed NJIC being established it would attend meetings in Scotland and take part in the affairs of the SJIC. The Scottish Alliance, on the other hand, told the Constitutional Subcommittee it was unlikely to accept the SJIC becoming a branch of the NJIC as this could mean Scottish affairs might be forwarded 'on appeal' for settlement south of the border.[1] The subcommittee, by the summer of 1960, had failed to agree a revision of the NJIC because of difficulties over defining objectives. The difficulty was that the BFMP and the Scottish Alliance wanted Clause Two 'to secure complete organisation of employers and employees throughout the trade' – removed from the constitution whilst the unions argued it should stay since its removal, after being part of the constitution for forty years, could lead to misunderstanding.

Concurrent with the discussions over a reform of the constitution of the NJIC the trade unions sought to have recognition in its constitution that the organisation clause covered the organisation of clerical workers. The policy of the Scottish Alliance on this issue was clear cut. The objects of the NJIC, as drafted in 1919, had never been intended to cover clerical workers or any other occupation not peculiar to printing. For the Scottish Alliance, the NJIC could not, even if employers wanted to, give constitutional recognition of the right of unions to organise clerical employees in the UK or Scottish printing industries. By the time the Scottish Alliance changed its name in March 1960, the negotiations to reform the NJIC were continuing business.

The Scottish Typographical Association (STA)
In June 1954 the Scottish Alliance/STA Rotary Committee made recommendations with respect to a multi-unit:

(1) it be staffed on the basis of one letterpress machine manager and one auxiliary workers,
(2) the rate paid to the machine manager in charge of the machine be 17s 6d a week above the basic rate when operating up to, and including, two colours,
(3) an increase of 1s 6d be paid per week for each colour above two.

A further extra of 5s 0d was paid when running four colours because of the excessive heat on the top deck of such machines.

At its December 1954 meeting the Scottish Alliance Executive Board was informed the STA was seeking information on the working of incentive schemes in Scotland to develop a policy on such schemes at its next delegate meeting. The STA was informed it would be appropriate if information as to the working of incentives schemes was collected via the Incentives Subcommittee set up by the Alliance and the STA.

At the same meeting it was reported at a conference held in London the BFMP had proposed:

> …in the case of male workers over 18, 10/- be added to the basic weekly rate for the purpose of calculation of overtime payments for all hours worked in excess of the normal shift, whether day or night or double day shift or the normal period worked under special casual arrangements…

The Scottish Alliance considered the proposal be not implemented until after the individual unions had given the matter consideration. The STA indicated they were not prepared to accept the offer but decided to drop the matter.[2]

During 1956 and 1958, the Scottish Alliance/STA committees examined working conditions for two photogravure and two letterpress rotary machines so agreements could be reached with the STA on the staffing and machine extras acceptable to firms and appropriate to their particular circumstances. Agreements were reached with the STA which met these objectives. In late 1958, the Scottish Alliance and the STA signed an agreement covering the staffing and wage rates for five colour photogravure machines and a carton printing machine installed in a Glasgow firm.

The National Union of Printing, Bookbinding and Paperworkers (NUPB&PW)

For many years there had been agreements between the BFMP and the NUPB&PW covering extra rates paid to employees working on certain machines. The policy of the Scottish Alliance was that merit money be paid to men operating machines where it was considered extra skill and/or responsibility was involved. The NUPB&PW claimed this policy had led to anomalies so its Scottish Group District Council approached the Scottish Alliance to clarify the position. On 6 October 1953, a conference between the Scottish Alliance and the NUPB&PW took place at which the union was asked for evidence to support their claim for an agreement on machine extras which would provide the same rates as the Power Machine Agreement in England. In subsequent discussions it was clear the information given to the NUPB&PW by its members was not, in some cases, accurate. The union agreed to re-examine their information and bring to the notice of the Scottish Alliance specific cases where they considered their members were being treated unfairly.

Case Room at
Waterston's, Edinburgh.
Reproduced courtesy of the SAPPHIRE
Project, Scottish Centre for the Book,
Edinburgh Napier University.

The Alliance emphasised it would be a grave mistake to alter its long-standing practice that extra payments above the basic rate be given on the account of merit.

The claim by the NUPB&PW for an agreement on machine extras was subjected to two conferences in 1958. Proposals were put before the union for an agreement to deal with specialist machines which might be introduced in the future and to provide reasonable extras for a limited range of automatic machines already operated by their members. In March 1959 the Scottish Alliance and the NUPB&PW agreed proposals for machine extras. The proposed agreement went to a ballot vote of the union's members in Scotland. When a favourable result was known, the national wage negotiations of 1959, and subsequent stoppage, prevented any agreement between the Scottish Alliance and the union being signed and implemented.

A new agreement on machine extras became effective the week beginning 29 February 1960. This provided a reasonable period in which the firms concerned could make any necessary adjustments in piece-work schemes. If difficulty was experienced with these adjustments reference was in the first instance to be to the secretaries of the parties to the agreement. Members of the NUPB&PW who were in receipt of wages in excess of those provided by the agreement, were not entitled to claim an increase. So that this could be fairly operated in houses, where piece-work, work measurement incentive schemes, production bonus or merit rating schemes were in operation the firms concerned, after consultation with the chapels, could make such adjustments as were fair and reasonable in the circumstances. If no agreement could be reached at shop floor level, reference was made in the first instance to the Secretaries of the Scottish Alliance (Barrie Abbott) and the Scottish District Council of the union (R H Hetherington) and if necessary to an appropriate joint committee, consisting of six members (three nominated by the Alliance and three by the union) together with the Secretary of the Alliance and the Secretary of the Scottish District Council.

Under the February 1960 agreement, 15s 0d minimum payment in addition to the basic weekly rate was paid to craftsmen in charge of automatic and semi-automatic rounding and jointing machines, lining and headbanding machines, casing-in machines, case-making machines, thermoplastic perfect binders, two-unit forwarding machines and continuous trimmers. A minimum payment of 7s 6d above the basic weekly rate was to be paid to craftsmen in charge of Krause continuous trimmers, Johne continuous trimmer and auto-fed blocking machines such as the Chandler and Price, Sheridan and Crabtree. A minimum of 5s 0d per week above the basic rate was paid to journeymen in charge of double-sided disc ruling machines, fed by reel or automatic feed with pile delivery, and 'L' disc ruling machines, with automatic pile feed and delivery.

Where an automatic or semi-automatic machine operated by a member of the NUPB&PW, of a fundamental design new in Scotland was introduced by a member firm of the Scottish Alliance, there was often a case for extra payment for the operative. If there was a dispute over whether a payment was justified or high enough, it was referred to a joint committee consisting of six members (three nominated by the Scottish Alliance and three nominated by the union) together the Secretary of the Alliance and the Secretary of the Scottish District Council. This committee, at the request, either of the Scottish Alliance or of the union inspected the machine. The joint committee made recommendations on staffing and machine extras subject to approval by the Scottish Alliance and the NUPB&PW.

In August 1954 the Scottish Alliance and the NUPB&PW reached an agreement providing for notice on leaving a situation and for the introduction and ending of shift work. No NUPB&PW member would resign from their existing employment without giving, or receiving, a fortnight's notice. NUPB&PW members employed in an office for four consecutive weeks became permanent employees covered by the appropriate collective agreements. All wages due, including payment in lieu of holidays, were paid at termination of notice. These provisions covering voluntary resignation from an existing job put NUPB&PW members in the same position as regards due notice as the members of the STA and other unions in Scotland.

Under the shift working clauses of the agreement an employer was required to give one week's notice of intention to start a regular double-day shift or regular night shift. When an employee had worked on a regular double-day shift or a regular shift night shift they were to receive two week's notice if the employer wished to end their shift work. Double day shifts or night shifts operating for four consecutive weeks were classed as regular shifts. The agreement provided when a double shift or night shift operated for one week or more but for less than four weeks, two working days notice of intention to start the shift was necessary. This agreement providing for notice with reference to shift working did not change the clause in the November 1939 agreement which provided where night shifts and double-day shifts were introduced to operate for less than one week time and half was paid for hours worked outside the normal hours of employment.

The National Society of Electrotypers and Stereotypers (NSES)

In June 1956 the Scottish Alliance and the NSES reached agreement providing for a special trade work payment in recognition that in Scotland there existed no employers' association comprised of firms undertaking trade work in electrotyping and stereotyping.[3] They were to receive a trade work payment additional to the basic rate of 30s 0d for each week, or part of a week, in which they were engaged on such work. This additional flat rate payment was paid in houses where incentive schemes operated. No NSES member had their wage reduced solely because of the operation of the agreement. By the same token members in receipt of wages in excess of those provided above were not entitled by the agreement to claim an increase. The agreement had become effective on 2 July 1956.

In 1958, a difficult case in the Glasgow area, which was amicably settled, related to the 1919 agreement between the Scottish Alliance and the Scottish District Council of the NSES. The union suggested that now was the appropriate time to review it. The Scottish Alliance agreed to review the 1919 agreement but making it clear to the NSES they regarded that agreement as still being in force. Following the joint review, both parties accepted the 1919 agreement still operated and no changes were required to its provisions.

The Amalgamated Society of Lithographic Printers (ASLP)

The by-laws affecting working conditions in the litho sector of the Scottish printing industry were first negotiated between the Scottish Alliance and the Scottish District Council of the ASLP in November 1925. They were amended in November 1931, again in April 1936 and yet again in October 1937. Further changes were negotiated in March 1953. One of the main changes was the introduction of double-day shift working. Where a member of the ASLP was employed on a double-day shift they received, for a shift averaging up to forty two hours per week, an hourly rate premium of 20%. Hours worked above forty two were paid at the appropriate overtime rate above the shift hourly rate. A second important amendment was machine men responsible for, and other ASLP members engaged on, bronzing received 2d per hour extra above the minimum rate of the branch for each hour, or part thereof, when engaged on that work. The ASLP had pressed in the negotiations the tea allowance be increased from 1s 0d but the Alliance refused to concede the claim. It did, however, advise members firms that, so far as possible, notice of their needs for overtime working be given the previous day.

In 1957 the ASLP presented a claim to the Scottish Alliance that the clause in the by-laws covering bronzing be changed to provide a payment on the same hourly basis as existed in England. The Alliance considered the proposal inappropriate to Scotland and the Scottish practice regarding payment for bronzing be retained. At a meeting of the two parties held on 22 May 1957 the Alliance proposed to increase from 2d to 3d the extra hourly rate for undertaking bronzing work.

The Alliance made clear to the ASLP it would only agree to either the existing English position or to the continuance of the Scottish practice but not to a mixture of both. In November 1957 the ASLP accepted the Alliance offer the existing clause in the ASLP by-laws regarding bronzing be modified by substituting 3d for 2d in the hourly rate thereby putting the extra on the same basis as applying in other sections of the printing trade in Scotland.

In October 1957 two new machine extras were agreed. These were in respect of the R20 Rotaprint and other small offset machines capable of producing a sheet with an area of over 400 square inches and the Dufa and similar proofing presses. The extra payment per week was 15s 0d for operating machines capable of producing an area of over 400 square inches and 12s 6d per week when working on the Dufa and similar machines.

In January 1958 at a conference between the ASLP and the Scottish Alliance the former put forward a claim the basic rate for plate grainers be increased from £8 17s 6d per week to £9 5s 0d. The claim was based on the alleged special skill required of plate grainers and on the recognition of this by the BFMP in agreeing in late 1957 to an increase of 7s 6d per week in the rate for such workers in England and Wales. It was made clear to the ASLP by the Alliance Negotiating Committee that it would resist any attempt to bring wages of ASLP general assistants into line with those of auxiliary workers in membership of the NUPB&PW and the STA. The Scottish Alliance did offer to accept the claim provided it was clearly recognised the increase in the basic rate be subject to absorption where merit money was being paid. In March 1958 formal agreement was reached between the ASLP and the Alliance providing for a new basic rate of £9 5s 0d per week for plate grainers with effect from 17 February 1958.

In 1956, the ASLP approached the Scottish Alliance seeking reclassification of stone and plate preparers to improve their status and enhance their basic weekly wage. In Scotland the rate for stone and plate preparers was settled so that the rate gave parity with the male auxiliary rate and the anomaly in connection with members of the ASLP who did auxiliary work, but not stone and plate preparing, be removed.

Manpower Shortages

Throughout the lifetime of the Scottish Alliance of Master Printers shortages of labour were a cause of concern. Its *Manpower Returns* and the *Registers of Apprentices* kept at head office provided evidence to show the unions that an increase in the supply of skilled labour was essential not only in the interests of the employers but also their own. In 1953, there were negotiations between the BFMP and the ASLP, but although the union admitted a shortage of skilled craftsmen it would not waive its existing quota of apprentices to journeymen. The supply of skilled labour problem was not helped by the failure of some Scottish Alliance member firms to take up their full quota of apprentices and to send relevant information on each apprentice started to the Scottish Alliance head office. In 1954 agreement was reached with SLADE to introduce twenty further bonus apprentices in Great Britain, four of which were allocated to member firms of the Alliance.[4] A conference was held in November 1954, with the STA to discuss the situation arising from that union's refusal to allow daily newspapers in Aberdeen, Edinburgh and Glasgow to train adequate numbers of apprentices to meet their manpower needs.

The agreements the Scottish Alliance concluded in 1956 provided for the introduction of additional apprentices outside the ratio. An additional 110 STA apprentices, (eighty in the composing room and thirty in the machine room) and forty additional NUPB&PW apprentices became available in 1956. The NSES co-operated with the introduction of apprentices outside the normal ratio where the circumstances of individual firms justified such action and adequate training facilities were available. The STA agreement contained provision that a special intake of fifteen composing room apprentices be admitted to the industry during 1957 to offset the loss of skilled labour suffered by the general printing trade due to the drain of skilled journeymen to the daily newspapers. The Scottish Alliance again reminded its member firms of the value of completing the labour force inquiry forms as it provided the Alliance with valuable information with which to argue the case for an increase in the supply of skilled labour to the industry.

The allocation of the forty additional NUPB&PW apprentices caused difficulties and in a number of firms the allocation was carried forward. The ASLP settlement provided for an altered ratio of apprentices to journeymen more appropriate to the needs of the lithographic section of the industry. In addition twenty apprentices outside of the ratio were started throughout Great Britain in each of the years 1957-1961 inclusive. The NSES restated its policy of dealing with any case of a shortage of labour supply by allowing additional apprentices where necessary in the light of the individual circumstances of each printing shop. In 1956, the BFMP and SLADE agreed where it was shown production requirements could not be met with the skilled workforce available, additional apprenticeships could be introduced.

By mid-1957, the labour shortage in the industry was easier than at any time since 1945 although in letterpress a shortage of machine managers was still generally being experienced.[5] On average, the amount of overtime worked in the industry was considerably down especially in Edinburgh and Glasgow. By 1958 the labour shortage was mainly confined to the composing and the letterpress machine room sections. Vacancies for compositors were little changed from 1957 but the position for letterpress managers was easing. Both in Glasgow and Edinburgh there were instances of small letterpress firms closing down or being absorbed but the comparatively few journeymen displaced soon found employment elsewhere. In the Dundee area the closure of a small lithographic department and consequent unemployment for some months of one recently qualified journeyman gave rise to a claim by the ASLP for a redundancy payment. The Scottish Alliance view was compensation for redundancy was, apart from normal notice of termination of employment, outside the ASLP Scottish Alliance by-laws agreement.

1958 also saw the allocation of the fifteen special additional apprentice vacancies which were provided for in the 1956 agreement between the STA and the Alliance. Claims for four additional apprentices in accordance with the May 1956 agreement with the ASLP were submitted to the union in September 1958. It indicated its branches were reluctant to accept the claims, largely because of the difficult employment situation. In January 1959, the Scottish Alliance advised the Scottish District Council in the circumstances it would not press its claims, provided the four places made available under the 1956 agreement were regarded by the council as being available if necessary.

The Scottish Alliance Executive Board report to the 1959 annual general meeting again reminded members of the necessity to take up the full quota of apprentices to which they were entitled. If any firm did not wish to take on apprentices to which it was entitled the Alliance could take steps for the vacancies to be transferred to other firms. The Scottish Alliance had made a special check during the summer of 1958 to ensure that the *Register of Apprentices* were accurate. Unfortunately the check disclosed some member firms had failed to follow the Executive Board's repeated request that information regarding the selection of apprentices be sent to the Scottish Alliance head office. Members were advised that unless their co-operation in this simple but important matter was regular, unnecessary work was created and difficulties with the unions could arise.

The 1960 *Manpower Inquiry* showed the progress of the last few years towards a more balanced labour force had not been maintained, particularly in the composing room where there remained a serious shortage of journeymen. In addition, to make up for the period of the 1959 stoppage, the industry had to deal with an increased volume of work caused by the October 1959 general election and a general increase in demand from that date. Accordingly, from August 1959 substantial amounts of overtime were being worked in all sections of the industry. Allocation of the special block intake of thirty five composing room and twenty machine room apprentices was virtually completed and in many cases apprentices had already started in accordance with this allocation. These additional apprentices had not in themselves filled the gap then existing between the number of staff required and the number actually available in the trade.

In the lithographic section there were, in 1960, difficulties in Glasgow area but it was possible for firms employing ASLP labour to apply for additional apprentices and to seek to upgrade suitable male auxiliary workers to full craft status. This latter possibility was a feature of the 1960 Alliance/ASLP agreement and the Scottish Alliance urged its members to operate upgrading whenever possible.

Summary

Between 1953 and 1958, the SJIC and NJIC functioned in general in a satisfactory manner. In 1957 protracted discussions began over revising the NJIC constitution, particularly the operation of its conciliation procedures in UK-wide disputes. In 1957, a revised conciliation procedure was agreed but did not operate effectively in the 1959 wages and hours dispute. Both sides of the NJIC argued in the light of this experience, the NJIC be subject to a searching review. By March 1960, no agreement had been reached on a reformed NJIC because of differences over its Clause Two objective – 'to secure complete organisation of employers and employees throughout the trade'. The Scottish Alliance wished to remove the Clause whilst the unions wished to retain it.

There were no disputes over mutual working conditions rules between the Scottish Alliance and the STA and the NUPB&PW. A new agreement on machine extras was negotiated with the last named union in February 1960. In mid-1956, the Scottish Alliance made an agreement providing for a special trade work payment to NSES members when employed in Alliance member firms. This was in recognition that in Scotland there existed no employers' association for firms solely engaged in electrotyping and stereotyping work. The by-laws regulating working conditions in the litho sector of the industry were initially negotiated between the Scottish Alliance and the ASLP in November 1925. During the lifetime of the Scottish Alliance of Master Printers there were further amendments to these by-laws covering the introduction of double day shifts and extra payments for bronzing work.

Shortages of skilled labour, particularly compositors, were of great concern to the Scottish Alliance. They managed the situation by persuading the unions to agree a bonus intake of apprentices over and above the normal apprenticeship ratio.

Notes

[1] See Minutes of the Executive Board Meeting 7 July 1960.

[2] See Minutes of the Executive Board Meeting 15 December 1954

[3] The definition of trade work covered the production of electros, stereos, or moulds, produced for, or supplied to other establishments for printing purposes in other than the office in which the electros, stereos or moulds were produced.

[4] See Report by the Executive Board to the Forty Fourth Annual General Meeting, Edinburgh, March 1955.

[5] See Report by the Executive Board to the Forty Seventh Annual General Meeting, Glasgow, March 1958.

Chapter 12

WAGES, HOURS AND WORKING CONDITIONS: UK, 1952 – 1960

This chapter analyses changes in wages and other employment conditions in the printing industry negotiated at the UK level and their implementation in Scotland. It starts by examining P&KTF attempts to persuade the BFMP to agree a transferable industrial pension scheme. The second section considers the impact of the cost-of-living bonus scheme contained in the 1951 collective agreements on pay rates and pay differentials. The next section outlines the negotiations between the print unions and the Scottish Alliance in the general printing industry. The final part of the chapter analyses one of the most traumatic industrial relations events in the history of the UK and the Scottish printing industry, namely the 1959 dispute over the unions' claim for a reduction in the working week and an increase in wages.

The Industrial Pension Scheme

At the end of November 1951, the P&KTF met with the Joint Labour Committee of the BFMP and the Newspaper Society to consider a possible pension scheme for the printing industry as a whole. The issue had been raised by the unions before the Second World War and in 1938 the National Joint Industrial Council had prepared a draft scheme which had to be dropped at the onset of the war[1]. In 1948 the P&KTF set up a subcommittee to investigate and report on 'the desirability of giving early consideration to the formulation of an Industrial Pension Scheme'. There followed early in 1950 informal discussions with the BFMP on the subject.

Further discussion did not take place until November 1951 largely because of the industry's preoccupation with trying to fashion a stable wage structure.

Progress during these informal negotiations was slow but by late 1953 had reached the point where the P&KTF had to decide whether to make a formal claim for the introduction of an industry-wide pension scheme or allow the issue to drop from their bargaining agenda. At a conference between the BFMP and the P&KTF held on 18 November 1953 the latter requested there be agreement in principle as to the desirability of the establishment of a national pension scheme. The P&KTF pointed out in 1953 25% of those employed in the industry were covered by pension schemes in firms and the remaining 75% could be catered for if a suitable scheme could be devised. The P&KTF accepted firms which already offered schemes would be considered as outside the proposals for an industry-wide scheme. It was unlikely they would agree to merge into such a scheme or that those paying better benefits would merge.

The P&KTF proposed *Industrial Pension Scheme* was based on three principles – inclusiveness, uniformity of contributions and benefits, and transferability. Participation in the scheme was to be voluntary for both employers and employees. The former were to provide the national pension scheme but existing private schemes would be excluded. The scheme would cover all employees in the industry whatever their age when entering the scheme. It would cover men, women and older workers, defined as whose age fifty one or over when joining the scheme. The retirement age was to be sixty five for men and sixty for women.

There was to be a flat rate payable into the scheme by the employer and by the employee irrespective of age of entry. The rate of contribution would be the same for all members of the same sex, irrespective of age. Each employer would make a contribution of 3s 0d per week for each of their employees who elected to join the scheme. Employees would pay a variable rate according to age of entry ranging from 1s 6d at age twenty/twenty one up to a maximum of 3s 0d per week payable by all entering at age fifty or over. In short, employees would contribute one half the joint weekly contribution according to their age of entry into the scheme. The pension benefit was to be 9d per week per year of service with a minimum pension of 10s 0d per week applicable to all employees who joined the scheme when over fifty one years of age. Without this provision older workers would receive only small amounts for each year of contribution. The standard pension rate payable per week would be 30s 0d for men and 20s 0d for women.

The P&KTF argued the pension scheme should provide that an employee changing their job take with them their pension rights. Employees in firms already providing pension schemes were to be excluded but could participate in changing their employment to a firm participating in the industry pension scheme. The P&KTF did not want a scheme that tied the employee to any individual employer. If they went to work for another firm within the ambit of the scheme they would take this right with them as though their employment had not changed in any way. An employee who, before reaching retirement age, died or moved to a firm outside the scheme, would have their past contributions to the scheme repaid plus compound interest at 2.5%. The BFMP said it would give later a considered reply to the P&KTF claim later.

In spring 1954, the BFMP gave their reply. They said that after a great deal of thought they had concluded they were opposed to an industrial pension scheme. They were not against the principle of pensions but considered the best way of extending the number of employees covered by a pension scheme was to encourage individual companies to introduce house pension schemes. The BFMP would offer guidance and advice to its member firms on a simple house scheme which could be applied in small offices as well as in medium-sized and larger establishments.

The BFMP main objections to the pension scheme were the principle of transferability and the detrimental effect of a further increase in the industry's cost base. The employers favoured house pension schemes, as they rewarded loyalty and long service amongst employees and reduced labour turnover. Scottish print firms were therefore reluctant to replace their house scheme by a transferable scheme, which was considered unlikely to foster loyalty and long service amongst employees. The matter of cost was important to every printing firm at a time when product market competition was becoming more intense. The cost of providing a transferable industrial pension scheme would fall partly on the employer increasing their production costs. BFMP and Scottish Alliance were naturally reluctant to accept further cost burdens.

The Scottish Alliance attitude towards an industrial pension scheme was decided at its Executive Board Meeting on 17 December 1953.[2] Opposition was based on some member firms already operating pension schemes for their employees and the number of such schemes would increase. Others expressed opposition saying such a scheme should not be considered whilst the unions provided superannuation benefit schemes for their members even though not every union did so and the rates of contributions and benefits paid by union members varied from union to union. Some members of the Executive Board considered the principle of a national pension scheme was sound and would benefit the whole industry. This was evidenced by some member firms providing pensions for long-serving employees even where they operated no specific scheme. Those supporting this view argued the contributions by employers and employees and the benefits envisaged should a national pension scheme be introduced could only be judged under specific conditions.

The Scottish Alliance was informed the P&KTF had now formally laid a claim for the introduction of a national pension scheme arguing the time was now opportune. Alliance members drew attention to the dangers which might result from the introduction of such a scheme, particularly with the present shortage of labour and the relatively large number of craftsmen in the industry over sixty years of age. The view was also expressed by nearly all printing unions and by a number of member firms, that because of the provision of pensions by the state there was no need for a scheme, particularly when any increase in the costs of production might have serious repercussions on the industry. The Scottish Alliance Executive Board did not vote on a national pension scheme but reported the wide-ranging view of its members to the BFMP's Labour Committee.

After considering the BFMP response the P&KTF made a further request the employers accept the principle of establishing a pension scheme with transferable rights for every male and female with union membership in the industry at the age of sixty five for males and sixty for females. A further conference took place at which the P&KTF expressed disappointment at the employers' refusal to accept transferability of pension rights from one firm to another. It did express satisfaction that the employers offered to give advice to member firms regarding the introduction of house pension schemes. The BFMP agreed to give further consideration to the matter but the P&KTF received a reply in mid-March 1955 the view previously taken by the BFMP members that they did not agree in principle to the introduction of an industrial pension scheme had been confirmed. The P&KTF then asked the BFMP to provide details of the extent to which they would assist the unions in their effort to persuade employers to inaugurate house-based pension schemes.

In 1957, the P&KTF set up a subcommittee to review the efforts made over the last few years to achieve a national pension scheme. It decided the BFMP again be approached and a reiteration of the unions' original request for a transferable industrial pension scheme be made. The BFMP and the P&KTF met in October 1957 at the end of which the former said it would consider the P&KTF's case and give them a written reply. In January 1958, the P&KTF received this written reply in which the employers made clear there was no change in their policy and they remained opposed to the introduction of a national pension scheme based on the principle of transferability and it would damage the competitiveness of the industry by increasing production costs. The P&KTF *Industrial Pension Scheme* Subcommittee concluded it was pointless to continue to try and persuade the BFMP and the Scottish Alliance to adopt the type of scheme for which the P&KTF had long been pressing. It recognised to continue to press the employers would only delay the adoption of some provision which, whilst not so broad in its application as the proposed national pension scheme, would benefit a considerable number of workers.[3]

The Cost-of-Living Bonus 1952-1956

The wage agreements implemented in Scotland in 1951 were characterised by an increase in basic wages, additional apprentices, co-operation with measures to promote increase in production, a five-year stabilisation period from November

1950 and a cost-of-living sliding-scale bonus. This bonus provided for each point increase or decrease in the Retail Price Index figure of 114 an increase/decrease by 1s 0d for men and 9d for women. The bonus was adjusted every six months. By November 1955 when the 1951 agreements terminated, the cost-of-living bonus for males over eighteen years of age was 33s 0d per week and for women 24s 9d per week. There had been no increase in basic rates since the implementation of the 1951 agreements. Basic rates had remained unchanged for five years which meant that so had shift, overtime rates and machine extras.

In December 1953, the P&KTF claimed 20s 0d (men) and 15s 0d (women) of the cost-of-living bonus be consolidated into basic rates justified on the grounds that in the 1951 negotiations, employers had hinted if the Retail Price Index rose steeply that overtime rates became unattractive in comparison to day rates, they would review matters. The Scottish Alliance advised the BFMP Labour Committee to have a further meeting with the P&KTF although it believed the claim for consolidation of part of the cost-of-living bonus be rejected. When the Scottish Alliance considered its attitude to the P&KTF claim, it noted the STA supported the claim but overtime rates in Scotland were more attractive to employees than in England. The overtime premium in England was +25% for the first two hours but in Scotland it commenced at +50%. The Scottish Alliance told the BFMP there was little evidence to support the union's contention that overtime was unattractive and therefore the claim for consolidation could not be accepted. In addition, the Alliance pointed out to consolidate part of the cost-of-living bonus would increase the costs of overtime and shift working and the industry's cost base. The P&KTF decided in late 1954 not to continue with its consolidation claim.

Prior to the 1956 wage negotiations (see below), the Scottish Alliance reviewed the operation of the cost-of-living bonus and concluded it had not been as successful as hoped. There had been a sharper rise in the Retail Price Index than anticipated. The 33s 0d flat rate additional weekly payment to basic rates meant the percentage wage differential between craft and non-craft employees narrowed. This disturbance of the wage structure concerned the STA and other craft unions in Scotland. Their chapels pressed for 'unofficial action' to re-establish traditional craft/non-craft differentials. On the employer side, some Alliance member firms addressed the issue by making merit payments to their craft employers but this in reality undermined the regulatory function of the national agreements. There were many on both the union and the employer side who saw the problem lying not with the cost-of-living bonus but with the length of the stabilisation period. Five years had been simply too long.

The 1955/1956 Wage Agreements
In Scotland the five year wage stabilisation agreements with the various unions (see Chapter 9) with the exception of SLADE terminated in November 1955, at which time the craft basic weekly rate was 143s 6d per week with the cost-of-living bonus for journeymen of 33s 0d per week. In June 1955

the Scottish Alliance gave thought to its bargaining objectives for the renewal of the agreements expiring in the following November. At its meeting on 13 June 1955 the Scottish Alliance Negotiating Committee established six major objectives for the forthcoming bargaining rounds with the unions:

(1) any increase in the costs of production be kept to a minimum

(2) an increase in the supply of labour be achieved by changes in the apprenticeship ratio, by a block intake of bonus apprentices, by the upgrading of auxiliary workers, by a reduced apprenticeship period and by the replacement of apprentices called up to National Service after serving five years at the trade

(3) the continued use, and introduction of, incentive payment schemes to increase productivity. There was a desire to alter existing 'mutual rules' to reduce the costs of production, for example, the ending of treble-time payment and permitting composing room apprentices to be trained as Linotype operators after two years of their apprenticeship

(4) active co-operation by the unions to ensure craftsmen were employed only on work suitable for craftsmen

(5) continuation of stabilisation of agreements but for a shorter period than five years and

(6) continuance of a cost-of-living bonus on a sliding scale.

Meanwhile, in March 1955, eleven unions, including the STA, NUPB&PW, ASLP and NSES, met in a conference to seek a common policy for approaching the BFMP and the Scottish Alliance when the existing agreements terminated in November 1955. The unions decided on the following claim:

(1) incorporation of the cost-of-living bonus into basic wages

(2) a wage structure based on:
- London craft rate (£11 1s 6d)
- Provincial craft rate (£10 10s 0d)
- Semi-skilled rate (87% of craft rate)
- General assistants (85% of craft rate)
- Women (75% of male Class III)

(3) one grade for all employees in the provinces

(4) a proposal for a percentage increase on the weekly rate for shift working instead of the hourly rate.

Nine of the unions favoured a cost-of-living bonus, realising this would include a stabilisation period but two unions were against the continuation of a cost-of-living bonus.

In July 1955, a group of six unions (NUPB&PW, TA, NATSOPA, STA, NSES and MCTS) presented a claim to the BFMP for a minimum craft rate of £10 10s 0d outside London, elimination of grading in the provinces and other concessions. The employers indicated were prepared to make a wage offer provided the unions helped overcome the acute shortage of skilled workers and that arrangements be agreed for the more efficient use of available labour. As the manpower shortage was different for each union, the six held separate negotiations with the employers on restrictive working practices and labour intake. A long series of negotiations followed resulting in new agreements concluded in November 1955 by the Scottish Alliance with the STA, NSES and NUPB&PW. These provided for a minimum craft rate of 195s 0d per week, a semi-skilled wage of 167s 0d, a rate for women after training of 114s 9d and of 124s 9d for women with four years experience after training. They covered working conditions, cost-of-living bonus, stabilisation period of three years and a substantial increase in manpower by way of bonus apprenticeships. These agreements were accepted by ballot votes by members of the STA, NUPB&PW and NSES and were to operate from January 1956.

No settlement was reached in the national negotiations between the BFMP and the ASLP despite references to the NJIC. An NJIC conciliation committee suggested the appointment of an advisory panel consisting of representatives from each side of the industry, in addition to the Chair and Vice-Chair of the NJIC. This suggested procedure was accepted by both sides and following further discussions between the ASLP and the BFMP a number of recommendations were made. The ASLP felt they did not form a basis for a settlement and requested a full meeting of the JIC. All those associated with the NJIC felt no useful purpose would be served by calling a full meeting. Subsequently, the ASLP and the Scottish Alliance concluded in November 1955 an agreement similar to that for the STA, NSES and NUPB&PW but in which there was, unlike in the other agreements, provision for increases in machine extras and for some absorption of merit money.

Throughout the wage negotiations following the end of stabilisation in November 1955 the LTS and the Association of the Correctors of the Press (ACP) acted independently of the other print unions. Their request to the London Master Printers' Association (LMPA) was for a new basic rate of £12. When the employers refused to concede this, the LTS and the ACP instructed their members to 'work to rule'. The LMPA discharged the members of the two unions as they considered working to rule was a breach of their employment contracts. The dispute was reported to the Ministry of Labour which on 16 February 1956 set up a Court of Inquiry into the causes and circumstances of disputes between the London Master Printers' Association and the LTS and ACP.

The separate negotiations decided upon by the TA[4] did not lead to a settlement of their wages difficulty and the union-imposed aggressive action, including the banning of overtime, against BFMP member firms. As the difficulty remained unresolved the Ministry of Labour referred the matter to a Court of Inquiry similar to the one to consider the difficulties between the LMPA and the LTS and ACP. During the early stages of the inquiry the BFMP and the TA agreed to resume negotiations under the chairmanship of a conciliation officer of the Ministry of Labour immediately following the publication of the Court of Inquiry report on the London disputes. The TA then lifted sanctions which had been imposed on 18 January 1956 and normal working was resumed on 22 February 1956.

The report of the Court of Inquiry into the London disputes was published in March 1956.[5] It recommended as a basis for agreement the following:

(1) apprentices be admitted in the number suggested by the London Typographical Society

(2) new basic minimum rate of £10 5s 6d incorporated the 33s 0d weekly addition due under the old cost-of-living sliding bonus

(3) new cost-of-living sliding bonus of 1s 0d per point rise over the figure in the Retail Price Index as operating upon the day the parties reach a settlement of the present dispute

(4) any settlement reached be embodied in an agreement operative from its date for a minimum period of three years

(5) a further effort be made to establish comprehensive national machinery on a two-tier basis for the negotiation of wages and conditions in the industry.

The Court of Inquiry report resulted in four unions (LTS, ACP, TA and ASLP) coming together to make an agreement with the BFMP. This was achieved in May 1956 when the four unions accepted a new basic weekly craft rate of £11 in London, of £10 5s 6d in the provincial Grade I towns and £10 in Grade II towns. In all cases, a cash increase of at least 27s 6d a week was paid to every craftsman irrespective of the wage they were currently earning. There was to be a cost-of-living bonus of 1s 0d per point the Retail Price Index was above the present figure of 155. The new agreements stabilised for three years and there were proposals including arrangements for increases in the craft labour force and for the revision of certain machine and other extras. All increases in extras were absorbed against house rates and/or merit money. The agreements operated from 20 April 1956.

A letter was then received by the P&KTF from the BFMP relating to the possible consequences of this settlement to the five unions which had settled in January 1956. The BFMP indicated their intention to achieve uniformity between the two groups of unions on the basis of the Retail Price Index figure of 155 for calculation of the cost-of-living bonus. With regards to the claim from the 'January unions' following the April 1956 settlement the BFMP said its policy was to hear the claims, to consider the arguments and to negotiate any alterations which could be regarded as just and fair. A meeting of the Scottish Alliance Negotiating Committee was held on 24 April 1956 to consider the situation arising from the four union settlement following the report of the Court of Inquiry into the dispute between the LMPA and the LTS and ACP. The Negotiations Committee accepted the craft basic rate in Scotland would require adjustment to come into line with the rate in the English provinces. But, in view of possible complications arising from the Court of Inquiry suggestion that a two-tier wage negotiating machinery be established for the UK, negotiations with the STA and NUPB&PW need not open until after the P&KTF had the opportunity to discuss the situation.

On 24 May 1956, the five January settlement unions which included the STA, met the BFMP and claimed their craft members expected adjustments to bring the rates up to those accepted by the four May settlement unions. For the non-craft members of the five January unions the request was for the percentages agreed upon when the unions' collective wage movement started, namely 87.5% of the craft rate for the semi-skilled workers, 85% for general assistants and 75% of the Class III rate for women. A conference between representatives of the Scottish Alliance and the STA was held on 3 July but on 7 July 1956 the STA announced it would not take part in any further negotiations in London but seek agreement directly with the Scottish Alliance. A conference of the January 1956 unions, other than the STA, was held in London on 11 July as a result of which the NSES accepted the offer of a weekly craft rate of £10 5s 6d outside of London effective from 6 August 1956. A conference with the NUPB&PW was held in London on 18 July but no settlement was reached because of difficulties over non-craft and female rates. Eventually an agreement was reached providing for, outside London, cash increases additional to those granted in January 1956 of 4s 0d a week for craftsmen, 2s 6d a week for semi-skilled male workers and 1s 6d for women. In addition 5s 0d of the present cost-of-living bonus for men and 3s 9d of the present bonus for women was consolidated in the new basic rates and the future cost-of-living bonus would be paid above an index figure of 155.

The STA continued separate negotiations with the Scottish Alliance. After careful consideration the Alliance agreed not to deny the STA the right to negotiate directly with it and it was not in the interests of Scottish Alliance member firms to prolong the negotiations. It accepted the autonomy of Scotland under the BFMP Constitution had now to be exercised. The Scottish Alliance thereby met on 2 August 1956 with the STA to reach agreement. This objective was achieved and the settlement provided for:
(1) a weekly craft rate of £10 5s 6d
(2) a weekly rate for male auxiliaries of £8 14s 6d
(3) a weekly rate for women workers, after completing training, of £6
(4) a weekly rate for women workers with four years experience after training of £6 10s 0d
(5) the extension of the stabilisation period to 20 April 1959 and
(6) cost-of-living adjustments as previously agreed but based on an index figure of 155 instead of 150.

Settlements on the same lines were also made with the Scottish District Councils of the NUPB&PW, ASLP and NSES. An agreement was subsequently reached with SLADE on a similar basis to those with the STA, NSES, NUPB&PW and ASLP, with the new rates of pay and other employment conditions effective from October 1956. Whilst the negative spotters' rate was fixed at the normal craft rate, the majority of SLADE craftsmen received a basic weekly rate of £12 15s 0d. SLADE did not give any firm undertaking on the intake of extra apprentices but merely agreed to consider cases put forward where there was a recognised shortage of craftsmen which SLADE could not satisfy.

The series of wage agreements covering the Scottish printing industry made in 1956 were stabilised until April 1959. This meant no changes in basic rates of pay for three years but there were improvements in pay stemming from the operation of the cost-of-living bonus which was reviewed every six months. By November 1958, the cost-of-living bonus stood at 13s 0d per week for journeymen and of proportionately smaller amounts for female workers and apprentices

The Scottish Alliance was pleased with the outcome of the 1955/56 national agreement negotiations. The agreements with the individual unions demonstrated the less rigid attitude of the unions to increasing the supply of labour to the Scottish printing industry expressed in the 1951 agreements was continuing. Long-established union rules could now be 'bought out' in return for wage improvements.

The 1959 Dispute and Settlement
a. Events Leading up to the Dispute
In September 1958, the Scottish Alliance Negotiating Committee under the chairmanship of W Hope Collins, discussed bargaining strategy to be adopted when the current collective agreements with the unions (except for SLADE) expired in April 1959. The committee was informed the P&KTF had made little progress in developing a two-tier negotiating body, as recommended by the 1956 Court of Inquiry, NATSOPA had given notice to terminate its membership of the P&KTF but the STA was likely in the forthcoming negotiations to work through the P&KTF. The Negotiating Committee agreed the Scottish Alliance representatives on BFMP Labour Committee be authorised to inform the various unions via the P&KTF, they favoured the continuation of the existing agreements until April 1960. If the unions accepted this the Scottish Alliance would agree limited consolidation of the cost-of-living bonus into basic rates. The Negotiating Committee instructed the Alliance Secretary to obtain information from member firms regarding the operation of their sick pay schemes and their continuance in their present form. In addition if the STA claim included changes in existing mutual rules these would be considered when known. If the present national agreements were to continue for a further year or negotiation on basic wages and hours started, no settlement on mutual rules, involving increased costs, should be concluded with the STA.

On 4 October 1958, the STA, NSES, ASLP and NUPB&PW met the Scottish Alliance. The current agreement with SLADE did not terminate until October 1959. The BFMP warned the P&KTF of the inadvisability of entering negotiations during the now difficult trading conditions and suggested the present agreements might be extended for twelve months. This suggestion was not accepted by the unions. At the October1958 meeting of the BFMP's Council the position of the Scottish Alliance in connection with the Joint Labour Committee's approach to the forthcoming negotiations was made clear as follows:[6]

(1) approval was given for a common policy on wages and hours and holidays within the limits set by the Scottish Alliance constitution, the BFMP constitution and the BFMP Council decision of January 1958 on negotiating procedure

(2) the Scottish Alliance would continue to discuss, and where appropriate settle, with the STA and other unions, matters covered by the 'mutual rules'

(3) there would be no lack of resolution by Scottish Alliance member firms in meeting unjustified union pressure from whatever source it came.

In December 1958, the P&KTF (acting on behalf of the unions including the STA) gave notification of claims for increases in wages and for shorter hours. These were formally tabled at a conference in January 1959. The claims, as they related to Scotland, were as follows:

(1) reduction in the normal working week from forty three and a half hours to forty hours

(2) increased basic rates:

a) journeymen – from £10 5s 6d per week to £11 11s 0d per week, ie an increase of £1 5s 6d.

b) male auxiliaries – from £8 14s 6d per week to £10 2s 1d per week, ie an increase of £1 7s 7d per week.

c) women workers after training – from £6 per week to £7 14s 0d per week – an increase of £1 14s 0d.

(3) cost-of-living bonus and stabilisation. The present cost-of-living bonus (13s 0d for men and 9s 9d for women) continue to be paid subject to variations in the index figure. Bonus of 1s 0d per point for men to continue but the bonus of 9d per point for women be increased to 1s 0d per point. Stabilisation period be three years from April 1959.

It was also intimated claims for amendment of the mutual rules would be received from individual unions including the STA, NSES, ASLP and NUPB&PW but not all domestic claims from the last two unions would affect Scotland.

Both the BFMP and the Scottish Alliance considered the P&KTF claims unrealistic given the adverse economic conditions affecting the industry. In February 1959, a detailed reply to the unions' case was given by Ralph Jackson, Chair of the BFMP Joint Labour Committee. He argued the basis of unions' claim was unsound and pointed out the employees in the industry already had higher wage rates and average earnings and shorter hours than found in other comparable industries. Detailed reference was made to competition from printers in other countries where in many cases hours were longer and wages lower than in this country. In such circumstances the BFMP considered the claims were economically impracticable and would, if conceded, endanger the future viability of the industry. Mr Jackson concluded his case by saying:-

> …It is because your claims both in regard to hours and basic wages and other matters, must mean increased costs if they were accepted that I must say quite firmly that we cannot, and do not, accept them…

On 4 March 1959, the unions again endeavoured to produce valid arguments in support of their claims. They argued the downward trends in profits did not give a fair picture and a longer term period of analysis including years prior to 1956 put the matter into perspective. They argued book production had increased in volume and general printing exports had risen steadily over the past five years and exceeded substantially the total imports of printed products. In the course of a fairly long statement the unions said they did not accept the 'excuse' given by employers of adverse change in the economic situation of the industry in the past three years. The unions were confident the basic prosperity of the industry would offer improvements in the standard of living of 'those who create this industry's wealth'. In mid-March the BFMP reiterated the suggestion that the present agreements continue after 20 April 1959, its refusal to accept the unions' claims and the two sides investigate ways by which costs could be reduced and the volume of work increased. The unions expressed strong disappointment at the BFMP's failure to make an 'offer' in response to their claims. Both parties accepted deadlock had been reached. No further meetings had been arranged.

At the annual general meeting of the Scottish Alliance held in Edinburgh on 25 March 1959 W Hope Collins, Chair of the Alliance Negotiating Committee, gave a full report of the developments arising since the unions had given the six months notice to terminate the 1956 agreements. He reported the unions persisted with their claims in full, deadlock had been reached in negotiations with the unions which now intended to ballot their members for industrial action to persuade the BFMP's to make any 'offer' other than continuance of the present agreements. Following Hope Collins' full report and discussion, the Scottish Alliance General Meeting adopted the following policy:

> The present claim by the unions regarding shorter hours, increased basic rates, stabilisation and cost of living bonus, cannot and will not be accepted. There will be no lack of solidarity or resolution by Alliance members in meeting unjustified union pressure from whatever source it may come.

In April 1959, the STA instructed its members to refuse to work emergency overtime, to refuse the introduction of double-day or night shift working and to cease the transfer of men on days off from one office to another to assist production in the general trade. The other print unions issued similar instructions to their Scottish members. The Scottish Alliance informed the unions their proposed actions were contrary to the letter and spirit of their 'mutual agreements'. The industrial sanctions would operate whilst the unions balloted their members, seeking authority to impose on print employers various forms of pressure including strike action. In early May 1959 the nine unions (including the STA, ASLP, NSES and NUPB&PW) announced that by a four to one majority their members had given authority to call various forms of industrial action, including strike action against BFMP and the Scottish Alliance. At the request of the P&KTF a meeting was held with the BFMP but the latter explained there was no change in the view of employers throughout the country the claims could not possibly be granted. The unions were asked to consider the suggestion that in the attempt to break the deadlock the dispute be referred to arbitration thereby avoiding open conflict which could only injure the interests of both employers and employees.[7] The 9 May 1959 Scottish Alliance Circular to members told them:

> …I, unhappily, have to report that the union representatives made it very clear that they will not agree to arbitration at the present time. It was stated that arbitration might have to take place later, probably after further aggressive action had taken place. Union representatives did not make it clear why arbitration is possible only after harm to the industry and the people in it has actually been done, unless there is a mistaken impression amongst the unions that the employers will concede the various claims after they have had to face further 'pressure…'

On 22 May 1959, a further meeting between the BFMP and the nine unions took place. It was a long conference. The unions again pressed for acceptance by the employers of a forty-hour working week and for a wage offer without conditions. Ralph Jackson, on behalf of the BFMP, again emphasised the danger to the industry and to the security of employment of union members, of increases in cost. He told the unions firmly the only sound basis for a settlement was one under which the unions agreed to co-operate fully in ensuring adequate labour supply and in increasing efficiency in the industry. On that basis the BFMP proposed to the nine unions:

(1) a forty-two-and-a-half hour working week on day work, subject to agreement on adjustment in apprentice quotas, reduction in the period of apprenticeship, and of acceptance of adult apprentices. There was no change in weekly hours for night and double-day shifts.

(2) an increase of 2.5% on present basic rates subject to agreement on the introduction of methods for improved efficiency under the broad headings of demarcation problems, productivity techniques, new processes and method study.

(3) the cost-of-living bonus to continue without consolidation and the new agreements be subject to six months notice but not fixed for any specific period of years.

(4) the employers could not consider meeting the domestic claims submitted by the individual unions.

The unions rejected this conditional offer describing it as 'totally inadequate', arguing the industry could afford a greater reduction of hours and a greater increase in wages and the unions could not accept the employers' rejection of their claims.

On 26 May 1959, the Scottish Alliance called an extraordinary general meeting to receive a progress report on the wage and hours negotiations. The meeting was told the current position was:

(1) the unions persisted with their claims for a forty-hour week, a 10% increase in basic rates, a three year stabilisation period with a cost-of-living bonus and domestic claims

(2) the employers had offered a forty-two-and-a-half-hour week on condition the labour supply problem was eased and an increase of 2.5% on basic rates conditional on some action by the unions to ease demarcation problem and to help employers prevent a further increase in costs

(3) the unions had been pressed to settle the current difficulties by arbitration and

(4) the unions had refused the suggestion of arbitration, believing they could achieve their objectives by force.

Following discussion in which criticism was expressed of the BFMP conditional offer the extraordinary general meeting approved unanimously the following resolution:

> The Alliance is gravely concerned regarding the conditional offers made to the unions last year. It appears that these offers, if accepted, would lead to increased costs of production for the Alliance membership as a whole and were, therefore, made contrary to the intentions and instructions of that membership.

> The Alliance reiterates its view that any increase in costs at the present time is against the best interests of all engaged in the industry.

> The Alliance trusts that if the unions refuse the present offers these offers will be withdrawn.

At a meeting held 28 May 1959 involving the BFMP and the P&KTF, the latter stated in their view 'the hours and wages discussions had broken down' and they would proceed 'to take the steps authorised by ballot vote of their members' despite the offers made on wages and hours and the BFMP's request the dispute be referred to arbitration. The only modification of the P&KTF previous position was their suggestion that a reduction in hours and increase in wages be by instalments over two years. The BFMP took the constitutional step of reporting the dispute to the JIC. The constitution of that body required the parties to refer to conciliation or arbitration any dispute which could lead to industrial action. The unions, however, categorically rejected the suggestion of arbitration.

On 3 June 1959, union members in Scotland (and in England and Wales) were instructed to take further industrial action. This included a ban on all overtime working, a policy of non-cooperation in the workplace, a ban on the introduction of new apprentices, a ban on union members leaving one office to take up work in another and withdrawal from incentives schemes. The ban on the introduction or extension of shift working already in force continued. In response, the Alliance advised its members to vary the conditions of employment of their production employees, whether union members or not. This involved giving employees two weeks notice they would be engaged on a day-to-day basis at their present rates of pay because employers could not continue to carry responsibility to pay two weeks wages when the unions were prepared to impose industrial sanctions without notice. In response the unions instructed their members not to accept day-to-day employment and called on them to withdraw their labour. At least 90% of production employees of Alliance member firms received protective notice of change in conditions of employment from their employer.[8] The 10 June 1959 *Circular* from the Scottish Alliance told member firms:

> ...I reported to you in my letter of two days ago that there had been a 'magnificent response' to the call on all members to issue notices of change in conditions of employment to production employees involved in the present dispute. We have now been able to make a detailed analysis of the response. This analysis shows that at yesterday's date, at least 90 per cent of employees concerned had received the notice. The response from all areas and all sections of the Scottish Alliance and the Scottish Newspaper Proprietors' Association membership had been uniformly solid. We wish to thank members for their co-operation in carrying out instructions so promptly and effectively when there was such genuine and widespread regret that the issue of these instructions had proved necessary...

On 12 June 1959, all unions with members in Scotland issued instructions to their members to withdraw their labour immediately after 19 June 1959 in five-day week houses and after 21 June 1959 in five-and-a-half-day houses. The majority of employees in these firms did not report for work on Monday 22 June 1959.

b. The Strike

The Scottish Alliance called an extraordinary general meeting in Edinburgh on 18 June 1959 to give members an opportunity to hear a further report on the wage and hours negotiations. A full report of the position facing the general printing and weekly newspaper industries, not only in Scotland but in England and Wales and in London, was given to the meeting at which over 200 representatives of member firms of the Scottish Alliance were present. The meeting was told all attempts by the employers to find a peaceful solution to the dispute had failed because the unions persisted with their original demands. Given the threatened aggressive action, including strike action, member firms of the BFMP had put their employees on a day-to-day employment basis and this had also been done almost without exception in Scotland. The unions instructed their members to withdraw their labour from 20 June 1959, except in cases where the employer had conceded a forty-hour week and a 10% increase in wage rates. Following discussion the extraordinary general meeting approved unanimously the following resolution:

> In view of the long standing tradition in Scotland of peaceful settlement of disputes, the Scottish Alliance deplores the attempts by unions affiliated to the P&KTF to obtain their demands by means of aggression and calls on all members to continue their united resistance to such aggression.
>
> The Scottish Alliance welcomes and endorses the many efforts being made to end the present national dispute by reference to independent arbitration.

The Scottish Alliance *Circular* to members on 18 June 1958 spelt out the situation. Were the employers, because of the threat or fact of aggression, to make concessions to the unions which the industry as a whole could not afford or were they prepared, in the interests of the future of the industry, to make it plain that the Scottish Alliance would stand united in the difficult days that lie ahead?

Print union members throughout Scotland obeyed, with very few exceptions, the instruction to withdraw their labour from general printing and newspaper firms. There were rumours circulating over the weekend before the strike was due to start firms had 'bought peace' on the unions' term. The Scottish Alliance conducted an investigation of the position and found the few firms which had acceded to the unions' terms employed less than 4% of the total number of employees who normally worked in Alliance member firms. Nearly half of the 4% was accounted for by one firm, Waterlow & Sons, a security printer who could not afford the penalty clause payments for non-delivering on its contracts, especially that for printing the *Radio Times*.[9] In early July Glasgow Corporation 'bought peace' with the unions by agreeing to a forty-hour working week and a 10% increase in basic rates. The impact of the Glasgow Corporation defection was to increase to 5.4% the number of the industry's employees employed by firms which in Scotland had bought peace. The Scottish Alliance had never wanted a strike and it told member firms in a *Circular* dated 24 June 1959:

> ...There has never been any wish by the employers to 'fight it out' and the sincere efforts by the employers' organisations to reach settlement by reasonable means are on record. If the unions wished to avoid a stoppage it need never have happened. It has become very clear, however, that the unions have acted as they have simply because they wrongly believed that their demands will be more readily accepted if force rather than reason is used... we believe that our employees are sincere in the wish for shorter hours and higher wages. The employees should realise that their employers are just as sincere and honest in their point of view.

Some Scottish Alliance member firms during the strike continued production in a limited form and were threatened with various reprisals by the unions. Neither bribes nor threats had been used by the employers to make their employees resign from union membership. The Scottish Alliance supported the view of the Joint Labour Committee of the BFMP that satisfactory safeguards against 'victimisation' of those who worked during the strike be part of any agreed terms for resumption of work.

As the strike continued public concern was being shown at the situation resulting from the unions' action not only against the printing and weekly newspaper industry but against the printing ink manufacture industry and indirectly against the national newspapers. NATSOPA was threatening industrial action against member firms of the Association of Printing Ink Manufacturers who supplied ink to the national newspaper industry. This led to TUC intervention in the dispute and by the Ministry of Labour. The TUC met the ten unions in early July. The BFMP said they would accept any TUC suggestion of a referee provided both sides agreed to accept an independent decision on the final terms of settlement.

A special meeting between a small number of employers and union representatives was held at the Ministry of Labour on 4 July. W Hope Collins was one of the employers' representatives. The meeting was unsuccessful. The one aim of the unions, apart from discussion on 'misunderstandings' about the conditions attached to the last employer offer of a forty-two-and-a-half-hour week and a 2.5% increase in basic rates, was to press strongly their original claim for a forty-hour working week and a basic wage increase of £11 5s 6d for a craftsman in Scotland without including in any agreement methods of meeting the increased costs involved. The union representatives spoke again of spreading the total wage increase and reduction to forty hours over a period but they would do no more than say they were willing to discuss with the employers, after the agreement came into force, ways of improving productivity. After the meeting, Ralph Jackson, Chair of the BFMP and Newspaper Society Joint Labour Committee, announced the employers would agree to the TUC suggestion for an independent referee, who would assist or guide the parties in negotiations, provided it was understood in the event of difficulties the parties would accept their advice on the terms of settlement. The employers also said they would discuss in detail with individual unions or groups of unions suggestions which would lead to increased productivity or to greater efficiency. The BFMP made it clear there be some improved productivity to balance the cost of any improvement in hours and wages.

On 10 July 1959 the unions agreed an independent chairperson be invited to preside at a preliminary meeting of the two sides to guide and advise and to get negotiations resumed. The unions agreed the chair continue as chair of a smaller body should the preliminary talks consider this desirable. On the same day the BFMP told the Ministry of Labour they would accept an independent and neutral chair to advise and guide the negotiations but there must be acceptance from both sides that any negotiations started under an independent chair result in a final settlement and if difficulties arise in the negotiations they be resolved by the chair's decision. On 10 July, the BFMP (including W Hope Collins) and the unions met at the Ministry of Labour under the chairmanship of the Chief Industrial Commissioner. The meeting was an attempt to reach some agreement on the appointment of an independent referee and their duties and power. The meeting lasted nearly eleven hours but terms were agreed for the resumption of negotiations.

Both employers and unions proposed Lord Birkett be appointed independent chairman, an invitation which he accepted. His role was to preside at joint meetings between the parties to assist them towards a solution of that dispute. His terms of reference provided for a complete settlement involving the BFMP and the ten unions and covering the issue of hours, wages, domestic claims, staffing problems and questions of improved efficiency. The terms of reference provided for the submission by the chairman on any points on which no agreement could be reached to members of the unions and to member firms of the employers' organisations as part of the final settlement for acceptance or refusal. Hope Collins and the Scottish Alliance Secretary, Barrie Abbott attended, on behalf of the Alliance, appropriate meetings held under the chairmanship of Lord Birkett, who was a noted British lawyer and judge who had served as the alternative British judge during the Nuremberg Trials after the Second World War. Born in 1883, he had been made a judge of the King's Bench Division in 1941. In 1950, he had become a Lord Justice of Appeal. He returned as a judge in 1957 but in the following year he was given a peerage. He died in 1963.

c. The Final Settlement

On 14 July 1959, the BFMP and P&KTF met with Lord Birkett at the Ministry of Labour for over three hours. On the next day the parties met at the BFMP offices for nearly seven hours. Both sides agreed official reports on the progress of the negotiations would be issued at appropriate stages and no separate reports by individual parties or their representatives would be made. The negotiations took the form of meetings at which all parties in the dispute met together so the principal issues could be bargained. It was subsequently decided six groups, or 'working parties' be formed to discuss in detail methods of increasing productivity and the domestic claims put forward by the unions at the same time as their principal claims. Five out of the six groups met in London but the Scottish Alliance representatives and those of the STA met in Edinburgh. Although their meeting made satisfactory progress, a great deal of time was taken up with assessing from Edinburgh the progress made by the working parties meeting in London.

The BFMP made one more effort to reach a negotiated settlement. Ralph Jackson told the unions although some of the suggestions which had been put forward by them were helpful, many were edged around with conditions and others were not firm proposals. He point out it was essential to have definite acceptance from all the unions of a number of 'basic requirements' details which were handed to the unions. These requirements covered the use of craft skill to maximum effect, shifts, work study, dockets and recording systems and new processes. He said all of them had already been accepted by one or more of the unions, or were generally common practice. Mr Jackson then said in return for acceptance of these basic requirements the BFMP would propose a forty-two-hour working week and a 3.5% increase in basic rates on condition there be no further change in hours and basic rates for three years. The unions, including the STA following a short adjournment, indicated the offer was still unsatisfactory. The Scottish Alliance told its members in a *Circular* dated 23 July 1959:

> It is very difficult to keep all members fully involved in these extraordinarily difficult negotiations under Lord Birkett…

Lord Birkett suggested an increase of 4.5% instead of 3.5% and that a 'judicial inquiry' be held in September 1961 on both hours and wages, if the unions wished to claim further improvements at that time. If no such claims were made it would be assumed wage rates and hours now agreed be effective for a stabilisation period of three years. Any findings of a 'judicial inquiry' would be binding on all parties within the stabilisation period. The BFMP made clear to Lord Birkett and to the unions no settlement could be agreed until its member firms had an opportunity to express views on specific proposed agreements.

At the extraordinary general meeting of the Scottish Alliance held in Edinburgh on 29 July 1959 a full report was given by Hope Collins on the negotiations which had taken place under Lord Birkett's chairmanship. He also outlined the proposals for new agreements between the Scottish Alliance and the four unions (STA, ASLP, NSES and NUPB&PW) and the conditions for a return to work. In the discussion that followed dissatisfaction was expressed with the proposed terms of settlement of the dispute.[10] It was formally moved, and agreed, that in view of all the circumstances the settlement be accepted. The principal terms of settlement accepted by the BFMP, the Scottish Alliance and nine unions, including the STA, ASLP and NUPB&PW were:

(1) there be a normal working week of forty two hours compared with forty three and a half a week which had operated since 1946
(2) there be an increase in basic rates of 4.5% to give a rate of £10 5s 6d to £10 14s 9d per week for journeymen
(3) a cost-of-living bonus to operate on the basis settled in 1956
(4) there be a stabilisation period of three years but in 1961 consideration be given to a reduction of hours and/or an increase in basic rates to operate from September 1961, and that failing a negotiated settlement by 30 June 1961 there be reference to a judicial inquiry whose decision shall be binding on the various parties

(5) there be effective measures in new agreements to provide for 'greater productive efficiency'. These included a flexible block intake of composing and machine apprentices, co-operation on method study and on shift working, and further introduction of incentive schemes where mutually agreed. In the case of the STA incentive schemes were on a group basis.

The NSES did not initially accept these terms due to a clause which permitted the introduction of auxiliary workers into stereo departments to perform only menial tasks.

It was agreed between the BFMP and the ten unions the date of return to work be Thursday 6 August 1959. Hope Collins and Barrie Abbott tried to ensure the date for return to work in Scotland should not be affected by the August Bank Holiday in England and Wales. Not for the first time the special position and interests of Scottish employers and employees were ignored by the UK-wide interest.[11] Agreements between the Scottish Alliance and the STA, NSES, ASLP and NUPB&PW were completed and signed by the end of 1959.

During the 1959 dispute, the Alliance had kept its member firms fully informed of all developments in connection with the unions' claim. It is interesting to note that some forty circular letters were sent to members of the Alliance and the Scottish Newspaper Proprietors' Association during the period April to July 1959 inclusive. Three extraordinary general meetings were held during the dispute and associations held special meetings whenever necessary.

The Scottish Alliance had little doubt if print firms all over Scotland, and throughout the UK, had not taken the stand they did, the unrealistic demands of the unions would have been forced on the industry, with the consequence that the future livelihood of all engaged in the industry might have been put in jeopardy. The Scottish Alliance Executive Board put on record its thanks for the co-operation received from members before, during and after the dispute and its special thanks to the office bearers of local associations.[12]

The print unions had been aggressive in pursuing their claim. They imposed a whole range of industrial sanctions against BFMP and the Scottish Alliance and refused to go to arbitration. They were determined to gain a reduction in hours of work because they believed it would help to sustain employment in the face of the technological developments expected to hit the industry in the 1960s. They genuinely believed the balance of bargaining power lay with them relative to the employers. For the unions there was an acute labour shortage, a high demand for print products, little import penetration and relatively high profitability in the industry. The unions had loyal memberships and the closed shop was the ultimate weapon to keep members in line. The unions were confident they could 'pick off' employers by isolating firms by selected strike action and watch the economic pressures intensify on them as their competitors took over their customers and markets. The unions felt 1959 provided a set of circumstances in which obtaining the forty-hour working week and a significant wage increase was highly probable and if industrial sanctions had to be imposed there was a high probability they would be effective. The six-week strike put strain on the finances of the unions, all of which provided relatively generous strike benefit. Large numbers of their members were involved in the strike so their income stream was lowered. Their members, after six weeks on strike, were feeling financial pressures on their weekly budgets. External pressures, for example from the TUC, to settle the dispute began to mount on the unions.

The 1959 strike had been traumatic for the Scottish Alliance and the print unions. There was a strong feeling the situation should never be allowed to arise again. Many, on both sides, thought in retrospect, the dispute had been a self-inflicted wound since in the final analysis both sides had had to settle their differences round the table under the chairmanship of an independent person. The member firms of the Scottish Alliance were upset by the unions' refusal to use the industry's conciliation machinery or to submit their claim to independent arbitration. The STA, on the other hand, was annoyed by what they regarded as the stubborn and rigid attitude of the employers in the early stages of bargaining. Both the Scottish Alliance and the unions realised now the dispute was over they had to continue to live together and there was little purpose in laying the blame for what had happened.

Summary
Between 1952 and 1958, the Scottish Alliance via its affiliation with the BFMP was involved in formal and informal discussions with the P&KTF over the introduction of an industry-wide pension scheme based on the principles of transferability, inclusiveness and uniformity of contributions and benefits. The BFMP and the Scottish Alliance opposed the introduction of such a scheme arguing it would damage the competitiveness of the industry by increasing its production costs and a number of their member firms operated their own occupational schemes. In light of this opposition, the P&KTF decided, in January 1958, to drop its claim.

The 1951 agreements between the Scottish Alliance and the individual print unions which were to operate for five years, provided for a flat rate cost-of-living bonus to be paid as an addition to basic rates. For five years there were no changes in basic rates. Between 1951 and November 1955 the Retail Price Index rose faster than anticipated. The cost-of-living bonus by November 1955 had reached for an adult man 34s 0d per week. This bonus disturbed the percentage differential between craft and non craft employees resulting in dissatisfaction and frustration amongst craft employees.

In July 1955, six unions (including STA, NSES and NUPB&PW) presented a claim for a minimum craft rate of £10 10s 0d and the abolition of the 'Wage Grading' system. A long and protracted set of negotiations followed resulting in agreements between the Scottish Alliance and the STA and the Scottish District Councils of NSES and NUPB&PW. These provided for a basic craft rate of £9 7s

---

6d, a cost-of-living bonus, stabilisation for three years and a substantial increase in manpower by means of bonus apprenticeships. These agreements became operative in January 1956. The London print unions (LTS and ACP) and the TA acted independently of the other unions and became involved in industrial disputes with the BFMP and the London Master Printers Association. The London dispute became the subject of a Court of Inquiry which reported in March 1956 and recommended, inter alia, the continuation of a cost-of-living bonus, increase in the number of apprentices admitted to the industry and a basic weekly craft rate of £11 in London and £10 5s 6d outside London. Following the Court's report, the LTS, ACP, TA and ASLP made agreements, operative from May 1956, with the BFMP and the LMPA providing for these proposed basic weekly craft rates, for a cost-of-living bonus, a three-year stabilisation period and arrangements for increases in the supply of skilled labour. The print employers moved quickly to achieve uniformity of pay rates for the two groups of unions. In August 1956, the Scottish Alliance made an agreement with the STA providing for a craft rate of £10 5s 6d per week followed quickly by similar agreements with the NSES, ASLP and NUPB&PW.

In January 1959, the P&KTF acting on behalf of the print unions put forward a claim for a working week of forty hours, a 5% increase in pay, a cost-of-living bonus and stabilisation for three years. The BFMP and the Scottish Alliance rejected the claim describing it as 'unrealistic' given the adverse economic conditions affecting the industry. In April 1959, the STA and the other print unions in Scotland refused to work emergency overtime working or to accept the introduction of double-day or night shifts. In May, the unions received the approval of their members to impose a series of industrial sanctions, including strike action. The Scottish Alliance, along with the BFMP, pressed for the unions to agree the differences be settled by independent arbitration. In an attempt to resolve the dispute, the print employers offered a forty-two-and-a-half-hour working week subject to increases in the labour supply to the industry, a 2½% pay increase conditional on accepting methods to improve efficiency and a cost-of-living bonus. This was rejected by the P&KTF-affiliated unions.

In June 1959, the unions imposed industrial sanctions on Scottish Alliance member firms, and on 19 June, called their members out on strike. The member firms of the Scottish Alliance maintained solidarity during the strike and few firms acceded to the unions' terms. On 10 July, negotiations were resumed under the independent chairmanship of Lord Birkett whose role was to assist the parties towards a solution to the dispute. This led to a settlement of the dispute and on 6 August 1959, work was resumed in the Scottish printing industry. It provided for a working week of forty two hours, a wage increase of 4.5%, a cost-of-living bonus, a stabilisation period of three years and the introduction of effective measures to provide for greater production efficiency. In addition, separate agreements were negotiated with the STA, NSES, ASLP and NUPB&PW to increase the supply of labour to member firms of the Scottish Alliance.

Notes

[1] See Annual Report 1952 and Report of Administrative Council, May 1953 Printing and Kindred Trades Federation.

[2] See Minutes of the meeting of the Executive Board, 17 December 1953.

[3] See Annual Report 1957 and Report of the Administrative Council, May 1958, Printing and Kindred Trades Federation.

[4] During the final stages of the negotiations, the TA decided not to remain in the six union movement but to bargain unilaterally with the BFMP and the Newspaper Society.

[5] See Report of a Court of Inquiry into the causes and circumstances of disputes between the London Master Printers' Association and the London Typographical Society and the Association of the Correctors of the Press, Cmd 9717, HMSO, London, March 1956.

[6] See Report by the Scottish Alliance Executive Board to the Forty Eighth Annual General Meeting, Edinburgh, March 1959 and see Minutes of the meeting of the Executive Board, 8 October 1958.

[7] See 'Wage etc Negotiations', Scottish Alliance of Master Printers, *Circular Letter*, 9 May, 1959.

[8] See 'Wage etc Negotiations', Scottish Alliance of Master Printers, *Circular Letter,* 10 June 1959.

[9] See 'Wage etc Negotiations', Scottish Alliance of Master Printers, *Circular Letter,* 22 June 1959. The same press release stated that in England and Wales the firms that had brought peace on the unions' terms accounted for only 5% of total employment in BFMP member firms.

[10] See Minutes of the Extraordinary General Meeting held in Edinburgh on 29 July 1959.

[11] See 'Wages etc Negotiations, Return to Work', Scottish Alliance of Master Printers, *Circular Letter,* 1 August 1959.

[12] See Report by the Scottish Alliance Executive Board to the Forty Ninth Annual General Meeting, Glasgow, April 1960.

Part 3

THE SOCIETY OF MASTER
PRINTERS OF SCOTLAND,
1960-1990

Chapter 13

THE GROWTH AND DEVELOPMENT OF THE SOCIETY OF MASTER PRINTERS OF SCOTLAND: THE EXTERNAL ENVIRONMENT

This chapter examines the external environment in which the SMPS operated during its lifetime (1960-1990). The first section outlines the changes in production technology with emphasis on the rise of photocomposition, computerised origination, offset litho and automation in the finishing and binding sectors. The second part examines the further growth of the alternative printing industry based on in-plant printing in non-print companies, import penetration and a communications industry based on electronic devices. The chapter then outlines the economic environment of the Scottish printing industry, 1960-1990. The period 1960 to 1979 witnessed the UK government's attempt to achieve price stability and a balance of payment surplus by direct interference in company price-setting and the outcome of collective bargaining by productivity, prices and incomes policies. The government's macroeconomic policy priority from 1979-1990 was the control of inflation via interest rate changes, incentives to increase productivity by, inter alia, privatisation, and 'liberalising' of the labour market to reduce trade union market power. The final section explains why over the lifetime of the SMPS the number of unions in the industry was reduced from five (STA, ASLP, NSES, SLADE and NUPB&PW) to two (NGA and SOGAT).

Technological Developments

For almost 400 years, production technology in the Scottish printing industry remained unchanged. In the composing room, hand composition was virtually unchanged since its introduction in 1508. In the machine room the major technological development since 1508 was the replacement of hand-powered wooden presses by mechanical (power-driven) iron built printing presses. The first major technological revolution in the Scottish printing industry came at the turn of the twentieth century when mechanical composition (Linotype and Monotype) replaced hand composition. Letterpress printing remained the dominant process over lithography and photogravure.

Within sixty years of the advent of mechanical composition, the Scottish printing industry experienced another major revolution in production technology. The period 1960 to 1990 saw the pace of change in the technology of production accelerate[1] with the expansion of lithography at the expense of letterpress. The 1960s and 1970s printing production technology revolution was based on the introduction of photocomposition in the origination area and offset litho in the machine room. Photocomposition involved the use of film unlike the hot metal associated with letterpress.

The 1980s witnessed a further production technology revolution in the Scottish printing industry based on computer techniques. Computerised typesetting was introduced into the industry on a commercial basis along with electronic colour scanning by which the separation and correction of colours in preparing plates for colour printing could now be done electronically rather than photomechanically. In the machine room, computerisation meant more productive multi-unit machines. In the bindery and finishing areas computer techniques led towards automation. Printing methods based on the computer obscured the boundaries between printing and other industries in that they enabled print origination work to be done outside the industry.

These technological revolutions initially impacted on larger firms in the industry employing 100 or more production workers. Over time they spread to smaller firms. The novelty of these technological revolutions was the rapidity with which they occurred and their impact on the industry's labour force in relation both to skills and the quantity of staffing required. For example by 1970, a unit known as the Photon 901 produced film-set type at a rate equivalent to the output of 200 Linotype operators.

a. The Origination Area

By the early 1960s, photocomposition was starting to be used in the industry. In the 1970s the number of photocomposing installations grew along with the degree of sophistication of the equipment. Before photocomposition the origination process for the production of a page for a magazine involved five steps. First the main body of text of the article was set in hot metal type by Linotype or Monotype. Second the pictures or illustrations were drawn by artists or originated photographically. Thirdly the main headings were set in hot metal or possibly drawn by an artist.

The fourth step was the insertion of subheadings. The final step was the insertion of the dropped capital which might be specified for the opening letter of the text.

Two systems that 'revolutionised' this process were Letraset and the Typositor machine. Letraset was introduced in the 1960s. It was a type image produced in the form of a paper transfer which could be stripped in as individual letters to form words for producing headings, subheadings and dropped capitals. The process was simple and avoided the need to set the copy in hot metal and produce a print for reproduction and subsequent assembly. The Typositor produced strips of letters photographically. These were black or white and ready for assembly and platemaking without any involvement of the composing room.

The 1970s saw the introduction into the industry of computer typesetting. In this the text was set on a tape or disc by the operation of 'qwerty' keyboard on which the keys were arranged differently to a Linotype or teletypesetter machine. The tape or disc was then fed through a computer which output a 'process-control tape', which in turn produced type by hot metal casting or by photocomposition. In producing the 'process-control tape' the computer made decisions normally made by a compositor, for example spacing, justification (the production of lines of type of a uniform length) and the make up of pages. Computerised typesetting was particularly useful for the production of classified publications such as directories and timetables. In the 1970s and 1980s as computer technology advanced, so did improvements in computer-based composition machinery. Visual display units (VDUs) were introduced which allowed operators to see what they had keyed and enabled alterations and corrections to the words/images. A VDU was essentially a typewriter with a television screen instead of paper and could be operated by anyone with a little training.

Different methods of producing printing plates developed in conjunction with the expansion of photographic and computerised origination systems. In the traditional rotary letterpress process type and plates were converted into curved stereos for locking onto the presses by firstly taking an impression of the page with a papier maché flong on a moulding press. The flong was then placed in a stereo casting machine and molten type-metal injected to cast the plate. With the introduction of web offset and photopolymer plates in the 1960s, stereotyping began to decline. Photopolymer plates such as Nyloprint were made by directing light through a negative onto a precoated photosensitive aluminium, steel or polyester plate. The polymer exposed to the light hardened and the remainder was washed off with water or a solvent to leave a relief printing surface. These plates were a fraction of the weight of traditional stereo plates. The 1970s saw the introduction of lasers in platemaking. These systems offered significant advantages through the absence of need for photosensitive emulsions.

The composing room escaped the effects of the implementation of technological change in 1950s and 1960s but in the 1970s, it was adversely affected.

The radical changes in production techniques introduced in the 1970s and the 1980s removed the skills needed to perform traditional composing work. Computer-based origination meant work could be done outside the industry in art and advertising studios or in publishing houses etc and performed competently by lesser-skilled employees who were either non-unionists or members of non-print unions. That origination work could then be sent to a printing firm for printing. The composing room had been bypassed.

There were a number of sources from which origination work could be done outside the printing industry and then returned to the industry for printing.[2] Computers allowed copy which would normally have gone to the composing room to be put on a magnetic tape or disc and transmitted straight to the composing machine, bypassing the Intertype or Monotype operator. Magnetic tapes were particularly attractive to producers of directories and indexes since they enabled updating to take place more easily and this led publishers, authors and automatic data processing (ADP) companies to produce their own material. Another source of origination work from outside the industry was microfilm. The ADP industry used film for record purposes but microfilm and microfiche could be put to other uses which impinged on work normally undertaken by the printing industry. By the mid-1970s it was common for parts of catalogues, price lists, library lists etc to be produced on microfilm. The boundaries between data processing and printing became increasingly blurred. In the late 1970s the word processor became another route whereby origination work could be produced outside a printing office. By linking a typewriter through a minicomputer and a visual display unit, a composition system was produced. Word processors used by authors and publishers became a threat to the book printing industry.

By the 1980s much work was printed by litho which allowed the complete image of the job to be prepared exactly as required before reproduction began. Preparation of copy could be done before work reached the printing plant from either 'original' copy or from film. Modern photographic techniques were now available to studios within publishing companies, advertising agencies and independent businesses. Whereas studios were once concerned solely with the creation of original design and illustration work they now prepared and assembled copy and corrected work to its final form bypassing the processes traditionally undertaken in a printing shop. Computer-based print origination techniques gave more power to the publisher than the printer.

b. The Machine Room
In the late 1960s to early 1970s, some Scottish printing firms gave preference to offset litho when buying new machinery. Web offset and sheet-fed litho machines were installed to do work previously done on letterpress machines and undertake some work which was carried out by photogravure.

Technical developments in litho made it more economical than letterpress for many kinds of work, but especially colour work of medium to long runs due to its higher production speed and lower downtime. Litho had great attractions to magazine and periodical publishers as it produced very good quality colour work economically. Litho had been traditionally carried out on sheet-fed rotaries as it was not thought practical to use web-fed machines (ie those fed by a continuous reel or web of paper). Web offset machines comprised a number of units, each capable of printing one colour on one side of the paper, or of perfecting units which comprised pairs of units printing on both sides of the paper.

Web offset presses were mechanically similar to web-fed letterpress and photogravure machines. They required those operating the presses to maintain the correct tension and register of the paper web and to monitor the reel stands, electronic controls and folders. Web offset presses incorporated the technology of sheet-fed litho presses which required the machine operator to deal with problems associated with the process such as the maintenance of correct damping and ink balance. In Scotland web-fed letterpress and photogravure presses were normally operated by craftsmen who were members of the STA assisted by members of the NUPB&PW (later SOGAT). Sheet-fed lithographic presses were usually operated by ASLP (later NGA) members also assisted by members of the NUPB&PW. Web-offset presses required the pooling of two kinds of experience. Those transferred to them who had been working on sheet-fed litho presses had to learn web-fed techniques whilst those whose experience was on letterpress had to learn the techniques of lithography. Although members of the NUPB&PW worked as assistants on both letterpress and lithographic machines it was unusual for individual members of that union to have experience of both.

Throughout the 1970s and 1980s, letterpress printing declined. Offset and gravure continued to grow through the advantages derived from improved reproduction methods and the ability to print on lower quality materials. Offset litho maintained a dominant position because of its flexibility and the growth of miniwebs which were often substituted for larger sheet-fed presses. The main trend in machine room production technology in the late 1970s and in the 1980s was automation, aimed at reducing the ratio of make-ready to run time and the introduction of multi-unit presses of five and six or more colours running at increasingly faster speeds. Automation on the printing press fell into two principal areas – automation of job change and set up procedures and automation of monitoring, including 'on the run' procedures. By the end of the 1980s, medium and large presses, particularly web installations, had preprogrammed fully automated routines for set up and job change. Prestored job data could be fed in for automatic press setting. Presses were equipped with data capture devices linked to production monitoring systems providing closed loops for production control, stock control and checks on production costs. By 1990 Scottish printing employers recognised the implementation of technological change in the press room had removed the need for semi-skilled labour. Employers required a team of skilled employees who could handle any job on the press and those ancillary to it.

c. Binding and Finishing

The binding and finishing area was the most labour intensive section of the industry. It was serviced by a wide variety of suppliers and had not been subjected to concentrated inputs of high technology compared with the origination and press rooms. Prior to the 1970s there was little technological development but during the period 1970 to 1990 the warehouse and finishing departments witnessed many changes. Guillotines were upgraded to computer control. Bookbinding departments, which previously had been predominantly hand work gradually became integrated into general finishing departments. The art and craft of bookbinding slowly diminished and mechanical collating and binding became the norm. Work previously done by pen or disc ruling machines became printed by lithography. Bookbinding sewing machine speeds increased over the thirty year period (1960-1990) by four to five times.

A major bookbinding innovation during the lifetime of the SMPS was perfect binding as an alternative to sewn binding. This involved grinding off the back folds of a collated book to expose the edges of the individual pages. Glue was then applied to the spine to hold the pages together. A second application of glue secured the cover to the book. It was then three-side trimmed on an automated three knife trimmer. This created a clean book with a flat spine. Perfect binding grew significantly as the popularity of paperback books, which were much cheaper than case-bound (hardback) books, grew.

Throughout the 1970s and 1980s, there were increasing pressures to lower costs in binding and finishing. There was a significant growth in the use of inline systems in finishing departments together with the application of programmable control for setting up and operating equipment, particularly in areas such as automatic inserting and automatic packing and addressing. Automation led over the period 1970 to 1990 to a reduction in the number of separate binding operations and to more in-line working. The late 1980s also witnessed the use of new technology such as inkjet printing, to labelling.

d. Inter-Union Problems

The printing technological 'revolutions' blurred the clear, and relatively unchallenged, demarcation between jobs within and between the main printing processes. They presented a challenge to inter-craft and craft/non-craft jobs in the composing, process, foundry and printing departments. The introduction of web-offset and developments in photocomposition and offset printing disturbed the previously clear demarcation between the letterpress and lithographic craft unions. In Scotland this caused in the 1970s and 1980s demarcation disputes between the National Graphical Association[3] and the Scottish Graphical Association, subsequently the Scottish Graphical Division of SOGAT,[4] over whose members should undertake the duties of machine minding when purely letterpress houses switched to the litho process.

The STA (later SGA) staffed letterpress houses in Scotland whilst litho houses were staffed by the ASLP and then on its merger with the NGA, by that union. The NGA claimed to be the litho union in Scotland and as litho machines entered letterpress houses staffed by the SGA, the union claimed the right to staff these. In the early 1970s the two unions challenged each other's claims to operate litho machines introduced into letterpress houses in Scotland. Attempts to reach an agreement failed. Matters were not improved when the NGA pronounced that if the SGA was not prepared to accept the traditional demarcation lines, neither would the NGA and it intended to recruit in Scotland amongst compositors and machine managers. The NGA suggested the issue be resolved by a merger of the two unions but in February 1974 the SGA rejected this option as it was in merger negotiations with SOGAT.

The SMPS Executive Board regretted the two unions were incapable of reaching a solution which would protect not only their members' interests but also those of employers. It made the strongest representation to both unions and predicted if accommodation was not quickly reached the competitive position of the Scottish printing industry would be prejudiced.[5] By one means or another the more acute individual house situations arising from NGA/SGA conflict were settled without interruption of production but without a permanent settlement to the inter-union 'battles', the industry would suffer long term damage. In January 1973 the NGA/SGA difficulties became more acute when the SGA withdrew all its members from the employment of Waddies, an Edinburgh company because, it claimed, certain of its members threatened with redundancy had not been permitted to operate litho machines. The strike lasted three weeks during which the SGA Executive Council threatened industrial action against the whole SMPS membership. Renewed efforts to get the two unions to come together failed and the Executive Board issued the following statement:

> …The SMPS recognises the involvement of both the National Graphical Association and the Scottish Typographical Association in the operation of lithographic equipment in Scotland. Practice is clear in houses where either the STA or the NGA is the sole union
>
> In other houses where there are conflicting claims as to rights to man lithographic equipment the claims shall be reported to the Secretary of the Scottish TUC for adjudication…

Heidelberg platen press

The proposed Scotland-wide action threatened by the SGA was withdrawn whilst the NGA instructed its members not to take any action which could make a solution more difficult. The General Secretary of the STUC confirmed his willingness to assist in the way indicated in the statement.

The NGA/SGA demarcation issue continued. Two cases were referred to the STUC which ruled the operation of litho machines in Scotland go to the SGA. There was an acute position in a member company in Hawick where there was a threat of withdrawal of SGA labour. It proved possible to avoid interruption of production. In October 1973 the SMPS held a meeting of member firms with both SGA and NGA employees to give those members the opportunity to explain and discuss the problems which they were facing on account of SGA/NGA demarcation issues. An invitation to attend the meeting was sent to forty two mixed houses but only ten sent representatives.[6] At the meeting a full report was given of the action taken by the Executive Board since the January 1973 Edinburgh dispute. The NGA had suggested the SMPS support more tripartite discussions. The Society was prepared to do this but the NGA requested their representatives make in the first instance, a direct approach to the SGA. The SMPS agreed this action even though its members were saying investment decisions were adversely affected by the SGA/NGA demarcation problems. Matters were contained after the NGA approached the SGA with an amalgamation proposal. Although no new areas of difficulty had emerged since the 'mixed' members' meeting of 17 October 1973 no progress had been made towards a solution of the NGA/SGA demarcation problems.

The problems continued though not to the point of disruption. In August 1974 a problem arose at a Glasgow member firm creating a potentially difficult situation. On the initiative of the Chair of the SMPS Negotiating Committee, T R Ballard, a meeting took place in August 1974 with the General Secretaries of the two unions at SMPS headquarters and a tentative agreement between the two unions was reached which assured for one year there would be no further problems. This interim agreement was based on a joint committee dealing with litho installations in Scotland and which had maximum flexibility to deal with any SGA/NGA conflicts that might arise. The committee operated within three guidelines:

(1) both unions adhere to the TUC *Disputes Principles and Procedures* with regards to the transfer of members
(2) SGA members currently operating litho machines, and, those required to operate them in the future, be given the opportunity to become NGA members
(3) the NGA will bring pressure to bear with respect to NGA membership of SGA members operating litho machines in solely letterpress houses or those required to operate them in the future who declined to join the NGA.

Although the interim agreement was to last for twelve months it could be terminated earlier by agreement between the two unions. It proved impossible to gain mutual acceptance of the interim agreement and in the months prior to its amalgamation in 1975 with SOGAT the SGA declined to acknowledge, let alone reply, to NGA correspondence.

Differences between the NGA and the Scottish Graphical Division (SGD) of SOGAT over the staffing of litho machines became even more acute. The NGA continued to reserve the right to recruit in Scotland all those categories of workers for whom it catered elsewhere in the UK unless the SGD agreed to recognise its traditional rights in the litho field. The SGD continued to argue the principle of the custom of the house prevail. In the spring of 1976 the NGA and the SGD reached agreement on union membership in the lithographic field. This agreement, which became known as the *Perth Agreement*, provided the traditional jurisdictional areas of the NGA in Scotland were recognised and accepted by SOGAT (SGD). Where existing letterpress houses changed to litho printing, members of the SGD affected were to remain in membership of SOGAT but that union would pay a licence fee of 15p in respect of such members. If SGD members covered by the licence fee went to a traditional litho establishment the NGA was the appropriate union. SOGAT accepted their members must, in such circumstances, transfer to the NGA. SOGAT agreed not to intrude into the litho agreement held between the SMPS and the NGA. Under the *Perth Agreement* any matters arising, in the future, concerning its operation were to be referred to the headquarters of both unions. Agreement at long last between the SGD and the NGA regarding letterpress/litho transfer had been reached.

The *Perth Agreement* operated satisfactorily until 1982 when two strikes resulted in appreciable lost working time. In both cases they resulted from, and had their roots in, the failure of the SGD and the NGA to reach mutual understanding on the staffing of litho equipment. One of the two disputes affected Holmes McDougall and was a costly and lengthy strike. It concerned the union membership of four members of the SGD who had been transferred, together with four litho machines, from the York Street, Glasgow plant of Holmes McDougall to the Clydeholm Road, Glasgow plant of the company. The NGA claimed the individuals become their members. SOGAT argued they remain in membership of SOGAT, but other wider issues were also involved in the dispute. In October 1982 a TUC dispute committee awarded the NGA was the appropriate union for workers employed on litho operation at the Clydeholm Road plant of Holmes McDougall. SOGAT was instructed to facilitate the transfer of membership into the NGA of the four workers who, together with the four litho machines, came from York Street to the Clydeholm Road plant.[7] Even after this finding a quick resumption of work did not happen until both unions said they accepted the TUC's ruling which effectively gave its support to the *Perth Agreement*.

e. Photocomposition

Many SMPS member firms began introducing phototypesetting equipment. The consequential house agreements, although made on an ad hoc basis, did in general operate in a satisfactory manner. The need for an industry-wide photocomposition agreement on fair and reasonable terms remained. The first formal proposal for a SMPS/SGD *Photocomposing Agreement* was made in 1974. Up to August 1978 there were references in SMPS annual reports, at meetings of its negotiating committee, at meetings of the Executive Board, at all local association and annual general meetings to lack of progress, in this field. At no stage had it been suggested by SMPS member firms that the proposed agreement with the SGD was unnecessary. No commitment had been made with the SGD regarding an industry wide photocomposition agreement although many house agreements had been made, some with SMPS authority, but some by members acting independently. By 1980 no industry-wide photocomposition agreement had been entered into to regulate both staffing and machine extras.

In February 1986 the SMPS and SGB reached an *Accord* on the introduction of advanced technology. The *Accord*, announced at the 'Scottish Printing Exhibition' was a joint statement committing both parties to the adoption of advanced technology in the long-term interests of customers, employees and companies. To encourage individual companies and their employees to meet the challenge of advanced technology both SMPS and SGB specified six major topics for bargaining. They were:
(1) the clear definition of the technology involved
(2) future employment implications
(3) job flexibility and redeployment

---

(4) education and training requirements

(5) rewards and benefits from the agreement and

(6) time schedule for implementation.

The *Accord* provided for a joint training initiative to give SGB members and the industry's managers a greater appreciation of the benefits of implementation of sophisticated technical developments. The *Accord*, the first between a printing union and a major employers' organisation, was expected to benefit the marketing of the Scottish commercial printing industry. Although this *Accord* on advanced technology between the SMPS and the SGB was not in itself an agreement guaranteeing the implementation of new technology, it did remove the uncertainty for SMPS member firms wishing to introduce changes in their production technology. A *Guide for Negotiators* was prepared to assist bargainers arrive at sensible practical agreements.

f. Origination Work From Outside the Industry

The advent of the computer into the Scottish printing industry enabled work originally performed in the pre-press area to be undertaken by staff employed, for example in art and advertising agency studios, and in publishing houses. In the mid-1970s the NGA and SLADE refused to handle work coming into a printing house from so-called 'unrecognised sources of work'. Initially the position in the Scottish printing industry was uncertain and the number of cases of real difficulty arising in Scotland was small. In 1977 the SMPS Executive Board was informed of a number of cases of interference with print work stemming from the NGA/SLADE action but in most cases suitable action by employers prevented continued difficulties. Many members of the Executive Board, however, emphasised that the current situation was far from satisfactory.

Whilst the impact of the action taken by the NGA and SLADE not to handle work from unrecognised sources was less serious than at one time feared, there remained substantial areas of difficulty. The SMPS was concerned by the impact of SLADE's organising activities in advertising agencies and design studios. In June 1977 its Executive Board agreed action be taken to ensure close co-operation with other employers' organisations, for example, the Institute of Practitioners in Advertising, on the matter. It agreed since a period of grace had been allowed by SLADE in England and Wales a similar period be permitted in Scotland. The Board advised all SMPS member firms employing SLADE members to pay the wage rate currently operating in the collective agreement between the SMPS and SLADE.

Growth of Alternative Products to the Printing Industry

In the 1960s, 1970s and 1980s the Scottish printing industry experienced greater product market competition from three sources. First the continued expansion of in-plant printing, second increased import penetration and third the rise of competitive outlets for advertising instead of solely newspapers and magazines. The first two were a major threat to the general printing industry. When the simplifications of pre-press techniques were taken into account with the wider availability of litho printing, reasons for an expansion of in-plant printing were not hard to find. In-plant printing in local government, nationalised industries, the civil service and the private financial sector had long been a problem for SMPS member firms. The 1970s saw the spread of in-plant printing into food processing and engineering companies as well as more building societies, banks and other financial companies. This spread of in-plant printing increasingly involved the installation of full-size presses. By the late 1970s engineering companies were not only producing copy for technical booklets and pamphlets but were typesetting and assembling pages. A further market challenge to the industry in the 1970s and 1980s was the development of 'instant print' shops in town centres. They took work away from the traditional printing industry by offering customers a speedy and convenient print service.

The period 1960 to 1990 saw a sharp increase in the amount of imported print work into Scotland from outside the UK. Although throughout the period the value of exports by the Scottish printing industry exceeded imports, its trade balance deteriorated. The share of imports in the Scottish printing market increased over the period from 5% in 1960 to 9% in 1990. The book printing sector was particularly affected by the loss of work abroad. By the late 1970s many books, particularly children's books, were being typeset and printed in Hong Kong, Spain, the Canary Islands and Czechoslovakia. In Scotland there was a further loss of book work from the increasing concentration of book printing in southern England. Until the late 1950s Scotland had been the leading UK centre for book printing but by the mid-1980s the specialist capabilities of the Scottish industry were much wider. Throughout the 1970s an increasing volume of mail order catalogues, cardboard cartons and travel brochures printing was transferred from Scottish firms for printing overseas.

There were many reasons for the expansion of imported print matter but amongst the more significant were technological change, higher inflation in the UK relative to other countries in the 1970s, the strong value, in the early 1980s, of the pound on foreign exchanges and the high interest rate policy adopted by the incoming Conservative government in 1979. To re-establish competitiveness, publishers turned to low cost non-traditional methods of origination. The increasing use of word processors and of author-generated copy meant an increasing amount of origination work for books was produced as camera-ready copy. The SMPS argued whilst this work was subject to a union ban on handling work from alleged unrecognised sources it was increasingly likely more work would be sent overseas. Cold composition techniques also meant it was easy to have a book typeset in one country and printed and bound in another. An increasing number of companies were importing origination from South East Asia and India, having established their own typesetting and origination departments in those parts of the world.

The 1970s and early 1980s saw further market challenges to the Scottish general printing industry. Non-paper modes of communications developed giving rise to a communications industry based on electronic devices – teletext, Prestel Ceefax, video cassettes, video discs and cable television. This new communications world brought increasing competition to the general print industry. It was not something SMPS member firms could ignore. The expansion of electronic-based communications industries turned out not to have the adverse effect on the paper-based communications industry expected. The communications industry as a whole expanded rapidly and although the printing-based share of the total communications market fell, in absolute terms it continued to expand. Many electronic communications devices and printing communications techniques turned out to be complementary, rather than substitutes, to the printed word.

The Economic Environment
a. Incomes Policy 1960-1970

From 1960 to 1979, UK governments managed the economy in accordance with the views of the economist John Maynard Keynes. He argued unemployment in the inter-war years resulted from a lack of spending power on the part of individuals and of companies. He advocated the government should intervene into the economy by increasing its own expenditure thereby creating employment. The confidence of individuals and companies would increase and they would start spending again. At this stage, the government would withdraw its intervention and balance its income and expenditure. A consequence of increasing spending power in the economy was the demand for goods and services could outstrip their supply, causing inflation and a loss of competitiveness in product markets. The Keynesian policy solution to inflation was the direct interference by the central government into company price-setting (price restraint) and into the outcome of collective bargaining to influence the size of the increases in money incomes. This was the basic approach of both Conservative and Labour governments in the period 1960 to 1979.

In 1961 the Conservative government of Harold Macmillan announced a 'pay pause' to be enforced in the public sector and anticipated this 'pay pause' would lead to a long term policy. This resulted in 1962 in the government introducing a 'guiding light' of 2-2.5% per year for general increases in pay. A National Incomes Commission (NIC) was established to consider any reference to it by the government of specific wage claims or settlements. In October 1964, a Labour government was elected under Harold Wilson, committed to implement a productivity, prices and incomes policy. It established a National Board for Prices and Incomes (NBP&I) to police the policy and to advise whether or not the changes of prices or of wages and salaries were in the national interest as defined by the government's criteria for the movements of prices and incomes. From April 1965 to July 1966, pay was not to increase by more than 3-3.5% per year except for pay increases linked to improvements in productivity, to ensure the distribution of staff from non-essential to essential industries, to enhance wage levels too low to give a reasonable standard of living and where there was widespread recognition the pay of a certain group of workers had fallen seriously out of line with the levels for similar work. In July 1966, the Labour government imposed a statutory pay freeze, and from January 1967 to end of July 1967 a zero norm for pay increases unless collective bargainers could show the proposed wage increase would improve efficiency and productivity, or would raise pay to levels providing a decent living, or would improve the allocation of labour or would rectify pay levels which had fallen seriously out of line with other groups. After 30 June 1967, the zero pay norm continued with four exceptions outlined above. The NPB&I had power to delay for up to three months pay deals outside the government's pay guidelines. If a trade union took industrial action to force an employer to pay a delayed pay deal, it committed a criminal offence. For pay increases in 1968 and 1969, the zero norm and the four exceptions continued. In the case of the exceptions there was a ceiling of 3-3.5% on the possible increase. The pay guideline for collective bargainers after 1969 was pay rises should not exceed a range of 2.5-4.5% per year. There were circumstances in which this range could be exceeded. These included increases in productivity, the reorganisation of pay structures and equal pay for women to comply with the Equal Pay Act (1970). The Labour government lost the 1970 general election and was replaced by the Conservatives under the premiership of Edward Heath.

b. Incomes Policy 1972-1974

The Heath government at first rejected pay policy as an anti-inflation measure, preferring to allow market forces to determine pay levels. In November 1972 it returned to incomes policy when its counter-inflationary policy imposed a standstill on pay increases. It set up a Pay Board to monitor and enforce the policy. The second stage of the policy, introduced in mid-1973, laid down a pay norm increase of 4% plus £1 for any group of employees with no individual receiving an increase greater than £250 per year. There was to be a minimum period of twelve months between pay increases. In November 1973, the Conservative government announced pay for employees could increase by up to 7% or, if negotiators preferred, an award of £2.25 a week for each member of the group with a maximum annual increase of £350 for any individual. There was a flexibility component providing for a further 1% in pay to remove anomalies from pay structures and obstacles to better use of manpower. There were exceptions to the pay criteria for productivity agreements which reduced unit costs and for increases to allow progress to equal pay for women. There was to be an automatic increase of 40p per week when the Retail Price Index rose by seven points from its November 1973 level and by another 40p per week for every point rise in the Index thereafter. Pay restraint was unpopular and in early 1974 the National Union of Mineworkers called its members out on strike to obtain a pay increase outside the limits of Stage Three. In February 1974, the Conservative government called a general election. Although it gained a larger number of seats than any other party, it did not gain an overall majority. It resigned, replaced by a minority Labour government under the leadership of Harold Wilson.

c. The Social Contract

The new Labour government implemented, as its major anti-inflation policy instrument, a 'social contract' negotiated when it was the main opposition party with the trade union movement via the Trade Union/Labour Party Liaison Committee. Under this agreement, the government introduced certain tax, monetary, industrial and social policies in return for union bargainers restricting pay settlements to guidelines set by the TUC. Inflation increased sharply following an increase in oil prices following the Arab/Israeli 1973 war. In July 1975, the UK inflation rate reached 25% and the government and the TUC agreed a maximum pay increase of £6 per week, paid as a supplement to existing earnings and a minimum period between pay increases be twelve months. In 1976, the 'social contract' was further modified. Pay increases were restricted to 5% per annum with a minimum weekly increase of £2.25 and a maximum of £4. These increases were a supplement to existing earnings and the twelve months minimum period between pay increases continued. In mid-1977, the government introduced a 10% guideline but with a kitty principle enabling negotiators to structure their settlements in whatever way suited their circumstances. By now, support for the 'social contract' amongst rank and file trade unionists was waning and the TUC told the Labour government it could no longer be a partner in the 'social contract' policy. The Labour government continued with its wage restraint policy, rejecting the union view there be a return to free collective bargaining. The government from 1 August 1978, applied a pay increase guideline of 5% with exceptions for productivity agreements and increases where the result would give a weekly pay of not more than £44.50. There was opposition to this policy, especially from public sector workers, resulting in industrial action in the so-called 'winter of discontent' of 1978/79. In April 1979, the Labour government lost a confidence vote in the House of Commons and was defeated by the Conservatives in the ensuing election held on 3 May 1979.

d. 1979-1990

The Margaret Thatcher-led Conservative government was convinced pay policies were not a permanent solution to inflation. It rejected Keynesian economics, adopting instead the economic philosophy of monetarism which advocated control of inflation by adjustments of interest rates. If inflation was rising then interest rates were to increase and vice versa. It saw non-inflationary growth coming from increased product and labour market competition, from injecting market forces into the supply of local authority services (eg compulsory competitive tendering), by lowering indirect taxes and corporation taxes and by privatising (selling to private owners) the nationalised industries. For the monetarists, the responsibility of government is to provide a non-inflationary environment in which industry, commerce and entrepreneurship flourish. They did not see the government's role was to ensure full employment. This was the responsibility of the buyers and sellers of labour services. If employees secured wages higher than the market would bear, they would 'price themselves' out of jobs. The price of labour was to be flexible downwards and upwards.

The monetarists believed the government could influence the price of labour and employment levels by removing obstacles in the labour market preventing wages being flexible downwards. The Thatcher and Major governments of 1979-1997 saw unions' behaviour in labour markets as a serious obstacle to flexible wages. Their governments introduced major pieces of legislation – for example the Employment Act (1980), the Employment Act (1982), the Trade Union Act (1984) and the Employment Act (1988) to reduce the influence of unions in labour markets. This was done by progressively reducing the circumstances in which unions could undertake industrial action in which those adversely affected by that action could not sue the union for compensatory damages. For example, the 1984 Trade Union Act said unions could only conduct a legal strike if they gained the consent of their members to the action via a secret ballot.

Trade Union Merger[8]

In 1950 there were thirteen major trade unions in the UK printing industry with a total membership of 273,000. The demarcation of jobs between these unions' members was clear. In letterpress printing the craft composing and reading functions involved five unions of which two were confined to London and one to Scotland. The London Society of Compositors (LSC) which had 14,000 members organised compositors and readers in London, defined as a fifteen mile radius from Charing Cross. The Association of the Correctors of the Press (1,500 members) organised readers in London. To become readers, its members passed the ACP entrance examination and had been readers' assistants (or copyholders) and as such, members of the National Society of Operative Printers and Assistants. The Monotype Casters and Typefounders Society (MCTS) had 939 members and organising Monotype caster attendants in London, Wales and the English provinces. 75% of its membership was employed in London. The Typographical Association (63,000 members) organised compositors, caster attendants and readers in the English provinces, Wales, Northern Ireland and the Irish Republic, except Dublin. The Scottish Typographical Association (STA) with 5,000 members organised the same groups in Scotland. Technological developments threatened the STA's members' employment as they were mostly hot metal compositors and letterpress machine managers. Its 1973 delegate meeting feeling this title was outdated, retitled this union the Scottish Graphical Association (SGA).

The production of duplicate letterpress printing plates was undertaken by the National Society of Electrotypers and Stereotypers (NSES) which had 5,000 members employed in the foundry departments of newspapers, general print companies and ad-setting trade houses. Although many stereotypers worked in newspapers the more common situation was their employment in ones or twos. Many general printing establishments did not have the volume of work to justify employing a stereotyper. The NSES had members in Scotland, but a significant number of SMPS members with stereotyping equipment operated it by STA members. This often led to ill-feeling between the two unions. Letterpress printing took place in the machine room staffed by machine managers who in London were organised into the Printing Machine Managers Trade Society (PMMTS) which had 5,700 members. In 1955 it amalgamated with the London Society of Compositors to form the London Typographical Society (26,000 members). In England, Wales and the whole of Ireland, except for Dublin, letterpress machine managers were organised into the TA but in Scotland in the STA.

In non-craft occupations in the letterpress printing process were two unions – NATSOPA and the NUPB&PW. The former organised readers' assistants, machine room assistants, some warehouse workers and clerical employees. Outside of printing it organised employees in ink manufacture. Although NATSOPA had a presence in Scotland it did not have any collective agreement with the SMPS. NUPB&PW had 171,000 members and its members were bookbinders, machine rulers, warehousemen, cutters, general assistants and employees in paper and paper board mills. After the printing process the jobs held by NUPB&PW members included folding, collating, gathering, stitching, binding, trimming, packing and despatch. By the mid-1950s the hand binding craft skills of NUPB&PW members were only found in establishments producing high quality presentation books. Most books were now bound by machine. Printing firms kept large stocks of paper cared for by warehousemen who knew all the papers' different sizes and qualities, how papers could be matched for a job and how to cut the paper to the right sizes. Warehousemen counted the correct amounts of paper required for a job and delivered it to the printing department. Work in despatching involved the receipt, wrapping, labelling and despatch of the printed product. The bulk of these tasks were done mechanically.

In the lithographic printing process the two craft unions were national, with members in Scotland. Origination work in litho was organised by the Society of Lithographic Artists, Designers and Process Workers (SLADE) which had 12,000 members. They included camera operators, colour retouchers and dark room workers. It operated a pre-entry closed shop under which the employee had to be already a member of the union to obtain the job, and an apprentice entry system. It manipulated the allocation of labour and wage levels through a 'white card system' under which a vacancy in a branch of the union was offered first to an unemployed member in that branch and then to an unemployed member in another branch and finally to an employed member in the branch where the vacancy existed. In litho platemaking and printing, the dominant union was the Amalgamated Society of Lithographic Printers and Auxiliaries of Great Britain and Ireland. It had 11,000 members who operated the lithographic printing process, not only on paper but also tin. The main occupations of its members were litho platemakers and litho machine managers. It had two other sections – the Plate Preparers and the Small Offset which consisted of male and female operators of small offset printing machines. In lithography the non-craft manual workers were organised by the

NUPB&PW and by NATSOPA. There were four main unions with an interest in lithographic printing compared to eleven in the letterpress process. The dominant non-craft print union in Scotland, the NUPB&PW organised across the printing processes. The craft unions, on the other hand, organised across particular jobs within the main printing processes. In the mid-1950s of the eight letterpress craft unions, three had memberships confined to London and one to Scotland. Of the four national unions, their London branches accounted for a significant proportion of their total membership.

The printing unions recognised the need to speak collectively on many matters and to have a means of settling their inter-union problems. In 1901 the printing unions formed the Printing and Kindred Trades Federation (P&KTF) to co-ordinate their activities.[9] In the mid-1950s the P&KTF had 240,000 members in seventeen affiliated unions. Its objectives included the establishment of uniform working conditions in different branches of the industry, co-ordination of union policies, the prevention and settlement of disputes, and unity of action amongst its affiliates. It spoke collectively to the TUC and the UK government and conducted research and enquiry work for its affiliated unions either collectively or individually. The P&KTF constitution stated that 'the Federation shall not interfere in the national management of any union nor its rules and customs'. Nevertheless it had powers to deal with demarcation disputes between affiliated unions via an Arbitration Board whose decision was binding on the parties. In May 1973, in the light of ongoing print union mergers, the P&KTF was dissolved.

In 1953 the demarcation between the job boundaries of the print unions was relatively unchallenged. Over the period 1960 to 1990 the implementation of technological developments in the industry blurred this unchallenged demarcation between jobs. These developments centred around an expansion of litho printing at the expense of the letterpress process, the growth of photocomposition and the rise of computer-based print origination, including origination work outside of the industry. These changes led to demarcation problems between the craft unions and between the craft and non-craft unions. The inter-union problems led the unions to recognise if they were to have any influence on the present, and future, developments of the industry then mergers were essential.

Under the Trade Union Amalgamation Act (1964) there are two processes whereby unions can merge. They can amalgamate, which involves the unions creating a new union with a new name and a new rule book all of which have been approved by ballot of the members of each union. The second process is a transfer of engagements under which one or more unions transfers its membership and finances to another union and accept the rule book and the industrial priorities of that union. In this type of merger only the members of the union wishing to transfer into the other union give their approval in a ballot. The members of the receiving union do not vote.

By 1989 there were two unions in the Scottish printing industry – the National Graphical Association (1982) and the Society of Graphical and Allied Trades (1982). In 1962 the MCTS amalgamated with the NUPB&PW. In 1966 the NUPB&PW and NATSOPA amalgamated to form the Society of Graphical and Allied Trades (SOGAT). Attempts by SOGAT to produce a common rule book failed and in 1970 the merger ended in divorce. The former NUPB&PW retained the name SOGAT but NATSOPA adopted the title, National Society of Operative Printers, Graphical and Media Personnel. In 1975 SOGAT and the Scottish Graphical Association amalgamated to create SOGAT (75) in which the SGA had autonomous status as the Scottish Graphical Division. In 1982 NATSOPA and SOGAT (75) amalgamated to form the Society of Graphical and Allied Trades (1982). In 1984, the Scottish Graphical Division fully integrated into SOGAT, becoming its Scottish Graphical Branch.

The National Graphical Association (1982) resulted from the merger of ten separate print unions. In 1955 the LSC and the PMMTS amalgamated to form the London Typographical Society (LTS) which in 1964 amalgamated with the Typographical Association to form the National Graphical Association. In 1965 the ACP and the NUPT transferred their engagements into the NGA followed in 1967 by the NSES. In 1969 the ASLP transferred its engagements into the NGA. Ten years later the National Union of Wallcovering, Decorative and Allied Trades (NUWDAT) transferred its engagements into the NGA. NUWDAT had 4,000 members (none in Scotland) and was an industrial union. It represented in the wallcovering industry, the skilled and unskilled workers, in the origination, production, warehousing and finishing stages of the wallcovering industries. It also organised the white collar employees of the industry. The family tree of the NGA was completed when it amalgamated in 1982 with SLADE to form the NGA (1982). One production worker print union was achieved in October 1991 when the NGA (82) and SOGAT (82) amalgamated to form the Graphical, Paper and Media Union (GPMU).

In Scotland in the 1970s and 1980s, there were three main unions – SOGAT, NGA and SLADE. SOGAT was the dominant union in terms of numbers. The main set of negotiations in Scotland were between SOGAT and SMPS. NGA and SLADE followed that agreement. There were cultural differences between the NGA and SLADE on the one hand and SOGAT on the other. SOGAT was an industrial union prepared to recruit into membership any employee in the industry regardless of job. It had in membership craft workers, semi-skilled and unskilled workers and women. It sought one union for the industry and was prepared to merge with any union in the printing industry. In terms of collective agreements in Scotland, SOGAT members were predominantly Grade D employees. The NGA and SLADE were craft unions recruiting only craft employees. Both unions supported the creation of a single production union but believed before this happened there be the creation of a single craft workers union. NGA members, along with former SGA members, were Grade B employees in the main collective agreements in Scotland.

Summary

Between 1960 to 1990, the pace of change accelerated with an expansion of litho at the expense of the letterpress. The 1960s and 1970s technology changes centred on photocomposition in the origination area and offset. in the machine room. The 1980s saw the implementation of computerised typesetting whilst in the press room machines became bigger, faster and capable of printing in six or more colours. In the binding and finishing area, there was the introduction of perfect binding which glued the pages of a book into the spine rather than sew them.

The growth of litho led to inter-union disputes between the SGA subsequently the SGD of SOGAT, and the NGA. The inter-union problems were acute in letterpress houses changing to litho with the NGA claiming in these circumstances it be the recognised union, and SOGAT claiming the 'custom and practice' of the house. A short-term solution to the NGA/SGD inter-union problems was provided by the *Perth Agreement* which broke down in early 1983 leading to stoppages of work at Waddie & Co in Edinburgh and at Holmes McDougall in Glasgow. The union membership rights issue was finally settled by a TUC Disputes Committee Award in 1983 in favour of the NGA.

Over the period 1960 to 1979 the economic environment in which the industry operated was dominated by successive UK government attempts to control inflation and achieve a balance of payment surplus by prices and incomes policy backed at times by parliamentary legislation. The government's intervention in the outcome of collective bargaining set out criteria for movements in pay, enforced through first the National Board for Prices and Incomes and then the Pay Board. In the face of accelerating inflation, incomes policies collapsed and post-1979 UK governments rejected incomes policies as a policy instrument to curb inflation. Instead, governments gave priority to controlling inflation by changes in interest rates and improving productivity by increasing product market competition through, for example, privatising public sector assets. It sought to increase employment levels by liberalising labour markets through legal measures to restrict the bargaining power of unions.

In 1960, there were five main unions operating in Scotland – the STA, the ASLP, the NSES, SLADE and the NUPB&PW. The demarcation between their job boundaries was clear and rarey unchallenged. Over the next twenty years the technological changes implemented in the industry changed this situation and the unions realised if they were to influence the future development of the industry, mergers were essential. To continue as separate unions would see them competing with each other for jobs and members. The ASLP, the NSES and SLADE merged with the NGA which had been formed in 1964. The NUPB&PW became SOGAT in 1972 after an unsuccessful merger with NATSOPA. The STA amalgamated with SOGAT in 1975. By the end of the lifetime of the SMPS, there were two unions – NGA and SOGAT – in the Scottish printing industry.

Notes

[1]   For an explanation of these see Report of a Court of Inquiry into the problems caused by the introduction, and the problems arising from the introduction of other modern printing techniques and the arrangements which should be adopted within the industry for dealing with them, Cmnd 3184, HMSO, London, 1967.

[2]   For a more detailed description of these see J Gennard (1990), *A History of the National Graphical Association.* London: Unwin Hyman, pp120-124.

[3]   In Scotland the main letterpress craft unions were the Scottish Typographical Association (STA) and the National Society of Electrotypers and Stereotypers (NSES). Given the development of lithography at the expense of letterpress the STA changed its name in 1970 to the Scottish Graphical Association (SGA). The major lithographic craft unions in Scotland were SLADE in origination and the Amalgamated Society of Lithographic Printers and Auxiliaries of Great Britain and Ireland (ASLP) in the machine room. The ASLP transferred its engagements (merged) to the National Graphical Association (NGA) in 1969.

[4]   In 1975 the SGA merged with the Society of Graphical and Allied Trades (SOGAT) to form SOGAT (75) and become the Scottish Graphical Division (SGD) of SOGAT with its own rules, funds and retention of its traditional industrial practices. In 1984 the SGD became the Scottish Graphical Branch and became fully integrated into SOGAT.

[5]   See *Annual Report and Accounts, 1971-72*, Society of Master Printers of Scotland.

[6]   See minutes of the SMPS Executive Board Meeting, 25 October, 1973.

[7]   See the TUC General Council Report to the 1983 Trades Union Congress, pp6-7.

[8]   For a detailed description of these trade unions and their reasons for merger see J Gennard (1990), *A History of the National Graphical Association.* London: Unwin Hyman, chapters 3, 4, 5 and 6, and J. Gennard and P. Bain (1995), *A History of the Society of Graphical and Allied Trades.* London: Routledge, Chapters 3, 4, 7 and 8.

[9]   For a fuller description of the P&KTF activities see *Sixty Years of Service, 1901-1961.* The Printing and Kindred Trades Federation, 1961.

Chapter 14

THE GROWTH AND DEVELOPMENT OF THE SOCIETY OF MASTER
PRINTERS OF SCOTLAND, 1960-1990

This chapter begins by tracing the characteristics of the Scottish printing industry (size of firms, products, number of employed, etc). It then examines the membership of the SMPS in terms of number of firms, location, ownership, and attempts to recruit new members. The third part considers the decision-making structures of the SMPS, particularly developments in its local associations, the Constitutional Committee, the Forward Policy Committee, the development of direct links with member firms and YMP activities. The fourth section explains attempts to ensure the SMPS finances remained sound with appropriate action taken to eliminate operating deficits, including changes to the subscription structure and the sales of York Place and Edinburgh House. The chapter concludes by analysing the core services provided by the SMPS to its member firms – industrial relations, education and training, management consultancy and political lobbying.

The Scottish Printing Industry

At the end of 1980s, the Scottish printing industry employed 20,000 people in 400 firms. The majority were general printers and small in size. Over 80% of print employment was in more specialised larger firms employing at least fifty people. By 1990 print specialisations had changed substantially since the days when Scotland was the leading UK centre for book printing and binding[1]. By the early 1980s the specialist capabilities of the industry were much wider and included business forms, security printing, stationery, cartons and labels as well as books, maps and diaries. General printing was the major employer, accounting for over two thirds of all printing employment.

In Scotland in the early 1980s the industry was typified by the general jobbing printer with relatively few employees but in every sector there were larger, more specialised firms. In general, the smaller firms were dependent on the Scottish market for their work whereas larger firms competed within the UK market. Export orders accounted for a small percentage of sales in all but a handful of firms. Most small firms were Scottish-owned with external ownership becoming more common as firm size increased. There were by the late 1970s a number of printing firms with more than one production plant. Prominent amongst these were George Outram & Co (fourteen plants), Wm Thyne (three plants), SUITS (three plants), Gilmour & Dean (three plants), Hunter & Foulis (three plants) and Typesetting Services (three plants). MacLehose, Dunn & Wilson, Inglis Paul, Aberdeen University Press, Charles Letts, Glasgow Numerical and McCorquodales all had two production plants.

Throughout the 1960s and 1970s, employment became increasingly concentrated in the larger specialised firms. Print plants existed throughout the whole of Scotland. Small firms were widely dispersed throughout the country meeting the needs of local communities whilst the larger firms were concentrated in central Scotland, from where they could enter the bigger regional and UK markets. Excellent road, rail and air connections and developments in telecommunications technology enabled Scottish print firms to remain close to customers in England and Wales and to compete effectively with print firms in other parts of the UK.

Diversity and specialisation were also characteristics of the Scottish print industry during the lifetime of the SMPS. It boasted household names, such as Collins for books, including the Holy Bible, Letts for diaries, Bartholomew for maps and atlases and Valentine's for greeting cards. Print specialisations included cartons, labels (both conventional and self-adhesive) and flexible packaging. Carton and label manufacturers were diversifying from servicing the Scottish whisky market into other markets, such as electronics, soft drinks, food and pharmaceuticals. Flexible packaging was widely adopted and applied successfully to a range of products from food and sweets to cosmetics.[2]

Membership of the SMPS
On its formation the SMPS had 331 firms in membership. By 1986 the number had fallen to 230. (See Table 14:1). The decline was due to smaller firms going bankrupt and/or being taken over by larger firms. Resignation of firms from membership was not a significant problem although some small firms were expelled for arrears of subscriptions. The only major company resigning from membership was Wm Collins Sons & Co in May 1980. Forty percent of member firms employed less than ten people. Only 20% employed over fifty employees.

Although there were many member firms specialising in book production, bank note and cheque printing, carton and packaging printing, printing tickets and the manufacture of envelopes, the majority were jobbing printers some of whom also printed weekly newspapers. In 1961 54% of member firms were located in either Glasgow (32%) or Edinburgh (22%). By 1990, the figure had risen to 59% with Glasgow accounting for 40% of member firms (see Table 14:2).

Table 14:1
Firms in Membership of SMPS

Date	Number of Firms
1961	331
1962	328
1963	329
1964	326
1968	307
1970	307
1975	298
1983	240
1986	230

Table 14:2
SMPS Membership of Firms by Local Association

Association	January 1963	February 1986
Aberdeen	25	20
Ayrshire	20	12
Central Counties	13	18
Dumfries	8	4
Dundee	18	9
Edinburgh	74	47
Fife	15	7
Glasgow	104	90
Greenock	6	-
Perth	8	10
Scottish Borders	10	-
Northern Counties	13	13
Lanarkshire	15	-
TOTAL	**329**	**230**

Source: SMPS, Executive Board, April 1987

During the lifetime of the SMPS, the membership subscription of company groups was a recurring issue. Each plant of such companies, having a separate physical identity, was treated for membership purposes as a separate firm whether it traded under the 'group name' or under a separate name. Separate membership meant company groups were in membership of different local associations and that the subscription payable to the SMPS in respect of the group was calculated separately for each 'firm'.

The SMPS was conscious of the need to increase its membership. In the summer of 1970, it considered how the membership and its local associations might be strengthened. Its office bearers held a meeting with local association presidents at which a number of matters needing attention were identified, including the introduction of more new members and adequate follow up to new member firms to ensure they were aware of the services the SMPS offered. Local association presidents undertook a survey in their own areas as to potential new members. In late 1972, the SMPS considered recruitment of new members was still not receiving the attention it deserved so a booklet was produced to explain to potential members, to other trade associations, to government, to local authorities and to existing members what the SMPS did and how it achieved its objectives.

In the light of the continued growth of in-plant/instant printing establishments in competition to the traditional Scottish printing firm the SMPS considered introducing two-tier membership. In the ensuing discussion no practical way was found of providing a two-tier membership without upsetting the basis of SMPS membership as a whole. It was decided applications for membership from in-plant printers be treated on their merits. There was no case to create a special category of membership for such a group.

In recruiting new members the SMPS stressed one of the many advantages was the opportunity afforded for print companies in Scotland to get to know their competitor firms as a partner, a neighbour and a friend.[3] The basis of its organisation was local associations in which individual firms were active participants. The majority of the problems experienced by Scottish printing firms could be dealt with on the spot by the local association or the member directly. The SMPS sought to recruit members by explaining many problems never came to its notice because of local understanding between member firms. Paper membership was not enough. Benefits of membership could only be gained through active liaison with the local association and fellow member firms. The SMPS gave priority to making available to its members information about matters affecting their business and always stressed to potential members it was not the SMPS's function to interfere into the internal affairs of its members as these were their own concern.

Constitutional Issues

The decision-making structure of the SMPS was based on a members' general meeting, an Executive Board with standing and ad hoc committees, local associations and a secretariat headed by the Director. During its lifetime the SMPS undertook a number of reviews of its constitution and rules. In May 1962 it set up, under the chairmanship of J J Thompson, a constitutional committee to review its constitution and rules and to propose such amendments as necessary to bring them up to date. In January 1978 the Executive Board established two subcommittees. One examined the structure of the Society and its staffing in the light of the services required by member firms. The other reviewed communications within the SMPS with respect to whom to communicate and what should be communicated to them. In November 1985 the Society examined the size of its Executive Board which had been agreed when the number of companies in membership was greater than the 1985 figure of 230. In November 1971 the Executive Board established a Forward Policy Committee to take a strategic approach to relationships with the print unions. The details of the recommendations of the bodies reviewing these constitutional issues are outlined later in the chapter.

a. Local Associations

Active local associations were essential to the health of the SMPS. Their activities were mainly of local interest. Control of membership was one of their prime responsibilities. Member firm requests for assistance other than those of a purely local concern were directed to the appropriate departments at SMPS head office. Local matters were dealt with by the local association secretary. Representation on the Executive Board by local associations was in accordance with agreed membership ratios. The control of the SMPS's activities was the collective concern of the local associations through the Executive Board. The local associations received their funding from SMPS headquarters.[4]

At the time of its creation the SMPS had thirteen local associations (see Table 14:2). In 1962 the membership in Banff, Keith and Peterhead was transferred from the Northern Counties to the Aberdeen Association. In 1963 the number of local associations was reduced to twelve by the amalgamation of the Scottish Borders Association with the Edinburgh Association. This merger was necessary because of the reduction in the number of firms in the Borders. A satisfactory attendance at its meetings proved, in the end, impossible. The merger was accepted by the Executive Board on the condition the Edinburgh Association gave the Borders representation on its Executive Board. In 1964 the number of local associations was reduced to eleven when the Greenock Association for the same reason as the Scottish Borders Association, and on the same conditions, merged with the Glasgow Association. In 1969 the Lanarkshire Association merged with the Glasgow Association. In 1987 the Ayrshire Association and the Dumfries Association consented to join an enlarged Glasgow Association. The Dumfries Association had been inactive since mid-1982, matters not having been

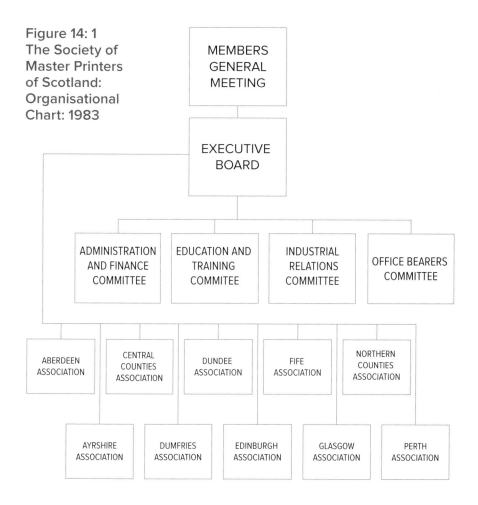

Figure 14: 1
The Society of
Master Printers
of Scotland:
Organisational
Chart: 1983

MEMBERS GENERAL MEETING

EXECUTIVE BOARD

ADMINISTRATION AND FINANCE COMMITTEE

EDUCATION AND TRAINING COMMITEE

INDUSTRIAL RELATIONS COMMITTEE

OFFICE BEARERS COMMITTEE

ABERDEEN ASSOCIATION

CENTRAL COUNTIES ASSOCIATION

DUNDEE ASSOCIATION

FIFE ASSOCIATION

NORTHERN COUNTIES ASSOCIATION

AYRSHIRE ASSOCIATION

DUMFRIES ASSOCIATION

EDINBURGH ASSOCIATION

GLASGOW ASSOCIATION

PERTH ASSOCIATION

helped by the scattered geographical nature of its membership, that its secretary was employed by a company not in membership of the SMPS and its president no longer worked in the area covered by the local association. The Edinburgh Association had for some time been administered by the SMPS head office, but in 1972 the Glasgow Association also became managed from, and by, a member of the SMPS head office staff. The number of local associations was reduced in April 1988 to seven with the Fife Association merger with the Edinburgh Association on the understanding the latter was allocated a seat on the Executive Board to be offered to a representative of a Fife company.

In 1969 the SMPS President, N D MacLehose began a consultative exercise with the presidents of local associations to consider ways of improving the service to members, of attracting new members and of ensuring existing members were fully involved in the work of the local associations. In this connection the Central Countries Association introduced an informal lunch for its members on a bi-monthly basis. In 1974 the Dundee Association held a number of lunchtime meetings during the course of the year following the pattern set by the Northern Counties Association which had held such meetings since 1969. It was also usual practice for the SMPS President, accompanied by the Director, to attend the annual general meeting of each local association. These meetings provided an informal forum in which to discuss various topics, an opportunity for more activity at local association level regarding membership matters and communications to, and from, SMPS headquarters and local associations.

b. The Constitutional Committee

In November 1962, J J Thompson, the SMPS Vice-President, became the Chairman of the Constitutional Committee, established in May, whose membership in addition to the chair and the office bearers, was ten members of the Executive Board. At its first meeting in February 1963 the committee identified three key areas for urgent review – the membership and subscription position of groups of companies, the appointment of the Executive Board and voting at the general meeting.

i. Membership – Groups

There was general agreement there be separate membership for individual units belonging to the one company group so the strength of the local association was maintained. There was a view this should not apply to those plants which had no office on site, ie units where the administration was done elsewhere. The point was made that the SMPS should not become involved in the way individual groups of companies chose to run their affairs. There was no case for distinguishing, for example, between units of production which traded under the group name and those that traded under separate names. The point was also made firms employing union members in all sectors of the industry probably created more work for the SMPS than those firms which employ union members in the same sector, but in different areas.

On subscription rates for group members, the committee was guided by the need to provide for an equitable subscription between one member and another. There was a strong view in the committee the current maximum subscription was too low and gave rise to anomalies. There were views ranging from 'each unit be treated quite separately for subscription purposes' to 'the way members organise their affairs should not affect their subscription' and the number of plants should have no effect on subscription levels. It was argued subscription rules be as simple as possible.

The committee finally recommended where members of the SMPS had more than one separate plant in Scotland, each unit must become a member of the appropriate local association of the SMPS. On the issue of subscriptions the committee recommended the annual subscription be of 10s 0d per £100 (from 1d per £) of the wages paid by the member firm and that the maximum annual subscription payable by any member be raised from £250 to £500. The minimum subscription would remain at £5. The Executive Board accepted all these proposals as did the SMPS annual general meeting held on 24 March 1965.

ii. Representation on the Executive Board

The board comprised forty five representatives of local associations, four representatives of the Scottish Newspaper Proprietors' Association and the Scottish YMP Group as well as fourteen ex-officio members (present office bearers and Past Presidents). Board members represented not their firms but their local association. SMPS head office was represented by the office bearers and its Past Presidents. Due to inflation in money values since 1919, the membership of the board in 1963 should have been 223 if the constitution and rules had been strictly applied. The size of the board had been 'frozen' for many years without objection from the membership but the present situation was unsatisfactory.[5]

There was general agreement the size of the present board should not be increased. Whilst views were expressed that the size of the board might be reduced to forty members, the majority view was a 'fixed size' board was the most advantageous. The composition of the board would continue to be based on a 'money formula' so changes in the various areas would automatically bring changes in board representation. Those in favour of a 'fixed' board pointed out a 'money value' basis would lead to change when none was required, any change in the position of one area against another was unlikely except over a long period and any necessary change in the board representation involving a change in the constitution would present little difficulty.

The Constitution Committee recommended the board consist of the President, Vice-President and Treasurer as ex officios, of Past Presidents, of forty representatives from the local associations, of three representatives from the SNPA, of one from the Scottish YMP and additional members, not greater than five, when necessary from time to time. The board members were to be appointed annually. The committee's recommendations were accepted by the Executive Board and the 1965 annual general meeting.

iii. Poll Voting – General Meeting

The SMPS constitution and rules provided for each member to have of one vote, plus one additional vote for every £1 of aggregate subscription paid. This so-called 'poll' vote had never been taken at a general meeting, voting being by show of hands only, as a guide to the wishes of the meeting. If a 'poll' vote were required it was estimated it would take two hours to be completed and the result ascertained. The purpose of 'poll' voting was to ensure that in a broad sense the members who paid the piper called the tune. Their power was restricted because the maximum subscriber paying £100 per year was allowed a maximum of twenty five votes. Changes in money values since 1919 and increases in the maximum subscription to £250 meant the intention of 'poll' voting was not being carried out. All member firms with a wage bill for subscription purposes of £5,760 or more per annum (ie paying an annual subscription of more than £24) had the same voting power.

In the committee the majority view was 'poll' voting was unnecessary but if it were to be retained there would have to be adjustments in the present scale of votes per member. Suggestions included substituting an amount in the range £10 – £50 for the £1 at present in the constitution and rules. There was a suggestion the maximum number of votes should not exceed five for any member. After discussion the committee recommended at each general meeting each member have one vote plus one additional vote for every £50 of aggregate subscription paid. This was accepted by the Executive Board and the 1965 annual general meeting.

c. The Forward Policy Committee

The business of the SMPS was managed by the Executive Board. By long practice and tradition, the Board decided in broad terms the policy of the SMPS in general or in any particular field and indicated the action to be taken to further that policy. It expected that policy to be implemented unless advised to the contrary. This principle of management by exception was widely favoured. Each year the board elected members to three standing committees - Finance (chaired by the Treasurer) Negotiating and Cost – set out in the SMPS constitution and rules. The Finance Committee received the annual accounts, authorised the budget, considered the SMPS investment policy, advised on levels of subscriptions, oversaw local association expenditure and advised on financial aspects of the BPIF/SMPS and SMPS/SNPA relationships. The Negotiating Committee advised on industrial relations matters, considered any substantial claims by the unions for changes to employment conditions referred to it by the Executive Board or by office bearers or by the Chairman and reported accordingly and requested information it deemed necessary to achieve its objectives. The Negotiating and Costing Committees subsequently became known as the Industrial Relations and Management Accounting Committees respectively.

The Executive Board also appointed other committees. It established a YMP Group Committee and an Education Committee with responsibility for matters relating to technical education in the Scottish printing industry. The Executive Board subsequently authorised the formation of an Education and Training Committee as a standing committee. It also established a standing committee on Forward Policy (in 1970), on Information (in 1977), and a President's Committee. By custom and practice the Office Bearers' Committee acted as a standing committee. The broad role of an Executive Board's committee chairman was to ensure the committee worked properly in the areas prescribed by the Board. They ensured that specific matters received attention but they could only bring to the Executive Board matters which their committee had examined or wish to have examined further. Unless the remit was given to a committee with 'powers' the authority for action rested with the Executive Board. The Forward Policy Committee and the President's Committee had no executive authority.

The Executive Board established a Forward Policy Committee under the chairmanship of Allan K Waterston to develop a more pro-active attitude by the SMPS in its dealing with the unions. In its *Interim Report*[6] the committee set out four basic principles to guide SMPS industrial relations strategy:

(1) the future of the Scottish printing industry depended upon relationships with customers, who demanded the services and products of the industry
(2) the industry have a sound relationship with its customers, and between employees and employers
(3) profitability be safeguarded and a contented labour force obtained and maintained
(4) in the national context of union negotiations, the objective be to secure an adequate supply of efficient and flexible labour at a fair cost.

The *Interim Report* argued the present demarcations between letterpress and litho unions mitigated against efficiency and steps be taken to convince the unions their members' interests would be best served by a joint pursuit of efficiency and flexibility. The report recognised a more flexible utilisation of labour required less numbers to be employed for a given volume of production, the Equal Pay Act (1970) would become increasingly relevant and employers accept the challenge they were employing an increasingly better trained, educated and informed workforce. It recommended improvement in the status of the foremen to be achieved by involving them more closely in management responsibility and problems and by increasing their pay rates. On the question of house agreements the *Interim Report* recommended appropriate agreements at this level be made but only within the overall policy approved by the Executive Board which would mean in most cases the involvement of SMPS staff in the settlement of house agreements. The *Interim Report* was approved by the Executive Board in March 1971. In May 1971 it was considered by local associations. This exercise demonstrated no need for significant modification to the *Interim Report*. Over the period June 1971 to mid-June 1973 action was taken to implement the report, particularly the provision of foremen's training courses, the control of house agreements and improvement of the facilities at SMPS head office. There had been little success in regard to STA/NGA flexibility and fundamental problems regarding communications and employer solidarity still remained. The fundamental principles set out in the *Interim Report* were still valid whilst certain sections of the industry were, in the mid-1970s busy, peaceful and prosperous.

By 1976 criticism was mounting against the Forward Policy Committee. Most of its time was spent debating tactics for use by the Negotiating Committee and there was a view this begged the real issues facing the SMPS. Discussions were repetitive and negotiating ploys available were limited by the then Labour government pay policy (see Chapter 12). The committee was unclear of its relationship to the Negotiating Committee or to the Executive Board. The committee was considered to have not produced any new thinking and nor studied any problems in depth. In 1977 the Forward Policy Committee was reconstituted so its main function became acting as the policy/planning arm of the SMPS, making proposals to the Executive Board on the future and undertaking investigations as requested by the board. The reconstituted committee comprised ten members – three YMPS, two Past Presidents, the chair of the Negotiating Committee and four others – all appointed by the Executive Board. The SMPS full-time secretariat were involved in an administrative capacity. It was chaired by J Harry Allen. The reformed committee's remit was to examine the present SMPS committee structure, function and operation including the role of the directorate, to undertake research projects into possible areas of policy change, to investigate areas proposed by the Executive Board, to provide employee relations advice and training and to examine the public relations activities of the Society.

At its initial meeting the reconstituted committee established two subcommittees. One to review the structure of the SMPS and its staff in the light of the services required by the members. The other to look at communications, the Executive Board having already agreed the appointment of an Information Committee. The Forward Policy Committee's subcommittee on communications had a broader remit. The Information Committee held its first meeting on 4 October 1978 and established four priorities. First, the improvement of communications within the SMPS, second enhancement of communications with outside bodies, for example central government, third sales and marketing and four communications with the general public.

The Forward Policy Committee's structure subcommittee report was approved in May 1978 and subsequently implemented. It recommended the establishment of four departments – Industrial Relations comprising a director and industrial relations officers; Training and Communications under the control of a director; Management Accounting directed by a management accountant and Administration managed by a secretary. The IR Department dealt with matters concerning negotiations with the unions and employment legislation. The Training and Communications department dealt with education and training, including the Industrial Training Boards, apprentice selection, careers information and advice; information services and liaison with local authorities, central government and other agencies. The Management Accounting Department was took responsibility for costing services and liaison with HMSO and the British Printing Industries' Federation (BPIF).

The Forward Policy Committee remained increasingly active in the late 1970s and the early 1980s. Principal matters upon which it took action included the formation of the Printing Industries Sector Working Party, the administration of which was undertaken by the National Economic Development Office (NEDO), strengthening the industrial relations directorate, membership, services and premises, new technology, relationships with the BPIF and industrial relations policy.

By 1982 it was clear the SMPS committee structure, built up over the years, was not as effective as it should be. Modification was required[7]. The subcommittee on structure and functions considered it not only needed to examine the present position of committees and how they operated but to reassess aims, motives and goals of the SMPS as a whole. Its report to the Executive Board in early 1982 contained seven conclusions:

(1) a strong, effective SMPS continued to maintain stability and efficiency of operation in the Scottish printing industry

(2) the SMPS continue as an independent body representing Scottish interests although closer working with the BPIF should always be sought

(3) links with the SNPA be not weakened whilst those with the publishing industry and other relevant bodies be strengthened

(4) there was no evidence any significant area of present, or potential, SMPS activity had been neglected by the present committee structure. However, it recommended the structure be streamlined, the role of committee chairs be more clearly defined, the function of standing committees be restated and the method of appointing committees be changed

(5) the role of the office bearers be restated and the Office Bearers' Committee become a standing committee

(6) there was a need for continuing the work of the Forward Policy Committee

(7) the SMPS constitution, last revised in 1965, no longer reflected the conditions in which members and potential member firms operated.

The subcommittee, in the light of these conclusions, made a number of recommendations. The standing committees be reduced to four – Industrial Relations, Education and Training, Administration and Finance, and Office Bearers. The President's Committee did not, and should not, operate on a standing committee basis, the President being entitled any time to seek advice on any matter of consequence from Past Presidents, who were members ex-officio of the Executive Board. The general role of the committees was to assist and advise the Executive Board on the formulation of policy and to oversee action in that area taken on the authority of the board. The role of committee chairs was to lead the committee's work and to liaise with the members of SMPS senior staff. The standing committees should consider regularly and report upon forward policy in the relevant area and suggest action the committee considered need be authorised by the Executive Board. Each committee was to consist of up to twenty members reflecting various interests making up the SMPS membership. The chair of a standing committee would be appointed by the Executive Board on the nomination of the office bearers and their term of office be not normally less than five years or more than ten. Committee members were to be appointed by the Executive Board as currently, on the nomination of the office bearers. In future the office bearers would obtain the advice of local association Presidents prior to making committee membership nominations to the Executive Board. The Scottish YMP Group would continue to operate as set out in its present constitution. The Executive Board accepted these recommendations of the Forward Policy Committee subcommittee and the SMPS constitution and rules were altered accordingly at the 1982 annual eneral meeting.

d. Review of the Executive Board
The SMPS Executive Board meeting of November 1985 remitted to the Office Bearers' Committee a suggestion the size of the Board be reviewed prior to wider consultation at local association meetings on any proposals arising from the review. It was initiated in the context that if members generally were given the opportunity of greater participation in the SMPS affairs through general/consultative meetings, then an Executive Board of some fifty members was unnecessarily large in a membership of 230 companies. An examination of the twenty four board meetings held over the five year period 1981-1985 revealed the average attendance was under twenty four, about 45%, with no single meeting drawing more than thirty. Whilst at first sight this indicated significant scope for bringing the number of places more in line with the average attendance, closer examination suggested no significant change could be achieved without either reducing the representation of certain groups or changing the structure of the board.

The Office Bearers' Committee put forward two possible approaches for reforming the Executive Board as a basis for discussion with local associations. The first approach proposed no change in the representation on the Executive Board for office bearers, the Scottish YMP Group and co-opted members. It proposed the SNPA representation be reduced from three to two places and that of the local associations be lowered from thirty nine to twenty three.[8] The second approach involved limiting Past President representation to the immediate Past President and reorganising the local associations into three regions covering the whole of Scotland – the North (covering Grampian, Highland and Tayside Regional Councils and Orkney, Shetland and Western Isles Council), East (Fife, Lothian and Borders Regions and Falkirk and Clackmannan Districts of the Central Region) and the West (Strathclyde, Dumfries and Galloway Regions and Stirling District of Central Region). The North Region would have four seats on the Executive Board, the East six, and the West seven, to give an Executive Board of twenty six seats. This second approach was more radical and meant the dissolution of existing local associations. The justification for a change of this nature was a regional structure would increase the active participation of members. The Office Bearers' Committee was at pains to stress that given the long history of local associations their winding up would not happen unless it met with the clearly expressed consent of the members. The committee also suggested with the exception of serving office bearers' no member remain on the board for more than five years consecutively, to ensure the rotation of representation from different companies.

There was unanimous support for the first approach as the local associations did not see a regional structure as a satisfactory arrangement. The local associations favoured retaining their representation on the Executive Board. The proposal one member remain on the board for no more than five years consecutively was also received favourably. The Dundee, Glasgow and Edinburgh Associations and the SNPA accepted the proposal their representation on the Executive Board be reduced. The Ayrshire Association explained it was seeking a merger with the Glasgow Association. In anticipation of this one representative additional to that originally proposed was allocated to Glasgow on the understanding that Ayrshire interests were accommodated within Glasgow's representation on the Executive Board. In the event of the Glasgow and Ayrshire Associations merger coming about members in Dumfries and Galloway where the local association was moribund should likewise merge with Glasgow. In consultations with Past Presidents it was agreed their representation on the Executive Board be confined to the immediate Past President.

e. Staff and Premises

The SMPS Director and head office staff implemented the policy of the Executive Board which had been decided on advice received from its various committees. If the committees were to work effectively a close liaison between its chairman and the member of senior staff responsible for its operation was necessary. An important role for the chairman was to guide the senior staff in the performance of their duties whilst in return the chairman relied on that individual for information and guidance to ensure the committee was operating effectively.

In 1966/67, Barrie Abbott's position as the chief official of SMPS was redesignated as Director although he continued his duties as Secretary to the Society. In January 1984, James Blair Raeburn became Director Designate succeeding Barrie Abbott as Director in May 1984. James Raeburn had previously been Secretary of the Electrical Contractors Association of Scotland. In 1966/67, George W Llewellyn was appointed an SMPS Assistant Secretary. He retired from the position on 31 December 1971 but was re-engaged as Deputy Secretary on a part-time basis from 10 January 1972. On the formation of the SMPS its Assistant Secretary was Mr T Lorimer, a post he held for over twenty years, retiring in October 1979. In 1972 he was appointed Secretary of the SMPS. His successor was Michael Brown who was replaced in 1980 by Michael Jeffrey. Mr Lorimer had acted as Assistant Secretary of the SNPA with special responsibility for the advertising field and had acted as secretary of the Edinburgh local association.

Barrie Abbott in 1984. He was Secretary to the Scottish Alliance of Master Printers and Director of the Society of Master Printers of Scotland between 1954 and 1984

On 5 January 1972, Desmond Doyle became Training and Technical Officer responsible for training, manpower, machine manning, rating matters and advice on technical issues including factory layout and the installation of new equipment. He left the SMPS at the end of July 1974 to continue business as a trade typesetter in the Republic of Ireland. He was succeeded by Jim Keppie who remained with the Society until February 1984. In November 1978, R M Littlejohn, Assistant Director (Industrial Relations) resigned and was succeeded in mid-1979 by Gordon Stewart who became Industrial Relations Director. He had been persuaded to return from Canada to the service of the SMPS as his experience there included important work in industrial relations. In November 1980 he was succeeded as Industrial Relations Director by James Graham who in turn was succeeded in 1981 by Bill Kidd. The SMPS at times suffered a high turnover of senior staff which made it difficult to maintain continuity of administration. The constant increase in the range of activities in which the Society engaged on behalf of its members required increases in staff. A substantial financial deficit incurred in 1983 and the forecast of a worsening situation for 1984 meant the Executive Board reduced expenditure and one economies was the elimination of the post of Director (Information and Communications).

For some time the SMPS office bearers, as Trustees of the Society had under consideration the need to find office accommodation more suitable than Hill Street. The Society's work had expanded since 1946 and this trend was likely to continue. Parking within easy reach of Hill Street was difficult whilst rail services to Princes Street (Caley) had been cut and eventually would cease. Despite improvements and changes made at Hill Street to use the available space in the best possible way, accommodation was inadequate. No additional staff could be accommodated without major changes to present arrangements. The caretaker's premises were substandard.

An opportunity arose to purchase 8 and 10 York Place, Edinburgh and an offer to buy them for £39,000 was accepted. The property at 8 York Place was sold in November 1964 for £19,500, as the property at Number 10 was adequate for the Society's present and future needs. In June 1965 Hill Street was sold for £11,000. In May 1980 the Executive Board agreed new premises for the head office of the SMPS be obtained on a long lease to be followed by the sale of York Place. New premises were necessary if the SMPS were to provide a better service to its member firms. There had been two serious interruptions in service to members in the past few years. One had been in Industrial Relations and the other in the Management Accounting department. It was necessary to increase staffing levels by 50% if the member firms were to be serviced effectively. York Place was no longer big enough. The Executive Board recommended that York Place be sold and a twenty-five-year lease be taken on premises in Edinburgh House, North St Andrews Street. York Place was sold on 1 December 1980 the transfer of operations to Edinburgh House having been successfully completed over the weekend of 15/16 November 1980. Edinburgh House officially opened to members on 25 March 1981.

During 1988 the SMPS received an approach from agents acting on behalf of the Co-operative Insurance Society, the Edinburgh House landlords, seeking the Society's agreement to surrender of its lease, entered into in 1980 for twenty five years, to allow demolition and the construction of a high quality building to proceed. After lengthy negotiations agreement was reached that on vacating the property by 30 June 1989 the SMPS receive the sum of £250,000. These successful negotiations were undertaken by David Henderson and Freddie Johnston.

The Executive Board delegated powers to the Office Bearers' Committee for the acquisition of new premises. In February 1989 the SMPS made a successful offer of £360,000 for the purchase of 48 Palmerston Place in the west end of Edinburgh. It had over 3,500 square feet of office space. A further £110,000 was needed for refurbishment. The funding for the purchase and refurbishment came from three sources. First there was the £250,000 due on leaving Edinburgh House. Second, the realisation of half the SMPS's investments and third a loan of £150,000 repayable over twenty years. As well as providing suitable offices 48 Palmerston Place represented a valuable asset at a net cost to the SMPS of five times the prospective annual rental of comparable leased accommodation. Palmerston Place was officially opened on 21 October 1989 by the Secretary of State for Scotland, Malcolm Rifkind.

f. Links with Members

The SMPS was concerned to involve its members, particularly those in the more rural areas of Scotland, more in its affairs. One instrument for doing this was the annual visit of the President to the annual general meetings of the local associations. This provided an opportunity for a two way exchange of views and information. In January 1961 the SMPS sought to communicate with its members via the launch of a quarterly publication entitled the *Scottish Digest*. Its purpose was to simplify for members the reams of notes, minutes, publications, discussions and speeches to present them in an attractive form for quick and easy consumption.[9] The quarterly publication assisted member firms who, because of distance lacked the opportunity to meet regularly with other members and exchange information and ideas on the current state of the industry. The launch of the *Digest* meant the report of the Executive Board to the annual general meeting could be shorter than would otherwise have been the case. By 1964 difficulties emerged with the continued publication of the *Scottish Digest* on a quarterly basis. These proved impossible to overcome and May 1964 saw the publication of its final issue.

Another way in which the SMPS communicated directly with its members was via ad hoc weekend conferences open to all SMPS members, wives and guests. In October 1963 such a conference was to be held in the Turnberry Hotel but the poor response from member firms caused its postponement. Such conferences, had, however, been held in 1936, 1937, 1959, 1960 and 1961. In 1979 a successful weekend conference was held in October and a further conference was scheduled for the autumn of 1982, but it proved impractical to proceed. In November 1984 the first conference open to all SMPS members was held at Peebles Hydro. It was a mixture of business and social events.

The SMPS also involved its members directly through 'member consultative meetings' the first of which was held in 1986 and attracted some sixty members. It took the form of short presentations by respective committee chairpersons and the Director followed by question and answer sessions. At subsequent meetings of the Executive Board it was suggested if members were given the opportunity of greater participation at consultative meetings, then an Executive Board of fifty members was unnecessarily large. Consultation at local association meetings in early 1986 indicated widespread support for a reduction in the size of the Executive Board. The SMPS held another successful consultative meeting around the theme 'Meeting the Challenge' at which the Scottish Office Industry Minister Ian Lang headed an impressive list of speakers addressing members on the development of markets, people, technology and unions. A further successful consultative meeting was held at the Peebles Hydro Hotel over the weekend 2/4 November 1990.

g. YMP Group
This group provided an opportunity for young managerial staff to take advantage of the only organisation in the Scottish printing industry catering directly to their development needs. It offered involvement in the affairs of a group that formed an important body of opinion within the SMPS. Membership of the YMP Group was through the SMPS organisation and open to those in

management positions between the ages of eighteen and thirty five who were members of, or in firms, that were members of the SMPS and whose training was focussed towards them qualifying for the position of Master Printer, partner or director, general manager etc. Members of the Group reaching the age of thirty five could retain their membership for a reasonable period at the invitation of the YMP Group Committee. The membership of the Scottish YMP Group over the life time of the SMPS is shown in Table 14.3. The main objectives of the group included providing the means whereby members became acquainted with the organisation and methods of the SMPS and the BFMP, enabling members to meet together, for conferences on technical, industrial, commercial and administrative matters connected with Scottish printing industry, focussing opinions to lay such opinions before the Executive Board and investigating as a group, any matter referred to it by the Executive Board or by the YMP Group Committee with concerted action if and when necessary.

Table 14:3
Membership of the Scottish YMP Group

Date	Number of Members
1961	80
1962	82
1963	91
1964	89
1975	125
1976	141
1977	117
1978	107
1979	116
1980	104
1981	119
1982	106
1983	116
1986	123
1988	122

Source: SMPS: Annual Report and Accounts

The highlight of the Scottish YMP Group calendar was its annual conference which was a working weekend focussing on a different aspect of management development, for example the turnover of apprentices, management development techniques and processes, management games and managing technological change. The Group's affairs were managed by a committee consisting of the President and Vice-President of the Group and four others. The Group had a secretary and held an annual general meeting open to all members. The 1985 annual general meeting changed the title of the Group from Scottish Young Master Printers' Group to the Scottish YMP Group with the subheading Management Development for Printing Industries. In October 1978 the Group held a dinner at the Roxburgh Hotel, Edinburgh to celebrate its golden jubilee. Of the ninety six people attending, twenty five were past Chairmen, whilst five attendees were at the Group's first conference held at St. Andrews in 1928.

There were local YMP Groups at Aberdeen, Glasgow, Edinburgh and Tayside. The last named Group was formed in 1971 and operated under the chairmanship of Hamish Milne, who later became Chief Executive of Spirax Binding of Perth, and a President of SPEF. By the late 1970s the Tayside Group was poorly supported and meeting attendance was low. It went into temporary suspension. These local groups ran a programme of evening meetings with guest speakers and discussion embracing a wide range of industrial and social topics of current concern to young people drawn from a broad spectrum of management disciplines. Works visits were frequently organised to printing works and paper mills and these provided an excellent form of technical training. Even more important was the opportunity YMP local group meetings provided for YMPs to make the acquaintance of their contemporaries in the Scottish printing industry. This 'getting together' was an important factor in the future of the SMPS whose affairs would, it was hoped, one day be controlled by former YMPs. Although the attendance at local and Scottish-wide YMP meetings was satisfactory the annual reports of the Executive Board frequently appealed for more active members to be recruited, for member firms to ensure present members of the Group attended its meetings and its annual conference and to ensure eligible members of their staff had the opportunity to join the group and participate in all its activities. Members of the Scottish YMP Group also played an active part in the YMP national organisation and in February 1984 John Crerar, President of the Scottish YMP accepted the Alden Trophy on behalf of Scotland which was presented by the YMP national Chair to the outstanding YMP Group of the year.[10] He later became President of the Scottish Printing Employers' Federation for the years 1997-1999.

Finances

The income and expenditure of the SMPS is shown in Table 14:.4. There were operating deficits in 1964, 1967, 1975, 1976, 1978, 1980, 1981 and 1983. The largest operating deficit was in 1978 (-£12,795). However, the SMPS finances remained sound with appropriate action being taken when operating deficits arose. The main source of income was membership subscriptions which accounted for 95% of total income. The main items of expenditure were staff salaries, travelling expenses and office accommodation. The major asset was the Society's head office. By May 1990 the SMPS had members' funds to the value of £497,731.

On the formation of the SMPS the annual subscription was 1d per £ of wage paid by the member firm, payable quarterly. The maximum annual subscription payable by any member firm was £250 and the minimum £5. As we have seen, an immediate issue was the membership subscription for multi-plant members. George Outram & Co, which had plants in six local associations, argued only one subscription should be payable in respect of the firm's organisation. The company was advised the long-standing practice of the SMPS was that firms or companies eligible for membership and in common ownership should all be in membership, a separate subscription payable for parts of a firm's organisation which had separate physical facilities and that firms or companies with separate identities were not entitled to 'aggregate' for the purposes of subscription calculation. The Executive Board asked the Constitution Committee to examine the issue (see above). Its recommendation, approved by both the Executive Board and the General Meeting was that where members of the SMPS had more than one separate unit of production each unit must be a member of the appropriate local association.

The issue of group subscriptions was raised again in 1971 and the Executive Board established a Groups Subscription Committee to review the matter. There was a substantial, but not unanimous, view in the committee that members having an appropriate element of common ownership with other members be permitted to aggregate wages paid for subscription purposes. The subscription payable be then the wage scale plus some additional sum to cover more than one unit of production was involved. The committee felt the 'non-aggregation' rule coupled with the traditional practice of having a relatively low maximum subscription was inequitable. It was thought desirable member firms wishing to aggregate be allowed to do so but only on request. The committee recommended 'aggregation' be permitted where there was significant elements of common ownership in respect of two or more members, provided notification was given to the SMPS Secretary and appropriate arrangements for payment of subscription made. The committee recommended in addition to paying their subscriptions on an aggregation basis such companies pay an additional lump sum contribution of £100. These recommendations were accepted by the Executive Board and the 1975 annual general meeting. The effect of this change was that the amount of subscription was the same for groups as for single operation units with the exception a member with more than one unit who would pay £100 more than a member with the same number of employees within one unit.

Table 14:4
Society of Master Printers of Scotland: Income/Expenditure 1961 – 1990

Date	Income (£)	Expenditure (£)	Surplus/Deficit
1961	21,465	18,425	+3,040
1962	22,196	21,383	+513
1963	22,702	21,042	+1,660
1964	23,434	24,419	-985
1965	30,711	30,266	+445
1966	36,216	31,911	+4,305
1967	35,622	36,342	-702
1968	36,318	34,204	+2,114
1969	36,379	35,936	+443
1970	38,349	36,903	+1,446
1971	45,413	41,797	+3,616
1972	47,946	45,486	+2,459
1973	54,717	51,805	+2,912
1974	64,458	60,022	+4,436
1975	74,126	74,353	-227
1976	86,218	86,862	-644
1977	96,236	93,577	+2,659
1978	108,562	121,357	-12,795
1979	149,055	148,509	+546
1980	189,118	198,291	-9,173
1981	225,452	259,343	-3,891
1982	280,787	267,961	+12,826
1983	262,687	273,263	-10,576
1984	328,634	311,175	+17,459
1985			
1986*	448,928	401,183	+47,745
1987	348,326	329,293	+19,293
1988	351,045	333,366	+17,679
1989	371,807	343,579	+ 28,228
1990	396,023	364,772	+31,281

Source: SMPS Annual Report and Accounts

*Figures for 1986 are for a period of 15 months, because of a change to the accounting year.

The 1965 General Meeting agreed the annual subscription be increased to 10s 0d per £100 of wages paid with a maximum subscription of £500 and a minimum of £5. It accepted the maximum subscription be reviewed within five years. Following this increase there was a marked increase in inflation, an extension of the SMPS general role in the interests of the members, increases in the scope of services the Society provided and a substantial increase in wage costs occasioned mainly by government action. In March 1970 the Finance Committee recommended the maximum subscription be increased from £500 to £650 per year from the subscriptions due in January 1971. This recommendation was accepted by the Executive Board and the 1970 annual general meeting. The 1976 annual general meeting approved the following wages scale for calculating the annual subscription payable by a member firm, as follows:

-	First £100,000 of wages paid	-	50p per £100
-	Next £200,000 of wages paid	-	25p per £100
-	Next £500,000 of wages paid	-	10p per £100

The maximum annual subscription was set at £1,500 and the minimum at £20.

In March 1978 the Finance Committee was informed the budget for that year was likely to be a deficit of £10,000 instead of the expected £6,000. The committee decided it was necessary, and equitable, that all members contributed towards the additional income required to bring the projected deficit back into line. Increases in subscription were therefore proposed to 1978 annual general meeting. The maximum subscription was increased to £1,800 and the minimum to £25. The scale of contributions per wages paid increased to 60p, 30p and 15p whilst for contributions on the basis of aggregate wages the additional lump sum payment was raised from £100 to £150 per annum. The 1979 annual general meeting approved further increases in subscriptions. The 60p per £1 on the first £100,000 of wage paid was increased to 70p, on the next £200,000 raised to 35p and on the next £400,000 uplifted to 20p. The maximum annual subscription was raised to £2,200 and the minimum to £40 whilst for contributions on the basis of aggregated wages the additional payment was increased from £180 to £200.

Further increases in subscriptions were required in 1980. In comparison with 1980 projected expenditure showed substantial increases in the cost of office premises, of staff and of operating costs totalling some £60 – 65,000 per year whilst the bank overdraft at mid-June 1980 had increased to £38,773. This level of indebtedness was not sustainable. The SMPS capital base was declining at an increasing rate. Given that a strong SMPS was necessary to protect the interests of its members the Finance Committee proposed a substantial increase in income by a general increase in subscriptions of 40% throughout the banding of the subscriptions and the minimum and maximum annual contributions. The Executive Board accepted the proposal as did a special general meeting held on 18 September 1980. There were further increases in 1981 when the subscription per wage banding increased to £1, 50p and 30p respectively whilst the maximum subscription became £3,840 and the minimum at £60. The additional payment for membership on the basis of aggregated wages increased to £280. In 1983 the maximum subscription was increased to £4,250, the aggregation fee to £350 and subscription rates became subject to annual review.

The Administration and Finance Committee, under the chairmanship of Freddie Johnston of the Johnston Press, Falkirk, in 1984 proposed radical changes to the SMPS subscription income. It recommended for the first two quarters of 1985 commencing 1 January and 1 April subscriptions be calculated, and paid, on the present basis and the annual general meeting of March 1985 be asked to change from quarterly payment of subscriptions to an annual payment. This would apply to subscriptions payable from 1 July 1986 and be based on wages and salaries paid to all those employed in any productive capacity for the twelve months ending 5 April. This annual subscription could be paid either in a lump sum, with a discount if paid before a certain date or in ten equal instalments under a direct debit mandate payable on the first day of each month. All companies due to pay an annual subscription of less than £300 would pay a lump sum. Annual subscriptions thereafter were calculated by reference to wages paid in the fiscal year. The Executive Board approved the Administration and Finance Committee's recommendations. In the following year the Society adopted the long-term objective that its financial resources be accumulated until they represented six months' subscription income.

By 1987, the minimum membership subscription had not been reviewed since 1980 when it increased from £50 to £60. The maximum subscription had been reviewed in 1983 when maximum subscriber member firms indicated rather than face sudden step increases they preferred to budget for regular but modest increases. In April 1987 the Administration and Finance Committee gave effect to this suggestion for 1987/88. The preliminary budget for 1987/88 projected a modest surplus but it was expected to be boosted by capital gains from share transactions. These represented one-off profits and were not regular income from which recurrent expenditure could be financed. The committee suggested the maximum subscription be increased by £200 to £4,450, an increase of 4.7% and the increase be implemented in the following way to avoid disturbing the actual subscription rate bands of £1, 50p and 30p.

First £120,000 of wages at £1 per £100	£1,200	
Next £250,000 of wages at 50p per £100	£1,250	
Next £666,667 of wages at 30p per £100	£1,850	
	£4,450	

In addition the aggregation fee was increased by £50 to £400 and by staged increases of £10 per annum the minimum subscription of £60 to £100. The effect of these changes increased the SMPS subscription income by £4,500 per year. The proposals were accepted by the 1988 annual general meeting. The 1990 annual general meeting approved further increases in subscriptions. The banding rates of £1,50p and 30p remained unchanged. The second and third bands were adjusted the effect of which was to increase the maximum subscription by £250 to £4,850 whilst the aggregation fee increased by £100 to £600. Members paying by lump sum were offered a discount of 6% for payment before 15 May or 4% before 30 June.

Services to Members
a. Industrial Relations Services
The SMPS negotiated with the print unions basic terms and conditions of production employees within member companies. Using the national agreement as a basis for sound industrial relations practice, the Society's staff provided an advisory service ranging from telephone consultation to representing the member's interest at meetings or negotiations with the unions. By the application of the nationally agreed disputes procedure and local conciliation procedure the SMPS helped resolve any disputes arising between a member company and its employees. With its wide range of contacts the SMPS offered members sound practical advice on all aspects of employment including contracts of employment, disciplinary matters, statutory rights of employees and appearing before Industrial Tribunals. The smaller company members which had no access to a personnel/human resource management department found this service particularly useful. The SMPS's staff arranged for member companies consultative meetings and training sessions designed to enable them to acquire and develop employee relations skills.

The Society's industrial relations policy assisted its members to achieve high levels of commitment, motivation and effectiveness from their employees. The policy aimed to create, and maintain, an industrial relations environment enabling its member firms to operate profitably and efficiently at any level of technology in both current and future markets. To achieve this aim the SMPS dealt fairly, reasonably and consistently with any industrial relations matter referred to it, reached collective agreements giving the maximum flexibility to member firms in the operation of their businesses, developed effective leadership within the industry at both management and employee representative level. It maintained member firm awareness of good industrial relations practice via information and training and ensured membership of the Society adhered to its collective agreements, seen as a positive benefit in industrial relations.

In the early 1980s the Industrial Relations Committee felt, in preparing for negotiations with the unions, the interest groups consulted need to be widened. It felt that making more use of a wider range of knowledge and experience existing within the SMPS would provide the Industrial Relations Committee and negotiating teams with adequate information and intelligence to devise a more effective negotiations strategy. The membership of the SMPS represented a wide range of activities within the printing and newspaper industries. Of necessity any national agreement needed to encompass as wide a range of interests as possible. To achieve this meant ensuring the view of the various interest groups were collected to determine the options available for incorporation into the negotiating strategy. There were benefits having technical knowledge available to the negotiating team when complex issues were being bargained. On 3 November 1982 the Executive Board accepted proposals from the Industrial Relations Committee for the establishment of interest groups to operate in an informal manner, meeting only when necessary and providing comment by correspondence when requested. Each group had a convenor and a deputy convenor both of whom were members of the Industrial Relations Committee. The remaining members of the group were drawn from within or from outwith the Industrial Relations Committee on a voluntary basis. The point of contact was the IR Department staff and convenor. The IR Committee chairman and the interest group convenors acted as an 'emergency committee' available for short notice consultation. This system further strengthened the SMPS negotiating team by providing access to experience in less demanding situations than national negotiations. Post-November 1982 a number of ad hoc interest groups were established, reporting to the Industrial Relations Committee. These interest groups gave valued service. The Binding and Print Finishing interest group, for example, successfully concluded its examination of machine classification and grading with the result agreement was made with SOGAT on these issues.

b. Management Consultancy Services

In the final analysis, profit determined the success of any printing business and thereby its future. Through its Management Accounting Service, provided by a qualified accountant with extensive knowledge of the industry, the SMPS assisted member companies to improve their performance and their profitability in a number of ways. These included determining accurate cost recovery rates, fundamental to a soundly based estimating system, a management ratio scheme, a computer service, the design and installation of budgetary control procedures and reporting systems, manual or computerised, targeting profitable work and highlighting less profitable work. The SMPS management accounting service was customised to meet the needs of the individual printing business. A confidential report was prepared, containing essential information, to assist member companies make important marketing and financial decisions.

The SMPS installed the Costing System in member firms and revised the system in those companies already operating the system. 1963 saw the fiftieth anniversary of the introduction of the Costing System during which time there had been comparatively little change to its original principles.[11] From the start some member firms saw the system as a means of controlling and checking costs but the majority who adopted the system used it mainly to establish selling prices and to improve the profitability of their businesses. Gradually, as statistics were compiled, it became possible to prepare standard hourly cost rates for various processes and such rates were an influence on the industry generally and were an enormous benefit to the smaller print companies. The costing system enabled the printer to identify the cost of any job in the peculiar circumstances of the production of that job. With that fact known the printer could determine the price to be charged for the job and the profit from it. Gradually it was realised that the ratio of costs to sales, profit to sales, and profit to capital employed in the business, were all clues to how efficiently the business was managed. The SMPS costing system enabled member firms who adopted the system to obtain monthly profit statements and to compare actual expenses throughout the year with the budgeted figure and begin to control such costs. Levels of production, the efficient use of plant, the cost savings effected by the introduction of new plant could be calculated from figures revealed by the use of the costing system.

The Management Accounting Service provided general services for member firms. These included the calculation of cost rates for special machines, advice regarding method study, work measurement, production control problems, calculation of cost increases due to changes in wage settlements, assistance in the preparation of integrated financial and cost accounts, advice on the purchase of another business, advice on bookkeeping systems and tendering for specific HMSO contracts. The Cost Accountant maintained contact with a large number of member firms by visits, and by attending annual general meetings of local associations. Special visits were made to particular areas from time to time. These visits kept touch with member firms using the Management Accounting Service intermittently, and informed members about the benefits from its use. Apart from the Costing and Technical Committee meetings of the BFMP, the SMPS Cost Accountant regularly attended meetings of the BFMP Cost Accountants in London.

The Management Accounting Service encouraged member companies to participate, initially at no cost, in the BFMP Management Ratio Scheme which allowed them to assess their use of resources and profitability in comparison with their competitors of similar size involved in similar markets. In 1963 thirty two firms participated in the scheme. By 1969 the participation rate had fallen to twenty companies. The cause of the decline was the introduction in January 1968, of the £7 charge by the BFMP for participation in the scheme. The charge also covered the report sent to each participant. The number of participating SMPS firms fell to seven in 1970 when the charge increased to £15. Matters were not helped by difficulties over the length of time taken in processing and returning information. By 1979 the number of participating companies was thirteen and the service improved with the ratios being returned from the BPIF within one week of data being supplied. Interest in the scheme began to decline again and by 1982 only five users, who were within specialist fields, were participating in the scheme. The SMPS decided to do nothing to revive interest.[12] In the main the fall in interest was due to the inordinate length of time SMPS staff spent in following up previous users and new users.

In early 1967 the SMPS introduced a Computer Service for its members and initially seven used the service. The computer was programmed for sales and purchasing as well as costing data but firms only participated in respect of job costing and pricing. The interest of member firms in the service indicated its usefulness but despite efforts continually to recruit member firms, participation remained limited. In 1980, the SMPS Accounting Service made several visits to the BPIF to provide assistance in the design of a complete suite of computer programmes comprising an integrated system of accounting, job costing, stock control and invoicing. It was decided use be made of the machine manufacturers and software houses offering computerised systems suitable to printers, embodying principles of accounting and costing systems as laid down by the BPIF.

The study of computer systems was an important part of the SMPS's management accounting service. In 1981 it was decided, for various reasons, to recommend to members the system offered by Create System of Perth, this being at the time the only software house offering a complete suite of programmes with printing and estimating packages. Subsequently an alternative package of systems on the same basis was developed and made available by a company from Livingston, RAAND Systems. It was designed to the specification of an SMPS member firm. 1982 saw an increase in the number of companies purchasing small micro systems for specific applications, but only a few companies made the capital outlay for larger, more sophisticated systems. The industry still lacked an efficient, adaptable system for estimating at a price related to that of micro-computers.

In the late 1980s, interest in quality assurance gained momentum amongst member firms. They began to seek registration to BS:5750 standards. The achievement of these standards made for greater internal efficiency as well as being a valuable marketing tool. The SMPS role, from the day the concept was introduced to Scottish printing in 1986, was to act as a catalyst. As one of three constituent members of the Printing Industries Quality Assurance Council the SMPS sponsored the production of a video demonstrating the application of quality assurance specifically in the industry. The video assisted employee communications and was well received by member firms.

c. Education and Training
A major aspect of the SMPS's work ensured basic provision of training facilities for use by entrants to the industry. The SMPS strategy in the field of training and education is analysed in Chapter 15. The Society promoted the industry with individual further education colleges and was represented in qualification awarding bodies such as City and Guilds and SCOTVEC. Specialist courses in subjects as diverse as print salesmanship and supervisory skills were organised by the SMPS whilst training in changes in legislation or working practices were arranged when necessary. Where a member company had a training or education need the Society's staff assisted in the preparation of a training programme.

d. Political Lobbying
The SMPS either individually or jointly with the BPIF and the Confederation of British Industry (CBI), influenced UK government legislation in the interests of member firms. It tried to persuade government to introduce legislation favourable to its members or to amend proposed legislation to limit the damage to its members interests. The Purchase Tax Joint Standing Committee continually pursued efforts to reduce anomalies caused by Purchase Tax regulations as they affected printing and stationery. Useful amendments were obtained in connection with compliment

---

slips, printed envelopes and partly printed leaflets. The SMPS argued unsuccessfully that the Scottish printing industry be relieved of the tax. When the Conservative government of Edward Heath (1970-1974) replaced Purchase Tax with Value Added Tax (VAT) books, newspapers and periodicals were taxed at a zero rate. In the late 1980s under pressure from the European Community the UK government threatened to raise the VAT rate on books, newspapers and periodicals. The SMPS, together with other printing and publishing trade associations persuaded the government to retain zero rating. It was a campaign from the grass roots to the highest ranking politicians in Brussels.

In 1970, a Joint Liaison Committee consisting of representatives of all the employers' organisations connected with printing and newspaper production and of the CBI was set up to exchange information about their industrial relations activities. The committee in 1970 made representations to the government concerning aspects of the Industrial Relations Bill and especially about the right to suspend employees who were prevented from working on account of industrial disputes in another section or outside the industry The SMPS made representation to the UK government to prevent further distortion of the objectives of the Redundancy Payments Act (1965) and the Conservative government's counter-inflation policy (1971-74). The work of the Joint Liaison Committee provided a forum for discussion of policy and practice adopted by organisations of employers connected with the printing industry and through the CBI with other industries.

In 1984, the Conservative government announced its intention to require local authorities to invite competitive tenders for particular types of work and with other designated activities/services such as printing, undertake value for money comparisons against the cost of provision other than by the authority itself. The SMPS responded that unless the proposed legislation provided effective sanctions, offending local authorities would find negative reasons for taking no action on value for money comparison results. The Society strongly recommended compulsory tendering be extended to printing services so local authority in-plant print departments would be put to the test in the market place. The Society unsuccessfully pressed its case at a meeting with Scottish Conservative MPs.

Summary
The membership of the SMPS fell during its lifetime. This was due to smaller companies going bankrupt and/or being taken over by the larger firms. Resignation from membership was not a problem. The only major company resigning was Wm Collins Sons & Co in May 1980. Despite its high degree of membership, the SMPS constantly sought, with varying degrees of success, to recruit new members.

The SMPS undertook a number of revisions of its constitution and rules. In May 1962, a Constitutional Committee recommended changes to membership contributions of groups of companies, representation on the Executive Board and voting at the annual general meeting. In the 1970s, a Forward Policy Committee was established to develop a proactive role in relationships with the unions. By the mid-1970s, the committee was spending too much time debating negotiation tactics. In 1977, the committee was reconstituted as a policy, planning and strategic thinking arm of the SMPS. In 1985, the size of the Executive Board was reduced. In 1964, the Society moved from Hill Street to York Place, which was sold in 1980 when it moved to Edinburgh House. In February 1989, the SMPS purchased 48 Palmerston Place which became functional on 21 October 1989. The YMP Group was an important body of opinion within the SMPS catering directly to the development needs of young printing managers. In October 1978, the Scottish YMP Group celebrated its golden jubilee.

In 1985, the SMPS accepted radical changes to the basis of its subscription income. In future, membership fees were paid annually rather than quarterly and paid in a lump sum with a discount if paid before a certain date. Using the national wage agreement as a basis for sound industrial relations practice, SMPS provided an advisory service ranging from a telephone consultation to representing the member company at meetings with the trade unions. The Society's Management Accounting Service was customised to the needs of individual printing businesses. It provided members with a confidential report containing essential information to help make important marketing and financial decisions. 1963 saw the fiftieth anniversary of the introduction of the cost system. There had been comparatively little change to its original principles.

Notes

[1] See *Printing in Scotland: The Market Challenge,* Scottish Development Agency/SMPS, 1981.

[2] On a smaller scale the Scottish printing industry was the home of several firms specialising in binding and finishing, spiral binding (Spirax Binders of Perth), books, journals, business forms and military and sporting targets (McQueens in the Scottish borders).

[3] See *The Scottish Digest*, Vol. 1, Number 2, Society of Master Printers of Scotland, May 1961.

[4] In 1964 the allocation from head office to the Ayrshire Association was £60, to the Dundee Association £175, to the Edinburgh Association £1,100 and to the Glasgow Association £1,400.

[5] See Minutes of the Meeting of the Constitution Committee held on 8 February 1963.

[6] See *Interim Report* by Forward Policy Committee to Executive Board Meeting, 31 March 1971.

[7] See Report and Recommendations by the Subcommittee of the Forward Policy Committee on the Structure and Functions of the SMPS Committees to the Executive Board, 1 February 1982.

8   The Northern Counties Association had not claimed its place on the Executive Board since 1982 whilst the Dumfries Association had been moribund for some time. The Edinburgh and Glasgow Associations currently held fourteen and fifteen places respectively on the Executive Board but were sending only six or seven representatives to meetings. It was proposed therefore their representation be reduced to seven (Edinburgh) and eight (Glasgow).

9   See *The Scottish Digest,* Vol. 1, No. 1, Society of Master Printers of Scotland, January 1961.

10 See *Report and Accounts, 1983/84,* Society of Master Printers of Scotland, 1984.

11 See 'Fifty Years of Costing', *Scottish Digest,* Vol. 111, No. 1, Society of Master Printers of Scotland, May 1963.

12 See *SMPS Report and Accounts, 1981-82,* Society of Master Printers of Scotland.

Chapter 15

EDUCATION AND TRAINING

The first section of this chapter examines the selection of apprentices and the content, location (on the job/off the job, etc) and assessment of their training. The second part outlines the industry's training arrangements for other production workers. It then describes the impact of the Printing and Publishing Industry Training Board (PPITB) in its objective of assisting the printing industry increase the quantity and quality of its industrial training. The final section of the chapter deals with the provision within the industry of training for non-production workers such as supervisors and clerical employees.

Introduction

A major activity of the SMPS was to facilitate the provision of training and retraining and to secure recruitment of employees to the industry. The future viability of the industry depended on a well-trained and well-informed workforce. To this end the SMPS in 1961 appointed an Education Committee to deal with technical training for the industry in Scotland. It had broad terms of reference covering apprenticeship selection and training, and ensuring that technical education in Scotland did not fall behind current developments elsewhere in the UK. Its membership contained at least one representative from each local associations. In 1965 the committee was retitled the Education and Training Committee.

In the early 1980s the SMPS conducted a review of its activities in education and training and reorganised its staff resources in the area. From September 1982 education and training activities were integrated with those of industrial relations. These new arrangements ensured member firms received training advice on a wide range of occupations and facilitated negotiations on education and training matters with the UK government, educational establishments, qualification awarding bodies and trade unions[1]. The unions had an interest in the quantity and quality of training available to their members and regarded training as a core collective bargaining issue. In the 1988 national negotiations however, both the NGA and SOGAT accepted training matters in future be discussed outwith the annual wages negotiations. This, it was hoped, would make desirable changes to training programmes more achievable. The intense pressures of wage negotiations carried the danger training issues might quickly fall from the bargaining agenda.

On the formation of the SMPS the training philosophy of employers in the industry was to train for the industry. The wide diversity of processes, equipment and techniques were broken down into four craft areas, namely graphic reproduction, typesetting and composition, machine printing, and binding and finishing. This was a convenient arrangement which served the industry well. During the lifetime of the SMPS technological advances challenged this arrangement and there was talk of training being upon a wider basis such as 'pre-machine' and 'post-origination'. One drawback to a wider base of occupations for training was it frequently did not match the short-term needs of print employers whose main priority with developing only those skills which they needed within their own business. With the advent of more specialised equipment Scottish printing employers were unlikely to have the hardware to support a broader training base. By 1990 greater specialisation within individual companies resulted in a change in training philosophy from one of training for the industry to one of training for company needs.

Craft Training

There was no formal restriction regarding age or academic qualification for an individual to apply for craft training but in practice most apprentices started their training between the ages of sixteen and eighteen. Although there were no mandatory academic qualifications for entry into the production side, many employers looked for the attainment of some 'O' or Standard Grades, particularly in English, arithmetic, art or a science subject. Entry requirements varied according to the vacancy. By the 1980s the industry was experiencing difficulties in attracting high calibre young people. There were a number of reasons for this, including the government encouraging more sixteen year olds to continue in full-time education, and the image of the industry. It was viewed, as the IT revolution gathered pace, as part of the 'old economy' rather than the 'new' and was also perceived as a male-dominated preserve. A further problem in attracting young people was the demographic trend of the late 1980s and that expected in the 1990s, namely sharp decline in the number of sixteen year olds entering the labour market. When the industry was expecting its greatest demand for qualified personnel it would experience the loss through retirement of the post-war intake of the 1950s and have difficulty in replacing them with young people who would be in short supply. The only alternative source of labour would be those who left school in the late 1970s and failed to find apprenticeships and, in many cases, started their working lives 'on the dole'. To help the industry compete for young people with the required talents the SMPS improved its careers presentation material and produced a film entitled *Print Your Own Future*. In 1989 the Executive Board approved the production of a career video with supporting literature for use by member companies and by the careers service.[2]

a. Selection

Potential craft trainees applied to be a printing craft apprentice in a number of ways, for example, through the Careers Office and job adverts but the most common method was direct application to a company. The SMPS received each year a limited number of applications from prospective apprentices and their details were circulated to member firms. Applicants completed an application form to undertake four years of training and related experience. Craft training was offered in four areas – composition, graphic reproduction, machine printing and bookbinding/print finishing. Compositors were the first in the chain of production operations. They turned the customer's copy into type or film. The planning and decisions made by compositors were crucial to the final appearance of the printed work. The customer's text was set on computer-controlled equipment linked to a phototypesetter which produced a photographic image on film or paper. After processing, the film or paper was cut and assembled with pre-set display lines, illustrations and other elements into pages. These were assembled in correct position and sequence, ready for the camera and platemaking operations. A compositor required a good command of English, proficiency in spelling and punctuation, the ability to work accurately, and with care and attention to detail. A liking for design and colour was essential.

The graphic reproduction area covered a wide range of specialist operations associated with the reproduction of illustrations and their preparation for the printing process. The main jobs were a camera operator, retoucher and assembler. A camera operator produced negatives or positives from drawings or photographs, calculated the reduction or enlargement needed, worked out lens apertures and exposures, selected filters and illuminated the subject correctly. The retoucher's work required a steady hand to remove blemishes from photographs, negatives and positives or adjust the tones. They worked with a brush or fine spray using dyes, opaques, acids and other chemicals to improve the image on the film.

Some retouchers operated electronic scanners which separated a colour picture into the printing colours. Assemblers worked with negatives and positives and combined the elements of a job prior to the production of a printing plate. Trainees in graphic reproduction required a knowledge of science and/or mathematics, the ability to work accurately and perfect colour vision. They required good eyesight and not to suffer from allergies which might be affected by fumes from solvents or contact with chemicals.

A machine printer positioned, and secured, the plates, selected and mixed, if necessary, the correct colour of ink, adjusted the machine so all parts of the image received the appropriate pressure, loaded the press with paper and ensured the machine settings were correct for the material being printed. Machine settings were checked by taking trial prints until the printer was satisfied the finished product matched the specification. During printing the machine printer kept watch to maintain the quality of each sheet or copy. After each job was completed, the printed sheets were off-loaded and the press prepared for the next job. On the larger printing presses machine printers worked as a team. Applicants for machine printing needed the ability to work accurately in what could be a noisy environment, have mechanical aptitude and excellent colour vision. A machine printer needed average physical strength and agility without any physical disability which could prevent long periods of standing or any allergy to fumes from solvents or contact with chemicals.

Although a bookbinder could be employed in a firm restoring old books and hand binding new expensive volumes, most were employed in the manufacture of books using machines which produced books mechanically. Various machines folded the sheets, put the sections into correct order, stitched the leaves, and made the case for the book or applied the lettering. The final operation brought all the parts together to form the finished book. Some bookbinders performed all operations involved in binding books and print finishing, whilst others specialised in particular operations. In some areas, local arrangements allowed for a separate apprenticeship in print finishing. This meant the trainee was not expected to become proficient in the skills of bookbinding but to concentrate on operations concerned with the finishing of general printing or stationery products, mainly folding, cutting and stitching. A bookbinder/print finisher required mechanical aptitude. For hand bookbinding an aptitude for working with hand tools was essential. Reasonable physical strength and agility was necessary coupled with the ability to work in a noisy environment. Good eyesight and normal colour vision were required.

If, on the basis of the application form, a print company wished to sponsor an individual as an apprentice, that individual sat the SMPS aptitude and colour vision test which provided indicators of their suitability for a particular craft area. The SMPS tested no more than two candidates for each apprenticeship

---

vacancy. If the individual test result showed they were a suitable candidate for a craft apprentice then an interview took place between the employer and the candidate after which the company made its final decision. If the company decided to sponsor the individual as an apprentice it returned an 'Apprentice Registration Form' to the SMPS stating, inter alia, the occupation area in which the apprentice would be trained during their in-company experience in the first year of their apprenticeship. The ideal candidate for a craft apprenticeship was under eighteen years of age, had a reasonable standard of numeracy and literacy, normal colour vision and could demonstrate an interest in a career in the industry. About one third of applicants for a craft apprenticeship were successful in gaining sponsorship. Unsuccessful candidates with suitable academic qualifications were advised of other career or educational opportunities within the industry. The above selection procedure operated in the urban areas of Scotland and ensured uniform standards in the selection of apprentices. In the more isolated parts of the country there were no formal methods of selection. Each company did its own thing.

b. The Content of the Training

The content of craft training delivered through a system of on, and off the job training developed individuals so that they could make a positive and effective contribution at their place of work. The normal period of training and related experience was four years, after which the trainee qualified for the full craft rate of pay. The training programme covered the main elements of skill training and related further education given within the first two years, with the remaining training concentrating on the application of the skills learned to a range of practical experiences.

Apprentices attended printing colleges on a day release basis but in 1967 the Edinburgh local association introduced full-time day release for the first year of training followed by block release in subsequent years. In 1968 the Education and Training Committee, chaired by Bob Thomson, recommended the printing colleges have a greater involvement in the apprenticeship selection process and in the first year of training there be full-time release for all apprentices in the industry. The balance of content between skills acquisition and development and further education (and agreed between the print colleges and the industry) was 60%/40%. Following the agreement of the Scottish Education Department of the Scottish Office to the introduction, throughout Scotland, of first year full-time courses for all print craft apprentices, a meeting took place in 1970 between the SMPS and the print colleges to establish a suitable syllabus. This emerged from the meeting, and was approved by the Scottish Office, and delivered in training programmes available only in the Glasgow College of Printing and Napier College of Science and Technology, Edinburgh. The change in attendance from day release to block release required consideration to when apprentices began their employment. The SMPS proposed during the interim period all craft apprentices completing their apprenticeship during 1971 and in January and February 1972 be replaced by apprentices starting in July/August 1971. Thereafter apprentices finishing their apprenticeships from 1 March in any year to the following 28 February be replaced in the July/August period of the year. After the interim period craft apprentices started their training in each July or August. These arrangements were accepted by the unions.

Duncan of Jordanstone College of Art, Dundee was one of five colleges chosen to run the 'pilot' course provided by the Printing and Publishing Industrial Training Board. Relative to the Glasgow and Edinburgh colleges' courses this 'pilot' course had a higher practical content. If the 'pilot' was successful it would form, in the future, the basis for all first year full-time courses for craft apprentices. In 1972 the SMPS Education and Training Committee concluded the standard of apprentice training following from the introduction of the first year full-time course in all three colleges had, relative to the previous scheme, improved substantially whether on a further education basis (Glasgow and Edinburgh) or on the more practical based PPITB programme. The Glasgow local association whilst recognising the improvement in the quality of training, requested the educational content following the first year of the apprenticeship be on a day release basis as opposed to block release. It recognised for geographical reasons, it was essential the Dundee College continued to provide block release after the first year as there was little desire in the Edinburgh local association for a change from block release. The SMPS recognised many advantages in the highly practical content of the Dundee 'pilot' course relative to the Edinburgh and Glasgow further education courses and became keen the 'pilot' course be adopted by those. Following discussions involving the SMPS, the unions, the printing colleges and the Printing and Publishing Industry Training Board, from the 1973/74 academic year, the PPITB first year full-time highly practical-based integrated course was extended to the Edinburgh and Glasgow colleges.[3]

In the early 1980s in response to rising school leaver unemployment the Conservative government introduced the Youth Training Scheme (YTS) to give young people some work experience, some systematic training and the opportunity to continue further education. The government provided grants to encourage employers to offer YTS training opportunities. The Manpower Services Commission (MSC) provided funds to 'managing agents'. The SMPS was recognised as a managing agent and amended the craft apprenticeship system to meet the conditions of the YTS. This scheme, known as the Scottish Print Training Scheme, became operative in 1983. Under it, if a member firm recruited a sixteen year old school leaver or a seventeen year old as a production apprentice, grant funding was available through the Scottish Print Training Scheme. Apprentices meeting the criteria set by the MSC were eligible for a grant of nearly £2,000 per year over two years if he/she started YTS at sixteen years of age and was a recent school leaver. Trainees under the Scottish Print Training Scheme remained employees of the sponsoring company paid according to the industry's national agreements. The SMPS administered the scheme as a managing agent and used YTS funds to pay for items such as college fees, trainer training and to contribute towards the employer's training costs.[4] In 1983 the SMPS successfully obtained over £70,000 of MSC funding for members recruiting apprentices and an additional £4,000 from the same source to cover its own administrative costs.

The conditions of YTS funding called for an individual training plan covering an agreed training content, off the job training in job-related and common core skills, along with assessment and monitoring of the training given. Printing skills trainees were given further education input designed to improve their skills in communications, numeracy, problem-solving and personal effectiveness, each of which helped the trainee adjust to the working environment. SMPS staff undertook monitoring and gave advice on training as an integral part of the scheme. MSC staff monitored both the trainee and their trainers to ensure the YTS contract was being fulfilled. The Scottish Print Training Scheme did not produce radical change in either the mode, content or method of training. It defined the core skills required in the various craft areas along with the development of a system of delivery which met the criteria of the MSC.

Whilst no MSC monitoring took place of non-YTS trainees, the SMPS maintained high standards for all trainees and training advice and monitoring of standards was offered. The majority of entrants in the 1980s to apprenticeships acquired some YTS funding. In 1983 there were thirty eight in this position and by 1988 the number was 125. Non-YTS trainees undertook a programme of study requiring the successful completion of twenty six modules leading to the National Certificate. Each student received detailed documentation outlining the areas in which they had demonstrated competency in their acquired skill and knowledge. College attendance was, in the first year, twelve weeks of full-time attendance followed in subsequent years by forty days of day release. The scheme provided common training in key skills for the four main craft areas. All trainees had the opportunity to gain the nationally recognised craft qualification provided by SCOTVEC or by City and Guilds. Over and above the common skills, individual employers, in assessing training standards achieved by their trainees, applied the craft standards expected within their company. Each trainee on the scheme was given a log book in which they recorded weekly the progress of their training but there was provision for monthly assessments of progress. On completion of training the log book remained the property of the trainee and was evidence of the standards attained.

In the late 1980s, the effects of recession made themselves felt in shortages of skilled staff required to operate sophisticated, and expensive, equipment. SMPS member firms realised the importance of training to the future prosperity of the industry. The efficient use of such equipment demonstrated, apart from traditional manual skills, there was a need to develop and broaden the knowledge base of production employees. In recognition of this the SMPS established in 1989, a Production Worker Training Working Party to establish what, if any, changes were needed to the current approach to print production worker training to meet the expected economic, demographic and technological change the industry faced over the next decade. The working party examined thoroughly the factors involved in updating the methods of production worker training, took account of UK government policy, of workplace-based Scottish Vocational Qualifications (SVQs) and of the likely shortfall in the numbers of school leavers. The working party identified seven areas of concern:

(1) the absence of a formal mechanism for the upgrading of non craft employees
(2) the uneven availability of the vocational qualification throughout Scotland and the absence of workplace standards of competence as a basis for its award
(3) changes to government-funded training arrangements with the advent of Local Enterprise Companies. The government expected employers to shoulder more of the burden of the cost of training and had announced a sizeable cut in training grants
(4) there was anxiety over the probably shortage of young entrants leading to a greater need for adult training and re-training
(5) the increasing pace of technological change would mean in the future shorter periods of training
(6) the need to accredit relevant training completed before entering the printing industry
(7) the working party was apprehensive about finding ways of ensuring a more equitable approach to meeting the costs of training.

The working party recommended the SMPS accept the principle that the SVQ be available for all production workers and that a realistic timetable be set to achieve this aim. The SMPS was urged to adopt a common set of nationally agreed workplace standards of competence as the basis for the development of the SVQ. In establishing this qualification, full recognition was given to attainments gained in advance of employment in the industry, provided such achievement met the nationally agreed standards of competence. The working party proposed all future training be based on defined achievements and not on specific periods of time and the pay of trainees be based on increments reflecting progress made towards meeting national standards. The SMPS sought formal agreement with the unions that future production worker training be based on a two-tier structure leading to the award of the SVQs and open to all without restriction based upon age, sex or previous employment. The SMPS stated that, wherever possible retraining for production workers in the industry be to nationally accepted standards of competence and be assessable towards the requirements of SVQs, and embarked on a promotional campaign to encourage the recruitment and systematic training of production workers.

The working party, in addition, suggested the SMPS set recommended standards of equipment and personnel for those companies giving training in basic skills and they produce a model scheme for those companies offering basic training along with training for those required to administer it. The SMPS promoted its own course in instructional techniques for those responsible for providing instruction to production workers.

The working party recommendations on production worker training were accepted by the Executive Board and the recommendations received the broad support of member firms at local association meetings. The next stage in the modernisation of the industry's production worker training was the establishment of SVQs primarily based on workplace standards of competence but sufficiently flexible to enable all production employees to gain the qualification at the level appropriate to the individual. This new system of production worker training encouraged individuals to upgrade to higher levels of skill during their working lives.

c. Off the Job Training

Printing education in Scotland was available throughout most of the twentieth century in the major cities of Edinburgh, Glasgow and Dundee. Further education for the print industry in Edinburgh was recorded as early as 1912 but the curriculum content was marginal to enhanced knowledge of craft skills needed by the industry. By the late 1920s, a printing department was established in Heriot-Watt College in Chambers Street, Edinburgh, offering further education to apprentices employed in the industry. This provided both theoretical and practical subjects directly related to the apprenticeship and classes were normally taught in the evening. This mode of attendance continued until the 1950s when as a result of a government initiative, day release attendance at a further education college became the norm. When Heriot-Watt College became a university in 1964 printing education was transferred to Napier Technical College in Merchiston where the Department of Printing and Photography was replaced with a new department named Print Media, Publishing and Communications. This title more accurately reflected the range of courses then being offered at further and higher education levels.[5]

Although further education for the industry existed on an evening-only basis before the First World War formal printing education commenced at Stow College of Printing in Cowcaddens, Glasgow in 1928, offering programmes of study directly related to the craft apprenticeship of the time. As in Edinburgh courses were originally offered on an evening basis only. With changes to the national education structure in the 1950s they moved to day release provision. In 1964 new premises, shared with Glasgow College of Building were opened in North Hanover Street and Stow College of Printing became the Glasgow College of Printing. The Departments of Printing Technology and Printing Management and Science offered courses in printing studies at both further and higher education levels.

In 1972 the Colleges of Building and Printing merged to form the Glasgow College of Building and Printing. In the following thirty years, many changes to the structure of the college took place. There were still two departments which offered courses directly, and peripherally, related to the printing industry, namely the Departments of Printing Studies and of Visual Communication.

Records show there was printing education at Dundee Technical College and School of Art as early as 1926. Printing education centred around the Duncan of Jordonstone College of Art where in 1959 the Printing Studies Department was established in the college's new premises in Perth Road. Teaching focussed on the day release training of apprentices from Dundee and the surrounding area. Later apprentices from Aberdeen and further afield in the Highlands were taught on a block release/residential basis under the auspices of the Printing and Publishing Industry Training Board. With the changes in apprenticeship patterns resulting from the introduction of new technology in the mid-1980s and the subsequent decline in the numbers applying for formal training, the Department of Printing as a separate entity closed in 1986. Credited to this college was the establishment of the first distance learning course in print within the UK. This HNC in Printing was devised and all 131 units written and produced by the staff long before digital imaging and web CT were teaching mediums.

For some years concern was expressed by member firms that trainees from outside the central belt of Scotland were disadvantaged as regards access to college facilities in Glasgow and Edinburgh. In 1985, following a joint initiative by the Aberdeen Master Printers Association and SMPS head office staff, arrangements were made with the Grampian Regional Council and the Glasgow College of Building and Printing for the accommodation of trainees from the north east of Scotland in Edinburgh and Glasgow. The arrangement was later extended to include trainees from as widely separated as Orkney and Dumfries.

In maintaining and developing closer links with the Glasgow and Edinburgh printing colleges, the SMPS Education and Training Committee held regular meetings with the staff. These provided a valuable exchange of views with college staff and the opportunity to see at first hand changes coming about in the colleges. One problem for the colleges was obtaining the latest production technologies. Technology was changing very rapidly but the new equipment was expensive to purchase. In 1988 the Scottish printing industry undertook to re-equip the colleges with the help of the Department of Trade and the Industry/ Printing Equipment Educational Trust (PEET). The SMPS and some member firms via donations could rightly claim a major role in the two print colleges. The period 1989-91 saw equipment installed to the value of approximately £1.5 million not including gifts of equipment from a number of manufacturers and suppliers. Whilst there was a continuing need to update equipment, the industry's late 1980's initiative to re-equip the colleges enhanced the quality of training provided by Napier College and the Glasgow College of Building and Printing. One disappointment of the initiative was the large number of printing/publishing firms throughout the UK who ignored the appeals for a contribution to PEET. Given this the SMPS approved a donation of £2,500 to PEET.

d. Assessment of the Training

While there was no reason to suppose the traditional approach to training failed to produce excellent craftsmen there was no doubt the lack of a regular and formal system of assessment often resulted in individual trainees failing to achieve the required standard in some aspects of their craft. Post-1983 the craft training scheme provided for regular and systematic assessment of the trainee. This ensured any failure to meet the defined standards was identified before any damage was done to the trainee or the trainer. The assessment was a two-way process and when properly conducted revealed shortcomings in a number of areas including the training scheme itself. The trainee's log books contained three different types of assessment documents. White sheets were completed weekly, initiated by the trainee and after discussion with the trainer or the supervisor completed by both parties. A blue document was completed on a monthly basis and was a review of progress between trainee and trainer and on completion indicated where progress had been made and which areas were to be concentrated upon over the next month. A yellow sheet was completed quarterly. This document summarised all the assessments which had taken place in the previous quarter and provided a broad picture of the trainee's progress.

The off the job training in the printing colleges was assessed by examination. Up until 1985, print apprentices received academic qualifications awarded by the City and Guilds of London Institute, founded in 1873 to encourage education and training in and for the workplace. The City and Guilds awarded qualifications for the printing industry at the Intermediate and Final Certification level as well as advanced awards like the Full Technological Certificate in Printing. In 1974 the SMPS successfully opposed proposals from the Joint Advisory Committee of the City and Guilds of London Institute to abolish the two-tier examination system in favour of a single course which required increases in the minimum hours of attendance at college. To have accepted the Joint Advisory Committee's proposal would have abolished the then basic and advanced craft certificate, introduced one examination and minimum attendance at college of three years for all apprentices. In 1985 the Secretary of State for Scotland amalgamated the former SCOTEC and SCOTBEC organisations into one awarding body, called SCOTVEC, providing a national framework for qualifications in the Scottish printing and graphic communications industry. SCOTVEC assessed and awarded qualifications at SVQ and HNC/HND level. SVQ were qualifications combining skills, knowledge and ability within a specific occupational area. They were based on National Occupational Standards produced by the National Training Organisation (on which the SMPS had representation) for the printing industry.

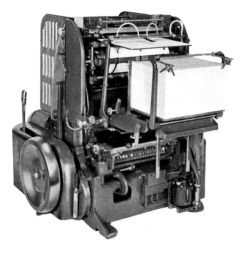

Vertical Miehle press

Other Production Worker Training

In 1970 arrangements were made between the SMPS and Stevenson College, Edinburgh to run regular four week introductory courses for female entrants into the printing industry. In 1981 the combined initiatives of the Printing and Publishing Industry Training Board, the Scottish Graphical Division of SOGAT and the SMPS persuaded the MSC to provide retraining courses for unemployed hot metal compositors. The course consisted of training in photocomposition and make-up techniques to improve the marketable skills of those attending. Agreement was also reached with the MSC to provide a similar course for the retraining of letterpress machine managers to acquire and develop skills to manage litho machines. Both courses were funded under the MSC Training Opportunities Scheme (TOPs).

The SMPS agreement with SOGAT contained provision for adult apprentices by upgrading of auxiliary staff already in post, usually machine assistants to machine manager. This approach was taken by print companies recruiting female keyboard/word-processor operators and was used by unions and employers to overcome local skill shortages and at the same time circumvent legislative barriers. In the former SLADE area (reproduction), although the 'wage for age' agreement allowed for the recruitment of adults, the prohibitive cost of this was a big disincentive to take advantage of the provision.

In the SOGAT Equal Pay Agreement (1973) there was no distinction made between craft and non-craft operations. All operations could be carried out by any individual provided they received the appropriate grade rate and 'time-served' employees received the same rate. In Edinburgh there was a recognised craft group of print finishers while in Glasgow only bookbinders were recognised as craftsmen. The common feature of all these routes into craft status was the four year period of service covering training and experience. In the majority of cases, skill training was confined to the first two years of employment with the remainder of the apprenticeship being confined to gaining experience. No credit was given to relevant pre-employment education and training and no differentiation made between training and experience.

The Printing and Publishing Industry Training Board (PPITB)

By the mid-1950s the system of vocational training which had evolved in the UK relied mainly on voluntary efforts by individual companies. The pattern of training standards in an industry was far from uniform. There were those employers whose training arrangements were comprehensive and thorough but a large number who did no training at all but relied for their skilled employees on poaching from those with good training arrangements. In between these extremes lay the greater part of industry. In 1956 the Conservative government set up a committee to investigate the vocational training situation in the UK. The committee, under the chairmanship of Robert Carr, Parliamentary Secretary to the Minister of Labour, consisted of representatives of employers and unions together with a number of other related organisations. The committee's report, entitled *Training for Skills,* concluded:

> Neither is the cost of training fairly shared by firms, nor is the amount and quality of training being done in the country enough to keep pace with the rapidly changing development and the rapidly changing technology which we need in order to keep ourselves alive in this island.

The Carr Committee appealed to industry to put its house in order but its appeal, based on pious hope, had little effect. Those who had always trained increased their efforts, but those who had not saw no reason to change their policy of 'poaching' skilled employees from wherever they could. In December 1962 the government issued a White Paper outlining a bill to put industrial training on an organised basis at a time when the UK, alone in Europe, had no legislation on the subject. The White Paper outlined a method of collecting a statutory levy from firms but paying back by way of a grant either less, the same or more than the amount collected in levy according to the quality and amount of training undertaken. The Industrial Training Act received Royal Assent in March 1964 and was the first Act of Parliament since 1563 relating to industrial training.

The Industrial Training Act took responsibility for training away from individual companies and transferred it to Industrial Training Boards. The Act had three objectives. First, to ensure an adequate supply of properly trained men and women at all levels of industry and second to secure an improvement in the quality of industrial training. The third objective was to share the cost of training more evenly between firms. The Act permitted the Minister of Labour to set up Training Boards to improve the provision for the training of people in any activities of industry or commerce. If an employer did not wish to train they would not be forced to. Where the size and training needs of a company made training necessary, the levy and grant system made it uneconomic for a firm to neglect its responsibility to train its own employees.

On 29 May 1968 the Printing and Publishing Industry Training Board was established under the chairmanship of Norman Fisher. It covered 400,000 employees. Its terms of reference were:

> …to assist the printing and publishing industry to increase its efficiency and prospects through effective training, thereby developing the industry's potential for the benefit of those who own it, those who work in it and its customers.

The levy imposed by the Training Board on printing companies was 1% of payroll. Training was based on the industry's national requirements rather than any individual company and was delivered for the Training Board by the printing schools in the further education sector. The levy was used to pay a grant to offset some of the cost of employing a trainer during their period of training. The remainder of the finance raised by the levy funded the operating costs of the PPITB and helped the FE colleges upgrade their industrial equipment.

The training programme commenced with a young person taking up a craft apprenticeship with a recognised printing company. The trainee attended a printing college full-time over the next year (forty weeks, times five days per week) where they received education and training based on a curriculum of general printing theory, technical printing theory based on their area of specialism and practical workshops based on their specialisms. At the end of this period of study trainees who had successfully completed the year were awarded a certificate of merit. On their return to their workplace they and their employer were encouraged to enhance the apprentice's education and training by attendance at the FE college for a further two years at the end of which they were assessed externally. Those who successfully completed this pattern were awarded a National Certificate from an awarding body such as the City and Guilds Institute or SCOTVEC. The Training Board gave a priority to retraining and development programmes to meet the need for the implementation of new production technologies.

The PPITB had two representatives from the Scottish printing industry – one on behalf of the employers and one on behalf of the print unions. Bob Thomson, chair of the SMPS Education and Training Committee, was co-opted onto the Training Board's Production Worker Training Committee. In 1972 the government published a White Paper on training dealing with the future of Industrial Training Boards in which it proposed the establishment of a National Training Agency to monitor

Industrial Training Boards. The emergence of the Training Services Agency (TSA) in 1975 resulted in changes to the nature and operation of the PPITB. The TSA had overall authority over the work of industrial training boards. The structure of the PPITB remained unchanged but its plans now required the sanction of the TSA which in turn answered to the Manpower Services Commission. The TSA approved the board's financial budget since the administrative costs of training boards were now to be met from central government funds rather than the levy paid by employers. The Employment and Training Act (1973) required training boards to exempt from levy payment all firms which reached an acceptable standard of training. In 1975 the PPITB introduced an exemption scheme and in that year 1,000 of the 3,887 establishments paying the levy applied for exemption and about half were approved.

In 1981, the future of the PPITB was in jeopardy when the Conservative government reduced public expenditure, inter alia, through staff reduction and by withdrawing their statutory duties of existing training boards. Voluntary training arrangements replaced statutory industrial training boards and the obligation on employers to finance training was removed. When in 1982 the Secretary of State for Employment, Norman Tebbit, announced the withdrawal of government financial support for the administration of industrial training boards, the PPITB was wound up. The SMPS opposed this arguing a statutory training board – albeit with reduced powers – was in the best interests of the Scottish printing industry. This view was at variance with that of the major employers' organisation in other industries.[6]

Non-Production Worker Training
The SMPS provided via conferences, seminars and short courses, training and development opportunities for the management teams in its member companies. In 1981 a residential course on 'Marketing for small businesses' was organised in co-operation with Paisley College of Technology together with courses on negotiation and managing technological change. From the mid-1980s the SMPS organised a series of short courses on supervisory skills, estimating, print sales, managing discipline and energy conservation. Member firms benefited from financial assistance by means of grants available through the SMPS and the Manpower Services Commission. Specific grants were available in respect of computer skills. The Manpower Services Commission funded courses covering print sales, supervisory management and statutory sick pay as well as computer staff training and supported the completion of the training of apprentices who had been made redundant. The Health and Safety at Work Act (1974) provided the impetus for courses for management representatives. These were held in the Glasgow College of Building and Printing.

Training was provided for instructors. In 1968 day conferences in 'Planning Systematic Training' were held in Edinburgh, Glasgow and Perth for representatives of top management. Following these conferences the Industrial Training Service prepared plans for training bindery instructors in the skills and job analysis for women operatives in the department. The courses each comprised ten days' classroom study with in-plant project work. In spring 1969, the Industrial Training Service ran a course for training present and potential training officers in the industry.

Several courses were arranged for senior managers. In June 1971, eleven executives representing nine firms attended a two-day course on 'Organisational development' run by the Industrial Training Service. It also ran four courses, each of three days duration, for senior managers and their supervisors from member firms. The theme of these residential courses was human relations. In the early 1970s the SMPS in conjunction with the BFMP arranged six seminars on VAT attended by nearly 300 people. In 1989, following agreement with the Training Services Agency, the SMPS and the BPIF co-operated in areas of management development and non-production employee training.

Summary

The typical candidate admitted to an apprenticeship was under eighteen years of age, had a reasonable standard of numeracy and literacy, normal colour vision and a real interest in a career in the industry. The content of their training covered the acquisition and development of skills to carry out the job competently and opportunities to continue further education. In 1983, to ensure apprenticeship training complied with the requirements for funding under the government's Youth Training Scheme, the SMPS introduced the Scottish Print Training Scheme. In 1989, the Society modernised apprenticeship training to one based on the principle of a common set of nationally agreed workplace standards of competence. Based on these standards, Scottish Vocational Qualifications (SVQs) were devised for production workers in the industry. The SVQ standards were flexible, enabling production employees to gain qualification at the particular level appropriate to their needs. This new system encouraged individuals to upgrade to higher skill levels.

Concerned about the lack of adequate provision for industrial training in the UK, the government introduced the Industrial Training Act (1964) to improve the quality and quantity of industrial training and, via a levy/grant system, make the sharing of the costs of industrial training more equitable. The Act took responsibility for training away from individual companies and transferred it to Industrial Training Boards (ITBs). In May 1968, the Printing and Publishing Industry Training Board (PPITB) was established and a training levy imposed on Scottish print firms of 1% of payroll. Training became based on the industry's national requirements rather than that of individual companies. In 1982 when the government withdrew its financial support for the administration of Industrial Training Boards and ended statutory obligations on employers to finance training, the PPITB was ended.

The SMPS provided via conferences, seminars and short courses, training and development opportunities for the management teams in its member companies. Programmes offered included negotiating techniques, management of change, marketing, supervisory skills, estimating print sales and computer skills.

Notes

[1] See SMPS, *Reports and Accounts, 1982/83,* Society of Master Printers of Scotland.

[2] See SMPS *Reports and Accounts, 1989-90,* Society of Master Printers of Scotland.

[3] The Printing and Publishing Industry Training Board's 'pilot' course had been running for two year at the Duncan of Jordanstone College of Art, Dundee when it was adopted as standard for the first year of training of print craft apprentices.

[4] The situation was helped, when in the 1982 wage negotiations SOGAT agreed a reduction of the first year apprentice rate to a level which enabled employers to claim a £16 per week award under the YTS. The combined effect of this award and the reduced wage fully compensated individual employers of apprentices from the loss of grants aid from the Printing and Publishing Industry Training Board in respect of fees the SMPS negotiated with colleges.

[5] In 1992 as a result of diminishing numbers of apprentices attending printing courses and a change in the structure of educational provision offered, Napier University withdrew from printing education at FE level.

[6] See SMPS, *Report and Accounts, 1981/82,* Society of Master Printers of Scotland.

Chapter 16

RELATIONSHIPS WITH THE BRITISH FEDERATION OF MASTER PRINTERS

This chapter examines relationships between the SMPS and the BFMP in terms of finance, labour negotiations, and constitutional matters following the implementation by the BFMP in 1967, of its first major reform of its operations since 1931. The main theme of the chapter is an examination of the attempts in 1968/69 and between 1981-1984 to establish a new basis for the relationship when it reached new low points.

Financial Relationships

a. SMPS Contribution

On the formation of the SMPS its annual subscription to the BFMP was £1,000, a figure agreed in 1956. In November 1963 the Society agreed that its President propose to the BFMP a 10% increase in the SMPS subscription. When the SMPS made this offer, the BFMP regarded it as derisory. The SMPS Finance Committee, arguing the subscription to the BFMP was a matter of policy rather than finance, decided the issue be examined by the President's Committee. In March 1965 the Executive Board agreed the SMPS annual subscription to the BFMP increase to £1,250, and be again reviewed in 1966 and thereafter at three year intervals.

In the 1966 negotiations, the basis of the subscription was altered so the BFMP received a fixed percentage of the SMPS subscription income, the intention being to remove the necessity of regular reviews which had led to antagonistic bargaining positions in the past. The 1969 review was complicated in that, in April 1969, the SMPS withdrew from participation in the main committees of the BFMP (see below). Given the importance to SMPS members of BFMP links, especially the Joint Labour Committee, the Society considered special circumstances prevailed and the 5% subscription rate be reviewed.

In October 1969 the Office Bearers of the SMPS therefore decided the annual subscription from April 1969 to the BFMP be reduced to 2.5% of subscription income. To say the least, the BFMP was unhappy with this proposal. After further negotiation it was agreed that for 1969 the SMPS subscription contribution to the BFMP should remain 5% (£1,103 in absolute terms) but from 1 January 1970 the annual subscription be 4% of SMPS total subscription income and the situation be reviewed in three years time.

In February 1980 the British Printing Industries Federation (BPIF see below) proposed a substantial increase in the SMPS annual subscription, from its current 4% of SMPS subscription income to 10%. This was resisted by the SMPS but in July 1980 the BPIF President again raised the proposal. The SMPS sought a meeting with the BPIF so misunderstanding did not arise. The SMPS President, Harry McNab and the Director Barrie Abbott met with the BPIF President, Bill Snell and its Director, Henry Kendall in London on 21 October. This meeting agreed that from the BPIF accounting year 1981-82 (SMPS accounting year 1981), the SMPS subscription rate to the BPIF be 5% of its annual subscription income. Interim arrangements were required to phase in the increased rate of 5% in respect of the SMPS fiscal year 1980-81 so the agreed subscription was set at £8,500. Under the *Carlisle Agreement* of 12 October 1981 between the SMPS and the BPIF, the basis of the SMPS subscription was in future related to the services carried out by the BPIF on behalf of the SMPS.

The 7 July 1981 meeting of the Executive Board confirmed the BPIF call for subscriptions in respect of 1982/3 could not be accepted because it had ceased, as of December 1981, to be a member organisation. It was prepared to pay for actual services received by SMPS members from the BPIF if the costs were properly identified and would not otherwise have been incurred by the BPIF. The Executive Board expected BPIF and SMPS co-operation wherever possible in action towards the benefits of the industry throughout the UK.[1] In October 1983, the SMPS and the BPIF established a liaison committee to consider the future relationship between the two bodies, including quantifying the amount of subscriptions which, in future, the SMPS should pay the BFMP. In the same month the BFMP accepted all SMPS financial commitments to it based on past agreements and extending from April 1982 to April 1984 be satisfied by a payment of £10,000 by the SMPS.

In July 1984, a meeting between the BPIF and the SMPS took place at York, to settle the basis of financial arrangements between the two bodies. Finding a mutually acceptable basis to regulate financial relationships proved difficult. It was eventually agreed SMPS recommend to their Office Bearers' Committee and to its Executive Board, that in future the annual subscription payable by the Society to the BPIF, starting from the year ending 31 December 1984, be 5% of the SMPS total membership subscriptions of the previous year and that the payment already made of £10,000 plus VAT be accepted as settlement for the SMPS contributions to the years ending 31 December 1983. In discussing the proposal the Executive Board stressed the SMPS remain independent, questioned what benefits would be received in return for the 5% payment, argued if a financial settlement could not be reached there was a possibility of ending relations with the BPIF and any agreement contain provision for reviewing the formula after a fixed period of time. After further discussion the Executive Board accepted in future the annual subscription payable to the BFIP be 5% of the previous year's subscription income with the proviso it be emphasised to the BPIF the SMPS remain independent for the foreseeable future. It agreed to seek an agreement with the BPIF on a reduction on the payment due for 1984. In November 1984 the BPIF agreed a subscription from the SMPS of £10,185 in respect of 1984. This represented 4% of the SMPS annual subscription income.[2]

b. Disputes Assistance Fund

In 1955, in anticipation of the wage negotiations with the unions in the following year, the BFMP established a Disputes Assistance Fund to provide financial assistance to member firms finding themselves in the forthcoming negotiations in dispute with the unions. In 1961, the SMPS made no payment into the fund as the BFMP had indicated the fund be frozen at a level not much above its existing one. It accepted if the BFMP did freeze the fund it would pay 10% of its BPIF contribution to bring the fund up to the limit proposed by the BFMP. So in February 1962, £500 was paid into the Disputes Assistance Fund by the SMPS for the year 1961/62.

In 1969, following the separation of the SMPS negotiating machinery from that of the BFMP the SMPS requested its share of the Disputes Assistance Fund be returned so the purpose for which the fund's had been set up could be implemented in Scotland if, and when necessary. The SMPS estimated this amounted to £15,785 plus interest until the time when the level of the fund was stabilised. The £15,785 was made up of £11,636 accruing from the Special Levy on all members of 1d per £1 wages paid during 1965 and of £5,000 from direct contributions from Scottish member firms over the period 1957-1962 inclusive. From this sum £850 was deducted, being the grants received from the Disputes Assistance Fund by SMPS member firms during the 1959 dispute. In March 1970, the BFMP transferred the Disputes Assistance Fund's Scottish portion to SMPS funds. The sum involved was over £10,000 and the SMPS invested this in fixed interest stock and equities.

The BFMP Commission on Labour Negotiations

In 1965, the BFMP established a Commission on Labour Negotiations to review its negotiating procedures with the unions. In October 1965, the SMPS submitted recommendations to the commission making four principal points.[3] First, the relationship between the two organisations was not the usual one of BFMP and constituent alliance. The BFMP constitution provided the SMPS was a member organisation but retained control of all matters affecting the industry in Scotland, of its own finances and conditions of membership. BFMP constitution gave Scotland autonomy in return for general co-operation on a UK basis. There was recognition of a UK interest with the need to preserve Scottish 'freedom'. It enabled the BFMP to speak as a UK organisation but maintained the freedom of the Scots. The SMPS memorandum to the Commission stressed that Scottish 'independence' must be preserved.

Second the SMPS, had its own agreements with five unions - ASLP, NSES, NUPB&PW, SLADE and STA – and also participated with the BFMP in the UK-wide negotiations on wages, hours, holidays and other matters discussed directly with the unions. The SMPS saw no reason to change this arrangement. It told the commission whatever happens in the future by way of union mergers the SMPS would wish to negotiate in Scotland with the appropriate unions. Its reason was in the relatively small Scottish printing industry points of difference were more easily overcome, than in the larger English and Welsh industry. For example, problems such as machine rating and staffing were generally solved quicker without hindrance to production.

Third, the memorandum argued while difficulties had arisen, and could do again, between the BFMP and the SMPS they were usually caused by problems of time and distance. It was recognised they could be minimised by good liaison between office bearers and officials of the two organisations. As neither the BFMP Labour Committee nor the BFMP Council controlled the SMPS, Scottish representation was not problematic provided it ensured proper liaison. There was no wish in Scotland for the size of its representation on the Labour Committee, or other BFMP decision-making bodies to change. In the SMPS there was no difficulty about representation on its Executive Board, committees etc. of different types of firms (for example, large, medium, small or group). All types accepted the SMPS representatives and the decisions they made. Consultation with the member firms was achieved during periods of negotiations by circulars, and special or emergency meetings of committees, the Board, and all members. There was relatively little criticism of the methods used nor of their effectiveness.

Fourth, it was the SMPS view if negotiations were to be conducted effectively, they be left to a small body. This view was based on experience in Scotland and had been referred to in a letter to Leonard Kenyon, Director of the BFMP, in June 1957 when consideration was given to revising the then negotiating procedures. The recent increase in the size of the BFMP negotiating team was seen as a retrograde step but was no reflection on the individuals involved. The SMPS memorandum stated the strength of a negotiating team was in inverse ratio to the number of its members. A team of five would have more strength than one of the present size but this could be difficult to achieve when Scotland, and presumably London, required to be represented when wages, hours and holidays were being bargained. The SMPS submission stressed members should have confidence in their appointed representatives in negotiations and a minimum number of them be allowed to do the difficult and unrewarding task of bargaining with employees. The BFMP Commission on Labour Negotiations reported in March 1966. It was accepted by the BFMP Council. Its main recommendation affecting the SMPS was reducing the size of the BFMP Joint Labour Committee such that in future Scotland would have one representative (instead of the current two) together with its Director. This situation was acceptable to the Executive Board.

Review of the BFMP Constitution

In April 1966, the BFMP Council set up a working party whose terms of reference were 'to review the constitution of the Federation and its member organisations in the light of the current circumstances and to report'. The BFMP constitution had remained substantially in its existing form since 1931. The Chair of the working party was Sir Max Bemrose. The SMPS submitted evidence to the working party in a memorandum dated 22 September 1966. The view in Scotland of the application of the BFMP constitution to the SMPS was that the footnote to Section II (Constitution) provided for control of Scottish affairs by the SMPS. The plenary powers of the BFMP Council in the management of the affairs of the BFMP related to England and Wales, but not to Scotland where authority rested with the Society's Executive Board. The SMPS evidence emphasised its representatives on the BFMP Council and committees in practice did not vote or intervene in matters which did not directly affect Scotland.

The memorandum pointed out the BFMP's standing committees' personnel, except for the General Purposes and President's Committee, was made up of members of 'alliances' with nominations from BFMP Council, etc. Scotland was treated 'de facto' as an alliance but the SMPS evidence stated that the SMPS autonomous position should remain. The SMPS argued there was a widespread recognition of the benefits to both organisations of close co-operation in matters of mutual concern but the unique relationship between the two organisations was not always understood. The SMPS suggested two changes to the existing BFMP constitution. First, its position be dealt with in the main body of the constitution and not by way of a footnote. Second, that on standing committees, the position of representatives from the SMPS be provided for explicitly.

The Constitution Working Party presented its report on 23 February 1967 and contained seven main recommendations. The name of the BFMP be changed to the British Print Employers Federation and its objectives revised. The BFMP would continue to comprise regional alliances and associations but their number be reduced. Other recommendations included individual firms should be members of the BFMP, the number of committees be reduced, the term 'Young Master Printer' be changed and the number of office bearers be increased by the appointment of another Vice-President. Under 'minor changes' the Constitution Working Party recommended the SMPS retain control of all matters affecting the industry in Scotland be stated in the body of the constitution and not in a footnote.[4]

In March 1967, the Executive Board debated the BFMP Constitution Working Party report. It noted three recommendations of that affected the SMPS directly. First there was the recommendation Scotland's constitutional position in the BFMP be shown in the main body of its constitution instead of by a footnote. The second was the proposal firms be in direct membership of the BFMP. Currently they were members of alliances which in turn were members of the BFMP. The third relevant recommendation was the BFMP change its name to the British Printing Employers Federation. After discussion the Executive Board unanimously agreed to inform the BFMP Council the SMPS did not accept that 'alliances' be taken to include the SMPS even for the purposes of the report and it rejected the proposal that member firms become direct members of the BFMP. In addition the BFMP be informed if it changed its name, the SMPS would not feel obliged to change its own name.

The recommendation that the SMPS's unique position be set out in the main body of the BFMP constitution rather than in a footnote, was welcomed by the Executive Board although it said it needed to study the details of the proposed change before acceptance. The Board expected to be given adequate time to examine specific changes proposed to the BFMP constitution before being asked whether or not the changes were acceptable. The Report of the Constitutional Working Party was accepted at the April 1967 BFMP Council meeting, except for the recommendation the BFMP change its name. The BFMP revised constitution and the new committee structure operated from autumn of 1967.

New Basis to the SMPS/BFMP Relationship
a. The 1969 Settlement
On 31 December 1966, the print unions gave notice to terminate their wage agreements with the SMPS and the BFMP. In view of the government's prices and incomes policy, it was unlikely any new agreements would be implemented before July 1967. It was hoped the intervening period be used to conclude new agreements in good time. This hope was not realised and by

August 1967 little progress had been made in the UK collective negotiations. At the end of August the STA indicated it wished to settle directly with the SMPS. It was possible to conclude an agreement in line with the objectives laid down by the Executive Board namely, elimination of the cost-of-living bonus, an improved apprentice intake, measures to increase productivity, an increase in the minimum journeyman rate of 25s 0d per week (including consolidation of 9s 0d cost-of-living bonus) and no fixed time duration to the agreement. In September 1967, a settlement with SOGAT was reached on similar terms and by end October with the NSES which had recently merged with the NGA.

By the end of October 1967, aggressive action by the unions, particularly against newspaper houses in the English provinces appeared to be leading to a complete stoppage in the newspaper and general printing industry in England and Wales. Urgent meetings resulted in a settlement between, on the one hand, the BFMP and the Newspaper Society and the unions, except for SLADE, on the other. The settlement contained measures to increase productivity but was not otherwise in line with the agreement made in Scotland. There was no provision for additional manpower, the increase in rates was 39s 0d for craftsmen (including consolidation of the cost of living bonus) payable in November 1967 and 14s 0d payable a year later. The agreement stabilised until end October 1969. The ASLP, which was a party to the BFMP settlement, approached the SMPS for similar terms but agreement was reached on the same terms as applied in Scotland to the other unions.

The unilateral action of the SMPS was regarded by the BFMP as so serious as to endanger relations between the two organisations. The BFMP office bearers held a meeting in London on 23 October 1967 with those of the SMPS to settle for future negotiations 'the exact relationship and responsibility of the parties'. For the SMPS, it was non-negotiable that the autonomy of Scotland should be preserved but it recognised the employers throughout the UK needed to work together as closely as possible in their common interests. The BFMP pressed the SMPS to give a written undertaking that in any circumstances in which the two organisations for some reason declined to act collectively in negotiations, they would pursue a common policy throughout their separate negotiations. The SMPS would not give such an undertaking and in November 1967 its Executive Board considered four options concerning future relationships with the BFMP: the status quo, accept the BFMP proposal, secede from the BFMP or negotiate some different basis of relationship with the BFMP.

The Executive Board considered the status quo unacceptable despite the occasions when autonomy had been exercised by Scotland in an undesirable manner by the BFMP were outnumbered by the occasions when the BFMP had taken action contrary to Scottish interests. The SMPS position – a BFMP member organisation but with full autonomy – led to misunderstandings and difficulties. Events proved neither organisation 'consulted' the other at all times in the manner in which the BFMP expected. It was impossible to accept the BFMP proposal. It had to be understood Scotland was a different country with different traditions as regards working conditions. Scottish printing labour relations were relatively good in comparison with England and Wales. The option of leaving the BFMP was harmful to one or other organisation and possibly both and was a course of action that might play into union hands. The achievement of unity on broad principles was regarded by both organisations as desirable. Despite difficulties from time to time there was a record of co-operation between the two organisations lasting some fifty years and neither the SMPS nor the BFMP wanted to 'turn back the clock'. The SMPS argued it should devise a method of working with the BFMP so both knew exactly where they stood with each other on some basis of partnership.

Following meetings between the office bearers of the two organisations held on 12 December 1967 and 12 March 1968 it was hoped the following agreement would prevent misunderstanding in the future.

> ...In any circumstances in which the Federation and the Society receive a common approach from trade unions involving basic wages, hours, holidays (or for any other reasons wish to associate in negotiations) the two employers' organisations will consult for the purposes of agreeing a common policy and the way in which it would be pursued. Any policy and procedure so agreed will be binding on the Federation Council and the SMPS Executive Board until the negotiations in question are completed...[5]

This statement was approved by the SMPS on 27 March 1968 and by the BFMP in April 1968.

The 1968 SMPS negotiations with the unions resulted in settlements but not without difficulty. Although their content was uniform, the SMPS was unable to harmonise the start dates of the different agreements. The main provisions of the agreements included stabilisation until 31 March 1970, an increase in rates for journeymen of £1 above the rate established in 1967, methods for dealing with manpower shortages, particularly in the lithographic section, the right to use female labour on non-traditional setting equipment and a procedure for productivity bargaining. The 1968 settlements by the SMPS did not arise from a common approach by the unions to the SMPS and to the BFMP but followed a decision of the BFMP that the SMPS no longer have representation on the Joint Labour Committee of the BFMP. The Chair of the Joint Labour Committee considered it too early to judge what results might flow from the divergence of the agreements between Scotland and England and Wales. The SMPS considered its wage settlements satisfactory in all the circumstances including the increase in wages due in England and Wales at the end of October 1968.

The BFMP considered the matter again in October 1968. However ten days before this meeting was due to take place, the Director of the BFMP was advised the Midland Alliance had passed the following resolution which they would submit to the 22 October meeting.

> ...The Midland Alliance proposes that Scotland should be asked to resign completely from the BFMP in consequence of making separate agreements with the Scottish Unions which are not considered to be in the interests of members in England and Wales. Under the circumstances there seems little point in Scotland retaining membership of the national organisation...

The office bearers of the SMPS met urgently in London with its six representatives on the BFMP Council on the evening before the 22 October Council meeting. This meeting agreed the SMPS President, N D MacLehose make a short statement to the Council in which he would offer the SMPS 'come off' the Joint Labour Committee. At the 22 October BFMP Council the Midland Alliance resolution was put to the meeting after the Chair of the Joint Labour Committee had reported the Scottish position and hinted the SMPS no longer be represented on the Joint Labour Committee. In his statement to the BFMP Council the SMPS President put forward two main arguments. First, the settlements made by the SMPS in both 1967 and 1968 were not entirely against the interests of BFMP members in England and Wales as suggested by the Midland resolution. Many aspects of the settlements, for example additional recruitment, females operating non-traditional keyboards and work measurement in SLADE departments, would be useful to include in future BFMP agreements. The SMPS was anxious to preserve unity with the BFMP but considered that body have regard to the interests of members, not only in different parts of England and of Wales but in Scotland and Ireland. Secondly, the BFMP Council was reminded SMPS office bearers had had special meetings with their counterparts in the BFMP and with the Joint Labour Committee to keep them informed of Scottish developments. These meetings had agreed the two organisations act together so far as was consistent with the BFMP constitution and with the different conditions of the two countries. The SMPS President concluded his statement by saying he could not see how the Midland resolution contributed anything to the two organisations working together. He made clear the SMPS would not resign from the BFMP as this would only create more divisions when it was essential the two organisations worked together as closely as circumstances permitted. In the ensuing debate there was some support for the SMPS position and hope expressed that maximum co-operation between the two organisations be sought in future negotiations.

Relationships continued to deteriorate, reaching a new low in December 1968 and January 1969 when the SMPS objected to a minute of the meeting of the Organisation Committee of 11 December 1968 and of the BFMP Council meeting of 22 October 1968. With regards to the latter the SMPS pointed out the minutes omitted the sentence from the SMPS presentation to the council stating the Midland Alliance motion contributed nothing to the objective of maximum co-operation between the two organisations in negotiations with the unions. The SMPS was concerned the minute made no reference to the number of speakers expressing understanding and support for its position, failed to note the SMPS had acted in accordance with the BFMP constitution and did not mention the Midland Alliance had offered to withdraw its motion. In addition, the minutes stated the report of the Labour Committee had been approved when it had been moved, seconded and agreed on the condition a small, but vital, amendment to that report was made. The BFMP said they had re-examined the minutes and found it difficult to see how, as they stood, they could result in any misunderstanding. The minute of the Organisation Committee recorded that:

> the Labour Officers have expressed the view that Scotland should not be represented on the Labour Committee for the time being but the SMPS would be welcomed back to the Labour Committee when they decide that they wish to come in line with the Federation in negotiations.

The SMPS also questioned the reference to Scotland 'coming into line with the Federation in negotiations'. The BFMP argued the reference to Scotland 'coming into line' with the Federation was more a question of intention than anything else. If the SMPS decided it was in their best interests to make agreement with the unions which were in line with the BFMP agreements, there would be a feeling of greater unity of purpose than there was at present.

At the BFMP January 1969 Council meeting the SMPS dissent from the relevant section of the minutes of the 22 October meeting of the Organisation Committee was noted. The Organisation Committee had unanimously accepted the recommendation of the labour officers that SMPS be not represented on the Joint Labour Committee until the SMPS agreements were brought into line with those of the BFMP. At the January Council meeting the SMPS representatives persuaded the Council to refer back the Organisation Committee decision the SMPS have in future no representation on the Joint Labour Committee. The BFMP and the SMPS then agreed to discuss a firmer basis for their future relationship. The SMPS suggested, prior to this meeting, that instead of representation on the Joint Labour Committee they have observer status with no power to vote. This status allow the Society to hear the views and to acquaint the Labour Committee with SMPS views on any matter. It would be made clear the BFMP labour officers could 'disown' Scotland on any appropriate occasion. The office bearers of both organisations met in London on 11 March 1969 but it became clear there were still many points of difference.

At the BFMP April Council meeting its President reported office bearers of the BFMP and members of its Labour Committee had had a discussion on the matter with the President (N D MacLehose) and Director (Barrie Abbott) of the SMPS on 11 March. At this meeting, the SMPS representatives took the view that some form of continued representation of Scotland on the Joint Labour Committee (possibly through an observer) was necessary to maintain liaison. The opinion of the BFMP office bearers was if there were to be a continuing divergence of policy between the two bodies, and if their respective collective agreements were to remain out of kilter it would be embarrassing to the BFMP in its own negotiations if the SMPS were present on the committee. The BFMP was prepared to accept a Scottish observer on the Labour Committee if the SMPS guaranteed it wished to work toward similar agreements with similar timing to those of the BFMP in regard to wages, hours and holidays. The BFMP, nevertheless, wished to set up a joint ad hoc committee of its Labour Officers and those of the SMPS to meet as and when necessary to exchange views and information and to co-ordinate policy.

The Presidents of the BFMP and SMPS both made statements to the April 1969 Council meeting. The BFMP President said he hoped Scotland would work towards similar agreements to the BFMP and at least maintain an acceptable level of exchange of views and information on labour matters, leading to a co-ordination of policy. He was sorry the SMPS did not hold this view but recognised it was autonomous and had not acted in breach of the BFMP constitution. He hoped the Council would agree Scotland continue to have six representatives on the BFMP Council and that in the future the BFMP resume the links which had existed previously with the SMPS. In the meantime, he said the BFMP Council would close this chapter, accepting the decisions of the SMPS Executive Board.

The SMPS President (N D MacLehose) told the meeting the Scots understood that the stance of the Labour Committee could only work if Scotland's autonomy was restricted by some undertaking as to its future action. This approach, the SMPS President argued, was in direct opposition to the BFMP's constitution and unacceptable to the SMPS. He continued:

> ...Let me be perfectly plain that despite their best efforts the Federation Office Bearers and the Labour Officers have failed to convince us of the correctness of the recommendation which is now before you. We don't like it, we think it's wrong, we think it is punitive and we also regard it as an attack on our constitutional rights...[6]

He went on to say the SMPS accepted the recommendation a SMPS representative not be elected to the Joint Labour Committee. The Society considered this decision marked a fundamental change in the relationship between the organisations and their whole relationship had to be reviewed as to the best course of action, given they both wished to retain the closest possible links, but Scotland keep its autonomy.

An easy course of action for the SMPS would be to resign from the BFMP but this had been rejected as they did not want to be responsible for taking the word 'British' out of the BFMP with all that implied. The SMPS told the April BFMP Council meeting:

> ...We have therefore as a precaution decided that for the present we will withdraw a little from your affairs by not exercising our constitutional right of nominating members to your three main Committees, i.e. Finance, Management Services and General Services. We will, however, continue to nominate our own members of the Council and we hope that there will continue to be Scottish representation on the National YMP Committee. We most sincerely wish the young to get to know each other as much as possible in the hope that they may learn to avoid the mistakes made by their seniors...

The SMPS President concluded his statement to the BFMP Council by saying the Scots now envisaged a type of membership that would be similar to those of the Irish associations which had seats on the Council but in labour and other matters made their own arrangements. A membership arrangement where Scotland and England would not interfere into each other's affairs would, the SMPS President stated, remove points of friction.

Following discussion after the statements from the two Presidents the BFMP Council and the SMPS both subsequently accepted the following as the future basis of their relationship.
(1) The SMPS would no longer participate in the affairs of the BFMP Joint Labour Committee.
(2) The SMPS would cease to appoint representatives to the Finance, General Services and Management Services Committees of the BFMP.
(3) The SMPS would continue to have six representatives on the BFMP Council.
(4) The SMPS would continue to have representation on the National YMP Committee.
The two organisations agreed to work towards the restoration of confidence in each other by informal consultation at all levels and not only on labour matters.

In the short term the withdrawal of the SMPS from the main committees of the BFMP and from its labour negotiation procedure had no apparent adverse effect on its affairs. The extent of inter-office contact on a personal basis between the two organisations was negligible, but in such contact as there was there were no problems. Enquiries from SMPS member firms regarding BFMP affairs were few. In October 1973 the President of the SMPS (Walter B Dickson) met in Edinburgh with the BFMP Director and President. The Vice-President of the SMPS (Hamish Watt) and its Director were also present. The meeting agreed the office bearers of the two organisations meet at six-month intervals, one meeting held in Edinburgh on the day of the Edinburgh local association annual dinner and the other in London. Those to be involved in these meetings were the Presidents and Vice-Presidents of the organisations, together with their respective Directors. It was agreed there be, at three monthly intervals, a meeting between the Chair of the BFMP Labour Committee and the Chair of the SMPS Negotiating Committee accompanied by the organisations' Directors.

At this October meeting, the BFMP reported they had taken the first steps to change their name from 1 January 1974 to the British Printing Industries' Federation (BPIF) and it expected alliances in England and Wales to change their titles accordingly. The SMPS Executive Board agreed at its 26 October 1973 meeting, unanimously, the Society would not change its name. This meeting was also informed the National YMP Group had decided that the 'M' stand for 'Managing' and not 'Master' as hitherto. Subsequently the Scottish YMP Group made the same change to its title.

b. The Carlisle Agreement

As a result of discussion raised by the breakdown of the national wage negotiations in May 1980 in England and Wales, the British Printing Industries' Federation set up a review body under the chairmanship of Lord McGregor to examine the outcome of recent events and to consider the objectives and organisation of the Federation. Lord McGregor reported in December 1980.[7] At its meeting on 13 January 1981 the SMPS Forward Policy Committee appointed a subcommittee to study the *McGregor Report* and to ascertain whether anything contained in it could be adopted by the SMPS to improving its effectiveness. This subcommittee produced its report on 24 March 1981 although the BPIF Executive Council had accepted the *McGregor Report* in principle at its 19 January 1981 meeting. The subcommittee report recommended the Executive Committee be reduced in number, sectional interests be enhanced by the formation of appropriate groups, for example packaging and bookbinding, members of the YMP movement have the opportunity to offer themselves for election, and be considered when the composition of standing committees was selected and communications between members and the policy-making bodies be improved.

Part II of the *McGregor Report* considered the conduct of industrial relations and wage negotiations. The SMPS subcommittee did not consider a review of this section necessary. In normal circumstances wage negotiations conducted by the BPIF for England and Wales were completed before the SMPS started its negotiations with the unions. The SMPS could only negotiate within limited parameters but its influence on the BPIF in these negotiations was at best minimal.

In May 1981, the BPIF issued its new draft constitution and rules in consequence of the *McGregor Report*. The draft text made no reference to the position of the SMPS or to Scotland at all. The SMPS President (W F Cairns Smith) wrote to the BPIF stating the SMPS wished to maintain the status quo as the basis of the relationships between the two organisations. The new constitution and rules of the BPIF became effective on 1 December 1981. Before this representatives of the BPIF and the SMPS met in Carlisle on 12 October 1981 and agreed a new basis for the relationship between the two organisations. This became known as the *Carlisle Agreement* which was approved by the SMPS on 29 October 1981 and by the BPIF on 10 November 1981 and subsequently by its National Board of Management.

The *Carlisle Agreement* contained an agreement to amend the BPIF constitution by adding to Section 3 the following:

> ...The organisation of printers in Scotland should be provided by the Society of the Master Printers of Scotland as an autonomous body. The relationship to, and services provided by the Federation will be subject to regular review and agreement between the SMPS and the National Board of Management of the Federation...

The basic interests of the two organisations had much in common, in particular the relationship with the European Economic Communities, the UK government and the printing trade unions, which were merging with each other. Discussions were to continue towards the merger of the two organisations in a manner beneficial to Scottish interests. It was thought, however, inappropriate for a target date for this.[8]

At Carlisle it was agreed joint consultation take place twice a year at the highest levels on current and future policy Those present were the office bearers, members of the National Board of Management and the respective Directors. SMPS office bearers were to attend BPIF General Meetings as observers and the SMPS members attending BPIF National Consultation meetings had authority to contribute to debates. SMPS members would sit as observers on the BPIF standing committees. Likewise BPIF members were invited to appropriate committees of the SMPS. As observers they were entitled to participate in meetings although not entitled to vote. SMPS members would have full membership of BPIF Sections but would not be permitted to serve as section chairs, or on the Joint Sections' Committee or the National Board of Management. All BPIF services were offered to the SMPS, whose Executive Board would decide their appropriateness. The Scottish YMP Group would play a full part in the activities of the National YMP Committee with at least one Scottish nominee on that committee. The financial basis of the relationship between the SMPS and the BPIF was the SMPS subscription to the BPIF be 5% of its total subscription income, being related to the representational services the BPIF provided to SMPS members firms.

c. The 1984 Settlement

Despite the *Carlisle Agreement*, progress in restoring a sound relationship between the BPIF and the SMPS was very limited. There had been a long series of negotiations over BPIF/SMPS relationships starting in early 1981 when the new BPIF constitution was drawn up following the *McGregor Report*. For many reasons the negotiations failed to produce a settlement despite the expressed wish of both organisations to find some practical means whereby they could work together. It remained the SMPS intention that, despite the difficulties, the negotiations continue.

It was then, regrettable that without SMPS authority or adequate warning, the BPIF President, Peter Barker, approached directly the chief executives of SMPS member companies to inform them the BPIF could no longer provide any services, including advice and information, as the SMPS had refused to pay its 1982 subscription to the BPIF. The SMPS Director, Barrie Abbott, sent a circular to member firms pointing out the content of the letter was factually incorrect but little would be gained by a public rebuttal of the BPIF letter. The Presidents of the BFIP (Peter Barker) and SMPS (Bob Walker) met in October 1983 to settle differences between their two organisations, particularly the SMPS outstanding subscription. They reported back to their respective organisations. The SMPS Executive Board gave its approval, on the basis all SMPS financial commitments to the BFIP, based on past agreements and extending from April 1982 to April 1984, be satisfied by a payment of £10,000. When Jim Raeburn, Director Designate met BFIP Chief Executive, Stanley Bradley in London in early March 1984 it came to light there were serious differences of understanding on what had apparently been agreed by the two Presidents.

A meeting of senior representatives of the BPIF and the SMPS took place in York on 31 July 1984. To say the meeting proved difficult was an understatement. The polite description of some robust exchanges would be full and frank, with the new BPIF President, John Blackton, exploding at the SMPS offer of a subscription of £5,000 per annum on an ongoing basis. He was also critical of the SMPS appointing a new Director (Jim Raeburn) when the BPIF believed that under the *Carlisle Agreement* the retirement of Barrie Abbott would be an opportunity for the two organisations to merge. Following an adjournment, it was agreed to restore the 5% formula. Returning to Edinburgh, SMPS

Vice-President, Inglis McAulay and Director, Jim Raeburn, were de-railed just south of Newcastle, the final straw in a bad twenty four hours.

Jim Raeburn made a point of cultivating good working relationships with his counterparts at the BFIP – Stanley Bradley, Colin Stanley, Tom Machin and Michael Johnson – which established harmony between the SMPS and the BPIF over the twenty three years of his Directorate at the SMPS. He was, however, determined to reduce the 5% formula which he regarded as unjustifiably expensive and his persistence was rewarded when latterly he negotiated the subscription payment down to £2,000 per annum.

Summary

At the start of its lifetime the SMPS paid a fixed amount as its subscription to the BFMP. In 1966 this subscription became a fixed percentage of the SMPS subscriptions income so removing the necessity to bargain over the matter. The percentage was fixed at 5% but reduced to 4% in 1970. A decade later, the BPIF proposed 10% but the SMPS resisted and the 5% contribution was re-established in 1984.

In 1965, the BFMP reviewed its negotiating procedures with the print unions. In its evidence, the SMPS stressed the need for Scotland's independence in industrial relations matters to remain, that there be good liaison in the industrial relations affairs between the two organisations and that negotiations be conducted by a small body. As a result of the review, SMPS representation on the BFMP Joint Labour Committee was reduced from two to one.

In April 1966, the BFMP reviewed its constitution which had remained unchanged since 1931. The SMPS suggested two changes. First, its autonomous position be stated in the main body of the constitution and second, Scottish representation on BFMP standing committees be explicitly provided in the constitution. The review body accepted the first of these suggestions. The SMPS rejected the proposal member firms became direct members of the BFMP.

In 1967, the SMPS exercised its constitutional autonomy by negotiating collective agreements with the STA, SOGAT and the NSES which diverged in important respects from the agreements negotiated by the BFMP, for England and Wales with the print unions. This also happened in 1968. This caused tensions between the two organisations and in October 1968, the BFMP Midland Alliance proposed the SMPS resign from the BFMP. Relationships worsened but in 1969 a new basis for the relationship between the SMPS and the BFMP was agreed. The SMPS would no longer participate in the affairs of the Joint Labour Committee, would not appoint representatives to the BFMP Finance, General Services and Management Services Committee, would continue to have six seats on the BFMP Council and would be represented on the National YMP Committee. In late 1981, following a revision of the BPIF's Constitution a new basis for the relationship between the organisations (known as the *Carlisle Agreement*) was agreed. SMPS remained an autonomous body but the relationship of the BPIF and the SMPS would be reviewed regularly.

Notes

[1] See *Minutes of the Meeting of the Executive Board,* 7 July 1983.

[2] See *Minutes of the Meeting of the Executive Board*, 9 November 1984.

[3] See *Memorandum to BFMP Commission on Labour Negotiations*, Society of Master Printers of Scotland, 11 October 1965.

[4] See *Report of the Constitution Working Party*, British Federation of Master Printers, 1967, para 97, p16.

[5] See *Annual Report and Accounts, 1967/68*, Society of Master Printers of Scotland.

[6] See 'Relationship with the BFMP', *Notice to Members of the Executive Board, dated 24 April 1969*, Society of Master Printers of Scotland, April 1969.

[7] See First Report of the Review Body appointed by the British Printing Industries' Federation, December 1980.

[8] See *Minutes of the Meeting of the Executive Board*, 29 October 1981.

Chapter 17

RELATIONSHIPS WITH TRADE UNIONS :
WORKING CONDITIONS - SCOTLAND, 1960-1990

This chapter begins by examining the industrial relations institutions governing the Scottish printing industry and then analyses the SMPS attitude towards recognising unions organising clerical workers in the industry. The third part examines labour supply problems for the industry over a thirty year period. The chapter then examines the impact on the industry of the inter-union disputes between the NGA and the Scottish Graphical Division (formerly the STA) of SOGAT over the staffing of litho machines in letterpress houses converting to the lithographic process.

The Scottish Joint Industrial Council
of the Printing and Kindred Trades (SJIC)

The Scottish JIC had not met since the 1959 dispute, and in England and Wales the JIC's work had been limited to the operation, at district committee level, of its apprentice selection schemes. There were attempts to revive the NJIC but they were unsuccessful until mid-1963 because of a difference of view between employers and the unions over the wording of some clauses of a new constitution. The BFMP felt strongly certain sections of the previous constitution (particularly regarding conciliation) had been flouted by the unions who, in turn, accused the employers of failing to carry out the 'objects' clauses of the constitution affecting the closed shop and the organisation of clerical workers. During these attempts to revive the NJIC the SMPS made it clear that should a Scottish JIC be reformed it would not accept it operating as a branch of the NJIC.

Early in 1963, agreement was reached on a new constitution and its first meeting was held in October 1963. In Scotland apprentice selection was carried on by local committees which were independent of the JIC whilst conciliation procedures were contained in the agreements between the SMPS and the various trade unions. There was little pressure, at least from the SMPS, for a revival of the Scottish JIC. The SMPS was reluctant to take action which might hinder the revival of the National JIC but repeated its support for a revival of the Scottish JIC provided it was not a branch of the NJIC. When it became clear a new NJIC constitution would be agreed, the print unions in Scotland drafted a constitution for the Scottish JIC. This followed in general the new NJIC constitution. Although there were certain differences of emphasis, the majority were of detail. There was pressure from the unions to revive the Scottish JIC without delay.

At a meeting held in Edinburgh on 18 December 1963, twenty six representatives of the SMPS and of the unions affiliated to the P&KTF approved the constitution and rules for a Joint Industrial Council in the Scottish printing industry. The previous council had functioned from 1922 until the 1959 UK-wide dispute in the printing industry. The new SJIC was not a branch of the NJIC although there would be close co-operation between the two organisations principally in the fields of health, education and conciliation. The SJIC met three times (February, June and October) per year. Its first meeting was on 24 June 1964. The objects of the SJIC were threefold.
(1) To secure complete organisation of employees and employers throughout the trade although it was understood the council had no powers to 'secure' organisation of either employers or employees and that their organisation into appropriate trade bodies was the responsibility of those organisations
(2) To promote good relationships between employers and employees including the recognition of mutual interests, the selection and training of apprentices, the improvement of working conditions and settling any industrial differences peacefully.
(3) For administration, the SJIC had district committees and such standing committees as it decided from time to time.
The membership of the SJIC was a maximum of sixty, appointed as one half by the SMPS and the other half by the unions affiliated to P&KTF panel. Membership of the previous SJIC had been fifty two – twenty six from each panel. In each important Scottish town a district committee existed comprising an equal number of union and employers' representatives, with power to deal only with matters within their respective areas. The SJIC had four standing committees. The General Purpose Committee dealt with matters connected to employment, and with proposed legislation which might affect the industry.

Its Conciliation Committee consisted of the chair, vice-chair and joint secretaries of the SJIC together with six representatives (three from each panel) chosen by the respective chair and secretaries of each panel. The Council had a Health and Education Committee. The previous SJIC had an organisation committee but given the difference between the SMPS and the trade unions over the 'object' of the SJIC to secure complete organisation of the Scottish printing industry it was felt there was no need for such a committee. When the chair of a committee was an employer the vice-chair was a member of a union and vice versa. The chair and vice-chair of the SJIC passed from panel to panel annually.

Disputes arising from claims for the establishment, or revision, of agreements between the employers' organisation and unions were outside the scope of conciliation by the Council. In the case of disputes of a local character no strike, lockout or other coercive action was to be taken until the matter had been referred, with the consent of the parties, to a local conciliation committee or failing such consent to the Conciliation Committee of the SJIC. Pending consideration by the Conciliation Committee both parties continued normal working. Where the conciliation machinery was used in a dispute between a union and an SMPS member firm, its procedures were exhausted before the parties referred the matter to the SJIC. In cases where a dispute had not been settled locally the Joint Secretaries of the SJIC were to be notified immediately and to arrange for a meeting, within seven days, of the Conciliation Committee. If a settlement to the dispute were not reached the Joint Secretaries could convene a special meeting of the SJIC within fourteen days. Until the matter had been considered by a conciliation committee or by a special meeting of the Council, no strike, lockout or other coercive action was to be taken and normal working would continue. The Joint Secretaries drew up the terms of reference of a conciliation committee and/or a special meeting of the Council in consultation with the parties concerned. In a local dispute referred to the SJIC for settlement, if one or other party did not comply with the 'peace obligation', the Council's conciliation machinery were exhausted. Any member, either an employer or a union could withdraw from the SJIC by giving six months' notice in writing. The Council could be dissolved by the SMPS or the P&KTF giving six months' notice in writing to the Council of their intention to withdraw.

The SJIC worked well initially but its meetings then began to be less frequent. On 26 October 1966 it met after a lengthy gap to hear an address on safety at work by the industrial organiser in Scotland of the Royal Society for Prevention of Accidents. The SJIC agreed unanimously to continue to function despite the dissolution of the National JIC covering England and Wales earlier in 1966. The SJIC met for the final time in March 1967 when addressed by the Deputy Controller, Ministry of Labour, Scotland and by George Llewellyn of the SMPS on the Industrial Training Act (1964).

The Organisation of Clerical Workers

Until the late 1960s the policy of the SMPS was to deal with the conditions of employment of production workers and not those of clerical workers. This policy was based, with few exceptions, on clerical workers not being members of any union. SMPS members were free to set, for such employees, employment conditions as they felt appropriate. In 1963 without prior warning, NATSOPA organised the clerical workers in George Outram & Co, Perth. The SMPS would not recognise NATSOPA or any other union in the clerical field but was happy for its industrial relations staff to provide any assistance as might be required to member firms in this position. A house agreement was made between NATSOPA and Outrams on terms the SMPS considered acceptable.

The SMPS feared NATSOPA might exploit its success in Perth and it was known other unions had an eye to organising clerical workers in printing. SMPS held a special meeting on 8 October 1965 at which a decision was taken not to conclude any agreements with NATSOPA granting its recognition as an appropriate union for clerical workers but to give every assistance to member firms seeking help to prevent organisation amongst its clerical workers. This decision was confirmed by the Executive Board on 23 November 1965.[1] Within months of this decision, a house agreement was signed between NATSOPA and Arthur Guthrie & Sons, Ardrossan who were part of the Johnston Group of weekly newspapers, whilst the clerical staff in the Berwick office of the Tweeddale Press joined the clerical section of the Transport and General Workers Union. At the same time ASTMS approached Wm Collins Sons & Co for recognition as the appropriate union for its clerical staff. The company had been previously approached by USDAW. It became known that Waterlow & Sons, East Kilbride signed a clerical house agreement with NATSOPA. SOGAT (Division A) in early 1971 failed to gain recognition for clerical workers at Wm Collins Sons & Co, John Laird & Son and Simplicity Patterns.

The STA did not wish to organise clerical workers because its present rules prevented this. SOGAT had stated in writing it would not 'poach' from NATSOPA in the general printing industry in England and Wales or in the newspaper field but it regarded itself as the appropriate union to organise clerical workers in the Scottish general printing industry. The SMPS was convinced, sooner rather than later, there would be a union recruitment drive amongst clerical employees in the industry. The Industrial Relations Act (1971) which provided a statutory union recognition procedure would assist SOGAT to this end. The SOGAT Glasgow Branch Secretary announced publicly he was determined to make a breakthrough in clerical organisation in the Scottish print industry. The time was fast approaching when the SMPS would have to consider what policies should be adopted to union organisation campaigns in the clerical field.

By 31 August 1971, pressure was growing on certain firms in Glasgow to accept SOGAT be recognised as the appropriate union to organise and represent clerical workers. NATSOPA had secured complete organisation of the clerical and advertising staff in twenty, primarily weekly newspaper, houses in the west of Scotland. The T&GWU (Clerical Division) had organised the same staff in a weekly newspaper house in the Borders. On 26 August 1971, the General Secretary of SOGAT, Vincent Flyn, wrote to the SMPS pointing out the union, like the SMPS, did not wish to see a non-print union organising clerical workers. This would simply add to the number of unions within the industry. The letter also pointed out NATSOPA had never operated within general print in Scotland and did not hold any agreement with SMPS member firms covering any sizeable category of employees. The letter concluded by suggesting an agreement between SOGAT and the SMPS in which the former be the appropriate union for clerical workers in the Scottish printing industry. Following the letter there were several informal discussions with SOGAT in which SMPS emphasised its unwillingness to take any action which would expedite clerical organisation in their companies.

By late October 1972, the amount of organisation by SOGAT was limited and it was doubtful whether the union, at least in Scotland, had the resources to advance to issue.[2] In Simplicity Patterns, Blantyre, a 'Recognition and Procedure Agreement' was concluded with SOGAT on 2 May 1972 and a full wage agreement signed on 10 August 1972. It had organised the majority of clerical workers in William Thyne, Edinburgh, Inveresk Stationery, Edinburgh and Gilmour & Dean, Hamilton. All three companies signed 'Recognition and Procedure Agreements' and subsequently wage agreements with SOGAT which was unsuccessful in its efforts to recruit clerical workers in John Laird & Son and John Horn, both of Glasgow. At the request of SOGAT a meeting was held on 22 August 1972 at which the union pressed its claim for recognition by the SMPS on the grounds if this was not afforded a multi-union position could emerge with needless difficulties ensuing. With recognition they contended, organisation by SOGAT would proceed 'gently'. SOGAT pointed out if this recognition was not granted, a campaign involving approaches to individual member firms or their staff would happen. SMPS questioned whether recognition would prevent other unions from organising clerical employees in the industry in Scotland or whether SOGAT could keep its clerical and production workers' functions separate. The SMPS did not receive an answer to either question.

The immediate problem for SMPS was whether or not to accept SOGAT's claim for recognition. It considered the likely price of clerical organisation, the advantages and disadvantages of multi-union organisation, the affect of any decision on SOGAT's activities in the production field and the interests of particular groups such as publishers/printers etc. In October 1971, the SMPS assumed, in the interests of its members, the responsibilities in the clerical field which it had for many years in the production field. This meant the SMPS would assist any member company to resolve problems that might arise because of union activity in the clerical field. The SMPS considered clerical workers in members' offices generally were not interested in becoming union members. The SMPS had to consider the action necessary when a union approached a member firm or its clerical staff or when clerical staff joined unions without the knowledge of the member firm and the union concerned then sought recognition. It was increasingly clear the 'appropriate' union for clerical workers was either SOGAT or NATSOPA. SOGAT, not unreasonably, regarded itself as the appropriate union for clerical workers employed in the general printing industry in Scotland. NATSOPA already organised clerical workers successfully in the newspaper industry in Scotland. The STA restricted its activities in the clerical field, as provided in the mutual rules, namely to organising costing and estimating clerks and designers of layout who had been compositors and to machine men who had retained STA membership. Efforts by unions which did not have agreements with the SMPS, for example, TGWU, USDAW, GMB and ASTMS, to secure a foothold in general printing and in weekly newspapers in Scotland was unlikely to be in the best interests of the industry. The SMPS advised its members not to encourage such unions to seek recognition for their clerical workers.

SOGAT continued to seek an agreement whereby the SMPS recognised it as the appropriate union for clerical workers in the industry but such recognition was not afforded. SOGAT succeeded in a few cases in organising the majority of clerical workers and house agreements covering recognition were made with the employers concerned. In October 1973 there were further discussions with senior officials of SOGAT regarding their discussions with NATSOPA to settle spheres of influence regarding the organisation of clerical workers. The SMPS had hoped the newspaper field would be regarded as appropriate for NATSOPA and SOGAT for the general printing industry. Complications arose in that clerical workers in some weekly newspaper groups were already in both NATSOPA and SOGAT whilst clerical workers in another office joined the auxiliary section of the STA. Despite this, clerical organisation by SOGAT in SMPS member firms continued to increase in 1974 and 1975 with house agreements covering recognition and wages and other conditions of employment signed where appropriate. Clerical organisation by SOGAT now covered the biggest member firms in the Glasgow area and several significant member firms in the Edinburgh and east of Scotland area whilst NATSOPA retained its hold in newspapers in Ardrossan and Perth. A disturbing development was that in several cases SMPS members only discovered suddenly that their clerical workers had joined a union other than SOGAT, when they were of the opinion if they had to deal with a union covering their clerical employees they preferred SOGAT. So far in such cases, it had been possible to 'switch' into SOGAT but only with great difficulty and in one case the attempt to switch was unsuccessful.

In October 1975 the secretary of the SOGAT Glasgow branch requested the SMPS recognised SOGAT as the clerical union in the industry in the west of Scotland and the SMPS make an overall agreement with SOGAT Glasgow covering not only recognition but basic rates. It was by now clear SOGAT would establish itself as the clerical union in the industry and further organisation of clerical workers was inevitable. It had become impossible to take effective measures to ensure that clerical employees who joined unions other than SOGAT could be transferred into SOGAT. In an attempt to control clerical worker union organisation SMPS made a declaration which effectively channelled further clerical organisation towards SOGAT.

Working Conditions – Local Agreements

Prior to the 1967 wage settlement, in the case of general changes to employment conditions the SMPS and the STA participated in wage negotiations on a UK-wide basis. The SMPS did negotiate, and conclude collective agreements, with the STA, NSES, ASLP, SLADE and NUPB&PW/SOGAT (Division A) over working conditions to operate solely in Scotland.

a. The STA

Local agreements were negotiated with the STA over manning and machine extras, method study and work measurement, changes to working practices and the supply of labour. In 1961 special arrangements with the STA were made, after inspection by the Joint Committee, concerning staffing and machine extras of two new continuous stationery machines – an aniline machine and a five-colour gravure machine. A Monophoto photocomposition installation was also jointly inspected after which an appropriate staffing level was agreed. There were discussions with the STA regarding staffing and machine extras in connection with teletypesetter installations. The union claimed there be an agreement similar to that operating in Scottish daily newspaper houses. The SMPS rejected this claim but agreed in April 1962 the operation of supercasters need not be on a 'one man, one machine' basis except where the work involved made such staffing necessary. In 1963 and 1964 several agreements covering the staffing and rating of new machines were bargained with the STA. SMPS member firms intending to introduce equipment of a new type into Scotland were asked to advise, in confidence, SMPS head office. In the 1973 main wage negotiations it was agreed with effect from the date of the next main wage agreement, machine extras would increase in line with movements in the basic rate.

In 1961 the SMPS and the STA made an agreement for the operation of group incentive schemes in STA departments. In the following year several new work measurement incentive schemes were successively started in Aberdeen, Edinburgh and Glasgow with those involving STA members being on a group basis. 1964 witnessed further installations of work measurement incentive schemes and the Joint Incentive Committee of the SMPS and the STA agreed a procedure for dealing with such installations. At the same time the procedure for dealing with difficulties arising in the operation of incentive schemes was clarified. In 1969 agreement was reached with the STA establishing where new work measurement incentive schemes were introduced holiday pay would include the average incentive bonus. The STA requested holiday pay be paid on the basis of average earnings but this was rejected by the SMPS.

In 1966 the STA agreed to the proposal by the Chairman of the SMPS Negotiating Committee, Hope Collins, that a small joint committee be formed to find ways of bringing the changes in working conditions mentioned by the Prices and Incomes Board in 1965 (see Chapter 18). The committee dealt mainly with manpower and related matters including education and training. The discussions ranged over a wide range of issues. The SMPS was asked to provide information as to the probable investment by its members in new plant and building over the next three to four years whilst the STA agreed to define in specific terms the protective measures they regarded as necessary to give employment security for their members. The union suggested a detailed and expert investigation into operations in the composing room with a view to finding what improvements to present practice could be made. Both parties agreed the investment information be provided and the composing room investigation be carried out. The investment enquiry showed the employers had sufficient confidence in the future of the industry to plan expenditure which would provide for adequate replacement of plant and building and for considerable development.[3] On the manpower question the STA was willing to make additional staff available but only if the full facts of the particular case were known, preferably in advance of requirements. The Joint Working Practices Committee, however, had only limited success.[4]

The STA claim in 1961 that pay be included in the mutual rules agreements was rejected by the SMPS as were the union's requests for changes to the rules covering machine extras and overtime working. In June 1965 there were significant changes to the STA mutual rules. The standard working week for day and night workers in all printing departments was to be forty hours whilst only forty eight hours overtime were to be worked in any calendar month. Despite SMPS initial opposition, the STA demand that part of an hour count as one hour as regards overtime working was agreed. There were changes to shift-working. The approved hours for double-day shift were Monday to Friday, 6am to 2.30pm and 2.30pm to 11pm with a break of half an hour in each shift. Each shift was paid at forty nine hours, at the worker's normal day hourly rate of wages. There were substantial increases in machine extras and the rates for Monotype and Linotype operators and readers. The STA claimed the bronzing extra be raised from 3d to 6d per hour but the SMPS responded that whilst it had some sympathy with the claim, the increase was not justified. The SMPS eventually offered an increase to 4d per hour which was accepted by the STA.

b. The ASLP

In 1961 ASLP members in Dundee refused to co-operate in the introduction of method study or a work measurement incentive scheme. This continued despite the national agreement containing a procedure for the introduction, and operation, of such schemes. On 7 November 1962 the SMPS met with the Scottish District Council to obtain uniformity of practice concerning double-day shift. No agreement was reached because a printing house in Edinburgh operated a practice whereby ASLP members working double-day shift received paid meal breaks. The union was unwilling to accept an agreement which specifically stated meal breaks would not be paid. An agreement was concluded in September 1964 regarding the position of apprentices in connection with multicolour litho machines whilst in 1965 the first installation in Scotland of a work measurement incentive scheme in the lithographic machine room was successfully completed after lengthy negotiations. The second such scheme in Scotland was started in 1966 in the Edinburgh area. In 1968 agreement was reached with the ASLP providing where new work measurement incentive schemes were introduced holiday pay would include the average incentive bonus payment.

c. The NSES

In 1962, there was a one-week strike in a Glasgow firm by the electrotypers and stereotypers employed there which the SMPS claimed was a breach of the mutual rules between the Society and the NSES. Such action was unusual in the industry and was a matter of regret to the SMPS. In 1968 the NSES claim that holiday pay be on the basis of average earnings was rejected by the SMPS but the union accepted where new work measurement incentive schemes were introduced holiday pay would include average incentive bonus payments.

d. SLADE

In 1962, a new agreement with SLADE dealt with wages, hours, overtime, apprentice ratios and paid holiday entitlement. Hitherto no separate agreement had existed between SLADE and the SMPS. In 1963, SLADE proposed call money be provided in Scotland. There were indications a similar claim might come from the ASLP. The SMPS agreed both unions be informed call money had not, up to now, been part of the Scottish industry, overtime arrangements in Scotland were different from those in England and Wales and the claim was rejected. There were also problems with SLADE concerning the introduction of work measurement incentive schemes. Despite the existence of an agreement the SMPS found it impossible to ascertain whether SLADE was, in practice, prepared to permit its members to operate under incentive conditions.

In early 1970s, SLADE issued a circular to its branches instructing them that normal overtime working be limited to fifteen hours per month, the reason being the relatively large number of unemployed SLADE members in England. The SMPS was quick to point out this action was not appropriate in Scotland because the current agreement provided for a normal overtime limit of thirty hours per month.

e. NUPB&PW/SOGAT (Division A)

At a conference in November 1963 representatives of the Scottish District Council of the NUPB&PW put forward various proposals to secure uniformity of staffing and machine extras for folding machines and backed existing practice in support of their claim. SMPS member firms were asked to give information about folding machines in their houses so the Negotiating Committee could consider the relevant facts prior to a further meeting with the Scottish District Council. Conferences with the union were held in 1964 but at a conference in January 1965 an agreement on machines extras was reached. The journeyman rate was to be paid to operators whether journeymen, male auxiliaries or female auxiliaries who set/ran auto-fed folding machines capable of taking a sheet size above thirty by forty inches. The craft rate was to be paid to female auxiliaries responsible for setting and supervising the running of two folding machines capable of taking a sheet of size thirty by forty inches. Female auxiliaries setting and running a folding machine capable of taking a sheet size thirty by forty inches or under were to be paid the female rate plus 20% thereof when producing folds of 2x16 pages or 1x32 pages.

In 1966 the NUPB&PW proposed revision of the 1959 agreement on machine extras. The SMPS regretted the procedure provided by the agreement for the regulation of new machine extras had recently been undermined in the Edinburgh area. The Edinburgh branch of the union misunderstood the basic principle that guided the Joint Committee in that it wished the claim for revision of the agreement considered by the Joint Committee before the formal claim had been submitted. Early in 1966, agreement was reached providing a procedure for dealing with the payment of machine extras and staffing levels in the case of the introduction of a machine not covered by the 1959 machine extras agreement.

Following this agreement a conference was held between SOGAT (Division A) and the SMPS to consider the former's claim that average incentive earnings be paid in respect of holidays in printing houses with work measurement incentive schemes. The SMPS, whilst recognising the union claim had some merit, saw acceptance of it could have far-reaching consequences. Little progress was made on the claim but in 1966 agreement was reached with SOGAT (Division A), and with the STA, NSES and the ASLP, providing where new work measurement incentive schemes were introduced holiday pay would include the average incentive bonus payment. In July 1967, an agreement was concluded with SOGAT (Division A) enabling the revision of machine extras and the speedy settlement of staffing and rating of binding and ruling equipment which was of a new type to Scotland. The 1973 main wage agreement between SOGAT and the SMPS provided machine extras would, from the date of the next settlement, increase in accordance with movements in basic rates.

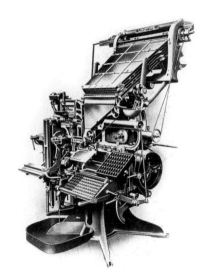

Linotype machine, model 4.

Reproduced courtesy of the Scottish
Centre for the Book, Edinburgh Napier University.

f. General Matters

The period 1970 to end of February 1974 saw industrial actions in the electricity supply and coal mining industries which caused serious disruption to the Scottish printing industry. During a work to rule in the electricity supply industry in December 1970 SMPS member firms were advised of their right to suspend employees when power supply ceased. In 1972 the curtailment of electric power supply to the industry occurred again this time occasioned by a strike of the National Union of Mineworkers. All possible action was taken by the SMPS to secure the objective of maintaining as far as possible both production and earnings of employees and to keep their member firms in touch with a situation which changed daily. In December 1973 the industry's electricity power supply was interrupted for a third time when the National Union of Mineworkers again called its members out on strike. This time the ensuing fuel and power crisis led the Conservative government to introduce a three-day working week as power supplies to industry were rationed. Scotland was permitted to work eight days from 17 December 1973 to 6 January 1974. The SMPS made various special arrangements with the print unions concerning the fuel and power crisis. The Executive Board set up an emergency committee to deal with the position and the arrangements made were in accordance with existing agreements which did not include any provisions for a guaranteed forty-hour working week. The three-day working week ended in March 1974 on the election of a Labour government.

From the mid-1970s into the mid-1980s it was SMPS policy to make clear to the unions by various means, including revision of the appropriate clauses in main agreements, satisfactory agreement on machine extras, staffing etc. could best be settled without ill-timed aggressive action by individuals or groups.

The SMPS emphasised strongly continuity of production and a constructive approach to the problems present in the introduction of new methods and machinery. SMPS 1980/81 Report stated:

> ...It is only in the monopolistic world of the daily newspaper that gross overmanning, absurd restrictive practices and foolishly high wage levels do not immediately bring normal economic consequences upon those responsible for them...[5]

SMPS policy continued to be ill-timed aggressive action by individuals or groups not be allowed to jeopardise agreements on machine extras and staffing.

Labour Supply Issues

On the creation of the SMPS its principal problem was a continuing labour shortage. There had been fears after the 1959 settlement that increased costs might lead to a lowering of demand for print products with a reduction in the demand for labour. Since August 1959 demand continued at a very high level so that even with the small intake of additional apprentices and lower National Service requirements, the shortage, particularly in letterpress departments, was a seriously limiting factor on production. Accordingly in 1960 the SMPS Negotiating Committee met with the STA to obtain local agreement as to the actual shortage of labour in the three cities – Aberdeen, Edinburgh and Glasgow. This was done in October 1960. It was agreed there were needs at that time in these centres for 135 compositors and forty five machinemen. On the assumption similar agreement could be reached in other centres, it was estimated there were vacancies throughout Scotland for 170 compositors and sixty machinemen. These figures were substantiated by the information obtained in the SMPS 1960 Labour Force Inquiry.

A conference was held with the STA on 5 January 1961. The agreed figures of shortage were disputed by the STA which pointed out 100 compositors and machinemen were on National Service and their return would help to meet the present labour shortage. The STA contended they would have difficulty persuading their members to accept measures to ease the labour shortage unless there was a quid pro quo from the employers regarding the union's new claim for higher wages, shorter hours and the establishment of a national pension scheme or unemployment scheme. In the lithographic section the shortage of SLADE employees was serious throughout Scotland. The shortage of ASLP journeymen in the Glasgow area had become more acute. The 1961 *Labour Force Inquiry* showed little change in the general printing industry position in Scotland.

The 1963 *Labour Force Inquiry* showed a drop in the number of compositors employed by SMPS member firms, disclosed the need for more manpower in lithographic departments and provided evidence that work which was capable of being done in Scotland had been lost because of staff shortages in the litho area.

The merger of the Edinburgh *Evening News* and *Dispatch* released a number of compositors for employment in the general printing trade and employment was quickly offered to all those displaced. The 1964 *Labour Force Inquiry* showed again a serious manpower shortage situation existed in several sectors of the industry, particularly in the composing rooms, the litho machine room and SLADE areas. By the mid-1960s there was evidence the print unions in Scotland realised the long-standing shortage of journeymen in certain sections of the industry operated against the best interests of their own members.[6] Interim measures had been agreed with each of the five unions but there was recognition regular attention to labour supply problems was essential. Although these measures improved the position it remained unsatisfactory. They brought an improvement in the numbers employed in litho departments accounted for by a substantial number of ASLP upgradings but which had little impact on the composing room labour shortages.

The shortage of skilled labour meant SMPS member firms suffered from a relatively high labour turnover as they sought to poach craft employees from each other. In 1967 the change to a five-year apprenticeship increased substantially the number of journeymen employed in member firms but the shortage of labour in lithographic machinerooms remained acute. The 1970 annual *Labour Force Inquiry* revealed the number of employees in the industry remained steady but a disturbing feature was the low intake of apprentices. There had been a reduction in the number of unfilled vacancies for journeymen but there was still a shortage of compositors. The SMPS/NGA Joint Panel, formed in 1968 continued to deal successfully with cases of serious shortages of lithographers. In 1970 a similar panel was set up with the STA and led to special measures to help SMPS member firms suffering serious labour supply problems.

The 1971 the annual *Labour Force Inquiry* showed the number of employees in the industry was the same as in previous years but that demand for additional journeymen was the lowest in all categories for many years, with the exception of litho machinemen. The amount of unfilled apprentice vacancies continued to give cause for concern. The STA was increasingly concerned about the number of unemployed journeymen, especially compositors, in the Glasgow area and imposed restrictions on its members working overtime. The union realised this unemployment resulted from events in the daily newspaper field but assured the SMPS the restriction would be applied with discretion in the general printing industry. The shortage of lithographers in Glasgow remained acute. The SMPS continued to reminded its members there were now adequate facilities for the introduction of adult apprentices and that shortages of STA or NGA craftsmen in specific cases could be considered by Joint Panels empowered to take appropriate action to deal with the shortage. By 1973 there had been a substantial improvement in the intake of apprentices but the number of unfilled apprentice vacancies was still higher than Scottish print employers would have liked.

The year 1980/81 saw the industry, or at least major sectors of it, experience the worst recession since 1945. UK government policy highlighted the effects of recessionary economic forces which had operated throughout the industrialised world. The industry witnessed redundancy and short time working. Over the period 1 July 1980 to 28 February 1981 the number of redundancies declared by SMPS member firms totalled 454 whilst the number of employees on short time was 1020.[7] There was confusion over 'permitted hours of overtime'. Local union representatives continued to use restrictions not to obtain or retain work but to seek an unrealistic price for their co-operation. Over the period 1980 to 1982 the total workforce in the industry was reduced overall by some 25%. The largest companies, and those engaged in book production, were the most affected whilst the specialist printing of dress patterns was lost.

In the mid-1980s output from the industry began to grow again but the market remained fiercely competitive in some sectors, especially those subject to penetration of the home market by foreign printers. In 1988 the output of the paper, printing and publishing industries rose by 9%, significantly outperforming manufacturing as a whole. The 1988/89 SMPS Annual Report remarked:

> …After six successive years of growth, an industry that entered the decade with serious problems, printing will leave the 80s as one of the top performers in Scottish manufacturing…

The implementation of technological change in the late 1970s and early 1980s led to a reduction in the number of production employees in the industry. This was accompanied however by an increase in the number of administrative, clerical and technical employees. A further impact of new technology was redrawing of the boundaries of 'who does what' leading to mergers amongst the printing unions. Developing technology gave productivity per head gains, and managing and negotiating redundancy became a major feature of SMPS industrial relations activities.

NGA/STA Demarcation

In the early 1970s, an important aspect of SMPS policy in bargaining with the various print unions was to increase flexibility in working arrangements and in particular find a workable solution to the problems arising from NGA/STA demarcation over the staffing of lithographic machines. In May 1972 the STA and the NGA signed a draft agreement under which STA members were authorised to operate lithographic machinery provided these members took up industrial membership of the NGA. This was never accepted by NGA members. On 27 December 1972 the STA meet with the SMPS to argue its members should not be excluded from employment on lithographic printing machines. The STA did not concede the argument that the NGA was the union with the sole prerogative of manning and negotiating for lithographic printers in Scotland. It pointed out STA members operated lithographic machines in more than seventy offices ranging through Aberdeen, Ayrshire, Edinburgh, Glasgow, Fife, Inverness, Perth, the Borders and elsewhere. The STA argued the full involvement of its members on lithographic machines would go a substantial way to obtaining the necessary flexibility in printing production which was required if the Scottish printing industry was to match developments in England and Wales and on the continent. The STA concluded its case by saying it required the SMPS to acknowledge its right to ensure its members full employment in the Scottish industry and for them not to be denied their birthright in the case of protecting the labour strategy of others.[8] The SMPS replied by stating it did not have the power to impose on the STA, the NGA or SLADE a radical change in working arrangements which had been acceptable to those unions and the Society.

On 22 January 1973 the SMPS warned its members a serious position was emerging in the NGA/STA demarcation problems. The tripartite (STA, NGA and SMPS) *Retraining and Transfer Agreement* had been abrogated by the two unions in 1969. It was a condition of the 1970 main wage agreement that a more effective procedure be agreed but it was only after considerable delay and acute difficulties in particular print houses that the unions were persuaded to try to seek a new agreement. A draft agreement was concluded in May 1972 which it was hoped would provide a basis of settlement for most, if not all, of the problems. Although the agreement was approved by the STA and eventually the NGA, the latter decided it should be put to a membership ballot vote in Scotland for ratification. This ballot never took place. In November 1972 the STA changed tack and decided the proposed agreement did not meet its requirements and sought the meeting outlined above with the SMPS.

On 4 January 1973, R & R Clark, Edinburgh said it needed to make redundant four journeymen machinemen and one male auxiliary. The STA stated the company had vacancies for litho journeymen. It was 'insisting the company place three STA printers on lithographic printing machines forthwith' and the reactions of another union to such a situation would be tested. The STA began to involve all its members employed by the company in industrial action to secure the involvement of its members on litho work and to obtain the withdrawal of the dismissal of five STA members. The company offered alternative employment for two minders, an apprentice and the auxiliary, in its parent company, William Thyne. The individuals involved rejected the proposed redeployment, joining other R & R Clark employees on strike. The SMPS expressed regret the STA's actions to gain a foothold in what had been traditionally NGA territory and for using the SMPS to achieve this end.[9] It pointed out the number of litho/letterpress houses were relatively small and it was only in these houses demarcation problems existed and there were over 1,000 NGA employees in SMPS member firms. There was no threat to the employment of STA journeymen, as the NGA was willing to allow STA members to operate litho equipment if they left the STA and joined the NGA.

By the end of January 1973, there had been little movement towards a settlement either at R & R Clark or in the general case of the STA/NGA demarcation. Whilst the objectives of the STA were clear in the R & R Clark situation, they continued to be ill-defined in general. On the one hand the STA objective was 'equal sovereignty with the NGA in respect of lithographic equipment' whilst on the other hand it claimed not to be seeking to invade NGA jurisdiction. The two positions were incompatible. On 9 February a settlement was reached in the R & R Clark dispute and there was a return to work on Monday 12 February 1973. As part of the settlement, the company agreed there be no redundancy of STA employees for a period of twelve months so discussion between the STA and the NGA to find a solution to their demarcation problems could continue. Agreement was eventually reached between the NGA and STA in 1974 and became known as the *Perth Agreement.* It set out which union would represent litho machine minders and platemakers in Scotland. The NGA would cover all litho in the general printing industry other than small offset which was held by the SGA (formerly the STA). The SGA would staff web offset litho machines in newspaper offices.

The *Perth Agreement* worked reasonably well for SMPS member firms until developing technology in typesetting moved litho from being a specialised area into general printing. The SGA was relaxed about the introduction of phototypesetting into local newspapers in Scotland and saw this as comparable with the web offset machinery being introduced in newspapers during the 1970s. The NGA was less sanguine as newspaper houses began using their web equipment for commercial printing. The SGA claimed sheet-fed litho in a newspaper house was their jurisdiction. The NGA which had only a token presence in local newspapers was unable to exert pressure on the SGA in this area but stiffened their resistance in general printing houses. In 1975 SGA amalgamated with the SOGAT to become its Scottish Graphical Division thereby strengthening the industrial muscle of the SGD as it was now possible to enlist the help of SOGAT chapels engaged in print finishing. Prior to this SOGAT and the NGA could 'black' litho output from houses where the NGA or the SGA were in dispute. With the SGA merger with SOGAT this sanction disappeared in relation to SGD output with SOGAT print finishers in Scotland remaining neutral in NGA/SGD disputes.

Sensing that the future of letterpress in a phototypesetting era was bleak the SGD abrogated the *Perth Agreement* and claimed where there was an NGA presence in any house contemplating the introduction of litho it would remain exclusively SGD. Where there was no existing NGA presence this did not create industrial relations problems for an individual company but did make the existing national agreement with the SMPS difficult to interpret. The SGD then decided to interpret 'follow the job' in a different way when letterpress was replaced by litho in houses already with an NGA presence. Retrained letterpress printers would remain in the SGD only seeking an NGA card when moving to a traditional litho house. This action by the SGD was seen by the NGA as an act of war and a series of strikes took place.

The first strike was at Waddie & Co, Edinburgh beginning 7 January 1982, when the SGD withdrew its members in the letterpress machine room and the continuous stationery department, in pursuit of its claim regarding current and future staffing of lithographic machines, normally operated in the company by NGA members. It followed up by withdrawing SGD members from the company's composing room on 14 January 1982. It was not in Waddie's power to grant the SGD demands as it already had agreements covering the staffing of machinery. The company argued any disputes should go through the laid down procedures and must be agreed by both unions. On 20 January Waddie's SOGAT employees were instructed to strike in support of SGD members. Supplies to NGA machinemen were cut off and on 22 January 1982 the company suspended its NGA employees. On 26 January the company met with SOGAT and SGD. They repeated their demands whilst the company restated their inability to arbitrate between the unions and their reluctance to break existing NGA agreements. No progress was made at the meeting but the company informed SOGAT and the SGD of the job losses incurred as a result of the dispute. Without SOGAT (SGD), the NGA and the company talking together, no purpose could be served by talks. Waddie's customers were finding their supplies disrupted and they were turning to other printers to meet their requirements. For many customers the dispute highlighted their vulnerability in having only one supplier and they took steps to ensure this did not happen again.

On 25 February 1982, normal working returned to Waddies following an agreement reached the day before after many hours of negotiation involving the company, the President of SOGAT, SGD, of the east of Scotland branch of SOGAT and SMPS Director, Barrie Abbott. The agreement contained the following clause:

> …The Parties (ie the Company and SOGAT) agree that their future relationship with each other should be conducted on the basis that continuity of production is essential and that if any demarcation or sphere of influence difficulty emerges the matter will be dealt with via the SMPS Joint Working Practices Committee procedure…

This clause was satisfactory from the perspective of the Scottish printing industry. Following the settlement of the Waddies dispute, SMPS staff were frequently engaged in assisting with the drawing up of house agreements allowing the introduction of phototypesetting and litho printing in commercial printing houses. It was a time of uncertainty as most house agreements involved some redundancies. The peace between the NGA and the SGD lasted five months. In July 1982 there was another outbreak of hostilities when the NGA called strike action in Holmes McDougall, Glasgow alleging provocation by SGD, with the threat to spread hostile action to the company's Edinburgh operations. Three machines lay idle meantime in Waddie's because each union threatened if men from the other operated the machines there would be another stoppage. The SMPS continued to complain it was not right for its members to be put in the position of deciding demarcation issues which could only be decided by the unions themselves. The NGA's action at Holmes McDougall led within days to the suspension of the SOGAT (including SGD) employees. The circumstances of the dispute concerning the staffing of litho machines transferred to Holmes McDougall's Clydeholm Road plant because of the closure of its York Street plant in Glasgow, have been explained in Chapter 13. Holmes McDougall had, without consulting the SMPS, signed an agreement with the SGD for its members to operate all litho equipment used in the company's printing of the magazine the *Scottish Farmer*. The stoppage in Edinburgh and Glasgow lasted for several weeks and resolved by a TUC Disputes Committee which forced an agreement between the two unions resulting in the house agreement between the company and the SGD being rescinded and the status quo resumed.

Summary

The SJIC had been created in 1922 and met regularly until the 1959 dispute after which it went into abeyance. In the early 1960s, there were attempts to revive the SJIC. In 1964 a revised constitution was agreed. The first meeting of the reformed SJIC took place in June 1964. It worked well initially but began to meet infrequently and met for the last time in March 1967.

In the 1960s, union organisation amongst clerical workers in the Scottish general printing industry began to emerge. This led to competition between NATSOPA and SOGAT. The latter tried to persuade the SMPS to recognise it as the appropriate union for clerical workers. The SMPS resisted this claim but by mid-1970 it was clear SOGAT would establish itself as the clerical union in the industry. In an attempt to control clerical worker union organisation, the SMPS made a declaration effectively channelling further clerical organisation towards SOGAT.

Negotiations were conducted with the STA, ASLP, NSES, SLADE and SOGAT over working conditions. In 1973, SMPS, the STA and SOGAT agreed increases in machine extras from 1974 be in line with changes in the basic rates of pay. In 1961 the STA accepted the introduction of group incentive schemes in the work areas of its members. Summer 1965 witnessed significant changes to the STA mutual rules, for example in future no more than forty eight hours would be worked per month. There were changes to the shift-working provisions for the Mutual Rules Agreement. In 1965, after lengthy negotiations, the first installation in Scotland of a work measurement incentive scheme in a litho machine room was introduced. In 1967, agreements were made with the STA, NSES and the ASLP providing where new work measurement incentive schemes were introduced, holiday pay would include the average incentive bonus payments.

In the 1960s and the 1970s, the industry suffered a serious manpower shortage in several sectors, particularly the composing rooms, the litho machine room and the SLADE areas. SMPS member firms experienced a relatively high labour turnover as they poached craft employees from each other. In the first half of the 1980s the industry witnessed redundancies and short-time working and the size of the workforce fell by 25%. The industry, in the late 1980s, improved its economic performance, exceeding that for manufacturing as a whole. The implementation of technological change in the late 1970s and early 1980s led to a reduction in the number of production employees in the industry but to an increase in the number of white collar employees.

Notes

[1] See Minutes of the Meeting of the Executive Board, 23 November 1965.

[2] Memorandum for meeting of the Negotiating Committee to be held on 19 October 1972, Society of Master Printers of Scotland.

[3] See Minutes of the Meeting of the Executive Board, 20 October 1966.

[4] See *Annual Report and Accounts, 1970-71*, Society of Master Printers of Scotland.

[5] See *Annual Report and Accounts, 1980-81*, Society of Master Printers of Scotland.

[6] See *Annual Report and Accounts, 1964-65*, Society of Master Printers of Scotland.

[7] See *Annual Report and Accounts, 1980-81*, Society of Master Printers of Scotland.

[8] See Statement by the Scottish Typographical Association to meeting with SMPS, 10 York Place Wednesday, 27 December 1972.

[9] See Press Release *General Statement to Shareholders, NGA, SOGAT, SGD, SMPS Employees and other interested parties*, Waddies of Edinburgh, 8 February 1982.

Chapter 18

WAGES AND CONDITIONS: 1960-1990

The first half of the chapter examines the collective wage agreements of the print unions over the period 1961 to 1966. This includes the introduction in 1962 of the forty-hour working week and in 1965 three weeks paid holiday entitlement. From 1967, the SMPS negotiated unilaterally with the main print unions rather than collectively on a UK basis with the BFMP. The chapter then explains the main outcomes, over the period 1967 to 1990, of the annual negotiations between the SMPS and the print unions. The final part of the chapter examines the implementation of the Equal Pay Act (1970).

The 1961 Collective Wage Agreement

The 1959 agreements contained provision for a stabilisation period of three years but also that in 1961 consideration be given to whether there was justification for a reduction of hours and/or an increase in basic rates to operate from September 1961. They provided if no negotiated settlement on such claims proved practicable by 30 April, then the claims be referred to a Judicial Inquiry to be conducted by Lord Birkett. The ten unions which took part in the 1959 dispute, including the four with which the SMPS had collective agreements (the STA, NSES, ASLP, and NUPB&PW) made claims on 15 December 1960 for a further reduction in hours from forty two to forty per week and for an increase in pay for craftsmen in Scotland of 16s 3d per week. The claim for female workers was for a £1 6s 3d per week increase together with significant increases for non-craft male auxiliaries. The hours aspect of the claim was a P&KTF/BFMP matter whilst the wages claim was an approach by a group of trade unions acting collectively with the P&KTF acting as the liaison. The employer negotiating team receiving the unions' claim consisted of the BFMP, Newspaper Society and SMPS representatives.

At the first bargaining session, the unions provided no evidence in support of the claims which were stated simply 'as the balance of the 1959 claims'. The employers stated they would approach the negotiations in 'a positive way' provided the unions would examine the extent of manpower shortages in the industry and co-operate in implementing measures to deal with the identified shortage. The BFMP told the unions they would conclude an agreement which would provide, by stages, for the introduction of a forty-hour week and for the balance of the 10% wage claim if they would move closer to their position on the labour shortage situation. On 8 May it was agreed separate meetings between employer representatives and those of the unions be held to assess whether progress could be made on the unions agreeing a substantial increase in the labour supply. A deadline of 11 May was set for the completion of these separate meetings after which full negotiations would resume. SMPS and the STA could not meet this deadline but agreed to meet in Glasgow on 12 May 1961.

On 11 May 1961 the BFMP and the unions involved discussed measures to increase manpower increases in wages and a reduction in weekly hours of work. All parties accepted a new agreement providing for a 5% increase in basic wages from the first week in September 1961 for craftsmen, auxiliary males and women workers. There was a reduction in standard weekly working hours to forty one in September 1961 and to forty hours in September 1962. On manpower issues, although there was no change in the existing apprenticeship ratios, there were to be substantial numbers of additional apprentices admitted to the letterpress, litho, binding and stereo departments.

In the circumstances, the SMPS in its negotiations on 17 May 1961 with the STA could do little other than agree an intake of additional, or bonus, apprentices and accept the settlement agreed by the BFMP and the other unions to increases in wage rates and reductions in weekly hours of work. On increasing the labour supply the STA agreed to 130 bonus apprentices over the next two years. In the case of additional composing and machine room apprentices, half would start after September 1961 and the other half as soon as possible after June 1962. Cases of hardship were the subject of national agreements between the STA branch and the SMPS member firm. An arrangement was reached whereby there would be no redundancy in firms recruiting bonus apprentices. As a result of the 1961 agreement the basic craft rate in Scotland became £11 6s 0d per week, for a male auxiliary £9 12s 0d and for a female auxiliary £6 17s 6d. Resulting from increases in the Retail Price Index, the cost-of-living bonus was increased in July 1961 and again in January 1962. The January figure was 24s 0d per week for adult male workers and 18s 0d for qualified female workers.

The SMPS Executive Board met on 16 May 1961 and agreed to implement the settlement agreed in the England and Wales. There was criticism of both the method, and the nature of the proposed settlement, particularly regarding manpower.[1] The possibility of a reference to Lord Birkett and of the SMPS exercising its industrial relations autonomy from the BFMP were considered. The Executive Board reluctantly approved the proposed settlement with the STA and similar settlements with the NUPB&PW, ASLP and NSES subject to satisfactory agreement on additional labour intake. SMPS members were informed on 3 July 1961 all ten unions, including the STA had, after membership ballots, accepted the 1961 settlement.

A new agreement between the SMPS and SLADE became effective from 1 January 1962 after negotiations spread over more than two years. It contained provisions on basic rates, hours, cost-of-living bonus and stabilisation similar to those provided by the 1959 agreements with other unions, as amended in 1961.

The Collective Wages and Holiday Movement, 1962

The 1959 agreements with the STA, NSES and the Scottish District Councils of the NUPB&PW and ASLP terminated in August 1962. Accordingly negotiations for new agreements between the employers' organisations and ten unions affiliated to the P&KTF opened in early 1962 but were only concluded after the terminal dates of the 1959 agreements. The ten unions presented their claim on 19 April 1962. It was for a third week's annual holiday, increases of 25s 0d per week for craft workers, consolidation of the cost-of-living bonus and its continuation at 1s 0d per point for both men and women, stabilisation for three years, improvement in shift payments and enhancement of apprentices' wages.

On 18 June 1962 the employers rejected the unions' claims and sought to end the cost-of-living bonus, suggesting one third of the present bonus be consolidated into basic wages. The negotiations were lengthy but SMPS kept its members informed of what was happening. Special meetings of the Executive Board were held and the views of local associations gathered concerning the content of any new agreements. The unions were reluctant to settle without a cost-of-living bonus provision but indicated they might accept such a settlement on a short-term basis providing the employers' offers on other terms were adequate. The unions stressed the third week's holiday was a key part of their claim whilst the employers made it clear no useful purpose would be served by discussing wages until the present position on the cost-of-living bonus had been settled. The BFMP proposed any settlement at this stage be short-term and that in

1963, and annually thereafter, wages be examined in the light of changes in the cost-of-living, productivity and profitability. In such a context it would be possible to review effectively measures to improve productivity away from the pressures of wage negotiations which had to be completed by a specific date. Although the abolition of the cost-of-living bonus was a major objective of the employers, the SMPS negotiators felt there was a lack of determination amongst BFMP membership regarding its abolition.[2] The view of the English and Welsh printers was while it might be possible to secure abolition it would be at a 'price higher than the industry could afford'.

On 10 August 1962, the employers and the unions reached agreement, of which the principal provisions were:
(1) staged increases (from January 1963 to January 1965) in basic wage rates totalling 15s 0d per week for craftsmen
(2) staged consolidation into basic rates of approximately two thirds (21s 0d in absolute terms for men) by three equal stages between September 1962 and January 1964 of the cost-of-living bonus
(3) modifications to the cost-of-living bonus including the use of the new Retail Price Index, and yearly in place of six-monthly reviews
(4) the present provisions for shift working continue to operate for the period of the new agreements
(5) stabilisation until 31 March 1965
(6) although the unions' annual holiday claim was not accepted either now or for any pre-determined date in the future the employers accepted that if at some time during the life of the agreement the unions considered circumstances warranted it, the employers would make an objective assessment of the position with them and consider whether there was justification for an additional week of holiday in some later period
(7) the parties undertook to review, periodically and jointly, the labour supply position and in the event of any surplus or shortage of labour arising to agree ways of dealing with the situation, including adjustments in labour intakes and in overtime limits. Should unemployment result from the introduction of new techniques or methods of production, the parties agreed to consider steps which would prevent or alleviate unemployment, including retraining of workers, shorter hours or additional holidays.

The SMPS was advised formally on 2 October 1962 all ten unions accepted the agreement. Whilst there had been a substantial majority in favour of acceptance there had been a small minority against the settlement in the case of the STA craft section. The STA had voted in favour overall as there was a substantial majority in its auxiliary section. In October 1962 the SMPS met with the NUPB&PW to clarify matters surrounding the new agreement, including dates for the cost-of-living bonus payments and in future female learner rates be calculated to the nearest 6d. By 1964, basic rates for craft employees, male auxiliary workers and qualified female workers has risen to

£12 19s 0d, £11 3s 0d and £8 2s 3d respectively; the cost-of-living bonus by 1964 was 11s 8d per week for adult male workers and 8s 10d per week for qualified female workers.

The Collective Wages Movement, 1965

In December 1964, nine unions collectively, including the STA, put forward a wage claim to replace existing agreements due to terminate on 31 March 1965. The unions tabled their claims in February 1965:

(1) stabilisation period of three years
(2) consolidation of cost-of-living bonus
(3) increase in craft rates of 17s 6d per week in each of the next three years to give new basic rates of £14 9s 6d (1965) to £16 4s 6d (1967)
(4) increase in the female basic rates to give them two thirds of the basic craft rate
(5) continuation of the cost-of-living bonus by payment per point being increased to 2s 0d for both men and women with adjustment half-yearly.

The SMPS told the BFMP it considered pay differentials be reduced and 'domestic' claims applicable to Scotland be dealt with directly between the SMPS and the unions concerned. The 1965 negotiations proved difficult, centring on the length of the stabilisation period, whether the claim was within the government incomes policy guidelines for movements in prices and incomes, the amount of pay increase and the unions' domestic claims. A settlement was reached on 17 May 1965 although it was not ratified until the first week in July 1965 following a ballot by all nine unions. The May settlement provided:

(1) on the implementation of the settlement
    (i)   there be a consolidation of the cost-of-living bonus to the amount of 7s 0d per week for men and proportionately for women, apprentices and female learners and
    (ii) an increase in basic rates of 10s 6d per week for craftsmen and proportionately for auxiliary workers, apprentices and female learners.
(2) the offset from the beginning of 1966 of
    (i)   a consolidation 7s 0d of the cost-of-living bonus
    (ii) an increase in basic rates of 12s 0d per week for craftsmen and proportionately for others
    (iii) an adjustment of the cost-of-living bonus in accordance with the movement of the Retail Price Index at the rate of 2s 0d per point for men and 1s 7d for women with the proviso there be no increase in the amount of bonus of the first three points above the figure of 108.
(3) stabilisation until 31 December 1966.

On 2 May 1965 the Minister for Economic Affairs, George Brown, referred the settlement to the newly-created National Board for Prices and Incomes because the agreement, he said, appeared to be out of line with the government policy on criteria for movement in prices and increases. The Board issued their report on 17 August 1965[3] the essence of which was the increase in earnings provided by the settlement was within the limits of the government's prices and incomes policy only if there was a major change in working practices providing the self-financing of the increases via productivity improvements. The report also recommended the cost-of-living bonus be eliminated, when the next national wage settlement was made, a joint manpower committee be set up with terms of reference specifically including the efficient use of manpower and both sides of the printing industry consider the introduction of an industrial pension scheme.

The Collective Wages Movement, 1966

In the summer of 1966, the unions including the STA gave notice of termination of the current agreements, due to end on 31 December 1966. By this date, the craft rate in Scotland was £14 18s 6d per week, the male auxiliary workers rate £13 and of the qualified female worker £9 10s 3d. There was a cost-of-living bonus payable at the rate of 9s 0d per week for adult male workers and 7s 8d per week for qualified female workers.

On 6 December 1966, the unions submitted the following claim:
(1) increases in the basic rate of 35s 0d for craftsmen, in two stages of 17s 6d on 1 January 1967 and 1 January 1968
(2) maintenance of the present male wage differentials but an increase in the women's rates to 75% of the craft rates
(3) from 1 January 1967, continuation of the current cost-of-living bonus provision but with 2s 0d per point for adult women as well as adult men and adjustments at six-monthly intervals rather than twelve
(4) a two-year agreement to run from 1 January 1967 until 31 December 1968
(5) domestic claims be notified separately by the unions concerned.
The employers, including the SMPS, intimated in January 1967 the claim be rejected. The SMPS were opposed to any continuation of the cost-of-living bonus and were not prepared in any new agreement for its continuation. This context of the negotiations meant it was unlikely new agreements could be implemented before 1 July 1967 when the 'period of severe restraint' of the government's prices and incomes policy (1 January to 31 July 1967) was due to end. It was expected the intervening period be used to conclude, in good time, new agreements. This expectation was not realised and by mid-August 1967 little progress had been made. The employers had rejected the union's claim, as a precondition to the negotiations, for an immediate payment to compensate their members for the fall in their real wages. Throughout the bargaining sessions, the unions continued to argue for the retention of the cost-of-living bonus. Its retention was just as vigorously resisted by the employers who repeatedly quoted the recommendation of the National Board for Prices and Incomes 1965 *Report* that 'the cost-of-living bonus in the printing industry should be eliminated when the next national wage agreement is made'. Whilst continuing to feel strongly it be retained, the unions set it aside until a later date. The SMPS made it clear as far as they were concerned, the cost-of-living bonus was at an end and they were not prepared to offer any wage increase not matched by measures designed to improve productivity. The SMPS productivity

proposals included a demand for greater flexibility of labour, the use of the disputes procedure, an assessment on staffing levels, the rating of equipment, the measurement of individual output, and the use of women on typewriters producing work for reproduction. These productivity improvement negotiations were to be the subject of separate union/employer talks.

Early in August 1967, the BFMP recommended a settlement based on consolidation of the current cost-of-living bonus (9s 0d for men and 7s 8d for women) and wage increases of 12s 6d per week for craftsmen, for 11s 0d to 11s 9d for non-craftsmen and 8s 0d for women provided their productivity proposals were met. The unions' response was to threaten industrial action unless the employers improved their wage offer. When the BFMP and the SMPS repeated they were not prepared to consider any improvement of their wages offer, the unions concluded the negotiations had broken down. In October 1967, the unions imposed an overtime ban in all provincial daily newspaper offices with effect from 16 October. At the end of August it emerged the STA wished to settle directly with the SMPS and it proved possible to conclude an agreement in line with the mandate the SMPS Executive Board gave to its negotiators. The agreement between SMPS and the STA included:
(1) abolition of the cost-of-living bonus
(2) no fixed term to the agreement
(3) improvement in apprentice intake
(4) measures to increase productivity
(5) increases in the minimum craft rate of 16s 0d per week (including consolidation of 9s 0d of the cost-of-living bonus) and proportionate increases to auxiliaries, apprentices and learners.
The SMPS informed the other unions with members in Scotland it would make agreements with them on similar lines. In September 1967, SOGAT (Division A) met with the SMPS at which settlement was reached. A settlement was also subsequently made with NSES, now part of the National Graphical Association. The ASLP did not take up the SMPS offer to make similar agreement to that made with the STA until a settlement had been made in England and Wales. A conference was held with the ASLP on 8 November 1967 and an agreement reached between the ASLP and the SMPS on the same terms as applied in Scotland to other unions.

By the end of October aggressive action by the unions, particularly directed against newspaper houses in the English provinces, looked like leading to a complete stoppage in the newspaper and general printing industry in England and Wales. A series of meetings resulted in a settlement between the BPMP and the unions, except for SLADE. Whereas the SMPS agreements provided for an increase in the craft rate of 16s 0d, for no stabilisation, measures to increase productivity and provisions for additional manpower, the BFMP agreements provided for an increase of 30s 0d in the craft rate over two years, namely 16s 0d increase in 1967 and a 14s 0d increase in 1968 and for measures to increase productivity.

The BFMP agreements contained a stabilisation clause for two years ending in October 1969. Again, unlike the SMPS agreements, it made no provision for additional manpower. The agreements made by the SMPS endangered seriously relations between the SMPS and the BFMP (see Chapter 15).

Third Week's Annual Holiday

In March 1963, the SMPS received notification from the STA it was desirable for a 'Scottish version' of the *Hours and Holiday Agreement*. Certain clauses in the UK-wide agreement did not apply in Scotland. The SMPS met with the STA but before doing so, produced its own draft Scottish version of the *Hours and Holiday Agreement*. This proposed no new principles but changes suggested for 2 January (a public holiday in Scotland) had implications for present practice in certain member firms and areas of Scotland. The Executive Board at its meeting of 11 July 1963 did not approve the terms of the draft. When the STA was informed of the decision, the union said it would pursue the matter in the future.

The 1962 settlement contained a clause permitting the unions, if the circumstances warranted, to ask the employers to consider jointly whether there was justification for an additional week of holiday or some lesser period. On 21 January 1964, the P&KTF formally presented a claim for a third week of annual holiday, to be taken in the winter months, namely between 1 October and 31 March. The employers argued the claim was unjustified but indicated they might grant some additional holidays on certain conditions. The SMPS considered effective measures to deal with the serious manpower shortage in several sections of the Scottish print industry be agreed with the unions before additional holidays could be granted. Negotiations continued for about a year without a significant breakthrough. A settlement was agreed on 8 December 1964 and ratified by union ballots on 27 January 1965.

The SMPS agreed with the five unions in Scotland three important changes.
(1) Three weeks annual holiday be given to all employees. The additional week's holiday to be taken between 1 October and 31 March unless otherwise mutually agreed. The actual dates the holiday was taken within this period was to be settled after consultation with the employer. In cases where a firm already allowed more than two weeks annual holiday, the extra week counted towards the additional week provided by the agreement. For the winter 1964/65 only, management had the option of providing a week's pay in lieu of the holiday.
(2) A *Retraining and Transfer Agreement* signed by the ASLP, STA and SMPS provided where expansion of the lithographic printing process accompanied the contraction of the letterpress process or vice versa the two unions would, with the co-operation of the SMPS and the management at the company, jointly take measures to avoid members of either union being declared redundant.

(3) Manpower issues be dealt with separately from the annual wage negotiations but measures to deal with the current labour shortages be agreed between the SMPS and each of the five unions by the end of February 1965.

The new agreement for increased holidays contained provisions the SMPS and each of the five unions make a joint study of the present and future manpower requirements.

a. The NSES

The union argued the apprentice intake provided by the present ratio be altered to reduce the number of apprentices coming into the industry in the next two to three years. Several of its members in Scotland were unemployed though this was in national daily newspapers rather than the general trade. The SMPS reassured the union it was not their policy to recruit more apprentices than the industry required. After negotiations, the present apprentice ratio was suspended for two years provided individual cases were considered if there was prima facie evidence in support of starting an apprentice.

b. SLADE

SLADE proposed one additional apprenticeship outwith the quota be allocated to firms employing fourteen or more SLADE members. Only three firms in Edinburgh could meet this criteria. SMPS advised SLADE this was unsatisfactory and action be taken to solve the labour shortage in the individual firms.

c. The ASLP

The union accepted employers could upgrade one auxiliary employee in each of the twenty printing houses in which there was an existing shortage for labour.

d. The NUPB&PW

The union accepted solutions to the labour supply problem be settled at branch and SMPS local association level and a 'fair gesture be made'. It drew to the SMPS attention the existing apprentice facilities whilst employers, to secure greater flexibility, asked NUPB&PW branches to examine the position of qualified cutters with over five years training in the industry. Both parties accepted that if these steps in the short-term did not produce the required result, further action be considered.

e. The STA

As a step to solving the current manpower shortage, the STA instructed branch secretaries to take into membership non-unionists in the various areas and to offer membership to ex-apprentices who had left the trade. The SMPS expressed disappointment greater progress could not be made to ease the manpower shortage in the composing room but continued to pressurise the STA to release skilled compositors from work which could easily be done by composing room auxiliaries. This view was strongly expressed at the 14 July

1965 meeting of the Executive Board which, after discussions unanimously approved the following resolution:

> ...This meeting of the Board, held on 14 July 1965, having noted the undertaking given by the Scottish Typographical Association, as part of the Additional Holidays Agreement, to deal with any current labour shortage by 28 February 1965, is gravely concerned that there is still a serious shortage of labour, particularly in the case room section, and that all steps taken so far have proved totally inadequate to meet the situation. It, therefore, demands that the Negotiating Committee asks the STA, when that Association intends effectively to implement its part of the Agreement of 22 January 1965.[4]

The only practical steps the STA had taken to implement the 22 January 1965 *Agreement* were to admit into membership non-unionists and to deal sympathetically with particular cases of hardship. The impact of these measures was limited. In May 1965, the STA agreed, in principle, to allow male auxiliaries to do certain jobs in the composing room provided they were paid the craft rate and there were adequate safeguards against redundancy. The union was reluctant to accept any general scheme for upgrading in the machine room and its policy towards auxiliaries in the composing room was, as far as the SMPS were concerned, limited. Most of the tasks the union was prepared to see upgraded did not come within the field of craft work. The growing view amongst SMPS member firms, was the only way to obtain additional labour supply from the STA was by a large block of bonus apprentices or by alteration of the present ratio. Unfortunately, action on these lines was long term and it remained SMPS policy that long-term proposals to deal with labour supply shortages could only be put to the STA after measures to deal effectively with the present shortage had been agreed.

Main Wage Agreements, 1968-1990

A consequence of the SMPS exercising its autonomy within the BFMP Constitution to conclude its own wage agreements, was it 'withdrew' from negotiations on a UK basis. From 1967 it negotiated agreements covering wages, hours of work, holidays, etc directly with the print unions having members employed in Scotland. These Scottish national agreements became referred to in SMPS publications as the main wage agreements. The SMPS negotiated separate agreements with the National Graphical Association (stereotypers, electrotypers and the litho machine area), SLADE, STA (later SGA, the SGD of SOGAT and the SGB of SOGAT) and SOGAT (Division A).

These Scottish national agreements became an annual landmark. Each union submitted its separate wages and other employment conditions claims.

Two problems for the SMPS were the rationalisation of the unions' various demands and until the early 1980s, the SMPS Negotiating Committee often operated without a clear negotiating strategy or picture of the direction the industry was moving over the next few years. From the 1983 main wage negotiations, the negotiating team entered the bargaining sessions with the unions with an agreed strategy. The main wages agreements classified employees as Grade B, C and D. There was a long term commitment to consider the introduction of a Grade A but neither the unions nor the SMPS were willing to address the issue. The grades were paid as B = 100 %, C = 90% and D = 87.5% of A. The majority of Grade D employees were female. Most Grade C employees were male and most Grade B employees were time-served males. The definitions of the grades were arbitrary and related little to the skills involved. The agreements also contained a complex and outdated system of 'machine extras' which were arbitrary in nature and did not reflect current technology.

a. The 1960s

The 1968 wage settlements with SOGAT, NGA (Stereo/Electrotypers), ASLP, STA and SLADE were not made without difficulty. It proved impossible to make all the agreements with the five unions operative from the same date but a uniform pattern of conditions was achieved. The main provisions of the agreements included stabilisation until 31 March 1970, an increase in the craft rate of £1 above the rate established in 1967, methods dealing with the labour shortage, particularly in the lithographic section, to use female labour on non-traditional setting equipment and a procedure for productivity bargaining.

b. The 1970s

The negotiations for new main wage agreements to replace those which terminated on 31 March 1970 started towards the end of 1969 and resulted in timeous settlements with the NGA and SOGAT. In the case of SLADE, although no serious difficulties emerged, settlement was not reached until June 1970. For the STA the terms offered by the SMPS were rejected in a ballot of the membership. A second ballot vote heavily supported industrial action. Further negotiations produced a reasonable settlement, by which time it had become increasingly clear the wage rates in England and Wales, stabilised by agreement until October 1971, would increase before that date in the light of union pressure including some industrial action. The settlement in Scotland had anticipated this as well as any action required in the event of any major change in general service conditions affecting the country as a whole. By the end of August, revised main wage agreements had been concluded with all unions and new wage rates operated from the end of September 1970. The revised agreements were stabilised until June 1972 and provided for wage increases in August 1971 of £2 for craft grades with lesser increases for other categories of employees. They dealt with various matters other than pay including holiday pay, shift work, overtime payments, manpower and conciliation procedures.

In mid-1971, bargaining started with the STA, NGA, SOGAT and SLADE to revise the terms of main wage agreements to replace those due to expire on 16 June 1972. It was not until August 1972 a final settlement was reached with all four unions with a common termination date of 12 October 1973. The settlements were also within the limits laid down by the then Conservative government's counter-inflation policy. Following the election of a minority Labour government in February 1974, the previous Conservative government pay code, introduced under its counter-inflation policy, was abolished in July 1974. The negotiations for revisions of the main wage agreements with the four unions due to terminate on 31 August 1974 were not completed before this date because of the reluctance of the unions to commence negotiations until the pay code had been abolished. Final settlement was reached in October entailing retrospective payments of increases of some six weeks or more. These new main wage agreements, effective from 2 September 1974, provided increases in basic rates and an additional threshold (cost-of-living) payment in anticipation of further increases in the cost of living together with percentage increases in machine extras agreed. Provision was made for consolidation of part of the threshold payment into the basic rate at the start of 1975. The agreements operated until the end of August 1975 but a revision in March 1975 was possible depending on cost-of-living increases.

In May 1975, the SMPS proposed bringing forward the termination date of the current main wage agreements in the hope of achieving a better settlement. By doing so, matters became complicated when the Labour government introduced in July 1975 a counter-inflation policy under which the maximum weekly wage increase was £6. The government accepted the 1975 settlements with each of the four unions was compatible with its anti-inflation policy and could be paid from January 1976. The Labour government remained in office until May 1979 during which time it continued to operate a counter-inflation policy which involved direct interference in the outcome of collective bargaining. A central pillar of this counter-inflation policy was there be at least a twelve-month interval between pay settlements. The policy was, in the last resort, enforced by the government applying sanctions on employers who breached its pay policy. These could include, as far as the Scottish printing industry was concerned, the loss of HMSO contracts, the loss of work from local authorities, restrictions on any increase in advertising rates and cover charges. In addition, grants for new premises, new plant, etc and the temporary employment subsidy could be withheld with consequences for new investment and continuity of employment.

The provisions of the settlements with the unions reached in February 1978 included measures to improve productivity as permitted under the counter-inflation policy and which in many respects proved beneficial. The main wage agreements with the production unions effective from the beginning of July 1978 were compatible with the existing counter-inflation policy. Subsequent attempts to eliminate the effectiveness of these productivity measures by SOGAT/SGD were successfully resisted by the SMPS.

The 1979 main wage agreements with the production unions provided for substantial increases in basic rates from the beginning of July. These increases were greater than regarded as satisfactory from an employer point of view. The increases gave a Class B (craft) rate of £55.57 plus a supplement of £8.48 to give a minimum earnings level of £64.05 per week. The Class D grade rate was £48.62 plus a supplement of £8.24. The 1979 agreements provided for a reduction in the standard working week from forty hours to thirty nine effective from 1 February 1980.

c. The 1980s

The 1980 main wage agreements concluded with the production unions provided for substantial increases in basic rates as from July of £13, partial consolidation of the flat supplementary payment (currently £8.48) with provision for bonus calculations, machine extras increased by 23.39% and minimum earnings level of £80 per week by 4 August 1980 for craft employees, of £72 for Class C employees and of £70 for Class D workers. The general level of the settlements were higher than many SMPS members wished but the agreements with the NGA, SOGAT/SGD and SOGAT did include provisions for improving efficiency and productivity to reduce unit costs. The alternative to accepting these agreements would have been widespread industrial chaos and a greater loss of customer confidence. The 1980 agreements contained provision for reduction in the standard working week from thirty nine to thirty seven and a half operative from 6 July in 1981 when double shift, night shift and treble shift hours were reduced to thirty six. The majority of SMPS member firms implemented the hours reduction by finishing work at the end of Friday morning.

In preparation for the 1981 negotiations, the SMPS planned an agreement with the unions providing cash increases at as low a figure as possible and concluded a quick and timeous settlement which reflected the economic circumstance of the industry. The 1981 main wage agreements concluded with each of the four production unions provided for wage increases more in line with what the industry could afford than had recently been the case. They were significantly below the rate of inflation. The craft rate became £85 per week, the Class C rate £76.50 and the Class D rate £75.20. The minimum earnings level for craft employees was set at £87.95 per week and £79.96 respectively for Class C and D employees.

On 2 November 1981, SOGAT/SGD took strike action against Bell & Bain in Glasgow in breach of the main SMPS/SOGAT agreement. The company introduced modern composing equipment needed to compete in its main field of book production. Such equipment was already operating successfully in

Scotland. The recent agreement with SOGAT (Division A), provided machine classification be on the same basis as the BPIF agreement and practice, with suitable modification for Scotland. The extra in England appropriate to this machine was £14 per week and Bell & Bain agreed to pay the extra. The SGD claim was for a payment of £300 per week spread over forty five people plus a reduction in the working week and additional holidays. The company decided, after careful consideration, it could not continue to operate profitably under the threat of such absurd claims and aggressive industrial action. It would close down with the loss of seventy SOGAT jobs and the jobs of members of other unions unless normal working was resumed and the union's claim withdrawn.[5]

After a strike lasting more than two weeks, SOGAT realised the company would cease operations rather than meet the its claim. In the ensuing negotiations, agreement was reached that a machine extra of £17 would be paid and wage increases given throughout the composing section costing over £100 per week, justified on the basis of promised productivity increases and the maintenance of acceptable quality standards. Much needed production and substantial amounts of wages had been lost and the public image of book production further tarnished by ill-conceived aggressive action by the SGD. The SMPS warned strikes and stoppages, especially the pursuit of unrealistic wage claims by small and selfish groups could only diminish hope of recovery from present economic constraints.[6]

The 1982 main wage negotiations with the NGA, SOGAT/SGD and SLADE took place at a time of economic difficulty for the industry and resulted in increases for Class B employees of £6.25 per week and minimum earnings levels of £94.20 as opposed to £82.43 for Class D employees. At the same time, a delayed new system of machine classification came into force covering SOGAT and SGD employees operating printing machinery, binding and print finishing equipment and photocomposition equipment. Both parties reiterated their commitment to settle disputes peacefully by using agreed procedures. Sick pay was increased from one third to one half of normal weekly wages (upper limit of £59) and entitlement extended to twelve weeks for employees with more than five years service with their present employer. There was no change in the provision that sick pay not be paid for the first two weeks of absence on account of illness.

In 1983, the main wage conditions agreements concluded with SOGAT and, for the first time, the NGA as a combined SLADE/NGA union, were at a level which placed them roughly in the middle range of settlements within the UK. More important, for the first time for many years, the subsequent house agreements were concluded without disruption and in a harmonious manner.[7] The 1984 negotiations witnessed new money increases of £6.10 per week for Class B employees of £5.49, for Class C employees and of £5.34 for Class D. On SOGAT's claim for the abolition of Class D, the SMPS said it would not contemplate such a change but would examine with the union any specific job classifications within the Equal Pay Agreement which it was felt were wrongly graded. Both the 1985 and 1986 main wage, etc negotiations resulted in a settlement of £6.65 on the craft rate. In addition to the cash awards, both agreements provided for additional annual holiday, the result of which was the introduction of a fifth week of holiday from 1 October 1986 with a corresponding reduction of the single day entitlement to six days. The single day holiday entitlement was to be restored to seven on 1 January 1988 and to eight on 1 January 1989. Additional days were subject to absorption where individual houses had entitlements in excess of the national entitlement.

The BPIF established a Joint Pensions Working Party with the unions. The SMPS Executive Board agreed a small ad hoc working group explore whether it would be advantageous for the substantial number of member companies presently without pension schemes to establish such schemes. The working party invited proposals for an industry scheme in which employee participation be on a voluntary basis, membership be open to non-production employees and production employees, any scheme be money purchase and benefits include a retirement pension, death-in-service payments and half pension for spouses where death occurred after retirement. The working party considered two options. First, there be a contracted-in scheme the same or similar to the English and Welsh Printing Industry Pension Scheme. Second, a contracted-out scheme offering benefits at least equal to the Printing Industry Pension Scheme plus a Supplementary Earnings Related Pension Scheme (SERPS) at a cost not exceeding 7% plus the National Insurance rebate available from contracting-out. In 1987, the Executive Board accepted the Joint Pension Working Party recommendations a voluntary scheme be introduced on the basis of a 4.67% contribution by the employer and 2.33% by the employee. The scheme was implemented in April 1988.

In 1987, the cash settlement in the main wage agreements with the NGA (82) and SOGAT (82) was, for the second successive year, below those of the BPIF settlement. This had been made possible by early communication to the unions of the problems facing the Scottish printing industry. The agreements included a strengthening of the productivity clauses and improved wording relating to absenteeism. In the 1988 negotiations, the SMPS stressed the economic situation facing the Scottish economy and the printing industry where certain sections continued to experience difficulties. For the third successive year, the unions accepted increases on the basic rate below those of the BPIF agreement representing a further stage in breaking the link between the respective national agreements. In 1990, the wage negotiations resulted in increases in £11.68 on the Grade B rate from July 1990. The SMPS, for the first time, met with a combined NGA/SOGAT team to discuss a consolidation claim.

In the late 1980s, both NGA and SOGAT laid increasing emphasis on improvements to the 'social wage' (maternity, bereavement, paternity leave, etc). The SMPS whilst acknowledging the right of unions to seek enhancements for their members in these areas, considered such matters were not appropriate for national agreements. It remained of the view national agreements suited the overwhelming majority of its member companies. Recognising not all companies wished to be parties to such arrangements the Executive Board offered an opting-out facility to accommodate those planning to conduct their own negotiations. Only a few companies were expected to take this route.[8]

The Equal Pay Act (1970)

The Equal Pay Act received Royal Assent on 29 May 1970 and its objective was to eliminate discrimination between men and women, as regards pay and other terms and conditions of employment. This was to be achieved in two main ways. One by establishing the right of the individual to equal treatment when she was employed (a) on work of the same or broadly similar nature to that of a man and (b) in a job which, though different from those of men, had been given an equal value to men's jobs under a job evaluation exercise. Second, by providing for the then Industrial Court to remove discrimination in collective agreements, employers' pay structures and statutory Wages Orders which contained any provisions applying specifically to men only or to women only. Any complaints alleging discrimination in remuneration on grounds of sex were considered by Industrial Tribunals (now Employment Tribunals). The Equal Pay Act came fully operative on 29 December 1975.

The proportion of female workers in the Scottish printing industry was higher than in the English and Welsh printing industry. Scotland employed nearly 20% of all female workers in the UK printing industry. Two thirds of the females working in the Scottish industry were engaged in the bindery, warehouse and despatch departments. Envelope and stationery manufacture accounted for 10% of the total number of women employed. The number of female feeders and machine assistants was falling. Few women were employed as copyholders, small offset operators, non-traditional keyboard operators and negative spotters. In general, men and women in the industry were not normally engaged in like work. To protect against equal value claims job evaluation or rating of jobs would be necessary. In the industry's collective agreements, the wage was governed solely by the sex of the person concerned and not the work done by the person. If agreements were kept in this form, they would be open to the unions insisting females were paid at least the lowest male rate in the agreement.

The Scottish YMP Group undertook, during the spring and summer of 1971, an extensive survey of occupations in the industry to establish the 'value' of one to another. The list of occupations used was that of the Printing and Publishing Industry Training Board. The sample surveys were sufficiently large to make an objective approach to a topic which was basically subjective.

The survey showed it was possible to 'classify' operations in the printing industry and state appropriate wage rates in accordance with the classification.[9] Towards the end of 1971, SOGAT made clear its determination to negotiate an equal pay agreement with the SMPS but the other unions 'did not want to know'. The vast majority of female employees were in SOGAT. The SMPS concluded it would be wise to make as much progress as possible with that union.

In December 1971, the differing approaches of SMPS and SOGAT were explored but as some common ground was established, the negotiations continued. A small joint subcommittee was set up to clarify the issues. It became clear there were three basic areas of bargaining:
(1) job classification and the number of grades,
(2) wage rates for each grade but particularly the lowest and
(3) phasing.
By April 1972, the SMPS approach to the implementation of the Act was clarified as
(1) establish a fair job classification with five grades - A to E
(2) establish a rate for the E grade below the present lowest male rate (87.5%) with the objective that E be 80% and
(3) in the event of the above matters being settled reasonably, phasing be straightforward.
The position became complicated because of wage negotiations with SOGAT and the STA to agree new pay rates effective from 16 June 1972. In the course of these negotiations, the current ratios between craft and male and female auxiliary rates were maintained. There were equal pay conferences in April, May, June, July, September and October 1972. While progress, mainly on classification, was steady there seemed no possibility of settlement on Grade E until 4 October 1972 when SOGAT representatives realised settlement would not be reached if they continued to insist on a Grade E rate of 87.5%. While a Grade E rate of 85% was higher than many SMPS members thought justified, it was a rate below which SOGAT was entitled to have in terms of the Act and represented a major concession on SOGAT's part.

On 31 October 1972, the SMPS Executive Board accepted an agreement with SOGAT over implementation of the Equal Pay Act. It provided a system of payment by job classification be introduced between 1 November 1972 and 1 August 1975. The job classification was based on a points system and devised with the help of the Advisory Conciliation and Arbitration Service. Detailed provision was made for job classification in specialist sectors – general printing, manufactured stationery and carton/fibreboard. Within each classification, there were three Grades B, C and D. With effect from 1 August 1975, the wage rate paid for the Grades were Grade A 100%, Grade B 100%, Grade C 90%, Grade D 85.5% and Grade E 85%. The rate for Grade

B was to be the craft basic rate. Basic weekly wage rates for female workers after training was increased by 80p with effect from the first pay day after 1 November 1972, by 85p on the first pay day after 1 October 1973 and by similar amounts on the first pay days after 1 September 1974 and 1 August 1975. The new rate for female workers immediately after training, was £18.10 and for those with two or more years experience after training £18.60 per week. In 1973, a similar agreement was concluded with the STA. Due to circumstances outside the control of the SMPS, SOGAT and the STA the classification of operations envisaged in the agreements of 1972 and 1973 were not completed until July 1975.

The final adjustments for full implementation of the Equal Pay (1970) came into effect on 4 August 1975. The adjustments were of two kinds. First, there were wage increases for female workers bringing their rates up to the 'lowest male rate', namely 87.5% of the craft rate and the establishment of a unisex entry rate. Second, the grading of all operatives into three grades – craft 100% (£40.70), non craft 90% and non craft 87.5%.

Summary

In 1961, the SMPS conceded the balance of the unions' 1959 claims on the condition they accepted measures to increase the supply of labour to the industry. As a result, the forty-hour working week was implemented from September 1962. The 1966 collective wage movement resulted in 1967 in industrial action in England and Wales provincial newspapers as the SMPS and the BFMP sought to eliminate from the collective agreements the cost-of-living bonus. To avoid in Scotland the disruption taking place in England and Wales, the SMPS in October 1967 concluded its own agreements with the STA and other unions in Scotland. The agreement with the STA provided, inter alia, the abolition of the cost-of-living bonus and no stabilisation period and was followed by similar agreements with the NSES, ASLP and NUPB&PW. The eventual agreements concluded by the BFMP provided for a higher wage than in Scotland, the continuation of the stabilisation clause and no provision for additional supplies of manpower.

In January 1964, the P&KTF presented a claim for a third week of paid holiday entitlement. The SMPS argued that measures to overcome the serious manpower shortages in the industry must be agreed before the granting of additional holidays. Negotiations proceeded for almost a year before a settlement was reached in December 1964. Under the agreement, the SMPS traded an increase in the supply of manpower for an additional week of annual leave.

In the 1970s, the provisions of the main agreements between the SMPS and the print trade unions complied with the limits of government policy for the movement of wages. In 1980, the standard working week in the Scottish printing industry was reduced to thirty seven and a half hours with effect from 6 July 1981. In October 1986, a fifth week of annual paid holiday entitlement was introduced into the industry. In April 1988, a voluntary industry-wide pension scheme was introduced. In the late 1980s, the SMPS faced claims from the unions for increases in the 'social wage' but it took the view these were matters inappropriate to national agreements.

In October 1972, the SMPS and SOGAT reached agreement on the implementation of the Equal Pay Act (1970). It provided a system of payments by job classification be introduced between 1 November 1972 and 1 August 1975. The job classification was based on a points system. Within each classification there were three grades, B, C and D.

Notes

[1] See the Minutes of the meeting of the Executive Board, 16 May 1961.
[2] See the Minutes of the meeting of the Executive Board, 7 August 1962.
[3] See 'Wages, Costs and Prices in the Printing Industry', *National Board for Prices and Incomes*, Department of Economic Affairs, Cmnd 2750, HMSO, London, 1965.
[4] See the Minutes of the meeting of the Executive Board, 14 July 1965.
[5] At a time when the book printing industry in the UK was under increasing product market competition and when the SMPS was making effective efforts to maintain what was left of it for Scotland, the disregard by SOGAT of its members' real interest caused the SMPS to doubt the real motives of those responsible for the union aggression.
[6] See circular to members 'Industrial Relations: SOGAT: Glasgow Dispute', *Society of Master Printers of Scotland*, 27 November 1981.
[7] See *Report and Accounts, 1983-84*, Society of Master Printers of Scotland.
[8] See *Report and Accounts, 1989-90*, Society of Master Printers of Scotland.
[9] See *Memorandum on Equal Pay Act 1970 and its effects on the printing industry in Scotland*, Society of Master Printers of Scotland, 30 August 1971.

Part 4

THE SCOTTISH PRINT EMPLOYERS FEDERATION, 1991-2009

Chapter 19

THE SCOTTISH PRINT EMPLOYERS FEDERATION, 1991-2009: THE EXTERNAL ENVIRONMENT

This chapter begins by explaining why the title the Scottish Print Employers Federation (SPEF) was adopted. It then outlines the economic environment in which SPEF operated over the period 1990 to 2009 – recession, pressures on margins, overcapacity and overvalued pound against the euro. The third part describes the political/legal environment, including the development of the social dialogue process in the European Union and the election in 1997 of a Labour government committed to providing a framework in which the development of partnerships at work could flourish as a way of improving fairness at work. The next section analyses the major technological developments in the Scottish printing industry in the 1990s and the first decade of the twenty-first century with reference to the rise of the digital printing. The chapter concludes by examining the reasons for the creation of the Graphical, Paper and Media Union which brought together in a single print production union 30,000 general print, packaging, publishing and papermaking employees.

The Creation of Scottish Print Employers Federation

Early in his Directorship, Jim Raeburn had attempted to change the name from the Society of Master Printers of Scotland to the Scottish Print Employers Federation. He argued the title SMPS was more appropriate when printing companies were largely owner-managed. There was now a long tradition attached to the term 'master printer' and the attempt at a name change was resisted by member firms. Jim Raeburn bided his time but by 1990 had the backing for a name change of the then President, David Henderson, and the office bearers. Discussion on the suitability of the SMPS's name began in early 1990. Consultation with members at local association annual general meetings showed general support for change of name. It was felt the title SMPS was regularly misused and failed to communicate accurately who the Society represented. Few employers in the industry now described themselves as master printers.

The Office Bearers' Committee considered several possibilities including in March 1990 an Executive Board suggestion of SMPS on the grounds the adaptation of initials as a title in its own right was a growing practice amongst major organisation. As the Society was not in the same league as Imperial Chemical Industries which received immediate recognition as ICI, it would leave the question of 'who or what is SMPS?' A change of title to initials was considered inappropriate. After further discussion the Office Bearers' Committee unanimously favoured the title Scottish Print Employers Federation. 'Scottish' was preferable as the first word in any title but the words 'print or printing' were also essential. It was also thought the inclusion of the word 'employers' was desirable since its omission would reduce the descriptive value of the title. 'Association' and 'society' were considered as alternatives to 'federation' but the latter was more appropriate for an organisation embracing a number of local associations.

The May 1990 Executive Board meeting approved the change of name which was then submitted to a special general meeting held at Peebles Hydro on 4 November 1990 when many members were attending the Society's biennial conference. After consultation with the local associations there was support from member firms for changing the name of the Society and the most suitable title was the Scottish Print Employers' Federation (SPEF). The special general meeting resolved that:

> ...the name of the Society of Master Printers of Scotland be changed to the Scottish Print Employers Federation with effect from 1 January 1991...[1]

The Economic Environment
The first half of the 1990s saw the Scottish printing industry suffer a lengthy recession leading to company closures, job losses and reduced profits. From the Federation's own half-yearly 'state of trade' enquiries and information from other sources it was clear in comparative terms the industry performed relatively better in this period than the industry in the rest of the UK. While the downturn was less pronounced than for the UK as a whole recessionary conditions in Scotland endured longer than expected. Members' forecasts, expressed in the state of trade enquiries, of anticipated improvements in volumes of sales consistently failed to materialise.

In 1994/1995 there was evidence a modest if uneven economic recovery was underway. A growing number of Scottish printing companies reported a rise in the

Jim Raeburn, Director of the Scottish
Print Employers Federation 1984-2007

level of trading activity, helping to absorb the excess capacity that had resulted from the downturn. Prices and profit margins remained under downward pressures in an environment which remained more competitive than ever and in which it proved impossible to prevent further plant closures and redundancies. By the mid-1990s the Federation's 'state of trade' enquiries suggested print companies were experiencing mixed fortunes. Early indications of stronger growth in demand and output gave way to disappointment as the economy again slowed. The 'bull' market in paper prices and film came to an end. The flexible packaging sector saw the closure of three Scottish plants with a loss of nearly 200 jobs. There was considerable stability in employment levels but profit margins continued to narrow in an intensely competitive industry.

By the late 1990s the Scottish industry's performance lagged behind that of the rest of the UK and there was a reduction of companies in membership of the Federation. There was growth in the level of activity in the industry but its capacity continued at a level that often required increased sales volumes to compensate for the pressure on prices and margins. Matters were not helped by the government's policy of containing inflation through high interest rates, which slowed down domestic demand. The impact of this policy was compounded by an erosion of the industry's competitiveness in international markets by the high value of the pound sterling relative to other currencies and global events such as the economic downturn in south east Asia and Japan.

The new millennium year was a troubled one for the industry. It was a period of unrelenting pressure on margins with falling demand, notably from the electronics sector, overcapacity, a strong pound against the euro and e-procurement – all factors in driving down prices to levels offering unsatisfactory returns.[2] Despite this deteriorating confidence about the short term outlook evidence pointed, in the longer term, to continuing growth in the market for printed products. In 2001, the Scottish Executive's *Index of Production for Paper, Printing and Publishing* fell by over 8% relative to 2000. This was caused by overcapacity depressing prices to the point of wafer-thin margins, by the downturn in advertising and electronics sector and by work being lost to international competitors in countries with lower labour costs and in others by the weakness of the euro. The consequence was company closures and job losses. This difficult situation was exacerbated by the procurement problems of some major customers. Internet auctions and print services management companies were succeeding in driving down prices to sub-economic levels.

The industry experienced another challenging year in 2002/03. Overcapacity combined with weak demand translated into a continuing trend of narrow margins and poor profitability. There was a disconcerting divergence between the paper, printing and publishing industries in Scotland and in the UK. Whereas the UK-level *Index of Production for Paper, Printing and Publishing* showed little change over the period 2000-2002 inclusive the *Index* for Scotland fall by 16% over the same period. The effect of overcapacity, weak demand, and downward pressure on print product prices was illustrated by the BPIF/SPEF *Printing for Profit* report which showed by 2002/03 the average profit margin on sales had fallen to 3.83%. By 2005 it had become evident the industry landscape had changed significantly as the established relationship between the demand for print and the economic cycle had been broken as a result of structural change. The loss of print to internet delivery, globalisation and outsourcing had been part of this irresistible tide of change. The message from the Federation's senior management conference held in 2004 was, with pricing forecast to remain extremely competitive, the industry needed to become more entrepreneurial and innovative, providing a total service for its customers in print and information management from creation to delivery.[3]

In 2000 the BPIF, the European Flexographic Technical Association, SPEF, PIRA and the GPMU participated in a study commissioned by the Department of Trade and Industry into the competitiveness of the UK printing industry. Its report entitled *Print 21: Coming of Age* published in 2001, identified a positive future for printing as part of the communications cluster of industries if it could resolve its problems. It proposed seven key future initiatives by industry bodies and government. These were:
(1) improve margins through better performance and reduced costs,
(2) achieve a stable and competitive exchange rate,
(3) improve the industry's quality of management,
(4) strengthen the industry's education and training infrastructure,
(5) create a more positive external image,
(6) reduce environmental impacts through cost effective initiatives and
(7) strengthen the industry's technical competence and domestic supplier base.
The *Print 21* study was taken forward in 2002 with the launch of 'Vision in Print' as a new organisation dedicated to improving productivity and competitiveness in the workplace. It was one of a number of forums established for different industries for the purpose of enabling the transfer of best practice between companies and was an unprecedented step to bring change based on collaboration for mutual success.

The Department of Trade and Industry committed funding of £2.3 million over a period of four years to help Vision in Print[4] implement its programme which included performance benchmarking and international productivity comparisons. SPEF took an active interest in the agenda of Vision in Print as part of an ongoing drive for greater competitiveness through improved efficiency and unit labour costs. It involved participation in the Print Education Forum which dealt with skills and training issues and with the BPIF in the Industry Representatives Group responsible for representation and partnership. SPEF was involved in, and party to, the print industry strategic plan entitled *World Class Printing*, published in 2006, to strengthen the UK, including the Scottish, printing industry. The plan was based on three pillars – Vision in Print (productivity and competitiveness), Proskills (education and skills) and the BPIF together with other industrial organisations (representation and partnership) and set out a blueprint for the industry's future. It provided a radical agenda which the industry had to address if it were not to be marginalised.

Political/Legal Environment

When SPEF came into being, the UK government was Conservative under Prime Minister John Major, later re-elected in the 1992 general election. It managed the economy giving the highest priority to controlling inflation by the adjustment of interest rates. It continued the policies of previous Conservative governments over the period 1979 to 1992 of reducing the influence of trade unions and the government itself in labour markets. The Major government was voted from office in the 1997 general election. A Labour government under the premiership of Tony Blair took office, pledged to introduce some new minimum labour market standards including the introduction of a national minimum wage and legal procedures whereby individual workers could have their interests represented by a trade union. It introduced a number of constitutional changes including the Scotland Act (1998) which devolved inter alia, control of health, education and local government to a directly elected Scottish parliament in Edinburgh. The Blair government was re-elected at the 2001 and 2005 general elections.

The 1990s saw a significant development in the introduction of procedures (known as social dialogue process) whereby the European Union could harmonise minimum employment and social standards across member states. The Single European Act (1987) removed the right of member states to veto the introduction of Europe-wide legislation by introducing a system of qualified majority voting whereby member states were assigned a certain number of votes, up to a maximum of ten, depending on the size of their population. The ending of the member state veto brought the Single European Market (SEM), in which goods, people, capital and services could move freely, into being on 1 January 1993. A meeting of heads of government of EU member states at Maastricht in 1991 resulted in the Treaty on the European Union (1993). As well as providing for the introduction of a common currency (the euro), it introduced a detailed social dimension to the single market, including the social dialogue procedure under which EU employer and trade union bodies could negotiate framework (collective) agreements.

If the social partners failed to make an agreement or decided not to negotiate a framework agreement, the European Commission could propose a draft directive for consideration by the European Parliament and for approval by the Council of Ministers. The Major government of 1992-1997 negotiated at Maastricht an opt-out from implementing the outcome of the social dimension to the single market. One of the first acts of the Blair government (1997-2001) was to end this opt-out and sign up to the social dimension procedures agreed in the Treaty on the European Union.

a. Domestic Legislation

The major piece of employment legislation of the Major government (1992 to 1997) was the Trade Union Reform and Employment Rights Act (1993). This contained provisions covering union elections and ballots, new requirements for the disclosure of information by unions to their members, measures to limit the enforceability of the TUC's disputes principles and procedures (commonly referred to as the Bridlington principles), new regulations on the collection of union subscriptions through payroll deduction and the abolition of Wages Councils, which set wage rates in low-paid industries. It also created a new right for individuals deprived of goods or services to apply to the courts to restrain unlawful industrial action and the removal from the terms of reference of ACAS of the objective to promote collective bargaining. The Act provided all union industrial action ballots had to be postal to the members' home and unions must notify employers of their intention to hold the ballot, the date when it would be held and the outcome as well as the names of those members entitled to vote in the ballot.

SPEF took a relaxed view of the 1993 Act believing most of its provision would not alter significantly employment relationships in the Scottish printing industry. The creation of one production union for the industry in September 1991 meant inter-union disputes would be a thing of the past. Wages Councils did not exist in the industry and unlawful industrial action was not a problem. SPEF welcomed the changes to the statutory strike ballot procedure believing employees would be protected from intimidation by militant chapel officials. It regarded the reform to the collection of union subscription through the payroll whereby union members had to re-authorise the deduction of their union subscription from their wages as an irritant which its members could do without.

The major employment legislation of the Blair government (1997-2001) was the Employment Relations Act (1999) which provided a framework in which the development of partnerships at work could flourish and improve fairness at work. The Act was designed to develop a culture in businesses in which fairness was second nature and underpinned competitiveness. There were three elements of the framework. (1) Policies to enhance family life by making it easier for both men and women to go to work with less conflict between their responsibilities at work and at home.

(2) Provisions for the basic fair treatment of employees.

(3) By new procedures for collective representation at work enabling unions to be recognised for collective bargaining purposes where the workforce chose such representation.

In the area of family-friendly policy, the Act provided for parental leave, the extension of maternity leave to eighteen weeks, the right to extend maternity leave and to parental leave after one year's service with the same employer and a right to reasonable time off for family emergencies for all employees regardless of length of service. The Act raised the maximum compensation for unfair dismissal to £50,000, lowered the qualifying period of service with an employer to gain unfair dismissal rights from two years to one year and prohibited employers from asking employees on fixed term contracts of more than one year's duration to waive their right to claim unfair dismissal on expiry or non-renewal of the contract. For part-time workers the Act provided they received no less favourable treatment than full-time workers and where a worker was required or invited to attend a discipline or grievance hearing they had the right to be accompanied by a person of their choice including a trade union representative.

In the field of collective rights, the Act gave protection against dismissal for those participating in lawful industrial action. Dismissal within the first eight weeks of lawful industrial action became automatically unfair. The Act provided several routes for collective representation at work to be achieved. It provided for statutory trade union recognition but this right applied only in workplaces with at least twenty one workers, thereby excluding most Scottish printing workplaces. Union recognition could be achieved through three routes:

(1) recognition by voluntary agreement,

(2) second recognition from the Central Arbitration Committee (CAC) and

(3) through a recognition ballot.

The employer was obliged to co-operate with the ballot and if at least 40% of those eligible to vote supported union recognition, the CAC declared the union was recognised.

The first Blair government passed the National Minimum Wage Act (1998) which introduced for the first time a national minimum wage covering every region of the UK and all sections of the economy. The Act came into force on 1 April 1999 providing a minimum wage of £3.60 per hour for workers aged twenty two or above and £3.00 per hour for those aged eighteen to twenty one. Workers aged sixteen or seventeen were exempt. By 2008 the minimum wage for adult workers had risen to £5.86 per hour.

The main piece of employment legislation of the second Blair government was the Employment Act (2002). It covered parental rights at work, dispute resolution in the workplace, improvements to employment tribunals procedures, the Fixed Term Work Directive and a new right to time off work for union learning representatives. The Act provided a balanced package of support for working parents, at the same time aimed to reduce red tape for employers by simplifying rules governing maternity, paternity and adoption leave and pay, and by making it easier to settle workplace disputes. From April 2003, for the first time, mothers and fathers of young children under six or disabled children under eighteen could request more flexible working arrangements. Employers could only refuse such requests where there were business reasons for doing so. The Act introduced the right for fixed term employees not to be treated less favourably than permanent staff working for the same employer. It introduced time off for trade union learning representatives to ensure they were properly trained to carry out their duties. The Act sought to help working mothers by entitling them to twenty six weeks paid and a further twenty six weeks unpaid maternity leave.

The Act introduced statutory minimum dismissal, disciplinary and grievance procedures. It set minimum standards to be followed but did not replace existing standards for disciplinary and grievance procedures where they were better than the minimum. The standard dismissal and disciplinary procedure contained three stages. Stage one was a statement of grounds of action in which the employer set out the circumstances leading to contemplate dismissal or action short of dismissal. Stage two was the meeting, after which the employer informed the employee of its outcome and notified the employee of the right to appeal. Stage three was the appeal stage. If the employer did not comply with this three stage procedure, any resulting dismissal was automatically unfair. The standard statutory grievance procedure contained three stages – statement of the grievance, the meeting and the appeal stage.

SPEF took a relaxed view of the employment legislation of the Blair years. Its member firms were unionised and pay levels in the industry were well above the proposed minimum wage. Its team of industrial relations advisers ensured member firms, when disciplining and dismissing their workforce, adopted best practice by acting with just cause after a thorough investigation and if there was a case for action, behaved in a fair, reasonable and consistent manner. Being a relatively highly unionised industry, in disciplinary hearings and appeals employees were invariably represented by an FOC and/or MOC. Industrial disputes occurred very infrequently in the Scottish printing industry.

b. Legislation from the European Union[5]

Over the period 1992 to 2007 inclusive there were nine main EU Directives in the employment field – two covered equal opportunities, four related to employment protection and working conditions, two covered employee relations and one health and safety. In 1996 the EU social partners (Business Europe [formerly UNICE], CEEP and ETUC) concluded a framework agreement on parental leave which was then issued as a directive. It provided the right for parents to have three months' unpaid leave after the birth or adoption of a child before its eighth birthday. The directive entitled individuals to a number of days off work for urgent family reasons in the case of sickness or accident. The UK government transposed this directive into national legislation via the Maternity and Parental Leave Regulations (1999). The Sex Discrimination

Directive (1997) provides where a complaint to a tribunal established 'facts' from which it could be presumed there had been direct or indirect discrimination, it placed the burden of proof on the employer to demonstrate the principle of equal treatment had not been breached. This directive was implemented in the UK in October 2001 by the Sex Discrimination (Indirect Discrimination and Burden of Proof) Regulations.

In 1997 the EU multi-sector social partners negotiated a framework agreement on part-time work to remove discrimination against part-time workers, to improve the quality of part-time work and to develop part-time work on a voluntary basis. Under this directive part-time workers were to receive, relative to full-time employees, the same rate of pay, annual leave, sick pay, access to company pension schemes and maternity/parental leave on a pro rata basis. This directive was transposed into UK legislation by the Part-time Workers (Prevention of Less Favourable Treatment) Regulations. In 1999 the EU social partners concluded a framework agreement on fixed term contracts discouraging the use of fixed term contracts. The UK gave effect to this directive in 2002 via the Fixed Term Employees (Prevention of Less Favourable Treatment) Regulations. The Proof of an Employment Relationship Directive (1992) required employees working over eight hours per week for more than one month to receive written confirmation of the main terms and conditions of their employment within two months of starting work. Implementation of this directive in the UK was via the Employment Rights Act 1996. The Posting of Workers Directive (1999) gave protection to workers posted temporarily to a member state other than the one in which they normally worked. A posted worker was guaranteed the terms and conditions laid down by law and by collective agreements in the member state to which he/she was posted. This directive was transposed into UK law via the Employment Relations Act (1999) and the Equal Opportunities (Employment Legislation) (Territorial Limits) Regulations (1999).

The European Works Council Directive (1994) and its extension to include the UK in 1998, required a Europe-level information and consultation system be set up in organisations with more than 1,000 employees in member states and employing more than 150 people in each of two or more of these. A Works Council was negotiated between the central European-level management of the organisation and a Special Negotiating Body (SNB) of employee representatives. The directive was transposed into UK legislation by the Transnational Information and Consultation of Employees Regulations (1999). Given the lack of multi-national companies in the Scottish printing industry this directive had little impact. The Information and Consultation Directive (2002) established a general framework setting out minimum rights of employees to information and consultation in undertaking or establishments within EU member states. Its requirements applied to undertakings employing at least fifty employees in any one member state, or establishments employing at least twenty employees in more than one state. The right to information and consultation covered information on the recent, and probable, developments of the undertakings or the establishment's activities and economic situation; on the structure, situation and probable development of employment within the undertaking/establishment and on any anticipated measures envisaged where there was a threat to employment and on decisions likely to lead to substantial changes in work organisation or in contractual relations.

An important EU measure in the field of health and safety was the Working Time Directive which was transposed into UK legislation by the Working Time Regulations (1998).[6] The Directive established a maximum weekly working time of forty eight hours, including overtime, a minimum period of paid leave of four weeks per year, a minimum of eleven consecutive hours rest in each twenty four hour period worked by employees, a 'rest break' for all workers whose working day was longer than six hours and the maximum hours of a night shift be eight hours. In the UK individuals could opt out from the forty eight hour maximum working week whilst groups of workers could do so through the negotiation of workforce agreements. The Directive's provision for rest breaks, night work and reference periods for ascertaining the average weekly working time worked by employees could be abrogated by means of legislation or collective bargaining. For example, the Directive provided for a maximum reference period of up to four months but this could be extended to twelve months if the provisions of the directive were implemented via a collective agreement.

The Technological Environment

The 1960s and the 1970 technological developments centred on the introduction of photocomposition and the expansion of the lithographic printing process. The late 1980s saw the introduction of computer-based production techniques at all stages of the printing process. The major technological development of the late 1990s and the first decade of the twenty first century was the rapid rise of digital printing. Nevertheless the dominant printing process in 2010 remained lithography but its share of the total print market in the UK and Scotland had fallen.

In the pre-press area the major technological innovations included computer to plate, computer to press and digital photography. Digital technology enabled corrections or colour changes required to be done immediately and colour separation and conversion from photographic images to the four printing colours speeded up. Digital plate-making ensured exact reproduction occurred every time with the same information being transferred to the quality check system on the machine. During the life time of the Scottish Print Employers Federation the pre-press area consisted almost completely of computerised and digital equipment. This continued computerisation made it easier for the customer, whether a publisher or an advertising agency to undertake much of their own pre-press work. By mid-2005 in terms of the skills required by pre-press employees, the balance had shifted from manual techniques to understanding of graphics, software, design skills and knowledge of the overall print process.

Digital printing developed dramatically in the late 1990s, producing finished copies without plates by the use of toners or inks allied to electronic image generation. Its benefits included short production times (on-demand printing), cost effective short-runs, shorter supply chains and the ability to print variable data. Digital printing had low set up costs, making it feasible to print single copies 'on demand' even tailored to the customer's interests. It made possible personalised products including letters, leaflets, parts manuals, books, through to facsimile reprints of old books and manuscripts, calendars, point of sale posters etc. Graphic examples were the ability to produce a parts manual in full colour, perfect bound with personalisation, from output on a personal computer to the finished product in half an hour. This meant shorter runs and a larger number of small jobs.

Printing on demand complemented 'conventional' printing processes in which there were also technological innovations in the 1990s and the first decade of the twenty first century. These provided employers with higher productivity, increased quality and maximum flexibility. Make-ready and setting up times were dramatically reduced in the press room and machine speeds increased more than 50% between 1990 and 1995. Allied to the increased speeds was improved quality and reduced waste coupled with greater efficiency. Developments in the press area saw movement towards greater automation with the gradual elimination of unskilled and semi-skilled operations. Employees working in the press room were required to become more computer literate and acquire electronic and electrical engineering skills. During the period 1991-2010 the running speed of web-offset machines increased from 50,000 copies per hour in 1991 to a capability of 100,000 copies per hour by 1996. Technological developments meant plate changing could be done automatically. This meant that a new plate was automatically positioned with the old plate stripped off allowing for a six colour press to change six plates with full register mounting within minutes.

Automatic plate changing systems on the presses reduced make-ready times. These were further reduced by the increasing use of computerisation for machine setting and colour control. Automatic make-ready systems provided automatic washing up, setting changes to the feeder, delivery and printing units to accept new paper sizes and thicknesses. Along with automatic pallet handling there was little need for manual intervention. The central control of presses through digital console technology became, in the period 1991 to 2010, a common feature of the Scottish printing industry press room. These systems encompassed job preparation, central job storage, control and monitoring of all major press functions, and press diagnostics.

The demand for printed corrugated packaging in Scotland increased because the big supermarket chains sought to reduce costs in their own supply chain. They wanted goods which could go straight onto the supermarket shelves with minimum preparation and labour time. They demanded more sophisticated packaging with more printing needed on the packaging which was no longer just a humble cardboard tray but a piece of marketing material. Packaging had to be easy to find, easy to open and put on the supermarket shelf, easy for the shopper, easy to throw away and easy to identify (the so-called 'five easies' of packaging). Packaging companies became known as packagers rather than printers per se.

In the post-press production stage new technology arrived in what had, over the past two decades, been the most labour intensive section of the industry. During the period 1991 to 2010 equipment in the post-press (finishing) area moved towards being completely computerised and automated. Integrated stitching units ensured a smooth transfer from the press to print finishing. Technical developments in the guillotine sector improved precision, a quick cut, high safety standards and fast job size changes. Features included automated knife changes giving greater operator safety and eliminating knife chipping in changeover together with automatic programmer and card-reading devices and automated waste disposal.

Over the period 1991-2010 these technological changes in the three stages of print production underscored the notion that revenue sources changed. In the 1970s, pre-press capabilities allowed printers to differentiate themselves from the competition. By 2000, it was in the post-press stage that most value was added to producing the printed product. By 2006 print customers sought a printer that could quickly finish a piece of print work and transform it from ink on paper, to a communications vehicle. The technological developments implemented post-1991 meant the development of the Scottish printing industry was about more than putting ink on paper and board. That would have left it as a commodity subject to the low prices that come with overcapacity in a fragmented industry. This route was exploited by opportunistic print brokers who with the capacity to obtain dozens of tenders through their web sites, further eroded profit margins. More than ever before the initiative had to be taken by print companies working closely with their customers to identify their wider needs and how these could be delivered effectively and profitably. By 2000 printing was an old established industry, but for those Scottish printing companies with the vision and vitality to accept the challenges of the new millennium the prospects were positive.[7]

The Creation of the Graphical, Paper and Media Union (GPMU)[8]

The GPMU came into being on 30 September 1991 following an amalgamation between the National Graphical Association (82) and the Society of Graphical and Allied Trades (82). The GPMU brought together in a single print production union 300,000 trade unionists in the UK and Republic of Ireland and which included those working in the printing, papermaking, packaging and publishing industries. Its members performed a wide range of jobs as paper workers, ink makers, graphic reproduction workers, planners and plate-makers, printers, artists, designers, photographers, keyboard and desk top publishing operators, bookbinders, print finishers, packers and warehouse staff, dispatch and delivery drivers, clerical, administrative and managerial staff, estimators and sales staff. 40,000 (20%) of its members were women. At the time of its formation it was the seventh largest union in the Trades Union Congress and the biggest graphical and paper union in the world.

A reason for the merger of was technological change introduced into the printing and publishing industry during the 1980s. These resulted in the NGA and SOGAT competing with each other for influence with employers, for members and control of jobs. The inter-union rivalry was particularly intense in provincial newspapers and web-offset commercial printing houses with, on occasions, each union 'co-operating' with the employer to undermine the industrial interests of the other. Both unions realised to continue like this would simply benefit the interests of employers. A further reason behind the marriage of the NGA and SOGAT was the need for the print unions to speak with a single voice to the TUC and to the Labour Party and to take a high profile in these two organisations if they were to influence the content of legislation repealing the trade union laws of the Conservative governments of the 1980s. As separate unions they had often put forward different opinions on employment and proposed legislation to the TUC and to the Labour Party with the result that, for the fear of offending either union, the TUC and the Labour Party merely noted their views and, at worst, ignored them. The ability to speak with one voice to the European Union decision-making bodies – the Commission, the Council of Ministers and the European Parliament and to international graphical trade union bodies such as the European Graphical Federation (subsequently UNI-Europa Graphical) was a necessity, if UK printing and paper unions were to increase their influence on the development of a social dimension to the European Single Market.

SPEF welcomed the overwhelming votes of SOGAT and NGA members in favour of the amalgamation. They regarded the creation of the GPMU as a positive step as it would remove inter-union differences and lead to increased efficiency with opportunities for a more flexible workforce. It provided an opportunity for a single collective agreement in Scotland covering all production workers and for an examination of the machine extra payments system operating with a view to a consolidating the machine classification agreement.

Summary

In 1990, the title SMPS was changed to Scottish Print Employers Federation (SPEF). SMPS was regularly misused and failed to indicate accurately who the organisation represented.

In the period 1990 to 2010, the economic environment in which SPEF operated was unrelenting pressure on margins, falling demand, a strong pound against the euro, over capacity, downward pressure on prices and e-procurement. The political/legal environment was dominated by the Trade Union Reform and Employment Rights Act (1993), the Employment Relations Act (1999), the National Minimum Wage Act (1998) and the Employment Act (2002). SPEF took a relaxed view of these Acts of Parliament as they did not require much change to existing behaviour. Over the same period, there were nine main directives in the employment field from the European Union. The Working Time Directive laid down minimum standards of working time. Its provisions were incorporated into the national agreement between SPEF and the GPMU thereby allowing the balance of working time and rest periods to be achieved over a twelve month period rather than four months as provided for in the Directive. The major technological development of the 1990s and the first decade of the twenty first century was the rise of digital printing. This acompanied the implementation of computer to plate, computer to machine, digital cameras, sharp declines in make-ready times, automatic plate changing and shorter run times.

The creation of Graphical, Paper and Media Union (GPMU) as a result of merger between NGA (82) and SOGAT (82) on 31 September 1991, brought to the industry one union for production employees. SPEF welcomed this development offering the removal of inter-union differences, improved efficiency and a more flexible workforce.

Notes

[1] See Minutes of the meeting of the Executive Board, 5 September 1990 and *Annual Report and Accounts, 1990/1991,* Scottish Print Employers Federation.

[2] See *Annual Report and Accounts, 2000/2001,* Scottish Print Employers Federation.

[3] See *Annual Report and Accounts, 2004/2005,* Scottish Print Employers Federation.

[4] 'Vision in Print' was an independent organisation governed by a board which included representatives of small businesses and the GPMU as well as directors of several large groups. The SPEF was represented on the board by its Vice-President.

[5] For a more detailed explanation of the European Union (EU) decision-making processes and the impact of the social dimension of the EU on UK employee relations see J Gennard and G Judge, *Managing Employment Relations*, Chartered Institute of Personnel and Development, 2004, chapter 5.

[6] The UK government's application in 1996 to the European Court of Justice to have the Directive annulled, on the grounds its provisions were not about health and safety but employment issues was rejected on 12 November 1996. Being brought forward as a health and safety matter meant it could be approved by the Council of Ministers by qualified majority voting instead of by unanimous agreement.

[7] See *Annual Report and Accounts, 1999/2000,* Scottish Print Employers Federation.

[8] For a more detailed description and analysis of the creation of this union see J Gennard and G Hayward *A History of the Graphical, Paper and Media Union*, London, 2008.

Chapter 20

THE EVOLUTION AND DEVELOPMENT OF THE SCOTTISH PRINT EMPLOYERS FEDERATION 1991 - 2009

This chapter deals with internal developments within SPEF. It begins by examining constitutional issues, including the level of membership, its governance and links with member firms. The chapter then explains the financial structure and difficulties of SPEF after which it outlines developments in services provided to members. These were wide-ranging and included political lobbying in Scotland, the UK and Europe, management accounting, education and training, health and safety, employment relations help and advice and collective agreements with the GPMU.

The Scottish Print Employers' Federation, was created on 1 January 1991. This was simply a change of name. Its objectives included the protection, promotion, defence and the furtherance of the interests of its members, and to provide the means so policies to achieve these ends could be implemented. The Federation secured mutual support and co-operation throughout its area of industrial activity covering origination, printing, bookbinding, finishing, stationery manufacture and other related activities. SPEF co-operated to make agreements with employees or trade unions on matters affecting general and common interests or specific activities. It played a major role in the settlement of differences between member firms and their employees whether by conference, arbitration, agreement or otherwise and secured the equitable application of agreements concluded with employees and/or their trade union. An important objective of the Federation was to collect and circulate amongst its member firms information on matters relating to its specific activities and to promote, watch over, or take action in regard to governmental legislative measures, affecting, or likely to affect these. In 1991, the Federation adopted the following mission statement:

> The purpose of the Scottish Print Employers Federation is to help create the commercial and industrial conditions in which its member companies can achieve profitable growth for the benefit of their shareholders, employees and customers.

Constitutional Issues
a. Membership
Membership of the Federation was open to firms, partnerships and companies engaged in printing activities in Scotland. The Federation's 2000 annual general meeting approved 'associate membership' open to companies engaged in the supply of equipment, materials or services to the industry. In 1991, the Federation had 230 printing and SNPA companies in membership but by the end of 2007, due to company closures and an overvalued pound sterling, the number of printing companies had fallen to forty five. There were few resignations or expulsions from the Federation and those who resigned did so to cut costs at a time of economic recession. Member firms resigned by giving six months' written notice. Any member firm failing to pay its subscription, acting contrary to the constitution and rules, acting against the Federation's interests or failing to comply with Federation policies, was liable to expulsion. It could appeal to the Executive Board but the final court of appeal was the annual general meeting.

b. Local Associations
The governance of the Federation was the same as that of SMPS, namely local associations, the Executive Board and its committees and general meetings. These decision-making bodies were serviced by a Director who managed a small but dedicated professional staff. The Federation provided services to its member companies. To do this successfully it needed its member firms to play an active part in discussing and determining its policies. To this end, it hoped to draw on the knowledge and expertise of senior managers of its member companies. Fortunately for the Federation, many of the senior personnel of its members did participate in its affairs through its Executive Board and its committees. Some senior executives served the Federation, unpaid, for many years. For example, in 1994, Patrick Mark stood down as Chairman of the Industrial Relations Committee after nine years of dedicated service.[1] In the following year, Jim Crone stood down having, inter alia, chaired the Education and Training Committee for five years.

All member firms were members of a local association. On the creation of the Federation there were seven such associations – Aberdeen, Central Counties, Dundee, Edinburgh, Glasgow, Northern Countries and Perth. The Federation President and Director together visited each local association on the occasion of its annual general meeting. This provided a valuable opportunity for the Federation to consult and to canvas the opinions of a wide cross-section of its membership on a wide range of issues.

In March 1994, the annual general meeting of the Central Counties Local Association agreed its members be balloted on disbanding itself. The subsequent ballot was in favour of disbandment. The western half of the Central Counties Local Association joined the Glasgow Local Association and its eastern half the Edinburgh Association on the understanding these associations would nominate as one of their representatives on the Federation Executive Board a representative from the former Central Counties Association. In 1996, the Perth and Dundee Associations elected to merge to form the Perth and Dundee Print Employers Association with two representatives on the Federation's Executive Board. In 2000, the number of local associations fell to four – Aberdeen, Edinburgh, Glasgow and Perth and Dundee – when the Northern Counties Local Association disbanded and its members transferred to the Aberdeen Local Association.

c. The Executive Board

The business of the Federation was managed by the Executive Board which consisted of the President, Vice-President and Treasurer ex-officio; the immediate Past President, if eligible for election to the Board; representatives from each of the local associations and the Scottish YMP Group; representatives from the SNPA and up to five members as the Board deemed necessary. Board members represented their local associations and not the interests of their companies. No representative could serve as a Board member for more than five consecutive years. The Board appointed the Federation's Director and its auditor, who had to be a professional accountant, or a firm of professional accountants. In practice, the Board was responsible for determining all matters of policy taking account, where appropriate, of recommendations from its committees. In 1997, the Federation's annual general meeting accepted the disaffiliation of the SNPA making it no longer appropriate for that body to have representation on the Executive Board. It was agreed to provide continued representation of the SNPA on the Federation's Executive Board and the Office Bearer's Committee under the co-option powers contained in the constitution and rules.

The November 1996 Executive Board meeting approved the arrangements whereby SNPA disaffiliated from SPEF. The SNPA would pay an annual management fee of £51,000 payable quarterly on the basis the overall level of staff involvement remained broadly unchanged from that currently provided. This management

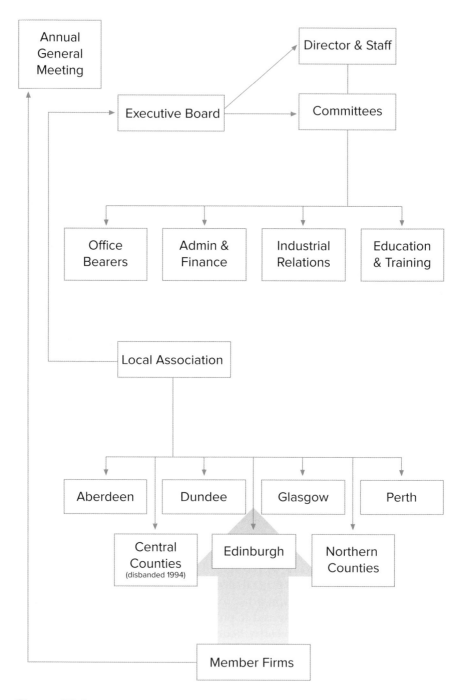

Figure 20:1
Scottish Print Employers Federation – Organisation Chart

fee would be adjusted annually in line with movement in average earnings as published for December each year. Any withdrawal from these arrangements would apply from 31 March following notice in writing of not less than twelve months. Constitutionally SNPA members were not members of SPEF after disaffiliation, but were de facto treated as members. Their subscriptions were covered by the management fee unless they withdrew from membership of the Federation. Whilst in terms of the SPEF constitution and rules, SNPA would no longer have representation on the Executive Board or the Office Bearers' Committee the Executive Board maintained the relationship by co-opting SNPA representatives.

The SNPA disaffiliated from the Federation on 1 August 1997 following amicable discussions between the two bodies and by agreement the SNPA continue to be serviced, despite now being a completely separate organisation, by the Federation's secretariat. The increasing concentration of ownership in recent years of Scottish weekly newspapers meant the number of individual newspaper proprietors with integrated commercial printing interests had diminished. Most of the large and medium-sized companies now considered themselves specialist newspaper publishers and their interests and the service they sought were increasingly different from other Federation member firms. Scottish newspaper publishers now gave greater priority to marketing than to industrial relations issues. The financial arrangements, given the changed relationship between the two organisations, were of critical importance to the Federation. In the financial year 1996/97, SNPA members paid £15,000 in membership contributions to the Federation, including the subscriptions of those members who retained general print interests. A study of financial information showing an allocation of costs between SNPA and SPEF, taking into account the time Federation staff spent on SNPA duties suggested, after excluding SPEF costs of £62,000 attributable to print interests, the existing financial arrangements were fair to both organisations.[2]

On 12 February 1998, the Federation held a special general meeting at Stirling at which it was agreed the size of the Executive Board be reduced. Its membership was reduced from a potential maximum of thirty three to twenty four. The 1998 annual general meeting, amended Rule 17(3) so that the number of representatives appointed to the Executive Board be reduced from eight to four in the case of the Edinburgh Association and that of the Glasgow Association from nine to five.

The Executive Board elected as standing committees an Administration and Finance Committee of which the Treasurer was Chairman, an Industrial Relations Committee and an Education and Training Committee. It had power to appoint other committees for specific purposes. By the mid-1990s, this obligation on the Executive Board was too prescriptive, in that it specified certain standing committees that it must establish. The 1997 annual general meeting amended the rules so the Board need only establish such committees as it deemed necessary. Throughout the lifetime of SPEF, its Executive Board had four major standing committees – Administration and Finance, Education and Training, Industrial Relations Committee and Office Bearers'.

The Administration and Finance Committee managed the Federation's finances and received financial statements and other financial information the committee required for that purpose. It monitored and managed the performance of the Federation's investments and recommended membership subscription rates. The committee was committed to generate, on an annual basis, a maximum surplus of £20,000 or 5% of income whichever was the greater and to maintain a cash resource, not less than 50% of annual expenditure.

The Education and Training Committee assessed, and responded to, the education, training and development needs of the industry. It promoted employer investment in people as essential to competitive business performance, promoted careers in the industry and ensured appropriate universities/colleges met the education and training needs of the industry. The committee also represented the industry's interests to the Scottish Office, the Scottish Qualifications Authority, Local Enterprise Companies, the Scottish Council of National Training Organisations, the Glasgow College of Building and Printing and Napier University.

The Industrial Relations Committee ensured national agreements with the unions remained relevant to the needs of employers and recommended to the Executive Board a brief for bargaining with the GPMU. It also advised member firms on employment legislation and practices, made suggestions to improve the industry's competitiveness and monitored industrial relations developments which might have implications for the industry. The Office Bearers' Committee submitted nominations for appointments as office bearers, committee chairmen and to standing committees, promoted relations with organisations such as the BPIF, and planned the biennial conference programme. Other important functions of this committee included the determination of conditions of employment for Federation senior staff, appointment of the Federation's Director and policy matters not within the remit of other standing committees.

d. Strategic Review

The future direction of the Federation was considered at a special general meeting held at Stirling in February 1997. Members were invited to review the performance of SPEF and to debate whether current policies effectively addressed the industry's and members' needs. Attention focussed on the role and structure of the Executive Board and its relationship with local associations.[3] There was consensus the Executive Board was too large and the practice of most local associations of holding one meeting per year provided no proper basis for those serving on the Executive Board to represent the views of their associations. In seeking the approval of the annual general meeting to reduce the size of the Executive Board to a maximum of twenty four, it was recognised increased activity at local association level was a key element to the proposed new arrangements operating effectively. It was expected grass roots participation in a two-way flow of thinking would enhance the value of membership and strengthen SPEF.

e. General Meetings

The annual general meetings of the Federation were held at intervals not exceeding eighteen months. It was policy to alternate meetings between Glasgow and Edinburgh. The meeting received, and approved, the work of the Executive Board, received an audited statement of accounts for the preceding year and elected the office bearers. The office bearers held office until the next annual general meeting. No office bearer, other than the Treasurer, could hold the same office for more than three consecutive years. At general meetings, each member had one vote, plus an additional vote for every £50 of aggregate subscription paid by each member in respect of the preceding year. Every partner or director of a member firm or any individual appointed and empowered to represent a firm or company and approved by the Executive Board, could attend and participate in the general meeting but the vote of any member firm could only be exercised by one individual.

f. Links with Member Firms

Members could also attend the Federation's biennial conference to which they could bring guests and partners. The biennial conference was arranged around a theme. In 1992, the conference included a ministerial presentation on the Scottish economy and others by leading experts on industrial relations, technological developments and on implications of German laws on the recycling of paper and packaging waste if similar arrangements were adopted by the European Union. The theme of the 1994 conference was 'Competing for the Future' and addressed challenges facing the industry by examining developments in markets, technology and people. In 1996, the theme was 'Towards Business Excellence' reflecting a forward-looking programme with examples of best practice in supplier partnering, the use of technology to develop business opportunities, measuring company performance and achieving the effective use of staff through team-working.

The 1992, 1994 and 1996 biennial conference took place at Peebles Hydro but in 1998 the conference venue was moved to Crieff Hydro. The 1998 theme 'Towards the Millennium' embraced several key issues with eminent speakers addressing the future of printed media, the internet, the implications of the introduction of the euro, the Scottish Parliament and human resource issues in the workplace. After the 1998 biennial conference, because of declining membership and economic recession, no further conferences were held.

g. Staff and Premises

Over the period 1991 to 2009 inclusive, SPEF was located at 48 Palmerston Place, Edinburgh and its Director, Jim Raeburn, was on 1 July 1996 designated Director and Secretary of the Federation. The previous SPEF Secretary was Michael Jeffrey, a position he held until December 1995 when this post became redundant. Amongst his duties was leading the secretariat which serviced the Administration and Finance Committee. Douglas Robertson was appointed Accountant, a post he took up in December 1995 and whose duties included servicing the Administration and Finance Committee. He held the post until his resignation in 1997 when it was retitled Finance Secretary and Jill Fleming appointed to the post. She resigned in early 2004 replaced by Alan Sharp who took the title Federation Secretary with Jim Raeburn reverting to the sole title of Director.

On the formation of the Federation, Michael Heggie held the position of Management Accountant. Following his resignation the Federation contracted its management accounting services, with effect from October 1991, to Hunter Lynch Associates. Bill Kidd was the Federation's first Director of Manpower working with Bob McAllister as Industrial Relations Advisor and George Roxburgh as Training Adviser. At the end of 1992, Bill Kidd left his post as Director of Manpower three years ahead of his scheduled retirement. He had worked for the Federation and the SMPS for nearly eleven years, during which time he made a valued input to the work of those organisations. Bob McAllister, who had joined the staff of the SMPS in 1987, was promoted from 1 January 1993 to the position of Head of Industrial Relations and Aileen Hay became Industrial Relations Advisor. Bob McAllister subsequently became Deputy Director of the SPEF, retaining the title of Head of Industrial Relations. When George Roxburgh retired, he was replaced by Graham Wilson and later by Bill Stark who served as Training and Safety Advisor for nine years until he retired in 2008. As the membership of the Federation declined, so did the number of staff employed at Palmerston Place but the diminishing number of staff remained committed and motivated, and delivered a high quality service to member firms and their customers.

h. The Scottish YMP Group

This group played an important role in the development of the industry's young managers as well as providing opportunities for networking. During the 1990s the membership of the group remained steady at 160. In December 1993, the Executive Board approved a proposed marketing brochure to promote the YMP Group amongst potential members and member companies. It refused the suggestion that Scottish employers follow the example of some English companies and make attendance at YMP meetings a condition of employment.[4] In 2000 the Executive Board, to strengthen the YMP Group, accepted the group's proposals to increase the age limit of membership to forty, to redefine

Presidents of the Scottish Young Master Printers Group, photographed in 1991.

Back Row: Alan Wilson, Donald Ferguson, Bernulf Clegg, Ronnie MacMillan, Hamish Milne, Alan Davidson **Middle Row:** Scott Gillespie, Malcolm Spiers, John Crerar, James Collins, Tony Cormack, Frank Gow **Front Row:** Eric Deane, Allan Waterston, Geoffrey Waterston, David Henderson, John McGee

the industry as the 'printing and graphic communications industry', to admit eligible staff from SPEF associate members and to allow individuals from non-member companies to attend the group's monthly meetings.

By 2002, the group was experiencing difficulties. Its activities at both Scotland-wide and local level were declining resulting in limited activity and fewer meetings. A number of reasons explained this situation. For example fewer young people entering the industry saw it as a long term career. The make-up of the industry was changing involving a reduction in the number of family-owned business and competing interests for people's leisure time. The YMP Group sought additional financial resources from SPEF and there was discussion meetings might be open to HND printing students. The Federation maintained its view member companies encouraging the participation of eligible employees was the best way to strengthen the group rather than providing additional financial support. Some members of the Executive Board believed that the group did not require additional resources from SPEF given the relatively large surplus generated by the group's annual conference.

At the Scotland level, the group undertook many activities. It held workshops on marketing and selling, production, finance and human resource management. In 1994, it launched a management training programme, offering opportunities for young managers of the industry to broaden their skills at a modest cost. It involved itself in projects, the reports of which were considered by the Executive Board. Two such projects included the development of a training strategy and of a market strategy. The main event of the group at the Scotland-wide level was its annual conference which was a mixture of business and social activity. It was always organised around a theme. Such themes included the 'Role of the

Individual in Team Setting', 'Improving Personal Performance', 'Improving Communications', 'The Challenge of Change', 'Leading Teams' and 'Make Teams Work'. The group's fiftieth annual conference was held at Stirling in April 1991 and its theme was 'Success Through Teamwork'.

The chief officers of the YMP Group were its president, vice-president and secretary. During the lifetime of the Federation, the group's president was always a man. In May 1992 the steady increase in the number of young women entering the industry and joining the YMP Group was recognised with the election of Gillian Lyall of Nevisprint as Vice-President, the first woman office bearer in the group's history. The group also awarded annually the accolade of 'YMP of the Year' to a member on the basis of their high level of commitment and development and participation in the group's activities.

The Scottish YMP Group had three local branches – Aberdeen, Edinburgh and Glasgow. Local branches ran a varied programme of evening meetings and guest speakers and scheduled visits to companies, including non-print. The local branches provided an opportunity for young managers to further their knowledge of the industry, not least for an exchange of views and ideas with their contemporaries, to the ultimate benefit of their companies. Regular branch meetings enjoyed solid support in Edinburgh and Glasgow although, regrettably, reduced YMP membership in Aberdeen meant meetings there were often not viable. Throughout the early 1990s, the Aberdeen branch struggled to attain a reasonable level of attendance. By mid-1995, concern regarding its future was high because of the few times it met. Given that SPEF companies in the Aberdeen local association employed some 1,000 employees within travelling distance of Aberdeen there was the basis for a viable branch but attempts to reactivate it were unsuccessful.

Financial Issues

All members of the Federation paid an annual subscription. The amount was based, until 1994, on wages paid in the fiscal year ending five days after the start of the Federation's financial year. From the 1994/95 financial year, the annual subscription was based on wages paid in the calendar year immediately preceding the commencement of the Federation's financial year. The change improved the efficiency of the Federation's budgeting and subscription procedures. Wages for the calculation of the annual subscription were those of production workers, apprentices, supervisory and managerial staff employed by the member firms in productive activity in origination, the press room, bookbinding and finishing, stationery manufacture and warehouse staff. The wages of general management, office and sales staff were excluded from the calculation. Initially the rates for the calculation of the annual subscription were determined by the annual general meeting. Under these arrangements the annual general meeting only formally approved an Executive Board recommendation on financial matters after they had been implemented.

To overcome this, the 1994 annual general meeting vested authority in the Executive Board to determine subscription bands and rates.

There were four elements to the structure of the annual membership subscription.
(1) three bandings of wage levels to each of which was assigned a subscription rate (see Table 20:1)
(2) a maximum annual contribution and a minimum annual contribution
(3) there was the aggregated fee applied to member firms having more than one separate production unit in Scotland. Companies paying on the basis of aggregated wages paid the sum required under (1) above, plus an aggregated fee decided by, until the end of the 1993/94 financial year, the annual general meeting but subsequently by the Executive Board. This change took into account the effect of the trend towards consolidation of ownership in the industry.
(4) there was a discount on the annual subscription, if paid in a lump sum, before a certain date. Subscriptions not paid in a lump sum were payable in ten equal instalments by direct debit mandate.

Table 20:1
SPEF : Structure of Annual Subscriptions

Production Employee Wages	Subscription Rate
First £120,000 wages paid	£0.95
Next £330,000 wages paid	£0.50
Next £850,000 wages paid	£0.30
Maximum Subscription	£5,340.00
Minimum Subscription	£120.00
Aggregation Fee (Annual)	£600.00
Discount – lump sum payment by 31/5/92	4%

The income, expenditure and operating surplus of the Federation over the period 1991 to 2007 is shown in Table 20:2. In 1991, the Executive Board approved members whose subscriptions were fully paid at 31 March 1992 receive a credit note to the value of 5% of their annual subscription for 1991/92 and the subscription rates and wage banding remain unchanged for 1992/93 relative to 1991/92. The maximum subscription and the aggregation fee was frozen at £5,340 and £600 respectively. In 1993, against a healthy financial background, the Executive Board proposed subscription rates and wage bands remain unchanged for the third consecutive year but that the discount offered to member firms paying their annual subscription in a lump sum prior to 31 May be reduced from 4% to 3%. It was agreed the £150 YTS managing agency fee be reimbursed to member companies employing apprentices. Further good news for member companies was they would again receive a credit note to the value of 5% of their annual subscriptions for 1992/93 for use against their 1993/94 subscription.

Table 20:2
Scottish Print Employers Federation: Income/Expenditure
(1991 – 2007)

Year	Income (£)	Expenditure (£)	Surplus (£)
1991	423,375	374,204	+49,171
1992	400,162	374,404	+25,758
1993	410,025	377,793	+32,232
1994	383,118	357,289	+25,829
1995	378,497	342,258	+36,239
1996	375,302	348,366	+26,836
1997	397,244	352,782	+26,462
1998	469,737	447,243	+22,494
1999	500,607	487,470	+13,137
2000	461,976	453,826	+8,150
2001	477,393	477,560	-167
2002	472,717	470,364	+2,353
2003	500,522	476,210	+24,312
2004	550,849	529,571	+21,278
2005	481,904	451,648	+30,256
2006	487,685	468,817	+18,868

Source: Scottish Print Employers' Federation, Annual Reports and Accounts.

In 1994, the SPEF increased the wage bandings for the second and third tiers to £350,000 and £870,000 respectively. The impact was to increase the maximum subscription level by 3% to £5,500 from £5,340 and the minimum annual subscription payable from £80 to £135. The aggregation fee remained at £600. It was further accepted that the discount for payment in a lump sum before 31 May be increased from 3% to 4%. Following the decision of the 1994 annual general meeting to give authority to the Executive Board to determine subscription rates and the wage bandings, the Board made no major changes for 1995/96. Making a small adjustment in the two higher subscription bands, increased the maximum annual subscription for a member company operating on a single site by £140 to £5,640, an increase of 2.5%. At the same time, the minimum subscription was raised from £135 to £145 and the discount offered to member firms paying in a lump sum by 31 May raised from 4% to 5%. In March 1996, given the Federation's strengthened financial position, the Executive Board decided the subscription rates and the wage bandings to apply for 1 April 1996 remain unchanged from those applying for 1995/96 but the discount for the payment of the annual subscription in full by 31 May be reduced from 5% to 3%.

In March 1997, given the continuing strength of SPEF's financial position the Executive Board accepted for the year 1997/98 the subscription rate applicable to the first wage bandings of £120,000 be reduced from 95p to 90p giving, for the smaller member companies an annual saving of £60. The other subscription rates and wage bandings remained unchanged. Given the healthy financial position, the Executive Board approved, for the third time, each member company be given a credit note to the value of 5% of its annual subscription for 1996/97 for use against its 1997/98 subscriptions. The 1997/98 financial year saw a further strengthening of the financial position through a 23% rise in the value of the Federation's investment portfolio enabling the Executive Board to leave subscription rates and wage banding thresholds unchanged for the 1998/99 financial year. In 1999, the Executive Board, by adjusting the top wage banding, sanctioned the first increase (+2.7%) in the maximum subscription for member firms for four years. Subscription rates and bandings remained unchanged for the year 1999/2000.

In March 2000, the Executive Board agreed subscription rates remain unchanged for 2000/01. The rates had never increased since the early 1980s and first rate of 90p per cent applicable to the first £120,000 of payroll had been reached after two 5p reductions. As a consequence of increasing the third wage banding level, the maximum annual subscription by a member firm increased for only the second time in six years by £150 or 2.6%. The Executive Board held subscription rates and wage bandings unchanged from the year beginning 1 April 2002. In the year 2002/03, the Federation suffered a decline in subscription income illustrating it was not immune from the adverse business pressures affecting the industry.[5] Action was taken to reduce expenditure by cutting staff costs and the subscription to BPIF. The Federation thereby held the subscription rates unchanged for the 2003/04 year but adjusted the top wage banding, the net effect being an increase of £100 in the maximum subscription, the first increase in three years.

A decline in subscription income in 2003/04 was offset by increases in management fees and by rental income from letting surplus office space. The Executive Board, nevertheless, restructured the wage banding and subscription rates for the 2004/05 year which reduced subscriptions by 22% for small companies with a production payroll of up to £24,000. The measure was calculated, at modest cost to the Federation, to make it more attractive for companies, particularly the smaller ones, to become members. Whilst leaving subscription rates unchanged for the 2005/06 year the Executive Board agreed a 2.5% increase in the maximum subscription to £6,150, the first increase for over two years. By the end of 2005/06 year, the market value of the Federation's investment portfolio stood at £275,000 whilst its balance sheet revealed a worth of over £1 million (see Table 20:3). The Federation was in a sound position to withstand any additional costs in the financial year 2006/07. The Executive Board while again leaving subscription rates unchanged, approved a 2.4% rise in the maximum annual subscription rate to £6,300 for 2006/07. By 2007 the wage bands and the accompanying subscription rates were:

- First £250,000 of wages 70p
- Next £250,000 (ie £250,000 to £500,000) of wages 50p
- Next £1,000,000 (ie £500,000 to £1,500,000) 30p
- Maximum subscription was £6,300

Table 20:3
Scottish Print Employers Federation (1991 – 2007)
Members' Funds : Balance

Year	Balance
1991	529,515
1992	554,976
1993	576,445
1994	593,151
1995	627,937
1996	647,423
1997	668,431
1998	685,453
1999	631,967
2000	656,467
2001	664,723
2002	667,348
2003	669,306
2004	925,603
2005	949,450
2006	973,075

Source: Scottish Print Employers' Federation, Annual Reports and Accounts.

SPEF also received income from management fees, bank interest, training boards and interest from investments. In 1991, the Federation adopted the policy of building, over a period time, investments to the level where they equated to six months' expenditure which at that time amounted to about £200,000. It decided that to achieve a more balanced investment portfolio, up to £20,000 of funds next available for investment be placed in a money market deposit while continuing with the existing policy of investing in equities. By 1997, the market value of the Federation's investment portfolio was £170,706. Shareholdings were held with, inter alia, Marks and Spencer, Royal Bank of Scotland, British Telecom, Unilever, General Electric, British Airports Authority (BAA), Glaxo Smith Kline, Cadbury Schweppes and the Vodafone Group.

After the bombing of the twin towers in New York on 11 September 2001, the market value of the Federation's investment portfolio declined by £22,000 in

2000/01, by £23,000 in 2001/02 and by nearly £79,000 in 2002/03. In absolute terms, the market value had declined from £246,911 in 2000/01, to £144,300 in the year 2002/03. This relatively poor performance reflected the decline in equity markets. From financial year 2003/04 the market value of the Federation's investment portfolio began to increase again. By end March 2006, the market value of the investment portfolio stood at £275,000. The Federation had a strong balance sheet worth nearly £1 million. Although the its industry suffered badly in the first decade of the twenty first century and membership declined, the Federation remained financially sound and a wealthy organisation.

In 1999, the working party appointed by the Executive Board to consider the present and future needs of the Federation concluded that whilst the Palmerston Place premises might not be ideal, they remained suitable in terms of location and in satisfying members and staff needs. No benefit was seen in seeking other premises but the position of Palmerston Place was to be reviewed periodically. At the end of the financial year 2005/06, the premises at Palmerston Place were revalued at £750,000. The property was put on the market at the end of 2008 for over £800,000. An offer for this amount was made but the potential purchasers proved unable to go through with the sale.

Services to Members

Membership of the Federation gave members access to a range of services – pension and business insurance schemes, legal advice, health and safety, management accounting, education and training, employment relations and representation of the industry's interests to governments, public bodies and the European Union via the Federation's membership of various industry bodies including the CBI and Intergraf. The Federation undertook surveys on the state of the trade (six monthly), productivity, profitability, and wages and salaries. It provided members with advice on the Scottish Print Pension Scheme and business insurance. Technical and legal advice was provided for members as was informed guidance on all aspects of health and safety relating to the printing industry. SPEF had a responsibility to promote a training culture to help ensure the skills needs of the industry were met. As a member of the Printing and Graphic Communications National Training Organisation, the Federation ensured national occupational standards in the sector met both current and future training needs. It assisted companies in the selection of their apprentices and organised short course management training programmes. Member firms had access to an employment relations service which provided advice and expertise on employment law and working practices. This service included national and house level negotiations with the GPMU, liaison with the union, representing member firms at an Employment Tribunal in dismissal and disciplinary cases, in redundancy situations, and in managing employee grievances. The Federation provided a management accounting service for which it charged fees. An important SPEF service to members was political lobbying involving representing the industry's interests to the decision-making institutions of the European Union, the UK Parliament, from 1999 the Scottish Parliament and local authorities.

The Federation performed this function through its affiliation to BPIF, the Confederation of British Industry (the CBI) and by joining the EU-wide print employer body (Intergraf).

a. Health and Safety

In the 1990s, increasing health and safety obligations upon employers, resulted in greater calls for advice and assistance from the Federation. A seminar outlining the provisions of new regulations which came into force on 1 January 1993 attracted substantial support as did regular courses on COSHH Regulations. By the mid-1990s, printing industry management recognition of the importance of good practice combined with increasing regulation and growth in claims for industrial injuries generated calls for assistance on a range of health and safety issues. By the 1990s, health and safety and environmental matters were subjects upon which the Federation was increasingly called upon for advice. The Federation, through its representation on the Health and Safety Commission's Printing Industry Advisory Committee, helped shape regulations and guidance. Much of the environmental regulation such as pollution and packaging waste, originated from Europe where the Federation's interests were represented by Intergraf which played an invaluable role in lobbying the EU decision-making bodies.

The importance of providing a safe working environment was to the forefront in the first half of the first decade of the twenty first century. The Federation's expertise in health and safety was called upon with increasing frequency as the Health and Safety Executive conducted an 'enforcement-led blitz' on manual handing. While Scottish printing employers recognised the importance of providing a safe working environment, there was, by 2006, a growing concern amongst SPEF members that the demands of the HSE inspectors were becoming unreasonably excessive.[6] By 2008, health and safety and environmental issues were high on the agenda of all responsible Scottish printing companies. This was particularly the case with manual handling, risk assessment and noise measurement.

b. Management Accounting

The Federation offered a management accounting service for which it charged member firms. On the creation of the Federation, the daily charge was £200 plus VAT which was regarded by member firms as representing outstanding value for professional consultancy. In 1991, the total income for management accounting fees was £23,000. In the same year, the management accountant retired. Whilst demand for the service was not expanding, it represented an important service provided by the Federation. The options for the Federation were either make a new appointment to the post or enter a contractual arrangement to meet actual demand. After discussion, the Executive Board went for the contractual option. The Federation contracted with Hunter Lynch Associates, whose principal, Jim Hunter, was a former employee of the Federation, to provide, from October 1991, the management accounting service on an as-and-when basis. These new arrangements, which involved no fixed costs for the Federation, were considered to be mutually beneficial, whilst maintaining an important service to member firms. In 1992, the Federation participated in the BPIF *Productivity and Profitability Survey*. It was an exercise enabling respondents to compare their company's performance with other companies in the same sector and with the industry as a whole. Individual company reports analysed key measures of productivity in terms of sales, value of output, value added, wages and employees. Profitability was analysed as a percentage to operating assets, sales and value added. In 1993, the second year of participation it attracted growing interest with forty five respondents.

A first meeting of the Benchmarking Interest Group was held in May 1996 extended performance measurement and comparison into areas beyond profitability and productivity ratios. The objective was to establish common benchmarking standards in selected areas to enable participants to make meaningful comparisons irrespective of the sector in which they operated and to identify improvement opportunities. The Benchmarking Interest Group finalised its proposals in 1997. These proved useful to member firms in measuring their relative performance in selected areas outwith productivity and profitability.

The Federation assisted member companies in ascertaining BS:5750 accreditation. The Printing Industries Quality Assurance Council, on which SPEF was one of four constituent bodies, published in 1994 guidance notes for the application of ISO:9002 (1994) to the printing industry replacing the previous guidance notes for BS:5750. The list of member companies accredited grew throughout the mid-1990s as the industry and Federation demonstrated a continuing interest in quality assurance. In some cases, pressure from a leading customer led a member firm to seek BS:5750 standards. Unless the company gained accreditation, the major customer threatened to take their business to another firm.

c. Political Lobbying
The Federation represented the industry's interests where a collective voice transcended what its members could achieve individually.

i. Within the UK
In carrying out this function, SPEF liaised, and co-operated, with the Confederation of British Industry (CBI), BPIF and other employer organisations. In 1991, after years of representation, the Federation and the BPIF finally persuaded the Lord Chancellor that the defence of innocent dissemination be available to printers to defend libel cases based on defamatory content of which they were unaware and could not reasonably have been expected to be aware. The Federation's efforts were rewarded when the government, in 1995, introduced the Defamation Bill providing a defence of reasonable care in defamation proceedings for persons, such as printers, not primarily responsible for the publications of the defamatory statement. The Bill received Royal Assent in 1996. It recognised that in an era

where the printer did not have the same requirement to examine copy submitted by customers they should not be liable for defamatory statements of others.

There was mounting concern by 1993, given the government's growing public sector borrowing requirement, that the Chancellor of the Exchequer would impose VAT on books, newspapers and magazines in his March 1993 budget. It was widely held the campaign and lobbying conducted by the representative bodies was the influential factor in dissuading the Chancellor from ending zero rating. In a joint letter signed by the Presidents and Chairmen of sixteen trade associations and related bodies, including the SPEF President (Hamish Milne), the Chancellor Norman Lamont was urged to reject reversing a policy stretching back to 1860 against taxing knowledge, reading and the demand for literacy and information. Many member firms made valuable individual contributions in pursuing the issue with their constituency MPs.[7] While the immediate threat had been lifted, concern remained over the government's future intentions.

This concern was not unfounded and the campaign mounted against the imposition of VAT on books, magazines and newspapers prior to the March 1993 budget was revived when the new Chancellor of the Exchequer, Kenneth Clarke, contemplated such a measure in the November 1993 budget. With the support of the opposition parties, the Federation took its case to Scottish Conservative MPs who, given the government's narrow majority in the Commons, were in a position to influence the Chancellor's thinking. The successful outcome was due to the lobbying of constituency MPs by printers and publishers throughout the country.

Not all lobbying of the UK government was successful. In 1991, the combined strength of Britain's trade bodies proved insufficient to deter the government from transferring part of the cost of state sick pay benefits to employers. In 1993, in response to the government's consultative paper on measures to address late payment of commercial debt, the Federation favoured legislation giving a statutory right to interest payment on such debts. Whilst recognising it was not a panacea and the reluctance of companies to take action against debtors though fear of jeopardising future business, the Executive Board favoured legislation providing an effective backstop for those who had ceased to hold such concerns. The Conservative government did not legislate along these lines.

The Scotland Act (1997) devolved, from 1 July 1999, a wide range of matters, for example education, health and local government to the Scottish Parliament. 'The Scottish Parliament adjourned on 25 March 1707 is hereby reconvened' were the words whereby Scotland's first Parliament in nearly 300 years, opened on 12 May 1999 as its members took their seats. The SPEF Director (Jim Raeburn) wrote to each of the 129 Members of the Scottish Parliament congratulating them on their election and giving a brief introduction to SPEF and the printing industry. He offered to arrange visits to member companies for those interested.

The Federation was uniquely placed to represent the Scottish printing industry's interests to the Scottish Executive and MSPs and to develop a working relationship with each of the main political parties – Conservative, Labour, Liberal-Democrats and the Scottish Nationalist Party. Within Scotland, the Federation lobbied the Scottish Executive, Scottish Enterprise and the financial sector that it was in the best long-term interests of the Scottish economy to support an industry central to most people's lives.

ii. Within the European Union

In the European Union, the initiator of legislation is the European Union Commission. To influence EU legislation, the Commission and the European Parliament have to be lobbied. The Commission will only consider representations from EU-wide institutions. It will not deal with individual companies. The EU-wide private multi-sector employers' body was the Union of Industrial and Employers' Confederations of Europe (UNICE) which in 2006 changed its name to Business Europe. Its membership was the central employers' organisation in member states. The Federation's membership of UNICE was indirect, via its membership of the Confederation of British Industry through its affiliation to the BPIF. The EU Commission received representation from sector EU-wide employer bodies. The appropriate body for the printing industry was Intergraf. The Federation's application to join Intergraf was accepted in Brussels in November 1991. Intergraf represented twenty six printing employers' federations in twenty three countries. In 2002, BPIF resigned from Intergraf, leading the Federation to review its own membership. The review concluded given the strengthening role of the European Commission and Parliament, the printing industry's interests needed effective representation at the European level and continued membership of Intergraf was necessary.[8] It was an honour for the Scottish printing industry that the Federation's President, Bob Hodgson, was elected President of Intergraf at its General Assembly held in Edinburgh in June 2006. The ability of Intergraf to influence EU measures affecting the printing industry before they were required to be implemented in legislation by member states, remained a key role for the Federation.

Lobbying in Brussels on behalf of member federations on proposed EU environmental Directives for Integrated Pollution Prevention and Control (IPPC) and Reduction of Emissions of Volatile Organic Components (VOC) which, as originally drafted, would have covered even small print companies, formed a substantial part of Intergraf's workload in the early 1990s. Its representation obtained the removal of the requirements for permits for small operations and the raising of low levels on the consumption of organic solvents. Without these amendments, there was a danger unless references to capacity to use organic solvents were replaced by threshold figures based on actual consumption, even the smallest printing companies would be caught up in bureaucratic licensing procedures.

One example of the value of the Federation's membership of Intergraf was, in the 1990s, related to environmental issues. Intergraf, in conjunction with the

European Graphical Federation, undertook a project on behalf of the European Commission to produce and publish guidance on Best Available Techniques (BAT) in the printing industry in relation to meeting the requirements of the Integrated Pollution Prevention and Control and Volatile Organic Components Directives. In addition to the assistance they offered to print companies, they also helped harmonise interpretations of the directives by local authorities.

Intergraf won European Commission recognition of the problems experienced by the industry through the loss of business to China and persuaded the Commission to fund a study on this issue. It actively lobbied the EU to ensure fair operating conditions for the industry as a result of the constraints imposed by the Commission's chemical strategy and, supported by the paper and publishing industries, contested moves to introduce an eco-label for printed products. Intergraf co-operated with the Commission on a voluntary industry declaration to increase the recovery and recycling of paper to avoid EU legislation on the matter. Intergraf supported a Europe-wide project led by the European Association of Fine Paper Manufacturers, to promote the advantages of print.

SPEF, represented by the President (Bob Hodgson) and Director (Jim Raeburn), participated in a workshop organised in 2003 by the EU, the European Centre for Monitoring Change and Intergraf on the drivers for competitiveness in the printing industry. It proved a valuable opportunity not only to inform those parties about the problems arising from overcapacity, resulting mainly from increased performance of printing equipment against stable or slowing demand but to debate opportunities for the industry. Whilst by 2004 Intergraf's member Federations, including SPEF, believed the interests of the printing industry should be represented at European level, there was a widely-held view that Intergraf required to change if it were to be effective in that aim. Following the presentation of a consultant's report, Intergraf concentrated on its core business of lobbying, information and network with its main commercial activities being moved to a separate entity.

The British and Irish Printing Industries Council (BIPIC), comprising SPEF, BPIF and the Irish Printing Federation (IPF), was an initiative launched in 2004 for co-operation in areas of common interest and to share knowledge in serving the interests of member companies. SPEF was the only Federation of the three still in membership of Intergraf, the BPIF and IPF having resigned on grounds of cost. IPIC was a means of facilitating the BPIF's return to membership of Intergraf at less cost than when a member in its own right. BIPIC joined Intergraf, providing print specific European lobbying on EU legislation such as the REACH chemical Directive. The BIPIC arrangement was an extension of the co-operation between the three federations with the added benefit of cost savings for the three parties. SPEF President, Bob Hodgson, was nominated by BIPIC as its first employer representative to serve on the Intergraf Board.

Summary

On its formation, the SPEF had seven local associations but by 2008 the number had fallen to four (Glasgow, Edinburgh, Perth and Dundee). In August 1997, the SNPA disaffiliated from SPEF, but SPEF's staff remained the secretariat of the SNPA who paid a management fee to SPEF for this service. In 1998, the size of the Executive Board was reduced, whilst twelve months beforehand the Board had agreed only to appoint such subcommittees as it felt appropriate, rather than specific subcommittees set out in the SPEF constitution and rules. The head office of SPEF developed a number of direct links with member firms of which the most important was the biennial conference, organised around a particular theme. 1991 saw the fiftieth annual conference of the YMP held at Stirling whilst in the following year Gillian Lyall became the YMP Vice-President, the first woman office bearer in the YMP Group's history.

There were four elements to the structure of the annual subscription to SPEF – three bandings of wages levels to each of which was assigned a subscription rate; a maximum and minimum annual contribution; an aggregating fee applied to member firms having more than one separate unit of production in Scotland and a discount if the annual contribution was paid as a lump sum before a certain date. By the end of 1997, the market value of SPEF's investments was nearly £200,000. Its policy was to build up, over a period of time, investments to the level where they equalled six months' expenditure.

SPEF offered a management accounting service for which it charged fees. In 1991 the service was subcontracted to Hunter Lynch Associates and offered to members on an 'as and when' basis. It represented the industry's interests where a collective voice transcended what its members could achieve individually. This involved lobbying the UK government, the Scottish Parliament and local authorities. It was part of a successful campaign to persuade the UK government not to raise the rate of VAT on books, newspapers and magazines. SPEF influenced the political decision makers in the European Union indirectly via its membership of the CBI through affiliation to the BPIF and through its membership of Intergraf.

Notes

[1] See *Annual Report and Accounts, 1993-94*, Scottish Print Employers Federation.
[2] See Minutes of the Meeting of the Executive Board, 1 November 1996.
[3] For more details, see *Annual Report and Accounts, 1997-98*, Scottish Print Employers Federation, p3.
[4] See Minutes of the Meeting of the Executive Board, 25 March 1993.
[5] See *Annual Report and Accounts, 2002-03*, Scottish Print Employers Federation, p5.
[6] See *Annual Report and Accounts, 2004-05*, Scottish Print Employers Federation, p5.
[7] See *Annual Report and Accounts, 1992-93*, Scottish Print Employers Federation.
[8] See *Annual Report and Accounts, 2002-03*, Scottish Print Employers Federation.

Chapter 21

EDUCATION AND TRAINING

This chapter begins by tracing public policy initiatives over the period 1990 to 2008 to encourage employers to invest in the training and development of their employees and to help individuals improve their employability. The second part of the chapter outlines training and development programmes provided for new entrants into the Scottish printing industry whilst the third deals with production worker training in terms of standard setting and the location of training. The next part of the chapter examines non-production worker training whilst the final part assesses the extent to which training and development matters were the subject of collective bargaining between SPEF and the GPMU.

Public Policy Initiatives

Voluntarism was the traditional philosophy of the Federation's members and of UK governments in their approach towards vocational training. It was the responsibility of individual companies to make decisions as they saw fit in investing in the education, training and development of their employees. Many SPEF resources were invested in education and training services to members but most of it was 'below the line' activity, results often only seen in the longer term. The Federation made a substantial contribution to the development of competency standards for Scottish Vocational Qualifications (SVQs) in printing but the 'dividend' was not seen for three years when the first young people completed their modern apprenticeship with SVQs at Level 3. The UK government promoted, via a number of agencies, incentives, to encourage private and public organisations to invest in the training and development of their employees. These agencies changed their names, if not their nature, with great frequency. For example, Local Enterprise Companies (LECs), set up in 1990, were replaced in 1998 by a network of National Training Organisations (NTOs), replaced in April 2001 by Learning and Skills Councils.

Local Enterprise Companies (LECs) were set up in 1990 to improve vocational training for young people, to raise training standards in smaller businesses and to promote local economic growth. Twenty two Local Enterprise Companies were established in Scotland with responsibility for supporting local businesses or individuals in business development, to help with business planning, market advice, financial help for product development, quality improvement, skills development, support for individual or company training and environmental improvements. The twenty two were autonomous but for the Federation this had disadvantages. The devolving of decision-making to the LECs, meant the Federation, instead of having a single contract as previously with the Training Agency, covering the whole of Scotland, now entered into contracts on a variety of terms with each individual LEC. The introduction of LECs meant SPEF approached each LEC individually to put in place administrative, and contractual arrangements for the continuation, for example, of Youth Training after 1 April 1991.

This new arrangement was less than satisfactory but, by the Federation absorbing the problems, it maintained the benefits for member firms. There were four elements to the Federation's approach to co-ordinating moves to LECs for funds for the training and re-training of employees.[1]
(1) The Federation entered into contracts with those LECs prepared to offer one.
(2) In other areas, the Federation sought a 'sympathetic' managing agent who would accept print trainees as an addition to their contract with the LEC but otherwise acted as a post office between the Federation and the LEC.
(3) The Federation paid companies the actual sum received from the LEC concerned, less its managing agency and college fees.
(4) The Federation paid college fees directly to the college except in those cases where the LEC contribution was insufficient, for example in Lanarkshire.
Member firms were encouraged to become involved locally in the work of LECs and several SPEF representatives secured places on the Executive Board of LECs which comprised personnel from member firms, industry, local government and the training profession. The LECs had a key role in the UK training system.

In 1996, BPIF and SPEF entered discussions on setting up a National Training Organisation (NTO) for the UK print sector. This was in response to the then Conservative government's plans to establish a network of NTOs. They took a primary role in co-ordinating employer involvement in the development and uptake of education, training and qualifications to improve businesses' competitiveness. A Scottish committee of the print NTO was established with the expectation in due course it would replace the Federation's own Education and Training Committee. Representation on this committee was offered to the GPMU, in response to the union's repeated request for the establishment of a joint SPEF/GPMU training council. After much preparatory work, the bid submitted by the BPIF, SPEF and other partners for the establishment of a UK printing and graphics communications NTO was approved. Tom Domke, Chairman of the Federation's Education and Training Committee, served as the Federation's representative on the NTO Council whose structure included a Scottish committee with representation from the various partner organisations.

National Training Organisations strengthened the sectoral dimensions in identifying and meeting skill needs. They identified the industrial sector's training needs, established occupational standards and qualifications, provided information on training capacity and ensured the sector had the relevant training capacity. The Print and Graphic Communications NTO established in 1998, promoted training throughout the sector, identified skill needs and led the development of qualifications in the sector. SPEF played a leading role in the Print and Graphic Communication NTO which brought together the printing industry's employer and employee organisations and others to represent, and promote their education and training interests across the UK. The Federation organised the NTO's Scottish committee whose remit covered the separate and distinct education and training arrangements of Scotland.

The Print and Graphic Communication NTO soon established its presence in representing the interests of the UK-wide printing industry in education and training. It was involved with a large number of projects, each designed to provide essential information on industry training needs or to provide help in facilitating training and qualifications. The Federation sponsored the Scottish team for the Priesthill competition organised by the NTO as part of is Manpower Skills Festival held in 1999 in Birmingham. In 2000, the Labour government began consultation with industry and commerce over the future of National Training Organisations. The government was keen to reduce their number but the Federation's Executive Board expressed concern if this were achieved by merging the Print and Graphic Communications NTO into a large amorphous body, print employers would be less likely to identify with that body.[2]

From April 2001, LECs were replaced by Learning and Skills Councils which also took over the role of the NTOs. The Blair Labour government promoted greater labour market flexibility based on minimum standards and security of employment for all employees. Two principles underpinned this approach. First, every person at work was guaranteed properly enforced basic minimum standards. Second, labour market security for the employee within more flexible labour markets came from improving their employability through training and development.

The Blair government placed sector skills high on the political agenda with a view to improving the competitiveness and productivity of UK economy. It rated the performance of NTOs as uneven and replaced the seventy three NTOs with a reduced number of Sector Skills Councils (SSCs). The objectives of these councils included the reduction of skills shortages and the anticipation of future skill needs in their sector, improved productivity through specific action and to enhance the training and education system, for example by developing the training frameworks. They increased the opportunities to develop the productivity of all employees in the sector, to promote industry action to address equal opportunities and to improve access to training. They were employer-dominated and created by 'business for business', it being believed employers were best able to identify skill gaps and devise strategies, and related policies, to fill them. The government provided more funding for Sector Skills Councils than it did for NTOs on the condition they covered at least 500,000 workers and there was stronger employer involvement. The Print and Graphic Communications NTO was too small for recognition as a Sector Skills Council. It was inevitable it would be replaced by a council embracing other sectors.

The Print and Graphic Communication NTO entered discussions with possible allies with whom a bid for Sector Skills Council status could be made. The Federation's preferred option was that the NTO became a semi-independent division of the proposed Process and Manufacturing Sector Skills Council which would include paper, surface coatings, glass, furniture manufacture and the extractive industries. In 2002, the Print Education Forum (PEF), on which Graham Ellis served as the SPEF-nominated representative, was established with the remit of strengthening the industry's competitiveness through investment in skills development and training. Following extensive discussions, the PEF Board decided against joining the proposed Proskills Sector Skills Council, representing five different manufacturing activities, on the grounds its business plan did not meet the needs of the printing industry. The protracted negotiations concerning the printing industry's possible participation ended when, in late 2002, the PEF joined the Proskills Sector Skills Council from 2003. This council's primary responsibility was to strengthen the industry's competitiveness through skills development. Its vision became the driving force for the training and development of the skills of the workforce to make a significant contribution to the increased productivity of the UK process and manufacturing industry. Within the Proskills Sector Skills Council, industry groups were established to advise on strategic priorities for that industry, hence Proskills Print. The Scottish launch of Proskills was in March 2006 with the Federation arguing although support for Proskills was essential, the body must demonstrate it could deliver meaningful benefits to SPEF member firms.

The 1997-2005 Labour governments pursued a policy of creating what it described as the 'Learning Age' to create a culture of lifelong learning in the UK. The basic theory behind this initiative was by encouraging everyone to get involved in learning activity, not necessarily job-related, a better educated, more confident workforce, would be created to meet the changing demands of the workplace. The government's drive to create a 'learning society' not only involved training and development initiatives at the workplace but initiatives such as the University for Industry and Individual Learning Accounts.

a. University for Industry (UFI)

The University for Industry did not provide education directly. It had two main objectives. It stimulated demand for lifelong learning amongst businesses and individuals, and promoted the availability of high quality learning and improved access to, and information about, learning opportunities. The University for Industry, open to everyone, made educational provision flexible and accessible, by stimulating new markets to reduce costs, by offering information and advice and by providing opportunities for people to learn at their own pace and in a convenient location.

b. Individual Learning Accounts

These were established in 2000 to pay for learning of the individual's choice. As part of piloting individual learning accounts, people opened learning accounts in a bank or building society with a contribution of £150 from TEC funds. Individuals made a similar contribution from their own resources.

c. National Skills Task Force

The National Skills Task Force was to develop a National Skills Agenda. Its remit included examining the extent and outcome of skill shortages and skill gaps, how these be measured, monitored and overcome and how best to ensure the education and training system responded effectively to the need to increase key skills and employability within the workforce.

Entrants into the Industry

Despite being amongst the most technologically advanced industries, the Scottish printing industry failed to project its vibrant and forward-thinking nature. When this was combined with need to avoid, during difficult trading periods, non-essential costs it meant the industry struggled to attract young people to enter its various sectors. This was reflected in an ageing workforce. In 1993, apprentice recruitment reached an all time low when only forty young people were recruited in the whole of Scotland. In 1995, the situation was even worse: the total intake of print apprentices for Scotland was only twenty nine. In 1996, the total intake was even lower at twenty five. In the period 1994-1996 inclusive, only ninety four print apprentices were recruited throughout Scotland. In future years, apprentice recruitment remained a problem. Matters were made worse in that there was a 9% drop out rate amongst apprentices. Although nearly one in ten of the new young entrants into the industry left before they completed their training, the record in Scotland in other sectors was even worse.[3]

In 1995, the 'intake of apprentices' problem led the Federation's Education and Training Committee to make recommendations to address the situation.

It recommended the fixed-term, four-year apprenticeship be abolished. Apart from the virtual abandonment of pre-press apprenticeships, the committee felt the introduction into the industry of a set of SVQ standards accredited by SCOTVEC recognised time-serving was no longer appropriate. The essence of SVQs was that an individual demonstrated their ability to work to standards set by the industry and the achievement of these standards was the key to the completion of an apprenticeship. The acceptance of the committee's recommendations meant in future apprenticeship would be of variable duration although it would probably take three years for a trainee to attain the Level 3 qualification required under the standards of a modern apprenticeship. After much discussion, the Executive Board approved, in future, the completion of an apprenticeship be the attainment of an SVQ Level 3 qualification or four years on-the-job training, whichever was the earlier. It accepted the SPEF/GPMU Working Party, agreed during the 1995 wage negotiations, should examine the industry's skill requirements and the Industrial Relations Committee review apprentices' pay. The new arrangements applied to apprentices starting employment in the industry from 1 April 1996.

The Federation was involved in a number of other initiatives to encourage young people to consider a career in the industry including raising their awareness of its high tech nature. In November 1990, the Federation launched a video entitled *Scottish Print – the Career for you* together with a supporting poster and brochure. Copies were distributed to secondary schools in Scotland. This decision was taken in the knowledge print employers were experiencing increasing competition from other sectors to attract young people of the right calibre. Research-based evidence showed, for the decade of the 1990s, the number of young people entering the Scottish labour market would be less than in 1990. In 2002, the Federation, through the Print and Graphic Communication NTO, secured Department of Trade and Industry funding for a part-time appointment who was to explain printing careers opportunities in the Scottish printing industry to schools throughout central Scotland. Craig Russell worked during the autumn of 2003 with Glasgow College of Building and Printing in promoting its programmes as a route to a career in the industry. The initiative proved worthwhile with twelve visits to address pupils in secondary schools in west and central Scotland and with participation in careers fairs. He described the *Print Team* literature as a spectacular success, succinctly communicating the employment opportunities in the sector. In further attempts to encourage young people to take up employment in the industry, SPEF increased the profile of the industry in schools and colleges, improved, and delivered, more up-to-date and comprehensive print related teaching materials for use in schools and colleges. The Federation exposed students and schoolchildren to the various sectors of the printing industry and increased their knowledge and understanding of the sectors, processes and career opportunities existing within the industry.

Production Worker Training

a. Standard Setting

Scottish Vocational Qualifications (SVQs) were developed in the late 1980s to establish a range of employer-led vocational qualifications with national accreditation. The SVQ concept was based on four principles – industry-led, performance on the job rather than entirely on knowledge, accessibility and transferability. The successful completion of an SVQ was determined by assessment in the workplace with the candidate being observed carrying out the job. The system was based on competence doing the job, rather than sitting examinations at a further education college and serving time as a trainee. SVQ standards were set by a lead body in the industry responsible for awarding the SVQ certificates. A major element of the Federation's work in the early 1990s was developing a Scottish Vocational Qualification for print production workers. The Federation and BPIF, as partners in the industry lead body, were responsible for the specification of standards of competence and with SCOTVEC developing those standards into appropriate awards. SVQ and, in England, Wales and Northern Ireland, National Vocational Qualifications (NVQs) were recognised throughout the UK as mutually compatible and based on common standards. With the active participation of member firms, the Federation oversaw the development work associated with the print finishing sector.

Progress on developing SVQs for print production workers was painfully slow despite the set date of 1993 for their introduction. The steering group responsible for co-ordinating the task, published in 1991/early 1992 consultative documents seeking views from interested parties on draft standards for occupations in origination, machine printing, print/finishing/mechanised binding and carton converting. In the light of industry comments, the standards were revised and piloted in selected companies in the spring of 1992. A meeting took place with the GPMU to address their concerns over SVQ standards and dilution of craft employment, the age of entering into employment in the industry, adult training, the availability of trainers and assessors and the ability of print employers to provide workplace training. The Federation, with considerable assistance from member companies, played a full part at each stage of the lengthy but important exercise. The slow progress in preparing standards for accreditation by the National Council for Vocational Qualifications and SCOTVEC continued into 1993 although it had been agreed SCOTVEC and the Federation be the joint awarding partners for SVQs. There was delay in obtaining approval from the National Council for Vocational Qualifications for the standards submitted by the Printing Industry Lead Body as the National Council doubted whether the proposed Printing Industries Council of England, Wales and Northern Ireland was an appropriate awarding body.

After long development work, a set of SVQs for print production workers received accreditation in 1994 and was implemented in autumn 1995. The SVQs were awarded in occupations such as origination, machine printing, print finishing/mechanised binding and carton conversion. The SVQs existed at three levels. Level 1 was defined as competence in performing a range of routine tasks. Level 2 was defined as competence in a range of varied tasks carried out in a variety of different situations. Some were non-routine and involved some individual responsibility and required working in co-operation with others. Level 3 required the trainee to demonstrate competence in a wide range of varied work activities performed in a variety of situations. Most of these skills were complex and non-routine. They involved considerable responsibility and decision-making and required the control or guidance of other workers. Workplace assessments were carried out by experienced employers familiar with the work or by supervisor, or by line mangers. Assessors were trained and accredited by the SVQ awarding body and had, or were working towards, an assessment qualification. In some Scottish print companies, external assessors were used but they required to have sufficient experience and knowledge of the work being assessed and to be accredited by the SVQ awarding body. The Federation established a network of workplace assessors through a training programme arranged in conjunction with the Glasgow College of Building and Printing.

One consequence of the introduction of SVQs was that the Print Training Scheme had to be put on an SVQ basis if funding for it from the LECs were to continue. The Federation remained committed to the Scottish Print Training Scheme despite the administrative inefficiencies of contracting with individual LECs on a multitude of different terms. Finance for the Print Training Scheme continued to cover college fees and to make a contribution to the employment cost of apprentices. In November 1993, the Conservative government introduced a modern apprenticeship system based on the SVQ system. They were aimed at people aged between sixteen and seventeen but their objective was to achieve SVQ Level 3 in the subjects relevant to the apprentice's chosen area of work. Additional SVQ units had to be acquired to give the apprentice a balanced range of skills to meet the specific needs of the company.

Modern apprentices were introduced in the industry in the autumn of 1995 and were managed by LECs. They provided young people starting in the industry with a breadth of foundation knowledge and skills building up to a skilled and qualified operator. The training programme provided continuous development of the apprentice through skills training in the workplace and through learning at college and at the same time had the flexibility to incorporate the individual's development needs and their employer's specialist requirements. For apprentices starting in 1996 the fixed four-year period of training and relevant experience was replaced by an apprenticeship of variable length related to the completion of the appropriate SVQ at Level 3.

The Scottish Qualifications Authority granted the Federation 'Approved Centre' status, the only centre in Scotland authorised to offer all print-related SVQs. SPEF was uniquely placed to offer training and appropriate qualifications for each specialist occupation, preferable to a system based on time-serving. SPEF worked in conjunction with the colleges with the latter providing the underpinning knowledge and assessment to enable apprentices to achieve the relevant SVQ. In 1998 the Federation in its role as an Approved Centre was granted approval to offer new SVQs in non-impact printing and desktop publishing. The Federation's *Annual Report* for 1999/2000 reported it would be difficult to claim SVQs met with unbridled enthusiasm amongst its member firms.[4] The report pointed out a great deal of work had gone into producing revised standards which were more user-friendly. This measure combined with the Federation's initiative to train workplace assessors and reduce the industry's dependence on Glasgow College of Building and Printing made a major contribution to the understanding and the promotion of SVQs amongst member firms.

Following extensive discussions between the Federation and Glasgow College of Building and Printing, the first year common course for modern apprenticeships was revised to start with the 2001/2002 academic year. Attendance was reduced from sixteen to ten weeks with a corresponding saving in fees. From April 2002, Scottish Enterprise awarded the Federation a single contract to replace the several it held with individual LECs all on different terms. Only after several meetings, did SPEF succeed in persuading Scottish Enterprise to increase its contribution from £5,500 to £7,000 for modern apprenticeships in printing. In 2004, the Federation persuaded Scottish Enterprise to raise its contribution by a further £500 to £7,500. Scottish Enterprise agreed, in principle, to a limited number of adult apprenticeships attracting a contribution of £3,500 to assist the industry address its skills needs. The Federation's case was based, in part, on the need to persuade companies Scottish Enterprise funding made a meaningful contribution to the cost of apprentice education and training and assisted the recruitment of more young people into the industry. The Federation, by applying modest management charges with regard to modern apprentices employed by a number of companies, encouraged such recruitment. The Federation continued, unsuccessfully, to press Scottish Enterprise to bring the funding contribution for modern apprenticeships up to the level provided within England by the Learning and Skills Councils. In 2000, in recognition of the high quality of service the Federation had consistently delivered to its member companies, Scottish Enterprise awarded it a three-year contract for modern apprenticeship training.

A study of 132 modern apprentices recruited between 1996 and 1999 showed a success rate of 87% with 115 completing SVQs at Level 3.[5] The others had left the industry. A survey of apprentices gave the Scottish Print Training Scheme a high rating. The scheme had been the subject of positive reports by the Scottish Qualifications Authority and by the Scottish Quality Management System.

Building and maintaining a training infrastructure was a key role of the Federation in meeting the industry's present and future skilled manpower requirements. It worked closely with Danapak, Dundee in pioneering adult apprenticeships with a successful outcome when three gravure printing assistants, after eighteen months training, achieved skilled status. All sixteen places on a pilot contract between the Federation and Scottish Enterprise, providing a financial contribution of £3,500, were taken up early in 2006. This was a welcome means of assisting the industry address its skill needs, with other companies following the development with interest. Scottish Enterprise ran up a well-publicised deficit and, despite strong representations from the Federation, further funding for adult apprenticeships was not forthcoming.

b. Printing Colleges

The training of apprentices had elements of on-the-job and off-the-job activities. The latter was undertaken in printing colleges. There were two main printing colleges in Scotland – Napier Polytechnic and the Glasgow College of Building and Printing. In 1991 the future of craft apprentice courses at Napier was called into doubt when the Federation was advised to plan for only one more intake of apprentices to Napier under the then SCOTVEC arrangements. Falling apprentice numbers were causing an unacceptably low student/staff ratio. It was clear, as a non-advanced course, the National Certificate was no longer regarded by the Polytechnic as appropriate given its elevation to university status. The Federation and its Edinburgh Local Association expressed serious concern about the possible loss of an important training facility. The Federation succeeded in persuading Napier University to reverse its decision to close the craft apprentice course. Its Principal agreed an extension guaranteeing an intake of apprentices up to and including September 1994 on the basis of introducing a general course to be followed by all apprentices. The Federation warned its member firms the case for keeping two training centres in Scotland was not assisted by their continuing weakness in apprentice recruitment.[6]

In 1995, after more than a decade of uncertainty over the print apprentices' course at Napier University, the Federation decided, given the continuing reduction in apprentice intake across Scotland, the industry should concentrate future course provision at the Glasgow College of Building and Printing. From academic year 1996/97 all first year apprentices attended college in Glasgow. The Napier course was phased out progressively ending in 1998. Other reforms accompanied the Glasgow College becoming the sole off-the-job training provider for apprentice training. All first year apprentices attended for four blocks of four weeks in 1997/98. The second year was switched from day release to four blocks of two weeks. These changes facilitated progress with SVQs in conjunction with the college which purchased, with the assistance of £10,000 from the residue funds of the Printing Equipment Educational Trust, six simulators for training on sheet-fed presses.

In 2002, the Federation responded to a consultation document on the proposed merger of the Glasgow College of Building and Printing, the Glasgow College of Food Technology and Glasgow Central College of Commerce, by stressing the need for continuation of printing courses for craft apprentice to HND level in the merged set up. It explained how crucial the Glasgow college was, as the only college in Scotland offering such courses, to the future competitiveness of the industry. The Federation asked the merged college recognise printing courses were capital intensive and it should be prepared to make regular investment in advanced technology to ensure its courses meet industry needs. The merger was approved and implemented from January 2004 with the printing courses remaining intact.

Non-Production Worker Training

SPEF continued to offer a programme, for member firms, of specialist training events ranging from supervisor skills, sales, production control, estimating and health and safety, topics for which take-up was high. In some instances, courses tailored to meet their specific need were arranged for individual companies. The Federation received a growing number of requests to provide in-company courses. Its initiative to offer, in conjunction with Glasgow College of Building and Printing, the NEBOSH Certificate in Occupational Safety and Health met with particularly good support. This was timely with the Health and Safety Executive Inspectorate taking closer interest in the requirements for 'competent people' and risk assessments. In 2004, the Federation held its first ever senior management conference at Stirling and which proved a success and was repeated in subsequent years.

The Federation welcomed the introduction from September 1991, by Napier Polytechnic, of a three-year BA degree in Graphic Communications Management. Industry representatives had participated in the validation of the course which replaced the old HND Printing (Administration and Production). A modified HND which, in accordance with SCOTVEC policy, was reduced from three to two years, was offered by the Glasgow College of Building and Printing. In 2000, meetings were held with Napier University to underline the importance the Scottish printing industry attached to its Graphic Communications Management degree course which was under threat because of downward trends in enrolments. The concern was the potential loss of a course that was a regular source of well-qualified graduates for junior management positions. SPEF pressed that greater emphasis in the course content be placed on digital communications and business administration as well as the need for improved marketing of the course. In 2001 Napier University announced due to insufficient demand from potential students, its Graphic Communications Management degree course was withdrawn even though it was unique in Scotland. The Federation considered the decision had more to do with the University's own commercial interests than any considerations of what it might mean for the future of the Scottish printing industry.[7]

In 1992, the Federation's Education and Training Committee, working with Glasgow College of Building and Printing, established a professional qualification for print sales representatives, namely a SCOTVEC-accredited HNC in Print Sales and Marketing. The course was offered by the Glasgow College of Building and Printing as a full-time, day release or evening studies. The course content balanced sales and marketing skills and the technical knowledge expected of a competent sales representative.

Training and Collective Bargaining

In the National Agreement between SPEF and the GPMU, both parties recognised the need to complement the industry's investment in technological developments with high quality training for its employees. The agreement accepted training should take account of nationally agreed standards of competence and lead to credits towards a vocational qualification recognised by the industry. To improve the quantity and quality of training, both SPEF and the GPMU recognised their common interests in having a single training agreement covering all production workers. Such an agreement, although never concluded, was to concentrate on the content, quality and means of delivery of training. Wages and other conditions of employment for apprentices remained a matter for the *Wages and Conditions National Agreement*. First year apprentices received 40% of the craft rate whilst those in second year received 65%. Third year apprentices were paid 75% of the craft rate whilst those in their final (fourth) year received 85% of the craft rate. A final year apprentice operating a machine or, in the case of multi-colour machines, fully trained and a recognised member of the press room, received 50% of the machine classification payment.

A proposal to increase the intake of trainees was discussed at a meeting in March 1996 between SPEF, BPIF, the GPMU and the then Labour Party spokesman on employment, Stephen Byers. The proposal offered employment and training to young people aged eighteen to twenty four with the cost of a £60 per week subsidy for six months met from the windfall tax on the profits of privatised utilities. A handicap from the Federation's perspective of the proposal was the qualification trainees be recruited from those who had been unemployed for at least six months.

In 1994 the Federation, in response to the GPMU claim to establish a Scottish Joint Training Council, appointed a joint working party to review, during the lifetime of the 1995/96 National Agreement, the skill requirements of the industry and how these might be met. Of common concern was the falling intake of apprentices. An agreed target of fifty for 1995 was considered feasible by both the Federation and the GPMU so long as Scottish print companies remained confident there would be no economic downturn. The joint working party considered a labour market assessment undertaken by Howard Affiliates for the Federation in 1994. The assessment found while the low employment turnover of recent years was welcomed, there was fear it could lead to stagnation unless new blood and new ideas were brought into the industry. The study concluded although valuable development and training work was done by many companies others needed encouragement to progress towards best practice. The joint working party noted the report. The GPMU argued for a joint SPEF/GPMU training council, whilst the Federation maintained support for an ad hoc joint working group to assess and discuss future training and manpower requirements of the industry. It maintained that to establish a permanent body was an unjustifiable duplication of the Print and Graphic Communication NTO.

The GPMU, arguing every voluntary effort to increase the employers' commitment to training had failed, sought Federation support in 2000 to establish a Training and Development Fund with statutory authority for employer contributions. SPEF was against accepting any form of compulsion in the funding of vocational training. It had reservations about the practicalities of the union's proposal and what it could deliver but admitted this did not mean there were no problems with the existing quality and quantity of vocational training in the industry. It accepted some member companies had a good record on investment in training but there were too many others with a less enlightened attitude.[8] In the 2002 negotiations for the revision of the National Agreement, the union again raised the issue of vocational training seeking the right to five days training per annum for every employee. The Federation rejected the claim arguing they would not bear the costs of such a provision. They further said any investment in training and development was a matter for individual companies to be determined by the training needs of its workforce.

In 2000, the Federation considered its position in the light of the support declared by BPIF and the GPMU for a statutory levy of 0.2% of payroll on all printing companies to enable the Print and Graphic Communication NTO to become independent financially and to provide additional funding for training to meet the industry's skill needs. The Executive Board, while agreeing in principle to seek fair and equitable funding arrangements to enable the NTO to achieve financial independence, held serious reservations about the practicalities of collecting relatively small sums of money from thousands of small printing companies and what such funding might be expected to deliver.

The *Print 21 Report* identified low levels of training and the decline in print education as problems which could hinder the future development of the UK printing industry. The ageing workforce and the reduced number of young people entering printing, pointed to the industry failing to address longer term skill needs. The GPMU argued voluntary training arrangements had failed and the industry should generate funding through a statutory training levy on all firms in the industry. The Executive Board accepted the industry's record on training and development could be improved and the intake of apprentices was low despite the availability of funding of £7,000 for each trainee on a modern apprenticeship. SPEF said it would need hard evidence to persuade it a statutory levy provided the solution to the industry's training weaknesses. SPEF considered its decision not to support the introduction of a statutory training levy was fully vindicated by the rejection in a consultative ballot[9] on the introduction of such a scheme in England and Wales by BPIF members.

Summary

The UK government attempted, via a number of agencies, initiatives and incentives to encourage private and public organisations to invest in the training and development of their employees. The agencies frequently changed their names, if not their functions. For example, Local Enterprise Companies (LECs) were set up in 1990 to be replaced in 1998 by a network of National Training Organisations (NTOs) which were replaced in April 2001 by Sector Skills Councils.

In the period 1990 to 2008, the Scottish printing industry experienced problems in attracting young people to take up a career in the industry. In 1996, the total intake of apprentices for the whole of Scotland was twenty five and in future years the recruitment of apprentices continued as a problem. To address this, SPEF reformed the apprentice system from time serving to training to standards, launched a new video entitled *Scottish Print – the Career for You* and participated in careers fairs.

A major element of SPEF's work in the early 1990s was the development of Scottish Vocational Qualifications for print production workers. These qualifications established a range of employer-led vocational qualifications with national accreditation. After arduous development work, a set of SVQs for print production workers received accreditation in 1994 and was introduced in the autumn of 1995. SVQs for printing production workers put apprentice training on an SVQ basis (the Printing Training Scheme). Modern apprenticeships were introduced into the industry in the autumn of 1995. They provided a breadth of foundation knowledge and skills leading to an output of a highly skilled and qualified operator. The training of apprentices had elements of off-the-job and on-the-job training. The former was carried out in printing colleges in Glasgow and Edinburgh (Napier) but from the academic year 1996/97 off-the-job training only took place at the Glasgow College of Building and Printing. Non-production worker training involved specialised training events of a short duration covering topics such as supervisor training with courses usually customised to meet the specific needs of an individual company.

The national agreement between SPEF and the GPMU recognised the need to complement the industry's investment in technological developments with high quality training for its employees. SPEF resisted requests from the GPMU for a joint body to monitor training in the industry arguing such a body would duplicate the work of the National Training Organisation and subsequently the Sector Skills Councils. It resisted successfully the union's claim for the setting up of a Training and Development Fund with statutory authority to collect contributions from SPEF members.

Notes

[1] See Minutes of the Meeting of the Executive Board held on 28 March 1991.
[2] See *Annual Report and Accounts, 2000/01*, Scottish Print Employers Federation, p4.
[3] See *Annual Report and Accounts, 1992/93*, Scottish Print Employers Federation.
[4] See *Annual Report and Accounts, 1999/00*, Scottish Print Employers Federation. p4.
[5] See *Annual Report and Accounts, 2002/03*, Scottish Print Employers Federation, p4.
[6] See *Annual Report and Accounts, 1992/93*, Scottish Print Employers Federation.
[7] See *Annual Report and Accounts, 2001/02*, Scottish Print Employers Federation, p4.
[8] See *Annual Report and Accounts, 1999/00*, Scottish Print Employers Federation, p4.
[9] See *Annual Report and Accounts, 2003/04*, Scottish print Employers Federation, p4.

Chapter 22

WAGES AND CONDITIONS OF EMPLOYMENT 1991-2008

This chapter examines the employment relations service provided by the Federation to its members, particularly the negotiation of a national agreement with the GPMU. It provided them with industrial relations advice on UK and European Union legislation and on in-house company matters such as managing a redundancy situation, occupational pensions, harassment and bullying, and handling disciplinary matters. Member firms placed importance on having direct access to the Federation's staff specialist advice, particularly that enabling them to stay on the right side of the law. As well as a regular access to advice and assistance, member firms could participate, at no extra cost, in the BPIF/SPEF survey on production worker wages, on staff salaries and benefits, on productivity and on profitability.

This chapter begins by examining the case for a national agreement and for a separate Scottish agreement. It then describes the process of merging three separate collective agreements with three different unions into one agreement. The fourth section addresses wage movements, wage differentials and changes in working time. The chapter concludes by outlining changes between 1991 and 2008 in other employment conditions such as pensions and sick pay.

The National Agreement

Each year SPEF negotiated a national agreement with the GPMU setting out minimum standards of employment conditions applicable in all SPEF membership companies. The Federation's Executive Board reviewed regularly the case for maintaining this agreement. It took the view while there were issues on which it would be prepared to forego a national agreement, the arrangement had, on balance, served the industry well and provided industrial relations stability.[1] The Federation maintained this view, despite in the late 1980s/early 1990s, other employer organisations, notably the Engineering Employers Federation, withdrawing from national wage agreements.

Following the collapse of the BPIF/GPMU national agreement during their 1993 national negotiations, the SPEF Director sent a letter to member companies stating the Federation's policy towards the future of its national agreement with the GPMU. The letter said the Federation believed national agreements had served the industry well and helped provide an increase of stability over a long period. It concluded:

> …Accordingly, the Committee presently favours the retention of a national agreement but emphasises that its continuation will depend on a willingness to reach settlements which serve the best interests of the industry.

In short, the Federation's continued support for a national agreement depended upon it being achieved at an affordable cost.

In 2002, the Federation appointed a review group to consider its future direction including the importance of the SPEF/GPMU national agreement to member firms. Responses to the review group's questionnaire demonstrated the importance SPEF members attached to the national agreement. From the replies, its members felt the national agreement was in need of reform if in the future it was to address adequately the challenges facing the industry. SPEF members considered the agreement needed to address issues relating to skills developments and the work-life balance of people working in the industry, and to enable companies to respond to increasing competition from the growth of the new media and from the outsourcing of print overseas. The view amongst member companies that the national agreement required reform led SPEF to accept observer status at the Joint Review Body established by the GPMU and the BPIF as part of their 'Partnership at Work' initiative. In the meantime, the long-established national agreement, warts and all, continued to serve a useful purpose. In addition to saving an enormous amount of management time at company level, the national agreement offered stability and flexibility.[2]

The Separate Scottish Agreement

The implementation date of the BPIF/GPMU national agreement covering England and Wales was April. The national agreement between SPEF/GPMU became effective on 1 July each year. Bargaining over changes to the SPEF/GPMU national agreement took place after the BPIF/GPMU settlement. It was inevitable the outcome of these negotiations would have a significant influence on the Scottish negotiations, particularly as the same union officials were involved in both sets of negotiations. The Federation always resisted pressure from the GPMU to import into Scotland the BPIF/GPMU agreement, arguing bargaining be conducted in a Scottish context. As a result, there were important differences between the two national agreements some favourable to Scotland and some not. Call money, for example, was removed from the Scottish agreement in 1993 but not from the BPIF agreement until 2005. The Scottish agreement provided for lower pay levels relative to the BPIF agreement. Despite these differences, the content of the Scottish national agreement resulted from decisions made by Scottish employers and such control had been shown to be crucial on occasions, for example 1993, when there had been a breakdown in the BPIF/GPMU negotiations.

In March 1992, the Executive Board, arising from a debate at a meeting of the Dundee Local Association, discussed the value of the Scottish printing industry maintaining an agreement for Scotland, separate from that of other parts of the UK. In the discussion, the Federation Director observed suggestions to end the separate agreement for Scotland were based on nothing deeper than a comparison of SPEF Grade B/BPIF Class I wage awards. He explained that the negotiations between SPEF and the GPMU took place some two months after those between the BPIF and the union and offered Scottish printing companies breathing space in which to find a solution in the event of industrial action following any breakdown in negotiations for the English and Welsh agreement. Whilst such circumstances might only arise exceptionally, a study of the respective agreements revealed economic reasons in favour of retaining a separate Scottish agreement. The Federation Director cited two specific examples – one, apprentice/craft trainee wage rates where the BPIF had unsuccessfully attempted to negotiate a reduction in their higher remuneration rates in relation to Scotland and which they acknowledged had had an adverse effect on employers' recruitment intentions, and two, the payment of Class II (Grade C) rates for certain Class III (Grade D) jobs. The Director pointed out a separate Scottish agreement enabled Scottish employers to shape the agreement to meet the industry's needs whilst their ability, if they were to part of the BPIF/GPMU agreement to influence and shape the UK negotiations, would be minimal. The Executive Board, after discussion, considered the matter further at its September 1992 meeting asked the Industrial Relations Committee to review whether the Federation policy of maintaining its own separate agreement from that of the BPIF remained appropriate for the foreseeable future.

The Industrial Relations Committee report noted until the 1960s the BFMP and the SMPS conducted joint negotiations but strains developed in the relationship when the BFMP took exception to an agreement reached between the SMPS and the STA in August 1967, leading in 1969 to the SMPS withdrawing from the BFMP Joint Labour Committee. The paper also drew attention to the formation of the GPMU which meant there was now only one union covering the whole of the UK, thereby weakening the argument a substantially different union structure in Scotland justified separate agreements. A further change outlined in the Industrial Relations Committee report was the increased concentration of ownership making it not unreasonable to expect some large company groups, usually with head offices located in England, to press for their Scottish subsidiaries to operate under a common agreement. There had been no such pressure. SPEF settlements were not seen as detrimental to their interests. The report also pointed out there were many similarities in the two agreements which was inevitable given they covered employees performing the same duties only in different parts of the country. It did point to some significant differences between the two agreements.

The Industrial Relations Committee's report outlined at least three advantages in maintaining a separate Scottish agreement. First, BPIF negotiations took place in February with a settlement effective from 24 April whereas the outcome of the SPEF negotiations, conducted during April/May, were implemented from 1 July. While it was rare for negotiations in the south to break down, as Scotland had sovereign agreements it was possible to distance Scotland from any disruption. It gave SPEF breathing space in which to determine its policy and tactics for its later negotiations.

Second, a separate Scottish agreement meant negotiations could take account of economic and trading conditions in Scotland rather than influences affecting other parts of the UK. An example was seen in March 1992 when after consultation with its member firms, SPEF was left in no doubt they favoured a single rather than two stage implementation of the negotiated wage increase as had happened in England and Wales, even accepting in the short term it would prove more expensive. Third, and the main reason, for continuation of a separate agreement for Scotland was that SPEF member companies could have a direct influence on the outcome of the negotiations whereas the opportunity to influence UK negotiations would be modest. The reality was SPEF would be no more influential than any other Alliance of the BPIF. The Industrial Relations Committee recommended the Executive Board reaffirm the SPEF policy of maintaining its own industrial agreements with the GPMU but the policy be subject to three-yearly review.[3] The Executive Board accepted this recommendation.

The Single Agreement
On the formation of the GPMU, there were three national agreements. One covered SOGAT members, a second NGA members whilst a third related to the SLADE

members. This last agreement covered employees working in graphic reproduction. In September 1991, the Federation's Industrial Relations Committee appointed a working party to draft a single agreement covering all GPMU members. A single agreement was to incorporate common machine classification provisions. The Working Group examined social wage aspects to which the Federation had previously committed itself to hold joint discussions with the GPMU.

The 1992 national agreement contained a commitment from SPEF and the GPMU to reach a single agreement integrating the former NGA, SLADE and SOGAT agreements by 1 July 1993. By autumn 1992, substantial progress had been achieved but important differences remained. A contentious issue was how to accommodate employees whose terms and conditions were regulated by the agreement with the former SLADE section of the GPMU. The Federation's Industrial Relations Committee view was that with continuing technological advances leading to increased flexibility across all pre-press activities, and given the relatively small number of employees involved, SPEF should remove the former SLADE provisions, failing which the position be reconsidered. Other areas of difficult negotiation concerned overtime and machine classification payments. By the end of June 1993 a single agreement had been concluded to operate from 1 July 1993. It represented a simplification of those agreements it replaced. In integrating three agreements into one, some concessions were necessary if a common position was to be achieved.

Wage rates in the single agreement followed those established under the SOGAT and NGA agreements, giving three grades of employees – B (Craft), C and D (lesser skilled). The separate rates for the occupations defined in the former SLADE agreement were discontinued. All employees covered by that agreement now qualified for the Grade B craft rate of £175.90. A further payment of £38.73, representing the difference between the present former SLADE rate and the Grade B rate, was paid to those craftsmen and others who, until July 1993, qualified for the SLADE rate of £207.21. This payment applied only to employees continuing in the employment of their employer as at 1 July 1993. New employees working in graphic reproduction and those changing employer after 1 July 1993, received a negotiated house level payment. Apprentice wage rates were set in line with the scale under the former SOGAT agreement. Differences between the NGA and the SOGAT rates had been in relation to the first and second year. The latter provided for 40% and 65% of the craft rate whereas the former awarded 45% and 60% respectively. Any NGA apprentice about to enter their second year was paid 65% of the craft rate (Grade B).

There were significant changes to the previous agreements covering overtime working provisions. Subject to one qualification, the single agreement provided overtime worked during any one day be paid at time and a half for the first five hours and thereafter at double time. The qualification was those employees who immediately prior to July 1993 worked under the NGA agreement be paid double time for overtime worked after midnight so long as they remained in the employ of their present employer. With Sunday overtime working, the period of work offered was six hours which represented a compromise between the eight hours set down in the SOGAT agreement and the four hours in the NGA agreement. The single agreement encouraged voluntary overtime to meet customer needs and added, wherever practicable, employers give at least one day's notice of overtime working. Call money, paid where notice of overtime working had not been given the day before or prior to straight-on working for one hour or more after normal stopping time, was added as was payment for altering an employee's meal break.

Sick pay provisions in the single agreement continued with the arrangements established under SOGAT and NGA agreements. The sick pay provisions of the SLADE agreement providing payment for the fourth day of illness were ended apart from an understanding those presently enjoying such provision continue to do so whilst remaining with their employer as at 1 July 1993. Holiday pay was calculated in line with the formula established under the SOGAT and NGA agreements.

The three former agreements made reference to apprentice quotas. In the single agreement these were replaced by a statement there be sufficient craftsmen in proportion to the number of apprentices employed so that there was no undue production pressure on apprentices learning their craft. Machine classification payments were a major problem to be overcome in integrating the three agreements. There were differences in the payments in the NGA agreement relative to the SOGAT agreement. While the differences were long standing, the reality was actual wage rates for employees qualifying for machine payments were generally influenced by local competition for labour rather than which agreement regulated an individual's machine payment. In the end, the Single Agreement embraced former NGA and SOGAT employees subject to the proviso the agreement did not disturb machine extra arrangements existing immediately prior to July 1993. Separate payments based on letterpress and litho were removed from the unified agreement.

Wage Movements
a. Craft Rates
The 1991 wage negotiations were conducted against a backdrop of difficult trading conditions, falling inflation and a recent BPIF settlement of £10.45 per week increase on the craft rate. SPEF sought a straightforward cash settlement reflecting these circumstances. The settlement was an increase in the Grade B rate of £10.45 per week with other rates enhanced on a pro rata basis. Adjustments were made to current provisions on payment for the use of UV equipment and to the equal opportunities clause so it included reference to sexual harassment. Despite pressure from the GPMU for the introduction of 'social wage' items, the Federation refused to make any concession on these matters but did agree with the union consultation on the whole area.

In 1992, the GPMU claim was for a substantial pay increase, a pro rata increase in machine extras payments, an adjustment of the bonus calculator, six weeks holiday, a reduction in working week without loss of pay, enhanced holiday pay, improved sick pay and enhanced maternity/paternity leave. The Federation's negotiating team priority was a cash settlement at an acceptable level which would give the industry stability as the UK economy emerged from recession. It did accept there was scope for limited changes to sick pay provisions. The union believed, given the narrow majority vote by its members to accept the 1992 BPIF agreement, its Scottish members would not accept a two stage implementation when the Scottish print industry was performing relatively better than that down south, albeit in recessionary conditions. The 1992 agreement provided for an increase of £6.99 per week on the minimum grade rate for craft/Grade B employees. This was in line with the then inflation rate of 4.3%. Agreement was only reached after lengthy negotiations which had come close to breakdown. While the pay settlement was marginally above what the Federation would have wished, it was their belief the deal was the best in the circumstances. The Federation had resisted union pressure for an additional day of holiday.

The 1993 national wages negotiations were conducted in unusual circumstances in that they were not preceded by a national agreement for England and Wales. The breakdown of the BPIF/GPMU negotiations were followed by the union, threatening industrial action to establish an increase of £6.50 per week, 3.78% extra on machine classification payments and an additional days holiday from January 1994 as the pattern. Against this background the Executive Board received a recommendation of the Industrial Relations Committee for the national wage negotiation with the GPMU scheduled for 13 and 14 April. It recommended negotiating the continuation of a national agreement providing for an increase on the minimum grade rate plus corresponding percentage adjustments on machine classification payments. The negotiators were not mandated to offer additional paid holidays without referring the matter back to the Executive Board.

At the negotiations, the SPEF explained to the GPMU the severity of the continuing economic pressures on member companies. In offering an increase of £4.70 on the craft/Grade B rate, SPEF stressed the need for a moderate settlement if member firms were to see benefit in maintaining the national agreement. The offer was considered inadequate by the GPMU which would not contemplate an agreement that did not provide for, at some point in 1994, an additional day of holiday entitlement. Negotiations were adjourned to allow SPEF to consult with its members. Given developments in England and Wales following the breakdown of BPIF/GPMU negotiations the view of SPEF members firms was they were prepared, albeit reluctantly, to accept an additional day of holiday if it enabled the retention of a national agreement at an affordable level.[4] The Industrial Relations Committee explained the additional day was necessary if an agreement was to be reached but recommended its implementation be postponed to as late as possible in the year and be taken on a day decided by individual employers. The committee recommended the parameters of a settlement in terms of an increase on maximum grade rates in return for specific proposals, that would offset the corresponding increase in labour costs.

Settlement was finally reached on 18 May providing for an increase of £6 per week on the craft/Grade B rate, pro rata adjustment of machine classification payments by 3.53% and an additional day of holiday, at a date determined by the employer, in the holiday year commencing 1 October 1994 together with a number of measures, notably the abolition of call money, to offset the additional labour costs. While the outcome was at a greater cost than might have been forecast some months earlier, it was secured on the best terms consistent with the preference of both parties to maintain a national agreement. SPEF saw three benefits from the agreement:
(1) financial savings for member companies when measured against the alternative
(2) stability rather than disruption and deterioration of working relationships particularly in those companies resisting the union's terms for settlement, and
(3) facilitating the introduction of a single SPEF/GPMU Agreement from 1 July replacing the existing agreements with the former SOGAT, NGA and SLADE section of the NGA.

Prior to the annual wage negotiation with the GPMU in 1994, the Federation considered its strategy. The Industrial Relations Committee recommended any settlement be conditional on obtaining concessions corresponding to those achieved by the BPIF, progress be made on calculating overtime on a weekly rather than a daily basis and on reducing shift rates. The GPMU claimed a substantial increase in wages and adjustments to machine extras and sick pay. The Executive Board was reminded a similar claim had been presented to the BPIF and had been settled with a weekly increase of £15 together with clauses providing for full cost recovery, flexibility of working between all occupations and the elimination of demarcation lines. The negotiations resulted in an increase of £5.45 per week on the craft/Grade B rate and the adjustment of machine classification payments by 3.1% effective from July. The increase on actual wage rates paid in the industry, was close to the April Retail Price Index of 2.6%.

The Federation secured a full cost recovery clause, allowing the increased employment costs to be offset through productivity improvements agreed, and implemented, at company level, no later than 31 August 1994, by acceptance of full flexibility of working between all occupations and by the elimination of demarcation lines. SPEF member firms were urged to achieve new levels of efficiency through full use of these clauses. The Federation's negotiators pressed for a reduction in shift rates arguing shift payments in Scotland were higher than those paid in the rest of the UK. Progress was limited to the appointment of a joint working party to examine working hours and earnings of shift workers in member companies and in competitor companies outwith Scotland. The working party was to report during the lifetime of the 1994 agreement.

It was not until October 1994 the agreement was accepted by GPMU members when following two ballots narrowly rejecting a recommended settlement, a third for strike action or industrial action short of a strike was rejected. This was deemed by the GPMU as a mandate to accept the settlement on offer. Federation representatives had remained resolute throughout the protracted negotiations. They were not prepared to trade flexible working between all occupations and for full cost recovery. These were 'must haves' if the national agreement was to survive.

The Joint Working Party on shift rates made little progress. The Federation argument that Scottish print employers paid higher shift rates than their competitors was countered by the union contending there was little evidence to support the SPEF arguments. Part of the SPEF strategy for the 1995 annual pay negotiations, was to seek lower rates than presently applicable for companies which had not previously operated shift work, albeit this meant competing print companies applying different terms. The GPMU claimed a substantial increase in wages, an additional day's holiday, the abolition of the Grade D category, an improved sick pay scheme, apprentice intake targets and time off for trade union activities and training. The Federation adopted the bargaining position that if the GPMU made either additional holidays or the abolition of Grade D a condition of agreement then the negotiations would break down.

Against a background of rising inflation, GPMU acceptance the Scottish print industry was not performing as strongly as that in England and Wales and wage awards generally were running ahead of the previous year, the 1995 settlement of a £6.70 per week increase on the craft/Grade B was regarded as realistic. While no progress was made on shift rates and balancing time, the GPMU's demand for additional holidays was rejected as was their claim for improvements to the industry-wide sick pay scheme although the Federation did concede some minor changes to this (see below). The 1995 agreement made provision for management and chapels to implement efficiency and productivity measures sufficient to offset, in full, the additional employment costs arising from the wage award.

For the 1996 wage negotiations, the Federation adopted a negotiating mandate any wage settlement should not exceed a £7 per week increase on the craft/Grade B rates. The 1996 wage settlement provided an increase of £6.70 per week on the craft/Grade B rate. Measured against a trend of rising wage awards in industry generally the settlement, by holding the monetary increase on minimum grade rates to the same level as in 1995 but down in percentage terms (from 3.69 to 3.56), was considered satisfactory.

In March 1997, the Federation's Industrial Relations Committee set out its objectives for the forthcoming negotiations with the GPMU. It defined a range of settlement for the wage increase, continuing provision for full cost recovery, aim for a marginal widening of the Grade B/Grade D differential and seek an increase in apprentice intake. The negotiating team agreed to hold further discussions with the GPMU on the EU Working Time Directive and to discuss, without commitment, the GPMU proposal for a SVQ at Level 4. The strategy for the 1997 negotiations was also not to pursue changes to shift and overtime rates and balancing time, but secure the right of the Federation to return to these issues at a future date. The Industrial Relations Committee rejected the idea of an agreement with the GPMU for more than one year. When SPEF received the GPMU claim, an interesting feature was the absence of claims for a reduction in the working week, additional holiday and social wage items. The 1997 settlement offered an increase on the craft/Grade B rate of £6.90 per week, with continuing provision for full cost recovery. SPEF members considered the settlement a balanced one when account was taken of continuing competitive pressures and of the need to reward employees for their contribution to increased efficiency.

Table 22:1
Annual Weekly Increases in Grade B Rate : 1991-2007

Year	Increase (£)
1991	+10.45
1992	+6.99
1993	+6.00
1994	+5.45
1995	+6.70
1996	+6.70
1997	+6.90
1998	+8.05
1999	+5.20
2000	+6.40
2001	+6.70
2002	+4.95
2003	+6.99
2004	+6.60
2005	+7.45
2006	+6.35
2007	+8.59
2008	+9.07

The 1998 negotiations resulted in an increase of £8.05 per week on the Grade B basic rate but a restriction on the Grade D rate increase. The union's claim for an increase in the premium rate for permanent night shift working and for the introduction of paid paternity leave were rejected. The full cost recovery clause was maintained and Federation staff assisted members achieve efficiency savings in many different ways, including variations in shift working arrangements. The 1999 wage negotiations were difficult that the economic climate brought gloom to the Scottish printing industry. The Executive Board and the Industrial Relations Committee were resolute in their position that unless a settlement was reached which recognised the economic state of the industry, they would terminate the national agreement. The national agreement survived when, following extended negotiations, a settlement was concluded providing an increase of £5.20 on the Grade B rate, representing 2.48%. The GPMU claim to increase the minimum period of notice for shift changes from four weeks to ten was firmly rejected by SPEF.

Reconciling the GPMU insistence on a substantial pay rise and the widespread resistance of customers to accepting price increases made the 2000 wage negotiations difficult. That inflation rose from 2% in January 2000 to 3% in April did not assist the Federation's case. The eventual settlement provided an increase of £6.40 on the Grade B rate, representing 2.98%, and was only reached following resumption of talks after two days of negotiations had ended with the parties far apart. The GPMU claim for a reduced working week and additional holiday never had any prospect of succeeding. The Federation recognised these two items were high priorities on the GPMU bargaining agenda and there was always the threat they might withdraw from the national agreement if they judged there would never be scope for progress on these items. The union's argument for increased holidays and shorter working hours was based on the shorter hours enjoyed by employees in the printing industries of certain western European countries. SPEF countered by saying such an argument ignored printing was close to the top of league tables on both items in the UK.[5]

In the 2001 negotiations, the settlement was an increase of £6.70 per week for Grade B craft employees representing 3.03% on the minimum grade rate. The GPMU claims for paid paternity leave, improvements in the industry sick pay scheme and the rights of employees to five days training per annum were rejected. In the following year the settlement achieved provided an increase of £4.95 per week for Grade B employees representing 2.17% on the minimum grade rate. These negotiations had been preceded by discussions with GPMU officials on cost recovery issues which it was agreed should be based on 'efficiency and productivity measures' as set out in the clause on unit costs and competitiveness in the national agreement. Under this, companies were to examine the scope for greater efficiency. The GPMU expressed concern the clause was, in some cases, being used as a vehicle to reduce minimum employment terms and conditions. Both SPEF and the GPMU were aware some long-established terms in the national agreement were being questioned by employers taking the view if change cannot be achieved nationally, they would seek to do so by other ways. The GPMU and SPEF recommended such negotiations be kept separate from cost recovery bargaining. Cost recovery negotiations centred on the introduction of measures which would provide practicable improvements to productivity and competitiveness. They were not related to reduced holiday entitlement, longer hours or reduced overtime or shift premiums.

The two vote majority of GPMU members in approving the 2002 wages settlement together with signs of increased unrest provided advance notice to SPEF the negotiations in 2003 would be difficult. The union was determined to secure a settlement above the rate of inflation (3.1%), failing which it would pursue matters at house level. With SPEF equally determined any settlement take account of the poor trading conditions, the parties started the bargaining sessions far apart and the prospects for reaching a settlement doubtful. The implications for the industry and its customers in the event of a breakdown of negotiations were recognised by both sides. Compromises were required if an accommodation was to be reached. The SPEF negotiating team had no doubt the national settlement could not have survived at less cost than the agreed £6.99 per week increase on the Grade B rate plus eligibility for sick pay after three working days. The actual cost in payroll terms for companies was significantly below inflation. The full cost recovery clause remained. For SPEF members, this was a key part of the national agreement enabling them to identify 'efficiency and productivity measures' which could limit unit cost increases.

In 2004, a settlement with the GPMU providing an increase of £6.60 per week on the Grade B rate, representing 2.75% on the minimum grade rate, was a reflection of the troubled state of the industry. This was the final set of negotiations with the GPMU before that union's merger with AMICUS in November 2004 to become the Graphical, Paper and Media Sector of that union. In the first negotiations (May 2005) with AMICUS, agreement was reached on an increase of £7.45 per week on the Grade B rate, representing 3.02% on the minimum grade rate. The Federation bargained an increase in the Grade B/Grade D differential. In response to the GPMU's claim for a Partnership at Work Agreement along the lines of that negotiated with BPIF, the Federation was willing to enter discussions on the basis that they be held in a strictly Scottish context. There was no question of simply importing the BPIF/AMICUS (GPM) deal as it contained concessions to the union unpalatable to Scottish employers. These concessions to the union by BPIF were in return for, inter alia, the elimination of call money and the introduction of balancing time on a daily basis, which were already in the SPEF *National Agreement*, the latter since 1993. The reality was while the SPEF/GPMU agreement had scope for modernisation, Partnership at Work was little more than recognition of the arrangements on issues such as shift patterns and working hours which it had been possible to negotiate at company level for years. The Federation adopted a cautious attitude towards bargaining a Partnership Agreement with AMICUS (GPM Sector).

Heidelberg Speedmaster
6 colour printing machine,
photographed at Stewarts of
Edinburgh, Marionville Road

Reproduced courtesy of the Scottish
Centre for the Book, Edinburgh Napier
University.

During 2005, Partnership at Work discussions with the AMICUS (GPM) made slow progress as union officials were inhibited about negotiating anything at variance to the agreement reached with BPIF. SPEF supported the principle of Partnership at Work but believed the concept had yet to deliver tangible benefits, and so it would prove difficult, before any headway could be made in Scotland towards a similar agreement. While discussions continued, SPEF encouraged member companies to engage their workforce in delivering productivity improvements using the full cost recovery clause of the national agreement. In the meantime, the 2006 wage negotiations provided an increase of £6.35 per week for Grade B employees, representing 2.5% on the minimum grade rate. This was recognition of the adverse economic pressures on the industry. The overall increase on company payrolls was calculated at 2%, below both the benchmark Retail Price Index and average pay settlements in manufacturing.

b. Differentials
The SPEF/GPMU national agreement had three categories of occupation. These were Class B (skilled craft workers), Class C (semi-skilled employees) and Class D (lesser skilled). The traditional wage differentials were Class C employees received 90% of the Class B rate whilst Class D workers were paid 87.5% of Class B. SPEF member firms considered that Class D employees were paid above their market rate and the differential between Class B and Class D should be widened. In the 1995 wage negotiations SPEF put down a marker they would seek in future negotiations to widen the Grade B/Grade D differential and match any changes in corresponding grades in the BPIF/GPMU agreement.

In the 1996 negotiations, the Federation pursued their policy to restrict the increase on Grade D rate by presenting a proposal based on maintaining the traditional differential of 87.5% of the Grade B rate relative to the minimum earnings guarantee but applying a lower percentage increase to the graded basic rates. While no progress proved possible there were indications from the GPMU the proposal to widen the Grade B/Grade D differential might receive a more positive response in 1997. It was the 1998 negotiations which paved the way for the Grade D increase to be restricted to 85% of the Grade

B rate instead of the customary 87.5%. These negotiations resulted in weekly increases of £8.05 for Class B employees, of £7.25 for Class C workers and of £6.84 for Class D. The 2006 wage agreement saw the implementation, on a permanent basis, of a widening of the Grade B/Grade D differential from 15% to 17.5%. For many member firms this widening of the differential resulted in a relative fall in their payroll costs.

c. Working Time

The Working Time Directive (1993) restricted weekly working hours to a maximum of forty eight, provided for at least an eleven hour break between finishing work and restarting work, limited a night shift in principle to a maximum of eight hours, restricted Sunday working and provided for employees a minimum of three weeks, eventually rising to four, paid holiday. Under the Directive, these restrictions on working time could be balanced over a three month period. The Federation expressed its opposition to the Directive, pointing to its potentially harmful consequences for the industry, and emphasising as customers expect print companies to respond to ever shorter deadlines, shift working was essential for the profitable use of capital. The Federation also opposed the Directive on the grounds that unnecessarily restrictive limitations on working hours, especially night shift, could prejudice flexibility in the application of innovative working arrangements between employers and employees, even though these were usually agreed after meaningful consultation with the employees concerned.

In October 1998, SPEF alone, among mainstream employer organisations, concluded a collective agreement maximising the benefits from the application of the Working Time Regulations which were the transposition of the Working Time Directive into UK domestic legislation. A key consideration by SPEF in concluding a collective agreement was the GPMU acceptance that the forty-eight-hour working week and the maximum number of hours of a night shift be averaged over a fifty-two-week period as against a seventeen-week period stated in the Regulations. If the Working Time Regulations were implemented by collective bargaining, rather than by law, the reference period for the balancing of working time was twelve rather than the legal maximum of four months. The Federation viewed the Working Time Regulations as an example of a growing plethora of employment legislation in the late 1990s placing burdensome demands on its members who, in turn, looked to the Federation for advice and assistance on such matters.[6]

Other Employment Conditions

In the 1992 wage negotiations, SPEF agreed for employees who had completed three years of continuous service with their present employer, the waiting period for payment of sickness benefit be reduced from two weeks to one. The upper limit for sickness benefit increased to £110 per week but the period of entitlement remained unchanged at six weeks. Thereafter each individual's case was reviewed individually by their employer. In the 1995 negotiations, SPEF rejected the GPMU's claim for significant improvements in the sick pay scheme. It did offer to reduce the waiting period for sick pay from fourteen days to seven for employees with less than three years' service in return for completion of the basic working week before overtime rates applied. This was unacceptable to the GPMU. In the 1999 bargaining round, SPEF agreed in return for the introduction of a qualifying period of one year's service for employees starting on or after 1 July became eligible for sick pay, the waiting period be reduced from two weeks to one week for those with less than three years service.

In 1999 SPEF agreed with the GPMU pre-retirement arrangements to assist employees adjust to retirement and through the provision of counselling and training to those approaching retirement and by the introduction of a phased reduction of working time without loss of pay in the three months prior to retirement. The 2002 revision to the national agreement provided for the extension of cancer screening to all employees. In the same year, SPEF accepted the GPMU request for a 'Voluntary Trade Union Reorganisation and Access Procedure' as an alternative to the statutory union recognition procedures of the Employment Act (1999). A condition of acceptance by SPEF was it be regarded as a separate arrangement outside the national agreement.

In 1997, following a joint review with the GPMU, the Scottish Print Pension Scheme was converted from an occupational money purchase scheme into a group personal pension plan with effect from 1 August 1997. The flexibility of the new scheme, supervised by a joint SPEF/GPMU committee, attracted new interest from employers and employees. By 2000, the scheme had attracted further support and had fourteen participating employers, 737 active members and 190 paid up/deferred members. Annual premiums were £1.26 million and the estimated funds had reached £7.37 million.[7] By the end of 2001, they stood at £9 million. From 2001, employers without an occupational pension scheme were obliged to offer their employees access to a stakeholder pension and pass on contributions from their wages. To assist their respective members, the Joint SPEF/GPMU Management Committee reached agreement with Standard Life to offer a stakeholder pension plan for the Scottish printing industry. It facilitated the obligation placed on employers to offer employees access to such a scheme in the absence of an eligible occupational pension scheme.

Summary

SPEF supported the existence of a national agreement on the grounds it served, at an affordable cost, the industry well and had, over a long period, provided industrial relations stability. SPEF members valued a national agreement for Scotland separate from that for other parts of the UK. The separate agreement enabled Scottish employers to shape the agreement to meet the industry's needs whilst their ability, if they were part of the BPIF/GPMU agreement to influence the UK negotiations, would be minimal. While it was rare for negotiations between BPIF and the GPMU to break down the fact Scotland had a sovereign agreement meant it was possible to isolate Scotland from any disruption resulting from a breakdown.

On its formation, SPEF had three separate collective agreements – one covered SOGAT members, a second NGA members and a third former SLADE members. These three agreements were integrated into one between SPEF and the GPMU to operate from 1 July 1993. It represented a simplification of the three previous agreements. National agreements negotiated annually between the SPEF and the GPMU resulted in wage increases in return for increased flexibility of working between all occupations and a full cost recovery clause allowing increases in employment costs to be offset through productivity improvements agreed, and implemented, at company level.

The traditional wage differentials were that Class C employees received 90% of the Class B rate whilst Class D workers received 87.5%. SPEF member firms wished to see the pay differential between Class B and Class D widened. In the 1998 wage settlement, the Class B/Class D differential became +15% instead of +12.5% and in 2006, +17.5%. In 1998, SPEF became the first mainstream employers organisation in the UK to incorporate the provisions of the EU Working Time Directive into a nationwide collective agreement.

Notes

[1] See *Annual Report and Accounts, 1994/95*, Scottish Print Employers Federation.
[2] See *Annual Report and Accounts, 2005/06*, Scottish Print Employers Federation, p3.
[3] See the Minutes of the Meeting of the Executive Board, 24 September 1992.
[4] See the Minutes of the Meeting of the Executive Board, 14 May 1993.
[5] See *Annual Report and Accounts, 2004/05*, Scottish Print Employers Federation, p4.
[6] See *Annual Report and Accounts, 1988/99*, Scottish Print Employers Federation, p4
[7] See *Annual Report and Accounts, 1999/00*, Scottish Print Employers Federation, p4.

Part 5

GRAPHIC ENTERPRISE SCOTLAND, 2009 TO DATE

Chapter 23

GRAPHIC ENTERPRISE SCOTLAND

This chapter begins by explaining the SPEF 'Review of Operations' and the reasons behind the change of name to Graphic Enterprise Scotland (GES). It then outlines the economic environment in which the GES came into being. The third part of the chapter concentrates on the governance of the GES and then analysing the financial structure of the organisation. The chapter concludes by outlining the main developments in two important services to GES members – employment relations and vocational training.

The Strategy

The 2007 annual general meeting of SPEF called for a strategic review of its operations and resources. The recommendations were instrumental in the Executive Board repositioning SPEF for the future. At its meeting of 23 May 2007 the Executive Board ratified a Mission Statement, and a series of values for SPEF. These were approved on 5 December 2007 following discussion and consultation through the strategy programme. The mission for SPEF became 'to be recognised as Scotland's most cohesive, representative and persuasive force in the creative industries sector'.

In spelling out its values SPEF committed itself, whenever appropriate, to comply with the combined *Code on Corporate Governance* and every member company was expected to pursue similar standards. It declared no deliberate action or policy of the Federation would secure direct commercial advantage for SPEF over any member company. Further values included staff, management and the Executive Board would strive to secure and sustain productive working relationships with the supply chain companies and to stimulate opportunities for regular, open communication amongst the membership. Central to SPEF's mission was its work to reposition printing and related industries more appropriately within the context of Scotland's communications industry. Such a strategy called for a new name. Thus, from the summer 2008 the face of the Scottish Print Employers Federation became Graphic Enterprise Scotland. The story of SPEF was at an end. It was not, however, until September 2009 that the Executive Board formally approved this new name.

The strategic review had involved rebranding, deciding to sell 48 Palmerston Place, reducing operating costs, defining member benefits, increasing revenues and growing a services menu. Palmerston Place was regarded no longer appropriate to the needs of either the organisation or its member companies, although it was recognised it had served the organisation well over the years and, judged by its valuation, represented a sound investment. It was now simply too big for GES which was seeking to trim back its own costs. The focus was, and remained on gearing organisational resources to match demand from the membership. It was a question of cutting the GES's cloth to suit. The future would require a reform of the GES decision-making structure, devising a new subscription revenue model, the consideration of new membership benefits and confirmation of a development plan.

In 1992 membership of SPEF had been over 150 companies but by 2008 was only forty five. The strategic review suggested five options for the future of GES:
(1) the status quo
(2) a leaner and smarter SPEF
(3) go it alone
(4) reposition itself and
(5) seek a marriage with another employers' organisation.
By early 2009, however, it was apparent that continuing with the present strategy was no longer appropriate to the circumstances and a new strategy was required. The Executive Board in March 2009 discussed three options for the future.
(1) GES be dissolved and its assets distributed throughout the current membership by a predetermined formula.
(2) Dissolve the organisation and link up in some way with the BPIF. Although discussions took place it was recognised this option would mean only limited funds, if any, would be available to distribute to the members.
(3) Run a reduced GES operation servicing the membership for two years allowing the property and financial market to return to reasonable levels and review in December 2010 whether the organisation be wound up.

An extraordinary meeting of the Executive Board took place on 6 May 2009. There was much discussion over the future of SPEF/GES around four options:
(1) dissolution and planned distribution of assets
(2) a merger with the BPIF
(3) a partnership with the BPIF and
(4) consolidation.
The meeting agreed the consolidation option although revised budgets were to be prepared for two situations. First there be a new part-time post of Director who would work with a part-time Deputy Director, a full-time Personal Assistant, a part-time Financial Consultant and a part-time SNPA Director. Second, a new full-time Director be appointed who would have a staff consisting of a part-time Deputy Director, full-time Personal Assistant, a part-time Financial Consultant and a part-time SNPA Director. The meeting finally decided on the new part-time Director option. The meeting made five other important decisions:
(1) a fixed period of two years be set in which to try and turn round the fortunes of GES.
(2) the President contact Bob Hodgson to discuss with them the GES position and circumstances with a view to becoming employees of the GES.
(3) Simon Fairclough be asked to stand down from being Director but if he was agreeable, be retained on a fixed contract to service the SNPA until February 2010.
(4) the present staff be relocated to the basement of Palmerston Place thus benefiting from a significant reduction in business rates.
(5) pursue interested partners in renting the first and second floor of the building.
The May Executive Board also envisaged that with some further cost-cutting across the premises and the budget lines, in addition to the appointment of a part-time Director, a smarter, leaner organisation could possibly enable it to ride out the worst of the recession. In the meantime efforts were to be made to resume implementation of the repositioning strategy including the recruitment of industry partner/associate members. In terms of the staff establishment it was agreed this would break down as follows – part-time Director whose appointment would be up to three years, part-time Deputy Director (again a contract up to three years), full-time Executive Assistant to work five days a week and a part-time Financial Consultant who would work up to two days per week. This option was a flexible one allowing for the ongoing support of the SNPA if necessary, but would need approval by the members of GES in a special resolution. This was done and the September 2009 Executive Board meeting accepted a proposal from the Director to change the name of the organisation from SPEF to GES. On 6 June 2009 Simon Fairclough resigned the position of Director but agreed to work an average of two and a half days per week on SNPA business. On 1 July 2009 Bob Hodgson was appointed part-time Director of GES on a three day per week basis. He had been a past President of SPEF, past President of Intergraf and had over thirty years experience of work in the industry. He had an in-depth understanding of every corner of the print world.

The Economic Environment

The GES came into being just as the UK economy was to enter its deepest recession since the 1930s, caused by the collapse of financial markets in late 2008. This recession spread over to the labour market and the Scottish print economy experienced increased unemployment, redundancy and short-time working. In the UK by the end of March 2009 printing output was down some 13% relative to twelve months earlier. Even in the absence of this deep economic recession, the Scottish printing industry would still, in the period 2008-2010 inclusive, have experienced difficult economic times because of its fragmented markets, structured imbalance between supply and demand, overcapacity, falling prices and of the increasing competition from the internet.

Most Scottish printing employers saw it as a matter of survival (hanging on) by strict cost control and cost containment until sufficient firms had dropped out of the market to eliminate the excess capacity. Those with this view reviewed their operations constantly and did everything possible to retain skills at a sustainable level to survive the unprecedented downturn. Business failures, however, did take place. In the financial year 2008/09, for example, three major companies ceased to trade, underlining the severity of the recessionary climate.

GES members reported that the availability of credit from the banks was difficult. Companies seeking new or renewed finance found it was either not available or the costs of access (arrangement fees, interest rates and insurance) rose sharply relative to previously. Scottish print firms were being forced to cut prices to attract new business whilst at the same time facing price increases for raw materials, particularly paper. Margins were continually squeezed. Printers' lead times contracted as economic activity slowed. In other cases, the slow growth in demand resulted in mothballing production capacity as well as cuts in staffing levels. The environment in which GES came into being was well summarised in its 2008/09 annual report.

> ...Any considerations about the state of trade currently echo themes such as the inconsistency of demand, vicious and damaging price competition and rising supply chain costs. Equally there is something of a spirit of the blitz emerging, which sees companies renewing their operations and doing everything possible to retain skills at a sustainable level in order to survive this unprecedented downturn...[1]

In 2009 GES imposed a nationwide pay freeze when it informed the GMPU sector of Unite the Union there was no point in meeting to review the national agreement because its members could not afford any increase.

Constitutional Issues

The constitution and rules of the SPEF were also those of GES. Its decision-making machinery therefore consisted of local associations, the Executive Board and the annual general meetings. The decline in membership due to plant closures meant that the local associations had become moribund by the time of the formation of GES. The size of the Executive Board had also fallen and in 2010 consisted of only six members. The office bearers were the President (David McCormick), the Vice-President (Trevor Price) and the Treasurer (Jim Robertson)

Through rebranding itself GES hoped to broaden its appeal of membership and attract into membership organisations working along the supply chain – paper, ink suppliers, equipment manufacturers, publishing houses, agencies and direct mail houses. By March 2010, GES had met with only limited success in increasing its membership.[2] It had not attracted anybody into associate membership despite approaching eighty such potential members and a formal presentation to twenty one suppliers in Glasgow. Membership had been marketed by March 2010 to 419 potential members. The net result was that only three new members had been recruited along with two potential members. The response to say the very least was disappointing. There were a number of reasons why organisations were not attracted to membership of GES. There were the severe financial pressures on companies from the recession whilst other potential members said the benefits of membership were of limited value. Larger potential member companies said employment law advice and national agreements were not relevant to their needs. They were signatories to house agreements. Many potential small company members claimed the industrial relations services provided by GES were not relevant because they did not recognise, or operate, with the trade unions. Other potential members said they did not see membership as attractive because the subscription rates were too high for the services offered.

An important part of GES recruitment strategy was to affiliate with other organisations where this would result in a broadening of the services that could be offered to members and potential members. Discussions were being held at the time of writing with the General Insurance Group, with the Independent Printing Industry Association which could design, manage and administer training services, and Maclay Murray and Spens LLP to provide legal advice at reduced rates. Arrangements with Chiene + Tait, a firm of accountants have also been concluded and small business advice seminars have now been offered to members and non-members

In May 2008 the Scottish Newspaper Publishers Association (SNPA), which represented Scotland's 120 weekly newspaper titles, reached a new twelve-month rolling agreement with GES. An SNPA review group had concluded the organisation should continue to be allied with SPEF based on the heart rather than perceived potential synergy. SNPA membership was looking for a cost effective voice for its member companies for marketing and lobbying. The agreement was based on five components – reassurance regarding SPEF/GES financial viability, an agreed allocation of the Director time between SNPA and SPEF/GES, consultation on new initiatives, for example new premises, and clarity regarding a period of notice.

Under the agreement the SPEF/GES Director would devote half his time to SNPA business. SPEF/GES would continue to have its headquarters within the boundaries of the city of Edinburgh for at least twelve months and was to provide adequate accounting and administrative support as needed to ensure efficient delivery of the SNPA business plan. Specialist human resources and health and safety advice and assistance were to be made available to SNPA members on request on the same basis as that to SPEF/GES members. In return for these services SPEF/GES would receive a management fee of £65,000 plus VAT covering the period 1 January to 31 December 2008. Termination of the agreement by either party was subject to twelve months written notice.

The GES and its 'constituent organisation' relationship with the SNPA came to an end in October 2009. The challenges facing the Scottish newspaper publishing industry were every bit as serious as for Scottish print. SNPA's members faced declining circulations, substantial falls in advertising revenue, and government interventions which diverted public sector advertising away from the press, whilst readers were turning in increasing numbers to internet-based news sites. Against this background the SNPA decided that it must redouble its efforts to represent its members' interests as a single industry association. GES wished the SNPA well and hoped their lobbying endeavours would persuade public policy makers of the many advantages of news in print, not least the contribution which Scotland's local newspapers made to the democratic process

The loss of the SNPA management fee was offset at least partly by the appointment of the new GES Director on a part-time basis. This also heralded the opportunity to bring a new focus to the initial task of recruiting new members, broadening the membership criteria to attract supply chain partners, re-engineering existing member services and, importantly, developing new services.[3]

Finance
The main sources of income for the GES were subscriptions, income from investments and grant income from Skills Development Scotland. All firms joining the GES paid an entrance fee, based on wages paid by them during the twelve calendar months preceding the date of application, towards revising and maintaining the common fund. Into this fund, which covered the ordinary working expenses of the organisation (including the working expenses of local associations), member firms paid an annual subscription, based on wages paid in the calendar year immediately preceding the commencement of the GES

financial year. It was to be paid either in one lump sum or in ten equal monthly instalments by direct debit mandate or standing order. The rates for calculation of the annual subscription were determined by the Executive Board as were subscriptions of members having more than one separate unit of production engaged in printing activities in Scotland.

For the year ending 31 March 2008 subscription income was down on the previous year, reflecting consolidation and, unfortunately, further business failures. Income was also hard hit by the reduction in management fees previously paid by the SNPA and the Press Standards Board of Finance. While these losses had been anticipated, their absence significantly depleted the funds available to the Executive Board. The outcome at the end of the 2007/08 financial year was a deficit around £8,500 and a budget for a break-even position in 2008/09.[4] In the financial year 2008/09 subscription income was £118,190 compared with £113,432 for the previous year. However, the single largest contributor to overall income was represented by grant income received from Skills Development Scotland relating to the Scottish Print Training Scheme. This more than covered the payments returned to employers.

In the financial year 2007/08 investment income was some £9,000.[5] SPEF decided to crystallise some of its equity gains made in recent years. It also established a formal resources policy to help future decision-making, based on the ability to offer operational continuity in times of extreme difficulty. In the financial year 2008/09 investment income fell although not as dramatically as might have been the case, with yields remaining strong. The same could not be said of the portfolio's value. Although some stocks held or increased their value, most suffered losses. In discussions with the auditor, it was agreed that five holdings could reasonably be assessed as being permanently impaired. It was agreed, therefore, that a provision of £25,000 be incorporated within the financial statements to take account of such impairment.

The main items of GES expenditure were salaries, national insurance and pensions, administration and travel. A further important item of expenditure was a £5,057 payment to the BPIF for services, for example, surveys provided by that body. As announced at the 2008 annual general meeting, during the financial year 2008/09 costs were tightened up considerably with savings achieved in staffing costs and travel. Payments to employers related to the training scheme increased, but overall costs went up by around 5%, against a rise in overall revenues of 22.5%. Excluding the provision agreed for the impairment of the investment portfolio, GES ended the 2008/09 year with a deficit of £1,087, an improvement on the previous year's loss of £8,421.

GES's most significant asset, 48 Palmerston Place, was to have been sold in 2009. Failure, at the eleventh hour, of the buyer to secure funding proved a set-back. It had been hoped that in smaller, more appropriate premise the organisation might focus on the Executive Board's 'Repositioning and Member Service Extension Strategy'. However, SPEF/GES had negotiated and secured a non-refundable deposit from the purchaser, which covered all SPEF/GES legal and marketing costs. Unfortunately the SPEF/GES had served notice on its tenants in Palmerston Place and lost, albeit temporarily, a valuable income stream as a result. Given that the price negotiated for the building was well in excess of the October 2006 valuation recorded in the balance sheet it was judged unnecessary to provide for any reduction in the likely present market value of the building. In line with this the Executive Board approved modest investment in IT and telecomms, which allowed SPEF/GES to benefit from reduced staff costs as well as improving communication. As a result of the aborted sale of the building GES moved all the organisation's operations to the basement of 48 Palmerston Place and in doing so benefited from a significant reduction in business rates. In April 2010, the whole of 48 Palmerston Place, was let to one tenant on a ten-year lease with an option to buy at the end of year eight. The subsequent rental income has significantly reduced the projected deficit and has allowed the organisation to move forward on a firm footing.

Vocational Training

The main training scheme remained the modern apprentice scheme in conjunction with Glasgow Metropolitan College. This delivered twenty to twenty five new print professionals into the industry each year to ensure Scotland could maintain the skills necessary for the future needs of the industry. Industry training survived the double administrative onslaught of the determination of an incoming Scottish Government in 2007 to overhaul training, and a new SQA print qualification accreditation regime. The old challenges relating to lack of flexibility between vocational courses and qualifications, as well as financial restraints, remained unchanged when preparing annual funding applications to Scottish Enterprise. As an SQA approved centre, the SPEF/GES continued to run a busy Modern Apprentice Scheme with over 100 apprentices in receiving training in the 2007/08 financial year.

With the retirement of Bill Stark, the GES Training Manager for almost ten years, the opportunity was taken to find savings in the administration of the industry training scheme through the appointment of two supervised focus groups in spring 2009. At the time of writing GES was taking a fresh look at training given changes in the industry's requirements.

Wage Movements

Prior to the 2008 negotiations with the GPM section of Unite the Union, the Executive Board argued that, given that trading conditions were especially tight, with margins down and bad debts and production costs up, there was little room for a pay increase at the national level. The Executive Board also agreed that the cash equivalent to the increase granted by the BPIF be fixed as the upper limit of any offer from the SPEF/GES. This figure was £9.41 equivalent to 3.5% on the craft rate. It also agreed unanimously that negotiations be confined to money rather than other issues such as a Scottish 'Partnership at Work' agreement. The theme of the 2007 negotiations had been affordability whilst those of 2008 focused on stressing the real damage to jobs and corporate survival.

The resulting settlement, which union officials agreed to recommend to their members, was based on an increase in the Grade B rate of £9.07 equating to a percentage increase below that of the Retail Price Index inflation. This gave a minimum earnings level of £280.75 and a new basic weekly rate of £278. The increase in the Grade C rate was £8.16 giving a basic rate of £250.21. The increase in the Grade D rate was £7.48 to give a basic weekly rate of £256.86. Pay rates for apprentices and nationally agreed machine extras increased by 2.37%. From 1 July 2008 the amount of sick pay was increased by £5 per week to give a weekly rate of £173. The provision in the national agreement on unit costs and competitiveness, providing for full cost recovery remained in force.

Prior to the 2009 negotiations, the Executive Board agreed there be no increase in pay in 2009. Efforts were to concentrate on retention of jobs/skills and the Director was instructed to telephone the union and explain that negotiations were to be suspended for a year. A questionnaire and an email had been sent to member firms prior to the 2009 annual negotiations. Twenty three responses were received from sixty four emails in which the majority view was that there should be no pay increase in 2009, because job losses over the past twelve months indicated the industry was collapsing, negotiation should concentrate on retaining jobs, and any increase in pay could not be passed on to the customer. The highest priority, the survey results said, should be given to job security.

Paying heed to the results of this research the Executive Board decided not to offer any pay increase in 2009 but to retain the advantages relating to the stability the national agreement gave the industry. The union held a meeting of its FOCs/MOCs in Scotland at which it was decided to approach each company with a wage claim for an increase in line with the Consumer Prices Index (CPI), namely 2.3%. GES advised its members to refuse to concede this demand. The union responded by saying it would now ballot its members for industrial action. GES had taken the view it would be pointless to invite the union negotiating team to commit at least one day to travel to Edinburgh to hold pay talks when it was clear the employers could not afford to finance any pay increase.

The Executive Board remained resolute, that while employers could not afford to meet the costs of any wage increase, they would be very reluctant to shed jobs, preferring to look at a wage freeze, short-time working and/or any other appropriate changes to terms and conditions which could deliver efficiency savings. In the event, the union did not take any industrial action and had at best limited success in concluding company-wide deals. GES members remained, however, committed to retaining a national agreement. Having such an agreement in place undoubtedly saved participating employers many hours of unnecessary duplicated effort and worry as well as securing the best possible deal.[6] This pattern was repeated in 2010 and Unite the Union have pursued individual employers for wage increases of 3.7 %.

Member companies, struggling to survive the worst recession in living memory, looked at every aspect of other businesses to achieve leaner operations. In addition industrial relations work at GES continued to centre around restructuring, dispute resolution and regulatory compliance. In 2010, many member companies are now operating within their own house agreements, a number of which are now some way away from the basic terms and conditions of the National Agreement last negotiated in 2008.

Notes

[1] See Graphic Enterprise Scotland, *Annual Report and Accounts*, 2008/09, p1.
[2] See Minutes of the Executive Board meeting held on 3 March 2010.
[3] See Graphic Enterprise Scotland, *Annual Report and Accounts*, 2008/09, p2.
[4] Investment income came mainly from industrial equities. These include investments in Cadbury Schweppes, HBOS, Local Securities, Prudential, Royal Bank of Scotland Group, Royal Dutch Shell, Scottish and Southern Energy, Unilever, Vodafone Group and the Yell Group.
[5] See Minutes of the Executive Board meeting 10 December 2008.
[6] See Minutes of the Executive Board meeting held in June 2009.

Part 6

CONCLUSIONS

Chapter 24

THEMES

During its 100 year existence, the collective organisation of Scottish print employers had five names – the Scottish Alliance of Employers in the Printing and Kindred Trades, the Scottish Alliance of Master Printers, the Society of Master Printers of Scotland, the Scottish Print Employers Federation and Graphic Enterprise Scotland – and six Secretaries – F H Bisset, R T Wishart, W Barrie Abbott, Jim Raeburn, Simon Fairclough and Bob Hodgson. These five organisations worked on behalf of the Scottish industry, making a positive contribution to their members' businesses. Through their collective representation of the industry's interests at Scottish, UK and European levels and their hands-on assistance with services on an individual basis to member companies, the Scottish printing employers' collective voice added value to businesses.

What is now Graphic Enterprise Scotland, was formed in 1910/11. Its main purpose was to combine employers in the industry so they could counterbalance the growing power of the unions which at branch level (primarily Edinburgh and Glasgow) were increasingly threatening aggressive action. There had, for many years, been local associations of print employers, for example the Master Printers Associations of Glasgow, Edinburgh, Dundee, Greenock, Falkirk, Perth, Stirling and Kirkcaldy[1] but they were increasingly unsuccessful in containing strong union actions by the Scottish Typographical Association, formed in 1853. The new Scottish Alliance was in operation before the 1914-1918 World War started but a 'free bargaining' position did not occur until after the armistice of 1918.

This chapter analyses four common themes over the 100 year history of the Scottish printing employers collective organisation. These are:
1. coping with technological changes to methods of production
2. relationships with the British Federation of Master Printers and subsequently the British Printing Industries Federation
3. the relationship, after 1967, between the collective agreement covering England and Wales and that covering Scotland
4. the industrial peace of the industry.

Theme 1 : Technological Change

For the first sixty years of the Scottish print employers' collective organisation, the technology of production remained very stable, There was clear demarcation between the main printing processes – letterpress, lithography and gravure – and the tasks within these processes. Up to the 1960s, the dominant technology in the origination area was mechanical composition – Monotype (particularly for book production) and Linotype machines – combined with the letterpress printing process. The craft trade union structure was organised around the main printing processes. In Scotland, the STA represented compositors, readers and letterpress machine managers and the NSES represented letterpress duplicate platemakers. Lithographic origination craftsmen were members of SLADE whilst platemakers and machine managers were in membership of the ASLP.

The last forty years of the existence of the Scottish employers' collective body was a period of unprecedented change in which three major technological revolutions took place. In the 1960s, the dominance of letterpress began to decline as the 'litho revolution' hit the industry. Photocomposition began to replace mechanical composition. The former, referred to as cold composition, involved generating type images on film or paper rather than the casting and manipulation of metal type. The work of the compositor changed from assembling type and blocks to film assembly or paste up. Photocomposition was not easily compatible with the letterpress process and offset (both web- and sheet-fed) litho machines increasingly replaced the Wharfedale, Miehle, Heidelberg platen and other letterpress machines. By the late 1970s offset litho was producing high quality multi-coloured printed matter at high speeds.

Approximately fifteen years after the general implementation of photocomposition and offset litho, the industry experienced another major technological revolution with the introduction of computer based techniques into all stages of production – pre-press, press and post press. Computer technology enabled machines to make decisions traditionally made by a compositor on tasks such as spacing, justification and page make-up. It enabled the electronic production of plates through the process of computer to plate and later computer to machines rather than by hand.

In the machine room, this resulted in the introduction of faster machines capable of printing in five, six or more colours. Colour registration was computerised, reducing considerably the time and skill necessary to ensure colours were printed in the precisely correct position. In the post-press area, computer-based equipment automated many manual tasks and led to inline production.

Table 24:1
Scottish Printing Industry Industrial Revolutions : 1910-2010

Revolution	Dates	Printing Process	Length of Technology
Mechanical Composition	1910-1970	Letterpress	80 years
Photocomposition	1976-1985	Lithography	15 years
Computerisation	1985-1995	Lithography	10 years
Digital	1995 onwards	Digital/Litho	Almost Daily

The computerisation revolution was replaced within ten years when the industry experienced in the late 1990s a further – digital – printing revolution. Although digital printing spread rapidly, the major printing process in 2010 remained litho, but its share of the total Scottish print market fell relative to previous periods. Digital plate-making ensured exact reproduction occurred every time with the same information being transferred to the quality check system on the machine. Digital technology enabled scanning, proofing, corrections and additions to be done rapidly and without any hard copy. Colour separation of photographic images to the four printing colours was more quickly done than in the past. Digital printing produced finished copies using toners without plates. Its benefits included cost effective short-runs, shorter supply chains and the ability to print variable data. Low set-up costs made it economical to print even single copies 'on demand' tailored to the customers' individual needs. Printing on demand complemented 'conventional' printing processes in which, from the late 1990s, technological innovations, such as automatic plate changing systems, enabled faster printing speeds and greatly reduced down time between jobs.

These three 'technological revolutions' had a profound impact on the industry and the employers' collective organisation had to adjust to survive. By the centenary of that body, the industry was highly capital intensive. Over the 100 years, labour was substituted by capital but expansion of demand meant that initially employment levels in the industry increased in both relative and absolute terms. However, the technological revolutions changed the distribution of employment. Over the last forty years, the employment of those on direct printing production declined, whilst those employed to support production (administrative, clerical, technical and managerial) increased.

These technological developments contributed to radical changes in the corporate structure of the industry. In 1910, the industry was dominated by family owned firms such as Blackie; MacLehose; Bell & Bain; Wm Collins Sons & Co (all in Glasgow), R & R Clark, T & A Constable, Oliver & Boyd, Hunter & Foulis; Ballantyne (all in Edinburgh); Valentine; Burns & Harris (both in Dundee) and Farquhar & Son from Perth. By 2010, the industry was polarised between a small number of large companies, often multi-national, and a larger number of very small firms serving niche markets. Changing technology meant most of the family-owned firms existing in 1910 had by 2010 either gone out of business or been taken over by another print company. For example both Collins and Bartholomew (the map printers) were taken over by News International, a multinational company. Oliver & Boyd in 1962 was bought by the Financial Times, part of the Pearson Publishing Group. In 1987, Pillans & Wilson, established in Edinburgh in 1775 was taken over by Colorgraphic plc, an English-based company, but the merged entity did not survive. Valentine & Sons, a Dundee-based company, became part of the Waddington Group in 1960 but ceased operating in 1994. Aberdeen University Press in 1966 merged with Edmont and Spark (stationers and bookbinders) but in 1970 was taken over by the British Bank of Commerce. In 1978, Aberdeen University Press closed.

The industrial revolutions post-1980 in the Scottish industry resulted in employment losses in the production areas. They enabled printing companies to transfer origination work to locations outside the UK and then distribute it electronically back to the UK for printing and distribution. This was referred to as 'offshoring' leading to a 'distribution and print' business model as opposed to the conventional 'print and distribute' model. It became increasingly the case in book production that publishers had origination work undertaken outside the UK but then transmitted it electronically back to the UK for printing and distribution.

The technological revolutions of the past forty years, coming as they did in rapid succession, blurred the demarcation lines between the trade unions, initially causing inter-union problems which were resolved eventually by union mergers. At the beginning of the life of the Scottish employers collective organisation, there were five trade unions with members in Scotland – the STA, the NSES, the ASLP, SLADE and the NUPB&PW. As the letterpress process declined, the NSES transferred engagements into National Graphical Association which until 1965 had no members in Scotland. As litho expanded, the ASLP transferred its membership into the NGA. It preferred to see redundant letterpress craft workers retrained to undertake craft litho jobs. In 1982, SLADE amalgamated with the NGA to form NGA (82). The NUPB&PW merged in 1966 with NATSOPA to create SOGAT. This merger was dissolved in 1972, but the former NUPB&PW retained the title SOGAT. The STA became the Scottish Graphical Association in 1973, amalgamating with SOGAT in 1975, to become the Scottish Graphical Division of SOGAT (75). In 1982, SOGAT merged with NATSOPA which had few members in Scotland to form SOGAT (82), of which the Scottish Graphical Branch was the sucessor to the SGD of SOGAT (75). In 1991 NGA (82) and SOGAT (82) merged to form the GPMU, creating a single production workers union. Thus, the technological revolutions of the last forty years rationalised the trade union structure in the industry.

The growth of computerised production techniques meant origination work could be done effectively by non-print companies. The boundaries between the 'conventional' printing industry and other industries became blurred. Origination work by non-print employees was then sent to a print firm for printing. There were by 2010 a number of sources from which origination work could be done outside the industry, including art studios, advertising agencies, publishers and authors. This work could be delivered as a disc or memory stick, downloaded and passed to the press room. In the period 1910 to 1980 this would have been impossible. Then craft skills were embedded in the hands of the journeymen and alternative sources of labour supply were few. Computerisation and digitisation transferred these manual skills to expensive equipment.

Printing is a communications medium based on paper. Computerisation and digitisation gave birth to a communications industry based on electronic modes such as teletext, Ceefax, DVDs, cable television and the internet. The communications industry in the last two decades expanded greatly. Although printing's share of the total communications industry is relatively smaller today than in the 1960s and 1970s, in absolute terms it is bigger in output and sales. Communications based on electronics have proved to be complementary to communications based on the printed word. There is a bright future for the Scottish printing industry but it will operate in market situations very different than in the last 100 years, or indeed during the major technological revolutions of the past forty years.

Theme 2 : Relationships with the BFMP/BPIF

Relationships with the BFMP/BPIF were frequently strained. These difficulties arose from the unique constitutional position of the Scots, within the English and Welsh collective print employers' body, from their financial relationships and their status in industrial relations matters. To restore stable relationships between the Scots and the BFMP/BPIF, it was necessary at times over the last century to renegotiate the basis of the relationship. This happened in 1919, in 1969, in 1981 (the Carlisle Agreement) and in 1984 (the York Agreement).

The relationship between the Scottish print employers' collective body and the BFMP was not the usual one of Federation and its constituent alliances. The BFMP constitution provided that the Scots were a member of the organisation but had complete autonomy in financial, governance and labour relations matters. This autonomy was in return for general co-operation on a UK basis. This desire to represent a UK interest allied to the need to preserve Scottish 'freedom' was as old, at least, as 1707. The constitutional arrangement agreed in 1919 gave the BFMP the right to speak as a UK organisation but it maintained the 'freedom' of the Scots. The BFMP/BPIF Council had no authority over the Scottish Executive Board whereas the Alliances in England and Wales were bound by the decisions of that Council.

There were other ways in which there was no direct comparison between the Scottish Alliance and other Alliances of the BFMP. The Scots determined their own membership subscriptions, membership conditions, operated their own management accounting service, negotiated their own collective agreements with the unions and paid the expenses of their representatives to travel to London to represent Scotland's interests on the decision-making bodies of the BFMP/BPIF. The Scots jealously guarded this independence and would preserve it at all costs. They accepted the core interests of the Scottish and the English and Welsh organisations had much in common; in particular to lobby within Europe and the UK government. The printing unions were, for most part, UK structures. They also recognised the mutual benefits of the highest possible degree of consultation, for example on union demands for employment conditions improvement.

During the last century, there were a number of occasions when the Scots insisted on explaining their difference from other BFMP/BPIF Alliances. In 1956, the Scots agreed to increase their annual subscription to the BFMP on the condition in its annual accounts and in its rules and constitution, the BFMP inserted a footnote explaining the autonomy of the Scottish Alliance. The change of name in 1953 to the Scottish Alliance of Master Printers was because the previous title did not sufficiently denote the Scottish Alliance was different from the other BFMP Alliances. The change of title was sufficiently different from the titles of the Alliances in England and Wales, for example the Midlands Alliance, the Yorkshire Alliance, to denote a Scottish Alliance, given its financial and industrial relations autonomy, was different from other organisations affiliated to the BFMP. This change of name did not remove misunderstanding in England and Wales of the special position of the Scottish Alliance so in 1960 the Scottish organisation was retitled the Society of Master Printers in Scotland (SMPS). Twenty one years later (1981) the BPIF amended its constitution to make clear:

> The organisation of printers in Scotland should be provided by the Society of Master Printers of Scotland as an autonomous body.

The financial relationship between the Scottish printing employers' organisation and its equivalent in England and Wales was that the former paid an annual fee to the latter. Initially, this fee was negotiated annually but in 1965 it was agreed the fee be subject to re-negotiation every three years. In 1966, to remove the need for regular renegotiation of the annual fee, the Scots agreed to contribute a fixed proportion of its own membership subscriptions. This was set initially at 5%. After 1969, the Scots became genuinely autonomous in industrial relations matters and unsuccessfully sought to reduce their financial contribution, in the face of strong BFMP/BPIF resistance. In 1981, under the 'Carlisle Agreement', the Scots would pay an affiliation fee related to the services received from the BPIF. This was not without its problems and in 1984 the 'York Agreement' settled the future basis of financial arrangements between the two bodies. This agreement revived the principle of a percentage of the SPEF subscription income. The Scots were never happy with this. They considered the sum of £5,000 per annum too high given the quantity and quality of the services provided by the BPIF. By the early millennium, the fee was reduced to £2,000 per year.

At the end of the Second World War, negotiations to determine employment conditions in Scotland took place on a UK basis. The Scottish body participated with the BFMP and the Newspaper Society in negotiations with the unions. Local mutual rules agreements were made between the Scottish print employers' collective body and the individual unions. For bargaining purposes, the P&KTF was recognised by the BFMP but this was not a policy which commended itself to the Scottish employers body. During the 1950s and 1960s, higher wages, longer holidays, shorter hours of work were demanded with increasing frequency. The employers' policy to deal with the pressure by cost-of-living bonuses coupled with stabilisation of agreements was finally recognised as misguided and from the mid-1960s annual agreements became the norm. At the same time, employers tried to obtain relief from manpower shortages, restrictive practices and demarcation. It became clear no relief from these problems would be obtained, except as part of a wages or hours or holidays 'deal'. This fact exposed another weakness. It was extremely difficult to obtain a 'quid pro quo' which had relevance to Scottish conditions.

The Scots who took part in the UK negotiations found they could not influence greatly the concessions on wages, hours or holidays which were, for right or wrong, acceptable by those who represented 90% of the UK industry. Further, when they returned to Scotland to negotiate the 'quid pro quo', the unions did not feel obliged to make any concessions because the part of the bargain in which they were interested had been settled. Attempts were made to solve this problem by agreement amongst the employers none of them would 'pay' until all had settled the last comma but these attempts proved unrealistic. This position nearly came to a head in 1959 when there was a stoppage of six weeks duration throughout the UK. In fact, the then Scottish Alliance of Master Printers could have made a settlement without the stoppage on better terms than eventually emerged but it preserved the common UK front, albeit with difficulty. The negotiations for hours reductions in 1960-62 gave the Scots no comfort and when in 1967 a position similar to that in 1959 appeared likely to arise, the SMPS decided, with reluctance, the independence to which it was entitled under the BFMP constitution be exercised. From 1967, the Scottish print employers collective body negotiated their own national agreements with the appropriate print unions. The BFMP/BPIF continued to negotiate an agreement covering only England and Wales.

The exercise by the Scots of their autonomy in 1967 led to demands from the English Midlands Alliance that the Scots be asked to resign from the BFMP. Negotiations between the SMPS and the BFMP followed, resulting in a new basis for the relationship between the two organisations. The Scots withdrew from the BFMP affairs by not exercising their constitutional right to nominate members to its main committees (Finance, Management Services and General Services) and participating no longer on the BFMP Joint Labour Committee. It would still nominate six representatives to serve on the BFMP Council and continue with representation on the National YMP Committee.

Constitutional tension arose because of those in the BFMP/BPIF who thought Scotland could be treated like all other member organisations. They believed Scotland could be treated like a region or an English county. The Scots could be directed as to what they had to do and they would have to like it or leave it. The reality was Scotland would not be treated in this way. The Scots wanted the best of both worlds. They wanted autonomy (ie devolution) so they could make their own agreements with respect to Scotland but wanted the protection and benefits of a larger voice by being part of a UK organisation.

Theme 3 : Separate Agreements in Scotland and England and Wales

Since 1967, in the UK there have been two national agreements covering the printing industry. One was negotiated between the BFMP/BPIF and the print unions and covered print workers employed in England and Wales. Bargaining took place in the first quarter of the year and the agreement became operative in April. The second agreement involved the print unions and the Scottish print employers' collective body. Bargaining took place in late spring and the agreement was implemented in July. From 1967, Scotland negotiated national agreements on a satisfactory basis and unlike England and Wales, without interruptions in production. Whatever the theoretical advantages of UK solidarity on the part of print employers experience showed this was in fact illusory.

Although there were two separate negotiations, the English and Welsh negotiations and their outcome impacted on Scotland. There were links between the two agreements not least because on the union side the same people were involved in both sets of negotiations. The Scots, however, refused to copy slavishly the English and Welsh agreement and insisted bargaining took place in a Scottish context. This resulted in some important differences between the two agreements. For example, pay rates were lower in the Scottish agreement. The Scots insisted their negotiations were autonomous and by so doing obtained variations from the English and Welsh agreements. Scotland had 'independence' in industrial relations matters.

The English and Welsh negotiations took place first and this was advantageous to the Scots. They had forewarning of the claim they were likely to receive from the print unions. It enabled the Scots to observe the strategy and tactics of the union bargainers and gauge the strength of feeling as to their willingness to trade each of the items in their claims. That the BFMP negotiations were first meant if there was a breakdown in negotiations and the unions imposed industrial action, including strike action, the Scots would be isolated from this action. This was well illustrated by the major dispute between the print unions and the BPIF in 1980 over the union demand for a thirty-five-hour working week and in 1993 over, inter alia, the GPMU demand for sixth week paid holiday entitlement.

On the few occasions when the print union failed to make an agreement in England and Wales before negotiations were due to start with the Scots, union negotiators would come to Scottish negotiations in a spirit of compromise and a desire to conclude an agreement which could then be used as a bargaining tactic with the BPIF. In short, in these circumstances, the unions would make concessions to the Scots they were not prepared to make in England and Wales, and which they would have been unwilling to make in Scotland in normal circumstances. In a survey of its members in the 1980s, the SMPS was told by 70% of respondents that isolation from any industrial action taking place in the rest of the UK was the main reason for their membership. Although the issue was occasionally raised amongst the Scottish employers as to whether having a separate agreement for Scotland from the rest of the UK was beneficial to the industry there was always clear support for a separate agreement. There was no way the Scots could 'set the pace' as regards wages for the whole of the UK. If 90% of the industry (England and Wales) did not want to 'pay' it could not be made to by the 10% minority (Scotland). From a Scottish viewpoint, it would be unable to 'influence' the English and Welsh negotiations if it were a direct participant in them.

A further reason for continuing support for a separate agreement for Scotland was that the size of the collective employers body's Executive Board and its Industrial Relations Committee, unlike that of the BPIF, meant all major print companies in Scotland could be represented in these forums and when decisions were made they were deliverable. Given the heavy concentration of the industry in the central belt of Scotland, it was always possible, if a major problem arose, to summon interested parties around a table in one room, in either a formal or informal setting to deal with the question or problem. A good example occurred in the 1993 pay negotiations between SPEF and the GPMU. Pay negotiations broke down and the national agreement in England and Wales collapsed. The GPMU responded by pursuing its claim, in which one day's additional paid holiday was a 'must have' item, by imposing industrial sanctions against selected English and Welsh printing firms. This policy proved highly successful with the 'picked off' companies conceding the extra day's holiday. The GPMU claim to SPEF in 1993 also included the additional day's holiday. SPEF members were adamant there be no concessions by their negotiators on the paid holiday claim. When it looked highly probable that, if the SPEF negotiators held to this line, the Scottish negotiations would break down and the national agreement collapse, the SPEF office bearers called a meeting to which key personnel from member firms, rather than just members of the Executive Board, were invited. At this meeting, SPEF office bearers told their member firms if they wished to retain the national agreement, they would have to concede a day's additional holiday but this could be offset by gaining concessions elsewhere from the union. The alternative would be the GPMU taking industrial action against selected companies, with those companies being unlikely in isolation to avoid conceding an additional day's holiday but gaining nothing in return from the union. Given this, member firms gave their negotiators a mandate to grant an extra day's holiday.

Theme 4 : A Peaceful Industry

Over the last century, including the second half in which there was dramatic technological change, relationships between employers and employees in the industry have been harmonious, with little open hostility. There were only two Scotland-wide disputes. One was in 1959 over the demand from the unions for a forty-hour working week and a 10% pay increase. The other was the General Strike of 1926 which was not against print employers but a sympathy strike in support of striking coal miners. There were only a handful of disputes involving stoppages against a whole company, for example John Horn in 1914, Waddie & Co (1986), Holmes McDougall (1987) and Bell & Bain (1993). The relationship between employers and their employees and their union officials were on the whole of a friendly character and negotiations, either locally or nationally, were nearly always conducted in a spirit of moderation. The Scottish print employers built up a reputation with their employees and the print unions of dealing in a fair, reasonable and consistent manner in bargaining, grievance handling, managing redundancy, dealing with disciplinary issues and informing and consulting about the workforce situations. This did not mean there were never occasions when the settlement of differences required careful handling and wise heads on the part of employers and employees and their representatives.

One reason for the industry experiencing good relationships over the last 100 years was it developed mechanisms for the resolution of disputes in a peaceful manner. Working conditions and working rules agreements with the STA, ASLP, NUPB&PW and NSES provided for conciliation committees of equal numbers of employer and employee representatives to help resolve disputes. They were successful bodies in this regard. They dealt with a great variety of subjects but the main differences with which they dealt were over the interpretation and application of existing agreements. These were dealt with quickly and efficiently and both the unions and employers showed a desire to uphold and carry out the intentions of the makers of the agreements.

Until the early 1960s, another important conflict resolution mechanism was the conciliation committees of the NJIC and of the SJIC. These bodies were established, after the First World War, and amongst their objectives was 'to devise ways and means of settling any differences that may arise'. Both the NJIC and the SJIC had standing committees of which one was a conciliation committee. After the 1959 dispute, the settlement of disputes arising from claims for the establishment, or revision of collective agreements between the employers' organisations and unions were outside the scope of conciliation by these councils. In the case of a dispute not settled locally, the joint secretaries of the councils arranged within seven days for a meeting of the Conciliation Committee. Whilst the Conciliation Committee was considering the matter, the status quo prevailed. If the Conciliation Committee recommendations failed to resolve the issue, the matter was referred to a full meeting of the NJIC and/or of the SJIC.

The Scottish national agreement contained a disputes and conciliation procedure to deal with disputes over the interpretation and application of the agreement. The first stage of the procedure was at house level and involved local company management and union chapel officials. If the matter was not resolved at house level the dispute went to the second stage – branch level – which involved the senior management of the company, assisted by SPEF and the union branch secretary. The third level was the national level which involved the national officials of the print employers' body and of the union who were obliged to endeavour to find an acceptable solution. Failing agreement at the national level, the matter could be referred to a joint panel representing the employers collective body and the trade union. This panel was convened under an independent chairperson agreed by the parties and who was to guide and advise the panel and assist them to resolve the dispute. No hostile action was to be taken by the parties whilst the dispute progressed through the various stages of the procedure.

Institutional arrangements of themselves do not guarantee peaceful resolution of disputes. There were other factors at work in explaining the relative lack of open conflict and warfare in the industry. One important factor was that print workers enjoyed good terms and conditions of employment relative to workers in other industries and had a reasonable lifestyle. Until the mid-1980s, there was a shortage of labour and market forces exercised upward pressure on wages and conditions. Print workers did not need to impose industrial action to gain increases in pay. Prior to the mid-1970s, production technology meant it was not easy for print employers to obtain alternative supplies of skilled print labour. Redundancy arising from technological change did not occur as a major issue in the industry until the late 1980s/early 1990s and was managed by retraining redundant workers, natural wastage, and voluntary, as opposed to compulsory, redundancy. An ageing workforce meant early retirement was an attractive option in redundancy situations helped by generous redundancy payments. In short, the peaceful adjustment in the Scottish printing industry to its technological revolutions came about by retraining, redeployment, voluntary redundancy and social dialogue, including meaningful consultation with their workforce by the print employers.

A further explanation of the relative industrial peace for over a century in the industry was the close common interest between the employers, employees and the unions the industry should grow, develop and prosper. It was to their mutual advantage for this to happen. Skilled print workers were well paid but could only utilise their skills in the printing industry. To gain employment outside the industry on print terms and conditions of employment was always going to be difficult. The craft employees had a self-interest along with the employers in seeing the industry was profitable, competitive and efficient. If the industry became uncompetitive and declined, print skilled workers as well as print employers would suffer.

Notes

[1]   There were also collective organisations of lithographic printers and of bookbinders. These included the Association of Master Printers and Lithographers of Dundee and District, Edinburgh and East of Scotland Master Lithographers Association, Glasgow and West of Scotland Master Lithographers Association, the Association of Edinburgh Master Binders and Machine Rulers and the Glasgow Master Bookbinders Association.

APPENDIX 1

Presidents

 1910 – 1913
Walter B Blaikie, LLD
T & A Constable

 1928 – 1930
John Wylie
Aird & Coghill

 1913 – 1916
James MacLehose
R MacLehose & Co

 1930 – 1932
Theodore Watt
The Rosemount Press

 1916 – 1919
James S Waterston
George Waterston
& Sons

 1932 – 1934
Robert Kilpatrick
T & A Constable

 1919 – 1922
James Paterson
Wm Collins Sons & Co

 1934 – 1936
Robert P Graham
Brownlie, Scandrett
& Graham

 1922 – 1924
Robert Wilson
H & J Pillans & Wilson

 1936 – 1938
John S. McQueen
J McQueen & Sons

 1924 – 1926
John Blackie
Blackie & Son

 1938 – 1940
Robert Wylie
Aird & Coghill

 1926 – 1928
William Maxwell
R & R Clark

 1940 – 1942
John Bartholomew
J Bartholomew & Son

1942 – 1944
W Hope Collins
Wm Collins Sons & Co

1960 – 1962
J Harry Allen
The Allen
Lithographic Co

1944 – 1946
Duncan C Sillars
Valentine & Sons

1962 – 1964
Blair Maxwell
R & R Clark

1946 – 1948
William C Todd
T & A Constable

1964 – 1966
J J Thomson
C L Wright

1948 – 1950
J Gilchrist Johnston
Wilson, Guthrie & Co

1966 – 1968
Alexander Brown
Hunter & Foulis

1950 – 1952
John N Milne
The Central Press

1968 – 1970
N D MacLehose
R MacLehose & Co

1952 – 1954
Alastair M Stewart
George Stewart & Co

1970 – 1972
James Gray
J McQueen & Sons

1954 – 1956
Frank L Paton
James Paton

1972 – 1974
Walter B Dickson
Harveys

1956 – 1958
James M Waterston
George Waterston
& Sons

1974 – 1976
H M R Watt
Aberdeen University
Press

1958 – 1960
John Murdoch
J & J Murdoch

1976 – 1977
T R Ballard
Wm Collins Sons & Co

1977 – 1979
Robert Thomson
R & R Clark

1979 – 1981
Harry McNab
James Paton

1981 – 1983
W F Cairns Smith
Smith Brothers
(Kilmarnock)

1983 – 1985
R B R Walker
Clark Constable (1982)

1985 – 1987
C Inglis McAulay
Inglis Paul

1987 – 1989
David C McCormick
John McCormick & Co

1989 – 1991
David J Henderson
George Stewart & Co

1991 – 1993
Hamish G R Milne
Spirax Binding
(Scotland)

1993 – 1995
Alf Downie
Bell & Bain

1995 – 1997
Patrick Mark
The Simpson Label Co

1997 – 1999
John A Crerar
Mackenzie & Storrie

1999 – 2001
Brian W Purves
Waddie & Co

2001 – 2003
Gordon B Cunningham
Ritchie (UK)

2003 – 2006
Bob Hodgson
Pillans & Waddies

2006 – 2008
Terry O'Hare
Stewarts of Edinburgh

2008 – 2010
David McCormick
John McCormick & Co

2010 –
Trevor Price
21 Colour

APPENDIX 2

Secretary/Director

Secretaries

F H Bisset	1911 – 1919
R T Wishart	1919 – 1954
W Barrie Abbott	1954 – 1966/7

Directors

W Barrie Abbott	1966/7 – 1984
James B Raeburn	1984 – 2007
Simon Fairclough	2007 – 2009
Bob Hodgson	2010 –

INDEX

A

Abbott, W Barrie   192, 195, 202, 226, 228, 269-270, 304, 313, 317, 336, 441: appointed Assistant Secretary, 56; appointed Secretary, 186

Aberdeen   3-4, 8-9, 14, 18, 29-30, 35, 57, 66, 81-82, 93, 118, 127, 148-150, 168, 170, 189, 193, 274, 295, 326, 331, 334, 384,

Aberdeen Breviary   2

Aberdeen Journal (later the *Press and Journal*)   4

Aberdeen Local Association (and predecessor bodies)   77, 79-80, 94, 183, 185, 260-261, 295, 377-378, 384: formation of, 52

Aberdeen Trade Society   19

Aberdeen University Press   9, 257, 444

ACP, see Association of Correctors of the Press

Adult apprenticeships, see under Apprentices

Advisory Conciliation and Arbitration Service (ACAS)   355, 365

Air raids, work during   136-138, 141

Albion press   10

Allen, J Harry   266

Alloa   14, 168

Alva   168

Amalgamated Society of Lithographic Printers (ASLP)   30, 34, 37, 95, 97-100, 110, 116-117, 170, 180, 182-183, 204-205, 239, 241, 253, 306, 309, 328-329, 331-332, 442, 444, 451: 1959 strike, 218-220, 227-228; apprentices, 66, 206-207, 346-347; dispute 1915-1916, 85-86; machine extras, 118-119; wage claims 1947-1951, 161-168; wage claims 1955-1956, 214-217; wage claims 1960s, 339-341, 345, 349; wage negotiations in World War I, 79-82

Amalgamated Society of Printers' Warehousemen   32

AMICUS (Graphical Paper and Media Sector)   461

Anderson, George   4

Anderson/Campbell monopoly   3, 5

Anglo-American Council on Productivity   59, 154

Anglo-American Letterpress Printing Productivity Team   59

Arbuthnot, Alexander   2

Index

Index

Index

Index

Index

Index

Index

Index

Index